Volvo 240 Series Owners Workshop Manual

by J H Haynes
Member of the Guild of Motoring Writers
and Bruce Gilmour

Models covered
All Volvo 240, 242, 244 and 245 models: DL, GL, GT, GLT & Turbo
2.0 liter (121 cu in), 2.1 liter (130 cu in) & 2.3 liter (141 cu in)

Does not cover Diesel engine variants

ISBN 1 85010 335 6

ABCDE
FGHIJ
KLMNO

Haynes Publishing Group
Sparkford Nr Yeovil
Somerset BA22 7JJ England

Haynes Publications, Inc
861 Lawrence Drive
Newbury Park
California 91320 USA

Acknowledgements

Special thanks are due to A B Volvo for the supply of technical information and some of the illustrations used in this manual. Castrol Limited provided lubrication data, and the Champion Sparking Plug Company supplied the illustrations showing the various spark plug conditions.

We are particularly grateful to John Tallis Motors Limited, Bathwick Hill, Bath, who supplied the Volvo 244 used as our project car.

Lastly thanks are due to all of those people at Sparkford who helped on the production of this manual.

About this manual

Its aim

The aim of this manual is to help you get the best value from your car. It can do so in several ways. It can help you decide what work must be done (even should you choose to get it done by a garage), provide information on routine maintenance and servicing, and give a logical course of action and diagnosis when random faults occur. However, it is hoped that you will use the manual by tackling the work yourself. On simpler jobs it may even be quicker than booking the car into a garage and going there twice to leave and collect it. Perhaps most important, a lot of money can be saved by avoiding the costs the garage must charge to cover its labour and overheads.

The manual has drawings and descriptions to show the function of the various components so that their layout can be understood. Then the tasks are described and photographed in a step-by-step sequence so that even a novice can do the work.

Its arrangement

The manual is divided into thirteen Chapters, each covering a logical sub-division of the vehicle. The Chapters are each divided into Sections, numbered with single figures, eg 5; and the Sections into paragraphs (or sub-sections), with decimal numbers following on from the Section they are in, eg 5.1, 5.2, 5.3 etc.

It is freely illustrated, especially in those parts where there is a detailed sequence of operations to be carried out. There are two forms of illustration: figures and photographs. The figures are numbered in sequence with decimal numbers, according to their position in the Chapter — eg Fig. 6.4 is the fourth drawing/illustration in Chapter 6. Photographs carry the same number (either individually or in related groups) as the Section or sub-section to which they relate.

There is an alphabetical index at the back of the manual as well as a contents list at the front. Each Chapter is also preceded by its own individual contents list.

References to the 'left' or 'right' of the vehicle are in the sense of a person in the driver's seat facing forwards.

Unless otherwise stated, nuts and bolts are removed by turning anti-clockwise, and tightened by turning clockwise.

Vehicle manufacturers continually make changes to specifications and recommendations, and these when notified are incorporated into our manuals at the earliest opportunity.

Whilst every care is taken to ensure that the information in this manual is correct, no liability can be accepted by the authors or publishers for loss, damage or injury caused by any errors in, or omissions from, the information given.

Introduction to the Volvo 240

With the introduction of the Volvo 240 series another quality vehicle of conventional design is added to the Volvo stable. It is available with carburettor or fuel injection engines.

There is a choice of many additional features: Manual gearbox, with overdrive, automatic transmission, power steering, limited slip differential and air conditioning.

Overhaul and repair operations to the car are not complicated and all major components are fairly accessible.

Contents

Volvo 244 DL - 1977 UK Specification

General dimensions, weights and capacities

For modifications, and information applicable to later models, see Supplement at end of manual

Dimensions

Overall length:
- 1975 to 1976   ...   .   192.8 in (4898 mm)
- 1977 to 1980   ...   .   192.1 in (4878 mm)
- 1981 on   ...   .   188.6 in (4790 mm)

Overall height:
- Saloon   ...   .   56.2 in (1427 mm)
- Estate ...   .   57.5 in (1460 mm)

Wheelbase:
- Manual steering   ...   .   103.9 in (2640 mm)
- Power steering   ...   .   104.3 in (2650 mm)

Front track:
- Early models ...   .   55.9 in (1420 mm)
- Later models ...   .   56.3 in (1430 mm)

Rear track:
- Early models ...   .   53.15 in (1350 mm)
- Later models ...   .   53.5 in (1360 mm)

Turning circle (between kerbs) ...   .   32 ft 6 in (9.8 m)

Weights

Kerb weights (approx):
- 242, 244 and 245 (UK)   ...   .   2830 lb (1285 kg)
- GT and DL (240 and 242) (US)   ...   .   2891 to 2999 lb (1312 to 1362 kg)
- GL (244) (US)   ...   .   2933 to 3065 lb (1332 to 1392 kg)
- Estate (245) (US)   ...   .   3129 to 3162 lb (1421 to 1436 kg)

Maximum trailer weight   ...   .   2000 lb (908 kg)

Capacities

Engine:
- B20 (ohv)   ...   .   6.6 Imp pints (4.0 US qt, 3.75 litres)
- B17, B19, B21 and B23   ...   .   6.8 Imp pints (4.1 US qt, 3.85 litres)

Manual transmission:
- M40, M45   ...   .   1.3 Imp pints (0.8 US qt, 0.75 litre)
- M41   ...   .   2.8 Imp pints (1.7 US qt, 1.6 litres)
- M46   ...   .   4.0 Imp pints (2.4 US qt, 2.3 litres)

Automatic transmission:
- BW 35   ...   .   11.3 Imp pints (6.8 US qt, 6.4 litres)
- BW55/AW55 (early models)   ...   .   11.4 Imp pints (6.85 US qt, 6.5 litres)
- BW55/AW55 (later models)   ...   .   12.1 Imp pints (7.3 US qt, 6.9 litres)
- AW70/AW71 ...   .   13.2 Imp pints (9.8 US qt, 7.5 litres)

Rear axle:
- Type 1030   ...   .   2.3 Imp pints (1.4 US qt, 1.3 litres)
- Type 1031   ...   .   2.8 Imp pints (1.7 US qt, 1.6 litres)

Cooling system:
- Manual gearbox models   ...   .   16.7 Imp pints (10.0 US qt, 9.5 litres)
- Automatic transmission models   ...   .   16.4 Imp pints (9.8 US qt, 9.3 litres)

Fuel tank ...   .   13.2 Imp gal (15.8 US gal, 60 litres)

Use of English

As this book has been written in England, it uses the appropriate English component names, phrases, and spelling. Some of these differ from those used in America. Normally, these cause no difficulty, but to make sure, a glossary is printed below. In ordering spare parts remember the parts list may use some of these words:

English	American	English	American
Accelerator	Gas pedal	Leading shoe (of brake)	Primary shoe
Aerial	Antenna	Locks	Latches
Anti-roll bar	Stabiliser or sway bar	Methylated spirit	Denatured alcohol
Big-end bearing	Rod bearing	Motorway	Freeway, turnpike etc
Bonnet (engine cover)	Hood	Number plate	License plate
Boot (luggage compartment)	Trunk	Paraffin	Kerosene
Bulkhead	Firewall	Petrol	Gasoline (gas)
Bush	Bushing	Petrol tank	Gas tank
Cam follower or tappet	Valve lifter or tappet	'Pinking'	'Pinging'
Carburettor	Carburetor	Prise (force apart)	Pry
Catch	Latch	Propeller shaft	Driveshaft
Choke/venturi	Barrel	Quarterlight	Quarter window
Circlip	Snap-ring	Retread	Recap
Clearance	Lash	Reverse	Back-up
Crownwheel	Ring gear (of differential)	Rocker cover	Valve cover
Damper	Shock absorber, shock	Saloon	Sedan
Disc (brake)	Rotor/disk	Seized	Frozen
Distance piece	Spacer	Sidelight	Parking light
Drop arm	Pitman arm	Silencer	Muffler
Drop head coupe	Convertible	Sill panel (beneath doors)	Rocker panel
Dynamo	Generator (DC)	Small end, little end	Piston pin or wrist pin
Earth (electrical)	Ground	Spanner	Wrench
Engineer's blue	Prussian blue	Split cotter (for valve spring cap)	Lock (for valve spring retainer)
Estate car	Station wagon	Split pin	Cotter pin
Exhaust manifold	Header	Steering arm	Spindle arm
Fault finding/diagnosis	Troubleshooting	Sump	Oil pan
Float chamber	Float bowl	Swarf	Metal chips or debris
Free-play	Lash	Tab washer	Tang or lock
Freewheel	Coast	Tappet	Valve lifter
Gearbox	Transmission	Thrust bearing	Throw-out bearing
Gearchange	Shift	Top gear	High
Grub screw	Setscrew, Allen screw	Trackrod (of steering)	Tie-rod (or connecting rod)
Gudgeon pin	Piston pin or wrist pin	Trailing shoe (of brake)	Secondary shoe
Halfshaft	Axleshaft	Transmission	Whole drive line
Handbrake	Parking brake	Tyre	Tire
Hood	Soft top	Van	Panel wagon/van
Hot spot	Heat riser	Vice	Vise
Indicator	Turn signal	Wheel nut	Lug nut
Interior light	Dome lamp	Windscreen	Windshield
Layshaft (of gearbox)	Countershaft	Wing/mudguard	Fender

Buying spare parts and vehicle identification numbers

Buying spare parts

Spare parts are available from many sources, for example: Volvo garages, other garages and accessory shops, and motor factors. Our advice regarding spare part sources is as follows:

Officially appointed Volvo garages - This is the best source of parts which are peculiar to your car and are otherwise not generally available (eg. complete cylinder heads, internal gearbox components, badges, interior trim etc). It is also the only place at which you should buy parts if your car is still under warranty - non-Volvo components may invalidate the warranty. To be sure of obtaining the correct parts it will always be necessary to give the storeman your car's engine and chassis number, and if possible, to take the 'old' part along for positive identification. Remember that many parts are available on a factory exchange scheme - any parts returned should always be clean! It obviously makes good sense to go straight to the specialists on your car for this type of part for they are best equipped to supply you.

Other garages and accessory shops - These are often very good places to buy materials and components needed for the maintenance of your car (eg. oil filters, spark plugs, bulbs, fanbelts, oils and greases, touch-up paint, filler paste etc). They also sell general accessories, usually have convenient opening hours, charge lower prices and can often be found not far from home.

Motor factors - Good factors will stock all of the more important components which wear out relatively quickly (eg. clutch, oil filters, pistons, valves, exhaust systems, brake cylinders/pipes/hoses/seals/shoes and pads etc). Motor factors will often provide new reconditioned components on a part exchange basis - this can save a considerable amount of money.

Vehicle identification numbers

1 Although many individual parts, and in some cases sub-assemblies fit a number of different models it is dangerous to assume that just because they look the same, they are the same. Differences are not always easy to detect except by serial numbers. Make sure therefore, that the appropriate identity number for the model or sub-assembly is known and quoted when a spare part is ordered.

2 The final drive assembly has a number of its own which is carried on a plate fastened to the left-hand side of the casing. This plate gives the drive ratio, part number and serial number of the unit. The gearbox carries a similar plate on its underside giving the type designation, part number and serial number. On automatic transmission the plate is on the left-hand side of the casing.

3 The engine serial number appears on the left-hand side of the engine at the lip of the cylinder block just below the cylinder head.

4 The type designation and chassis number of the vehicle is stamped on the right-hand front door pillar and on a plate mounted on the luggage compartment rear wall (242/244) or on the side section under the right-hand rear side window (245).

5 The type designation, chassis number and code numbers for colour and upholstery appear on a plate located on the right-hand side wheel housing.

The engine serial number is stamped on the left-hand side of the engine block

This plate gives the type designation, chassis number and code numbers for colour and upholstery

Tools and working facilities

Introduction

A selection of good tools is a fundamental requirement for anyone contemplating the maintenance and repair of a motor vehicle. For the owner who does not possess any, their purchase will prove a considerable expense, offsetting some of the savings made by doing-it-yourself. However, provided that the tools purchased are of good quality, they will last for many years and prove an extremely worthwhile investment.

To help the average owner to decide which tools are needed to carry out the various tasks detailed in this manual, we have compiled three lists of tools under the following headings: *Maintenance and minor repair, Repair and overhaul,* and *Special.* The newcomer to practical mechanics should start off with the *Maintenance and minor repair* tool kit and confine himself to the simpler jobs around the vehicle. Then, as his confidence and experience grow, he can undertake more difficult tasks, buying extra tools as, and when, they are needed. In this way, a *Maintenance and minor repair* tool kit can be built-up into a *Repair and overhaul* tool kit over a considerable period of time without any major cash outlays. The experienced do-it-yourselfer will have a tool kit good enough for most repair and overhaul procedures and will add tools from the *Special* category when he feels the expense is justified by the amount of use to which these tools will be put.

It is obviously not possible to cover the subject of tools fully here. For those who wish to learn more about tools and their use there is a book entitled *How to Choose and Use Car Tools* available from the publishers of this manual.

Maintenance and minor repair tool kit

The tools given in this list should be considered as a minimum requirement if routine maintenance, servicing and minor repair operations are to be undertaken. We recommend the purchase of combination spanners (ring one end, open-ended the other); although more expensive than open-ended ones, they do give the advantages of both types of spanner.

> Combination spanners - 10, 11, 12, 13, 14 & 17 mm
> Adjustable spanner - 9 inch
> Engine sump/gearbox/rear axle drain plug key
> Spark plug spanner (with rubber insert)
> Spark plug gap adjustment tool
> Set of feeler gauges
> Brake adjuster spanner
> Brake bleed nipple spanner
> Screwdriver - 4 in long x $\frac{1}{4}$ in dia (flat blade)
> Screwdriver - 4 in long x $\frac{1}{4}$ in dia (cross blade)
> Combination pliers - 6 inch
> Hacksaw (junior)
> Tyre pump
> Tyre pressure gauge
> Grease gun
> Oil can
> Fine emery cloth (1 sheet)
> Wire brush (small)
> Funnel (medium size)

Repair and overhaul tool kit

These tools are virtually essential for anyone undertaking any major repairs to a motor vehicle, and are additional to those given in the *Maintenance and minor repair* list. Included in this list is a comprehensive set of sockets. Although these are expensive they will be found invaluable as they are so versatile - particularly if various drives are included in the set. We recommend the $\frac{1}{2}$ in square-drive type, as this can be used with most proprietary torque wrenches. If you cannot afford a socket set, even bought piecemeal, then inexpensive tubular box spanners are a useful alternative.

The tools in this list will occasionally need to be supplemented by tools from the *Special* list.

> Sockets (or box spanners) to cover range in previous list
> Reversible ratchet drive (for use with sockets)
> Extension piece, 10 inch (for use with sockets)
> Universal joint (for use with sockets)
> Torque wrench (for use with sockets)
> 'Mole' wrench - 8 inch
> Ball pein hammer
> Soft-faced hammer, plastic or rubber
> Screwdriver - 6 in long x $\frac{5}{16}$ in dia (flat blade)
> Screwdriver - 2 in long x $\frac{5}{16}$ in square (flat blade)
> Screwdriver - 1$\frac{1}{2}$ in long x $\frac{1}{4}$ in dia (cross blade)
> Screwdriver - 3 in long x $\frac{1}{8}$ in dia (electricians)
> Pliers - electricians side cutters
> Pliers - needle nosed
> Pliers - circlip (internal and external)
> Cold chisel - $\frac{1}{2}$ inch
> Scriber
> Scraper
> Centre punch
> Pin punch
> Hacksaw
> Valve grinding tool
> Steel rule/straight-edge
> Allen keys
> Selection of files
> Wire brush (large)
> Axle-stands
> Jack (strong scissor or hydraulic type)

Special tools

The tools in this list are those which are not used regularly, are expensive to buy, or which need to be used in accordance with their manufacturers' instructions. Unless relatively difficult mechanical jobs are undertaken frequently, it will not be economic to buy many of these tools. Where this is the case, you could consider clubbing together with friends (or joining a motorists' club) to make a joint purchase, or borrowing the tools against a deposit from a local garage or tool hire specialist.

The following list contains only those tools and instruments freely available to the public, and not those special tools produced by the vehicle manufacturer specifically for its dealer network. You will find occasional references to these manufacturers' special tools in the text of this manual. Generally, an alternative method of doing the job without the vehicle manufacturers' special tool is given. However, sometimes, there is no alternative to using them. Where this is the case and the relevant tool cannot be bought or borrowed, you will have to entrust the work to a franchised garage.

Valve spring compressor (where applicable)
Piston ring compressor
Balljoint separator
Universal hub/bearing puller
Impact screwdriver
Micrometer and/or vernier gauge
Dial gauge
Stroboscopic timing light
Dwell angle meter/tachometer
Universal electrical multi-meter
Cylinder compression gauge
Lifting tackle
Trolley jack
Light with extension lead

Buying tools

For practically all tools, a tool factor is the best source since he will have a very comprehensive range compared with the average garage or accessory shop. Having said that, accessory shops often offer excellent quality tools at discount prices, so it pays to shop around.

Remember, you don't have to buy the most expensive items on the shelf, but it is always advisable to steer clear of the very cheap tools. There are plenty of good tools around at reasonable prices, so ask the proprietor or manager of the shop for advice before making a purchase.

Care and maintenance of tools

Having purchased a reasonable tool kit, it is necessary to keep the tools in a clean serviceable condition. After use, always wipe off any dirt, grease and metal particles using a clean, dry cloth, before putting the tools away. Never leave them lying around after they have been used. A simple tool rack on the garage or workshop wall, for items such as screwdrivers and pliers is a good idea. Store all normal wrenches and sockets in a metal box. Any measuring instruments, gauges, meters, etc, must be carefully stored where they cannot be damaged or become rusty.

Take a little care when tools are used. Hammer heads inevitably become marked and screwdrivers lose the keen edge on their blades from time to time. A little timely attention with emery cloth or a file will soon restore items like this to a good serviceable finish.

Working facilities

Not to be forgotten when discussing tools, is the workshop itself. If anything more than routine maintenance is to be carried out, some form of suitable working area becomes essential.

It is appreciated that many an owner mechanic is forced by circumstances to remove an engine or similar item, without the benefit of a garage or workshop. Having done this, any repairs should always be done under the cover of a roof.

Wherever possible, any dismantling should be done on a clean, flat workbench or table at a suitable working height.

Any workbench needs a vice: one with a jaw opening of 4 in (100 mm) is suitable for most jobs. As mentioned previously, some clean dry storage space is also required for tools, as well as for lubricants, cleaning fluids, touch-up paints and so on, which become necessary.

Another item which may be required, and which has a much more general usage, is an electric drill with a chuck capacity of at least $\frac{5}{16}$ in (8 mm). This, together with a good range of twist drills, is virtually essential for fitting accessories such as mirrors and reversing lights.

Last, but not least, always keep a supply of old newspapers and clean, lint-free rags available, and try to keep any working area as clean as possible.

Spanner jaw gap comparison table

Jaw gap (in)	Spanner size
0.250	$\frac{1}{4}$ in AF
0.276	7 mm
0.313	$\frac{5}{16}$ in AF
0.315	8 mm
0.344	$\frac{11}{32}$ in AF; $\frac{1}{8}$ in Whitworth
0.354	9 mm
0.375	$\frac{3}{8}$ in AF
0.394	10 mm
0.433	11 mm
0.438	$\frac{7}{16}$ in AF
0.445	$\frac{3}{16}$ in Whitworth; $\frac{1}{4}$ in BSF
0.472	12 mm
0.500	$\frac{1}{2}$ in AF
0.512	13 mm
0.525	$\frac{1}{4}$ in Whitworth; $\frac{5}{16}$ in BSF
0.551	14 mm
0.563	$\frac{9}{16}$ in AF
0.591	15 mm
0.600	$\frac{5}{16}$ in Whitworth; $\frac{3}{8}$ in BSF
0.625	$\frac{5}{8}$ in AF
0.630	16 mm
0.669	17 mm
0.686	$\frac{11}{16}$ in AF
0.709	18 mm
0.710	$\frac{3}{8}$ in Whitworth; $\frac{7}{16}$ in BSF
0.748	19 mm
0.750	$\frac{3}{4}$ in AF
0.813	$\frac{13}{16}$ in AF
0.820	$\frac{7}{16}$ in Whitworth; $\frac{1}{2}$ in BSF
0.866	22 mm
0.875	$\frac{7}{8}$ in AF
0.920	$\frac{1}{2}$ in Whitworth; $\frac{9}{16}$ in BSF
0.938	$\frac{15}{16}$ in AF
0.945	24 mm
1.000	1 in AF
1.010	$\frac{9}{16}$ in Whitworth; $\frac{5}{8}$ in BSF
1.024	26 mm
1.063	$1\frac{1}{16}$ in AF; 27 mm
1.100	$\frac{5}{8}$ in Whitworth; $\frac{11}{16}$ in BSF
1.125	$1\frac{1}{8}$ in AF
1.181	30 mm
1.200	$\frac{11}{16}$ in Whitworth; $\frac{3}{4}$ in BSF
1.250	$1\frac{1}{4}$ in AF
1.260	32 mm
1.300	$\frac{3}{4}$ in Whitworth; $\frac{7}{8}$ in BSF
1.313	$1\frac{5}{16}$ in AF
1.390	$\frac{13}{16}$ in Whitworth; $\frac{15}{16}$ in BSF
1.417	36 mm
1.438	$1\frac{7}{16}$ in AF
1.480	$\frac{7}{8}$ in Whitworth; 1 in BSF
1.500	$1\frac{1}{2}$ in AF
1.575	40 mm; $\frac{15}{16}$ in Whitworth
1.614	41 mm
1.625	$1\frac{5}{8}$ in AF
1.670	1 in Whitworth; $1\frac{1}{8}$ in BSF
1.688	$1\frac{11}{16}$ in AF
1.811	46 mm
1.813	$1\frac{13}{16}$ in AF
1.860	$1\frac{1}{8}$ in Whitworth; $1\frac{1}{4}$ in BSF
1.875	$1\frac{7}{8}$ in AF
1.969	50 mm
2.000	2 in AF
2.050	$1\frac{1}{4}$ in Whitworth; $1\frac{3}{8}$ in BSF
2.165	55 mm
2.362	60 mm

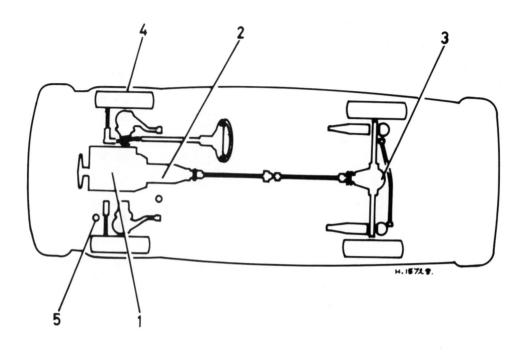

H.15719.

Recommended lubricants and fluids

Component or system	Lubricant type or specification
1 Engine	Multigrade engine oil (SAE 10W/30 or 10W/40)
2A Manual gearbox (with or without overdrive)	
M40 and M41	Hypoid gear oil (SAE 80 or 90)
M45, M46 and M47:	
All climates	Automatic transmission fluid type F or G
Temperature rarely below -10°C (14°F):	
Up to 1986	SAE 10W/40 or 10W/30
1986 on	Volvo Thermo oil P/N 1 161 243-9
2B Automatic transmission	Automatic transmission fluid type F or G
3 Rear axle*	Hypoid gear oil SAE 90
4 Front wheel bearings	Lithium-based grease
5 Power steering fluid reservoir	Automatic transmission fluid
Hydraulic system	Hydraulic fluid to SAE J1703

* If the vehicle is fitted with a limited slip differential a special lubricant is required. Consult your Volvo dealer.

Note: *The above are general recommendations only. Lubrication requirements vary from territory to territory. If in doubt, consult your nearest dealer or the operator's handbook supplied with the vehicle.*

Routine maintenance – models up to 1984

For information applicable to later models, see Routine maintenance at end of manual

Introduction

Routine maintenance is a chore - however enthusiastic an owner or ardent a car lover you may be. A better name for it is preventive maintenance. This does not make it any less of a chore, but it is one of those chores which pays off.

It does this in three ways:

a) *It reduces wear and lengthens car life by ensuring that all parts that need it are properly lubricated.*

b) *It ensures that all small adjustments which make so much difference to the performance of the car - and in some cases neglect of these may mean disaster - are always correct.*

c) *Most important of all, by carrying out maintenance you give your car a thorough inspection.*

The maintenance tasks described below are in the main those recommended by Volvo, but we have added a few more to the list which practical experience has convinced us are well worth doing.

The recommended time intervals are applicable in temperate climates where the roads are reasonably dust-free and for yearly distances of 12,000 - 24,000 miles (20,000 - 40,000 kms). They may need to be modified where environmental conditions are extreme or distances driven are very much greater.

2 Weekly, before a long journey, or every 250 miles (400 kms)

1 Check the engine oil level which should be up to the 'Max' mark on the dipstick. Top-up the oil in the sump if necessary. On no account allow the oil to fall below the 'Min' mark on the dipstick.

2 Check the battery electrolyte level and top-up as necessary with distilled water. Make sure that the top of the battery is always kept clean and free of moisture.

3 Check the coolant level in the radiator or expansion tank. Top-up if necessary with the same mixture as is already in there - do not top-up antifreeze solution with water. Persistent need to top-up indicates leakage somewhere and should be investigated without delay.

4 Check the tyre pressures - and that includes the spare. The correct tyre pressures depend on the type of tyre that is being used and the vehicle load carried. The local Volvo garage, or indeed, any garage which deals in the make of tyre that is fitted, will be able to give this information. Keep the spare tyre at the highest pressures used as it can always be let down a little when it is fitted.

5 Refill the windscreen washer container with perfectly clean water. If it is necessary to add an antifreeze always use the sort specially made for windscreen washers. Check that the jets are operating correctly.

6 Check the windscreen wipers for correct operation and the blades for signs of deterioration. Renew the blades if their condition is suspect.

7 Check all the lights - notably the brake lights. When the car brakes suddenly, the car behind it needs all the warning it can get.

8 Check the level of the brake and clutch (when the hydraulic system is used as opposed to cable operation) hydraulic fluid reservoir/s. Top-up to the 'Max' mark if necessary.

3 Every 6,000 miles (10,000 km) or 6 months

1 Carry out the service operations in the weekly check.

2 Run the engine until it is hot and drain the engine oil. Refill with fresh oil.

3 Renew the engine oil filter.

4 Wipe the top of the carburettor suction chamber and top-up the carburettor until the fluid is 0.25 in (6 mm) from the top. For further

information see Chapter 3.

5 Check the carburettor adjustments, as described in Chapter 3. When fuel injection is fitted, further information will also be found in Chapter 3, but it may be as well to leave this to the local Volvo garage.

6 Check the cooling and heater systems for signs of leakage. Be sure that all hose clips are tight and that none of the hoses shows signs of cracking.

7 *Carburettor engine only.* Clean the filter in the fuel pump. For further information, refer to Chapter 3.

8 Check the fanbelt for signs of wear. If necessary set the tension, as described in Chapter 2.

9 Lubricate all throttle and engine control linkages with a little engine oil.

10 Check the adjustment of the handbrake and footbrake. If it was necessary to make an appreciable adjustment to the handbrake inspect the linkage for wear. Full information will be found in Chapter 9.

11 Carefully examine all the brake hydraulic pipes, hoses and unions for signs of leakage. The flexible hoses must not rub against any part of the car when the steering is turned through both locks.

12 Lubricate all moving parts of the handbrake system.

13 Clean and adjust the spark plugs, as described in Chapter 4.

14 Check the state of charge of the battery with an hydrometer. If it is not fully charged, and there is no immediate explanation of this (as, for example a slack fanbelt), have the battery checked by a local garage or preferably a specialist. If it is not in very good shape, it may be wise to consider replacement, especially in the winter.

15 Clean the battery terminals and smear them with petroleum jelly (vaseline) to prevent corrosion.

16 Check the alignment of the headlights and adjust, if necessary, as described in Chapter 10.

17 Check the steering box for leaks. Check oil level in reservoir (power steering).

18 Check the tyre wear pattern as, if irregular, it can indicate that the front suspension is out of alignment. If this does appear to be the case, the remedy is obvious and expert advice should be sought as soon as possible.

19 Wipe around the filler plug of the final drive unit (differential) and remove the plug. Check the oil level which should come up to the filler hole. If necessary, top-up with the correct lubricant. Refit the plug.

20 Check the propeller shaft for wear, as described in Chapter 7. Generally speaking, if wear is evident it would already have made its presence felt by causing vibration in the transmission system.

21 For cars with manual gearboxes, whether or not they are fitted with overdrive, wipe round the filler plug and check the oil level which should be up to the filler hole. If necessary, top-up with the correct lubricant.

22 *Automatic transmission.* The dipstick and filler tube is located in front of the bulkhead on the right-hand side of the engine. To check the oil level drive the car for a few miles to bring the fluid up to its normal operating temperature. With the car on a level surface move the selector to the 'P' position and allow the engine to idle for two minutes. With the engine still running, remove the dipstick, wipe clean with a non-fluffy rag, quickly insert fully and withdraw. If necessary, add fluid of the correct type to bring the level up to the 'Max' mark but take care not to overfill.

23 Check the exhaust system for leaks. If small blow holes are found, these can be rectified with a proprietary repair kit. However, this is a sign that corrosion is well advanced and the pipe or system will require renewal shortly. Check all exhaust mountings for tightness.

24 Check and, if necessary, adjust the clutch free-play. Where a cable system is used check the condition of the cable and lubricate with a little engine oil.

25 Check and adjust the distributor contact breaker points. Full information will be found in Chapter 4.

Fig. 1. B21A carburettor engine

1 Data plate
2 Oil dipstick, automatic transmission
3 Oil dipstick, engine
4 Brake fluid reservoir
5 Ignition coil
6 Battery
7 Ignition distributor
8 Oil filler cap, engine
9 Expansion tank, cooling system
10 Windscreen washer reservoir

Oil sump drain plug

Topping up with engine oil

Fig. 2. Checking the carburettor damper oil level

Gearbox level/filler plug and drain plug

26 Check ignition timing and reset if necessary, as described in Chapter 4.
27 Ideally the front wheel alignment should be checked and reset if necessary. This is best left to the local Volvo garage. See Chapter 11 for further information.
28 Generally, check the suspension and steering attachments for security and wear.
29 Check the valve clearances (B 20 engine) and reset if necessary. Full information will be found in Chapter 1.

---

4   Every 12,000 miles (20,000 km) or 12 months

---

1   Carry out the service items for the 6,000 mile (10,000 km) service.
2   Renew the spark plugs. Refer to Chapter 4.
3   Generally lubricate all locks, catches and hinges.
4   Thoroughly examine all electrical connections and fuel lines for signs of deterioration and damage.
5   Check the pad thickness of the front wheel brakes with the help of a mirror and 0.12 in (3 mm) wire gauge. If less than 0.12 in remains (the wire gauge will not fit), the pads should be considered worn out. If the wire gauge fits but the clearance is small it should be noted that the pads will not last another 12,000 miles (20,000 km).
6   Check the pad thickness of the rear wheel brakes. When 0.04 in (1 mm) remains between the base plate of the lining and the tensioning spring, the pads are worn out.
7   Check the valve clearances and reset if necessary. Full information will be found in Chapter 1.

Fig. 3. Lubrication points - body

No.	Lubricating point
1	Engine bonnet lock
2	Bonnet hinges
3	Sliding roof wind deflector
4	Door check assy.
5	Striker plates
6	Boot lid hinges
7	Door hinges
8	Door hinges
	Door stops
9	Front seat slide rails and latch devices
10	Window winders
	Lock device (on the inside of the doors)
11	Keyholes
12	Boot lid lock
	Keyhole

8   Clean the recirculation valve, pipes and connection nipple in the exhaust manifold.

5   Every 15,000 miles (24,000 km) or 15 months

1   Clean the fuel tank filter (fuel injection - CI).
2   Clean EGR valve.
3   Renew Lambda-sond sensor.

6   Every 24,000 miles (40,000 km) or 18 months

1   Carry out the service items for the 6,000 and 12,000 mile service.
2   Drive the car until the oil in the transmission and final drive is thoroughly warm, drain and refill the systems.
3   Renew the air cleaner element, as described in Chapter 3.
4   *Fuel injection engine* - Change the fuel filter.
5   Check condition of crankcase ventilation hoses and for possible blockage. Remove and clean the nipple in the inlet manifold. Replace the flame guard.

7   Every 32,000 miles (48,000 km) or two years

1   Drain and refill the cooling system with fresh coolant as described in Chapter 2.
2   Renew EGR valve.

8   Every 36,000 miles (60,000 km)

Change the timing gears drivebelt on B21 engines. Full information is given in Chapter 1.

9   Every three years

Drain the brake hydraulic system, renew all rubber seals and refill with fresh fluid. Bleed the system.

Jacking and towing

Jacking

The jack supplied with the car tool kit should be used only for changing a roadwheel. Whenever repair or overhaul operations are being carried out jack the car in the following positions and always supplement the jack with axle stands placed under the body side frame.
Raising the front end. Place the jack under the front axle member.
Raising the rear end: Place the jack under the tubular section of the axle casing as close to the trailing arm as possible.

Towing

Towing eyes are fitted to the front and rear of the car and any towing hooks or ropes should always be attached to these points only. Always remember to unlock the steering wheel in order to steer the car.

Bear in mind that the servo assistance does not function when the engine is not running, so the brake pedal will have to be depressed with greater force.

For cars with automatic transmission the gear selector must be in position 'N' and the car must not be towed for a distance exceeding 20 miles (32 km) or at a speed in excess of 20 mph (32 kph).

If it is necessary to tow a car with automatic transmission for more than 20 miles (32 km), remove the propeller shaft.

Chapter 1 Part A : Overhead camshaft engines

For modifications, and information applicable to later models, see Supplement at end of manual

Contents

Specifications

Engine (B 21) - general

	B 21A	B 21E
Type		
Max output:*		
HP at rev/min DIN	100/5250	123/5500
KW at rev/min DIN	74/5280	90/5520
Max torque:*		
lbf ft at rev/min DIN	125/3000	125/3500
kgf m at rev/min DIN	17.3/3000	17.3/3500
Compression pressure at 250 - 300 rpm (warm engine turned over with starter)	128 - 156 psi (9 - 11 kg/sq cm)	128 - 156 psi (9 -11 kg/sq cm)
Compression ratio	8.5 : 1	9.3 : 1
Number of cylinders	4	4
Bore	3.622 in (92 mm)	3.622 in (92 mm)
Stroke	3.150 in (80 mm)	3.150 in (80 mm)
Capacity	130 cu in (2127 cc)	130 cu in (2127 cc)
Weight (approx.)	340 lb (155 kg)	365 lb (165 kg)

Typical figures which vary with emission control system and compression ratio

Pistons

Material	Light alloy
Permissible weight difference between pistons in same engine	0.35 oz (10 g)
Length	2.79 in (71 mm)
Clearance in bore	0.0004 - 0.0012 in (0.01 - 0.03 mm)
Compression rings:	
Number on each piston	2
Width	0.078 in (1.98 mm)
Gap	0.0138 - 0.0217 in (0.35 - 0.55 mm)
Side clearance in groove	0.0016 - 0.0028 in (0.040 - 0.072 mm)
Oil scraper ring:	
Number on each piston	1
Width	0.1566 - 0.1571 in (3.978 - 3.990 mm)
Gap	0.010 - 0.016 in (0.25 - 0.40 mm)
Side clearance in groove	0.0012 - 0.0024 in (0.030 - 0.062 mm)
Gudgeon pins (general):	
Arrangement	Fully floating with circlips at both ends
Fit in con-rod	Sliding fit
Fit in piston	Push fit
Gudgeon pin diameter:	
Standard	0.945 in (24.00 mm)
Oversize	0.947 in (24.05 mm)

Cylinder head

Material	Light alloy
Height between cylinder head joint face and face for bolt head	3.74 in (95.1 mm)

Valves

Inlet valves:	
Seat angle in cylinder head	45°
Valve seat angle	45.5°
Seat width in cylinder head	0.08 in (2 mm)
Valve head diameter	1.732 in (44 mm)
Stem diameter	0.3132 - 0.3138 in (7.955 - 7.970 mm)
Exhaust valves:	
Seat angle in cylinder head	45°
Valve seat angle	44.5°
Seat width in cylinder head	0.080 in (2 mm)
Valve head diameter	1.378 in (35 mm)
Stem diameter	0.3120 - 0.3126 in (7.925 - 7.940 mm)
Valve clearance - inlet and exhaust	
Adjusting cold	0.014 - 0.016 in (0.35 - 0.40 mm)
Adjusting hot	0.016 - 0.018 in (0.40 - 0.45 mm)

Valve guides

Length	2.047 (52 mm)
Inner diameter	0.3150 - 0.3159 in (8.000 - 8.022 mm)
Height above cylinder head face:	
Inlet	0.606 - 0.614 in (15.4 - 15.6 mm)
Exhaust	0.705 - 0.713 in (17.9 - 18.1 mm)

Valve springs

Free-length	1.77 in (45 mm)
With load of 62 - 70 lb (28 - 32 kg)	1.50 in (38 mm)
With load of 156 - 174 lb (72 - 80 kg)	1.06 in (27 mm)

Valve tappets

Diameter	1.4557 - 1.4565 in (36.975 - 36.995 mm)
Adjuster washer:	
Thickness	0.13 - 0.18 in (3.3 - 4.5 mm) in steps of 0.002 in (0.05 mm)

Crankshaft

Endfloat	0.0015 - 0.0058 in (0.037 - 0.147 mm)
Big-end bearing clearance	0.0009 - 0.0028 in (0.024 - 0.070 mm)
Main bearings clearance	0.0011 - 0.0033 in (0.028 - 0.083 mm)
Main bearing journals:	
Diameter:	
Standard	2.4981 - 2.4986 in (62.451 - 63.464 mm)
Undersize 1	2.4882 - 2.4886 in (63.197 - 63.210 mm)
Undersize 2	2.4781 - 2.4786 in (62.943 - 62.956 mm)
Width on crankshaft for flange bearing shell:	
Standard	1.5338 - 1.5351 in (38.960 - 39.000 mm)
Oversize 1	1.5438 - 1.5451 in (39.061 - 39.101 mm)
Oversize 2	1.5538 - 1.5551 in (39.163 - 39.203 mm)

Big-end bearing journals:
    Bearing seat width ... ...   1.179 - 1.183 in (29.95 - 30.05 mm)
    Diameter:
        Standard ... ...   2.1255 - 2.1260 in (53.987 - 54.000 mm)
        Undersize 1 ... ...   2.1155 - 2.1160 in (53.733 - 53.746 mm)
        Undersize 2 ... ...   2.1055 - 2.1060 in (53.479 - 53.492 mm)

Connecting rods

Endfloat on crankshaft ... ...   0.006 - 0.014 in (0.15 - 0.35 mm)
Length between centres ... ...   5.71 ± 0.0039 in (145 ± 1 mm)
Permissible weight difference between con-rods on same engine ...   35 oz (10 gramme)

Camshaft

Marking/MAX lift height:
    B21A 1975 ... ...   A/0.39 in (9.8 mm)
    B21A 1976 on ... ...   A/0.41 in (10.5 mm)
    B21E ... ...   D/0.44 in (11.2 mm)
Number of bearings   5
Journal diameter ... ...   1.1437 - 1.1445 in (29.050 - 29.070 mm)
Radial clearance ... ...   0.0012 - 0.0028 in (0.030 - 0.071 mm)
Endfloat ... ...   0.004 - 0.016 in (0.1 - 0.4 mm)
Valve clearance for camshaft setting (cold engine) ... ...   0.028 in (0.7 mm)
Inlet valve should then open at:
    B21A 1975 ... ...   5° btdc
    B21A 1976 on ... ...   13° btdc
    B21E ... ...   15° btdc
Diameter of camshaft bearings ... ...   1.1811 - 1.819 in (30.000 - 30.021 mm)

Timing gears

Number of teeth:
    Crankshaft gear   19
    Intermediate gear   38
    Camshaft gear   38
    Drivebelt   123

Intermediate shaft

Number of bearings   3
Diameter bearing journal:
    Front ... ...   1.8494 - 1.8504 in (46.975 - 47.000 mm)
    Intermediate ... ...   1.6939 - 1.6949 in (43.025 - 43.050 mm)
Radial clearance ... ...   0.0008 - 0.0030 in (0.020 - 0.75 mm)
Endfloat ... ...   0.008 - 0.018 in (0.20 - 0.46 mm)
Diameter of bearing in block:
    Front ... ...   1.8512 - 1.8524 in (47.020 - 47.050 mm)
    Intermediate ... ...   1.6957 - 1.6968 in (43.070 - 43.100 mm)
    Rear ... ...   1.6917 - 1.6929 in (42.970 - 43.000 mm)

Flywheel

Permissible axial throw (max) ... ...   0.002 in (0.05 mm) at diameter of 5.9 in (150 mm)

Lubrication system

Oil capacity:
    With oil filter ... ...   6.8 Imp pints (8.1 US pints : 3.85 litre)
    Without oil filter ... ...   5.9 Imp pints (7.1 US pints : 3.35 litre)
Oil pressure at 2000 rpm (engine warm) ... ...   37 - 85 psi (2.5 - 6.0 kg/cm^2)
Oil filter - type ... ...   Full flow
Oil pump:
    Type ... ...   Gear type pump
    Number of teeth on each gear   9
    Endfloat ... ...   0.0008 - 0.0047 in (0.02 - 0.12 mm)
    Radial clearance ... ...   0.0008 - 0.0035 in (0.02 - 0.09 mm)
    Backlash ... ...   0.0059 - 0.0138 in (0.15 - 0.35 mm)
Relief valve spring length:
    Free-length ... ...   1.54 in (39.2 mm)
    With load of 11 ± 0.8 lb (5 ± 0.4 kg) ... ...   1.03 in (26.25 mm)
    With load of 15 ± 1.8 lb (7 ± 0.8 kg) ... ...   0.83 in (21 mm)

Torque wrench settings

Cylinder head (cold):	lbf ft	kgf m
Stage 1	44	6
Stage 2	81	11
Main bearings	92	12.5
Big-end bearings	46	6.3
Flywheel	52	7
Spark plugs	18	2.5
Camshaft bearings	15	2
Camshaft gear bolt	37	5

Intermediate shaft gear bolt	...	...	...	...	...	...	...	37	5
Oil sump bolts	...	...	...	...	...	...	...	8	1.1
Crankshaft gear bolt	...	...	...	...	...	...	...	122	16.5
Tensioner retaining nut	...	...	...	...	...	...	...	37	5

1 General description

The B21 engine is an in-line, four cylinder, fluid cooled, overhead camshaft engine. The B21 has two versions - B21A and B21E. The primary difference between them is in the different fuel systems they use. The B21A is a carburettor engine and the B21E has a fuel injection system of the Bosch CI type.

The B21E has a higher output, not only due to the fuel injection but also because of the higher compression ratio and a different type of camshaft with greater lifting height. The greater compression ratio on the B21E is achieved through flat piston crowns, while the pistons on the B21A have concave tops. Otherwise, the basic engine is the same for both versions.

The cylinder block is made of cast iron, in one piece, with the cylinder bores drilled directly in the block. An intermediate shaft for driving the ignition distributor, the lubricating oil pump and the fuel pump (B21A engines) is carried in three bearings on the left-hand side.

The cylinder head is made of aluminium alloy and the camshaft is carried in five bearings machined in the head and bearing caps. The cams of the camshaft operate directly on the valve tappets. The camshaft is driven by a toothed rubber belt, which also drives the intermediate shaft, from a pinion on the crankshaft.

The crankshaft has five main bearings which run in replaceable bearing shells. The connecting rods are made of drop forged steel and have pressed-in bronze bushings which act as bearings for the gudgeon pins at the small end. The big-end bearings are replaceable shell bearings.

The pistons are made of light alloy and have two compression rings and one oil scraper ring. The upper compression ring is chromed in order to reduce cylinder wear.

The cylinder head is bolted to the block (ie there are no studs in the block). The combustion chambers are cast and have separate inlet and exhaust ports, one for each valve. The valves are made of special steel and run in replaceable valve guides. Rubber seals are fitted on the top side of the inlet valve guides to prevent excessive oil from penetrating down between the guides and the valve stems. The seals are fitted only on the inlet valve guides where risk of oil being sucked in is greatest.

The engine lubrication system is of the conventional type with pressure lubrication of the main and big-end bearings, the intermediate shaft bearings and the camshaft bearings, and splash lubrication of the gudgeon pins and pistons. The camshaft works in a bath of oil which is fed from the camshaft bearings. The lubrication channel to the camshaft bearings comes from the main oil line. The three bearings on the intermediate shaft are supplied with oil through oilways from the main bearing housings. The engine timing gears are mounted on the outside of the engine and do not require any lubrication.

The gear type oil pump is driven by a gear on the intermediate shaft and has a spring-loaded ball-type relief valve fitted in the pump. On the discharge side of the pump there is a bleeder valve. In the event of the oil pump taking in air (eg. when taking a sharp bend with a low oil level), the bleeder valve ensures that the pump resumes its delivery in spite of the air mixture.

All oil supplied by the oil pump passes through a filter, located

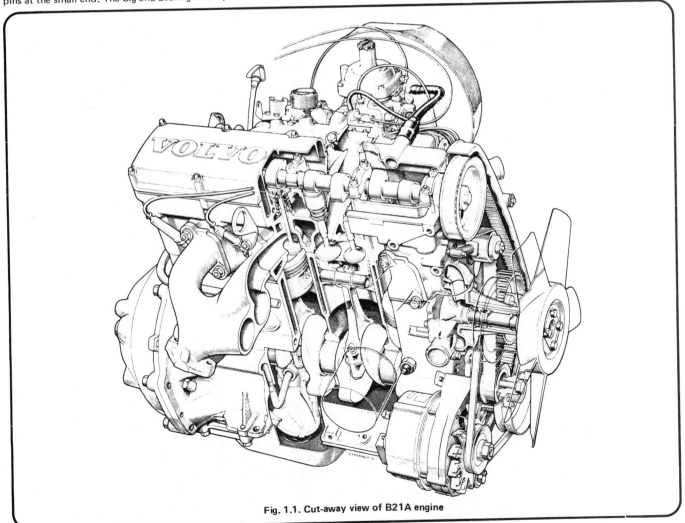

Fig. 1.1. Cut-away view of B21A engine

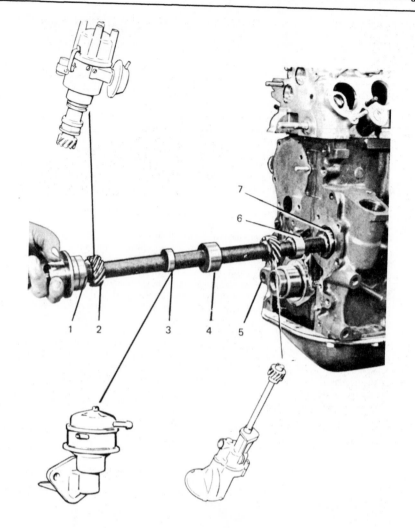

Fig. 1.2. The intermediate shaft

1 Front bearing
2 Gear for driving the ignition distributor
3 Cam for fuel pump
4 Intermediate bearing
5 Gear for driving oil pump
6 Support (used in manufacture)
7 Rear bearing

on the right-hand side of the engine, before going to the various lubricating points. The filter contains a bypass valve which allows oil to bypass the filter should resistance to flow become excessive (blocked filter) and a non-return valve which prevents the filter from being emptied when the engine is switched off.

2 Engine removal - when is it necessary?

1 Because engine removal is a bothersome job for the ordinary owner whose lifting tackle may well consist of nothing more than a barely adequate pulley block, he will naturally want to do all he can with the engine still in place. The Volvo owner is fortunate in that he can remove the complete front section of the car and this gives very good access to the front of the engine. This means that such jobs as replacing the camshaft or timing gears present no problems with the engine in the vehicle. Removing the sump is a little awkward and has a Section to itself later on (Section 38). Once it is removed, you can deal with the big-end bearings, and with these removed and the head off you can push the connecting rods up the cylinders and remove the pistons.
2 This means that you can get at the engine sufficiently well to give it a thorough examination in order to decide whether, for example, it needs a re-bore or the crankshaft needs grinding, to say nothing of carrying out quite a range of repairs, without having to take the engine out of the car. Nevertheless, if you are faced with replacing the crankshaft or main bearings or if you have got to do anything on the flywheel more difficult than straightforward replacement of the clutch assembly, you will have to take the engine out.

3 Engine - removal (general)

1 The engine can be removed and replaced quite easily with the gearbox attached. However, we recommend that the automatic transmission (where fitted) be removed before the engine because of the high weight factor.
2 It is not necessary to remove the front section of the body when removing the engine but to provide better access we removed the front grille, cover plate and stay.
3 Although Volvo instructions for removing the engine make no mention of dropping the front axle member slightly, we found this to be necessary when removing the engine from the car shown in the photographs. For this a mobile hoist, axle stands and a jack are required.

4 Engine (carburettor models) - removal

1 Disconnect the leads from the battery.
2 Disconnect the windscreen washer hose and the engine compartment light and cable from the bonnet. With the help of an assistant, take the weight of the bonnet and remove the bolts securing the bonnet to the bonnet hinges. Carefully lift the bonnet over the front of the car. Store in a safe place, away from the immediate work area, where it will not get scratched or damaged (photo).
3 Jack-up the front of the car and place axle stands or other secure supports at the jacking points behind the front wheels. Chock the rear wheels.
4 Remove the drain plug and drain off the oil into a container (photo).
5 Carefully drain the cooling system and remove the fan shroud and the radiator, as described in Chapter 2.

4.2 Bonnet securing bolts

4.4 Sump drain plug

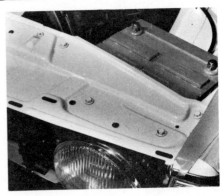
4.6a Remove the cover plate

4.6b Removing the cover plate stay

4.7 Removing the air cleaner

Fig. 1.3. Removing the servo pump (Sec. 4)

6   Remove the front grille, cover plate and stay (photo).
7   Remove the air cleaner, as described in Chapter 3 (photo).
8   *Cars with power steering:* remove the servo pump and bracket by removing the tensioning bolt and tilting up the pump. Lift off the belt and remove the bolts securing the bracket to the engine block.
9   *Cars with power steering and air-conditioning:* remove the servo pump by removing the bolts on the tensioning bar, lifting off the belt and placing the servo pump securely on the inside of the casing. Remove the pulley on the crankshaft, lift off the compressor belt and replace the pulley temporarily with two bolts. Remove the compressor and its bracket and place the compressor securely on the inside of the wheel arch (valance). *On no account disconnect the hoses from the compressor*, otherwise the air-conditioning system will have to be evacuated and this requires special equipment and may cause danger to health.
10 Disconnect the earth strap from the engine block, and the valve cover (photo).
11 Disconnect the low tension lead, and the high tension lead from the coil. Remove the distributor cap complete with plug leads (photo).
12 Disconnect the leads from the starter motor. Disconnect the lead from the charging regulator and remove the clamp (photo).
13 Disconnect the fuel inlet pipe from the fuel pump and blank-off the pipe.
14 Disconnect the servo brake hose from the engine and the heater hoses from the bulkhead at the rear of the engine block.
15 Disconnect the throttle and choke controls (photo).
16 Disconnect the leads from the water temperature and oil pressure switches.
17 Remove the pre-heating plate from the exhaust manifold.
18 Remove the nuts securing the exhaust pipe flanges (photo).
19 Remove the front engine mounting bolts (photo).
20 Remove the bracket for the front exhaust pipe clamp (photo).
21 Disconnect the clutch cable from the operating fork and its support on the clutch housing (cable actuation) or disconnect the hydraulic pipe from the slave cylinder (hydraulic actuation) (photo).
22 Release the rubber gaiter from the gearlever. Remove the retaining pin and the gearlever. Disconnect the lead for the reversing lights (photos).

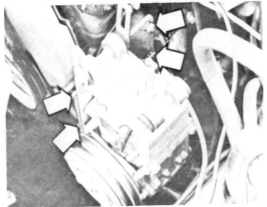
Fig. 1.4. Removing the air-conditioning compressor (Sec. 4)

23 Disconnect the speedometer cable from the gearbox (photo).
24 Remove the bolts from the front propeller shaft, and lower it to the ground.
25 Disconnect the link arm from the gearlever end, (5 mm Allen key) and from the gearbox. On cars with overdrive disconnect the cable to the gearlever (photos).
26 Position a jack under the gearbox and remove the gearbox support member (photos).
27 Using a hoist and a suitable sling, support the weight of the engine/gearbox. Check that all controls, cables and pipes have been disconnected and tucked out of the way.
28 Commence lifting the engine, lifting the rear downwards to clear the bulkhead until the sump clears the front axle member. At this stage we found it necessary to slacken off the front axle member retaining bolts and drop the front axle member slightly to allow the sump to clear the axle, when being pulled forward (photos).
29 Continue lifting the unit and pull it forward clear of the engine compartment. Lower the engine to the ground and support it so that it can't fall over.

4.10 Earth strap from valve cover to bulkhead

4.11a Ignition coil with HT lead removed

4.11b Removing the distributor cap and plug leads

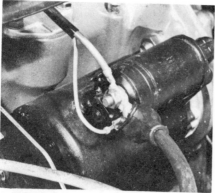
4.12 Disconnecting the leads from the starter motor

4.15 Disconnecting the throttle cable

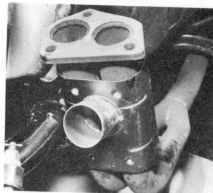
4.18 Exhaust pipe disconnected

4.19 Removing the front engine mounting bolts

4.20 Removing the bracket for the front exhaust pipe clamp

4.21 Disconnecting the clutch slave cylinder

4.22a Removing the gear lever retaining pin

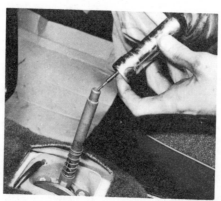
4.22b Lifting out the gear lever

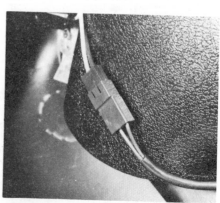
4.22c Disconnecting the lead for the reversing light switch

4.23 Disconnecting the speedometer cable from the gearbox

4.25a Disconnecting the link arm at the gear lever

4.25b Removing the link arm from the gearbox

4.25c Gearbox with propeller shaft, speedometer cable and link arm disconnected

4.26a Gearbox support member retaining bolts

4.26b Gearbox flexible mounting

4.26c Gearbox mounting retaining nut

4.28a Lifting out the engine

4.28b The front axle member retaining bolts

5 Engine (fuel injection models) - removal

1 The removal sequence is basically the same as that described in Section 4, but there are several points that should be noted, relative to the disconnecting of the fuel injection equipment.
2 Disconnect the crankcase ventilation hose.
3 Disconnect the four vacuum hoses from the engine.
4 Disconnect the clutch cable from the clamp on the starter motor.
5 Disconnect the cable to the air-conditioning from the solenoid valve on the shutter housing (where fitted) and pull the cable forward.
6 Remove the tank cap (to eliminate any over pressure in the system). Disconnect the hose from the filter and the return hose from the return pipe. Remove the guard plate for the pre-engaging resistor (Fig. 1.5). On later models the pre-engaging resistor is mounted behind the radiator grille.
7 Disconnect the plug contacts from the pre-engaging resistor, four on the cable harness and bands, two from the relay and one from the pre-engaging resistor switch.

6 Engine (automatic transmission models) - removal

When automatic transmission is fitted it is recommended that because of the weight involved, the automatic transmission unit should be removed first, as described in Chapter 6, and then the engine removed in the normal way.

7 Engine - dismantling (general)

1 The essential preliminary to dismantling an engine is cleaning. The ideal way to do this is to brush the engine all over with paraffin or, better, 'Gunk' or a similar commercial solvent. Allow it to stand for a while and then hose it down. Where the dirt is thick and deeply embedded, work the solvent into it with a wire brush. If the engine is very dirty a second application may be necessary here and there.

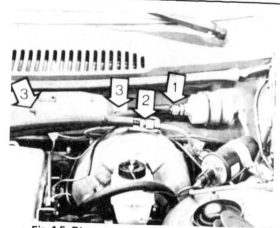

Fig. 1.5. Disconnecting the fuel hoses (Sec. 5)

1   Hose from filter
2   Return pipe hose
3   Guard plate retaining screws

Finally, wipe down the outside of the engine with a rag. If it is not possible to use a pressure hose to remove the dirt and solvent, cleaning will be much more laborious, but however laborious it is, it will pay in the long run. After all, the engine has got to be cleaned at the end of the dismantling process, so it might just as well be as clean as possible at the start.

2   Clean each part as the engine is stripped. Try to ensure that everything taken off - down to the smallest washer - goes back exactly where it came from and exactly the same way round. This means laying the various bits and pieces out in a tidy manner. Nuts, bolts and washers may often be replaced finger tight from where they were removed.

3   Most parts can easily be cleaned by washing them in paraffin and

wiping down with a cloth, but do not immerse parts with oilways in paraffin. They are best wiped down with a petrol or paraffin dampened cloth, and the oilways cleaned out with nylon pipe cleaners.

4   Re-use of old gaskets is false economy. Oil and water leaks will always result even if nothing worse. Always use genuine Volvo gaskets obtainable from Volvo garages. Volvo say that jointing compound should not be used with any of their gaskets.

5   Do not throw the old gaskets away as the engine is stripped down. These may be used for checking the pattern of new ones or as templates for making gaskets for which replacements are difficult to obtain. Hang up the old gaskets as they are removed.

6   In this Chapter we have described the order in which we stripped down the engine shown in most of the photographs. Where it seems necessary we have explained why we removed or did not remove certain parts at certain times. Generally speaking when stripping an engine it is best to work from the top down, at least once you have removed the gearbox. Support it with wood blocks so that it stands firmly on its sump or the base of the crankcase to start with. When the stage of removing the crankshaft and connecting rods is reached, turn it on its side and carry out all subsequent work with it in this position.

8   Engine - dismantling procedure

1   Remove the bolts securing the gearbox to the engine and separate the gearbox and engine (photo).
2   Remove the exhaust manifold (photo).
3   Disconnect the ignition setting sender (17 mm open ring spanner).
4   *Carburettor engines:* disconnect the fuel pump to carburettor pipe, the coolant hose to the inlet manifold, the vacuum hose and the crankcase ventilation hose. Remove the inlet manifold and fuel pump (photo).
5   *On fuel injection engines:* disconnect the crankcase ventilation hose, the lead and fuel line from the cold-start valve, the lead and hoses from the auxiliary air valve. Remove the cold-start valve (5 mm Allen key) and the auxiliary air valve. Remove the stay between the block and

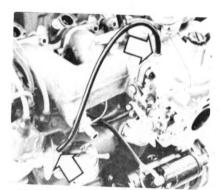

8.1 Separating the gearbox and engine

8.2 Removing the exhaust manifold

8.3 Disconnecting the ignition setting sender

Fig. 1.6. Disconnecting the vacuum hose (Sec. 8)

Fig. 1.7. Disconnecting the crankcase ventilation hose (Sec. 8)

8.4 Removing the fuel pump

inlet manifold and the vacuum hose, slacken the upper hose clamp at the rubber bellows and remove the inlet manifold. Disconnect the pipes to the injectors, the electrical connections and remove the fuel distributor and control pressure regulator.

6 Remove the starter motor, the temperature sensor and, on E type engines, the thermal timer sensor.

7 Remove the engine mountings. Remove the bolt securing the dipstick tube.

8 Disconnect the leads from the alternator, remove the bolts from the tensioning bar and lift off the belts. Remove the alternator and

bracket. Remove the fan (photos).

9 Remove the pulley from the water pump.

10 Disconnect the lead and remove the oil pressure sensor (photo).

11 Remove the oil filter (photo).

12 Remove the distributor (photo).

13 Remove the cover protecting the timing gears.

14 Remove the coolant pipe to the heater element and remove the water pump. Remove the thermostat housing, the thermostat and the lifting eye (photos).

15 Slacken the belt tensioner nut and slacken the belt by pushing the roller back against the spring. Lock the spring by inserting a 3 mm pin (eg. drill) in the hole on the thrust pin. Remove the toothed drive-belt.

16 Remove the retaining nut and washer and pull off the belt tensioner roller.

17 Restrain the camshaft from turning (a bar in one of the holes) and remove the camshaft gear retaining nut. The gear wheel and guide plates can be pulled off by hand.

18 Remove the six bolts securing the crankshaft pulley and lift off the pulley. Remove the centre bolt from the front of the crankshaft and remove the front hub (photo).

19 Remove the crankshaft gear and guide plate. Use a puller, if necessary.

20 Remove the retaining bolt and gearwheel from the intermediate shaft.

21 Remove the cable harness and the rear part of the belt guard. Remove the front sealing flange and press out the seals (photo).

22 Remove the oil pump pinion cover and lift out the oil pump pinion. Pull out the intermediate shaft taking care that the shaft gear does not damage the bearing bushing in the engine block (photo).

23 Remove the valve cover and gasket. Remove the cylinder head bolts,

Fig. 1.8. Removing the inlet manifold (Sec. 8)

Fig. 1.9. Removing the fuel distributor and control pressure regulator (Sec. 8)

1   *Electrical connections*   3   *Retaining bolts*
2   *Injectors*

Fig. 1.10. Removing the temperature sensor (Sec. 8)

1   *Temperature sensor*   2   *Thermal timer sensor (E engines)*

8.8a Alternator earth cable

8.8b Removing the alternator

8.10 Removing the oil pressure sensor

8.11 The oil filter

8.12 Removing the distributor

Fig. 1.11. Removing the drivebelt guard casing (Sec. 8)

8.14a Disconnecting the pipe from the water pump to the heater element

8.14b Removing the thermostat housing and the lifting eye

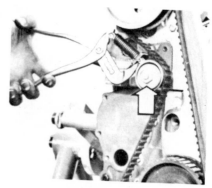

Fig. 1.12. Releasing the tension on the drivebelt and removing the tensioner roller and drivebelt (Sec. 8)

8.18 Removing the crankshaft gear and guide plate

8.21 Removing the bolts securing the rear part of the belt guard

8.22 Taking off the oil pump pinion cover and lifting out the oil pump pinion

Fig. 1.13. Withdrawing the intermediate shaft (Sec. 8)

8.24a Removing the clutch assembly

8.24b Pilot bearing retaining circlip

10 mm(3/8 in) Allen key, and lift off the head.

24 Unscrew the bolts holding the clutch assembly to the flywheel a little at a time, keeping them in step to avoid the risk of distorting the clutch cover. Mark the clutch assembly and flywheel to identify position for replacement and remove the clutch assembly. Remove the circlip retaining the pilot bearing and remove the washer and bearing (photos).

25 Restrain the flywheel from turning and remove the eight retaining bolts. Remove the flywheel taking care not to push in the ignition setting sender. On cars with automatic transmission a drive plate with ring gear, a support plate and flange are fitted in place of a flywheel (photo).

26 Remove the reinforcing bracket. Remove the rear sealing flange and press out the seal.

27 Remove the sump. Remove the oil pump and the 'O' ring seals from the block and also from the pipe, if fitted (photo).

28 Check the marking on the connecting rods and caps, and mark the pistons accordingly, so that they can be identified regarding their respective cylinders when being refitted. The five main bearing caps are marked 1 to 5 with No. 1 at the front. When removing bearing shells, mark them too, so that they can be refitted in the same location if they are not being renewed.

29 Remove the pistons and connecting rods by removing the bearing caps and shells and pushing the connecting rods through the cylinders and steadying the pistons as they emerge. Take care not to scratch or damage the pistons as they are removed (photo).

30 Remove the main bearing caps and lift out the crankshaft. Remove the spacer sleeve on the front end of the crankshaft. Remove the bearing shells from the engine block and caps (photos).

9 Cylinder head, valves and camshaft - overhaul

1 Remove the spark plugs and injectors (if fitted).

8.25 Removing the flywheel retaining bolts

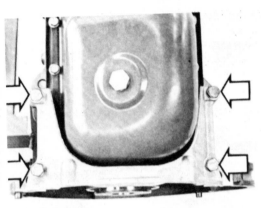

Fig. 1.14. Reinforcing bracket retaining bolts (Sec. 8)

8.27 Removing the oil pump

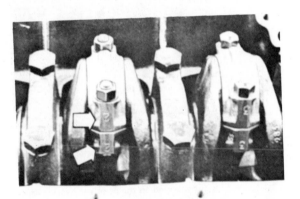

Fig. 1.15. Identification marking on connecting rods and caps (Sec. 8)

8.29 Removing the connecting rod caps

8.30a Lifting out the crankshaft

8.30b Remove the main bearing shells from the engine block

2   Check the marking on the camshaft bearing caps, they are numbered 1 - 5 from the front (Fig. 1.16). Slacken off the cap retaining nuts, evenly and in rotation till the tension is off the camshaft, then remove the bearing caps and the camshaft. Remove the front seal and the half-moon shaped rubber seal at the rear of the cylinder head.

3   Lift out the valve tappets and remove the rubber rings. Identify the tappets to their location so that they can be fitted in the same position on reassembly (photo).

4   Clean the oil and grease off the cylinder head and remove the carbon from the combustion chambers and valve heads with a scraper or a rotary wire brush.

5   Using a suitable valve spring compressing tool, compress the spring until the collets are free from their recess, remove the collets, release the pressure on the spring, lift off the upper spring retainer, the spring and the lower spring retainer. Push the valve through the valve guide and remove it. If the valve seems a tight fit in the guide, this may be because the upper part of the stem has carbon on it. Give it a clean in this case. Remove the valve stem seals from the inlet valve guides (photos).

6   Keep the valves lined up in the order you remove them, and place them with their springs and retainers together with their tappets.

7   With the valves removed, clean out any carbon from the ports. Examine the valve seats, if they are only slightly pitted it is possible to make them smooth again by grinding the valves against the seats, as described in Section 11. Where pitting is very deep they will have to be recut: a job for the specialist with the necessary equipment.

8   Check the valve guides with the valve stems to ensure that they are a good fit: the stems should move easily in the guides without side play. Worn guides can be extracted and new ones installed but this should be left to your Volvo agent.

9   Examine the valves, checking them for straightness and the condition of the face. Slight pitting can be removed by grinding-in, but if the pitting is deep the valve will have to be machine ground by a specialist.

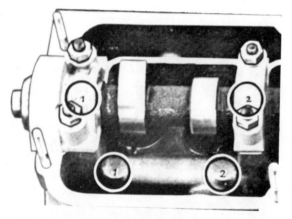

Fig. 1.16. Checking the marking on the camshaft bearing caps and cylinder head (Secs. 9 and 27)

10 The camshaft and its bearings in the cylinder head are part of the Volvo engine which seems virtually everlasting. If there should be noticeable play between the camshaft and its bearings, or if the bearings are damaged then the cylinder head will have to be renewed as the bearings are machined in the head. If very light scratches are present on the camshaft these can be removed by gently rubbing down with a very fine grade emery cloth or oil stone. The greatest care must be taken to keep the cam profiles smooth.

10 Tappets and adjuster washers - inspection

1   Examine the tappets for scoring or damage. Place them in the cylinder head and check that they move easily but have no noticeable side play.

2   Check the condition of the adjuster washers; if they show signs of wear they must be renewed.

11 Valves and valve seats - grinding-in

1   Grinding-in is essential when fitting valves whether these, or their seats, be new or old. As well as removing every trace of scoring, it ensures that the valve face and the seat have exactly the same slope and hence a reasonably wide area of contact. Where new valves are being fitted to correctly re-cut seats, grinding is still essential, because - as you can see from the specifications at the start of the Chapter - a valve face is cut to an angle which is very slightly less than that of the face in the cylinder head and consequently the contact area is very small. The correct area of contact is obtained by grinding.

2   Valve grinding is a simple matter, needing only fine and coarse carborundum paste, an inexpensive tool and a great deal of patience. Fig. 1.17 illustrates the procedure. Place the cylinder head upside down on a bench with a block of wood at each end to give clearance for the valve stems.

3   Smear a trace of coarse paste on the seat face, apply a suction tool to the valve head and insert the valve into the cylinder head. Press lightly on the tool using the palms of the hands and rotate the tool with a to-and-fro motion, then lift the valve from the seat and give it a quarter or half a turn before repeating the process. When a dull, matt, even surface finish is produced on both the valve seat and the valve, wipe off the coarse paste and carry on with the fine paste, lifting and turning the valve as before. When a smooth unbroken ring of light grey matt finish is produced on both valves and valve seat faces, the grinding operation is complete.

Aim to get a seat width in accordance with the Specifications at the start of the Chapter. If the seat is too wide, you can reduce the width by carefully rounding off the corners with an oil stone.

4   When the grinding is complete, clean away every trace of grinding compound with paraffin or petrol. Take great care that none is left in the ports or the valve guides.

12 Pistons and piston rings - examination and renovation

1   If the old pistons are to be refitted, carefully remove the piston

9.3 Lift out the tappets

9.5a Compressing the valve spring and removing the collets

9.5b Lifting out the valve spring

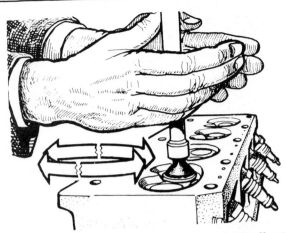

Fig. 1.17. Valve grinding, using hand suction tool. Lift off seat occasionally to spread grinding paste evenly over seat and valve face (Sec. 11)

Fig. 1.18. Measuring the piston ring gap with feeler gauge (Sec. 12)

Fig. 1.19. Measuring piston ring clearance in groove with feeler gauge (Sec. 12)

13.1 Slot on piston top (must face forward when piston is fitted in cylinder)

round the groove and inserting the feeler gauges (Fig. 1.19). For correct clearances, see Specifications at the beginning of this Chapter. Note that of the two compression rings, the chromium plated one goes at the top. The scraper ring, which is grooved fits in the bottom groove.
5   In engine manufacture the cylinders are all machined simultaneously and because of this have very slight differences in diameter. This is allowed for by selecting pistons to fit each bore; this is why it is so important when refitting old pistons that they should be replaced in the cylinders that they came from.

13 Gudgeon pins - general

1   The gudgeon pins are retained in the pistons by circlips and can easily be pushed out of the pistons when these are removed. When you separate the connecting rod from the piston, mark the connecting rod so that you can refit it the same way round. There is no need to mark the piston as this has a small slot (which must always face forwards when the piston is in the engine) on the top (photo).
2   The fit of the gudgeon pin in the connecting rod should be such that it can be pushed out with light thumb pressure but should have no noticeable looseness. It should fit in the piston so that you can push it through by hand, against light resistance. If the gudgeon pin hole in the piston is worn, an over-sized gudgeon pin must be fitted. In this case the holes must be reamed out in line to the correct measurement (see paragraph 4).
3   If the bush in the connecting rod is worn, it can be pressed out and a new bush pressed in. The new bush must be reamed to the correct fit.
4   Reaming is best carried out by someone who has suitable machinery and experience. If you do not come within this category, have it done through your Volvo agent.

14 Intermediate shaft - inspection

1   Examine the pinions for the distributor and oil pump for chipping or damage. Check the fuel pump operating cam for wear.
2   Fit the shaft in its bearings in the engine block. If there is noticeable play between the intermediate shaft and its bearings, they will have to be renewed, but this is a highly specialised job, involving the reaming of three bearings in line - definitely a task for the specialist.

15 Crankshaft and bearings - examination and renovation

1   Inspect the bearing shells for signs of general wear, scoring, pitting and scratches. The shells should be a matt grey in colour. If any trace of copper colour is noticed, it is an indication that the bearings are

rings and then thoroughly clean them. Take particular care to clean out the piston ring grooves. Do not scratch the comparatively soft material of the pistons in any way. Piston rings can be easily removed by raising one end and slipping a thin metal strip (such as an old feeler gauge of around 0.020 in (0.05 mm) underneath it. Slide the strip round the piston easing the ring out of the grooves as you go.
2   If new rings are to be fitted to the old pistons, then the top ring should be stepped so as to clear the ridge left above the previous top ring. If a normal but oversize new ring is fitted it will hit the ridge and break, because the new ring will not have worn in the same way as the old.
3   Before fitting the rings on the pistons, put them in the cylinder bore at a point below the bottom limit of their travel and check their gap (Fig. 1.18). This should be between 0.016 - 0.022 in (0.40 - 0.55 mm). If the ring gap is too small rub down the ends of the ring with a very fine file until it is correct. To keep the rings square in the bore for measurement, line them up with a piston in the bore.
4   Check the fit of the piston rings in the grooves by rolling them

badly worn, because the white metal is plated onto a copper coloured underlay.

2   The bearing shells will have figures stamped on them to indicate their size, and naturally ensure that the shells purchased are of the same size as the ones taken out.

3   Examine the bearing surfaces on the crankshaft for signs of scoring or scratches and check their ovality with a micrometer. Take measurements at a number of positions on each surface, paying particular attention to the surfaces of which the bearing shells show signs of wear. If there are differences in diameter of more than 0.002 in (0.05 mm) on the main bearing surfaces or 0.003 in (0.07 mm) on the big-end surfaces the crankshaft must be reground. It is probably worthwhile regrinding the crankshaft if it is found that the bearings are worn and the crankshaft ovality is appreciably more than half these figures.

4   Regrinding the crankshaft and subsequent fitting of under-sized bearing shells is a job for the specialist. If the reground crankshaft is returned with the bearing shells fitting to the surface, be sure not to change them round when refitting.

5   **Never** make any attempt to cure a noisy big-end by filing the bearing cap and/or working on the bearing shell.

16 Flywheel starter ring gear - renewal

1   The ring gear is a shrink fit on the flywheel. Replacing it needs care but is not really very difficult. Remove the old ring by drilling through it at the root of the gear teeth at two diametrically opposite points, being careful not to drill the actual flywheel. Drill as big a hole as possible and then break the ring gear with a hammer and cold chisel.

2   Heat up the new ring in the oven, setting the thermostat to 350°C (662°F). If possible, put the flywheel in the refrigerator or deep freeze for an hour or so at the same time.

3   Before the ring has time to cool, fit it over the flywheel and clamp it in position so that as it cools down it will be accurately positioned.

4   After refitting a ring, the flywheel (ideally the flywheel assembled to the crankshaft), should be balanced. Any out of balance is rectified by drilling on the flywheel close to, but not on, the joint between the wheel and the ring gear.

5   Do not be tempted to heat the ring gear with a flame. It is case-hardened and if the temperature is raised too much locally the casing will be softened.

17 Oil pump - overhaul

1   Dismantling the pump is straightforward: pull the delivery pipe out of its socket, remove the wire clip and take off the strainer. Remove the four bolts and remove the cover, the spring and ball. Remove the gears.

2   Clean the parts in petrol and wipe them dry with a non-fluffy cloth.

3   Examine the gears and housing for damage. Check the cover for wear. Fit the gears and check the backlash, this should be between 0.006 and 0.014 in (0.15 and 0.35 mm). Check the endfloat as shown in Fig. 1.22, this should be 0.0008 - 0.0047 in (0.02 - 0.12 mm). Check for wear by fitting the drive gear; the gear should rotate freely without side play. If wear is apparent the pump will have to be renewed.

4   Check the relief valve spring against the Specifications at the beginning of this Chapter, if it does not meet the specifications it must be renewed.

5   The sealing rings at each end of the delivery pipe are made of special rubber and are manufactured to very close tolerances. Use only Volvo parts when renewing them. When assembling the pump coat them with soapy water to ease fitment.

Fig. 1.20. Dismantling the oil pump (Sec. 17)

Fig. 1.21. Checking the backlash (Sec. 17)

Fig. 1.22. Checking the endfloat (Sec. 17)

Fig. 1.23. Replacing the relief valve ball and spring (Sec. 17)

18 Engine - reassembly (general)

1   To ensure maximum life with minimum trouble from a re-built engine, not only must every part be correctly assembled but everything must be spotlessly clean, all the oilways must be clear, locking washers and spring washers must always be fitted where needed and all bearings and other working surfaces must be thoroughly lubricated during assembly. Before assembly begins, renew any bolts or studs whose threads are in any way damaged and wherever possible use new spring washers.

2   All bearing caps should be assembled with new bolts.

3   Be sure that where the instructions call for pressing on bearings, pressing in bushes, pressing on gears and so forth, suitable tools are used for doing the job. In most cases these can be made up with suitable bolts, lengths of tubing washers, bridging pieces etc. The point is that taking things off is, generally speaking, easier than putting them on, and in any case when removing a bearing which has already been condemned it doesn't matter whether it is damaged further or not. When replacing things however, one does not want the replacement to be damaged in any way. In the case of replacement bearings or replacement gears, there is no reason why one cannot have a rehearsal with the old ones.

4   Be sure all the gaskets needed are to hand.

5   Finally, when reassembling this engine regard a torque wrench as a necessity, not a luxury. The bolts and nuts for the big-ends and main bearing caps do not carry washers or split pins; they rely on accurate torque setting to stretch them just enough to ensure a really shakeproof assembly.

19 Crankshaft - refitting

1   Make sure that the crankcase is thoroughly clean and that all the oilways are clear. Inject oil into the oilways at several points with a forcefeed oil can or plastic bottle: this will have the two-fold benefit of checking that the oilways are clear and getting oil into them before

you start assembly. Do the same with the crankshaft - it is particularly important to get as much oil as possible into the crankshaft oilways.

2   Remove every trace of protective grease from new bearing shells.

3   Wipe the seats of the main bearing shells in the crankcase clean and fit the appropriate shells in them. The rear shell incorporates thrust flanges. Note that the bearing shells have tabs on them which fit into grooves in the casing, so they can only be fitted the one way. If the old bearings are being refitted be sure to place them in their original positions (photo).

4   Oil the shells generously and place the crankshaft on top of them - be sure that it is the right way round (photo).

5   Wipe the bearing cap housings and fit their shells into them, keeping an eye on the order if necessary.

6   Oil the bearing surfaces of the crankshaft generously and fit the bearing caps over them, ensuring that they locate properly. The mating surfaces must be spotlessly clean or the caps will not seat correctly.

7   As each cap is fitted, put a new pair of fixing bolts through the holes and screw them up finger tight. Be sure the caps are fitted in their right order and the right way round.

8   When all the caps are fitted and the nuts finger-tight, check that the crankshaft rotates freely without any suggestion of high spots. If it does not, there is something wrong: do not go any further in the assembly until the cause has been found. The most likely cause is dirt on one of the bearing shells.

9   Tighten the bolts to a torque of 92 lb f ft (12.5 kg f m). Recheck the crankshaft for freedom of rotation (photo).

10 Check that the crankshaft endfloat lies within the Specifications at the beginning of this Chapter.

20 Pistons and connecting rods - reassembly

1   We have already considered the overhaul of the pistons, connecting rods and gudgeon pins and it only remains to assemble the connecting rods, gudgeon pins and pistons before fitting them into the cylinder block. Check that the connecting rods are the right way round and make sure that when the mark on the connecting rod lines up with the

19.3 Fitting the rear main bearing shell

19.4 Placing the crankshaft in the engine block

19.9 Tightening the main bearing cap bolts

20.1a Connecting rod big-end bearing assembly

20.1b Marking on connecting rod and cap

corresponding mark on the bearing cap, the cap itself is right way round, the piston is placed as in Fig. 1.24 with the slot in the head facing forwards (photos).

2   Assemble the connecting rods and gudgeon pins to the pistons, and fit the retaining circlips (photos). Heat the piston in hot water if the gudgeon pin is tight.

3   Check that the piston ring grooves and oilways are thoroughly clean and that the clearance between piston rings and the edges of the grooves is correct (see Section 12 and Fig. 1.25).

4   Fit the piston rings to the pistons, remembering that the top compression ring is chromium plated and the oil control ring with its ridges and slots goes at the bottom. Piston rings should always be fitted over the top of the piston and not from the bottom. A simple method is to place three narrow strips of thin metal - old feeler gauges of about 0.020 in (0.051 mm) are ideal - at equal distances round the

Fig. 1.24. Slot on piston head must point forward and numbers on connecting rod must face right-hand side of engine block (oil filter side (Sec. 20)

piston and slide the piston rings over these. Stagger the gaps in the piston rings equally round the piston. Be very careful not to scratch the piston or damage the grooves when fitting piston rings.
Mind too that you do not let the connecting rod bang against the piston as this may damage or distort it. Remember that the pistons are made of alloy and are comparatively soft.

5   Insert the pistons into the cylinders from the top, using a device like the one shown in the photograph to clamp the rings. If you haven't got the correct tool it is a very simple matter to make a substitute. We have used a large worm drive clip with success. Whatever you use, make sure that you do not scratch the piston. Gently tap the piston through the piston ring compressor into the cylinder. Ensure that each piston is the correct one for the bore and that the front of the piston (with the slot) faces forwards. Lubricate the piston well with clean engine oil.

6   As each piston is fitted, wipe the big-end bearing seat on the connecting rod perfectly clean and fit the shell bearing in position with its locating tab engaged with the corresponding groove in the connecting rod. The procedure and precautions are exactly the same as those needed for fitting big-end bearings as described in Section 19.

7   Generously lubricate the corresponding surfaces on the crankshaft with engine oil and draw the connecting rod on to it.

8   Fit the bearing shell to the connecting rod cap in the same way as with the connecting rod itself.

9   Generously lubricate the shell bearing and offer up the connecting rod bearing cap to the connecting rod. Join the cap to the rod with new fixing bolt and nuts (photo).

10 Tighten the retaining bolts evenly - in other words tighten each bolt a little at a time alternatively - to a torque of 46 lb f ft (6.3 kg f m) (photo).

21 Oil pump - refitting

Fit new sealing rings on both ends of the delivery pipe. Make sure the pipe is located properly in the crankcase and the pump. Fit the pump retaining bolts.

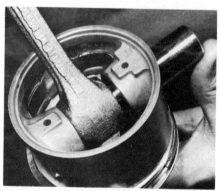

20.2a Assembling the connecting rod, gudgeon pin and piston

20.2b Fitting the gudgeon pin retaining circlip

Fig. 1.25. Correct fitting of piston rings (Sec. 20)

20.5 Use a piston ring clamp when inserting the pistons in the cylinders

20.9 Fitting the connecting rod bearing cap

20.10 Tightening the connecting rod big-end bearing bolts

22 Rear sealing flange - refitting

1   Press a new seal into the sealing flange.
2   Clean the surface of the block and using a smear of grease stick the new gasket in place on the block.
3   Grease the rubber lip on the sealing ring and opposite surface on the crankshaft with mineral grease.
4   Fit the sealing flange taking great care that the rubber lip is not damaged by the edge of the crankshaft or twisted so that the spring jumps out of its position (photo).
5   Trim off the projecting parts of the gasket with a knife (photo).

23 Intermediate shaft and front sealing flange - refitting

1   Oil the intermediate shaft journals. Fit the shaft in the block taking care that the gears do not damage the bearing bushings in the block. Fit the spacer sleeve on the crankshaft (photos).
2   Clean the joint faces of the block and sealing flange, and fit a new gasket and the front sealing flange (photo).
3   Cut off the projecting parts of the gasket and fit the rear part of the belt guard and the cable harness (photo).

24 Sump - refitting

1   Ensure that the sump is really clean and that all traces of the old gasket have been removed from the flanges of the sump and the crankcase. Fit the new gasket to the crankcase.
2   Lightly grease the flange on the sump. Place the sump in position and fit the spring washers and bolts. Tighten the bolts to a torque of 6 - 8 lb f ft (0.8 - 1.1 kg f m) (photo).

25 Water pump - refitting

1   The water pump is simply screwed to the cylinder block, a gasket being required even though there is no water outlet from the pump into the side of the block. A sealing ring is placed in the groove at the top of the pump and will be compressed by the cylinder head when it is fitted (photos).
2   Fitting the water pump when the head is removed as we are doing here is somewhat simpler than fitting it with the head in position, because you have to push the pump up against the head, ensuring that the ring is properly located, as you put in the bolts. This will have to be done of course, if the pump has been removed for some reason when the head has not been taken off.

26 Flywheel and clutch - refitting

1   Turn the crankshaft so that No. 1 cylinder is at tdc (top-dead-centre).
2   Position flywheel (or drive plate in the case of automatic transmissions) on the crankshaft so that pin (A) is approximately 15⁰ from the horizontal position and pointing away from the starter motor mounting as shown in Fig. 1.26. Note that there are two pins (A) and (B).
3   Fit the retaining bolts and tighten them to a torque of 53 lb f ft (7 kg f m) (photo).
4   Fit the input shaft bearing (packed with grease), the retaining washer and circlip. Fit the reinforcing bracket (photo).
5   Refit the clutch disc and pressure plate assembly and lightly secure it in position with its securing bolts (photo).
6   Carefully line-up the disc with the input bearing. This is ideally done by using the input shaft from the gearbox, if it is available, otherwise use a mandrel with a diameter the same as the disc hub and having a spigot on the end which fits in the pilot bearing (photo).
7   When the clutch disc is correctly aligned tighten the clutch assembly securing bolts in stages in a diagonal and progressive manner.

22.4 Fitting the rear sealing flange (oil seal retainer)

22.5 Cutting off the projecting parts of the rear sealing flange gasket

23.1a Fitting the intermediate shaft in the engine block

23.1b When fitting the spacer sleeve, fit it the opposite way round to what it was at removal

23.2 Fitting the front sealing flange (oil seal retainer)

23.3 Rear part of the drive belt guard fitted in position

24.2 Fitting the sump

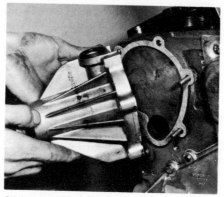
25.1a Fitting the water pump

25.1b Water pump in position and sealing ring fitted

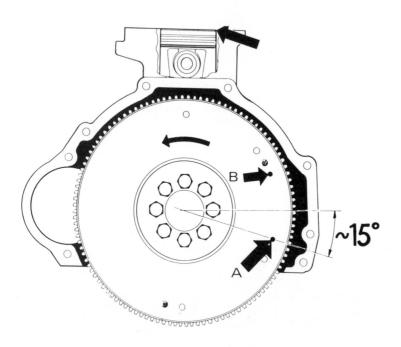
Fig. 1.26. Locating the flywheel in correct position on the crankshaft. Do not confuse pin A with pin B (Sec. 26)

26.3 Tightening the flywheel bolts

26.4 Fitting the reinforcing bracket

26.5 The clutch disc is marked to identify the side fitted towards the flywheel

26.6 Using the gearbox input shaft to align the clutch disc

27.1 Fit new valve stem seals on inlet valve guides

27 Cylinder head and camshaft - reassembly

1   Fit new valve stem seals on the inlet valve guides (photo).
2   Unless parts have been renewed, refit the valves, springs and tappets in the positions from which they were removed. Oil the valve stems before inserting them in the valve guides (photo).
3   Over each valve fit the lower spring retainer, the valve spring and the upper spring retainer. Using a valve spring compressing tool, compress the spring and fit the collets in the recess in the valve stem and release the compression tool. Fit the rubber ring, refer to Fig. 1.27. (photos).

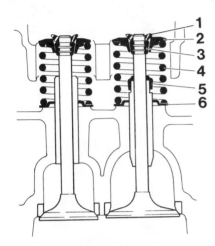

Fig. 1.27. Valve and valve spring assembly (Sec. 27)

1 Rubber ring	4 Valve spring
2 Upper spring retainer	5 Valve stem seal (inlet only)
3 Collets	6 Lower spring retainer

4   Oil the bearing seats for the camshaft, the bearing caps, the camshaft and the tappets. Fit the tappets and the adjuster washers. Place the camshaft in the cylinder head (photo).
5   Coat the face of the front cap that mates with the cylinder head with a sealing compound. Fit the caps, with the markings aligned as shown in Fig. 1.16, and the retaining nuts. Screw down the nuts in an even and progressive manner to compress the valves springs without putting uneven stress on the camshaft. Torque tighten the nuts to 15 lb f ft (2 kg f m).
6   Before fitting the camshaft seal apply mineral grease to the rubber lip of the seal and the corresponding surface on the camshaft. Take care not to damage the seal against the edge of the camshaft. Fit the seal so that a new wear surface is obtained against the camshaft.
7   Fit the rear guide plate, the gearwheel with the slot on the gear located on the pin on the camshaft end, then the front guide plate, washer and retaining bolt. Restrain the gear wheel from turning and torque tighten the bolt to 37 lb f ft (5 kg f m).
8   Fit the torque tighten the spark plugs to 18 - 22 lb f ft (2.5 - 3 kg f m) on carburettor engines or fit the retainers for the injectors and the injectors (fuel injection engines). Use new 'O' ring seals.

28 Cylinder head - refitting

1   Check that both cylinder block and cylinder head mating faces are perfectly clean.
2   Lubricate each cylinder with engine oil.
3   Always use a new cylinder head gasket. The old gasket will be compressed and incapable of giving a good seal. Do not smear grease or gasket cement on either side of the gasket.
4   Place the gasket on the cylinder block the right way up and carefully aligned with the bolt holes in the block.
5   Place the cylinder head in position, being careful to align the bolt holes accurately, and fit the cylinder head bolts (photo).
6   Tighten the cylinder head bolts, in two stages, in the numerical sequence shown in Fig. 1.28; tighten the bolts to the specified torque.

27.2 Fitting valve into cylinder head

27.3a Compressing the valve spring

27.3b Retaining collets fitted in position

27.3c Don't forget the rubber ring

27.4 Fit the tappets and adjuster washers

28.5 Fitting the cylinder head

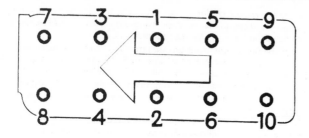

Fig. 1.28. Numerical tightening sequence for cylinder head bolts
(Secs. 28, 67 and 69)

29.3 Fitting the gear wheel on the intermediate shaft

29 Crankshaft and intermediate shaft seals and gears - refitting

1   Fit a new sealing ring on the crankshaft. Before fitting, grease the
seal rubber lip with mineral grease and take care not to damage the seal
against the edge of the spacer sleeve. If the spacer sleeve has not been
renewed, locate the seal so that a new contact surface is obtained.
2   Fit the intermediate shaft seal observing the same procedure.
3   Fit the gear wheel on the intermediate shaft, and restraining the
shaft from turning, fit the retaining bolt and tighten to a torque of
37 lb f ft (5 kg f m) (photo).
4   Fit the guide plate on the crankshaft, the gear, the front hub and
the centre bolt. Tighten the centre bolt to a torque of 122 lb f ft
(16.5 kg f m) while restraining the crankshaft from turning by blocking
the flywheel.

30 Toothed drivebelt - refitting

1   Fit the belt tensioner and retaining nut. Tighten the nut and remove
the pin (fitted at disassembly) compressing the spring.
2   Rotate the crankshaft to where the timing marks coincide, Fig. 1.29.
3   Rotate the intermediate shaft to where the marks coincide, Fig. 1.30.
4   Place the valve cover in position and rotate the camshaft to where the
marks coincide, Fig. 1.31.
5   Fit the toothed belt on the crankshaft gear. Ensure that the belt is
in good condition and clean, with no trace of oil or grease. New belts
have a colour marking. Set the double lines on the belt against the
crankshaft gear mark, the next line should then be opposite the
intermediate shaft mark and the other mark opposite the camshaft
mark.
6   Stretch the belt and fit it on the camshaft gear and belt tensioner.
Do not use any tools for this as they might damage the belt.
7   Slacken the tensioner retaining nut, so that the spring tensions
the belt and then re-tighten the nut (photo).
8   Rotate the engine clockwise and then check that the belt marks are
correctly aligned. Retension the belt and tighten the nut to a torque of

Fig. 1.29. Aligning the crankshaft timing mark (Sec. 30)

Fig. 1.30. Aligning the intermediate shaft timing mark (Sec. 30)

Fig. 1.31. Aligning the camshaft timing mark (Sec. 30)

37 lb f ft (5 kg f m).
9   Fit the pulley on the front hub (if the car has air-conditioning, fit
the pulley temporarily with two bolts).
10   Fit the belt guard casing.
11   Retension the belt after 600 miles (1000 km).

31 Valve clearance - adjustment

1   Lift off the valve cover and turn the engine to the firing position for
No. 1 cylinder (both cams on No. 1 cylinder pointing obliquely upwards
at equal angles, and the ignition mark on crankshaft pulley at 0°). Always
turn the crankshaft with the centre bolt.

2   Measure the valve clearance with a feeler gauge (photo).

Clearance when checking:

Cold engine: 0.012 - 0.018 in (0.30 - 0.45 mm)
Warm engine: 0.014 - 0.020 in (0.35 - 0.50 mm)

Clearance when adjusting:

Cold engine: 0.014 - 0.016 in (0.35 - 0.40 mm)
Warm engine: 0.016 - 0.018 in (0.40 - 0.45 mm)

The clearance is the same for inlet and exhaust valves.
3   To adjust the clearance turn the tappets so that the slots are at right

angles to the camshaft. Position the Volvo tool 5022 as shown in Fig. 1. 32, and depress the tappets so that the adjuster washers can be removed.
4   Remove the adjuster washer and fit a washer of the correct thickness to obtain the specified clearance. Adjuster washers are available in different thicknesses between 0.130 and 0.180 in (3.30 and 4.50 mm) in steps of 0.002 in (0.05 mm). The thickness of the washer is marked on one side; always fit the washer with the marked face downwards. Oil the washer before fitting it. Remove the tappet depressing tool.
5   Rotate the engine to No. 3 cylinder firing position and proceed as for No. 1 cylinder, then to No. 4 cylinder and No. 2 cylinder.
6   If the Volvo tappet depressing tool is not available the tappet can be depressed by turning the engine till the cam depresses the tappet, then fitting a wedge to hold the tappet down while you turn the camshaft to the checking position and lift out the washer, as shown in photograph.
7   Fit the halfmoon-shaped rubber seal at the rear of the cylinder head. Place the gasket in position. Oil the camshaft and fit the valve cover. Attach the ignition setting indicator to the valve cover with one of the nuts (photos).

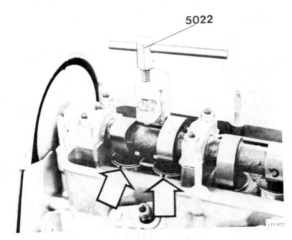

Fig. 1.32. Depressing the valve tappet. Note the position of the slots in the tappets. The tool bears upon the rim of the tappet (Sec. 31)

Fig. 1.33. Adjuster washer. Fit marked face downward (Sec. 31)

30.7 Tensioning the belt

31.2 Measuring the valve clearance with a feeler gauge

31.6 Keeping the tappet depressed with a suitable wedge and removing the adjuster washer

31.7a Fitting the valve cover gasket

31.7b Attaching the ignition setting sender to valve cover

32 Distributor - refitting

1   Rotate the crankshaft to the firing position for No. 1 cylinder. This
is checked by looking through the valve cover filler hole to see the
position of the camshaft cams, Fig. 1.34, and checking that the ignition
mark on the crankshaft finally is at 0° on the graduated scale on the
belt guard casing (photo).
2   Refer to Fig. 1.35. Turn the rotor clockwise so that the line
marked on it is approximately 60° from the mark on the
distributor housing.
3   Fit the distributor in position in the engine block and check that
the mark on the rotor and the mark on the distributor housing are
now opposite each other. Fit the distributor retaining screw.
4   Remove the rotor, fit the seal and replace the rotor. Do not fit
the distributor cap at this time as it may get damaged when refitting
the engine in the car.

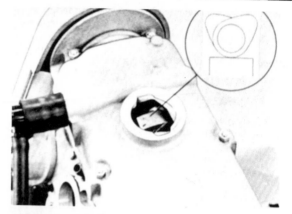

Fig. 1.34. Firing position for No. 1 cylinder (Sec. 32)

33 Fuel pump - refitting

1   Ensure that the mating faces of the cylinder block, spacer and fuel
pump are clean with no traces of old gaskets.
2   Fit the bolts in the pump flange and place a gasket, the spacer and
another gasket on the bolts.
3   Fit the assembly to the cylinder block and tighten the bolts.

34 Oil filter - refitting

1   When fitting the oil filter smear the filter rubber ring with oil.
Screw on the filter, by hand, until it just touches the block. Then
screw a further half turn by hand. Do not overtighten (photo) or
use a tool to tighten.

35 Other fitments - refitting

1   When replacing the other fitments the procedure is the reverse of
dismantling.
2   Don't forget the lifting brackets when fitting the thermostat housing,
the inlet manifold the exhaust manifold (photos).
3   When fitting the exhaust always use new gaskets and position
them with the marking 'UT' facing outwards. Centre the manifold
round No. 1 cylinder lower stud and fit washers so that the marking
UT/OUT faces outwards. Fit the lifting bracket at No. 3 cylinder.
Tighten the nuts to a torque of 15 lb f ft (2 kg f m) (photo).
4   When fitting the alternator, tension the belt, as described in Chapter 2.
5   When fitting the cold start valve (fuel injection engines) don't forget
to connect the earth lead at one of the retaining screws.
6   When fitting the water pump to heater pipe always fit new rubber
seals.
7   Fit the gearbox to the engine, this should be straightforward providing
the clutch disc has been correctly aligned.

32.1 Graduated scale on belt guard casing

36 Engine - refitting

1   Refitting of the engine and gearbox is the reverse of the removal
sequence. Make sure that all loose leads, hoses or pipes are tucked out
of the way where they won't get caught up as the engine is lowered into
position. If the front axle bolts have been slackened off don't forget to
retighten them.
2   When the engine has been refitted check that all the items removed
or disconnected at removal have been refitted and all connections made.
3   Check that the drain tap is closed, and drain plugs tightened.
Fill the cooling system with coolant and the engine with the specified
oil. Don't forget to check the gearbox oil level and fill as necessary. Make
sure that all tools, rags, etc have been removed from the engine
compartment (photo).

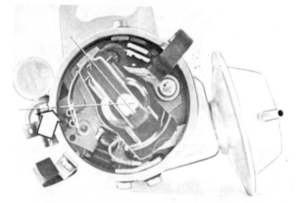

Fig. 1.35. Fitting the distributor (Sec. 32)

37 Engine - initial start-up after overhaul or major repair

1   Just have a quick look at the last item in the previous Section.
2   Make sure that your battery is fully charged - it may have to work
hard before the engine starts.
3   If the fuel system has been dismantled, it will require quite a lot of

engine revolutions to get the petrol up to the carburettors. With the
fuel injection engine, of course, this problem will not arise. If there is
doubt about the state of charge of the battery, take the plugs out and
the petrol will be pumped up with far less effort.
4   As soon as the engine fires and runs, keep it going at a fast tickover
only (no faster) and bring it up to normal working temperature.
5   As the engine warms up, there will be odd smells and some smoke
from parts getting hot and burning off oil deposits. Look for water or
oil leaks which will be obvious if serious, particularly as the engine is so

34.1 Oil filter fitted in position

35.2a Fitting the thermostat

35.2b Fitting the inlet manifold

35.3 Don't forget the lifting eye when fitting the exhaust manifold

36.3 Don't forget to fill up with engine oil

nice and clean.

6 When the engine running temperature has been reached, adjust the idling speed as described in Chapter 3.

7 Let the engine run at normal temperature for ten minutes. Then switch if off, allow it to cool for at least 30 minutes and check the torque of the cylinder head bolts. Slacken each bolt in sequence, a quarter turn before tightening it. Only release and retighten one bolt at a time.

8 Then check to see if there are any lubricant or coolant drips. or coolant drips.

9 By now the reader will hardly be able to wait to get the car on the road and check that the ignition timing is correct and gives the necessary smoothness and power. Don't forget that although the old pistons and crankshaft may still have been used, new bearing shells will have been fitted. Treat it as a new engine and run-in at reduced revolutions for 500 miles (800 kms).

38 Oil sump - removal and refitting (engine in car)

1 Fit a lifting attachment to the lifting bracket at the thermostat housing and take the weight of the engine without lifting it. Remove the left-hand engine mounting bolts. If the car has air-conditioning first remove the compressor as described in Section 4, paragraph 9.

2 Drain the engine oil. Refit the plug after draining and tighten to a torque of 45 lb f ft (6 kg f m).

3 Remove the guard plate under the engine. Hoist the engine slightly and remove the left-hand engine mounting.

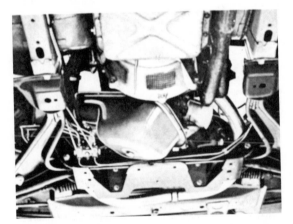

Fig. 1.36. Removing the sump with engine fitted in the car (Sec. 38)

4 Remove the reinforcing bracket and the sump bolts.

5 Release the sump, turn it as shown in Fig. 1.36 and take it out. Remove the gasket.

6 Refitting is the reverse of the removal sequence. Make sure the joint faces are clean. Always use a new gasket. Don't forget to refill with the specified engine oil.

See next page for 'Fault diagnosis - engine'.

39 Fault diagnosis - engine

When investigating starting and uneven running faults do not be tempted into snap diagnosis. Start from the beginning of the check procedure and follow it through. It will take less time in the long run. Poor performance from an engine in terms of power and economy is not normally diagnosed quickly. In any event the ignition and fuel systems must be checked first before assuming any further investigation needs to be made.

Symptom	Reason/s	Remedy
Engine will not turn over when starting switch is operated	Flat battery Bad battery connections Bad connections at solenoid switch and/or starter motor Defective solenoid Starter motor defective	Check that battery is fully charged and that all connections are clean and tight. Remove starter and check solenoid. Remove starter and overhaul.
Engine turns over normally but fails to fire and run	No spark at plugs No fuel reaching engine Too much fuel reaching the engine (flooding)	Check ignition system according to procedures given in Chapter 4. Check fuel system according to procedures given in Chapter 3. For carburettor engines: Slowly depress the accelerator pedal to floor and keep it there while operating starter motor until engine fires. Check fuel system if necessary as described in Chapter 3. For fuel injection engines: Flooding signifies malfunction of cold starting system - check cold start valve and thermal timer and their electrical connections.
Engine starts but runs unevenly and misfires	Ignition and/or fuel system faults Incorrect valve clearances Burnt out valves	Check the ignition and fuel systems as though the engine had failed to start. Check and reset clearances. Remove cylinder heads and examine and overhaul as necessary.
Lack of power	Ignition and/or fuel system faults Incorrect valve clearances Burnt out valves Worn out piston or cylinder bores	Check the ignition and fuel systems for correct ignition timing and carburettor settings. Check and reset the clearances. Remove cylinder heads and examine and overhaul as necessary. Remove cylinder head and examine and overhaul as necessary
Excessive oil consumption	Oil leaks from crankshaft oil seal, valve cover gasket, oil sump gasket, or sump plug washer Worn piston rings or cylinder bores resulting in oil being burnt by engine. Smoky exhaust is an indication Worn valve guides and/or defective valve stem seals	Identify source of leak and repair as appropriate. Fit new rings - or rebore cylinders and fit new pistons, depending on degree of wear. Remove cylinder heads and recondition valve stem bores and valves and seals as necessary.
Excessive mechanical noise from engine	Wrong valve clearances Worn crankshaft bearings Worn cylinders (piston slap)	Adjust valve clearances. Inspect and overhaul where necessary. Inspect and overhaul where necessary.
Unusual vibration	Misfiring on one or more cylinders Loose mounting bolts	Check ignition system. Check tightness of bolts and condition of flexible mountings.

Chapter 1 Part B : Overhead valve engines

Contents

Specifications

Engine (B20) - general

	B20A	B20E
Type		
Max. output:		
HP at rev/min DIN	82/4700	120/6000
KW at rev/min DIN	60/4680	73/6000
Max. torque:		
lb f ft at rev/min DIN	115/2300	110/3500
kg m at rev/min DIN	16/2300	15.2/3500
Compression pressure at 250-300 rpm (warm engine turned over with starter motor)	156 - 185 psi (11 - 13 kg/sq cm)	170 - 200 psi (12 - 14 kg/sq cm)
Number of cylinders	4	4
Compression ratio	8.7 : 1	10.5 : 1
Bore	3.5 in (88.9 mm)	3.5008 in (88.92 mm)
Stroke	3.150 in (80 mm)	3.150 in (80 mm)
Capacity	1986 cc	1986 cc
Weight (approx.)	341 lb (155 kg)	341 lb (155 kg)

Pistons

Material	Light alloy
Permissible weight difference between pistons on same engine	0.35 oz (10 g)
Length	2.79 in (71 mm)
Clearance in bore:	
B20A	0.0004 - 0.0012 in (0.01 - 0.03 mm)
B20E	0.0016 - 0.0024 in (0.04 - 0.06 mm)
Compression rings:	
Number on each piston	2
Width	0.078 in (1.98 mm)
Side clearance in groove	0.0016 - 0.0028 in (0.040 - 0.072 mm)
Oil scraper rings:	
Number on piston	1
Width	0.186 in (4.74 mm)
Side clearance in groove	0.0016 - 0.0028 in (0.040 - 0.072 mm)
Piston ring gap	0.016 - 0.022 in (0.40 - 0.55 mm)
Gudgeon pins (general):	
Arrangement	Fully floating with circlips at both ends
Fit in con-rod	Sliding fit
Fit in piston	Push fit

Gudgeon pin diameter:
  Standard ... ... 0.945 in (87.0 mm)
  Oversize ... ... 0.947 in (95.1 mm)

Cylinder head

Material ... ... Light alloy
Height between cylinder head joint face and face for bolt heads:
  B20A ... ... 3.42 in (87 mm)
  B20E ... ... 3.34 in (84.9 mm)

Valves

Inlet valves:
  Seat angle in cylinder head ... ... 45°
  Valve seat angle ... ... 45.5°
  Seat width in cylinder head ... ... 0.08 in (2 mm)
  Valve head diameter ... ... 1.732 in (44 mm)
  Stem diameter ... ... 0.3132 - 0.3138 in (7.955 - 7.970 mm)
  Valve clearance (cold and warm) ... ... 0.016 - 0.018 in (0.40 - 0.45 mm)
Exhaust valves:
  Seat angle in cylinder head ... ... 45°
  Valve seat angle ... ... 44.5°
  Seat width in cylinder head ... ... 0.080 in (2 mm)
  Valve head diameter ... ... 1.378 in (35 mm)
  Stem diameter ... ... 0.3120 - 0.3126 in (7.925 - 7.940 mm)
  Valve clearance (cold and warm) ... ... 0.016 - 0.018 in (0.40 - 0.45 mm)

Valve guides

Length:
  Inlet ... ... 2.047 in (52 mm)
  Exhaust ... ... 2.323 in (59 mm)
Inner diameter ... ... 0.320 - 0.321 in (8.000 - 8.022 mm)
Height above cylinder head face:
  B20A ... ... 0.689 (17.5 mm)
  B20E ... ... 0.705 in (17.9 mm)
Valve stem clearance:
  Inlet ... ... 0.0012 - 0.0026 in (0.030 - 0.067 mm)
  Exhaust ... ... 0.0024 - 0.0038 in (0.060 - 0.097 mm)

Valve springs

Free-length ... ... 1.81 in (46 mm)
With load of 60 ± 5 lb (29.5 ± 2.3 kg) ... ... 1.57 in (40 mm)
With load of 181 ± 10 lb (87 ± 4.5 kg) ... ... 1.18 in (30 mm)

Lubrication system

Oil capacity:
  With oil filter ... ... 6.6 Imp pints (8 US pints/3.75 litres)
  Without oil filter ... ... 5.75 Imp. pints (7 US pints/3.25 litres)
Oil pressure at 2000 rpm (engine warm) ... ... 36 - 85 psi (2.5 - 6.0 kg/cm^2)
Oil filter:
  Type ... ... Full flow
  Make ... ... Wix or Mann
Oil pump:
  Type ... ... Gear type pump
  Gear endfloat ... ... 0.0008 - 0.004 in (0.02 - 0.10 mm)
  Radial play ... ... 0.0032 - 0.0055 in (0.08 - 0.14 mm)
  Backlash ... ... 0.006 - 0.014 in (0.15 - 0.35 mm)
  Number of gearteeth 9
  Relief valve spring:
    Free-length ... ... 1.54 in (32.5 mm)
    With load of 11 ± 0.88 lb (5 ± 0.4 kg) ... ... 1.03 in (26.25 mm)
    With load of 15.4 ± 1.7 lb (7 ± 0.7 kg) ... ... 0.83 in (21 mm)

Crankshaft

Endfloat ... ... 0.0018 - 0.0054 in (0.047 - 0.137 mm)
Main bearing clearance ... ... 0.0011 - 0.0033 in (0.028 - 0.083 mm)
Big-end bearing clearance ... ... 0.0012 - 0.0028 in (0.029 - 0.071 mm)

Main bearings

Main bearing journals:
  Diameter:
    Standard ... ... 2.4981 - 1.4986 in (63.451 - 63.464 mm)
    Undersize ... ... 2.4881 - 2.4886 in (63.197 - 63.210 mm)
    Undersize ... ... 2.4781 - 2.4786 in (62.943 - 62.956 mm)

Big-end bearings
Big-end bearing journals:

Diameter:									
Standard	...	...	...	...	...	...	...	...	2.1255 - 2.1260 in (53.987 - 54.000 mm)
Undersize	...	...	...	...	...	...	...	...	2.1155 - 2.1160 in (53.733 - 53.746 mm)
Undersize	...	...	...	...	...	...	...	...	2.1055 - 2.1060 in (53.479 - 53.492 mm)

Connecting rods

Endfloat on journal	...	...	...	...	...	...	...	0.006 - 0.014 in (0.15 - 0.35 mm)
Permissible weight difference between con-rods of one engine			...	...				0.35 oz (10g)

Camshaft

Number of bearings	...	...	...	...	...	...	...	3
Running clearance	...	...	...	...	...	...	...	0.0008 - 0.0030 in (0.020 - 0.075 mm)
Endfloat	...	...	...	...	...	...	...	0.0008 - 0.0024 in (0.020 - 0.60 mm)
Camshaft marking:								
B20A	...	...	...	...	...	...	...	A
B20E	...	...	...	...	...	...	...	D
Bearing journal diameter:								
Front	...	...	...	...	...	...	...	1.8494 - 1.8504 in (46.975 - 47.000 mm)
Centre	...	...	...	...	...	...	...	1.6919 - 1.6929 in (42.975 - 43.000 mm)
Rear	...	...	...	...	...	...	...	1.4557 - 1.4567 in (36.975 - 37.000 mm)
Valve clearance for valve timing setting (cold engine):								
B20A	...	...	...	...	...	...	...	0.043 in (1.10 mm)
B20E	...	...	...	...	...	...	...	0.055 in (1.40 mm)
Inlet valve should then open at:								
B20A	...	...	...	...	...	...	...	10° ATDC
B20E	...	...	...	...	...	...	...	5.5° BTDC
Timing gear backlash	...	...	...	...	...	...	...	0.0016 - 0.0032 in (0.04 - 0.08 mm)

Flywheel

Permissible axial throw (max.)	...	...	...	...	...	...	0.002 in (0.05 mm) at a diameter of 5.9 in (150 mm)

Torque wrench settings

									lbf ft	kgf m
Cylinder head (see text):										
Stage 1	...	...	...	...	...	...	...	...	30	4.1
Stage 2	...	...	...	...	...	...	...	...	60	8
Stage 3	...	...	...	...	...	...	...	...	65	9
Main bearings	...	...	...	...	...	...	...	...	87 - 94	12 - 13
Big-end bearings	...	...	...	...	...	...	...	...	51 - 57	7 - 8
Flywheel	...	...	...	...	...	...	...	...	47 - 51	6.5 - 7
Spark plugs	...	...	...	...	...	...	...	...	25 - 29	3.5 - 4
Camshaft nut	...	...	...	...	...	...	...	...	94 - 108	13 - 15
Crankshaft pulley bolt	...	...	...	...	...	...	...	...	50 - 60	7 - 8
Oil sump bolts	...	...	...	...	...	...	...	...	6 - 8	0.8 - 1.1
Oil filter nipple	...	...	...	...	...	...	...	...	32 - 40	4.5 - 5.5

40 General description

The engine is a four cylinder, water-cooled, overhead valve unit, the valves being pushrod operated by a three bearing camshaft. It employs alloy pistons and a five bearing crankshaft. The big-end bearings are replaceable shells.

The three bearing camshaft is made of special grade cast iron and has case hardened cams. It operates the valves through the normal mechanism of tappets, pushrods and rockers. There are no inspection covers for the valve tappets since these are accessible after the cylinder head has been removed.

The connecting rods are made of drop forged steel and have precision machined bushes at the little end which act as bearings for the gudgeon pins.

The pistons are made of light alloy and have two compression rings and one oil scraper ring. The upper compression ring is chromed in order to reduce cylinder wear.

The cylinder head is bolted to the block (ie. there are no studs in the block). All the combustion chambers are machined throughout and have separate inlet and exhaust ports, one for each valve. The valves themselves have chromed stems and run in replaceable valve guides to which they are sealed with rubber seals.

The cylinder block is made of special cast iron and is cast as a single unit. The cylinder bores are machined directly in the block. The oilways in the block are arranged so that the oil filter, which is the full flow type, is directly attached to the right-hand side of the block.

The engine has a 'force' feed lubrication system. Pressure is provided by a gear pump driven from the camshaft and fitted under the crankshaft in the sump. The pump forces the oil past the relief valve (itself fitted inside the pump), through the oil filter and then through oilways out to the various lubrication points. All the oil supplied to the lubricating points first passes through the oil filter.

41 Engine - removal

The removal procedure is basically the same as for overhead camshaft engines, refer to Sections 3, 4 and 5 of Chapter 1/Part A.

42 Engine - dismantling procedure

1   Assuming that the engine is out of the car and on the work bench, first of all remove the inlet and exhaust manifolds for a carburettor engine or the inlet ducting and exhaust manifold in the case of a fuel injection engine and pull out the pipe that goes from the water pump along the side of the block to the heater. Once this is done there ceases to be any difference between fuel injection engines and carburettor engines, and the instructions which follow are equally applicable to both.

2   It is a good idea to start with the more cumbersome items as the remainder of the engine then gets progressively easier to handle. If the gearbox has not yet been removed, do so now by removing the bolts round the edge of the flywheel housing. Two of these anchor the starter motor which will now be freed.

3   Remove the rocker arm casing which is held down by small screws round its edges. Remove the four screws holding down the rocker arm

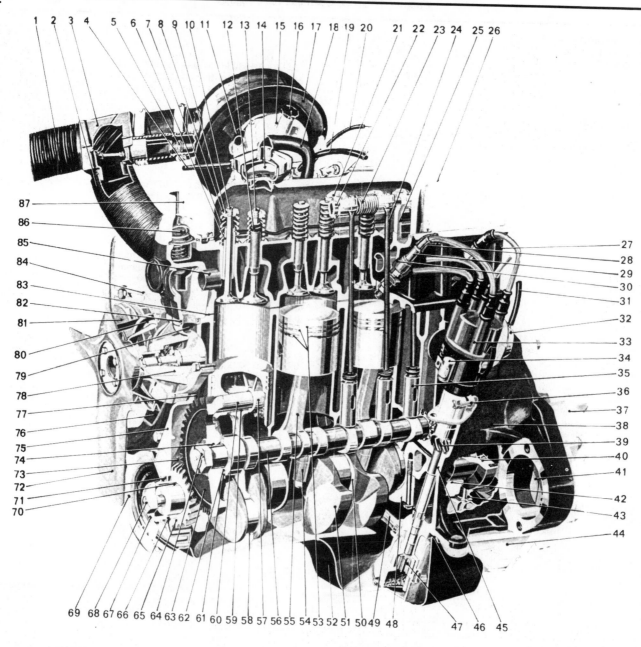

Fig. 1.37. Cut-away view of B20 engine

1	Cold air hose	22	Rocker arm shaft	44	Reinforcing bracket	66	Hub
2	Hot air hose	23	Spring	45	Bush	67	Washer
3	Flap, constant air temperature device	24	Pushrod	46	Seal	68	Bolt
4	Fuel line	25	Bearing bracket	47	Oil pump	69	Pulley
5	Thermostat	26	Rocker arm casing	48	Main bearing cap	70	Key
6	Valve tappet	27	Rubber seal	49	Delivery pipe	71	Seal
7	Valve spring	28	Rubber terminal	50	Main bearing shell	72	Fan
8	Washer	29	Rubber seal	51	Crankshaft	73	Oil nozzle
9	Valve collet	30	Cylinder head	52	Sump	74	Key
10	Exhaust valve	31	Vacuum hose	53	Piston rings	75	Timing gear cover
11	Connection for crankcase hose	32	Vacuum governor	54	Connecting rod cap	76	Coolant inlet
12	Valve tappet seal	33	Distributor	55	Connecting rod	77	Gasket
13	Intake valve	34	Condenser	56	Camshaft	78	Water pump
14	Oil filler cap	35	Valve tappet	57	Piston	79	Gasket
15	Carburettor	36	Retainer	58	Bush	80	Pulley
16	Damping device	37	Flywheel casing	59	Big-end bearing shell	81	Alternator
17	Air cleaner	38	Engine block	60	Gudgeon pin	82	Sealing ring
18	Hose for crankcase gases	39	Gear wheel	61	Washer	83	Cylinder head gasket
19	Vacuum hose for distributor	40	Pilot bearing	62	Spacing ring	84	Tensioner
20	Choke wire	41	Flywheel	63	Camshaft gear	85	Water distributing pipe
21	Rocker arm	42	Flange bearing shell	64	Nut	86	Thermostat
		43	Sealing flange	65	Crankshaft gear	87	Coolant outlet

42.3a Removing the rocker arm assembly

42.3b Lifting out the push rods

42.3c Removing the thermostat

42.3d Lifting out the tappets

42.4a The water pump has a gasket between it and the cylinder head

42.4b These rubber rings seal the water pump outlets to the cylinder head

42.5 Removing the crankcase breather

42.7 Timing marks on the crankshaft pulley

42.8 Remove the central bolt and the pulley will come off without difficulties

assembly and lift it off. Take out the pushrods and put them in a safe place. There is no advantage in keeping them in order though this is a good idea for valves. Remove the thermostat. Unscrew the bolts holding down the cylinder head and place it on one side. Lift out the tappets with pliers (photos).

4   It is now easy to remove the water pump. Notice how it is sealed to the cylinder head by two rings. It can of course be removed and fitted with the cylinder head in position (photos).

5   The fuel pump (on a carburettor engine) and the crankcase breather are easy to deal with. The crankcase breather is fastened to the case by a single screw (photo). The oil filter simply unscrews. The neat way in which the alternator is fixed makes its removal a simple matter.

6   As the distributor is timed, its removal is better left until the timing case has been taken off. This enables the position of the rotor arm shaft for a given timing setting to be noted and so ensure that the timing is the same when the distributor is replaced.

7   Before removing the crankshaft pulley, note the index mark on the timing cover and the figures on the edge of the pulley which indicate degrees before or after top dead centre for No. 1 (front) and No. 4

(back) pistons (see photo). This is not sufficient for checking the setting of the rotor arm in the distributor because it is not possible to determine which of these cylinders is firing without a further check.

8   Take out the central bolt and draw off the crankshaft pulley (photo).

9   Unscrew the timing cover bolts including the front sump bolts and withdraw the cover, taking care not to break the sump gasket (photo). Extract the spring clip, retaining washer and felt ring from the cover as the felt ring must be renewed.

10 With the timing cover removed, the timing can be set for checking the position of the distributor rotor arm. Rotate the crankshaft until the timing dot on the crankshaft gear comes opposite the mark on the camshaft gear as shown in the photograph.

11 Mark the position of the distributor shaft which carries the rotor arm and also mark the position that the distributor assembly occupies relative to its clamp - just in case it is necessary to loosen the clamp later on. Now undo the fastening bolts and lift out the clamp and assembly as a unit. Follow this by lifting out the driving gear which is operated by the camshaft (photos).

12 Remove the nut from the camshaft and pull off its timing gear as

42.9 Removing the timing gears cover

42.10 The timing marks aligned

42.11a Withdrawing the distributor assembly

42.11b Lifting out the distributor drive gear

42.12a Pulling off the timing gear (be careful - it is a fibre gear)

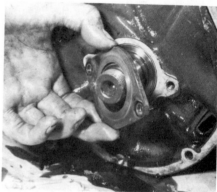

42.12b Removing the camshaft thrust flange and spacing ring

42.12c Withdrawing the camshaft

41.12d The sleeve or 'hub' that takes the crankshaft pulley. Note the key that also keys timing gear. Just under tip of thumb you can see the nipple which directs oil onto gears

42.14 Restraining the flywheel from turning

42.15 The wired bolts securing the sealing flange (oil seal retainer)

42.18a The rear main bearing cap and shell. This is the only one which has flanges

42.18b With the crankshaft out of the engine it is easy to pull off the timing gear

shown in the photograph. Be careful not to push the camshaft backwards - certainly do not hammer it - because the hole in which it runs at the back of the cylinder block is supposed to be sealed off for life and it certainly won't be if the camshaft is hammered against it. The seal (or most of it) can be seen in the top left-hand corner of photograph 42.15. Now remove the thrust flange and the spacer ring behind it, and then withdraw the camshaft (photos). Now pull off the sleeve (called by Volvo a 'hub'). Start it on its way by getting a bit of purchase under the two holes on the timing gear. These holes are threaded, and bolts screwed into them can form the basis of a simple device for pulling the timing gear off. If however the crankshaft is being removed one can easily take it off later, which is what we did.

13 Unscrew the bolts holding the clutch housing to the flywheel a little at a time, keeping them all in step to avoid the risk of distorting the clutch housing. Mark the clutch housing and flywheel to identify position for replacement, and remove the clutch assembly from the flywheel.

14 Stop the flywheel from turning by wedging it with a screwdriver as shown in the photograph, undo the six bolts holding it to the crankshaft and lift it away, marking flywheel and shaft to identify position.

15 Undo the wired bolts holding on the sealing flange and remove it.

16 Remove the reinforcing plate and the sump. Undo the bolts fastening the oil pipe to the crankcase and remove the oil pump. Its delivery pipe simply pushes into a hole in the crankcase and it is sealed by a rubber ring.

17 Before proceeding any further have a look at the bearing caps. They are marked, either with dots as are shown in several of our photographs or with stamped figures to indicate their positions. When the bearing caps are refitted they must be put back in the same places and the same way round as they were before. The big-ends are marked 1, 2, 3 and 4, the front one (in accordance with time-honoured convention) being No. 1. The five main bearings are marked 1 – 5, No. 1 being at the front. It is easy to see which way round the caps are meant to be

because of the shape of the pads which carry the dots. Often these pads are circular, in which case it may be more difficult to remember how the caps have to go. If in doubt, put marks on. There should also be a mark on one side of the connecting-rod and a corresponding mark on the same side of the bearing cap which ensures that the piston as well as the bearing cap, goes back the same way round as it came out. If such marks are not visible then make some. When removing the shells, mark them too, so that if a later inspection reveals faults, its location can be found.

18 Now for each of the connecting-rods in turn, remove the bearing cap and shell, and push the connecting-rod up the cylinder, steadying the piston with the other hand as it emerges. Take great care when doing this that things do not get banged about or scratched, and in particular that the skirt of the piston does not knock against the connecting-rod. Remove the main bearing caps with their shells, and the crankshaft can be lifted out of the crankcase. Pull off the timing gear, now a very simple matter (photos).

19 Removal of a retaining clip and protecting ring at the back end of the crankshaft reveals the pilot bearing for the clutch (photo). There is no need to remove this in order to inspect it thoroughly, and we suggest that it is only removed for renewal purposes. It then does not matter if the removal process damages the bearing. If a puller which will do the job is not available, a suggested method is to fill the cavity behind the bearing with thick grease, push a circular drift which is a pretty good fit into the bearing, and give the drift a good blow with a hammer. The pressure exerted by the grease will then drive the bearing out.

43 Cylinder head, valves and cylinder block - overhaul

1   Clean the oil and grease off the cylinder head and remove the carbon from the combustion chamber and valve heads with a scraper or rotary wire brush.

2   Remove the valves by compressing the valve springs until the collets are free of the recesses in the spring retainers, remove the collets, release the pressure on the spring, lift off the spring and its retainer. Push the valve through the valve guide and remove it. If the valve seems a tight fit in the guide, this may be because the upper part of the stem has dirt or carbon on it. Give it a clean in this case. Remove the rubber seal from the end of the valve guide (photos). Keep the valves in the order in which you removed them. A good idea is to stick them through holes in a piece of thick paper. We like to stand them up when we have done this, and slip the spring and retainer belonging to each valve over the stem. Then if we find anything amiss with a valve seat we know at once which valve and spring to look at.

3   With the valve removed, clean out any remaining carbon from the ports. This done, examine the valve seats. If they are only slightly pitted you will be able to make them smooth again by grinding the valves against the seats. Where bad pitting has occurred they will have to be re-cut - a job for the specialist. Grinding the valves is described in Section 11.

4   Check the valve guides with the valve stems to ensure that they are a good fit; the valve stems should move easily in the guides without slop or side play. Worn guides can be extracted and new ones installed. The guides should project above the adjacent surface of the cylinder head by the amount shown in Fig. 1.38. After fitting new guides, check that they are free from burrs and that the valves move easily in them.

42.19 The pilot bearing for the gearbox input shaft

43.2a Compressing the valve springs ...

43.2b ... and removing the collets

43.2c Removing the rubber seals

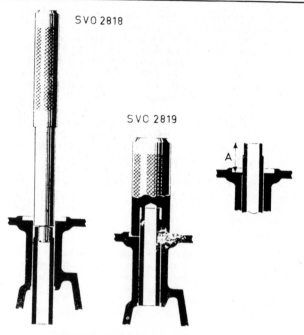

Fig. 1.38. Replacing valve guides (Sec. 43)

B20A engine: A = 0.689 in (17.5 mm)
B20E engine: A = 0.705 in (19.9 mm)

Be sure to have the step end of the guides at the top.

5   Examine the valves, checking them for straightness and noting the condition of their faces. Slight pitting can be removed by grinding in, but if it is serious the valves will have to be refaced by a specialist.

6   Remove the carbon at the tops of the cylinder bores and polish them. Now examine them for scoring, scratching and wear. Start by carefully examining the top of the bores. If they are worn you will detect a very slight ridge at the top of the cylinder at the highest point the piston reaches. Using an internal micrometer, measure the maximum diameter of the cylinder just below this ridge and compare it with the diameter at the bottom where no wear has taken place. If the difference between these diameters exceeds 0.010 in (0.025 mm) you need a rebore. If a micrometer is not available remove the rings from a piston and insert it in its cylinder about ¾ in (19 mm) below the top of the bore. If a 0.010 in (0.025 mm) feeler gauge can be slid between the top of the piston and the cylinder on the right-hand side just below the ridge, a rebore is required. If the wear is less, the diameter difference or feeler gauge thickness will be correspondingly reduced. If it is around 0.004 in (0.010 mm) it is possible to purchase and fit special rings designed to cope with small amounts of cylinder wear and stop the engine burning oil.

7   Reboring followed by the fitting of over-sized pistons is a job for specialists and the local Volvo agent will be able to arrange for this to be done.

44 Piston and piston rings - examination and renovation

Refer to Section 12 of Chapter 1, Part A.

45 Gudgeon pins - general

Refer to Section 13 of Chapter 1, Part A.

46 Rockers and rocker shaft - overhaul

1   Remove the circlips from the ends of the shaft and take off the springs and rockers. Remove the plugs from the ends of the shaft and give it a good clean paying special attention to the oil holes through which the rockers are lubricated. Check the shaft for straightness by rolling it on a flat surface, and for wear which will show as ridges where the rocker arms were running. If any wear is present or the shaft is

appreciably distorted, replace it. Wear is likely to have occurred only if the rocker shaft oil holes have become blocked.

2   Check the rocker arms for wear on the rocker arm bushes. There should be no appreciable play between the rocker arm and the shaft. If there is, the bushes in the rocker arms can be pressed out and replaced but after replacement they must be reamed to fit the shaft correctly. If the equipment is not available have this done by the local Volvo garage.

3   Check the tip of the rocker arm where it bears on the valve for cracking or serious wear. If none is present the rocker arm may be refitted. Otherwise replace it - grinding the face is only a short term remedy because the arm is case-hardened.

4   Check the pushrods for straightness. If bent they must be renewed.

47 Tappets (cam followers) - inspection

Clean these thoroughly and look them over for any indentation on the end that bears on the camshaft. Check that they are a reasonable fit in the cylinder block. It is very unusual to find anything wrong with the tappets.

48 Camshaft - inspection

1   The camshaft and its bearing bushes in the cylinder block are another part of the Volvo engine which seems virtually everlasting. If there is noticeable play between the camshaft and its bearings, they will have to be replaced, but this is a highly specialised job, involving as it does the reaming of three bushes in line - definitely a task for the specialist.

2   The camshaft itself should show no sign of wear. If very light scoring marks are present they can be removed by gently rubbing down with a very fine emery cloth or an oil stone. The greatest care must be taken to keep the cam profiles smooth.

49 Timing gear - overhaul

The Volvo timing system is simplicity itself; only two gears, nothing to adjust. If the fibre gear on the camshaft is worn, replace it. The only thing to notice is the oil spray nipple which can be seen just under the thumb in photo 42.12d. Take this out and give it a good clean.

50 Crankshaft and bearings - examination and renovation

Refer to Section 15 of Chapter 1, Part A.

51 Starter ring gear - renewal

Refer to Section 16 of Chapter 1, Part A.

52 Oil pump - overhaul

Refer to Section 17 of Chapter 1, Part A.

53 Engine - reassembly (general)

Refer to Section 18 of Chapter 1, Part A.

54 Crankshaft - refitting

Refer to Section 19 of Chapter 1, Part A.

55 Pistons and connecting rods - reassembly

Refer to Section 20 of Chapter 1, Part A.

56 Camshaft and timing gear - reassembly

1 Oil the camshaft well and insert it into the block, being careful to keep it straight so that the edges of the cams (which are very sharp) do not hit the bearing bushes and damage them. This is an operation that should be taken gently.

2 When the camshaft is in place, fit the spacing ring over the end and follow this by the retaining flange. Bolt the retaining flange to the block and bend the tab washers over the bolt.

3 Fit the camshaft gear to the shaft, not forgetting the Woodruff key. Press it on gently, using a tool which depends on a bolt screwing into the centre of the camshaft, see Fig. 1.39. Don't hammer it on - see Section 42, paragraph 12 for the reason. Take care with this gear - it is a fibre one and can easily be damaged. Put the nut on the camshaft (there is no washer) and tighten it to 94 - 108 lb f ft (13 - 15 kg fm). Do not try to prevent the gear from turning by putting a screwdriver between the teeth. Some sort of device carrying two bolts which can be pushed into two of the holes in the gear will do the trick with perfect safety.

4 Turn the camshaft and the crankshaft so that when you fit the crankshaft gear with the key in its correct position the timing marks will line up as shown in photo 42.10. Press the gear onto the crankshaft, noting that the key will stick out in front of the gear and engage with the sleeve which you fit next (see photo 42.12d).

57 Distributor - refitting

1 With the timing marks aligned, fit the drive pinion for the distributor in the position required for the distributor rotor to take up the position that was marked for it when the engine was taken apart (see Section 42, paragraph 10). Oil the pinion and its shaft well before fitting them. Fit the distributor flange, using a new gasket. This fitting is the reverse of the dismantling process.

2 Just to check the position of the rotor we mention here that when the timing marks are coincident cylinder No. 4 is at the top end of its compression stroke. Hence the rotor should be selecting the plug on No. 4 cylinder and the points should just have opened.

58 Oil pump - refitting

This is a very simple matter - the driving dog on the oil pump must engage with the dog on the shaft of the distributor drive spindle, and the delivery pipe must be pushed home into its socket in the crankcase. Oil the pump well before assembly and ensure that the flange on the pump is bedding against its mating surface in the crankcase before it is fastened down.

59 Rear sealing flange - refitting

1 Wipe the surface of the cylinder block clean, smear the new gasket very lightly with grease so that once placed on the surface it will not move about and carefully position the gasket on the cylinder block.

2 Refit the sealing flange, but do not at this stage have the felt ring fitted into the flange. Fit the bolts with their spring washers but do not tighten them for the moment.

3 Carefully centre the sealing flange, using feeler gauges to ensure that the distance between the sealing flange and the end of the crankshaft is the same all the way round. Be very careful when moving the flange not to damage the gasket.

4 When it is right, first of all do up the bolts finger-tight and then tighten them up with a spanner as with a cylinder head - each one a little at a time, in crosswise order. Finally, wire them up (see photo 42.15).

5 Oil the felt ring well and fit it into the flange, following it with the washer and circlip. Make sure that the circlip is properly embedded in its groove.

60 Sump - refitting

Refer to Section 24 of Chapter 1, Part A. However as the timing

SVO 2408

Fig. 1.39. Fitting the camshaft gear (Sec. 56)

cover is not fitted at this stage the front bolts cannot be inserted.

61 Fuel pump - refitting

Refer to Section 33 of Chapter 1, Part A.

62 Flywheel and clutch - refitting

1 Clean the mating faces of the crankshaft, flywheel and (in the case of automatic transmission), the spacing and support plates. Refit the flywheel (and support plates if present) to the crankshaft, taking note of any position marks you made when dismantling. Tighten the bolts to a torque of 36 - 40 lb f ft (5 - 5.5 kg fm) (see photo 42.14).

2 Refit the clutch disc and clutch assembly. Refer to Chapter 1, Part A, Section 26 paragraphs 5 to 7.

63 Oil filter - refitting

Refer to Section 34 of Chapter 1, Part A.

64 Valves and springs - refitting to cylinder head

1 Unless there has been some renewal, each valve and spring should be put back in the guide from which it was removed.

2 Fit each valve and valve spring in turn, wiping down and lubricating the valve stem as it is inserted into the guide.

3 As each valve is inserted, slip a new rubber sealing ring over the stem and onto the top of the valve guide.

4 Slip the spring over the stem of the valve and fit the retaining cap into the top of the spring. Position the compressor so that the bottom part of it bears on the head of the valve. Depending on what sort of compressor is being used it may be necessary to rig up some arrangement of wooden wedges or the like to achieve this. Whatever method is being used, be careful not to scratch the valve head, the combustion chamber or the mating surface of the cylinder head.

5 Compress the valve spring until the cotters can be slipped into place in the cotter grooves. It will be helpful to grease the cotters which sometimes had the annoying habit of falling out of the grooves at the critical moment and disappearing under the bench.

65 Water pump - refitting

Refer to Section 25 of Chapter 1, Part A. However as the timing cover is not fitted at this stage the water pump pulley must be removed.

66 Tappets (cam followers) - refitting

1 Lubricate the tappets generously, inside and out and insert them in the bores before fitting the cylinder head.

67 Cylinder head - refitting

1 Refit the cylinder head as described in Chapter 1, Part A, Section 28, paragraphs 1 to 5.
2 Tighten the cylinder head bolts in the order shown in Fig. 1.28 to the Stage 2 specified torque bringing them up to this in two stages. This is not the final tightening value: there will be further tightening after running the engine.

68 Rocker arms and rocker shaft - assembly and refitting

1 Assembling the rocker arms on the rocker shaft is simply a reversal of the dismantling process and calls for no particular comment. Squirt oil into the rocker shaft and oil all the bits and pieces generously.
2 Fit the pushrods, making sure that they are sitting in the top of the tappets.
3 Fit the rocker arm and shaft assembly to the cylinder head.
4 Volvo do not lay down a torque wrench setting for the rocker shaft fixing bolts. We feel that it is a good idea if they are evenly tightened with a torque wrench and suggest a setting of 25 lb f ft (3.4 kg fm).

69 Valve clearance adjustment and cylinder head tightening

1 Adjust the valve clearances between limits 0.002 in (0.05 mm) greater than those laid down in the Specifications. The correct setting will be made when the final cylinder head tightening is carried out after the engine has been run. The simplest method of setting the valve clearances is to use two feeler gauges, one for the lower limit and one for the upper limit. Adjust the clearances so that the thicker feeler gauge will not go between the rocker arm and the valve and the thinner one will fit in quite easily.
2 It is important that the clearance of a valve is set when the tappet operating it is well away from the peak of its cam. This can be done by carrying out the adjustments in the following order, which also avoids turning the crankshaft more than necessary.

Valve fully open	Check and adjust
Valve No. 8	Valve No. 1
Valve No. 6	Valve No. 3
Valve No. 4	Valve No. 5
Valve No. 7	Valve No. 2
Valve No. 1	Valve No. 8
Valve No. 3	Valve No. 6
Valve No. 5	Valve No. 4
Valve No. 2	Valve No. 7

3 Just in case one of our readers doesn't know how to set the valve clearances, we show a photograph of it being done. The locknut on the rocker arm is slackened off and the screw turned to raise or lower the rocker on the pushrod. If two feeler gauges are used as we have suggested, the reader will soon learn what the fit of the thin one feels like when the clearance has been set so that the thicker one won't go in.
4 If the valve clearances are being adjusted as a routine service with the engine in the car, first remove the air cleaner and the rocker arm casing (cover). The clearances may be adjusted cold or hot (see Specifications). Use a new gasket when refitting the rocker cover.

70 Timing gear cover and crankshaft pulley - refitting

1 Though we have fitted the timing gears we have not so far dealt with the timing case cover. The photo shows the preliminary to fitting it - a new gasket fitted to a clean surface very lightly smeared with grease. Fit the cover to the cylinder block, making sure that its mating surface is perfectly clean and very lightly greased, and also making sure that the sump gasket is not damaged. If necessary use a piece of card or a feeler blade to feed the cover over the gasket. Fit the *front* cover bolts finger-tight.
2 Align the cover so that the crankshaft extension is perfectly central in it. It should be possible to insert a 0.004 in (0.02 mm) feeler gauge comfortably all round it. Recheck this after fully tightening the fixing bolts.
3 Fit a new felt ring (well oiled). Follow this with the retaining washer and circlip. Check that the circlip is properly embedded in its groove.

69.3 Adjusting the valve clearance

70.1 Preparing to fit the timing case cover

71.3 Checking the fan belt tension

4   Insert the front sump bolts and tighten to the specified torque.

71 Other fitments - refitting

1   The remaining fitments call for no special instructions. Provided mating surfaces are absolutely clean, with no more than a thin smear of grease used to keep the thinner gaskets in position, you cannot go wrong. The fitting procedures are simply the reverse of dismantling.
2   When you fit the thermostat, remember to fit the clips that carry the clutch cable and the fuel pipe.
3   Fitting the alternator and water pump pulley brings us to the problem of tensioning the fanbelt. Settle for 0.5 in (13 mm) of lateral movement at the mid-point position between the alternator pulley and the crankshaft pulley. Don't have the belt too tight - if you do the alternator and water pump bearings wear rapidly. On the other hand, if the belt slips because it is too loose, it will get hot and very soon pack up. Proper maintenance will prevent this; the only point we are making here is that when tightening a fanbelt you should remember that fanbelts are cheaper and easier to replace than alternators and water pumps (photo). We have not yet mentioned the crankcase breather, which should be given a new seal ring and bolted down with its single bolt. The crankcase ventilation system is covered in Chapter 3.
4   Fit as much of the carburation or fuel injection system as was on the engine when you took it out of the car. We suggest that you don't fit the distributor cap and plug leads at this stage; distributor caps are all too easily damaged.
5   We suggested that in the beginning the engine should be put back in the car with the gearbox attached. If you now fit the gearbox and bellhousing you are at least ready to re-unite the car and engine which by now you are probably beginning to think had been parted for far too long.

72 Engine - refitting

Refer to Section 36 of Chapter 1, Part A.

73 Engine - initial start-up after overhaul or major repair

1   The procedure is the same as described in Section 37 with the exception of the torque loading of the cylinder head bolts, which is given in the Specifications (Stage 3 torque). With the rocker shaft assembly in position it will not be possible to use a socket on the left-hand side cylinder head bolts, and it will therefore be necessary to either obtain a crowfoot adaptor or alternatively to remove the rocker shaft assembly. The valve clearances should be re-checked after using either method.
2   It is recommended that the rocker shaft is removed in preference to using a crowfoot adaptor since the metered torque when using an adaptor has to be calculated using a special formula, and removal of the rocker shaft only involves unscrewing four bolts.

74 Sump - removal and refitting (engine in car)

Refer to Section 38 of Chapter 1, Part A.

75 Fault diagnosis - engine

Refer to Section 39 of Chapter 1, Part A.

Chapter 2 Cooling and heating systems

For modifications, and information applicable to later models, see Supplement at end of manual

Contents

Specifications

Type ... ... Sealed system with expansion tank

Pressure valve opens at
B20 engine ... ... 10 psi (0.7 kg/sq cm)
B21 engine ... ... 9.2 to 12 psi (0.65 to 0.85 kg/sq cm)

Capacity ... ... 16.0 to 16.7 Imp pints (9.6 to 10.0 US qts, 9.1 to 9.5 litres)

Thermostat (B20A)

	Type 1	Type 2
Type	Wax	Wax
Marking	170°	82°
Starts to open at	75 - 78°C (168 - 172°F)	81 - 83°C (177 - 181°F)
Fully open at	89°C (192°F)	90°C (195°F)

Thermostats (B21A & B21E)

	B21A	B21E
Type	Wax	Wax
Marking	92°C	82°C
Starts to open at	91 - 93°C (196 - 199°F)	81 - 83°C (177 - 181°F)
Fully open at	102°C (216°F)	92°C (198°F)

Fanbelts
B20A ... ... HC-38 x 888
B21A (35A alternator) ... ... HC-38 x 925
B21A (55A alternator) ... ... 2 x HC-38 x 925
B21E ... ... 2 x HC-38 x 925

1 General description - cooling system

1 A sealed type cooling system is used on engines fitted to the Volvo 240 series. A diagram of the cooling system is given in Fig. 2.1.

2 The engine coolant is circulated by a thermo-syphon, water pump assisted system, and the coolant is pressurised. This is primarily to prevent premature boiling in adverse conditions and to allow the engine to operate at its most efficient running temperature, this being just under the boiling point of water.

3 With this type of cooling system the overflow pipe from the radiator is connected to an expansion tank, which makes topping-up virtually unnecessary. The coolant expands when hot, and instead of being forced down an overflow pipe and lost, as with the earlier systems, it flows into the expansion tank. As the engine cools the coolant contracts and because of the pressure differential, flows back into the radiator.

4 The cap on the expansion tank is set at a pressure which will increase the boiling point of the coolant to just above that at normal atmospheric pressure.

5 The cooling system comprises the radiator, top and bottom hoses,

the expansion tank, the water pump, the fan and the thermostat. A drain tap is provided on the right-hand side of the cylinder block. The radiator does not have a cap as the system is filled through the expansion tank. The radiator is of the horizontal type having the tanks standing along the sides of the matrix.

6 The system functions as follows: Cold coolant from the radiator circulates up through the lower radiator hose to the water pump, where it is pushed round the water passages in the cylinder block helping to keep the cylinder bores and pistons cool. The coolant then travels up into the cylinder head and circulates around the combustion spaces and valve seats. Then, when the engine is at its normal operating temperature the water flows out of the cylinder head, past the now open thermostat, through the top hose and into the radiator. The coolant flowing down through the radiator matrix is cooled by the time it reaches the bottom hose when the cycle is repeated.

7 When the engine is cold, the thermostat (a valve which opens and closes according to coolant temperature), maintains the circulation of the same coolant in the engine and only when the correct minimum temperature is reached, as given in the Specifications, does the thermostat begin to open, allowing coolant to return to the radiator.

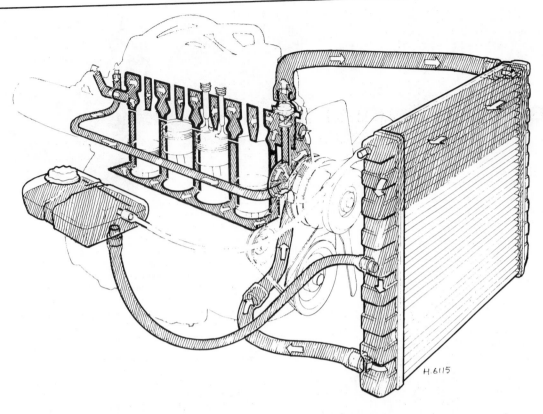

Fig. 2.1. The cooling system (Sec. 1)

2 Cooling system - draining and filling

Volvo recommend the use of a 50% Volvo antifreeze/water mixture all the year round as the antifreeze prevents rusting. The coolant should be changed every two years at the beginning of the winter. If water only is being used in the system, a rustproofing medium should be added.

1 With the cooling system cold remove the expansion tank cap and move the heater controls to hot. Do not remove the tank cap while the engine is hot, as the sudden drop in pressure will cause the coolant to boil.

2 If the system is being drained for reasons other than the renewal of the coolant, place containers to collect the coolant for re-use. Disconnect the bottom radiator hose and open the drain tap on the right-hand side of the engine.

3 Before filling flush the system with clean water. Close the drain tap and connect the bottom radiator hose. Set the heater control to maximum heat.

4 Fill the system with coolant until the level in the expansion tank is at the 'Max' mark or slightly higher. Run the engine for several minutes at different speeds. If necessary, top-up with more coolant and then refit the expansion tank cap. After driving for a short time, check the coolant level again and top-up with more coolant - it takes some time before the system is completely free of air.

Fig. 2.2. The expansion tank (Sec. 2)

3 Radiator - removal and refitting

1 Drain the cooling system, as described in Section 2.

2 Remove the two screws securing the fan shroud and move the shroud rearwards. Disconnect the top radiator hose at the radiator and the expansion tank hoses from the radiator (photo).

3 On cars with automatic transmission, disconnect the oil pipes from the radiator and blank-off the pipes.

4 Remove the two radiator retainers and lift out the radiator (photos).

5 Replacement of the radiator is the reverse of the removal sequence. Fill the cooling system, as described in Section 2. Run the engine at its normal operating temperature and check for leaks at the hose joints.

4 Radiator - inspection and cleaning

1 With the radiator out of the car, any leaks can be repaired by soldering or repaired with a fibre glass paste. Clean out the inside of the radiator by flushing with clean water, turn it upside-down and reverse flush the matrix. Clean the exterior of the radiator by hosing down with a strong jet of water to clean away road dirt and dead flies, etc., which may be lodged in the matrix.

2 Inspect the radiator hoses for cracks, internal or external perishing and damage caused by over-tightening of the hose clips. Renew defective

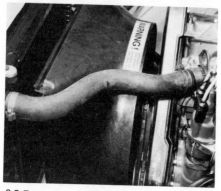

3.2 Removing the shroud securing screws and disconnecting the top radiator hose

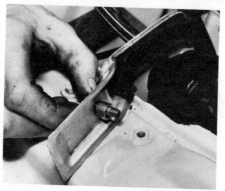

3.4a Removing the radiator retainers

3.4b Lifting out the radiator

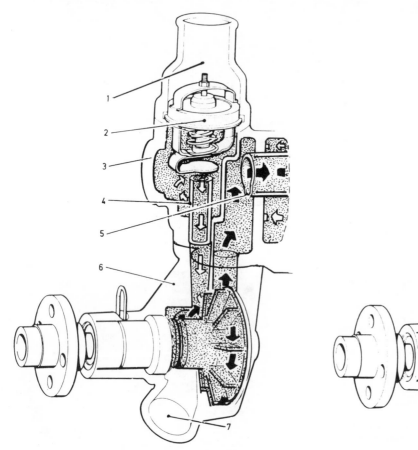

Fig. 2.3. Coolant path - (left) thermostat closed - (right) thermostat open (Sec. 5)

1 To radiator	3 Cylinder head	5 Distributor pipe	7 From radiator
2 Thermostat	4 By-pass	6 Water pump	

hoses. Examine the hose clips and renew them if they are rusted or distorted.

5 Thermostat - removal, testing and refitting

1   The action of the thermostat is shown in Fig. 2.3. Note the definite change-over action when the coolant is allowed to flow through the main hose which is connected from the top of the thermostat casing to the radiator: the circulation path to the water pump is closed up by the tongue on the bottom of the thermostat. For proper operation of the system, therefore, you should be careful not to bend or twist this tongue when removing or fitting the thermostat.

2   To replace a faulty thermostat, lower the level of the coolant in the engine by partially draining the system through the tap on the cylinder block. Collect the coolant in a clean container for using again.

3   Remove the nuts securing the thermostat housing and lifting eye. Lift off the housing and remove the thermostat.

4   Clean off the contact faces of the head and the housing, fit a new thermostat, in the identical position, and a new gasket. Refit the housing and the lifting eye. Refill the system through the expansion tank.

5   To check the performance of a suspect thermostat, suspend it in a container of water which can be heated. As the water warms up, note the temperature at which the thermostat begins to open and also that at which the fully open position is reached. Compare these with the figures in the Specifications at the beginning of this Chapter.

6   Generally speaking, when the thermostat fails it remains shut. This

leads to overheating, and if for any reason you are unable to replace the thermostat you should remove it and run the car without it. This is alright as a temporary measure, but in this situation the engine takes longer to warm up on starting and also there is no regulation of the coolant system to keep the engine at its optimum operating temperature. Therefore, always renew the thermostat at the first opportunity.

6 Water pump - removal and refitting

If the water pump starts to leak, shows signs of excessive movement of the shaft, or is noisy during operation, it should be renewed.
1   Drain the cooling system, as described in Section 2. Remove the two screws securing the fan shroud and push the shroud back over the fan.
2   Remove the fan centre bolt. Remove the fan and the shroud. Slacken the tensioner bolt and remove the belts from the alternator. Remove the fan hub retaining bolts, the fan spacer and pulley.
3   On B21A and B21E engines remove the timing gear cover. Disconnect the radiator hose and the return water pipe. Remove the bolts securing the pump and remove the pump.
4   Remove residue of old gasket on the cylinder block mating surface and also clean the rubber ring contact surface on the cylinder head. Fit a new rubber sealing ring on the new pump, ensure you fit the correct ring. Varying heights of rings are available to allow for different thickness of cylinder head gaskets.
5   Fit a new gasket against the cylinder block, use a smear of grease to hold it in position. Press the pump upwards against the cylinder head and fit the retaining bolts. Fit a new rubber ring on the water return pipe, fit the pipe and the retaining bolts. Connect the lower radiator hose.
6   Fit the timing gear casing (B21A and B21E engines). Fit the fan pulley. Fit and tension the belts, as described in Section 7. Position the fan shroud and fit the fan. Fit the fan shroud retaining screws. Fill the system as described in Section 2.

7 Fanbelts - general

1   According to the type of engine, either one or two fanbelts are fitted. Proper tensioning of the fanbelt will ensure that it has a long and useful life. Where twin belts are fitted always renew both at the same time, even if only one is defective.
2   Adjust the tension by slackening the tensioner bolt of the alternator. With a properly tensioned belt it should be possible to depress it 5/16 in (5 - 10 mm), midway between the fan and the alternator (see Fig. 2.5) with normal force (approx. 18 lb [8 kg]). Always check, and if necessary, adjust the tension on newly fitted belts after 300 miles (500 km) driving.
3   Check regularly to make sure that belts are in good condition and are clean. Worn or dirty belts can cause poor cooling and poor alternator output.

8 Cooling fan - general

1   The B20 and B21 engines have a fixed plastic cooling fan and a slipping viscous drive coupling.
2   At low speeds, the blades revolve at the same speed as the water pump shaft to which it is attached, but as the water pump speed increases the fan speed levels off and for shaft speeds of over 4000 rpm it actually drops as shown in Fig. 2.6.
3   Fig. 2.7. gives a diagram of the fan coupling. The central hub is bolted to a flange which is in turn bolted to the front of the water pump pulley. The fan itself is bolted to the back of the coupling unit with four bolts.
4   The disc attached to the central hub is covered with friction material which causes it to drag against the viscous liquid with which the coupling is filled. Because of the energy dissipated the liquid gets quite hot - hence the cooling fins.
5   It is highly unlikely that this unit will give trouble unless due to wear or mechanical damage the oil leaks out. It is unlikely that this leakage would pass undetected. You can check that all is well with the fan by turning the blades by hand and noting the slight resistance produced in the coupling. If you want to be really fussy you can mark

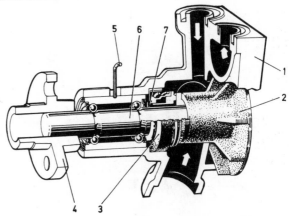

Fig. 2.4 The water pump on the B20 engine (Sec. 6)

1 Housing	*5 Lock spring*
2 Impellor	*6 Shaft with ball bearings*
3 Seal ring	*(integral unit)*
4 Flange	*7 Wear ring*

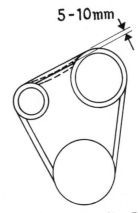

Fig. 2.5. Fan belt tension (Sec. 7)

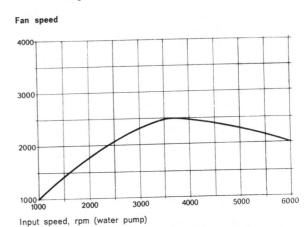

Fan speed

Fig. 2.6. Speed graph for viscous fan coupling (Sec. 8)

Input speed, rpm (water pump)

the fan pulley and the fan itself with chalk, and check their speeds with a stroboscope for comparison with Fig. 2.6.
6   If anything goes wrong with the fan coupling it is very unlikely that you will be able to repair it. The only remedy is renewal.

9   Pressurising of cooling system - general

1   The expansion tank filler cap is provided with a valve which opens at a pressure of 10 psi (0.7 kg/sq cm) above atmospheric on B20 engines or 9.2 to 12 psi (0.65 to 0.85 kg/sq cm) on B21 engines.

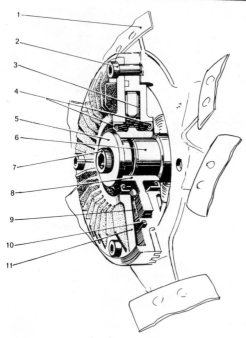

Fig. 2.7. Viscous slip coupling (Sec. 8)

1	Fan blade	7	Centre bolt
2	Bolt	8	Hub
3	Oil	9	Friction material
4	Seals	10	Rubber ring
5	Washer	11	Housing
6	Flange, water pump		

2　If for any reason the water in the system approaches boiling point, air and possibly steam will be driven out through the cap. When the system cools down again another valve in the cap opens to relieve the partial vacuum that would otherwise occur.

3　If the coolant is very close to boiling point, it will certainly start to boil when the expansion chamber cap is removed and coolant may well be forced out and make a mess in the engine compartment which needs to be wiped up as the glycol has a corrosive action. For this reason you should be very careful about opening the cap when the temperature gauge needle is reading high. Put a rag over it, turn it slightly and allow the pressure to dissipate before you remove the cap entirely.

10 Temperature gauge sensor unit - general

1　The sensor for the coolant temperature gauge is a semi-conductor device whose electrical resistance varies with temperature. It is supplied with a constant voltage via the temperature indicator on the instrument panel (see Chapter 10). The variations of resistance cause a varying current to pass through the sensor, and this current is registered on the indicator as a variation in temperature.

2　The sensor is located on the left-hand side of the cylinder head beside the rear inlet port.

3　To remove it, partially drain the cooling system through the tap in the cylinder block (removing the filler cap in the expansion tank) until the level has fallen to just below the cylinder head. To check this, unscrew the sensor slightly and see if there is any tendency for coolant to leak out. When enough coolant has been drained from the system the sensor can be unscrewed and removed for checking.

4　To check the sensor attach temporary extension leads to the device (one from the tag on the top to the lead in the cable harness, the other from the metal part to the frame of the car) and suspend it in a container of water which is then heated up to boiling point. You can check that the needle on the indicator rises smoothly as the water temperature rises, finishing up between normal and hot when the water starts to boil. Do not forget that the boiling point of water in free air is somewhat lower than the boiling point reached in the sealed system (see Section 9).

11 Fault diagnosis - cooling system

Symptom: excessive rise in coolant temperature.
　1　Broken or loose fanbelts.
　2　Low coolant level in system.
　3　Faulty thermostat.
　4　Ignition too far retarded.
　5　Incorrect fuel mixture.
　6　Blocked radiator tubes.
　7　Brakes binding.
Symptom: loss of coolant.
　1　Leaking hoses or joints.
　2　Leaking radiator or drain tap.
　3　Expansion tank cap defective.
　4　Defective cylinder head gasket.
Note: Unlike an open cooling system, the sealed system loses little or no coolant unless there is a definite leak somewhere or overheating is so pronounced that it would be detected quite apart from its effect on the coolant level.

12 Heating system - general description

1　The heating system is a combined warm air/fresh air system. Incoming air is blown by a fan through the miniature radiator in the heater unit and out into the car. The fresh air can be heated and directed to the required areas of the car by various controls.

2　The ducting system varies with the model and year, but all employ the same heating unit. A typical combined heater and fresh air unit is shown in Fig. 2.8. A heat control valve keeps the heated air at a predetermined and constant temperature. This is achieved by the thermostat which is incorporated in the control valve. If the coolant temperature increases, the thermostat capillary expands and acts on the valve in the control system to reduce the flow of coolant.

3　The heater has two separately controlled outputs - floor ducts and defrosters. These are regulated by flaps which are connected by cables to the control unit fixed to the dashboard. A similar cable arrangement from this unit operates the heat control valve. The heater unit is shown in Fig. 2.9.

13 Heater unit - removal and refitting

1　Disconnect the battery for safety reasons.

2　Remove the combined instrument panel (see Chapter 10).

3　Disconnect the hoses to the control valve, the defroster hoses and the control wires. Remove the switch for the fan and disconnect the cables to the fan motor.

4　Unbolt the fuse box from the heater, and then the control valve and the upper hose to the heater unit. Take great care with the control valve and the copper pipe attaching it to the heater as these are easily damaged.

5　Plug the outlets on the heater so that the remaining coolant does not run into the car - antifreeze is not good for paintwork. Disconnect the earthing cable from the right-hand bracket, remove the four screws which hold the heater unit to the brackets and free the drain hose. The heater unit and control valve can now be removed.

6　Refitting is a straightforward reversal of this procedure. Handle the control valve and its connecting pipe with care.

14 Heater unit - overhaul

1　Remove the four rubber bushes on the sides of the heater unit. Mark the fan casing so that you don't have to worry which way round it goes when reassembling. Remove the spring clips (Fig. 2.10) which hold the heater together and separate the two halves. This exposes the matrix system with its thermostatic control and the fan motor.

2　Inspect the matrix for signs of leakage and check that all is well with the flap system. Give it a drop of oil here and there. The only other overhaul procedure is replacement of the motor should its bearing be worn. The mounting plate for the motor is attached to the fan casing by bent over tabs. Straighten these carefully, and remove the mounting plate from the casing. The motor can then be unscrewed from the mounting plate.

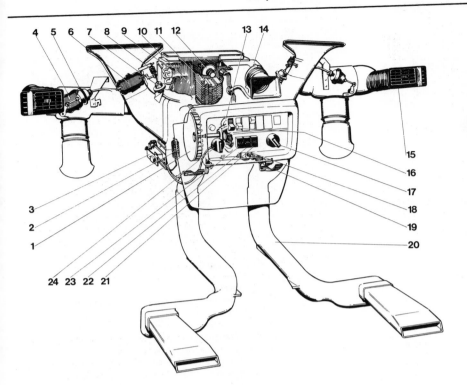

Fig. 2.8. Combined warm air/fresh air unit
(Sec. 12)

1 Turbine
2 Capillary tube for heater control valve
3 Heater control valve
4 Shutter, air vent left floor
5 Vacuum motor
6 Shutter, left defroster nozzle
7 Vacuum motor
8 Return spring for vacuum motor
9 Evaporator (only on vehicles with air
   conditioning)
10 Air intake cover
11 Heater matrix
12 Vacuum motor for air intake cover
13 Fan motor
14 Central unit
15 Blow-in valve
16 Air conditioning switch
17 Fan motor switch
18 Vacuum motor
19 Shutter, right air duct, rear floor
20 Air duct to rear floor
21 Knob, air intake cover
22 Knob, defroster shutter
23 Knob, floor shutter
24 Temperature controls

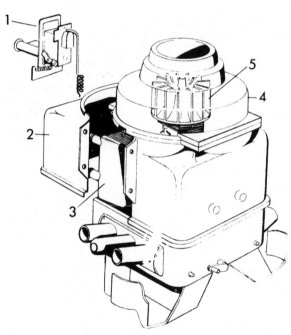

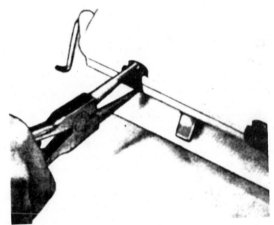

Fig. 2.10. Removing the spring clips on the heater (Sec. 14) (open
pliers to expand the clips)

Fig. 2.9. Heater unit (Sec. 12 and 13)

1 Heat control valve	4 Fan casing
2 Heater casing	5 Fan
3 Matrix	

3 On reassembly, scrape off the old sealing compound at the various
joints in the heater and replace this with a suitable soft sealing agent.
On reassembly use new spring clips and replace the rubber bushings.

15 Heater control unit - general

1 The complete unit is fixed to the dashboard with three nuts. To
remove it, first take out the panel below the dashboard and then free
the cables from the heater unit and control valve.
2 Pull the illuminating lamp and holders out of the unit, leaving them

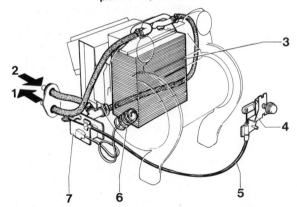

Fig. 2.11. Heater matrix system (Sec. 14)

1 Water hose, output	5 Control cable
2 Water hose, input	6 Capillary tube for heater
3 Matrix	control valve
4 TEMP control	7 Heater control valve

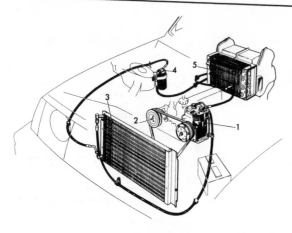

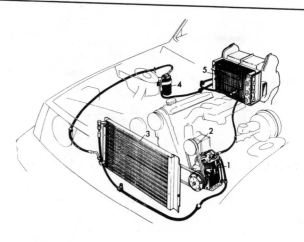

Fig. 2.13. Air conditioner installed - B21 engine (Sec. 16)

1	Compressor	4 Drier
2	Servo pump	5 Evaporator
3	Condenser	

1	Compressor	3	Condenser
2	Air pump or idler pulley	4	Drier
		5	Evaporator

suspended in the wiring, undo the nuts and lift out the unit.

3   Check that the wheels and cables are operating freely. Oil where necessary. Replace any damaged or worn parts.

16 Air-conditioning system - general

1   The air-conditioner is of the compressor type, which means that the refrigerant is circulated by a compressor.

2   Fig. 2.12 and 2.13 show the layout of the air-conditioning units. The system is divided into the main components as follows: condenser, receiver-drier, thermostatic expansion valve and the evaporator. The evaporator and expansion valve are placed in front of the heater matrix assembly inside the car and the other components in the engine compartment.

3   There is little that can be done to it by way of maintenance, apart from keeping one's eye on the compressor drivebelt and the pipeline connections. *Never disconnect any part of the refrigeration circuit*, but have the system discharged by your dealer. The escape of refrigerant gas can injure your health.

Chapter 3 Part A: Fuel system - carburettor models

For modifications, and information applicable to later models, see Supplement at end of manual

Contents

Specifications

Fuel pump

Type	Diaphragm pump
Make, designation	Pierburg APG
Fuel pressure, measured at same level as pump (1000 rpm)	1.5 - 3.5 psi (0.11 - 0.25 kg/sq cm)

Carburettors

	B20A	B21A
Make, designation	SU	Zenith-Stromberg
Designation	HIF-6	175 CD 2SE
Number	1	1
Size (air intake diameter)	1.75 in (44.5 mm)	1.75 in (44.5 mm)
Metering needle, designation	BCJ	B1 ED
Idling speed	700 rpm	850 rpm
Oil for damping cylinder	Automatic transmission fluid	

Max. exhaust CO content:*	Adjusting value	Checking value
B20A (1975)	2.5%	1.5 - 4%
B20A (1976)	1.5%	0.5 - 4%
B21A	2.5%	1.5 - 4%

Fuel type

USA models	RON 91, leaded or unleaded
All other models	RON 93 (3-Star)

Also refer to vehicle decal or handbook

1 General description

The basic fuel system comprises a single fuel tank, mounted at the rear of the car, from which petrol is pumped by a mechanical pump to the horizontally mounted carburettor. The air filter is of the replaceable paper type.

In order to meet air pollution regulations in North America, and elsewhere, modifications and improvements to the basic fuel system have been introduced over the years. Positive crankcase ventilation and improved fuel utilisation during initial warm-up deal with pollution due to products of combustion, while a recycling system prevents petrol vapour from reaching the atmosphere.

2 Fuel pump - general description

1 The fuel pump used in the 240 series is a Pierburg APG, diaphragm type pump.

2 The basic components of the fuel pump are:
A petrol chamber incorporating a filter
An outlet valve
An inlet valve
A diaphragm
A spring which pushes on the diaphragm
A lever which pulls the diaphragm
A small spring against which the lever operates
The inner end of the lever is linked to a rod attached to the diaphragm.

3 If there is no petrol in the pump the diaphragm is pushed up by the spring so that the space inside the fuel chamber is a minimum. In this case, the outer end of the lever is in its lowest position.

4 The lever is operated by a cam on the engine camshaft. The cam pushes the lever upwards, the diaphragm is drawn downwards, the space inside the fuel chamber increases and petrol is sucked in to fill the resulting vacuum. When the cam leaves the lever, the diaphragm

returns to its original position, but the inlet valve stops the petrol from returning to the tank.

5   As this operation is repeated, the fuel chamber soon fills with petrol which passes through the outlet valve and outlet pipe to the carburettor float chamber. When the float chamber is full, the carburettor needle valve closes and no more petrol can pass along the pipe.

6   When this happens, the diaphragm cannot return to its original position. Soon the pump becomes full of petrol and the diaphragm is extended downwards, holding the lever away from the cam on the camshaft which operates it.

7   When the level in the carburettor float chamber drops, the needle valve opens and petrol can once more pass along the outlet pipe. The diaphragm moves upwards as it pushes the petrol out, the lever moves closer to the cam and the diaphragm is operated until the pump is again filled up.

3   Fuel pump - importance of efficient operation

1   Fuel is only pumped to the carburettor when required by the level of fuel in the carburettor bowl. Although the pump arm works continuously, integral valves control the flow and pressure according to requirements.

2   Any air leakage on the inlet side will cause the pump to take in air and so reduce its efficiency. Very often mechanical pumps are fitted below the level of the petrol tank so that the inlet pipe does not empty back into the tank if there is air leakage. This means that there is no direct indication that leakage is occurring and causing the pump to work harder than it ought, so it is a good idea to check that all is well on the inlet side of the fuel pump from time to time.

4   Fuel pump - removal and refitting

1   Remove the fuel inlet and outlet connections from the fuel pump and plug the ends of the pipes to stop loss of fuel and the entrance of dirt.

2   Unscrew the bolts holding the pump body to the crankcase and lift it away.

3   Remove the fuel from the pump - by operating the lever a few times - before dismantling it.

4   Refitting is the reverse process to removal. Inspect the gaskets on either side of the insulating block and if they are damaged replace them with new ones.

5   Fuel pump - dismantling

1   Thoroughly clean the outside of the pump with paraffin or a proprietary solvent and then dry. To ensure correct reassembly mark the upper and lower body flanges.

2   Take off the cover and remove the gasket and fuel strainer.

3   Undo the six screws joining the upper and lower pump housing and separate these, freeing the diaphragm which is sandwiched between them. Be very careful not to damage the diaphragm in the process.

4   Remove the circlip from the lever shaft, push out the shaft, remove the lever and its return spring.

5   Remove the diaphragm with the spring, spring guide and rubber seal. The spring can be removed after the rubber seal has been levered over the nylon washer.

6   Remove the screw on the underside of the upper body section, take out the stop arm and the leaf spring inlet valve (see Fig. 3.1).

6   Fuel pump - inspection and reassembly

1   Thoroughly clean all parts in paraffin. Dry off and examine each part for signs of wear. As we have already pointed out, very little mechanical wear can be accepted. Look for it on the rocker arm pin or bearing holes, the face of the cam lever and the diaphragm pull rod. Renew any part about which you are doubtful.

2   The diaphragm and pull rod (a single assembly) must be renewed if there are any signs of wear or cracking in the diaphragm.

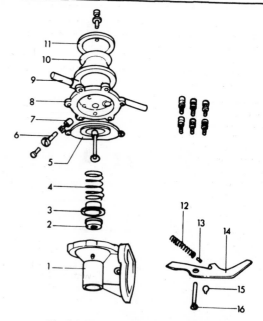

Fig. 3.1. Pierburg fuel pump (Sec. 5)

1	Lower pump housing	9	Inlet pipe
2	Rubber seal	10	Strainer
3	Guides	11	Cover with gasket
4	Diaphragm spring	12	Return spring
5	Diaphragm	13	Spring holder
6	Stop arm	14	Lever
7	Spring	15	Circlip
8	Upper pump housing	16	Lever shaft

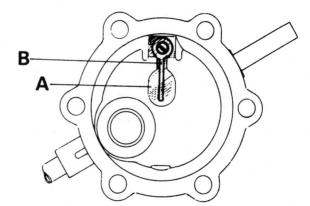

Fig. 3.2. Underside view of upper body, Pierburg fuel pump (Sec. 6)

A   Inlet valve   B   Stop arm

3   Check that the seating surface for the inlet valve spring is clean and smooth and that the port edges are free from burrs. There is no provision for removing the outlet valve, but it never seems to give any trouble. Ensure that it is clean before you reassemble the pump.

4   To reassemble, first install the cam lever and its pivot pin in the lower body. Replace the lever return spring.

5   Assemble the diaphragm spring, seal and washer in the order in which they were dismantled and centre the diaphragm in the return spring. Engage the diaphragm pull rod with the lever and position the diaphragm so that the holes round its edge are exactly in line with those on the body flange. When all is correctly positioned, check that the pull rod is properly seated in the lever fork and that everything operates smoothly.

6   To fit the upper half of the body, hold the diaphragm against the flange by pushing on the lever while placing the upper body in position, with the alignment marks made on the two flanges coinciding. Insert the six screws and tighten them until the heads just engage with the

spring washers. Check that the diaphragm is correctly centred and that it does not overlap the edge at any point. Then tighten the screws alternately until all are fully home.

7   Replace the filter gauze and refit the top cover using a new gasket. Do not overtighten the screw on the top cover or you may distort the cover and be troubled with leakage at the joint.

7   Fuel pump - testing

1   Hold the pump steady in the protected jaws of a vice. Fit two short lengths of plastic tube to the inlet and outlet pipes and take the inlet tube to a container of paraffin (much safer than petrol) set a short distance away, with the paraffin level slightly above that of the pump. Insert the end of the outlet pump into a measuring jar set a little below the pump. Pump with the lever arm until paraffin is coming through without bubbles. Once pumping is established the pump should deliver not less than 1.75 fl oz (50 cc) in 10 strokes. If the delivery is below this, it indicates a faulty valve or weak diaphragm return spring. If bubbles appear continuously in the output, an air leak somewhere in the chamber is the cause.

2   Empty the pump of paraffin and remove the plastic tubes. Push up the cam lever, cover the end of the inlet pipe with one finger and then release the cam lever - a distinct suction should be felt, the lever should return very slowly, and on removing the finger there should be an inrush of air as the lever springs back.

8   Fuel tank - cleaning filter, and removal and refitting

1   At the intervals specified in Routine Maintenance the fuel level sender unit must be removed from the fuel tank and the filter which is attached to it must be cleaned.

2   To remove the sender unit disconnect the battery earth terminal and lift the mat in the boot.

3   Remove the cover plate and disconnect the earth wire and the lead from the sender unit terminal.

4   Make up a tool similar to the one shown in Fig. 3.3 to engage in the sender unit cover plate cut-outs and turn it in an anticlockwise direction.

5   Refitting is the reversal of removal. Always fit a new gasket.

6   To remove the tank, refer to Part B, Section 30.

9   Carburettor (SU) - general description

1   The variable choke SU carburettor is a relatively simple instrument. It differs from most other carburettors in that instead of having a number of various fixed jets for different conditions, only one variable jet is fitted to deal with all possible conditions.

2   Air passing rapidly through the carburettor draws petrol from the jet so forming the petrol/air mixture. The amount of petrol drawn from the jet depends on the position of the tapered carburettor needle, which moves up and down the jet orifice according to the engine load and throttle opening, thus effectively altering the size of jet so that exactly the right amount of fuel is metered for the prevailing road conditions.

3   The position of the tapered needle in the jet is determined by engine vacuum. The shank of the needle is held at its top end in a piston which slides up and down the dashpot in response to the degree of manifold vacuum.

4   With the throttle fully open, the full effect of inlet manifold vacuum is felt by the piston which has an air bleed into the choke tube on the outside of the throttle. This causes the piston to rise fully, bringing the needle with it. With the accelerator partially closed, only slight inlet manifold vacuum is felt by the piston (although, of course, on the engine side of the throttle the vacuum is greater), and the piston only rises a little, blocking most of the jet orifice with the metering needle.

5   To prevent the piston fluttering and giving a richer mixture when the accelerator is suddenly depressed, an oil damper and light spring are fitted inside the dashpot.

6   The only portion of the piston assembly to come into contact with the piston chamber or dashpot is the actual central piston rod. All the other parts of the piston assembly, including the lower choke portion, have sufficient clearance to prevent any direct metal to metal contact which is essential if the carburettor is to function correctly.

Fig. 3.3. Fuel level sender unit

1   Filter

2   Tool for releasing sender unit flange

7   The correct level of the petrol in the carburettor is determined by the level of the float chamber. When the level is correct the float rises and, by means of a lever resting on top of it, closes the needle valve in the cover of the float chamber. This closes off the supply of fuel from the pump. When the level in the float chamber drops as fuel is used in the carburettor, the float drops. As it does, the float needle is unseated so allowing more fuel to enter the float chamber and restore the correct level.

10 Carburettor (SU-HIF6) - removal and refitting

1   Remove the air cleaner.

2   Detach the fuel pipe from the carburettor float chamber union.

3   Disconnect the distributor vacuum pipe from the carburettor.

4   Note the throttle and choke control connections and then disconnect them.

5   Remove the carburettor retaining nuts and withdraw the carburettor from the inlet manifold.

6   Cover the inlet manifold aperture with masking tape or blank off with a rag to prevent dirt ingress.

7   Refitting the carburettor is the reverse of the removal sequence. Always use new gaskets. Top-up the carburettor damper.

11 Carburettor (SU-HIF6) - dismantling, inspection and overhaul

1   Assuming that the carburettor is on the workbench, start by cleaning the exterior thoroughly with paraffin or a proprietary solvent, using a stiff brush where necessary.

2   Undo the cap at the top of the carburettor and withdraw it complete with the small damper piston. Empty the oil from the dashpot.

3   Mark the position of the float chamber cover relative to the body and remove it by unscrewing the four screws holding it down. Empty out any fuel still in the fuel chamber.

4   The float is held to the body by a spindle having a screw head on it (shown in Fig. 3.5). Unscrew and remove the spindle with its sealing washer, remove the float, unscrew the needle valve socket and remove it and the needle.

5   Dismantle the various control linkages, being sure that it is understood how the linkages work before they are taken off. It is an easy matter to sort this out before taking them apart, but much more difficult when they are in bits.

6   Unscrew the nut holding the fast idle cam - having first straightened its tab washer, take off the cam and its spring which is contained in a small housing behind it. Undo the two screws holding down this housing and pull on the spindle which held the fast idle cam and the whole cold start assembly will come out of the body. It is shown in Fig. 3.4.

7   Undo the screws holding the throttle disc into its shaft, being careful not to put too much pressure on the shaft in the process (support it with the other hand). Remove the disc and withdraw the throttle shaft.

8   Mark the flanges and remove the top part of the body (suction chamber) and the piston. Be careful of the needle on the end of the piston - a good idea is to stand the piston on a narrow-necked jar with the needle hanging inside it.

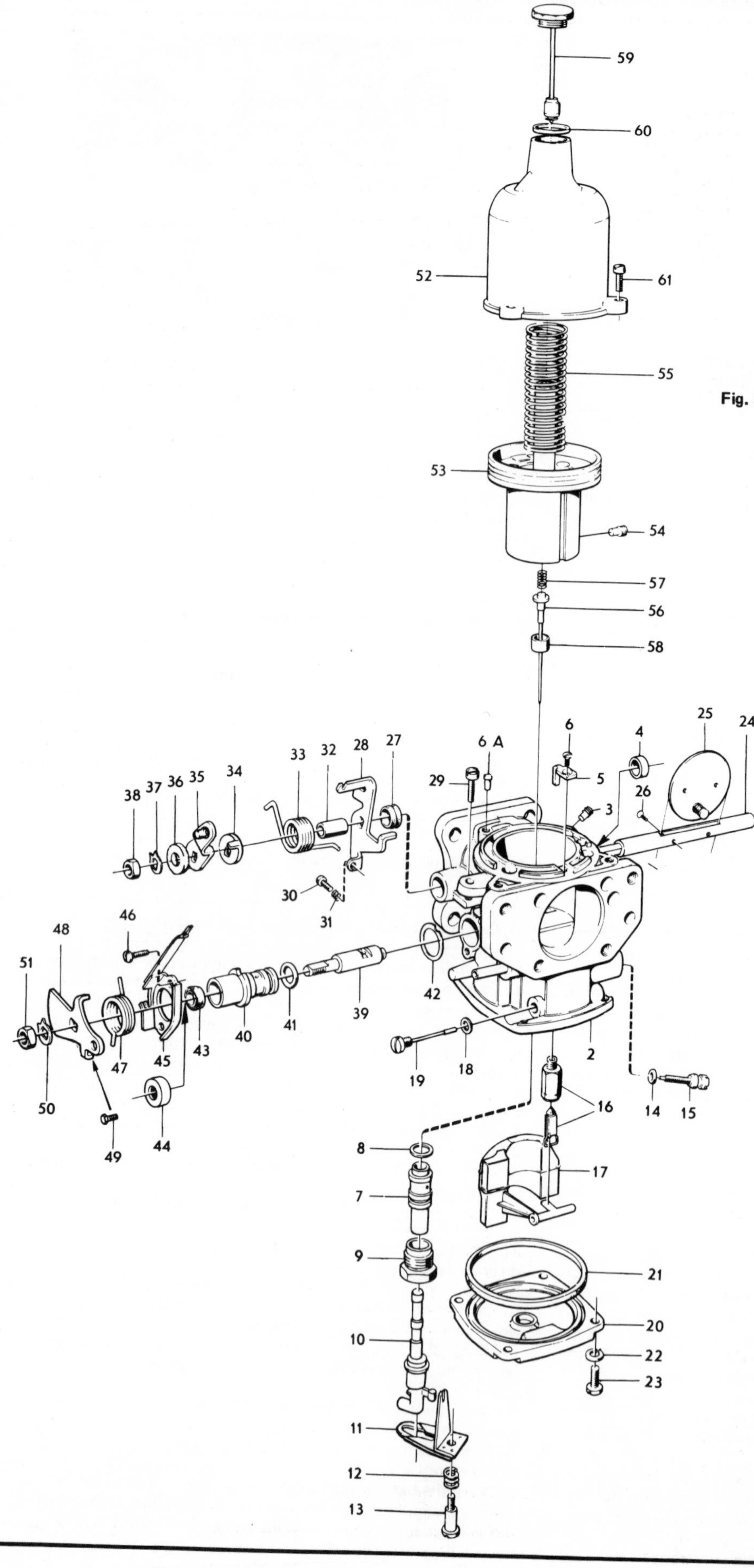

Fig. 3.4. SU HIF 6 carburettor - exploded view

2 Housing
3 Plug
4 Bushing
5 Key
6 Screw
6a Nipple
7 Bearing
8 Gasket
9 Screw
10 Jet
11 Bi-metal assembly
12 Spring
13 Screw
14 O-ring
15 Adjuster screw
16 Needle valve with seat
17 Float
18 Gasket
19 Spindle
20 Cover
21 Rubber ring
22 Spring washer
23 Screw
24 Spindle
25 Throttle disc
26 Screw
27 Seal ring
28 Throttle return lever
29 Adjuster screw
30 Adjuster screw
31 Spring
32 Distance sleeve
33 Spring
34 Throttle actuating lever
35 Throttle pick-up lever
36 Bushing
37 Lockwasher
38 Nut
39 Cold start device spindle
40 Valve sleeve
41 O-ring
42 Gasket
43 Seal ring
44 Guide
45 Retainer
46 Screw
47 Return spring
48 Fast idle cam
49 Screw
50 Lockwasher
51 Nut
52 Vacuum chamber
53 Piston
54 Screw
55 Spring
56 Jet needle
57 Spring
58 Guide
59 Damper
60 Gasket
61 Screw

Fig. 3.5. Jet and float assembly (Sec. 11)

1 Fixing screw for bi-metal   3 Bi-metal assembly
   assembly   4 Float valve retainer
2 Spring   5 Drilling to cold start valve

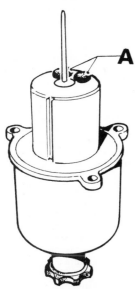

Fig. 3.6. Testing fit of piston in suction chamber (Sec. 11)

A Rubber or cork plugs

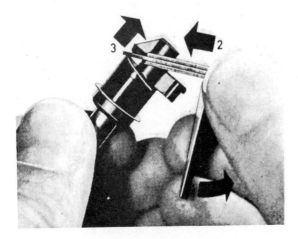

Fig. 3.7. Removal of bi-metal strip from jet (Sec. 11)

9 Unscrew the jet adjusting screw and remove the bi-metal assembly holding the jet.
10 The carburettor is now sufficiently dismantled for inspection to be carried out. One or two adjusting screws and the like have been left in the body, but it is recommended that these are only removed when actually ensuring that the various channels are clear. Generally speaking, the SU carburettor is very reliable but even so it may develop faults, which are not readily apparent unless a careful inspection is carried out, yet may nevertheless effect engine performance. So it is well worthwhile giving the carburettor a good look over when it has been dismantled.
11 Inspect the carburettor needle for ridging. If this is apparent it will probably be found that there is corresponding wear on the inside of the jet. If the needle is ridged, it must be replaced. Do not attempt to rub it down with abrasive paper as carburettor needles are made to very fine tolerances.
12 When replacing the needle locate it in the piston as shown in Fig. 3.6. The supporting stubs should be flush with the piston and the engraved line should point directly away from the channel in the piston face. Note that this makes the needle incline in the direction of the carburettor air cleaner flange when the piston is fitted.
13 Inspect the jet for wear. Wear inside the jet will accompany wear on the needle. If any wear is apparent on the jet, replace it. It may be unhooked from the bi-metal spring and this may be used again (see Fig. 3.7).
14 Inspect the piston and the carburettor body (suction chamber) carefully for signs that these have not been in contact. When the carburettor is operating the main piston should not come into contact with the carburettor body. The whole assembly is supported by the rod of the piston which slides in the centre guide tube, this rod being attached to the cap in the top of the carburettor body. It is possible for wear in the centre guide to allow the piston to touch the wall of the body. Check for this by assembling the small piston in the carburettor body and sliding the large one down, rotating it about the centre guide tube at the same time. If contact occurs and the cause is worn parts, replace them. In no circumstances try to correct piston sticking by altering the tension of the return spring, though very slight contact with the body may be cured - as a temporary measure - by polishing the offending portion of the body wall with metal polish or extremely fine wet and dry paper.
15 The fit of the piston in the suction chamber can be checked by plugging the air hole in the body and assembling the piston in the chamber without its return spring, fitting the damper piston without filling the dashpot with oil. If the assembly is now turned upside down as shown in Fig. 3.6 the piston would sink to the bottom in 5 - 7 seconds. If the time is appreciably less than this, the piston and suction chamber should both be replaced since they are matched to each other.
16 Check for wear on the throttle shaft and bushes through which it passes. Apart from the nuisance of a sticking throttle, excessive wear here can cause air leaks in the induction system adversely affecting engine performance. Worn bushes can be extracted and new bushes fitted if necessary. For inspection and overhaul of the cold start device see Section 12.
17 Reassembly is a straightforward reversal of the dismantling process. During reassembly the float level can be checked and adjusted if necessary as described in Section 13. When assembling the jet, screw up the adjusting screw so that the upper edge of the jet comes level with the bridge, then turn it 2½ turns clockwise. This gives the initial position for jet adjustment. Fig. 4.5 shows the jet assembled on the bi-metallic strip in the main body and also indicates the correct positioning of the float valve retainer on the tab on the float arm.
18 When the carburettor is assembled, the dashpot should be filled with automatic transmission fluid to within 0.25 in (6 mm) of the top of the cylinder before re-inserting the damper piston. Check that the piston is operating properly by lifting it with the lifting pin and letting it fall. It should hit the bridge of the carburettor with an audible metallic click. If it does not, perhaps the needle is fouling the jet (it is supposed to touch it lightly). This should not occur with careful assembly; there is no provision for centering the jet but if it is properly assembled this is not necessary.

12 Carburettor (SU-HIF6) - cold start device

1   The cold start device is shown assembled in Fig. 3.8 and a diagram is given in Fig. 3.9 from which it will be seen that as the spindle

(which also carries the fast idle cam) revolves, a 'V' shaped slot in the spindle progressively opens a channel between the float chamber and throttle chamber. At the same time a small air channel is opened so that a little air is mixed with the incoming vapour.

2   The fast idle cam operates the throttle by acting on a stop screw on a lever on the throttle shaft.

3   The whole device can be removed from the carburettor body (see

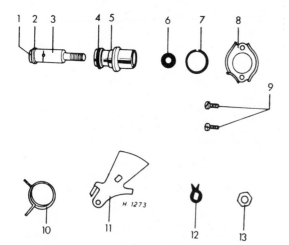

Fig. 3.8. SU HIF 6 carburettor - cold start device (Sec. 12)

1   Circlip
2   Washer
3   Spindle
4   Rubber ring
5   Housing
6   Rubber seal for spindle
7   Gasket
8   Spring retainer
9   Fixing screws
10 Return spring
11 Fast idle cam
12 Tab washer
13 Nut

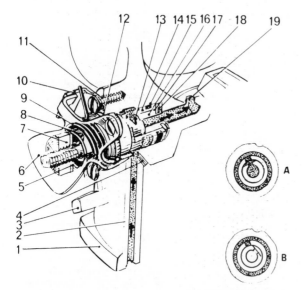

Fig. 3.9. SU HIF 6 - cold start device (Sec. 12)

A   Disengaged
B   Engaged
1   Carburettor housing
2   Channel from float chamber
3   Stop tab for lever
4   Channel for additional air
5   Tab washer
6   Cam for fast idle
7   Nut
8   Sealing
9   Return spring
10 Spring retainer
11 Screw
12 Packing
13 V-slot
14 Valve housing
15 Rubber ring
16 Spindle
17 Washer
18 Circlip
19 Channel to carburettor throttle chamber

Section 11, paragraph 6) and dismantled for cleaning and inspection. If kept oiled it should give no trouble. Should the spindle or the housing show signs of wear they should both be replaced.

13 Carburettor (SU-HIF6) - checking the float level

1   This is best checked with the carburettor body upside-down. The float will then be resting on the needle valve. The lowest part of the float should then be just a little higher than the face of the carburettor body, as illustrated in Fig. 3.10.

2   The distance between the float and the flange (measurement 'A' in Fig. 3.10) should be between 0.02 - 0.06 in (0.5 - 1.5 mm).

3   The level can be adjusted by carefully bending the metal tab on the float arm. Do not attempt to bend the arm itself. If there is a plastic tab instead of metal one, no adjustment is possible but it is unlikely to be needed.

4   There is no reason why this measurement should not be checked with the carburettor in-situ, holding the float against the flange whilst it is being done. It is awkward but possible.

14 Carburettor (SU-HIF6) - tuning

1   Before tuning the carburettor check that the valve clearances, spark plug gaps, contact breaker settings and ignition timing are all correct, that there is no air leak on the intake system and that the vacuum ignition advance tube is in place. Make the final adjustments with the engine at its normal running temperature and finish off by setting the throttle stop to give the proper idling speed when the air cleaner and crankcase ventilation pipes (which are removed when tuning so that you can check piston position etc.) have been refitted.

2   Unscrew the throttle adjusting screw until it is just clear of the throttle lever with the throttle closed. Check that the cold start lever is fully closed (cold start device out of action) and that the fast idle adjusting screw is well clear of the cam. Failure to observe this may result in the throttle being held open when, by external examination, it appears closed. Turn the throttle adjusting screw one and a half turns clockwise to open the throttle for a datum position.

3   Lift the piston with the piston lifting pin, checking that it falls freely when the pin is released.

4   Lift the piston high enough to reveal the bridge and jet. Turn the jet adjusting screw to bring the top of the jet flush with the bridge, or as near the top as possible. Turn the jet adjusting screw two turns clockwise to set the jet height to a datum position.

5   Start and run the engine until it reaches normal working temperature, and continue to run for approximately five minutes at the correct temperature until an even temperature is established.

6   Increase the engine speed to 2500 rpm for approximately 30 seconds. This will clear the plugs and any condensed fuel from the inlet manifold walls.

7   Adjust the throttle adjusting screw to obtain the correct idling speed as given in Specifications at the beginning of this Chapter.

8   Set the correct mixture strength by adjustment of the jet adjusting screw (turn clockwise to enrich and anticlockwise to weaken) until the fastest engine speed (with given throttle adjusting screw position) is obtained. The fastest engine speed must be obtained when adjusting from a weak setting and approaching a rich setting, so having found the correct setting, turn the screw anticlockwise until a small but perceptible

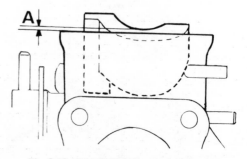

Fig. 3.10. SU HIF 6 - float level (Sec. 13)

A = 0.02 - 0.06 in (0.5 - 1.5 mm)

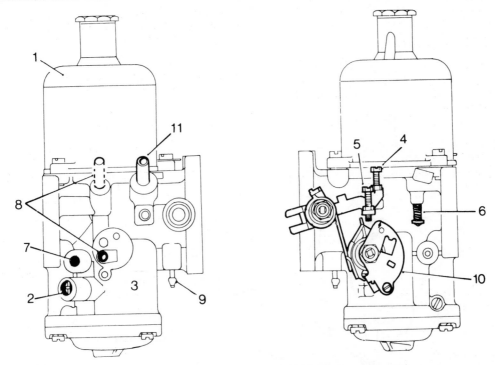

Fig. 3.11. SU HIF 6 carburettor - tuning and adjustment (Sec. 14)

1 Piston/suction chamber	5 Fast-idle adjusting screw
2 Jet adjusting screw	6 Piston lifting pin
3 Float chamber	7 Fuel inlet
4 Throttle adjusting screw	8 Vent tube (alternative positions)

9   Auto ignition connection
10 Cold start enrichment lever (cam lever)
11 Crankcase ventilation tube

fall in speed is noticed, then turn the screw clockwise very slowly until the maximum speed is regained. If the correct position is 'overshot', open the throttle to clear the engine, return to the weak setting and repeat the tuning procedure.

9   Following the mixture strength setting, the idling speed may need re-adjusting by adjustment of the throttle adjustment screw to restore the specified speed.

10 It is at this stage that the exhaust gas analysing test should be applied, if the tuning were being performed by an operator with this facility. The mixture strength obtained by very careful application of the procedures given above, gives only an approximation to correct carburation: final adjustment being made in conjunction with the exhaust analysis equipment to bring the carbon monoxide (CO) percentage within the specified limits. Therefore, in countries where stringent exhaust emission control laws exist, the foregoing tuning procedures must be regarded as for information or emergency use only.

11 To set the fast idle pull out the choke control on the instrument panel until the arrow marked on the cam is directly under the fast idle adjusting screw. Turn the screw to obtain a fast idle speed of 1100 to 1600 rpm. In very cold conditions it may be desirable to set the idling speed slightly faster.

12 Lock both adjusting screws, taking care not to disturb the settings. Refit the air cleaner.

15 Carburettor (Stromberg) - general description

1   The Stromberg type 175 CD-2SE carburettor is used on some models in the Volvo 240 series.

2   The carburettor has been specially designed to reduce exhaust emission to a minimum and to be compatible with other devices in the exhaust emission control system.

3   The carburettor is fitted with a temperature compensator which acts as an air valve during periods of high under-bonnet or fuel temperature levels.

4   A hot-start valve is fitted to offset the effects of accumulations of fuel vapour which occur in the carburettor intake during periods of high under-bonnet temperatures. This vapour originates from the carburettor float chamber and makes it difficult to start the engine in hot conditions. The valve discharges the fumes to atmosphere under throttle closed conditions and then deflects them into the air cleaner where they are drawn into the engine as soon as the engine starts running.

16 Carburettor (Stromberg) - removal and refitting

The sequence for the removal of the Stromberg carburettor is basically the same as that for the SU carburettor. Refer to Section 10 for removal procedure.

17 Carburettor (Stromberg) - dismantling, inspection and overhaul

1   With the carburettor removed from the car, clean away all external dirt.

2   Set the carburettor on the bench and arrange to have two or three small containers ready for screws and small components that can easily get lost.

3   Mark the position of the float chamber lid relative to the body and remove it by unscrewing the six screws holding it down. It is sealed to a blind plug which holds the jet in position. Ease it off carefully, turning it to-and-fro. Empty out any fuel still in the float chamber.

4   Carefully push out the pin on which the float is pivoted to the main body, take out the float and unscrew the needle valve assembly.

5   Dismantle the various linkages on the body and remove the temperature compensating device, the bypass valve and the cold start device (Figs. 3.14 - 3.17).

6   Undo the cap at the top of the body and remove it complete with the damper piston. Empty the oil from the dashpot. Remove the upper part of the carburettor body, marking the flanges so that you will not have to think twice about its position when replacing it. Remove and dismantle the piston, needle and diaphragm assembly. Treat this assembly carefully - a good idea is to stand the piston in the top of a jar with the needle hanging down inside.

7   Remove the blind plug from the main body, being careful not to

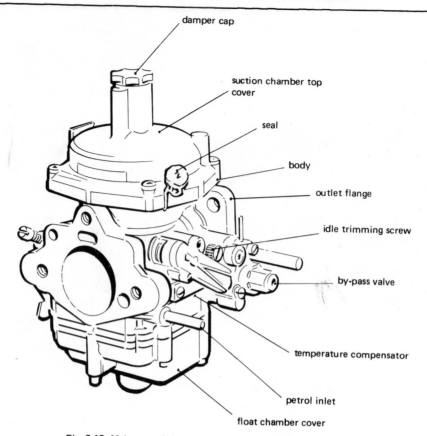

Fig. 3.12. Major components of Stromberg carburettor (Sec. 17)

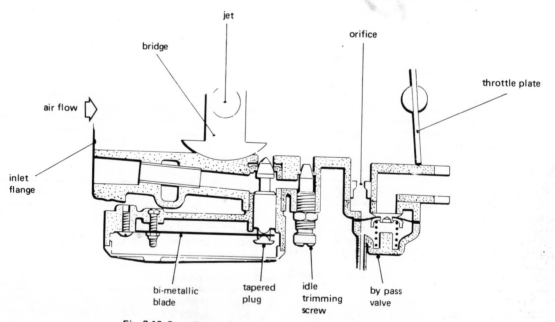

Fig. 3.13. Stromberg carburettor - cross-section through drive (Sec. 17)

damage the surface where it seals to the float chamber cover. Underneath it you will see a tube which is pressed into the main body and communicates with the jet. The jet itself is pressed into the body from the other end. Its removal and replacement is a matter for the specialist.

8   Undo the screws holding the throttle disc into its shaft, being careful not to put too much pressure on the shaft in the process (support it with the other hand). Remove the disc and withdraw the throttle shaft.

9   The carburettor is now sufficiently dismantled for inspection to take place. One or two adjusting screws still remain in the body, but these are best removed as you clean out the various airways and

replaced immediately. Generally speaking the Stromberg carburettor is very reliable but even so it may develop faults which are not readily apparent unless a careful inspection is carried out, yet may nevertheless affect engine performance. So giving the carburettor a good looking over when dismantled, is well worthwhile.

10 Start by cleaning the various parts, making sure that the air channels in the main body are completely clear. This is best achieved by blowing through them.

11 Inspect the carburettor needle for ridging. If the needle is ridged, it must be renewed - do not attempt to rub it down with abrasive paper as carburettor needles are made to very fine tolerances.

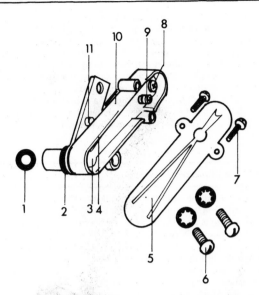

Fig. 3.14. Stromberg carburettor - temperature compensator (Sec. 17)

1 Rubber seal	7 Screw for cover
2 Rubber seal	8 Cross-slotted screw
3 Valve	9 Adjustment nut
4 Bi-metal spring	10 Housing
5 Cover	11 Identity label
6 Screw for temperature compensator	

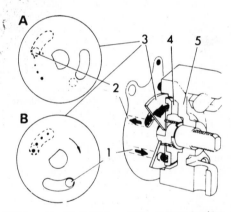

Fig. 3.15. Stromberg carburettor - cold start device (Sec. 17)

A Cold start device 'off'	B Cold start device fully 'on'
1 Passage from float chamber	3 Pierced disc
2 Passage to throttle chamber	4 Channel disc
	5 Housing

12 Where the jet is removable, inspect it for wear. Wear inside the jet may well accompany wear on the needle. If the jet is worn, replace it. Where the jet is pressed into the main body, it can be examined from above. Replacement, if worn, is a matter for the specialist.

13 Examine the diaphragm and replace it if it shows any sign of weakness or cracking. Examine the piston, in particular the dashpot cylinder on the top of it but unless there has been any maltreatment (such as dropping) it is unusual to find anything wrong. Check that the damper piston has a to-and-fro movement along its shaft of between 0.04 - 0.07 in (1.1 - 1.9 mm) and that it moves perfectly freely. This movement is essential for proper damping action. If there is any fault in the assembly, replace it complete.

14 Check for wear on the throttle shaft and the bushes through which it passes. Apart from the nuisance of a sticking throttle, excessive wear here can cause air leaks in the induction system (though this is less likely when the bushes are sealed) affecting the performance. Worn bushes can be extracted and new bushes fitted if necessary.

15 Reassembly is largely a reversal of the dismantling procedure, but the following internal adjustments and checks must be carried out during the process.

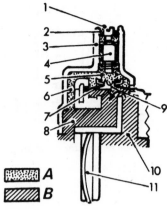

Fig. 3.16. Stromberg carburettor - bypass valve - diagram (Secs. 17 and 18)

1 Adjusting screw
2 Rubber ring
3 Cover
4 Nut
5 Spring
6 Drilling to underside of diaphragm
7 Diaphragm
8 Outlet channel for fuel/air fixing
9 Valve
10 Inlet channel for fuel/air mixing
11 Flap
Shading A = Vacuum   B = Fuel/air mixture

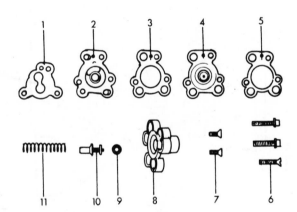

Fig. 3.17. Stromberg carburettor - bypass valve dismantled (Secs. 17 and 18)

1 Gasket	7 Cover screw
2 Housing	8 Cover
3 Gasket	9 Rubber ring
4 Diaphragm	10 Adjusting screw
5 Gasket	11 Spring
6 Fixing screws	

16 Thoroughly clean the channels of the bypass valve.

17 When refitting the cold start device to the carburettor, make sure that the mating surfaces are completely clean and smooth: there is no gasket. The outer end of the spindle carries a combined choke control lever and fast idling cam. The cam bears an engraved mark which should be set opposite the fast idle screw when the fast idling is adjusted.

18 Check that the temperature compensator valve moves easily in its housing. If necessary, it can be centred by slackening its crosshead screw which secures the bi-metallic strip and adjusting its position.

19 Float adjustment is illustrated in Fig. 3.18. It is achieved by bending the lug on the float arm which bears on the needle valve. With the carburettor body inverted, check the dimensions 'A' and 'B' and bend as necessary. It is possible to carry out this adjustment with the carburettor in-situ by pressing the float lightly against the needle valve, but a great deal more awkward. Do not try to bend the arm between the float and the needle valve.

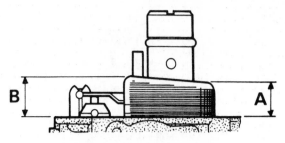

Fig. 3.18. Stromberg carburettor - float level (Sec. 17)

A = 0.35 - 0.51 in (9 - 13 mm)
B = 0.59 - 0.67 in (15 - 17 mm)

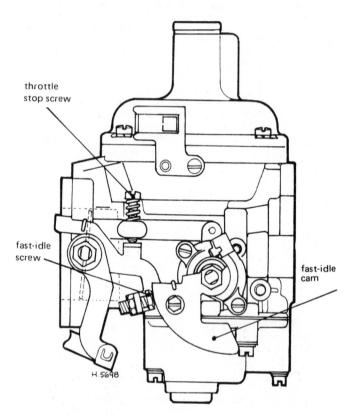

Fig. 3.19. Stromberg carburettor - tuning and adjustment (Sec. 19)

20 When refitting the flexible diaphragm, make sure that the lugs engage correctly in both the carburettor body and the piston.
21 Finally fill the dashpot with automatic transmission fluid to within 0.25 in (6 mm) of the top of the carburettor before inserting the damper piston.

18 Carburettor (Stromberg) - bypass valve

1   The purpose of this valve is to ensure that when the throttle is shut off with the engine running at high speed a certain amount of air still enters the engine, ensuring proper burning of the mixture and reducing noxious emissions from the exhaust. It is entirely self-contained, functioning automatically as the result of the high vacuum that occurs when the throttle is shut off under these conditions. In effect it slows up the rate at which the engine reduces speed when the throttle is closed. Once normal idling speed is reached, the valve ceases to operate.
2   It consists of a diaphragm clamped to a machined face on the wall of the unit by a cover. At the centre of the diaphragm is a combined metal valve plate and spring register, into which fits a compression

spring located at the other end over a spigot in the cover. The spring loads the valve plate to the closed position. The cover also forms a diaphragm control chamber, being connected to the engine intake manifold by a small bore pipe.
3   Depression, sensed in the diaphragm chamber, will lift the valve at a predetermined value, dictated by the compression spring preload, and admit air from the mixing chamber into the intake manifold, thus bypassing the throttle plate and limiting the depression. The maximum bleed flow is controlled by an orifice fitted in the bypass passage.
4   The bypass valve is preset and no attempt may be made to adjust it in service.

19 Carburettor (Stromberg) - tuning

1   Before adjusting the carburettor, check that the valve clearances, spark plug gaps, contact breaker settings and ignition timing are all correct, that there is no leakage in the intake manifold and that the vacuum ignition advance tube is in place. Make the final adjustments with the engine at its normal running temperature, and finish off by setting the throttle stop to give the specified idling speed when you have refitted the air cleaner and crankcase ventilation pipes.
2   Screw up the idling trimmer screw (see Fig. 3.12) as far as it will go and then undo it two full turns. Now run the engine until it reaches operational temperature, adjust the engine speed, to that given in Specifications at the beginning of this Chapter, by means of the throttle stop screw and then adjust the idling trimmer to give smoothest engine running on idling and good pick-up on acceleration. Should the idling speed increase when adjusting this screw, correct on the throttle stop screw.
3   Pull out the choke control on the instrument panel 0.9 - 1 in (23 - 25 mm) and adjust the cable so that the mark on the fast idle cam comes opposite the centre-line of the fast idle screw.
4   Jet adjustment should ideally (and in some parts of the world, by legal requirement) be set for minimum CO emission using the appropriate test gear and then sealed. In countries or states where stringent exhaust emission control laws exist the foregoing tuning procedure must be regarded as general information or for emergency use only.
5   When using a CO meter to set the carburettor, warm the engine up from cold and carry out the adjustment within eight minutes of the cooling thermostat opening. This can be ascertained by feeling the radiator top hose and when it suddenly turns warm, the thermostat will have opened.
6   The CO content should be as given in Specifications at the beginning of this Chapter and adjustment is carried out with the idling trimmer screw. If the CO content cannot be reduced to the specified level, suspect a fault in the temperature compensator on the front face of the carburettor.

20 Closed crankcase ventilation system - general

1   For efficient engine operation it is necessary that pressure should not build up in the crankcase. In times past this has been taken care of by providing a simple breathing device (sometimes, but not always, fitted with an oil trap) which vented the crankcase fumes to atmosphere. Such a device is found on early Volvo engines, but now all Volvo engines are fitted with a closed crankcase ventilation system in which the build-up of crankcase pressure is prevented without allowing it to breathe directly into the atmosphere.
2   Fig. 3.20 illustrates the system employed by Volvo on the B20 series. Clean air from a subsidiary filter in the air cleaner assembly is drawn into the crankcase via a small flame trap in the crankcase breather. The oil filler cap is connected to the inlet manifold through a nipple which restricts the amount of air drawn into the manifold while at the same time causing pressure in the crankcase to be lower than atmospheric, thus ensuring that air is drawn in from the air intake. When the throttle is fairly wide open, the vacuum in the inlet manifold is less than that in the air cleaner, and vapour flows out of the crankcase along both routes. Much of this enters the air cleaner via the subsidiary insert, where it is remixed with fuel vapour and again enters the engine.
3   The only attention the system requires is periodical cleaning of the nipple and flame guard. To ensure that pollution of the atmosphere is kept to a minimum, ensure that the flexible pipes and their clips are in good condition and airtight.

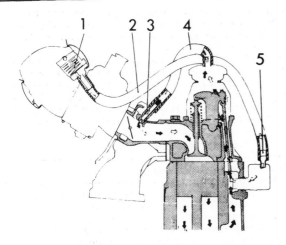

Fig. 3.20. Closed crankcase ventilation (Sec. 20)

1   Cleaner insert
2   Pipe for fresh air supply to crankcase
3   Nipple
4   Pipe for crankcase gases
5   Flame guard

21 Constant temperature air device - general

1   In order to ensure that the air entering the carburettor is rapidly raised to a temperature which thereafter remains constant, air at atmospheric temperature from an intake in the front of the car is mixed with air which has passed over a hot spot on the exhaust system, in a box which incorporates a flap controlled by a thermostat. A view of this box with the hose connections removed is given in Fig. 3.21.
2   Inside the box is a flap which in one extreme position completely blanks off the warm air intake and in the other blanks off the cool air intake. Fig. 3.22 shows the small tab found on either side of the box indicating the position of the flap. When it points to 'hot' the cold air intake is completely shut off and the warmest possible air is fed to the carburettor(s), the reverse happening when it points to 'cold'.
3   To check the operation of the thermostat, remove the unit from the car and test it in warm water. The flap should shut off the hot air intake (tab pointing to 'cold') at a temperature of 95 - 105°F (35 - 41°C) and shut off the cold air intake at 70 - 77°F (27 - 31°C).
4   The device is very unlikely to go out of adjustment, but the thermostat may possibly cease to function properly. If so, the complete device should be replaced.
5   When fitting, note that the thermostat should be in the middle of the air flow and that any hose clamp screws should be on top of the housing.

22 Evaporative fuel vapour control system - general description

1   In hot countries the problem of atmospheric pollution by evaporation of petrol, from motor cars, is a serious one. In California, it has been estimated that a car left out all day can lose as much as a gallon of

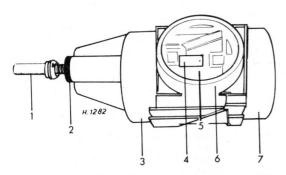

Fig. 3.21. Constant air temperature device (Sec. 21)

1 Thermostat	5 Flaps
2 Lock nut	6 Warm air intake
3 Air feeler connection	7 Cold air intake
4 Flap control	

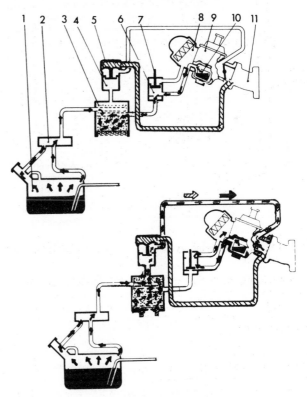

Fig. 3.23. Evaporative system (Sec. 22)

A Engine idling (top)	B Engine running (bottom)

1 Fuel tank	7 Control rod (connected to throttle)
2 Expansion tank	
3 Venting filter	8 Air cleaner
4 Air valve	9 Carburettor
5 Diaphragm	10 Float chamber
6 Hot start valve	11 Intake manifold

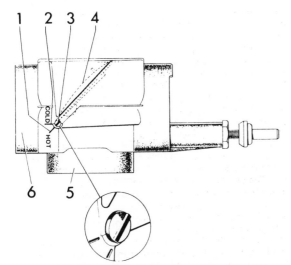

Fig. 3.22. Constant air temperature device (Sec. 21)

1 Hot - open for warm air	4 Shutter
2 Cold - open for cold air	5 Warm air intake
3 Tab	6 Cold air intake

fuel by evaporation. Even if the average figure is less than a hundredth of this, when one considers all the cars there are in California the fact that legislation has been introduced enforcing evaporation control is not surprising.

2   The sources of evaporation are:
   a) The carburettor float chambers
   b) The fuel tank

In the control system used by Volvo, when the engine is switched off or idling the vapour from these two sources is channeled into an absorptive element made up of active carbon granules which soak up the fumes like a sponge. When the engine is running, air is drawn through the active carbon element into the carburettor air intake, purging the element and drawing in vapour from the fuel tank as it is generated. At the same time the channel from the float chamber is diverted from the filter direct to the carburettor intake.

3   Fig. 3.23 shows how the system operates. When the engine is idling or switched off, the hot start valve has its plunger in the up position and any petrol vapour coming from the float chamber is fed into the filter. At the same time the main fuel tank can evaporate into an expansion tank where a certain amount of condensation can occur, the remaining vapour being passed to the filter also. The air valve on top of the filter, which is operated by engine vacuum, is closed when the engine is idling and the filter is cut off from the air intake. This is the position shown in Fig. 3.23.

4   When the engine is running normally the vacuum falls sufficiently to let the air valve open and at the same time the plunger of the hot start valve is lowered by its control lever. Vapour from the float chamber is now taken via the hot start valve into the air cleaner, while vapour from the circulation tank and the filter is sucked into the carburettor throttle chamber where it mixes with what is already being provided by the carburettor. The air drawn through the filter removes fuel fumes stored in the active carbon element.

23 Air cleaner - general description

1   There are two types of air cleaners fitted to carburettor engines. One type has a disposable element while the other is of sealed, throw-away type. Removal, dismantling, reassembly and refitting are obvious and straightforward. Attention to the air cleaner element is of paramount importance if engine efficiency is to be maintained. If operating conditions are particularly dusty, this component should be given frequent attention.

2   The complete filter or its element should be replaced every 24000 miles (40000 km).

24 Exhaust system (all models) - removal and refitting

See Section 58 of Chapter 3, Part B.

25 Fault diagnosis - fuel system and carburation

We give in the following table a few of the symptoms of carburettor or fuel system trouble, possible causes and remedies. Always bear in mind that it is very difficult to distinguish between ignition faults and carburettor faults in many cases. The golden rule should be - before starting on the carburettor, make 100% certain of the ignition. Ignition faults are easy to check, ignition adjustments, when required, are easy to make, and furthermore when adjustment is required as a result of normal wear and tear this adjustment is much more likely to be in the ignition than in the carburettor. The following table, therefore assumes that all is in order in the ignition system.

Symptom	Reason/s	Remedy
Smell of petrol when engine is stopped	Leaking pipes or unions Leaking fuel tank	Tighten or renew as necessary. Fill fuel tank to capacity and examine carefully at seams, unions and filler pipe connections. Renew tank.
Smell of petrol when engine is idling	Leaking fuel lines or unions between pump and carburettor Overflow of fuel from float chamber due to wrong level setting, ineffective needle valve or punctured float	Check lines and unions and tighten or repair. Check fuel level setting and condition of float and needle valve and renew if necessary.
Excessive fuel consumption for reasons not covered by leaks or float chamber faults	Worn needle and/or jet Sticking needle or piston	Replace. Check correct movement of needle and piston assembly, as detailed in this Chapter.
Difficult starting, uneven running, lack of power, cutting out	Blockages in carburettor Float chamber fuel level too low or needle valve sticking Fuel pump not delivering sufficient fuel Intake manifold gaskets leaking or manifold fractured	Clean out float chamber and body. Dismantle and check fuel level and needle valve. Check pump delivery and clean or repair as required. Check for blockage in fuel pipes. Check tightness of mounting nuts and inspect manifold.
Difficulty in starting not associated with faults already given	Over-rich mixture entering cylinders as a result of too much use of choke control or depressing the accelerator pedal when starting	Keep your foot off the accelerator pedal until the engine fires. If 'over-choking' has already occurred, push the pedal right down to the floor and operate the starter. Usually this will clear the fault. It will clear itself in time anyway.
Engine does not respond properly to throttle pedal	Sticking piston or needle Damper piston not working properly Oil level in dashpot low	Check correct movement of piston. Check free play or damper piston on its rod. Top-up.
Engine idling speed drops markedly after a long period of idling (in warm weather especially)	Defective temperature compensator (Stromberg) Hot start valves sticking in run position	Adjust or replace as necessary. Determine cause, adjust or replace as necessary.
Engine does not take up proper idling speed when throttle released	Sticking controls Defective bypass valve (Stromberg) or relief valve in throttle flap (SU)	Clean and oil as required. Correct defect or replace as necessary.

Chapter 3 Part B: Fuel system - fuel injection models

For modifications, and information applicable to later models, see Supplement at end of manual

Contents

Specifications

Pressure
System pressure	65 - 75 psi (4.6 - 5.3 kg/sq cm)
Closing pressure	24 psi (1.7 kg/sq cm)
Control pressure	53 ± 2.8 psi (3.7 ± 0.2 kg/sq cm)

Fuel pump
Type	Electric rotor pump
Capacity	1.32 to 1.52 Imp pint (1.58 to 1.82 US pints, 0.75 to 0.86 litres) per 30 sec at 71 psi (5 kg/sq cm)
Current consumption	8.5 amps (max)

Fuel filter
Type	Paper filter
Change interval	24,000 miles (40,000 km)

Auxiliary air valve
Fully open at	−30ºC (−22ºF)
Fully closed at	+70ºC (158ºF) (after 5 minutes driving with ambient temperature +20ºC (68ºF)

Air filter
Type	Paper filter
Change interval	24,000 miles (40.000 km)

Idling speed ... ...
900 rpm (manual), 800 rpm (automatic)

Maximum exhaust CO content* ... ...
1.7 to 2.3%

Refer also to individual vehicle decal or handbook

Fuel type
USA models	RON 91 (unleaded)
All other models	RON 98 (4-Star)

26 Fuel injection system - description of operation

1 The best way to an understanding of the working of the fuel injection engine is to consider the basic operation of the normal carburettor system.

Obviously, the more fuel an engine burns the more power it will give out. Notice that we say burns - fuel taken in and not burnt will add to your petrol consumption without doing anything to help you along.

To ensure that the fuel is properly burnt, it must be mixed with air in the right proportions. If the mixture is too rich, there will not be enough oxygen to support combustion, as every motorist who has ever used his choke too enthusiastically will realise. If it is too weak, the burning process is slow and irregular - sometimes it is still going on when the inlet valve opens and flames shoot through the carburettor/s as a result.

The basic function of the fuel system, then, is simply to provide the amount of fuel the engine needs at any given time, mixed with the amount of air required to ensure that it is properly burnt.

2 The modern carburettor solves this problem by reversing it. For a given throttle setting, the engine will suck in a certain amount of air per stroke. A measure of the amount of air going in is the amount of suck which occurs on the carburettor side of the throttle, ie. the degree of vacuum set up there. This pressure drop causes the carburettor to release an amount of petrol vapour suitable to the amount of air going in.

This is not an easy problem to solve, as is obvious when one looks at the complexity of a modern carburettor. Quite apart from the initial case when the engine is cold and the vapour starts to condense before it ever enters the cylinders, we find devices for modifying apparent size of jet (the vacuum controlled piston and needle arrangement used by the carburettors described in this manual) or various arrangements of subsidiary jets, tubes in which the petrol level rises and so on.

On top of this, we are faced with difficulties caused by temperature variations. The proportion of air to petrol varies with the temperature of the air being mixed in, basically because when air is warm the same weight of air occupies more space and it is weight of air to weight of fuel that we have to worry about, not volume to volume. Also, quite

apart from this, the required mixture depends on the temperature inside the cylinder and generally speaking the carburettor has no way of knowing what this is. In an ordinary carburettor system, these problems are to some extent side-stepped because the engine temperature and the air temperature stabilise themselves after the engine has been running for a while.

Elaborate arrangements are made for stabilising the temperature of the input air on carburettor engines; as we shall see, the problem is tackled in a different way in the fuel injection engine and the thermostatically operated flap and branch pipe to a hot spot on the exhaust system are conspicuous by their absence.

Cold starting is a problem on its own. The mixture is arbitrarily enriched so that in spite of condensation which may occur on the way there is a reasonable chance that some at least of the cylinders will receive mixture of a strength which will ignite when a spark appears. Where these devices are automatically controlled, they come off when the engine temperature has reached a certain level.

3 Over the years, the carburettor manufacturers have solved their various problems in different ways, all to some extent compromises, as is shown by the variety of carburettor designs. In the last few years, insistence on the reduction of atmospheric pollution has made the carburettor designers task more difficult. The electronic fuel injection system tackles these problems in an entirely different way from the traditional carburettor approach.

27 CI fuel system - control principle

1 The models in the Volvo 240 series having fuel injection engines are equipped with a CI system. CI stands for continuous injection, which means the injection valves of the system are always open, that is, are always injecting fuel when the engine is running. The amount of fuel is not controlled by variation of the injection time but through variation of the fuel flow through the injectors.

2 The CI system principle is to measure continuously the airflow into the engine and let this airflow control the amount of fuel fed to the engine. The measuring of the induced air and the control of the fuel flow is provided by an air-fuel control unit which is the 'heart' of the CI system. The air-fuel control unit consists of an airflow

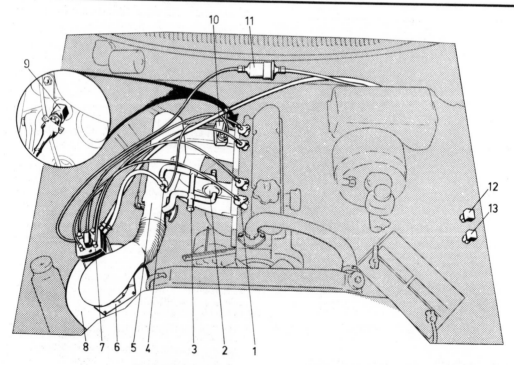

Fig. 3.24. Fuel injection system - general lay-out (Sec. 27)

1 Injector	5 Intake manifold	8 Air cleaner	11 Fuel filter
2 Auxiliary air valve	6 Air flow sensor	9 Thermal time switch	12 Safety relay
3 Idle adjustment screw	7 Fuel distributor	10 Control pressure regulator	13 Pump relay
4 Cold start injector			

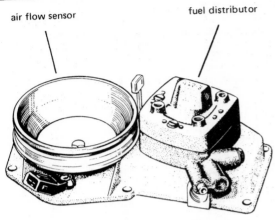

air flow sensor   fuel distributor

Fig. 3.25. Air-fuel control unit (Sec. 27)

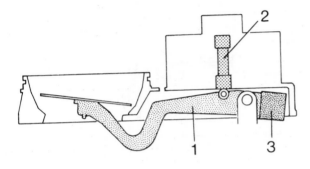

Fig. 3.26. The air flow sensor - operation (Sec. 27)

1 Lever
2 Control plunger
3 Balance weight

4 Metering slot
5 Control plunger

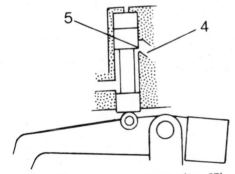

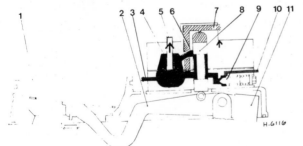

Fig. 3.27. Air-fuel control unit - schematic (Sec. 27)

1 Air flow sensor plate
2 Lever
3 From fuel pump
4 Pressure regulating valve
5 To injector
6 Control plunger head

7 To control pressure regulator
8 Plunger
9 Line pressure regulator
10 To fuel tank
11 Balance weight

sensor and a fuel distributor.

3   The airflow sensor consists of a plate in a venturi. The air flows upwards through the venturi and lifts the plate to let air pass through. A large airflow lifts the plate to a high position, a small airflow to a low position.

4   The movement of the airflow sensor plate is transferred by a lever to a control plunger in the fuel distributor. The lever is provided with a balance weight which equalizes the weight of the plate and the lever.

5   The control plunger is located in a cylinder which is provided with four metering slots, one for each engine cylinder. When lifted, the edge of the control plunger head uncovers the metering slots. A high airflow sensor plate position corresponds to a large uncovered metering slot area; a low position to a small area.

6   The difference between the fuel pressure ahead of the slot and after the slot must be constant in order to ensure that the quantity of fuel passing through the metering slots is proportional to the uncovered metering area. This is ensured by four pressure regulating valves, one for each metering slot, which maintain a constant pressure drop of 1.4 psi (0.1 kg/sq cm) over the slot.

7   Refer to Fig. 3.27. The dark shaded area shows the fuel flow to and from the slots, and the lightly shaded area shows a control pressure which prevents the control plunger from reacting too strongly to rapid increases of induced air.

28 Fuel injection system - general description

Air system

1   Besides the airflow control unit, the CI system consists of several other components. Figure 3.28 shows a diagram of the system.

2   The air cleaner has a replaceable paper type cartridge which should be replaced every 24,000 miles (40,000 km).

3   The airflow sensor controls the flow of air to provide a correct fuel-air mixture at all loads. The throttle is located in the intake manifold and is controlled by the throttle pedal. An idle adjustment screw is located in a channel bypassing the throttle. It increases or decreases the area of the bypass channel and thus controls the idling speed.

4   The auxiliary air valve is located on the intake manifold and like the idling adjustment screw, bypasses the throttle. A bi-metallic spring (Fig. 3.31) presses on the valve when the engine is cold and thereby the bypass air channel is kept open. Current flows through the coil when the starter motor is operated and when the engine is running. The coil heats the bi-metallic spring which decreases the pressure on the valve which is gradually closed by the coil spring.

Fuel system

5   The fuel system consists of the electric fuel pump, fuel accumulator, fuel filter, fuel distributor and injectors as well as the control pressure regulator and line pressure regulator. The components are described in the order the fuel travels through the system.

6   The fuel pump is a roller-type pump combined with an electric motor and is located in front of the fuel tank. If the fuel pressure should become excessive (pinched fuel line, etc.) a built-in relief valve allows the fuel to circulate inside the pump. In the rest position pressure is maintained in the system by a check valve in the fuel pump outlet (Fig. 3.32).

7   The fuel accumulator is located close to the fuel pump and helps accumulate and maintain pressure in the fuel system when the fuel pump check valve has closed (Fig. 3.33).

8   The fuel filter is located in the system between the fuel accumulator and the fuel distributor. The direction of flow is marked by arrows on the housing.

9   The fuel distributor controls the amount of fuel to the injectors in relation to the airflow. It consists of a line pressure regulator which controls the pressure to the fuel distributor; a control plunger, which controls and distributes the fuel to the injectors, and four pressure regulator valves which maintain a constant pressure difference between inlet and outlet of the control plunger (Fig. 3.34).

10 The line pressure regulator controls the fuel pressure to the fuel distributor. It closes the tank recirculation line if the fuel pressure is below 65.3 psi (4.6 kg/sq cm).

11 The fuel control unit plunger opens the metering slots according to the airflow sensor plate position, when the plate position is high more fuel is directed through the pressure regulating valves.

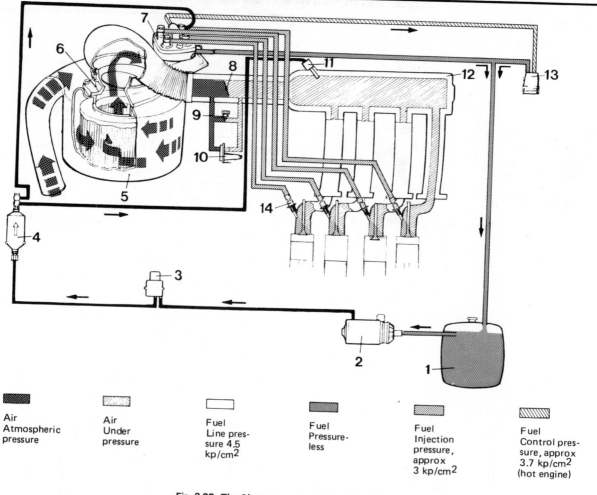

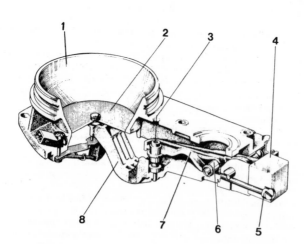

Air
Atmospheric
pressure

Air
Under
pressure

Fuel
Line pres-
sure 4.5
kp/cm^2

Fuel
Pressure-
less

Fuel
Injection
pressure,
approx
3 kp/cm^2

Fuel
Control pres-
sure, approx
3.7 kp/cm^2
(hot engine)

Fig. 3.28. The CI system - schematic diagram (Sec. 28)

1 Fuel tank	5 Air cleaner	9 Idle adjustment screw	13 Control pressure regulator
2 Fuel pump	6 Air flow sensor	10 Auxiliary air valve	14 Injector
3 Pressure accumulator	7 Fuel distributor	11 Cold start injector	
4 Fuel filter	8 Throttle	12 Intake manifold	

Fig. 3.29. Cut-away view of the air flow sensor (Sec. 28)

1 Venturi	5 Balance weight screw
2 Sensor plate	6 Roller
3 Adjustment screw	7 Link
4 Balance weight	8 Lever

Fig. 3.30. Location of idling adjustment screw (Sec. 28)

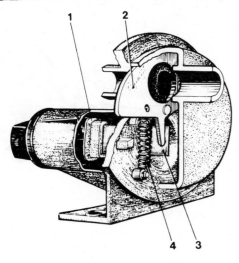

Fig. 3.31. Auxiliary air valve (Sec. 28)

1 Coil	3 Bi-metallic spring
2 Valve	4 Coil spring

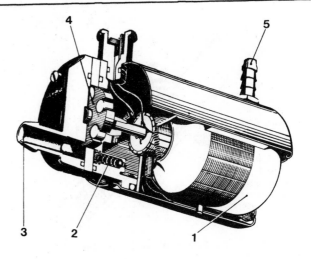

Fig. 3.32. Fuel pump (Sec. 28)

1 Armature	4 Pump rotor
2 Relief valve	5 Outlet
3 Inlet	

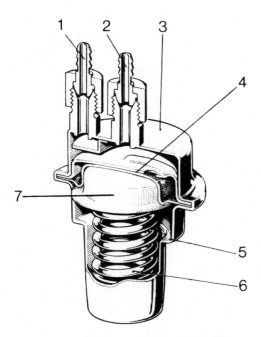

Fig. 3.33. The fuel accumulator (Sec. 28)

1 Inlet	5 Stop
2 Outlet	6 Spring
3 Pressure chamber	7 Plunger
4 Diaphragm	

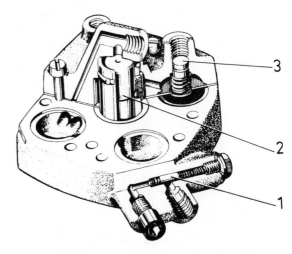

Fig. 3.34. The fuel distributor (Sec. 28)

1 Line pressure regulator	3 Pressure regulator valves
2 Control plunger	

15 The injectors have a spring-controlled valve which opens at a fuel pressure of 51 psi (3.6 kg/sq cm). The fuel pressure opens the valve and that makes the injection continuous, while the fuel flow varies according to the air inducted (Fig. 3.35).

16 The cold start injector supplies extra fuel for cold starting. The injection time is controlled by the thermal time switch and provides extra fuel for 12 seconds at −20ºC (5ºF). The cold start injector is injecting fuel only when the starter motor is operating. It stops injecting fuel if the engine starts, and the starter stops operating, before the time permitted by the thermal time switch is up (Fig. 3.36).

17 The thermal time switch determines the cold start injector operating time. It is a sealed unit, having contacts controlled by a bi-metallic spring. The bi-metallic spring has two coils one activated from the cold start injector and the other from the starter. The contacts are closed at below +35ºC (95ºF). When the starter operates current flows from the starter to the cold start injector and, via a coil and the contacts, to earth. At the same time current flows from the starter, via the second coil and the contacts, to earth. The cold start injector operates as long as the contacts are closed and the starter is operating. The current flowing from the starter to the coil heats the bi-metallic spring, the contacts open and the cold start injector stops operating. The heating time varies with the engine temperature: the warmer the engine the shorter the heating time for the bi-metallic spring and consequently also the injection time.

12 Some of the fuel from the fuel distributor inlet is diverted to the control plunger top side. From there it travels first to a control pressure regulator and then to the tank. The control pressure is controlled by the control pressure regulator and is normally 53 ± 2.8 psi (3.7 ± 0.2 kg/sq cm). The control pressure fuel acts on top of the control plunger and dampens the movement of the airflow sensor plate during fast acceleration.

13 The control pressure regulator controls, during the warm-up period, the control pressure in relation to the engine temperature so that the fuel mixture is enriched .

14 The pressure regulating valves provide a constant pressure drop across the metering slots, independent of the amount of fuel passing through the slots. This is necessary in order to achieve an injection rate proportional to the positions of the control plunger and the airflow sensor plate.

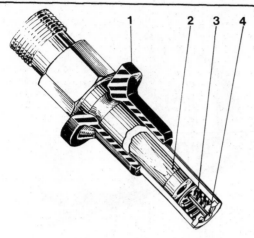

Fig. 3.35. Fuel injector (Sec. 28)

1 Retainer   3 Spring
2 Injector body   4 Valve

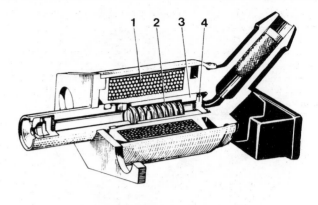

Fig. 3.36. Cold start injector (Sec. 28)

1 Solenoid coil   3 Actuator
2 Return spring   4 Gasket

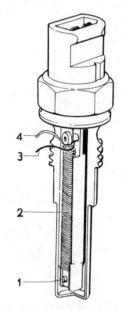

Fig. 3.37. Thermal time switch (Sec. 28)

1 Contacts   3 Lead to starter motor
2 Bi-metallic spring   4 Lead to cold start injector

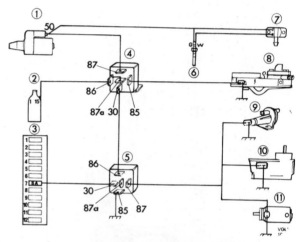

Fig. 3.38. Electrical system (Sec. 28)

1 Starter motor   7 Cold start injector
2 Ignition coil   8 Air-fuel control unit
3 Fuse box   9 Auxiliary air valve
4 Main relay   10 Control pressure regulator
5 Fuel pump relay   11 Fuel pump
6 Thermal time switch

Electrical system

18 Figure 3.38 shows the layout of the electrical system and the electrical system wiring diagram is shown in Fig. 3.39.

19 When the ignition is switched on, current flows from the ignition coil terminal '15' to the main relay terminal '86', through the relay coil to terminal '85' and finally to the air-fuel control unit and earth. The main relay is thus activated.

20 When the ignition key is turned to the starting position, current flows from the starter terminal '50' to the main relay terminal '87', through the closed contacts to terminal '30' and to the pump relay terminal '86'. From there through the relay coil to terminal '85' and earth. The pump relay is thus activated.

21 Current flows from fuse '7' to the pump relay terminal '30', through the closed contacts to terminal '87', to the fuel pump and earth. The fuel pump is thus activated and pumps fuel. The control pressure regulator and the auxiliary air valve are activated at the same time as the fuel pump.

22 When the starter motor is operating or after the engine has started, the contacts at the air-fuel control unit open, the earth circuit is opened, and the main relay is deactivated. Current now flows from terminal '86' to terminal '87a', through the contacts to terminal '30'. The fuel pump relay is still activated and the pump is operating.

There is no current flow to the main relay terminal '87' when the engine is running and the starter motor not operating.

23 If the engine stops (with the ignition still switched on), the contacts at the air-fuel control unit close. Main relay terminal '85' is earthed, the relay is activated, and terminal '30' is connected to terminal '87'. As there is no current flow to terminal '87', the pump relay is deactivated and the fuel pump stops working.

24 The cold start injector is activated only when the starter motor is operating and the engine temperature at the same time is so low that the thermal time switch cuts in.

25 The illustrations used are of a B20E engine which has the induction system on the right-hand side of the engine. On B21E engines the induction system is on the left-hand side of the engine, otherwise the two systems are basically the same.

29 Fuel tank filter - cleaning

1 The filter should be cleaned at intervals of 15,000 miles (25,000 km).
2 Empty the fuel tank by syphoning. Remove the plug from the bottom of the tank (Fig. 3.40) and clean it.
3 When refitting, ensure that the suction pipe is centred in the flange

hole, otherwise the filter can get damaged and, at worst, this could
shut off the fuel supply.

30 Fuel tank - description, removal and refitting

1 The fuel tank is mounted at the rear of the car and is of a fuel
evaporative control type. Empty the tank by syphoning.
2 To remove the tank, withdraw the floor panel from the boot, or

load area (Estate), disconnect all hoses and electrical leads from the
tank, unscrew and remove the mounting screws. Cut round the
sealing mastic and lift the tank out.
3 On cars fitted with a fuel evaporative control system the fumes
from the tank are stored in a canister charged with activated charcoal
until the engine is started when the fumes and vapour are drawn from
the canister into the inlet manifold or duct and burned during the
normal combustion cycle.
4 No maintenance is necessary except to occasionally check the
security of the connecting hoses.
5 Refitting of the tank is a reversal of removal but always renew the
sealing mastic round the edge of the fuel tank mounting.

31 Fuel tank sender unit - removal and refitting

Removal of the fuel tank sender unit is described in Section 8 of
Chapter 3, Part A.

32 Air-fuel control unit - removal and refitting

1 Clean round all the fuel connections before disconnecting them.
2 Remove the rubber bellows and the strap for the injector pipes.
3 Remove the injector pipes and the control pressure pipe from the
distributor.
4 Disconnect the cold start injector and recirculation pipe lines. Pull
at the electrical plug connection.
5 Disconnect the fuel line at the filter.
6 Remove the air-fuel control unit retaining screws and lift it out.
Collect the gasket.
7 Refitting is the reverse of the removal sequence. Always fit a new
gasket.

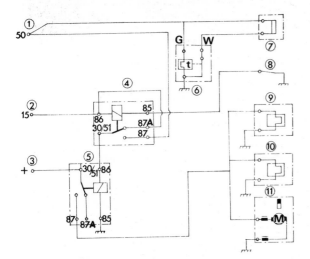

Fig. 3.39. CI fuel system wiring diagram (Sec. 28) (see caption to Fig. 3.38)

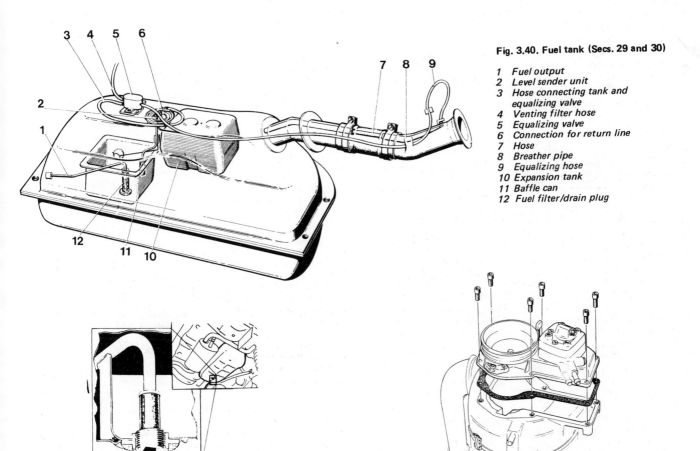

Fig. 3.40. Fuel tank (Secs. 29 and 30)

1 Fuel output
2 Level sender unit
3 Hose connecting tank and
   equalizing valve
4 Venting filter hose
5 Equalizing valve
6 Connection for return line
7 Hose
8 Breather pipe
9 Equalizing hose
10 Expansion tank
11 Baffle can
12 Fuel filter/drain plug

Fig. 3.40a. Fuel tank filter (Sec. 29)

Fig. 3.41. Removing the air-fuel control unit (Sec. 32)

33 Air-fuel control unit - dismantling and inspection

1 Clamp the unit lightly in a vice, do not use force or you are likely to damage it.
2 Remove the three securing screws and carefully lift off the fuel distributor taking care that the control plunger does not fall out and get damaged. **Note:** The fuel distributor must not be dismantled.
3 Remove the two retaining screws and lift off the bridge piece.
4 Remove the balance weight.
5 Remove the lever with the adjustment arm by removing the circlip, washer, rubber seal, springs and balls as well as the shaft.

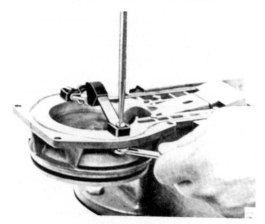

Fig. 3.42. Removing the bridge piece (Sec. 33)

Fig. 3.43. Undoing the screw to remove the balance weight (Sec. 33)

Fig. 3.44. Using circlip pliers when removing the adjustment arm shaft retaining circlip (Sec. 33)

6 Wash the control plunger in petrol and blow it off with compressed air. Check the plunger for damage. If the plunger is worn or damaged, the fuel distributor must be renewed; any attempt to clean the slots will do more harm than good. Renew any worn or damaged parts.

34 Air-fuel control unit - reassembly

1 Place the lever and adjustment arm in position. The adjustment arm should be positioned so that the roller for the control plunger is towards the fuel distributor. Fit the shaft, balls, spring, rubber seals, washers and circlips.
2 Fit the balance weight and centre the lever. Tighten the balance weight screw.
3 Fit the sensor plate stop so that the spring and contact are on the right side, Fig. 3.46.
4 Centre the airflow sensor plate. The sensor plate must not touch the venturi at any point. If adjustment is needed, loosen the plate screw and reposition the plate.
5 Check that with the airflow sensor plate at rest it is level with or no more than 0.039 in (1 mm) below the venturi edge. Adjust, if necessary, at 'A' in Fig. 3.47, with needle nosed pliers.
6 Check the sensor plate for freedom of movement from low to high positions.
7 Fit the fuel distributor, taking care to avoid damaging the central plunger and O-ring. Always fit a new gasket. Tighten the retaining screws to 2.3-2.7 lb f ft (0.31-0.37 kg f m).

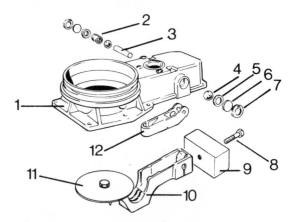

Fig. 3.45. Fitting the lever and adjusting arm (Sec. 34)

1	Housing	
2	Spring	7 Circlip
3	Shaft	8 Screw
4	Ball	9 Balance weight
5	Seal	10 Lever
6	Washer	11 Adjusting arm
		12 Sensor plate

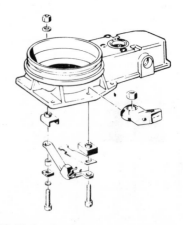

Fig. 3.46. Fitting the air flow sensor plate (Sec. 34)

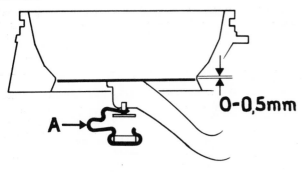

Fig. 3.47. Air flow sensor plate adjustment (Sec. 34)

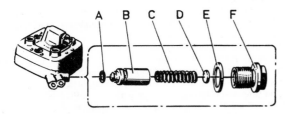

Fig. 3.48. Exploded view of line pressure regulator (Sec. 35)

A O-ring   D Shim
B Plunger   E Copper washer
C Spring   F Plug

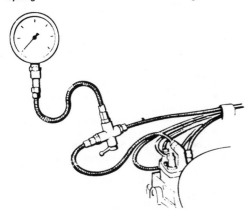

Fig. 3.49. Pressure gauge connected between the fuel distributor and the control pressure regulator (Sec. 36)

35 Line pressure regulator - testing

1 Refer to Fig. 3.48. Remove the plug taking care not to lose the shims in the plug.
2 Pull out the plunger and the spring. Remove the 'O' ring from the plunger.
3 Clean the parts and check them for damage. Renew defective parts, except the plunger which cannot be changed as it is matched with the fuel distributor. If it is defective change the distributor.
4 Fit a new 'O' ring on the plunger and refit the assembly using the same shims as were removed.

36 Line and rest pressure - testing

Line pressure
1 Connect a pressure gauge, with a three-way control lever as shown in Fig. 3.49, between the fuel distributor and the control pressure regulator.
2 Switch on the ignition and disconnect the lead at the airflow sensor, to start the fuel pump.
3 Check the line pressure on the gauge. It should be 65-75 psi (4.6-5.3 kg/sq cm).

4 If the line pressure is low the reasons could be as follows:

a) *Fuel line leakage. Check and rectify.*
b) *Line pressure regulator incorrectly adjusted. Adjust, as described in Section 37.*
c) *If there is no line pressure with the pump operating, check for blockage of the fuel lines, filters or fuel distributor.*
d) *Fuel pump defective.*

5 Excessively high pressure could be caused by:

a) *Blocked recirculation line.*
b) *Line pressure regulator incorrectly adjusted, refer to Section 37.*

Rest pressure
6 Reconnect the electrical lead to the airflow sensor.
7 After a few seconds check the rest pressure reading on the gauge. It should be 24 psi (1.7 kg/sq cm) minimum and 53 psi (3.7 kg/sq cm) maximum (injector opening pressure). Check that there is no noticeable drop in pressure within one minute. If the pressure is incorrect refer to Section 37, and adjust the line pressure regulator.
8 If the rest pressure drops too quickly check as follows:

a) *Turn the lever on the gauge towards the control pressure regulator. If the pressure still drops too fast the control pressure regulator or its fuel lines are leaking and should be replaced.*
b) *Block the fuel recirculation line after the fuel distributor. If the pressure stops dropping, the line pressure regulator or its 'O' ring is faulty. Refer to line pressure regulator checking, Section 35.*
c) *Turn the gauge lever at right-angles to the connection from the fuel distributor. Remove the airflow sensor lead for a few seconds to bring up the line pressure, then reconnect the lead. Pinch the fuel feed hose from the tank to the pump. If the fuel pressure stops falling the fuel pump check valve is defective.*
d) *Check the fuel lines for leaks.*

37 Line pressure regulator - adjustment

1 To adjust the line and rest pressure remove or add shims, as necessary, in the line pressure regulator.
2 There are two thicknesses of shims:

0.0039 in (0.1 mm) = 0.8 psi (0.06 kg/sq cm) pressure difference
C.0196 in (0.5 mm) = 4.3 psi (0.3 kg/sq cm) pressure difference

Use mainly the thick shims for adjustment. The thin shims are used when the line pressure is 69 psi (4.9 kg/sq cm) or more and the rest pressure at the same time is more than 24 psi (1.7 kg/sq cm).
Note: Both the line pressure and rest pressure are affected at the same time.

38 Control pressure - testing

The engine must be cold (at ambient temperature) when the control pressure is being checked.
1 Connect the pressure gauge between the fuel distributor and the control pressure regulator with the gauge lever at right-angles to the connection to the fuel distributor.
2 Switch on the ignition and start the fuel pump by disconnecting the lead at the airflow sensor.
3 Check the control pressure against the chart, Fig. 3.50. As you can see from the chart the control pressure at 20°C (68°F) should be 20.6-24.8 psi (1.45-1.75 kg/sq cm).
4 If the control pressure is too low, try a new control pressure regulator. If the pressure is too high, the recirculation line may be blocked. If it is open, try a new control pressure regulator.
5 Reconnect the lead at the airflow sensor and switch off the ignition.

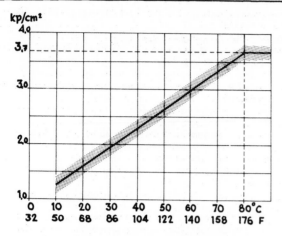

Fig. 3.50. Control pressure chart (Sec. 38)

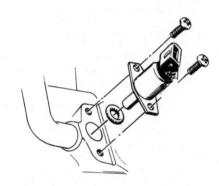

Fig. 3.51. Replacing the cold start injector (Sec. 41)

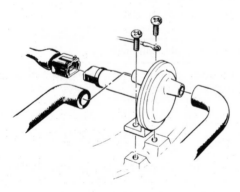

Fig. 3.52. Replacing the auxiliary air valve (Sec. 43)

39 Injector - removal and refitting

1   Clean round the fuel injector and fuel pipe. Disconnect the fuel pipe.
2   Remove the injector retainer and the injector.
3   When refitting the injector fit a new rubber seal.
4   Reconnect the fuel pipe. Start the engine and check for leaks.

40 Injectors - testing

1   Check the injectors at rest pressure.
2   Remove the injector with the fuel line connected.
3   Lift the airflow sensor plate so that the metering slots in the fuel distributor open.
4   Injectors must not leak more than one drop in 15 seconds. Renew

leaking injectors. **Note:** If all the injectors leak the reason may be an excessive rest pressure, see Section 36.

41 Cold start injector - removal and refitting

1   Disconnect the electrical plug. Clean round the fuel pipe connection and disconnect the pipe.
2   Remove the two retaining screws and the cold start injector and seal.
3   Refit the injector, use a new seal, and fit the retaining screws.
4   Reconnect the fuel pipe and electrical plug.

42 Cold start injector - testing

1   With the engine cold remove the cold start injector, leaving the fuel and electrical supply connected.
2   Hold the injector over a container (a glass jar is ideal), switch on the ignition and run the starter motor.
3   The cold start injector should spray for 12 seconds at an engine temperature of −20ºC (−4ºF), Higher temperatures decrease the injection time and it ceases completely above +35ºC (95ºF).
4   If no fuel appears, remove the plug and check that when the starter motor is turned, 12V appears across the socket pins. If it does the injector must be faulty and will have to be renewed. If there is no voltage the wiring or thermal time switch is faulty.

43 Auxiliary air valve - removal and refitting

1   Disconnect the plug and hoses.
2   Remove the retaining screws and the auxiliary air valve.
3   When replacing the valve do not forget to connect the earth wire to one of the retaining screws.
4   Reconnect the hoses and plug.

44 Auxiliary air valve - testing

1   Remove the hoses and electrical connection.
2   Check that the valve is open, it should be half open at +20ºC (68ºF). It is completely closed when the engine is hot. Use a mirror and a light to check.
3   Reconnect the electrical plug. The valve should close completely within 5 minutes.
4   If the valve has not closed, tap lightly on the valve, if it closes it is OK (engine vibrations normally contribute to closing).
5   If it stays open check for voltage at the plug; if the voltage is ok, replace the air auxiliary valve.

45 Control pressure regulator - removal and refitting

1   Clean round the fuel line connections.
2   Remove the straps from the fuel lines and disconnect the hose from the fuel distributor and the return hose. Remove the electrical plug connection.
3   Remove the two retaining screws and the control pressure regulator. Disconnect the fuel supply hose.
4   Refit the pressure regulator and connect the hoses and plug. Do not forget the earth wire which should be connected to one of the retaining screws.
5   Check the control pressure: refer to Section 38.

46 Fuel filter - removal and refitting

1   Clean round the hose connections.
2   Disconnect the hoses, remove the attaching screws and the filter.
3   Remove the unions and washers from the filter and fit them on the replacement filter.
4   Refit the filter and connect the pipe lines. An arrow on the filter casing shows the direction of flow, make sure it is the right way round.
5   Switch on the ignition. Disconnect the plug at the airflow sensor and check that the fuel filter connections are not leaking.

6 Reconnect the plug at the airflow sensor and switch off the ignition.

47 Thermal time switch - testing

1 Run the engine until the temperature is above +35°C (+95°F).

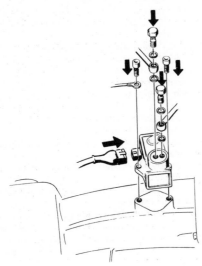

Fig. 3.53. Replacing the control pressure regulator

Fig. 3.54. Removing the fuel filter

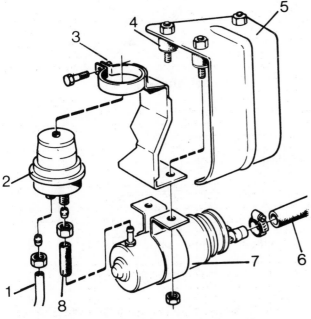

Fig. 3.55. Fuel pump and accumulator assembly

1 Outlet hose	5 Guard plate
2 Accumulator	6 Inlet hose
3 Bracket	7 Fuel pump
4 Rubber mounting	8 Pump to accumulator hose

2 Remove the cold start injector and hold it over a glass jar. Operate the starter motor.
3 The cold start injector should not spray, as the engine is hot. If it does spray, the thermal timer switch is faulty and should be renewed.
4 Refit the cold start injector.

48 Thermal time switch - removal and refitting

1 Disconnect the electrical lead.
2 Partly drain the coolant or have a small plug ready to block the orifice, then unscrew the timer from the block.
3 Replace the timer and reconnect the electrical lead.
4 Top-up the coolant system.

49 Fuel pump and accumulator - removal and refitting

1 Clean round all the hose connections so that dirt will not get into the pump.
2 Disconnect the battery earth terminal.
3 Pinch the fuel inlet hose with a clamp.
4 Disconnect the fuel inlet and outlet hoses.
5 Remove the retaining nuts, the fuel pump and accumulator, and the guard plate.
6 Disconnect the electrical plug and the fuel accumulator hoses.
7 Separate the bracket, rubber mountings, accumulator and fuel pump.
8 Refitting is the reverse of removal. Always fit a new fuel hose between the fuel accumulator and the fuel pump at every removal.

50 Fuel pump check valve - renewal

1 Remove the fuel pump, as described in Section 44.
2 Clamp the pump in a vice by its bracket. Never hold the pump other than by the bracket.
3 Screw out the check valve and make sure that no dirt enters the pump.
4 Refit the check valve, always use a new gasket. Torque tighten to 12 - 16 lb f ft (1.6 - 2.2 kg f m). Do not overtighten as you will damage the threads in the fuel pump housing.
5 Refit the fuel pump: refer to Section 49.

51 Throttle plate - adjustment

1 Loosen the locknut and turn the stop screw out until it is clear of the throttle lever stop (Fig. 3.57).
2 Turn the screw in, until it touches the stop, then a further ½ turn. Tighten the locknut.
3 Check that the throttle shaft lever touches the full throttle stop when the throttle pedal is fully depressed.

52 Idling speed - adjustment

1 Run the engine until it is at normal running temperature.
2 Adjust the idling speed to 900 rpm, manual transmission, or 800

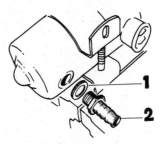

Fig. 3.56. Fuel pump check valve

1 Gasket	2 Check valve

rpm automatic transmission, with the throttle closed by turning the idling adjustment screw (see Fig. 3.30).

3 If the idling speed cannot be lowered to the specified speed, the throttle valve plate must be slightly open, check the setting, as described in Section 51.

53 Air filter - element renewal

1 Release the clamps securing the rubber bellows and remove the bellows.

2 Disconnect the electrical plug at the fuel distributor.

3 Undo the clips and remove the air cleaner upper part including the fuel distributor and move it to the side.

4 Remove the air cleaner element and fit a new replacement.

5 Refit the upper part of the cleaner and the rubber bellows. Reconnect the electrical plug at the fuel distributor.

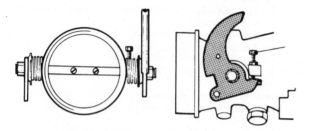

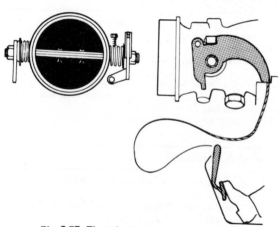

Fig. 3.57. Throttle plate adjustment (Sec. 51)

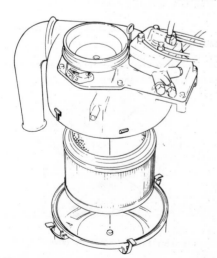

Fig. 3.58. Replacing the air cleaner filter element (Sec. 53)

54 Emission control systems - general description

1 In order to reduce engine and exhaust pollution to a minimum, various control systems are used. Certain devices (EGR; Air Injection System; Catalytic Converter; Lambda-sond sensor) are not fitted to all cars, but only to those vehicles destined for territories where stringent control regulations are in force.

2 The crankcase breather system and the fuel evaporative control system (see Sections 20 and 22) are integral parts of the overall emission control system.

3 The EGR (Exhaust Gas Recirculation) system is a method of re-cycling the engine exhaust gases by returning them to the combustion chambers where they reduce the combustion temperature and restrict the volume of noxious gases produced.

4 The arrangement includes a vacuum-operated valve, an air shutter and connecting pipes.

5 The Air Injection System is a method of injecting clean air to the exhaust ports in order to promote the complete combustion of exhaust gases before they are emitted from the exhaust system. The air supply is taken from the 'clean' side of the air cleaner, compressed by an air pump, which is driven by a belt from the engine crankshaft pulley and injected through a nozzle.

6 Components of the system include a diverter valve, an anti-backfire valve and an air manifold.

7 A Catalytic Converter is a device fitted to the exhaust system ahead of the silencer. It is made up of ceramic cores coated with platinum palladium which act as catalysts to absorb combustible elements remaining in the exhaust gases without being destroyed themselves.

8 See Section 59 for details of the Lambda-sond sensor.

Fig. 3.59. EGR valve (Sec. 54)

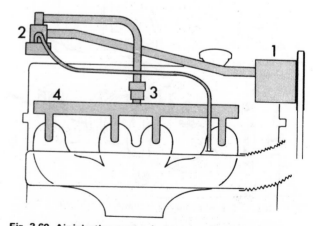

Fig. 3.60. Air injection system (exhaust emission control) (Sec. 54)

1 Air pump
2 Diverter valve
3 Backfire valve
4 Air manifold

55 EGR valve - servicing/mileage recorder - resetting

1   Every 15,000 miles (24,000 km) the EGR valve should be cleaned and checked. A mileage recorder is fitted under the fascia panel which causes two contacts to close at the specified mileage and to light up a warning lamp on the instrument panel as a reminder to the driver that the valve is due for servicing.

2   To clean the valve, disconnect the connecting pipes and unscrew and remove it. Using a wire brush clean away all the deposits, also clean the intake manifold nipple.

3   To reset the mileage recorder after having serviced the valve, remove the rear cover on the odometer and then depress the reset button (Fig. 3.64.

4   The EGR valve should be renewed at intervals of 30,000 miles (48,000 km).

5   To check the operation of the EGR system after refitting the valve, connect the distributor vacuum hose to the EGR vacuum chamber, start the engine and let it idle. The engine should run unevenly or stall. If this does not occur check that the return pipe and the EGR line are not blocked. If the pipes are clear and the engine still runs smoothly renew the valve complete.

56 Throttle and micro-switch - adjustment

1   Switch on the ignition (do not start the engine).

2   Disconnect the lead at the micro-switch (this is the lead connected between the micro-switch and the solenoid valve) and connect a test lamp in series between the disconnected lead and the micro-switch terminal.

3   Release the locknut on the throttle plate stop screw and back off its screw so it does not interfere with setting the throttle adjustment. The test light should go out and stay out for now.

4   Turn the throttle plate stop screw until it touches the stop, and then a further ½ turn. Tighten the locknut. Check that the throttle plate is free and does not stick in the closed position.

5   Insert a 0.060 in (1.5 mm) feeler gauge under the throttle stop screw, Fig. 3.66. The test light should still be out.

6   Screw in the micro-switch screw until the light just comes on. You will also hear the switch click. Tighten the locknut and remove the feeler gauge. Reconnect the micro-switch lead.

Note: Whenever the throttle plate adjustment screw is adjusted the micro-switch must also be adjusted.

7   To check the adjustment, insert a 0.056 in (1.4 mm) feeler gauge under the throttle plate stop screw - the test light should stay on. Insert a 0.072 in (1.8 mm) feeler gauge under the stop screw and the light should go out.

Fig. 3.61. Diverter valve (Sec. 54)

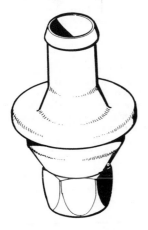

Fig. 3.62. Anti-backfire valve (flame trap) (Sec. 54)

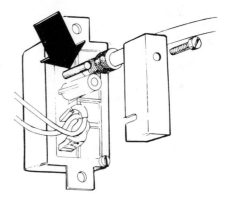

Fig. 3.64. Mileage recorder fitted in conjunction with EGR valve - arrow indicates reset button (Sec. 55)

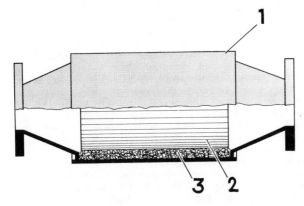

Fig. 3.63. Catalytic converter (Sec. 54)

1   *Stainless steel cover*   3   *Steel wool*
2   *Ceramic material*

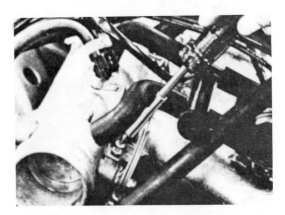

Fig. 3.65. Adjusting the throttle plate stop screw (Sec. 56)

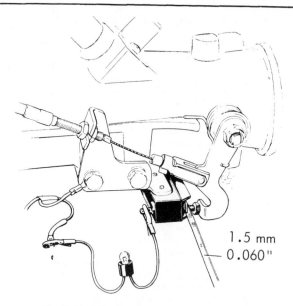

Fig. 3.66. Adjusting the micro switch (Sec. 56)

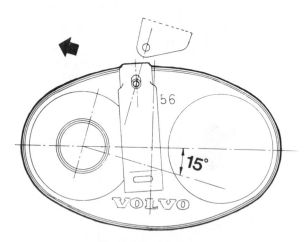

Fig. 3.67. Rear exhaust silencer installation diagram - arrow points to front of car (Secs. 24 and 58)

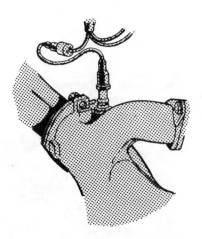

Fig. 3.68. Lambda-sond oxygen sensor (Sec. 59)

57 Air Injection System and Catalytic Converter - testing

1   Regular maintenance consists of maintaining the tension of the compressor drivebelt and the security of all hose connections. The compressor drivebelt should have a deflection of 0.5 in (12.7 mm) at the centre of its longest run. To adjust the belt, slacken the mounting and adjustment bolt. If the drivebelt breaks, the anti-backfire valve must be renewed.

2   The compressor is a lubricant-sealed type and when faulty must be exchanged for a new unit.

3   The diverter valve is located on the engine compartment rear bulkhead and the anti-backfire valve (flametrap) is mounted on the air manifold.

4   To check the anti-backfire valve disconnect the discharge hose at the diverter valve. Suck the hose and check for leakage. If leaking, renew the anti-backfire valve.

5   To check the diverter valve disconnect the discharge hose and block it with a plug (preventative measure). Check that air is blowing from the discharge hole when the engine is idling. (Do not attempt to block the outlet, especially at high speeds, as this could ruin the compressor if the diverter valve is defective). If the diverter valve is faulty it must be renewed.

6   A defective catalytic converter is indicated by excessive CO readings. It is renewed as a unit.

58 Exhaust system (all models) - removal and refitting

1   The exhaust system is suspended on rubber rings and shackles.

2   To remove the system, remove the pre-heater plate (carburettor engines) or the air cleaner, battery and EGR valve hose (fuel injection engines).

3   Disconnect the intermediate pipe from the front silencer. Plenty of freeing fluid will be required for this!

4   Remove the rubber suspension rings from the front silencer.

5   Remove the rubber suspension shackles from the rear silencer and lower the intermediate pipe, rear silencer and tailpipe, all joined together.

6   Disconnect the exhaust downpipe brackets from the transmission and unbolt the downpipe from the manifold.

7   The foregoing operations should be followed if only certain sections of the system are to be renewed. If the complete system must be renewed, then it will be much easier if the old pipes are sawn through with a hacksaw in short lengths for removal.

8   When installing the new system, de-burr the connecting sockets and smear them with grease. Fit new clamps and suspension components if necessary.

9   Refitting is a reversal of removal but make sure that the rear silencer is inclined forward as shown in the diagram before tightening the pipe clamps (Fig. 3.67).

59 Lambda-sond system

1   The system is fitted to North American vehicles having the B21 F/FT engine with CI fuel injection. Engines with LH Jetronic fuel injection do not have such an independent system, as the Lambda-sond functions are incorporated in the fuel injection system.

2   This device senses the level of oxygen in the exhaust gases. Should this level of oxygen exceed the optimum level the Lambda-sond unit triggers the fuel injection system to alter the air/fuel mixture being fed into the engine. This allows the Catalytic Converter to operate in optimum conditions and therefore ensures a really 'clean' exhaust.

3   The Lambda-sond oxygen sensor has an appearance somewhat similar to a spark plug and will be found screwed into the exhaust manifold, just above the downpipe flange. It is connected by a plug and electrical lead to an electronic module, then connected to a frequency valve on the fuel distributor.

4   The unit requires renewal at 15,000 miles (24,000 km) and the owner will be reminded of this when the 'EXH' light glows.

5   The indicator light switch is reset by referring to Section 55 as the light and switch are common to both the EGR and Lambda-sond systems.

6   Certain changes have been made to system components on later models - refer to Chapter 13.

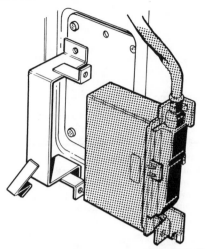

Fig. 3.69. Lambda-sond electronic module (Sec. 59)

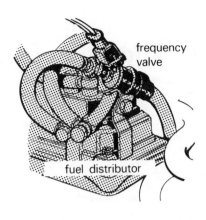

frequency valve

fuel distributor

Fig. 3.70. Lambda-sond frequency valve (Sec. 59)

60 Fault diagnosis - fuel injection system

We give in this Section a table detailing a few of the symptoms of fuel system trouble, possible causes and remedies. Always bear in mind that it is very difficult to distinguish between ignition faults and fuel system faults in many cases. The golden rule should be - before starting on the fuel system - make 100% certain of the ignition. Ignition faults are easy to check, ignition adjustments, when required, are easy to make, and furthermore when adjustment is required as a result of normal wear and tear this adjustment is much more likely to be in the ignition than in the fuel system. The following table assumes that all is in order in the ignition department.

Symptom	Reason/s
Smell of petrol when engine is stopped	Leaking fuel pipes or unions. Leaking fuel tank.
Smell of petrol when engine is idling	Leaking fuel lines or unions in fuel distribution system.
Difficult starting with cold engine	Leak in the intake system. Airflow sensor plate maladjusted. Fuel distributor or airflow sensor sticking or binding. Line pressure too low. Control pressure too high. Auxiliary air valve not opening. Cold start injector faulty. Thermal time switch faulty. Blocked fuel lines or filters.
Difficult starting with warm engine	Leak in the intake system. Airflow sensor plate maladjusted. Fuel distributor or airflow sensor sticking or binding. Line pressure too low. Cold start injector leaking. Air-fuel control unit leaking. Control pressure incorrect. Rest pressure incorrect. Injectors leaking.
Uneven running	Control pressure incorrect. Cold start injector leaking. Air-fuel control unit leaking. Auxiliary air valve not closing. Injectors leaking. Defective injector 'O'-ring seal. Air leak in intake system.
Poor performance, lack of power	Cold start injector leaking. Control pressure too high. Fuel starvation, blocked fuel lines, filters, injectors or fuel distributor. Intake system leaking.
Excessive fuel consumption not accounted for by external leaks	Control pressure too low. Cold start injector leaking. Faulty injectors.

Chapter 4 Ignition system

For modifications, and information applicable to later models, see Supplement at end of manual

Contents

Specifications

Ignition type

B20A, B21A	With breaker
B20E, B21E	Breakerless
Voltage	12 volts
Firing order	1 - 3 - 4 - 2

Ignition setting (vacuum disconnected)

At rev/min	700 - 800	2500
B20A	10º BTDC	23 - 27 BTDC
B20E	5º BTDC	
B21A 1975	12º BTDC	24 - 28 BTDC
B21A 1976 to 1978	15º BTDC	32 - 36 BTDC
B21E	8º BTDC	29 - 33 BTDC

Spark plugs

B20A	Bosch W 175T35
B20E	Bosch 200T35
B21A	Bosch W 175T30
B21E	Bosch W 200T30
Spark plug gap	0.028 - 0.031 in (0.7 - 0.8 mm)

Distributor

	B20A	B17A, B19A B21A, B23A	B20E	B21E
Type No.	JFU4	JFU4	—	JGFU4
Direction of rotation	Anticlockwise	Clockwise	Anticlockwise	Clockwise
Contact breaker gap, in (mm)	0.014 (0.35)	0.016 (0.40)	—	—
Dwell angle at 500 rev/min	62 ± 3º	62 ± 3º	—	—

Ignition coil
Ignition coil ... ...   Bosch 12V

Torque wrench setting
Spark plug ... ...   18 - 22 lb f ft (2.5 - 3 kg f m)

1 General description

1 Two types of ignition system are used on the Volvo 240 series: a conventional battery, coil and mechanical contact breaker type on carburettor engine, and on fuel injection engines a breakerless distributor is used. In the breakerless type the contact points have been replaced by an impulse sender. An electronic module has been added and triggering contacts are incorporated in the base of the distributor.

2 In order that the engine can run correctly it is necessary for an electrical spark to ignite the fuel/air mixture in the combustion chamber at exactly the right moment in relation to engine speed and load. The ignition system is based on feeding low tension (LT) voltage from the battery to the coil where it is converted to high tension (HT) voltage. The high tension voltage is powerful enough to jump the spark plug gap in the cylinders many times a second under high compression pressures, providing that the system is in good condition

and that all adjustments are correct.

3 The ignition system is divided into two circuits: the low tension circuit and the high tension circuit.

4 In the contact breaker type system, the low tension (sometimes known as the primary) circuit consists of the battery lead to the ignition switch, lead from the ignition switch to the low tension or primary coil windings, and the lead from the low tension coil windings to the contact breaker points and condenser in the distributor.

5 The high tension circuit consists of the high tension or secondary coil windings, the heavy ignition lead from the centre of the coil to the centre of the distributor cap, the rotor arm, and the spark plug leads and spark plugs.

6 The system functions in the following manner: Low tension voltage is changed in the coil into high tension voltage by the opening and closing of the contact breaker points in the low tension circuit. High tension voltage is then fed via the carbon brush in the centre of the distributor cap to the rotor arm of the distributor cap, and each time it

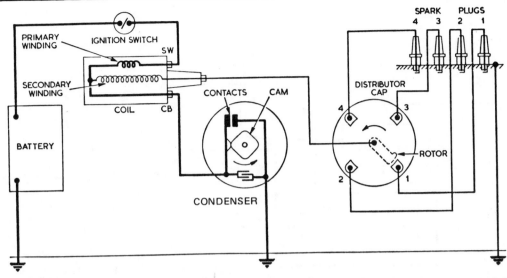

Fig. 4.1. B20A engine ignition system (distributor with contact breaker) (Sec. 1). LT circuit indicated by thick line

comes in line with one of the metal segments in the cap, which are connected to the spark plug leads, the opening and closing of the contact breaker points causes the high tension voltage to build up, jump the gap from the rotor arm to the appropriate metal segment and so via the spark plug lead to the spark plug, where it finally jumps the spark plug gap before going to earth.

7   The ignition is advanced and retarded automatically, to ensure the spark occurs at just the right instant for the particular load at the prevailing engine speed.

8   The ignition advance is controlled both mechanically and by a vacuum operated system. The mechanical governor mechanism comprises two weights, which move out from the distributor shaft, and so advance the spark. The weights are held in position by two light springs and it is the tension of the springs which is largly responsible for correct spark advancement.

9   The vacuum control consists of a diaphragm, one side of which is connected via a small bore tube to the carburettor, and the other side to the contact breaker plate. Depression in the inlet manifold and carburettor, which varies with engine speed and throttle opening, causes the diaphragm to move, so moving the contact breaker plate, and advancing or retarding the spark. A fine degree of control is achieved by a spring in the vacuum advance.

10   The various components of the breakerless electronic system are shown in Fig. 4.2. The distributor now contains a magnetic coil and a rotor disc which functions as an impulse sender.

11   An impulse goes from the distributor to the control unit. This closes and breaks the current to the ignition coil with the help of impulses from the impulse sender. Moreover, the dwell angle is regulated electronically. From the ignition coil the high tension impulse goes as usual to the spark plugs via the distributor rotor arm.

12   The ignition advance is still controlled by means of centrifugal weights and a vacuum chamber.

2   Contact breaker points - adjustment

1   Remove the distributor cap, the rotor arm and the protective cover. Clean the cap inside and out with a dry cloth. It is unlikely that the segments will be badly burned or scored, but if they are, the cap will have to be replaced.

2   Inspect the carbon brush in the top of the distributor cap and press it into its recess to test the spring.

3   Check the condition of the rotor arm and renew it if the metal contact is burned or loose. Slight burning can be cleaned up with a fine file.

4   Prise the contact breaker points apart and examine the condition of their faces. If they are rough, pitted or dirty, it will be necessary to remove them for resurfacing or for replacement points to be fitted.

5   With the points in a satisfactory condition, turn the engine till the heel of the breaker arm is on the highest point of one of the cams.

6   Measure the gap with a feeler gauge, it should be 0.014 in (0.35 mm)

2.6 Measuring the contact breaker gap

for B20A engines and 0.016 in (0.40 mm) for B21A engines (photo).

7   If the gap varies from this amount slacken the contact plate securing screw.

8   Place a screwdriver blade between the two 'pips' on the contact set and open or close the movable arm until the gap is correct. Tighten the securing screw.

9   On modern engines, setting the contact breaker gap in this way must be regarded as an initial setting only. For optimum engine performance, the dwell angle must be checked. The dwell angle is the number of degrees through which the distributor cam turns during the period between the instants of closure and opening of the contact breaker points. This can only be checked with a dwell meter. The correct dwell angle is as shown in Specifications. If the dwell angle is too large, increase the points gap; if it is too small, reduce the points gap.

10   With the gap correctly set, apply a smear of petroleum jelly to the high points of the distributor cam and refit the rotor arm and distributor cap. On some distributors an external lubricator is fitted into which two or three drops of engine oil should be injected.

3   Contact breaker points - renewal

1   Prise the springs which secure the distributor cap and withdraw the

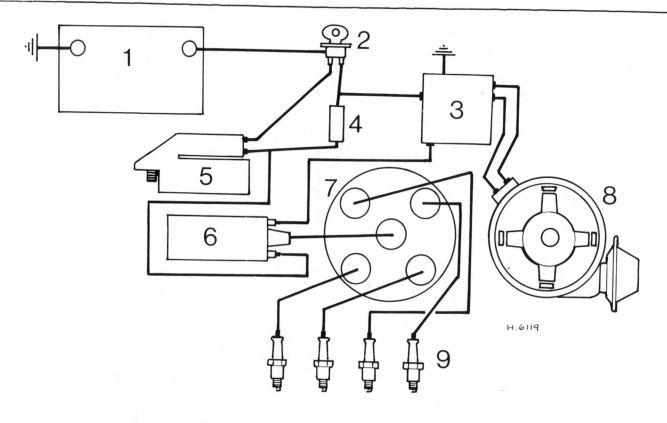

Fig. 4.2. Breakerless electronic ignition system (Sec. 1)

1 Battery
2 Ignition switch
3 Control unit

4 Pre-engaging resistance
5 Starter motor
6 Ignition coil

7 Distributor cap
8 Impulse sender
9 Spark plugs

cap and lay it to one side.

2 Pull off the rotor arm, and remove the protective cover (if fitted).

3 Disconnect the low tension (LT) lead from the terminal on the inside of the distributor body.

4 Unscrew and remove the contact breaker securing screw and lift the contact breaker assembly from the baseplate.

5 Inspect the faces of the contact points. If they are only lightly burned or pitted then they may be ground square on an oilstone or by rubbing a carborundum strip between them. Where the points are found to be severely burned or pitted, then they must be renewed and at the same time the cause of the erosion of the points established. This is most likely to be due to poor earth connections from the battery negative lead to body earth or the engine to earth strap. Remove the connecting bolts at these points, scrape the surfaces free from rust and corrosion and tighten the bolts using a star type lock washer. Other screws to check for security are: the baseplate to distributor body securing screws; the distributor body to lockplate bolt. Looseness in any of these could contribute to a poor earth connection. Check the condenser (Section 5).

6 Refitting the contact breaker assembly is a reversal of removal and when fitted, adjust the points gap as described in the preceding Section. Lubricate the high points of the cam and apply two or three drops of engine oil to the felt pad on top of the distributor shaft.

4 Distributor (breakerless type) - maintenance

1 No routine maintenance operations are required on this type of distributor except to check that all leads, connections and vacuum hoses are secure.

5 Condenser - removal and testing

1 The condenser ensures that with the contact breaker points open, the sparking between them is not excessive to cause severe pitting. The condenser is fitted in parallel and its failure will automatically cause failure of the ignition system as the points will be prevented from interrupting the low tension circuit.

2 Testing for an unserviceable condenser may be effected by switching on the ignition and separating the contact points by hand. If this action is accompanied by a blue flash then condenser failure is indicated. Difficult starting, missing of the engine after several miles running, or badly pitted points are other indications of a faulty condenser.

3 The surest test is by substitution of a new unit.

4 The condenser may be internally or externally mounted according to distributor type but is simply removed after withdrawing the single securing screw.

6 Distributor - removal and replacement

1 Remove the distributor cap (photo).

2 Disconnect the low tension lead and the vacuum hose from the distributor.

3 On cars equipped with fuel injection system, disconnect the leads from the triggering contact assembly.

4 Unscrew and remove the flange bolts and withdraw the distributor from the engine.

5 Replace the distributor as described in Chapter 13, Section 6.

6 Refit the distributor cap, reconnect the low tension lead and the

triggering contact lead, (if applicable). Refit the vacuum hose to the vacuum capsule.

7 Distributor (contact breaker type) - dismantling

1   Remove the rotor arm and the protective cover (if fitted).
2   Remove the circlip for the pull rod from the vacuum unit and take off the unit.
3   Mark the location of the spring clips for the distributor cap (to save trouble on assembly) and remove them. Remove the terminal from the low tension lead and the condenser. Your distributor may possibly be different from that shown in Fig. 4.4 but the principle is the same. The terminal is screwed through to the breaker plate and must be removed before this can be released (Fig. 4.5).
4   With the LT terminal removed, the breaker plate can be lifted out revealing the centrifugal advance mechansim.
5   Looking at this, you will see that the breaker cam is free to move relative to the distributor driveshaft. It has a plate integral with it with projections which engage with two small weights attached to the top of the distributor shaft. These weights and the top of the distributor shaft are clearly shown in Fig. 4.6. When the weights move outwards under centrifugal force as the distributor shaft rotates they move the distributor cam round and so advance the ignition. A pair of small, but important, springs provide opposition for the weights to push against; upon these springs the proper working of the mechanism depends and you should be careful not to distort them in any way when you remove them. In a number of cases they are not identical, so watch for this and note which spring goes where, marking the distributor if necessary to

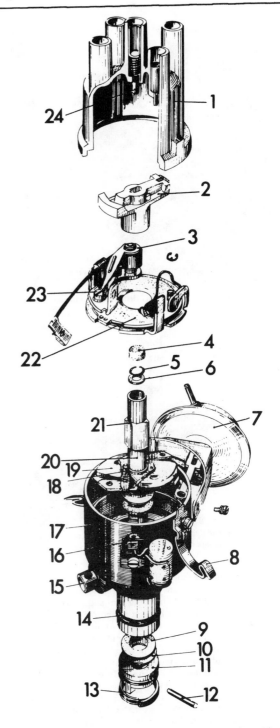

6.1 Location of distributor (ohc engine)

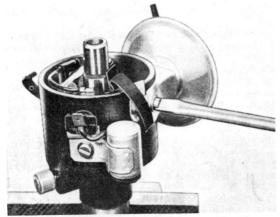

Fig. 4.3. Removing the vacuum capsule (Sec. 7)

Fig. 4.4. Distributor components, B20A engine (Sec. 7)

1 Distributor cap	14 Rubber seal
2 Distributor arm	15 Lubricator
3 Contact breaker	16 Primary connection
4 Lubricating felt	17 Distributor housing
5 Circlip	18 Centrifugal governor spring
6 Washer	19 Centrifugal weight
7 Vacuum regulator	20 Breaker camshaft
8 Cap clasp	21 Breaker cam
9 Fibre washer	22 Breaker plate
10 Steel washer	23 Lock screw for breaker
11 Driving collar	contacts
12 Lock pin	24 Rod brush (carbon)
13 Resilient ring	

Fig. 4.5. Removing the LT terminal and condenser (Sec. 7)

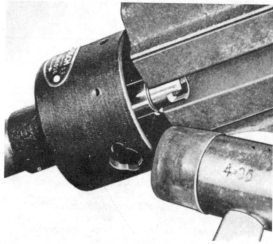

Fig. 4.7. Tapping the housing, releases the circlip holding the cam to the driveshaft (Sec. 7)

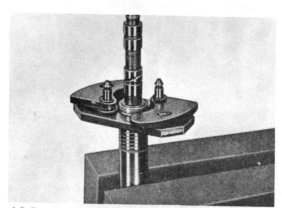

Fig. 4.6. Distributor driveshaft and weights (the cam and governor springs have been removed) (Sec. 7)

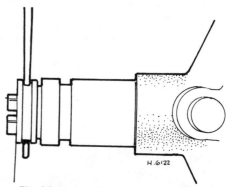

Fig. 4.8. Removal of driving collar (Sec. 7)

ensure that they go back in the right place. If you have to replace them, be sure that you get the right ones for your particular distributor.

6   With these springs removed, mark the cam and distributor shaft so that on reassembly the cam goes back in the correct position. Now hold the cam in a vice with protected jaws as shown in Fig. 4.7 and tap the distributor housing with a hide mallet or similar to release the breaker cam which is held in position by a clip. Draw the cam off the shaft, bringing with it the lubricating wick, the clip and a washer.

7   Undo the screws and remove the contact device where this is fitted.

8   Remove the resilient ring and mark the shaft and driving collar to ensure that when you put the collar back it is the correct way round. Drive out the pin and take the collar off the shaft (Fig. 4.8).

9   Take the shaft out of the housing, being careful not to lose any of the spacing washers on the shaft.

10 Remove the spring clips which hold the centrifugal weights to the shaft and take off the weights (Fig. 4.6).

8 Distributor (breakerless) - dismantling

1   Remove the rotor arm and protective cover.

2   Remove the vacuum capsule.

3   Remove the distributor cap clip assemblies. Note that the clip securing screws are of different lengths and if incorrectly replaced can project and damage moving parts. Always keep them with their respective clip assembly.

4   Remove the screw securing the impulse sender contact and pull it straight out (Fig. 4.10).

5   Using a pair of circlip pliers remove the circlip from the top of the distributor shaft and remove any shims located under it.

6   Remove the three screws which secure the impulse sender plate.

7   Lift off the reluctor and small lock pin (Fig. 4.12).

8   Remove the second circlip and withdraw the impulse sender plate. Separate the impulse sender from its plate by removing the three securing screws (Fig. 4.13).

9   The rest of the dismantling procedure follows that described in Section 7, paragraphs 5 to 10.

9 Distributor - inspection and repair

1   Thoroughly wash all mechanical parts in petrol or paraffin and wipe dry using a clean non-fluffy rag.

2   Check the contact breaker points (if applicable) as described in Section 3.

3   Check the distributor cap for signs of tracking, indicated by a thin black line between segments. Replace the cap if this is evident. Check that the carbon brush moves freely in the centre of the distributor cap and replace it if it is worn or in bad condition.

4   If the metal portion of the rotor arm is badly burned or loose, renew the arm. Slight burning can be cleaned up with a fine file.

5   Examine the fit of the contact breaker plate on the base plate and also check the breaker arm pivot for looseness or wear. If necessary replace the plate.

6   Examine the centrifugal weights and pivot pins for wear in particular, the holes in the centrifugal weights should not be oval or deformed in any other way. The importance of the springs has already been mentioned and these should be checked and replaced if necessary.

7   Check the fit of the breaker cam on the distributor shaft. Play between the distributor shaft and the breaker cam must not exceed 0.004 in (0.1 mm). If the breaker cam itself shows signs of wear or scoring, replace it.

8   The play between the distributor housing and the driveshaft should

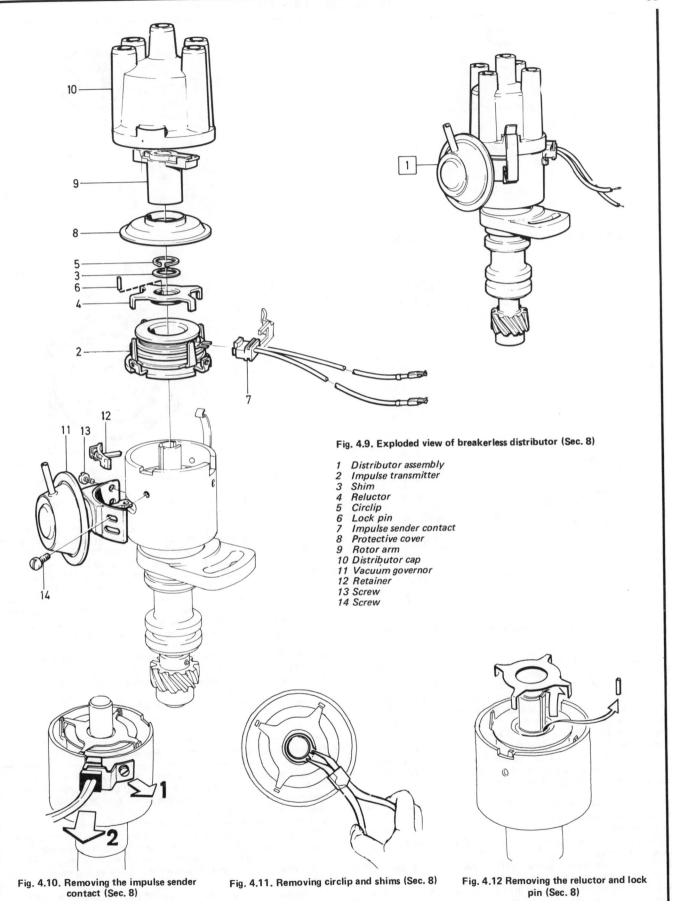

Fig. 4.9. Exploded view of breakerless distributor (Sec. 8)

1   Distributor assembly
2   Impulse transmitter
3   Shim
4   Reluctor
5   Circlip
6   Lock pin
7   Impulse sender contact
8   Protective cover
9   Rotor arm
10 Distributor cap
11 Vacuum governor
12 Retainer
13 Screw
14 Screw

Fig. 4.10. Removing the impulse sender contact (Sec. 8)

Fig. 4.11. Removing circlip and shims (Sec. 8)

Fig. 4.12 Removing the reluctor and lock pin (Sec. 8)

1   Securing screw   2   Contact

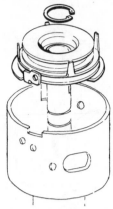

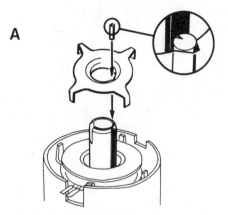

A

Fig. 4.13. Removal of the impulse sender and plate (Sec. 8)

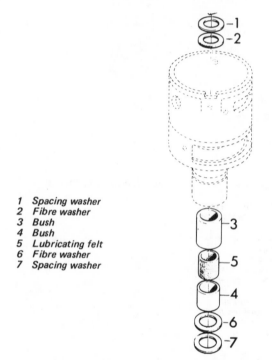

1 Spacing washer
2 Fibre washer
3 Bush
4 Bush
5 Lubricating felt
6 Fibre washer
7 Spacing washer

Fig. 4.14. Spacing washers and bushes for the driveshaft (Sec. 9)

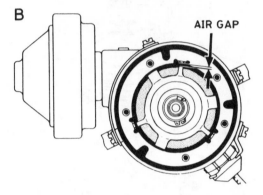

B

AIR GAP

Fig. 4.15 Breakerless type distributor (Sec 10)

A   Alignment of reluctor   B   Air gap
     and lock pin

3 On breakerless distributors the only lubrication permitted is applying a few drops of oil on the felt wick in the centre of the rotor shaft.
4 Assembly generally is a straightforward reversal of the dismantling procedure. To assemble the breaker cam on the drive shaft, slide the washer and circlip down the inside of the cam (using a suitable sleeve or two thin metal strips) until the circlip clicks into position. If you have replaced some of the parts whose position you marked when you were taking the distributor apart, be particularly careful about getting the new ones in the right position - you can easily be sure of this by checking with the old parts which you marked.
5 When fitting the reluctor on breakerless distributors the slot should be opposite the ridge on the distributor shaft. Fit the lock pin so that the slot faces the ridge on the shaft (Fig. 4.15), otherwise the lock pin may be sheared off.
6 With the reluctor and stator tips in alignment, the air gap should be 0.010 in (0.25 mm). Adjust if necessary.

not exceed 0.008 in (0.2 mm). If the play is excessive, replace the bushes and, if this is insufficient, also the shaft.
9 Fig. 4.14 shows the assembly of bushes and washers on the drive-shaft. Replacement of the old bushes is a matter of driving or pulling them out and pressing or gently tapping the new ones in, one from each end with the felt lubricator between them. The lubricator and the bushes should be soaked in oil for at least half an hour before fitting. The fibre washers at each end of the shaft should be next to the housing. The end play in the shaft should lie between 0.004 - 0.010 in (0.1 - 0.25 mm). If necessary this can be adjusted by altering the number of spacing washers on the distributor shaft.

10 Distributor - reassembly

1 Assemble the driving shaft into the housing as described in the previous paragraph (Section 9, paragraph 9).
2 One of the most important aspects of reassembly is lubrication. The cam lobes and the cam followers should all be lightly coated with grease and so should the weights. A touch of grease should also be applied where the pull rod from the vacuum regulator is attached to the breaker plate. Do not be too free with grease in this area - otherwise it may end up on the breaker contacts (mechanical breaker distributor).

11 Ignition timing (contact breaker distributor)

1 Turn the engine until No. 1 piston is at TDC on the compression stroke and the timing mark on the crankshaft pulley is opposite the appropriate mark (as given in Specifications at the beginning of this Chapter) on the timing scale.
2 Release the clamp bolt on the distributor mounting and with the distributor cap removed, turn the distributor housing until the contact breaker points are just opening. This can be checked by connecting a test lamp between the distributor low tension terminal and a good earth and switching on the ignition. When the points have just opened, the test lamp will light up.
3 Tighten the clamp bolt and remove the test lamp, switch off the ignition and refit the distributor cap.
4 It is recommended that the timing is now checked with a strobo-scope as described in the following Section.

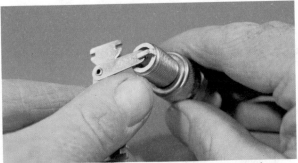

Measuring plug gap. A feeler gauge of the correct size (see ignition system specifications) should have a slight 'drag' when slid between the electrodes. Adjust gap if necessary

Adjusting plug gap. The plug gap is adjusted by bending the earth electrode inwards, or outwards, as necessary until the correct clearance is obtained. Note the use of the correct tool

Normal. Grey-brown deposits, lightly coated core nose. Gap increasing by around 0.001 in (0.025 mm) per 1000 miles (1600 km). Plugs ideally suited to engine, and engine in good condition

Carbon fouling. Dry, black, sooty deposits. Will cause weak spark and eventually misfire. Fault: over-rich fuel mixture. Check: carburettor mixture settings, float level and jet sizes; choke operation and cleanliness of air filter. Plugs can be re-used after cleaning

Oil fouling. Wet, oily deposits. Will cause weak spark and eventually misfire. Fault: worn bores/piston rings or valve guides; sometimes occurs (temporarily) during running-in period. Plugs can be re-used after thorough cleaning

Overheating. Electrodes have glazed appearance, core nose very white – few deposits. Fault: plug overheating. Check: plug value, ignition timing, fuel octane rating (too low) and fuel mixture (too weak). Discard plugs and cure fault immediately

Electrode damage. Electrodes burned away; core nose has burned, glazed appearance. Fault: pre-ignition. Check: as for 'Overheating' but may be more severe. Discard plugs and remedy fault before piston or valve damage occurs

Split core nose (may appear initially as a crack). Damage is self-evident, but cracks will only show after cleaning. Fault: pre-ignition or wrong gap-setting technique. Check: ignition timing, cooling system, fuel octane rating (too low) and fuel mixture (too weak). Discard plugs, rectify fault immediately

12 Ignition timing with a stroboscope

1   It is necessary to use this method where a breakerless type
distributor is fitted. The method is recommended for all types of
ignition.
2   Clean the timing mark on the crankshaft pulley and the timing
scale on the cover. Mark the appropriate setting with quick drying
white paint (or chalk).
3   Run the engine to normal operating temperature.
4   Disconnect the vacuum pipe from the distributor and plug it.
5   Connect a stroboscope in accordance with the manufacturer's
instructions, usually between No. 1 spark plug and No. 1 HT lead.
6   Make sure the engine idling speed is correctly set.
7   Start the engine and point the stroboscope at the white marks. They
will appear stationary and if the ignition timing is correctly set they
will be in alignment. If they are not directly opposite each other, release
the clamp bolt on the distributor mounting and turn the distributor
one way or the other until the marks line up. Tighten the clamp bolt.
8   If the engine is now revved up, the white mark will move away from
the fixed points indicating that the centrifugal advance mechanism is
operating correctly. If the vacuum pipe is reconnected, the movement
of the timing mark in relation to the fixed point will be greater when
the engine speed is increased. This indicates that the vacuum advance
is operating.

13 Ignition timing sender

1   In 1976 a new system for checking the firing position was introduced
for the 21 engine. Instead of a stroboscope, a special engine instrument
is used and is connected to a sender on the engine via a connection, and
to the spark plug cable for No. 1 cylinder. The firing position can then
be read off the instrument, (Volvo mono-tester - 999 9921).
2   The above makes it easier to check the firing position and adjustment can be more precise. It also reduces the risk of possible injury
from the fan and belts.
3   The system consists of an electro-magnetic sender mounted in the
engine block and two pins on the flywheel, Fig. 4.17. The position of
the pins in relation to the sender corresponds to 12° BTDC and 20°
ATDC for No. 1 cylinder.
4   The sender consists of a coil (resistance 15 ohms), wound round an
iron core, and a cable integrated with the sender. This coil is connected
to a connection terminal mounted on the valve cover.
5   To check the timing connect the tester to the battery positive
terminal, battery negative terminal, ignition coil terminal 1, the sender
connection on the valve cover and to the spark plug cable for No. 1
cylinder. The dial on the tester has a blue and a red scale. Push in the
button and read off the red scale. The tester indicates when a spark
is obtained in No. 1 cylinder, when the pins on the flywheel pass
the sender, the tester gives a reading which shows the actual firing
position.
Note: Although the 'timing sender' method of checking the timing
is more precise, the timing can effectively be checked using the
stroboscope as described in Section 12.

14 Spark plugs and HT leads

1   The correct functioning of the spark plugs is vital for the proper
running and efficient operation of the engine.
2   At intervals of 6000 miles (10000 km) the plugs should be removed,
examined, cleaned and if worn excessively, renewed. The condition of
the spark plug can tell much about the general condition of the engine
(see illustration).
3   If the insulator nose of the spark plug is clean and white, with no
deposits, this is indicative of a weak mixture, or too hot a plug (a hot
plug transfers heat away from the electrodes slowly - a cold plug
transfers heat away quickly).
4   If the insulator nose is covered with hard black looking deposits,
then this is indicative that the mixture is too rich. Should the plug be
black and oily then it is likely that the engine is fairly worn as well as
the mixture being too rich.
5   If the insulator nose is covered with light tan to greyish brown
deposits, then the mixture is correct, and it is likely that the engine is
in good condition.

6   If there are any traces of long brown tapering stains on the outside
of the white portion of the plug, then the plug will have to be renewed,
as this shows that there is a faulty joint between the plug body and the
insulator, and compression is being allowed to leak away.
7   Plugs should be cleaned by a sand blasting machine, which will free
them from carbon more completely than cleaning by hand. The machine
will also test the condition of the plugs under compression. Any plug
that fails to spark at the recommended pressure should be renewed.
8   The spark plug gap is of considerable importance, as, if it is too
large or too small the size of the spark and its efficiency will be
seriously impaired. The spark plug gap should be set to 0.028 - 0.032 in
(0.7 - 0.8 mm).
9   To set it, measure the gap with a feeler gauge, and then bend open
or close, the outer plug electrode until the correct gap is achieved. The
centre electrode should never be bent as this may crack the insulation
and cause plug failure, if nothing worse.
10 When replacing the plugs, remember to use new washers and replace
the leads from the distributor cap in the correct firing order which is
1, 3, 4, 2, No. 1 cylinder being the one nearest the fan.
11 The plug leads require no maintenance other than being kept clean
and wiped over regularly. At intervals of 6000 miles (10000 km)
however, pull each lead off the plug in turn and remove it from the
distributor cap. Water can seep down these joints giving rise to a white
corrosive deposit which must be carefully removed from the end of
each cable. At the same time, check that the suppressor connections
are in good condition. If cracked or damaged they should be renewed.

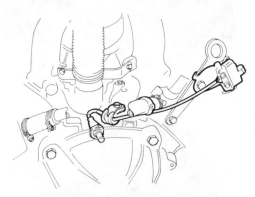

**Fig. 4.16. Ignition timing sender is mounted in front of the flywheel
(Sec. 13)**

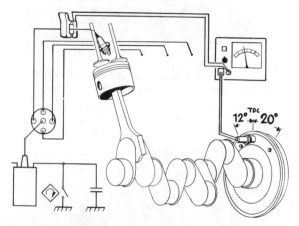

Fig. 4.17. Volvo Mono-tester connected to the engine (Sec. 13)

15 Fault diagnosis - ignition system (contact breaker type)

Failures of the ignition system will either be due to faults in the HT
or LT circuits. Initial check should be made by observing the security
of spark plug terminals, Lucar type terminals, coil and battery
connections. More detailed investigation and the explanation and
remedial action in respect of symptoms of ignition malfunction are
described in the following sub-Sections.

Engine fails to start

1 If the engine fails to start and the car was running normally when it was last used, first check there is fuel in the fuel tank. If the engine turns over normally on the starter motor and the battery is evidently well charged, then the fault may be in either the high or low tension circuits. First check the HT circuit. Note: If the battery is known to be fully charged, the ignition light comes on, and the starter motor fails to turn the engine check the tightness of the leads on the battery terminals and also the security of the earth leads to its connection on the body. It is quite common for the leads to have worked loose, even if they look and feel secure. If one of the battery terminal posts gets very hot when trying to work the starter motor this is a sure indication of a faulty connection to that terminal.

2 One of the commonest reasons for bad starting is wet or damp spark plug leads and distributor. Remove the distributor cap. If condensation is visible internally, dry the cap with a rag and also wipe over the leads. Replace the cap.

3 If the engine still fails to start, check that current is reaching the plugs, by disconnecting each plug lead in turn at the spark plug end, and hold the end of the cable about 3/16th inch (5 mm) away from the cylinder block. Spin the engine on the starter motor.

4 Sparking between the end of the cable and the block should be fairly strong with a regular blue spark. (Hold the lead with rubber to avoid electric shocks). If current is reaching the plugs, then remove them and clean and regap them. The engine should now start.

5 If there is no spark at the plug leads take off the HT lead from the centre of the distributor cap and hold it to the block as before. Spin the engine on the starter once more. A rapid succession of blue sparks between the end of the lead and the block indicate that the coil is in order and that the distributor cap is cracked, the rotor arm faulty, or the carbon brush in the top of the distributor cap is not making good contact with the spring on the rotor arm. Possibly the points are in bad condition. Clean and reset them as described in this Chapter.

6 If there are no sparks from the end of the lead from the coil, check the connections at the coil end of the lead. If it is in order start checking the low tension circuit.

7 Use a 12v voltmeter or a 12v bulb and two lengths of wire. With the ignition switch on and the points open test between the low tension wire to the coil (it is marked +) and earth. No reading indicates a break in the supply from the ignition switch. Check the connections at the switch to see if any are loose. Refit them and the engine should run. A reading shows a faulty coil or condenser, or broken lead between the coil and the distributor.

8 Take the condenser wire off the points assembly and with the points open, test between the moving point and earth. If there now is a reading, then the fault is in the condenser. Fit a new one and the fault is cleared.

9 With no reading from the moving point to earth, take a reading between earth and the (–) terminal of the coil. A reading here shows a broken wire which will need to be renewed between the coil and distributor. No reading confirms that the coil has failed and must be renewed, after which the engine will run once more. Remember to refit the condenser wire to the points assembly. For these tests it is sufficient to separate the points with a piece of dry paper while testing with the points open.

Engine misfires

10 If the engine misfires regularly, run it at a fast idling speed. Pull off each of the plug caps in turn and listen to the note of the engine. Hold the plug cap in a dry cloth or with a rubber glove as additional protection against a shock from the HT supply.

11 No difference in engine running will be noticed when the lead from the defective circuit is removed. Removing the lead from one of the good cylinders will accentuate the misfire.

12 Remove the plug lead from the end of the defective plug and hold it about 3/16 in (5.0 mm) away from the block. Restart the engine. If the sparking is fairly strong and regular the fault must lie in the spark plug.

13 The plug may be loose, the insulation may be cracked, or the points may have burnt away giving too wide a gap for the spark to jump. Worse still, one of the points may have broken off. Either renew the plug, or clean it, reset the gap, and then test it.

14 If there is no spark at the end of the plug lead, or if it is weak and intermittent, check the ignition lead from the distributor to the plug. If the insulation is cracked or perished, renew the lead. Check the connections at the distributor cap.

15 If there is still no spark, examine the distributor cap carefully for tracking. This can be recognised by a very thin black line running between two or more electrodes, or between an electrode and some other part of the distributor. These lines are paths which now conduct electricity across the cap thus letting it run to earth. The only answer is a new distributor cap.

16 Apart from the ignition timing being incorrect, other causes of misfiring have already been dealt with under the section dealing with the failure of the engine to start. To recap - these are that:

a) *The coil may be faulty giving an intermittent misfire.*
b) *There may be a damaged wire or loose connection in the low tension circuit.*
c) *The condenser may be short circuiting.*
d) *There may be a mechanical fault in the distributor (broken driving spindle or contact breaker spring).*

17 If the ignition timing is too far retarded, it should be noted that the engine will tend to overheat, and there will be a quite noticeable drop in power. If the engine is overheating and the power is down, and the ignition timing is correct, then the carburettor should be checked, as it is likely that this is where the fault lies.

16 Fault diagnosis - ignition system (breakerless type)

Symptom	Reason/s
Engine fails to start	Discharged battery or loose connections
	Fault in system component
	Disconnected system leads
	Incorrect air gap
Engine starts and runs but misfires	Faulty spark plug
	Cracked distributor cap
	Worn advance mechanism
	Incorrect timing
	Poor earth connections
	Incorrect air gap or faulty pick-up unit
Engine overheats	Incorrect timing
	Advance weights seized (retarded)
	Perforated vacuum pipe
Engine 'pinks'	Timing too advanced
	Advance weights seized (advanced)
	Broken weight spring

Chapter 5 Clutch

For modifications, and information applicable to later models, see Supplement at end of manual

Contents

Note: *For details on the hydraulic clutch used on right-hand drive models from 1975 onwards, see supplementary Chapter 13.*

Specifications

Type	Single dry plate, diaphragm spring
Size	8.5 in (215.9 mm)
Total friction area	68.2 in^2 (440 cm^2)
Throw-out fork free travel	
LH drive — cable-operated	0.12 - 0.16 in (3 - 4 mm)
RH drive — hydraulically-operated	Non-adjustable
Clutch pedal travel	
LH drive	6.0 in (150 mm)
RH drive	6.4 in (160 mm)

1 General description

1 The models covered by this manual which are fitted with manual transmission are fitted with an 8.5 in (215.9 mm) diameter diaphragm spring clutch operated by a cable connected between the release fork and the clutch pedal. On right-hand drive models from 1975 onwards, the clutch is hydraulically actuated. (Details of the hydraulic system appear in the supplementary Chapter 13). Two types of clutch are fitted which are interchangeable as complete assemblies, but not individual parts or friction discs.

2 A steel cover dowelled and bolted to the rear face of the flywheel has attached to it a pressure plate which (when the clutch is engaged) clamps a disc covered with high friction lining material to the flywheel. This disc has a central hub which engages with splines on the gearbox input shaft (first motion shaft). Thus when the clutch is engaged, the flywheel drives the gearbox through the disc and the whole assembly rotates at engine speed.

3 The gearbox input shaft is kept in alignment with the crankshaft because the end of it is held in a small bearing which is set in the end of the crankshaft. This bearing is known as the pilot bearing.

4 The pressure holding this sandwich together is exerted by a diaphragm spring fitted to the clutch cover. A diagram of this spring is given in Fig. 5.2. and you can see the central part of it quite clearly in the photograph.

In order to disengage the clutch, pressure is applied to the central part of the spring by a thrust bearing actuated by a lever attached to the flywheel housing. A look at Fig. 5.2 shows how this pressure acts to draw back the outer edge of the spring, so withdrawing the pressure plate. When the pressure plate is drawn back, the friction disc is no longer sandwiched between the flywheel and the pressure plate and ceases to be driven by the flywheel.

5 The thrust bearing is concentric with the gearbox input shaft, but in no way connected to it; the front part of the bearing revolves when it is in contact with the spring but the back part is stationary being attached to the release arm which is also stationary. When the clutch

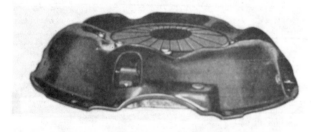

Fig. 5.1. Two types of clutch cover (Sec. 1)

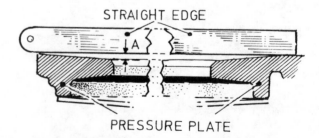

Fig. 5.2. Diagrammatic section through clutch assembly. Dimension 'A' representing deviation from flat on driving face, must not exceed 0.0012 in (0.03 mm) (Sec. 1)

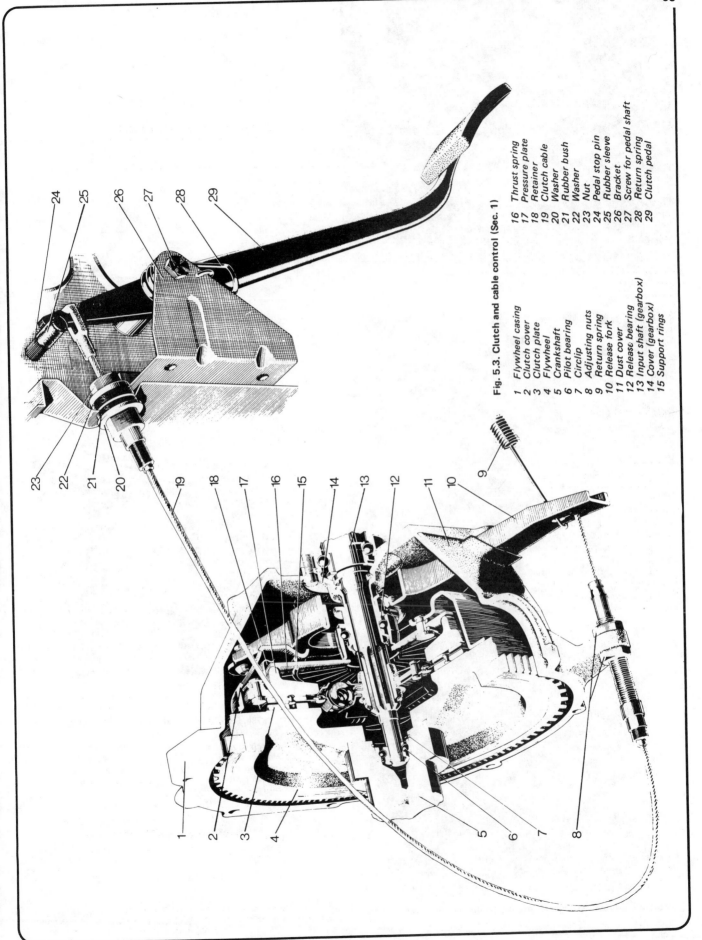

Fig. 5.3. Clutch and cable control (Sec. 1)

1 Flywheel casing
2 Clutch cover
3 Clutch plate
4 Flywheel
5 Crankshaft
6 Pilot bearing
7 Circlip
8 Adjusting nuts
9 Return spring
10 Release fork
11 Dust cover
12 Release bearing
13 Input shaft (gearbox)
14 Cover (gearbox)
15 Support rings
16 Thrust spring
17 Pressure plate
18 Retainer
19 Clutch cable
20 Washer
21 Rubber bush
22 Washer
23 Nut
24 Pedal stop pin
25 Rubber sleeve
26 Bracket
27 Screw for pedal shaft
28 Return spring
29 Clutch pedal

1.4 This view of the clutch in the car clearly shows the segmental diaphragm spring

5.3a Removing the clutch thrust bearing (cable actuation, M40 gearbox)

5.3b Clutch thrust bearing and fork (hydraulic actuation, M45 gearbox)

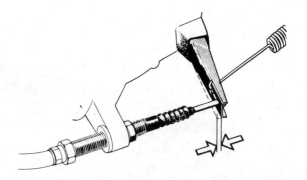

Fig. 5.4. Clutch fork free play adjustment - 0.12 - 0.16 in (3 - 4 mm) (Sec. 2)

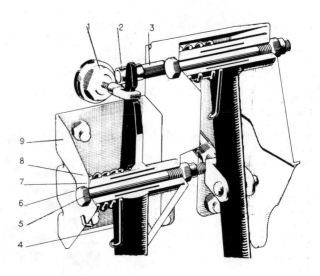

Fig. 5.5. Clutch pedal mounting (Sec. 4)

1	Clutch cable	6	Shaft
2	Rubber sleeve	7	Bush
3	Pedal stop	8	Return spring
4	Clutch pedal	9	Bracket
5	Bolt		

is engaged, the front of the bearing is not in contact with the spring and so does not revolve.

6   The central hub of the clutch friction disc is sprung in order to absorb transmission shocks and to help ensure a smooth take-off.

2   Clutch - adjustment

1   Engagement and disengagement of the clutch depends on the movement of the clutch lever which is actuated by the clutch cable. When the lever is pulled back, the clutch is disengaged, and when the lever is allowed to go forwards the bearing on the other end of it will move backwards and the centre part of the spring will also move backwards until the disc is firmly sandwiched between the plate and the flywheel. Once this has happened, the spring will cease to follow further movement of the bearing which will continue to move backward until the clutch cable is taut. It is obviously desirable that there should be some clearance between the spring and the bearing when the clutch is engaged.

2   The friction disc will wear in use and become thinner. When this has happened, the pressure plate will move a little closer to the flywheel when the clutch is engaged. The centre part of the spring will correspondingly move a little further backwards and the clearance between the spring and the thrust bearing will be reduced.

3   Clutch adjustment is effected by means of nuts which should be adjusted to give a clutch lever free travel of 0.12 - 0.16 in (3 - 4 mm). This free travel will be felt as free play movement of the clutch pedal. It is most important that this free play is always maintained. If you get to the stage where you cannot obtain it, then this is an indication that the friction disc is worn and requires replacement.

3   Clutch cable - removal and replacement

1   Unhook the return spring for the release lever.

2   Slacken off the two adjusting nuts that hold the outer cable sleeve to the housing boss and detach the inner cable from the clutch lever (photo).

3   Unscrew the rear adjustment nut from the cable sleeve and withdraw the cable from the housing boss.

4   Remove the clutch pedal bearing bolt and detach the inner cable from the pedal.

5   The cable can now be removed from the car.

6   Refitting the new cable assembly is the reverse sequence to removal. It will be necessary to adjust the cable as described in Section 2.

4   Clutch pedal and mounting - overhaul

1   Remove the panel under the dashboard which covers the pedal mounting. Details of the clutch pedal mounting are shown in Fig. 5.5.

2   Unhook the return spring for the pedal, slacken the nut and remove the pedal pivot bolt. Disconnect the pedal from the wire and remove the pedal.

3   The pedal runs on bushes bearing on a hollow shaft through which the bearing bolt passes. Take this shaft out, give the whole assembly a good clean and inspect for signs of wear and excessive play between the pedal and the shaft.

4   If necessary, drive out the bushes and replace them.

5   Inspect the tubular shaft for signs of wear (it is not very likely that you will find any) and replace if necessary.

6   Replace the return spring unless you are perfectly sure that it is all right. It is most annoying if you have to do the work all over again because a silly little spring breaks, only weeks after you have had an assembly like this to pieces.

7   Grease the shaft, bushes and spring generously and reassemble. Remember to hook the cable on to the pedal before you bolt it to the mounting.

5   Clutch release thrust bearing - removal, inspection and replacement

1   The classic symptom of wear in the clutch release bearing - and it is one which should not be disregarded - is clutch squeal, heard when

you depress the clutch pedal. Before getting to this stage you may hear a whirring noise when you have the clutch pedal down.

2   The thrust bearing only has to perform when your foot is on the clutch pedal. If you use the clutch pedal as a foot-rest the thrust bearing may well be revolving even though there is no clutch slip; this is a temptation which it is well worthwhile to resist.

3   To remove the thrust bearing, remove the gearbox as described in Chapter 6. The bearing can now be removed from the release fork. On M45 gearboxes the thrust bearing is retained by a spring clip (photos).

4   Check the bearing by placing it on the bench and rotating it under light pressure. The bearing should turn easily with no suspicion of binding and there should be no suspicion of play when it is under pressure. If there is any doubt about it, replace it. The whole assembly is replaced; there is no question of dismantling it and fitting a new bearing inside. Be sure when getting hold of a replacement to specify the clutch type as the thrust bearings are not the same for the different clutch types.

5   Replacement is the reverse of the removal sequence. Adjust the clutch lever free travel as described in Section 2.

6   Clutch - removal

1   Remove the gearbox complete with the bellhousing as described in Chapter 6. This will give you a view of the flywheel and clutch.

2   Undo the screws attaching the clutch housing to the flywheel cross-wise a couple of turns at a time to prevent possible warping of the clutch housing. Remove the clutch as shown in Fig. 5.6. The disc is not attached to anything at this stage, hence the thumb in the hole to keep hold of it.

7   Clutch - inspection and overhaul

1   The view of the friction disc in the photograph shows what this should look like when it is in good condition. Inspect the friction disc for wear and contamination by oil.

2   Wear on the linings is gauged by the depth of the rivet heads below the surface of the friction material. If this is less than 0.025 in (0.6 mm) the linings are worn enough to justify renewal.

3   When one considers how easy it is to slip on a polished floor, it is surprising that the highly polished surfaces of the clutch are able to generate so much friction. This is the case because there is - or should be - a complete absence of any form of lubricant between the mating surfaces. Under these conditions, the smoother the surface the better the contact and consequently the surface of the friction facings should have the appearance of smoothly finished wood - the grain of the material being clearly seen. It should be quite light in colour. If oil has penetrated to this surface, it will have been burnt off and it will darken the face. If however, the polish of the facing remains such that the grain of the material can still be distinguished clearly this will have little effect on clutch performance. Naturally, if you feel that oil is - or has been - present in the clutch you will take good care to find out how it got there and put a stop to it. If a more severe degree of oil contamination has occurred, the surface may be affected in two ways depending upon the nature of the oil:

Fig. 5.6. Removing the clutch (Sec. 6)

7.1 Clutch friction disc

9.2 Clutch friction disc marking

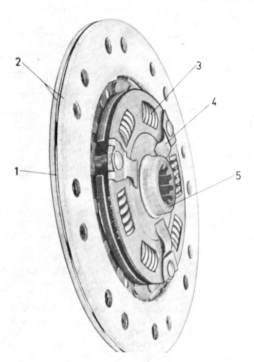

Fig. 5.7. Clutch disc assembly (Sec. 7)

1 Disc   4 Damper spring
2 Facings   5 Hub
3 Spring

a) The oil may burn off and leave a carbon deposit on the surface of
   the facings which become highly glazed and have a definite tendency
   to slip. In this condition the surfaces have the appearance of
   varnished wood and in general the grain of the material is hidden.
b) Oil may partially burn and leave a resinous deposit on the facings.
   This has a tendency to produce a fierce clutch and may also cause
   clutch spin due to the tendency of the face linings to stick to the
   surface of the flywheel or pressure plate.

4 If there are signs of severe overheating - brought about as a result
of clutch slip - it is well to replace the disc complete. It may be
distorted or the temper of the shock absorbing springs may have been
affected. If only the friction lining is affected, it is quite practicable
to replace this oneself rather than buy a complete replacement disc
assembly. Most people feel it is hardly worth doing and we would be

inclined to agree with this. Nevertheless the linings and rivets are
available as Volvo spares if you wish to have a go.

5 To replace the facings, first drill out the old rivets with an 0.14 in
(3.5 mm) drill. Then check the clutch plate. The indentations on the
tongues should be even. The clutch plate must not be warped. The
clutch springs and rivets in the hub should fit securely and not show
any signs of looseness. Check to make sure that there are no cracks. If
the plate does not pass all these tests with flying colours, replace it.

6 Rivet on the new facings (preferably in a rivet press). The rivets
should be inserted from the side on which the facing lies and riveted
up from the opposite direction against the disc. Use alternative holes
in the facing - the holes not occupied by rivets fixing one facing will
contain the rivets for the other. After riveting - the faces should be
quite flat and spaced from each other by the indentations on to the
clutch disc. This spacing is most important in order to achieve smooth
engagement of the clutch. Be sure that during these operations the
clutch facings are kept absolutely free from oil.

7 The pressure plate assembly should be replaced complete if faulty.
Check the pressure plate for damage by heat, cracks, scoring or other
damage on the friction surface. Check the curvature of the pressure
plate with a 9½ in (240 mm) steel straight edge placed diagonally
across the friction surface. It is permitted for the plate to be very
slightly concave, ie. the centre of the plate lies below the straight edge.
The distance between the plate and the straight edge must not exceed
0.0012 in (0.03 mm), check this with feeler gauges. If the plate is
convex, ie. the centre is higher than the edges, replace the assembly.
Check the pressure spring carefully; if cracked or damaged in any other
way, the assembly should be replaced.

8 Pilot bearing

1 This bearing is not all that easy to remove without damaging it.
For this reason we recommend that you wash it out and inspect it
while it is still in the crankshaft. This way you only have to remove it
if you have already decided to replace it and your problems are
simpler. Its removal is considered in Chapter 1.

2 Do not forget that the flywheel surface is an important component
of the clutch. If the surface of the flywheel in contact with the clutch
friction disc is uneven or burnt it should be reground. This is a job for
the specialist. We suggest that if this is necessary, you take the flywheel
and clutch assembly to the firm who is to do the grinding and have them
balanced as a unit after the grinding has been carried out.

9 Clutch - replacement

1 Before you start, ensure that the clutch assembly and friction disc
are completely free from oil. If necessary, wash in petrol and dry off
with a clean rag.

2 To refit the clutch, place the friction disc against the flywheel. Make sure it is the right way round as fitment the wrong way would result in non-operation of the clutch. The friction disc is marked as shown in the photograph.

3 Replace the clutch cover assembly loosely on the dowels, replace the six bolts and spring washers and tighten them finger-tight so that the clutch disc is gripped but can still be moved.

4 The clutch disc must now be centralised so that when the engine and gearbox are mated, the gearbox input shaft splines will pass through the splines in the centre of the hub.

5 Centralisation can be carried out quite easily by inserting a round bar or long screwdriver through the hole in the centre of the clutch, so that the end of the bar rests in the small hole in the end of the crankshaft containing the input shaft bearing bush. Moving the bar sideways or up and down will move the clutch disc in whichever direction is necessary to achieve centralisation.

6 Centralisation is easily judged by removing the bar and viewing the driven plate hub in relation to the hole in the centre of the clutch cover assembly. When the hub appears exactly in the centre of the release bearing hole all is correct. Alternatively if an old input shaft can be used, instant fitment will result.

7 Tighten the clutch bolts firmly in a diagonal sequence to ensure that the cover plate is pulled down evenly and without distortion of the flange.

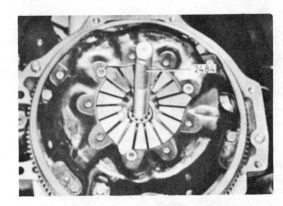

Fig. 5.8. Centralising the friction disc (Sec. 9)

8 Refit the gearbox as described in Chapter 6. Take care when inserting the input shaft into the clutch not to put any strain on the clutch assembly or input shaft.

9 Finally adjust the clutch cable as described in Section 2.

10 Fault diagnosis

Symptom	Reason/s	Remedy
Judder when taking up drive	Loose engine/gearbox mountings or over flexible mountings	Check and tighten all mounting bolts and replace any 'soft' or broken mountings.
	Badly worn friction surfaces or friction plate contaminated with oil deposits	Remove engine and replace clutch parts as required. Rectify any oil leakage points which may have caused contamination.
	Worn splines in the friction plate hub or on the gearbox input shaft	Renew friction plate and/or input shaft.
	Badly worn pilot bearing	Renew pilot bearing.
Clutch spin (failure to disengage) so that gears cannot be meshed	Clutch actuating cable clearance too great	Adjust clearance.
	Clutch hydraulic slave cylinder leaking	Renew seals
	Clutch friction disc sticking because of rust on lining or splines (usually apparent after standing idle for some length of time)	As temporary remedy engage top gear, apply handbrake, depress clutch and start engine. (If very badly stuck engine will not turn). When running rev up engine and slip clutch until disengagement is normally possible. Renew friction plate at earliest opportunity.
	Damaged or misaligned pressure plate assembly	Replace pressure plate assembly.
Clutch slip - (increase in engine speed does not result in increase in vehicle speed - especially on hills)	Clutch pedal free-play too little or non-existent resulting in partially disengaged clutch at all times	Adjust clearances.
	Clutch friction surfaces worn out (beyond further adjustment of operating cable) or clutch surfaces oil soaked	Replace friction plate and remedy source of oil leakage.
Clutch squeal when clutch is disengaged	Worn clutch release thrust bearing	Replace thrust bearing.

Chapter 6
Gearbox, overdrive and automatic transmission

For modifications, and information applicable to later models, see Supplement at end of manual

Contents

Specifications

Manual gearbox

Type

Without overdrive	M40	M45
With overdrive	M41	M46

Reduction ratios

1st gear	3.41 : 1	3.71 : 1
2nd gear	1.99 : 1	2.16 : 1
3rd gear	1.36 : 1	1.37 : 1
4th gear	1 : 1	1 : 1
Reverse	3.25 : 1	3.68 : 1
Overdrive	0.797 : 1	0.797 : 1

Lubrication

M40, M41	Gear oil, SAE 80W/90 or 80/90
M45, M46	Automatic transmission fluid Type F

Oil capacity

M40 and M45	0.75 litre (1.3 Imp pints - 1.6 US pints)
M41 (includes overdrive)	1.6 litre (2.8 Imp pints - 3.3 US pints)
M46 (includes overdrive)	2.3 litre (4 Imp pints - 4.8 US pints)

Tightening torques

Flange nuts - M40 and M45	69 - 76 lb f ft (9.5 - 10 kg fm)
- M41 and M46	119 - 130 lb f ft (16.5 - 18.0 kg fm)

Overdrive

Type	J
Application	Manual gearbox, type M41, M46
Ratio	0.8 : 1
Oil pressure	384 to 427 psi (27 to 30 kgf/cm^2)
Lubrication	In common with gearbox

Torque wrench settings

	lbf ft	kgf m
Casing nuts and bolts	7	1.0
Solenoid valve	37	5.0
Oil sump bolts	7	1.0
Relief valve plug	17	2.3
Oil pump plug	17	2.3
Pressure take-off plug	15	2.0
Output flange nut	135	18.6
Oil filter plug	17	2.3
Lubricating valve plug	10	1.3

Automatic transmission

Make and type	Borg-Warner, Type 35 and 55

Reduction ratios

	BW35	BW55
1st gear	2.39 : 1	2.45 : 1
2nd gear	1.45 : 1	1.45 : 1
3rd gear	1 : 1	1 : 1
Reverse	2.09 : 1	2.21 : 1

Size of torque converter	9.5 in (240 mm)
Torque ratio in converter	2 : 1 - 1 : 1

Weights

Gearbox	82 lb (37.2 kg)
Converter case	6.6 lb (3.0 kg)
Converter	24 lb (10.9 kg)
Total without fluid	112 lb (51 kg)
Total with fluid	126 lb (57.1 kg)

Fluid type	Automatic transmission fluid, Type F

Fluid capacity (from dry)

BW35	11.3 Imp pints (6.8 US qts, 6.4 litres)
BW55 (early)	11.4 Imp pints (6.95 US qts, 6.5 litres)
BW55 (later)	12.1 Imp pints (7.25 US qts, 6.9 litres)

Normal operating temperature of fluid	Approx. 230 - 240°F (110 - 115°C)

Approximate shift speeds

Engine	Throttle position	1st–2nd km/h	1st–2nd mile/h	2nd–3rd km/h	2nd–3rd mile/h	3rd–2nd km/h	3rd–2nd mile/h	3rd–1st km/h	3rd–1st mile/h
B20A	Full throttle	43	27	70	43				
	kick-down	60	37	95	59	86	53	49	30
B21A	kick-down	62	39	105	65	95	59	49	30
B21E	kick-down	60	37	108	67	98	61	49	30

Normal stall speeds

B20A	2200 rev/min
B21A	2200 rev/min
B21E	2550 rev/min

Torque wrench settings (BW35) - see Supplement for BW55 and AW55

	lb f ft	kg fm
Torque converter - drive plate	25 - 30	3.5 - 4.1
Transmission case - converter housing	8 - 13	1.1 - 1.8
Extension housing - transmission case	30 - 55	4.1 - 7.6
Oil pan - transmission case	8 - 13	1.1 - 1.8
Outer lever - manual valve shift	7 - 9	1 - 1.2
Pressure point	4 - 5	0.6 - 0.7
Oil pan drain plug	8 - 10	1.1 - 1.4

1 Gearbox - general description

1 The M40 type gearbox fitted to the Volvo 240 series is illustrated in Fig. 6.1. Later models in the series have an M45 type gearbox. When an overdrive is fitted to these gearboxes, the complete assemblies become the M41 and M46, the gearboxes being unchanged. Both gearboxes are very similar, the main difference being that the M45 casing is shaped differently, with external reinforcing ribbing and the reverse gear on the left side. Also the layshaft is journalled in taper roller bearings instead of needle bearings, and the rear cover is in one piece.

2 The gearbox has four forward speeds and reverse, with synchromesh on all forward gears. Its design is conventional and the problems associated with dismantling, inspection and assembly are in no way typical. Coping with these problems is well within the scope of the intelligent owner mechanic, even though he may never have tackled a gearbox before. If your experience is limited. (and after all, the average gearbox doesn't go wrong all that often), we suggest that you give a little thought to the working of your gearbox before starting to take it apart.

3 Start by taking a look at Fig. 6.2. Ignoring for the moment the arrow we see two clusters of gears, and looking more closely at these we see that four pairs of gears are actually in mesh. Another pair of

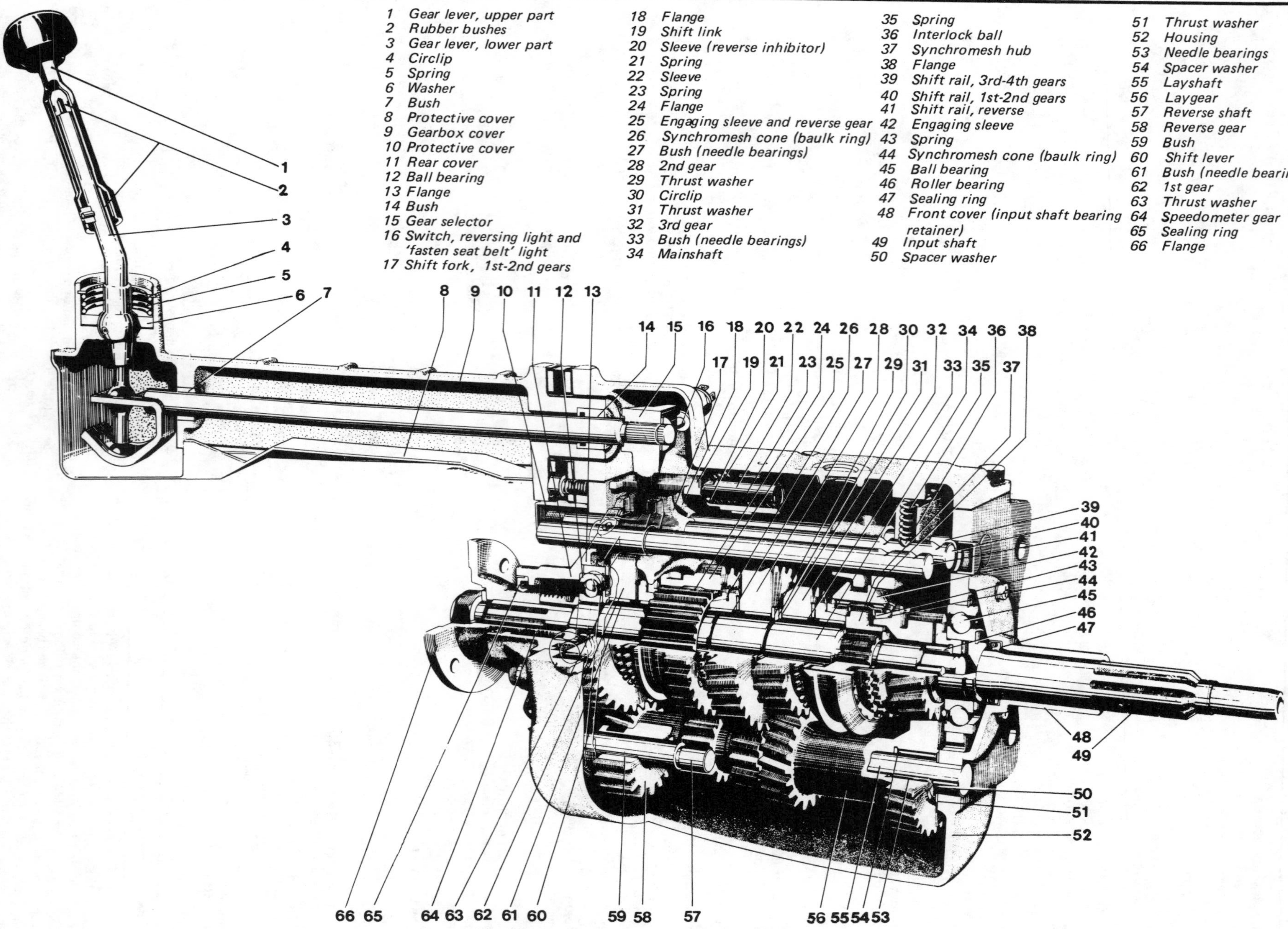

1 Gear lever, upper part
2 Rubber bushes
3 Gear lever, lower part
4 Circlip
5 Spring
6 Washer
7 Bush
8 Protective cover
9 Gearbox cover
10 Protective cover
11 Rear cover
12 Ball bearing
13 Flange
14 Bush
15 Gear selector
16 Switch, reversing light and 'fasten seat belt' light
17 Shift fork, 1st-2nd gears

18 Flange
19 Shift link
20 Sleeve (reverse inhibitor)
21 Spring
22 Sleeve
23 Spring
24 Flange
25 Engaging sleeve and reverse gear
26 Synchromesh cone (baulk ring)
27 Bush (needle bearings)
28 2nd gear
29 Thrust washer
30 Circlip
31 Thrust washer
32 3rd gear
33 Bush (needle bearings)
34 Mainshaft

35 Spring
36 Interlock ball
37 Synchromesh hub
38 Flange
39 Shift rail, 3rd-4th gears
40 Spring
41 Shift rail, 1st-2nd gears
42 Engaging sleeve
43 Spring
44 Synchromesh cone (baulk ring)
45 Ball bearing
46 Roller bearing
47 Sealing ring
48 Front cover (input shaft bearing retainer)
49 Input shaft
50 Spacer washer

51 Thrust washer
52 Housing
53 Needle bearings
54 Spacer washer
55 Layshaft
56 Laygear
57 Reverse shaft
58 Reverse gear
59 Bush
60 Shift lever
61 Bush (needle bearings)
62 1st gear
63 Thrust washer
64 Speedometer gear
65 Sealing ring
66 Flange

Fig. 6.1. Cut-away view of M40 gearbox (Sec. 1)

gears doesn't quite make it, and indeed they are not even exactly in line. We know better than to suppose that by now you haven't looked at Figs. 6.3, 6.4, 6.5 and 6.6 as well and you will have seen that the upper one of this particular pair of gears can move to-and-fro and gets linked up with its opposite number by a subsidiary gear to provide reverse.

4   If we now consider the arrow in Fig. 6.2 which shows the way the drive is transmitted in bottom gear we at once realise that the two shaft ends at the top of the figure must belong to different shafts, because they are rotating at different speeds. The shaft on the left which we will call the input shaft is quite short; it only carries one of the gears and fits into the other shaft about mid-way between the gear pair on the left and the gear pair next to it. The shaft on the right, which we will call the output shaft, or mainshaft, carries the three other gears of the upper set, any one of which can be locked to it as described later. The gear on the input shaft is integral with it.

5   The lower set of gears is all one piece. This assembly is known as the layshaft. In practice the assembly has a hole through the middle of it and revolves on needle bearings on a spindle as shown in Fig. 6.1.

The left-hand gear is driven by the gear on the input shaft, causing the whole layshaft to rotate with a speed that always bears the same ratio to the engine speed.

6   Although the various layshaft gears are all revolving at the same speed the gears they drive on the mainshaft all revolve at different speeds because each one is a different size and consequently has a

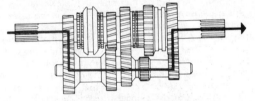

Fig. 6.2. Power path - 1st gear (Sec. 1)

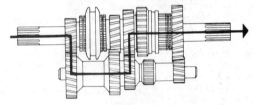

Fig. 6.3. Power path - 2nd gear (Sec. 1)

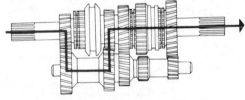

Fig. 6.4. Power path - 3rd gear (Sec. 1)

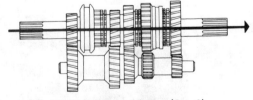

Fig. 6.5. Power path - 4th gear (Sec. 1)

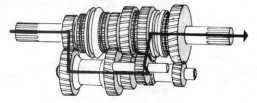

Fig. 6.6. Power path - reverse (Sec. 1)

different ratio to its opposite number on the layshaft. Gearbox ratios are selected by locking one or other of these gears to the mainshaft.

7   Details of the locking mechanism are considered later. At this stage it is sufficient to say that the locking is achieved by sliding operating sleeves along the mainshaft. If we look at Fig. 6.1 we see that there are two of these sleeves on the mainshaft. The one on the right is pushed over as far as it will go to the right and when it is in this position it locks the right-hand gear to the mainshaft. This gear now drives the mainshaft and we get the power transmission path indicated by the arrow. This particular gear is bigger than the other two, which means that its opposite number on the layshaft has got to be smaller than those driving its companions. Hence, this pair of gears has a larger reduction ratio than the others and gives us 'bottom gear'. In Fig. 6.3 we see the right-hand operating sleeve slid along the shaft as far as it will go to the left, in which position it locks the centre one of the three driven gears which is intermediate in size between the other two and gives us a reduced reduction ratio corresponding to 'second gear'. In Fig. 6.4 the right-hand operating sleeve is positioned mid-way between the two gears associated with it and in that position locks neither of them. The left-hand sleeve, however, has been moved over until it is close to the gear on its right, which it locks to the shaft. This is smaller than the other two driven gears and consequently gives less reduction - ie. 'third gear'. Fig. 6.5 shows the state of things for top gear. The left-hand sleeve is slid as far over to the left as it will go, and in this position it locks the input shaft direct to the output shaft. They operate as one shaft, not being driven through any gear train, hence the silence of top gear operation however rough the gearbox may be. Fig. 6.6 shows the set-up for reverse gear. Two gears set opposite each other on the mainshaft and the layshaft which do not engage directly are coupled together by a small pinion which is pushed into position when 'reverse' is selected. There is no particular significance in the fact that a driven gear for reverse forms part of an operating sleeve; this is simply a matter of engineering convenience. The sleeve is of course keyed to the shaft though it can slide along it freely.

8   The operating sleeves are pushed along the shafts by selector forks which are attached to selector rods. These rods carry dogs which are engaged by the gear lever. A simple interlock (described in Section 4, paragraph 3) prevents more than one selector rod being moved at a time. One selector rod is associated with each of the engaging sleeves and a third rod operates the lever that engages the reverse pinion.

9   Associated with the operating sleeves is the synchromesh mechanism which ensures that when a driven gear is about to be locked to the mainshaft - gear and mainshaft are rotating at the same speed. This is described in the next Section.

2   Synchromesh mechanism

1   We have already seen that when a gear is engaged, the gear wheel concerned is locked to the mainshaft by the engaging sleeve. Splines inside the engaging sleeve mesh with teeth on the hub of the gear wheel and simultaneously with the 'synchronising hub' on the mainshaft. In Fig. 6.2 the left-hand engaging sleeve is not locked to either of the gears on each side of it, but the right-hand sleeve is engaged with the gear on its right. You can see the synchronising hub on which it slides quite clearly on the left of it.

2   The purpose of the synchromesh is to provide an obstacle to travel of the engaging sleeve when the mainshaft (and hence the sleeve

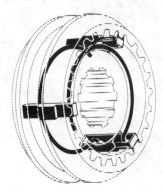

Fig. 6.7. Synchroniser sliding key and spring assembly (Secs. 2 and 10)

itself) is revolving at a different rate from the gear which it is desired to engage. The speed of this gear is determined by the engine speed via the layshaft. This obstacle is provided by the synchronising cone, which has teeth round its edge which get in the way of the synchronising hub when this is rotating faster or slower than the desired gear.

Photograph 5.5a gives a better idea of the mechanism than any drawing can. On the left we see the first speed gear (this photograph is the other way round to Figs. 6.2 - 6.6 which show the first speed gear on the right). It is displaced along the shaft - it would normally be running on the larger diameter portion. The hub of this gear has a taper on it and also carries the engaging teeth which do not show up well in this photograph but may be seen quite clearly in photograph 5.5b where this gear appears in the foreground. Returning to photograph 5.5a, it is easy to see that if the gear and the engaging sleeve are pressed together with the synchromesh cone between them the engaging sleeve will not get past the synchromesh cone unless the teeth on the cone line up with the splines inside the sleeve. If we now glance at Fig. 6.7 we see that the engaging sleeve has assembled inside it three sliding keys which are held in position by two circular springs. Two of these keys are clearly visible in photograph 5.5a, the one nearer the camera showing up very well as it has caught the light. Opposite this detent we can see a notch in the synchronising cone in which the key engages. If the cone is so positioned that one or other of the ends of the slot are touching the key the teeth on the cone get in the way of the splines on the engaging sleeve and this sleeve cannot get past. If the gear wheel revolves faster or slower than the engaging sleeve, friction between the tapered part of the gear hub and the cone will push it one way or the other until it comes to rest against the key. If the relationship reverses, the cone will start to move relative to the engaging sleeve in the other direction and the time will come when the sleeve can slip past it. As soon as this happens the splines on the engaging sleeve pick up the engaging teeth on the gear and the synchromesh cone just sits between them while they revolve as one unit.

3 Gearbox - removal

1 Disconnect the battery, the reverse light cable and the connection at the overdrive, if fitted.
2 Drain the oil from the gearbox into a clean container (photo).
3 Disconnect the shift selector rod from the gearlever by removing the lock bolt and pushing out the pivot pin.
4 Remove the four clips and release the rubber gaiter from the tunnel. Remove the reverse inhibitor bracket (4 mm Allen key). Remove the circlip and lift out the gearlever.
5 Disconnect the clutch cable or slave cylinder. Remove the bolts securing the exhaust bracket to the clutch housing and the nut at the exhaust pipe. Remove the bracket.
6 Place a jack under the engine sump and remove the gearbox support member (photo).
7 Remove the bolts securing the front propeller shaft to the gearbox flange and tie the propeller shaft up with a piece of wire to keep it out of the way.

8 Disconnect the speedometer cable (photo).
9 Lower the rear end of the engine slightly and remove all the bolts attaching the clutch housing to the engine except the right upper bolt. On the B20 engine, the starter motor can now be removed, on the B21 engine you must first remove the starter motor front support bracket.
10 Support the gearbox and remove the upper right attaching bolt. Withdraw the gearbox and turn it so that the casing goes free from the tunnel as it is pulled backwards. Take care not to place any strain on the input shaft as the gearbox is removed. An extra pair of hands makes this job a lot easier.

4 Gearbox - dismantling

1 Give the whole exterior a thorough clean with paraffin or a detergent such as Gunk. As well as making the job more pleasant it is the only way to be certain that you will not get dirt inside the gearbox at some stage in the proceedings.
2 As the gearbox has been dismantled complete with the bellhousing, the clutch thrust bearing and its withdrawal fork are easily removed for inspection as described in Chapter 5.
3 Remove the cover. On the underside of the cover you will see the interlock plate with square bosses, these lock all selectors except the selector that is being operated so that only that particular selector can move - this also ensures that the gearlever is properly positioned over the selector you want because if it is not you will not be able to move the selector. A look at the photograph of the selectors as seen from the top of the box will show you at once how the system fits together. The action of the spring on the interlock plate makes the gearlever return to the right-hand side of the box. When you select reverse, you have to give an extra push to make the interlock plate overcome the resistance of the plunger which is backed by a fairly strong spring (photo).
4 Remove the three springs (normally held in by the lid) which press on locating balls for the selector rods (see photo). The balls can be left in the holes for the time being if you keep an eye on them.
5 Engage two gears at once by pushing both the forward speed selector rods as far in one direction as they will go. This locks the gearbox and enables you to undo the nut holding the flange on the mainshaft with difficulty. Pull the flange off the shaft with a puller if it will not respond to very gentle taps with a hammer. Now is as good a time as any to remove the speedometer drive pinion by undoing the screw that retains it. Follow this by removing the screws which hold the mainshaft bearing housing - this gives the shaft freedom of movement at this stage and makes subsequent dismantling a little easier. Note the sealing washers on these screws which go right through into the gearbox (photos).
6 Remove the cap covering the ends of the selector rods, take out the locking screws holding the selector fork and the engaging dogs to the two outer rods (this will release the lever actuating the reverse pinion as well) and withdraw the rods. Be careful in your choice of screwdriver for undoing these screws - choose one that is a good fit in the slot.

3.2 Drain and filler plugs

Fig. 6.8. Removing the gaiter clips (Sec. 3)

Fig. 6.9. Removing the reverse inhibitor bracket (Sec. 3)

Fig. 6.10. Removing the gear lever retaining circlip (Sec. 3)

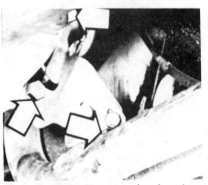
Fig. 6.11. Bolts and nuts securing the exhaust pipe bracket (Sec. 3)

3.6 Gearbox support member securing bolts

3.8 Disconnecting the speedometer cable

4.2a Disconnecting the selector rod (M45)

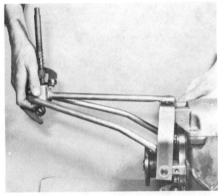
4.2b Removing the gear lever carrier bracket (M45)

4.3a Lifting off the cover (M45)

4.3b The locking plate, its return spring and the plunger that loads the reverse position

4.3c The selector rods showing the dogs that engage with the gear lever

4.4 Removing the springs that hold down the lock balls

4.5a Removing the flange ...

4.5b ... the speedometer drive pinion ...

4.5c ... and the fixing screws for the mainshaft bearing housing

4.6a The cap covering the ends of the selector rods

4.6b On M45 gearbox, a one piece rear cover is fitted in place of the bearing housing and cap

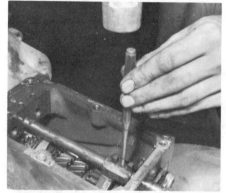
4.7a Drive out the lock pin ...

4.7b ... this is what it looks like ...

4.7c ... and pull out the selector rod

4.9a Layshaft, laygear and needle roller bearings

4.9b Layshaft taper roller bearing (M45)

4.10a Removing the input shaft housing ...

4.10b ... followed by the input shaft

4.10c The needle bearing in the input shaft which supports the front end of the mainshaft

4.10d The input shaft with its integral fourth gear pinion and engaging teeth, and their associated synchromesh baulk ring

These screws are screwed in tightly because a lot depends on them (photos).

Go easy when you take the rods out; keep the dogs and selectors parallel with the shaft as they may jam if they get slightly askew.

7　The dog on the centre shaft is held in by a lock pin because a screw would get in the way of the gearlever. Move the selector as close as you can to the side of the gearbox (ie. put it in the 'first speed' position). Drive the pin out a little way, but not so far as to foul the teeth of the first speed gear on the layshaft which is underneath it. Having started the pin on its way, take the selector back past the first speed gear when you have enough room to drive it out. Having done this, you can withdraw the rod. With the rods out of the way you can take out the dogs and selector forks (photos).

8　Remove the bellhousing, which until now will have been serving as a most useful stand, being careful to use a correctly fitting key for the Allen screws - which hold it to the gearbox. These screws should be done up tightly and trying to unscrew them with a key which is not quite right will almost certainly damage them.

9　The rear end of the layshaft is normally half concealed by the mainshaft housing. If you turn the housing slightly the layshaft can be driven out rearwards, but do not do it for a moment. If you just drive out the shaft, 42 needles will be scattered all over the place. The difficulty arises because you have to drive out the shaft and allow the laygear to fall to the bottom of the gearbox casing before you can remove the mainshaft.

The ideal solution to the problem is to have a shaft or tube 1-1¼ inches (2.5 - 3.1 cms) shorter than the layshaft, ie a bit shorter than the layshaft itself, and having a diameter equal or slightly less than that of the shaft. If this shaft were driven into the middle of the laygear, the layshaft being removed, the laygear would fall to the bottom of the gearbox with the substitute shaft inside it retaining the needle bearings in position. Volvo have produced such a rod (Tool no. SVO 2907) and if you can borrow it from a Volvo agent that is fine, but if you are faced with making something we suggest that you do not bother at this stage, but just push out the shaft and allow the whole lot to drop to the bottom of the gearbox. It will be much easier to devise something to use during

reassembly (where it is almost essential) when you have the layshaft and bearings available to try out your system and see if it works. This is what we did, and in Section 13 we describe how we went about it.

Whatever you do about retaining the bearings at this stage, you will have to push out the layshaft and let the laygear drop to the bottom of the gearbox before you can deal with the mainshaft. This problem does not arise with the M45 gearbox as the layshaft is mounted in taper roller bearings. Simply drive the shaft to the rear to release the outer bearing and then forward to remove the front outer bearing (photos).

10　Undo the three Allen screws which hold the input shaft bearing retainer (note their O-ring seals - these screws go right through to the inside of the gearbox) take off the housing and withdraw the input shaft with its bearing. The inner end of this shaft contains 14 rollers on which the mainshaft runs - watch out for them.

There is a synchromesh cone associated with this shaft - keep corresponding cones and gears together so that when you inspect the components you know which is associated with what (photos).

11　On M45 gearboxes there is no input shaft housing. Remove the input shaft seal and withdraw the input shaft with its bearing (photo).

12　Take out the mainshaft assembly complete with its bearing housing. With the mainshaft out, you can now lift out the layshaft. Check that you have got all those needle rollers from inside the casing (photos).

13　On the M45 gearbox the rear cover having been removed it is necessary to remove the mainshaft bearing. Two screwdrivers under the circlip will start it on its way. Lift the mainshaft and then the layshaft out through the top of the gearbox (photos).

5　Mainshaft - dismantling

1　The photograph shows a view of the mainshaft and its associated components. The right-hand end enters the input shaft and the engaging sleeve picks up the engaging teeth on this shaft in top gear. The left-hand end (sticking out of the housing) normally carries a flange which

4.11 Removing the input shaft (M45)

4.12a The mainshaft assembly being removed (M40)

4.12b Removing the laygear

4.13a Starting the bearing on its way (M45) ...

4.13b ... and removing the mainshaft bearing

4.13c Lifting out the mainshaft assembly (M45) ...

4.13d ... followed by the layshaft (M45)

5.1 Mainshaft assembly (M40)

Fig. 6.12. Mainshaft of gearbox with overdrive. The shaft is being pressed out of its bearing (Sec. 5)

5.2a Remove the circlip retaining the synchromesh hub ...

5.2b ... and slide off the hub and the engaging sleeve as a unit

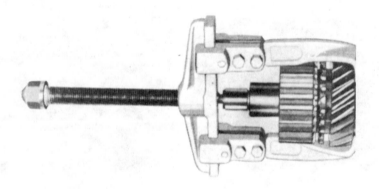
Fig. 6.13. Pulling off the front synchroniser (Sec. 5)

5.2c Then take off the synchronising baulk ring ...

5.2d ... the third gear pinion and the spacer ring behind it ...

5.3a ... revealing the circlip holding the second spacer gear

5.3b Remove the circlip and the spacing ring behind it

engages with the propeller shaft. Where overdrive is fitted, the left-hand end of the mainshaft is a lot longer and carries an eccentric for operating the overdrive oil pump. The bearing housing is different because it does not have to carry the speedometer drive. The bearing housing and rear end of this mainshaft are shown in Fig. 6.12. The eccentric for operating the pump is keyed on to the shaft just behind the shoulder. Once this is removed, the remainder of the instructions in this and the next Section apply equally to both types of shaft.

2   Remove the circlip at the end of the shaft remote from the bearing housing and slide off the synchronising hub and engaging sleeve as a single unit, then the synchronising cone and third speed gear. If the hub is a tight fit on the shaft, use a puller with its ends tucked behind the third speed gear as shown in Fig. 6.13. You know this is the third speed gear because it is the smallest of the three forward gears and so gives the least reduction ratio apart from the direct drive for top gear (photos).

3   Slide off the synchronising cone, the second speed gear and the spacing ring behind it. This brings you to the circlip retaining the second speed gear, and slide off the gear (photos).

Remove this circlip and spacing ring that lies between it and the second speed gear, and slide off the gear.

4   Slide off the synchronising cone and the engaging sleeve which also serves as a member of the reverse gear train. In this case you cannot take the synchronising hub with it as with the fourth speed/third speed engaging sleeve (paragraph 3) because the hub is in one piece with the shaft. When you pull it off, watch for the detents and spring which will fall out.

5   Using the first speed gear as a support, drive or push out the mainshaft from the bearing housing. A hide mallet carefully applied will do the trick or you can use a suitable puller or a home-made substitute.

The spacing ring and first speed gear can now be slid off the shaft, followed by the first speed synchronising cone (photos).

6   Remove the circlip from the mainshaft bearing housing and lift out the speedometer pinion unless you have the overdrive version in which the speedometer is naturally driven from the overdrive unit. Notice the way the friction drive spring for the pinion is fitted (photos).

7   Remove the oil seal from the other side of the bearing housing.

6   Input shaft - dismantling

1   The input shaft bearing is held on by a circlip and removal calls for no special comment. Note that this circlip comes in alternative thicknesses and is selected to be a snug fit in the groove. Bear this in mind if you have to renew the shaft or circlip.

7   Layshaft assembly (M45) - dismantling

1   Examine the taper roller bearings and renew if defective. Remove the defective bearings with a puller and press fit the replacement bearings (photo).

8   Gearbox components - examination

1   If the gearbox has been stripped because of some specific fault such as failure to stay in a selected gear, difficulty in engaging gear, or the sort of noise which can no longer be ignored, the cause of the fault will usually be pretty obvious (see also Fault Diagnosis, Section 18). A not so obvious cause of noise and trouble is bearing wear, which it is well worthwhile to rectify by replacing the bearings concerned before things get to such a state that you have to replace a shaft.

2   If you can detect slop in the bearings when they are still full of oil they are obvious candidates for the scrap heap, but otherwise you should give them a good wash in paraffin or cleaning fluid with a final rinse in White Spirit. You can then examine them for signs of wear, scoring, blueing or excessive play - ie. any play that you can actually feel. If you are in any doubt at all, replace them. In fact there is a lot to be said for replacing the bearings as a matter of course.

3   If the synchromesh cones show signs of wear or have a battered look around the slots that engage with the detents, they should be replaced. Once again, it is a good idea to replace them as a matter

5.3c Slide off the second gear pinion

5.5a The front gear and its baulk ring coming off the mainshaft. (Note the engaging sleeve is still in position)

5.5b Mainshaft components (engaging sleeves assembled on synchronising hubs)

5.6a Remove the circlip from the bearing housing ...

5.6b ... which is then easily pushed out

5.6c Removing the speedometer drive pinion ...

5.6d ... and its driving spring

7.1 Layshaft assembly (M45)

Fig. 6.14. Fitting the mainshaft bearing into its housing (M40) (Sec. 10)

of routine - they are not expensive.

4   Examine the teeth of all gears for signs of uneven/excessive wear and chipping. If a gear is in a bad state have a good look at the gear it engages with - you may have to replace this too, a nuisance if it happens to be on the layshaft which will then have to be replaced complete.

5   All the gears should be a good running fit on the shaft with no signs of rocking. The fourth/third speed synchronising hub should not be a sloppy fit on the shaft splines.

6   All parts of the selector mechanism should be examined for wear. This includes the selector forks - Volvo have thoughtfully fitted engaging pins on the first/second speed selector fork so that you do not have to replace the whole lot if these get worn.

7   We think it is false economy not to renew the oil seals, but if you intend to use the old ones again check that they are in good condition.

9   Gearbox - reassembly

1   Assembling the gearbox is a slightly tricky business, but there is nothing really to worry about. It is not the sort of job in which, if you make a mistake, you find out about it disastrously some months later. It is more like a jigsaw puzzle - once you have done it you know it is right. The chief precaution you need to take if you have not worked on a gearbox before is to allow yourself a lot more time than you think you can possibly need.

2   You may also like to give yourself a revision course on gearbox design before you start. Take a look first at Fig. 6.5. This shows the input shaft locked to the mainshaft by the synchronising sleeve on the left which is pushed over to the left as far as it will go. This is of course the forward end of the gearbox. Obviously as we change from fourth speed to third speed this is the synchronising sleeve that moves, so we know at once that the third speed gear is at the front end of the main-shaft, near where it joins the input shaft. The next two gears must be second and first, with the reverse gear forming part of the synchronising sleeve which slides between them. The gear stick comes backwards to engage second speed and forwards to engage first speed, so we know that the synchronising sleeve moves forwards to engage second speed and backwards to engage first speed, just as the other synchronising sleeve moves forwards to engage fourth speed and backwards to engage third speed. This means that the first speed gear (the biggest one, having the most reduction) must be at the back end of the mainshaft.

3   With the biggest gear at the back, naturally we have to have the smallest gear on the layshaft also at the back. So now we know which way round and in what order you have to put the various gears. Obviously the cone surfaces on each pair of gears have to face each other so we know which way round on the mainshaft the gears have to go. A look at the layshaft reveals that the reverse gear is close to the second speed gear; this tells you that the reverse gear teeth on the synchronising sleeve on the mainshaft must be near the second speed gear, ie. they must face the front. Once you have the logic of the thing in mind, you will not need to keep referring to Fig. 6.5 or any other figure to see which way round the various gears have to go.

4   Assembly of the M45 mainshaft is basically the same as described in Section 10 for the M40, except there is no bearing housing, the bearing being fitted on the shaft.

10   Mainshaft - reassembly

1   Where applicable, assemble the speedometer drive gear into the bearing housing (see photographs 5.6c and 5.6d).

2   Using a suitable drift, press the mainshaft bearing into the housing (see Fig. 6.14). You can easily make a substitute for the Volvo drift shown in the Figure and use your vice as a press. Smear the bearing and housing with oil and be sure that the bearing goes in perfectly straight.

3   Smear the oil seal with oil and fit it the correct way round, ie. the thin end towards the gearbox.

4   Before fitting the bearing housing to the shaft, assemble the first speed/second speed engaging sleeve with its detents and springs over the synchroniser hub on the shaft (photo and Fig. 6.7). The groove on the synchroniser faces the rear of the shaft, ie. the flange end or, if overdrive is fitted, the long splined end. Then slip the first gear and its synchronising cone on to the shaft (both gear and synchronising sleeve, of course, must have their tapered ends facing the synchronising hub), assemble the housing on to the shaft and fit the circlip. Assemble the second and third speed gears and the third/fourth speed synchron-iser on to the shaft, using the dismantling photo sequence 5.2, 5.3 and 5.5 in reverse order as guidance. The parts should be well smeared with oil before assembly. There is nothing particular to watch unless you are fitting new circlips, when you should be sure that these are selected to be a snug fit in the grooves; they are supplied in different thicknes-ses (photos).

11   Input shaft - reassembly

1   Press the bearing on to the input shaft, having smeared both with oil using a suitable substitute for the tool shown in Fig. 6.15.

2   Grease the 14 mainshaft bearing rollers and assemble these in the input shaft (see photo 49d). From now on the input shaft must be handled with a steady hand in order that the rollers do not get jolted out of place.

12   Reverse pinion - reassembly (M40)

1   If you have removed it, reassemble the idler pinion for the reverse train with its shaft into the casing. Note that the shaft end must protrude 0.28 - 0.30 in (7.0 - 7.6 mm) outside the housing (see Fig. 6.16).

13   Layshaft (M40) - assembly

1   Whatever you did on dismantling, you will have to have some sort of retainer for the needle bearings inside the laygear which you can rely on to hold them in place while you fiddle about with it during reassembly of the gearbox. We used a tube of slightly smaller diameter than the layshaft; slotting its ends and opening them out until they were a good fit inside the needle bearing assembly (photo).

2   Using the layshaft as a steady, fit the spacing washers and bearing needles into the laygear, using plenty of grease to anchor

10.4a The sliding keys are inserted between the engaging sleeve and the synchronising hub ...

10.4b ... backed by a spring at each end (see Fig. 6.7)

10.4c Select circlips which fit snugly in their grooves they are supplied in different thicknesses

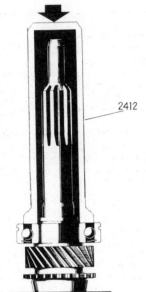

Fig. 6.15. Fitting the ball bearing on the input shaft (Sec. 11)

7,3 ±0,3 mm
0.29"±0.012"

Fig. 6.16. Fitting the reverse pinion shaft (M45) (Sec. 12)

1   Reverse shaft   2   Gearbox casing

13.1 A piece of copper tube with the ends flared out a little made a successful needle roller bearing retainer for the layshaft

13.2a To reassemble the layshaft needle bearings, first insert a spacing ring ...

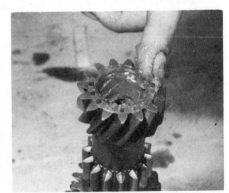

13.2b ... then using plenty of grease ...

them. The grease will stick better if the laygear is really clean and dry. Then slide the retainer in, letting it push the layshaft out of the laygear (photos).

14 Assembling components into gearbox casing (M40)

1   Press the input shaft bearing into the gear case as far as it will go (ie. until its retaining clip touches the case). Now stick the thrust washers for the layshafts to the inside of the case with grease. If the

case and washers are clean and dry they will stick all right.
2   Now comes the bit where a steady hand and deliberate movement is all important. Give things a jolt now, and they will come unstuck - literally. With the case standing upright on the bench, position the layshaft on the bottom of the case centrally and the right way round, ie. with the larger gears at the input shaft end.
3   Check that the rollers in the input shaft are properly in place and that the thrust washers are aligned with the holes for the layshaft. Slip the synchronising cone over the input shaft, and then pass the mainshaft through the hole in the end of the case (do not forget

13.2c ... and the layshaft as a steady, insert the needle roller bearings in the laygear ...

13.2d ... followed by the second spacer

13.2e Then insert the retainer, letting it push the shaft through the laygear

14.5 Fixing the mainshaft bearing housing

14.6 Don't cover up this hole when fitting the gasket for the input shaft housing

15.1 Be sure the selector forks are in place before you put the rods back

its gasket!) and gently engage it with the input shaft, pushing the housing into the hole in the casing as far as it will go.

4   Now comes the most ticklish bit. If it does not come off first time the penalty is not very severe - you will simply have to remove the mainshaft, reposition the thrust washers and if you are very unlucky take out the layshaft and reposition some of its rollers. To avoid this irritating frustration, proceed deliberately and gently. Get hold of the gear case, positioning your forefingers in the holes for the layshaft so that if necessary you can prevent the thrust washers from sliding right over the holes. Gently turn the case upside down so that the laygear comes to rest on the mainshaft with its ends more or less opposite the holes for the layshaft. If the thrust washers have moved slightly, align them with the holes and then insert the layshaft. Push the shaft through the laygear, letting it drive out the retaining tube. When the end of the shaft appears in the hole at the far end of the case, you have won.

5   Do not be tempted to pick up the gearbox from the bench until you have fixed the mainshaft bearing housing in its correct position - and for the overdrive gearbox this involves fitting the spacing flange for the overdrive unit with its gasket and the tab washers (new of course) for the bottom pair of fixing bolts. Do not forget the sealing washers for the fixing bolts (photo).

6   Slide the circular gasket over the input shaft, making sure that it is the proper way round - there is a hole in the gearbox casing which must be lined up with the hole in the gasket. This provides a path for oil to reach the input shaft bearing. Push the housing over the shaft and fasten to the gear case with its three fixing bolts, not forgetting their O-ring seals (photo).

7   Replace the speedometer drive pinion in the bearing housing where applicable.

15 Selectors (M40) - assembly

1   Place the two selector forks in their correct positions (the photo shows which way round they go) before you insert any of the selector rods.

2   Insert the centre rod and drive in the lock pin which anchors the

selector fork to it.

3   Insert the first/second speed rod, fitting the dog to it so that when positioned on the shaft by its grubscrew it slopes towards the dog on the centre shaft. Tighten the grubscrew for the fork and the dog (photo).

4   Fit the remaining selector rod whose dog operates the lever which moves the reverse idler gear.

5   Place the interlock balls and springs in position and fit on the gearbox cover. Check that all gears engage and disengage freely.

6   Fit the cover over the ends of the selector rods.

7   For a gearbox without overdrive, engage two gears at once, thus locking the output shaft and fit the flange. For a gearbox with over-drive, fit the eccentric which operates the oil pump on the mainshaft, using a circlip which fits snugly into the groove.

8   Assemble the clutch housing to the gearbox and fit the clutch release lever and thrust bearing.

16 Assembling components into gearbox casing (M45)

1   Fit the reverse gear selector rod and dog. Do not fit the dog lock pin yet.

2   Fit the reverse gear and shaft. Check and if necessary adjust reverse gear shaft position. The shaft must be flush with the housing $\pm$ 0.002 in (0.05 mm) (photo).

3   If necessary, adjust the clearance between reverse gear and selector. Adjust by driving in the shift selector bearing pin with a drift. Correct clearance 0.004 - 0.079 in (0.1 - 2.0 mm), see Fig. 6.17.

4   Place the layshaft in the bottom of the casing.

5   Place the mainshaft in the casing and fit the axial washer and bearing on the mainshaft. The spacer ring must be fitted on the bearing, Fig. 6.18.

6   Press the mainshaft bearing into position. Push the reverse gear towards the centre of the gearbox to prevent teeth from clashing and becoming damaged. The bearing spacer ring should be against the casing when bearing is in its correct position.

7   Grease and fit roller bearing in the input shaft. Place the 4th synchronising hub and fit the input shaft to the mainshaft. Press in the shaft

15.3 Use a suitable screwdriver for this important tightening operation

16.2 Fitting the reverse gear and shaft

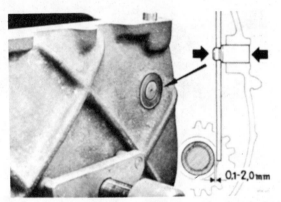

Fig. 6.17. Adjusting the clearance between reverse gear and selector (Sec. 16)

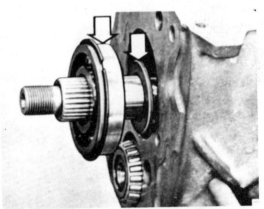

Fig. 6.18. Fitting the mainshaft bearing (M45) (Sec. 16)

Fig. 6.19. Input shaft with roller bearing in position (Sec. 16)

Fig. 6.20. Input shaft with spacer ring fitted (Sec. 16)

16.10 Fitting the layshaft outer bearings

as far as possible.

8   Place the layshaft so that the bearings are located in their housings.

9   Pull out the input shaft far enough, so that the spacer ring can be fitted on the bearing, then push in the shaft so that the spacer ring is against the casing.

10 Fit the layshaft outer bearing (photo).

11 Determine the thickness of shims for the input shaft by measuring (use a depth micrometer) the distance between the outer edge of the input shaft bearing and the casing, and the distance between the clutch housing contact face and the bottom of the bearing seat. The permitted axial clearance is 0.0004 - 0.0059 in (0.01 - 0.15 mm). When calculating the thickness of shim required do not forget to allow for a gasket thickness of 0.0098 in (0.25 mm) (Fig. 6.21).

12 Grease the gasket and shims to keep them in position on the casing and fit the clutch housing, tighten the retaining bolts to a torque of 25 - 36 lb ft (3.5 - 5.0 kg m) (Fig. 6.22). Fit the clutch withdrawal fork and thrust bearing as described in Chapter 5.

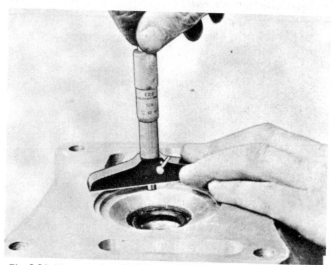

Fig. 6.21. Measuring the distance between the clutch housing contact face and bottom of bearing seat

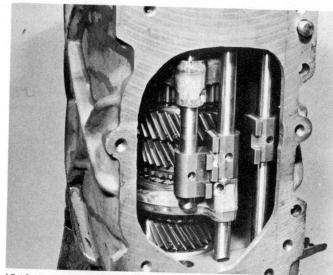

16.13a Fitting the selector rods and dogs

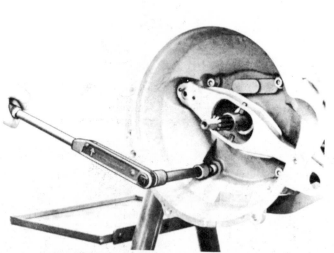

Fig. 6.22. Fitting the clutch housing (Sec. 16)

16.13b Fitting selector lock pin

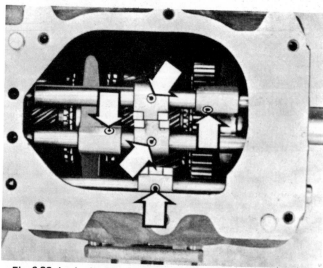

Fig. 6.23. Lock pins fitted flush in selector forks and dogs (Sec. 16)

16.15 Speedometer pinion fitted on mainshaft

13 Place the selector forks in position (they are both the same) and fit the selector rods and dogs. Fit the lock pins and drive them in flush with the upper edge of the dogs and selector forks, Fig. 6.23. Take care not to drive them in too far as they will foul the gears (photos).
14 Determine the thickness of shims for the layshaft and mainshaft by the same method as for the input shaft, paragraph 11 above. Permissible axial clearance:

> Layshaft:
>   Cast-iron casing   - 0.0009 to 0.0039 in (0.025 to 0.10 mm)
>   Aluminium casing - 0.0010 to 0.0030 in (0.03 to 0.08 mm)
> Mainshaft   - 0.0004 - 0.0060 in (0.01 to 0.15 mm)

Do not forget to include a gasket thickness of 0.0098 in (0.25 mm) in your calculations.
15 Fit the speedometer pinion with flange facing the bearing (photo).
16 Place the shims for layshaft on the bearing and the mainshaft shims in the rear cover, use grease to hold in position. Fit gasket and rear cover. Tighten rear cover bolts to a torque of 25-36 lb f ft (3.5-5 kg fm).

17 Engage two gears at the same time and fit the flange. Tighten to a torque of 67-88 lb f ft (9.3 - 12.2 kg f m) (photo).
18 Fit the speedometer drive and retainer.
19 Place the gasket, interlock balls and springs in position and fit the gearbox cover. Tighten the bolts to a torque of 11-18 lb f ft (1.5-2.5 kg f m). Check that all gears engage and disengage freely.
20 Fit the reverse light contact and the rear selector rod. Fit the gearlever carrier (photos).

17 Gearbox - refitting in vehicle

This calls for no special comment, being simply a reversal of the removal procedure which has already been described in Section 3. Do not forget the electrical connection to overdrive unit, if fitted, and the reversing light. Do not forget to fill up with oil and check the drain and filler/level plugs for tightness.

Fig. 6.24. Tightening the rear cover bolts (Sec. 16)

Fig. 6.25. The speedometer drive and retainer (Sec. 16)

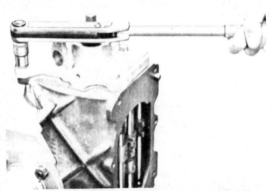

16.17 Fitting the gearbox flange

16.20a Fitting the reverse light contact

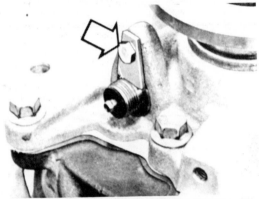

16.20b Fitting the gearlever carrier

18 Fault diagnosis - manual gearbox

Symptom	Reason/s
Weak or ineffective synchromesh	Synchronising cones worn, split or damaged. Baulk ring synchromesh dogs worn or damaged.
Jumps out of gear	Incorrectly assembled synchro units. Gearbox coupling dogs badly worn. Selector fork rod groove badly worn. Incorrect assembly of selector components.
Excessive noise	Incorrect grade of oil in gearbox or oil level too low. Bearings worn or damaged. Gear teeth excessively worn or damaged. Shimming of layshaft and/or mainshaft incorrect (M45 gearbox). Layshaft thrust washers worn (M40).
Excessive difficulty in engaging gear	Clutch pedal adjustment incorrect.

19 Overdrive - general description

1   The overdrive is essentially an extra gearbox, automatically controlled, driven by the output shaft of the main gearbox and producing on its own output shaft a step-up ratio of 0.797 : 1. The 'gear change' is controlled hydraulically, the hydraulic control valve being operated by a solenoid. The electrical connections to the solenoid are taken through a switch on the cover of the main gearbox which ensures that overdrive can only be brought into operation when the car is in top gear.

2   A cut-away illustration of the overdrive and an exploded view are shown in Figs. 6.26 and 6.27.

3   The heart of the overdrive is the epicyclic gear system whose components are shown in Fig. 6.27. These parts are assembled on the elongated mainshaft which extends from the main gearbox. Two of these parts, the planet carrier and the unidirectional clutch, are splined to the mainshaft and always revolve, therefore, at mainshaft speed. The unidirectional clutch sits inside the output shaft and ensures that if nothing else is driving the output shaft it will be driven by the gearbox mainshaft. In this manner, of course, the 1 : 1 ratio is obtained.

When this occurs, the planet carrier and the annulus on the output shaft are revolving at the same speed so the planet gears within the planet carrier are not being driven forwards or backwards and remain stationary on their splines. This means that the sun wheel must also be revolving at the same speed as the planet carrier and the annulus. The sun wheel is splined to the sliding clutch member and this too is revolving at the mainshaft speed. In practice the sliding clutch member is held against the tapered extension of the mainshaft when the 1 : 1 ratio is required and the whole gear system is locked together (Fig. 6.28).

4   To obtain the step-up ratio, the sliding clutch member is drawn away from the output shaft annulus and comes up against the outer casing of the gearbox which holds it stationary. It is still splined to the sun wheel, so this, too, is prevented from turning. This is shown in Fig. 6.28. The planet carrier continues to revolve at mainshaft speed, but because the sun wheel is stationary the planet wheels turn around their spindles in the planet carrier. This means that the outer teeth of the planet wheel (which mesh with the annulus) are moving relative to the planet carrier, and this makes the annulus move faster than the planet carrier.

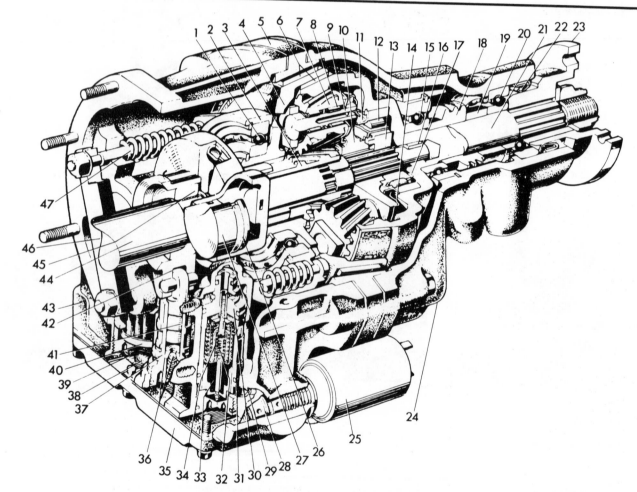

Fig. 6.26. Cut-away view of overdrive unit (Sec. 19)

1 Thrust bearing	13 Uni-directional clutch	25 Solenoid	37 Pump cylinder
2 Thrust bearing retainer	14 Oil trap	26 Piston seal	38 Magnet
3 Sunwheel	15 Ball bearing	27 Piston	39 Pre-filter
4 Clutch sliding member	16 Bush	28 Operating valve	40 Fine filter
5 Brake ring	17 Thrust washer	29 Orifice nozzle	41 Pump plunger
6 Clutch member linings	18 Speedometer driving gear	30 Cylinder top	42 Connecting rod
7 Planet gear	19 Spacer	31 Cylinder	43 Front casing
8 Needle bearing	20 Ball bearing	32 Spring	44 Input shaft (gearbox mainshaft)
9 Shaft	21 Output shaft	33 Large piston	
10 Planet carrier	22 Oil seal	34 Small piston	45 Eccentric
11 Oil thrower	23 Coupling flange	35 Base plate	46 Bridge piece
12 Uni-directional clutch rollers	24 Rear casing	36 Check valve for oil pump	47 Spring

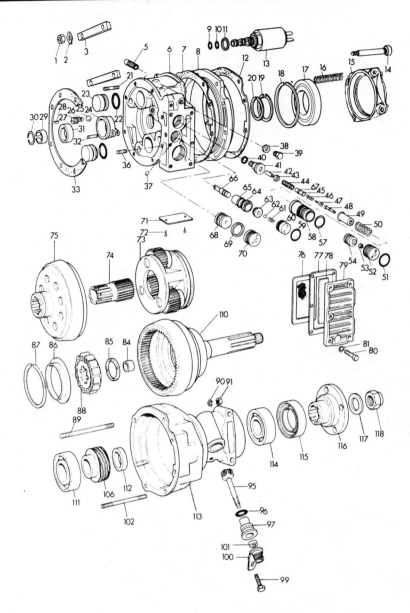

Fig. 6.27. Exploded view of overdrive unit (Secs. 19, 23, 24 and 26)

1	Nut	28	Key	57	O-ring	84	Bush
2	Lockwasher	29	Resilient ring	58	Cylinder	85	Thrust washer
3	Bridge piece	30	Circlip	59	O-ring	86	Oil thrower
5	Breather	31	Eccentric	60	Plug	87	Circlip
6	Front casing	32	Piston pin	61	Spring	88	Uni-directional clutch
7	Gasket	33	Gasket	62	Ball	89	Stud
8	Brake ring	36	Stud	63	Non-return body	90	Resilient washer
9	O-ring	37	Orifice nozzle	64	O-ring	91	Nut
10	O-ring	38	Seal	65	Pump body	95	Speedometer pinion
11	Seal	39	Plug	66	Pump plunger	96	O-ring
12	Gasket	40	O-ring	67	Washer	97	Bush
13	Solenoid	41	End piece	68	Fine filter	99	Bolt
14	Bolt	42	Piston	69	Seal	100	Retainer
15	Thrust bearing retainer	43	Washer	70	Plug	101	Oil seal
16	Spring	44	Spring	71	Data plate	102	Stud
17	Thrust bearing	45	Retainer	72	Screw	106	Speedometer driving gear
18	Circlip	46	Spring	73	Planet gear and carrier	110	Output shaft
19	Circlip	47	Screw	74	Sunwheel	111	Ball bearing
20	Circlip	48	Screw	75	Clutch sliding member	112	Spacer
21	Stud	49	Holder	76	Pre-filter	113	Rear casing
22	Piston seal	50	Spring	77	Gasket	114	Ball bearing
23	Piston	51	O-ring	78	Magnet	115	Oil seal
24	Connecting rod	52	Plug	79	Base plate	116	Flange
25	Non-return ball	53	Nut	80	Bolt	117	Washer
26	Non-return valve spring	54	Piston	81	Resilient washer	118	Nut
27	Plug						

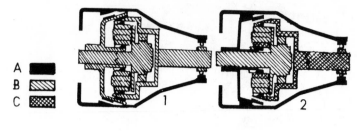

A
B
C

Fig. 6.28. Working principle of overdrive (Sec. 19)

1   Direct drive
2   Overdrive
A   Non-rotating parts
B   Parts rotating at the same speed as the input shaft
C   Parts rotating at a higher speed than the input shaft

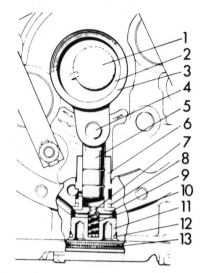

Fig. 6.29. Cut-away view of relief valve (Secs. 20 and 23)

1	Dashpot piston	9	Relief valve spindle
2	Dashpot sleeve	10	Residual spring
3	Dashpot spring cup	11	Relief valve spring cup
4	Dashpot spring	12	Relief valve spring
5	Relief valve for lubricating	13	Double dashpot spring
	oil pressure	14	Restrictor plug
6	Drilling from oil pump	15	Drilling from operating
7	Drilling to mainshaft		valve
8	Relief valve body	16	Dashpot plug

Note - lower dashpot and item 13 are omitted in later models

Fig. 6.30. Cut-away view of oil pump (Sec. 20)

1	Mainshaft	8	O-ring
2	Eccentric	9	Valve seat
3	Connecting rod	10	Spring
4	Gudgeon pin	11	Plug
5	Piston	12	O-ring
6	Cylinder	13	Pre-filter
7	Ball		

5   To 'change gear', therefore all that is necessary is to slide the clutch member along the mainshaft. This member is pushed forwards by four coil springs anchored by bridge pieces through a thrust bearing assembly. When the hydraulic system is actuated, two pistons push on the bridge pieces and draw the sliding member along the shaft until it comes up against the outer case. This changes the drive ratio as already described.

6   The sliding member is bolted to bridge pieces. Behind these bridge pieces are hydraulically operated pistons which are able to push the bridge pieces away from the case against the action of the clutch return springs when the hydraulic pressure is great enough. This means that changing gear is simply a matter of raising the oil pressure applied to the pistons. The oil pressure is generated in the first instance by a piston pump which is driven by an eccentric release shaft which gives either a low pressure or a high pressure according to whether the solenoid is energised or not (details of how this is done is given in Section 20). The oil reaches the pistons through oilways in the casing.

20 Hydraulic pressure control

1   The solenoid operated control valve is a simple double-ended affair which is sprung against a seating and blocks off the oil inlet to the valves when the solenoid is not energised. When voltage is applied to the solenoid, the valve is pushed against its spring until it comes up against a lower seating, allowing oil to flow through the control valve and into the relief valve via the orifice nozzle. To see how this affects the relief valve take a look at Fig. 6.29.

2   The key to this figure is the small piston which when pushed down by oil pressure building up in the inlet channel uncovers drillings in the body which allows oil to flow into channel and also to the relief valve, which sets a limit on the pressure that can build up. This cylinder acts against a complex arrangement of dashpots and springs which eventually all push against a large piston at the bottom of the valve. When oil is admitted into the lower input channel by the action of the control valve, this piston is pushed upwards compressing the springs and thus making it harder for the small piston to be pushed down. The oil pressure builds up until this piston eventually moves against the increased spring pressure and a new state of equilibrium is reached.

3   The oil pump (shown in Fig. 6.30) is simple in principle, oil being drawn in on the up stroke of the plunger and pushed past the ball valve into the outlet channel on the down stroke. It draws oil from the bottom of the case which acts as a sump and the system incorporates a filter, just like the oil system in a car engine.

4   As well as supplying the hydraulic system, the oil pump provides pressure lubrication via a drilling in the gearbox mainshaft which connects with the channel. The oil finds its way through the unidirectional clutch, and via the planet gear back to the bottom of the overdrive case.

21 Overdrive unit - removal and replacement

1   It is helpful, before removing the overdrive, to start the car and engage and disengage the overdrive with the clutch pedal depressed. This will avoid leaving any residual torque in the mainshaft, planet carrier and unidirectional clutch. If this has not been done, disconnect the propeller shaft and then, of course, achieve the same object without

moving the car.

2   Place a jack under the engine sump and remove the gearlever and gearbox support member as described in Section 3. Disconnect the propeller shaft, the exhaust pipe bracket, the electrical lead and the speedometer cable.

3   Lower the engine enough to let you get at the upper fixing nuts holding the overdrive unit to the spacing flange. Remove the nuts and withdraw the unit leaving the spacing flange on the gearbox.

4   Refitting to the gearbox is dealt with in Section 27.

22 Overdrive overhaul - preliminaries

1   Overhauling an overdrive presents special problems to the owner mechanic whose workshop facilities are limited. These arise from the fact that the unit incorporates a hydraulic mechanism which depends for its operation on the same oil that lubricates the gears. Absolute cleanliness is therefore essential. We recommend that for anything other than the simplest check the unit is removed from the vehicle, thoroughly cleaned, and then taken to a work place where scrupulous cleanliness can be maintained throughout the whole time that the unit is dismantled. Any lower standard than this is asking for trouble. Another set of problems is posed by the multiplicity of small parts in the hydraulic units. The best - almost the only - way to cope with these is to lay out the bits and pieces in order as they are disassembled, on a clean surface (a table covered with newspaper for example) where they can be covered over and left undisturbed. Putting them in small separate containers is very much a second best; if this is not done a lot of time will be wasted during reassembly making sure that everything is in the right place and the right way round.

2   Dismantling and reassembling the mechanical bits and pieces presents no special problem apart from the requirement for extreme cleanliness. Have the outside spotlessly clean before starting. This is more than just a good idea - it is essential. Smear all parts with oil as they are assembled.

3   Dismantling an overdrive unit is a job which needs better working conditions than the average owner has available and every bit of care and thoroughness that can be mustered.

4   If the overdrive is in working order prior to overhaul, it is worthwhile to check the oil pressure. Volvo recommend that this is done while the car is being driven and their agents have a special pressure gauge with suitable adaptors to fit to the different models of overdrive unit. When driving on direct drive at about 25 mph (40 kph) the pressure should be about 21 lb/sq in (1.5 kg/sq cm). When the overdrive is engaged, the pressure should rise to 380-425 lb/sq in (27-30 kg/sq cm). When the overdrive is disengaged, the pressure should drop to about 21 lb/sq in (1.5 kg/sq cm) within three seconds.

23 Solenoid, oil pump, hydraulic valves - dismantling

1   Remove the baseplate and the pre-filter and drain the oil into a perfectly clean container if you are proposing to use it again. **Warning:** If the overdrive has been running just before you drain it, the oil may be hot enough to scald you.

2   Remove the solenoid, using a 1 in (25 mm) open-ended spanner on the hexagon. The solenoid and operating valve form an integral unit which cannot be dismantled further and must be replaced complete if faulty.

3   Removing the baseplate and pre-filter will have revealed three plugs which retain the fine filter, oil pump and relief valve (see Fig. 6.31). To make a suitable tool for removing these plugs, get hold of two small bolts whose heads fit into the holes in the plugs and screw these into a pair of holes in a length of metal strip. If the surface of your strip rests against the plugs and the bolt heads are a reasonable fit in the holes you will be able to remove the plugs quite easily without trouble or damage (see Fig. 6.32). It is well worthwhile taking the trouble to make something like this rather than simply pushing bolts into the holes in the plugs - a method which will certainly lead to loss of time and loss of temper.

4   Remove the fine filter and its seal which are under the largest of the three plugs. Then turn your attention to the awe-inspiring assortment of bits and pieces which go to make up the relief valve. Check each part as it comes out against the exploded view in Fig. 6.27 and the cut-away view in Fig. 6.29, (the secondary dashpot is not present in later models). We strongly recommend that you lay the pieces out

Fig. 6.31. Three plugs under the baseplate and pre-filter hold the fine filter (shown dismantled), the relief valve and the oil pump (Sec. 23)

1   Filter   2   Seal   3   Plug

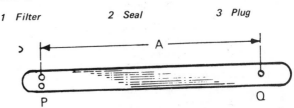

Fig. 6.32. Tool for applying correct torque when refitting plugs: To obtain correct tightening torque - connect spring balance to 'Q', keeping it at right angles to tool (Sec. 23)

'Q' - Balance hole   P - pegs for holes in plugs   A = 12 in (305 mm) Balance reading of 16 lbs (7.26 kg) = 16 lbs ft (2.2 kg m) of torque

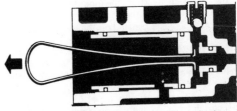

Fig. 6.33. Removal of relief valve with wire hook (Sec. 23)

somewhere where they will not be disturbed or get dirty. Draw out the body of the relief valve as shown in Fig. 6.33, which also illustrates the seating at the top of the valve for the small piston and the positioning of the ball valve which limits the pressure that can build up in the relief valve. The pump plunger can now be detached from the actuator and withdrawn through the pump body, which can then be withdrawn itself using a wire hook if necessary.

24 Overdrive mechanical components - dismantling

1   The numbers in brackets in this Section refer to Fig. 6.27.

2   Mount the unit vertically in a vice with wooden or copper jaw inserts, front end upwards. It is assumed that at this stage the solenoid and intermediate flange have been removed.

3   Straighten the locking tabs and unscrew the nuts for the piston bridge pieces (1,2,3) and remove the bridge pieces.

4   Unscrew the nuts holding together the front and rear sections of the casing (6,113) which have the brake ring (8) sandwiched between them. These should be slackened off gradually all round in case there is a difference in tension in the clutch sliding member return springs (16). The front casing and brake ring can now be lifted off the studs in the back case as shown in Fig. 6.34.

5   If necessary, use a copper drift to help free the brake ring from the casing.

6   Remove the clutch sliding member return springs and lift this member out complete with thrust bearing and sun wheel.

7   Lift out the planet carrier complete.

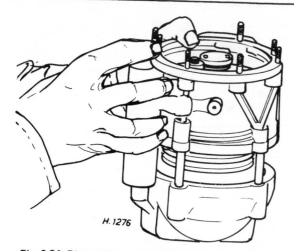

Fig. 6.34. Dismantling the overdrive (Secs. 24 and 26)

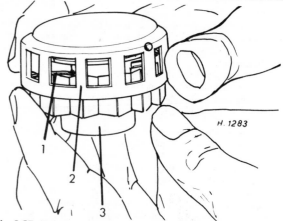

Fig. 6.35. Uni-directional clutch assembly (Secs. 24 and 26)

1 Spring	2 Cage	3 Hub

8 Removal of the pistons (23) from the front casing is best done with a small sucker (you can cut down one that is too big), unless you have compressed air available, when you can blow it out.

9 From the front casing remove the pump connecting rod (24).

10 To dismantle the clutch sliding member assembly, first remove circlip (20) and pull out the sun wheel. Then remove the circlip (19) and separate the bearing (17) and its housing (15) from the clutch sliding member. Finally, remove circlip (18) and press the bearing out of its housing.

11 Turning now to the rear casing, remove the bolt (99) and pull out the speedometer pinion and its associated bits and pieces.

12 Remove the flange nut and pull the flange off the shaft. Be sure that the centre part of your puller does not damage the thread at the end of the shaft - particularly if you are using a home-made device.

13 To disassemble the output shaft assembly, first press the output shaft out of the casing, then extract the inner bearing, freeing the speedometer pinion and spacer, then press out the rear bearing. These operations may make a bigger demand on the owner's workshop facilities than he is able to meet. We suggest, therefore, that having removed the oil seal (115) you check the assembly for lateral play after having washed all the oil out with paraffin followed by white spirit and if you find all is well leave it assembled; if not, have the bearings renewed at a local garage or workshop equipped for the job.

14 Remove circlip (87), take off oil thrower (86) and remove the unidirectional clutch from the annulus. Be doubly careful with the unidirectional clutch - make quite sure which way round it goes and mark it in some way to ensure that it goes back correctly, and watch the rollers as the clutch comes out - they are not attached in any way and like all such objects they have a wonderful instinct for concealment. Having got them all safely, have a good look at the way the spring and the cage are assembled in the outer frame of the unidirectional clutch. Compare the actual device with Fig. 6.35 which by itself may not be very revealing but will certainly serve as a reminder when you have seen the real thing.

15 Examine the bush (84) in the middle of the annulus before deciding to remove it, check that it is free from scores. Fit the output shaft to the gearbox mainshaft and check that there is no undue slop. If the bush is worn fit a new one. Be careful when fitting that it goes in straight and is not distorted or it will have to be reamed true.

25 Overdrive - inspection

1 No one will dismantle an overdrive unless he is certain that there is something wrong with it - excessive noise, failure to engage or disengage properly, or something of that sort. The nature of its shortcomings will have given a clue as to what to look for on dismantling and it may well be that the fault will be revealed before dismantling is complete. If this does happen, it still makes good sense to dismantle completely and give the whole thing a thorough inspection.

2 First of all, wash out all the passages in the casings and make sure that they are clean and dry. Two common domestic objects go a long way towards substituting for the compressed air so freely mentioned in service manuals and so rarely found in owner's workshops; the

ordinary hair drier and an empty plastic washing-up liquid container. This latter with its small rounded nozzle is a most useful device so long as it is clean and dry.

3 Give all the hydraulic bits and pieces a good wash and a good look over. Examine the seatings of all valves for possible scoring.

4 Wash the various bearings and the unidirectional clutch pieces in white spirit, dry them thoroughly with lint-free rag and inspect for excessive play and signs of wear.

5 Examine the various gears for signs of wear and damage. Make sure that the bush on the sun wheel is not worn. If it needs replacement, get a new sun wheel complete with bush - the bush must be concentric with the gear wheel and to achieve this is a factory job.

6 Check the pistons which act on the bridge pieces for signs of wear. Replace them if they are not perfect.

7 Check the brake ring for abrasion, cracks or wear.

8 Check the linings on the clutch sliding member for burning or wear.

9 Check the solenoid with a 12 volt battery and an ammeter. Current consumption should be about 2 amps and there should of course be no hesitation about its operation when it is disconnected from the unit. This should be checked again when the solenoid-operated control valve or control valve mechanism has been reassembled.

26 Overdrive - reassembly

1 Use new gaskets, O-rings, tab washers and oil seals when reassembling. If you are in any doubt about the filters, renew these too. The cost of these items is a small price to pay for peace of mind.

2 Absolute cleanliness is, of course, even more important during reassembly than during dismantling. Give every part a quick cleanliness check and smear it with oil as you reassemble it.

3 To assemble the rear casing and output shaft, press the front bearing on to the output shaft, followed by the speedometer spacers. Press the rear bearing into the rear casing using a drift similar to that shown in Fig. 6.36. Support the output shaft on a wooden block and then press the rear casing onto the shaft by pushing on the rear bearing with the same drift. Fig. 6.36 shows this process almost completed. As mentioned in Section 24, paragraph 13, this pressing operation may prove difficult for the average owner and it may be a good idea to have it done by a specialist.

4 Press in the oil seal, lubricating it well first. Get it the right way round - see Fig. 6.27.

5 Fit the coupling flange, washer and nut. Tighten the nut to a torque of 80-100 lb f ft (11-14 kg f m).

6 Assemble the unidirectional clutch cage on the hub with the spring as shown in Fig. 6.35, so that when viewed as in Fig. 6.37 the cage is sprung anticlockwise. Rotate the cage clockwise as far as it will go and lock it in this position with a temporary wedge. Position the rollers in the cage and tie them in with string.

7 Insert the thrust washer and follow this by the clutch in the centre of the output shaft, easing the string off the rollers when they are held by the mainshaft and removing the temporary wedge. Fit the oil

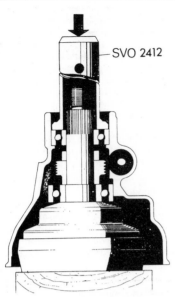

Fig. 6.36. Pressing the output shaft and its bearing into the rear casing
(Sec. 26)

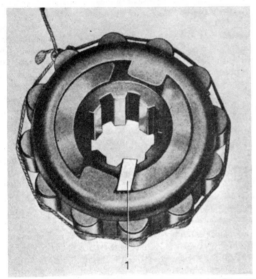

Fig. 6.37. Assembling the uni-directional clutch (Sec. 26)

1 Wedge

Fig. 6.38. Fitting the uni-directional clutch into the output shaft
(Sec. 26)

thrower and circlip.

8 Reassemble the speedometer pinion and bush in the casing.

9 Position the planet gear assembly in the output shaft annulus.
Note that when the overdrive is fitted to the gearbox the splines in the
planet carrier will have to line up with those in the unidirectional clutch
- both these items being splined to the gearbox mainshaft. Volvo make
a special splined tool for ensuring this and you may care to make something that will do the same thing - perhaps either a wooden dowel with
one or more 'splines' made of metal strip - but it can be done without
as there is no centering problem - it is simply a matter of getting the
splines lined up. You could do this at the last minute with a thin
screwdriver pushed up the middle of the assembly.

10 Turning now to the clutch unit, first press the ball bearing into its
retainer and fit the circlip (Fig. 6.27, Nos. 15, 17, 18 - numbers in
brackets in the following paragraphs also refer to this figure).

11 Put the bolts (14) through their holes on the retainer and press
the bearing with retainer on to the clutch sliding member. Fit the
circlip (19). Fit the sun wheel and its circlip (20).

12 Insert the sun wheel into the planet cluster and fit the four thrust
springs (16) on to the bolts. The clutch/output shaft assembly is now
complete.

13 Now is a good time to consider exactly how you are going to
ensure that those splines are lined up. It is better to solve this problem
on the bench than underneath the car.

14 Assembly of the hydraulic components in the front case calls for
no particular comment, being simply a reversal of the dismantling
process. Do not forget a light smear of oil on everything. Put the
actuating pistons (23) back in the case before assembling the valves
and pump to avoid possible trouble with air pressure behind them.

15 Install the brake ring on the front casing and reassemble the front
and rear casings with the brake ring between them exactly as they
were taken apart (see Fig. 6.34). Tighten the fixing nuts evenly, a
little at a time all round to avoid any possibility of distortion by the
tension in the clutch springs. Note that the two upper fixing nuts
have copper washers. Do not forget the tag washers on the nuts for the
bridge pieces.

16 Finally, fit the solenoid and check its operation.

27 Overdrive - refitting to gearbox

1 It is as important to preserve cleanliness during this operation
(carried out underneath the car in all probability) as it is when assembling the overdrive unit on a specially cleaned work bench. When working underneath the car it is easy to accidentally dislodge dirt from the
subframe; this dirt then rains down - and could enter the overdrive
unit if precautions are not taken during refitment. To avoid this problem, it is suggested that newspaper is stuck above the gearbox area so
that at least the fall-out does not descend all over the overdrive. If the
car is well jacked-up there will be more room to work and that is a
help.

2 Do not forget the gasket.

3 When the overdrive unit is offered up to the gearbox the splines on
the mainshaft will enter the unidirectional clutch at much the same
time as the eccentric enters the connecting rod for the pump. However,
thanks to the generous chamfer provided on this component it will
pull itself into line if it is not exactly right to start with. The secret
of success is to arrange matters by lining up the mainshaft splines,
their opposite numbers on the unidirectional clutch and the planet
gear cage and the pump connecting rod so that the unit can be slid
straight on to the intermediate flange (attached to the gearbox) and
pick up the holes on the flange with the studs - all this without having
to turn the overdrive unit. Careful alignment before starting and a
small amount of rocking just as the studs enter the intermediate
flange should do the trick. If it does not, the best thing to do
is to withdraw the unit and do the lining up again.

4 The rest of the installation is a simple reversal of the removal
procedure.

5 Finally, fill the gearbox with oil until it runs from the filler/level
plug. Allow time for the oil to flow into the overdrive (common
lubricant supply) before checking the level plug hole. Check the oil
level after a few miles road operation.

28 Fault diagnosis - overdrive

Listed overleaf are the commonest troubles experienced with overdrive and some possible causes. Start at the top of the list when looking for a fault and work through it. The overdrive is a well tried and well proven mechanism and - as the list reveals - trouble is more often due to causes outside the overdrive unit itself than within it.

Overdrive will not engage

1 *Faulty solenoid*
2 *Fault in electric wiring*
3 *Faulty gearbox switch*
4 *Faulty overdrive selector switch*
5 *Faulty relay (if fitted)*
6 *Low oil level in overdrive unit*
7 *Faulty non-return valve in oil pump*
8 *Blocked oil filter*

Overdrive will not release

Note: This fault should be attended to immediately. Above all, do not reverse when overdrive is engaged as this will cause considerable damage.

1 *Fault in electrical wiring, (voltage permanently on solenoid)*
2 *Control valve sticking*
3 *Mechanical damage in overdrive (note that when found this may be the result of the trouble and not its original cause)*
4 *Sticking unidirectional clutch*

Clutch slip in overdrive

1 *Low oil level in overdrive unit*
2 *Control valve incorrectly adjusted or not operating properly*
3 *Worn linings on clutch sliding member*

Noise

As the overdrive ages, normal wear may give rise to a certain amount of noise when the unit is in overdrive. Regard any harsh noise with the utmost suspicion. The only way you can be reasonably certain that the noise in your unit is significant or not is to consult someone who has the experience necessary to judge it.

29 Automatic transmission - general description

The Borg-Warner Model 35 automatic transmission fitted to the Volvo 240 series comprises two main components, a three element hydrokinetic torque converter coupling capable of torque multiplication at an infinitely variable ratio between 2 : 1 and 1 : 1 and a hydraulically operated epicyclic gearbox providing three forward ratios and reverse.

The automatic transmission is connected to an oil cooler which is housed in the bottom of the radiator. On some earlier models the oil cooler may not be fitted.

The control lever (which is mounted on the floor) has six positions: Position 'P' locks the transmission for parking; 'R' is reverse; 'N' is neutral; 'D' is the normal driving position; '2' stops the gearbox from engaging its third gear; '1' keeps the gearbox in first gear.

The BW55, introduced in 1977 has a different internal gearing system and the brake band systems have been replaced by multi-disc brake systems which do not require any adjustment. In respect of the operations dealt with in this manual both units are practically the same.

30 Automatic transmission - repair and maintenance

Because of the complexity of this unit, it is not recommended that the owner should attempt to dismantle it himself. If performance is not up to standard or some failure occurs, your Volvo garage should be called in. They will have special equipment for accurate fault diagnosis and rectification. Bear in mind that many tests of the unit are best carried out when it is still in the car, so if there is trouble, do not remove the unit from the car before placing it in the hands of the repairer.

The following Sections, therefore, confine themselves to adjustments and servicing information. Instruction for removal is given because this is an essential preliminary to removing the engine.

31 Fluid level - checking

1 Put gear selector in 'P'. Start the engine and allow it to idle. Shift into the various positions. Dwell in each position 4-5 seconds.
2 Shift back to 'P' and wait two minutes before checking the oil level.
3 Top up as necessary. The difference between the 'MIN' and 'MAX' levels is 1 pint (0.6 litre).

32 Speed selector linkage - adjustment

1 Place the control lever in '2'.
2 Disconnect the selector rod from the lever on the side of the transmission housing and then set the lever in position '2'. This is the first detent towards the rear of the car from the fully forward position.
3 Release the lock nut on the rod and adjust the length of the rod so that when it is reconnected there will be a clearance of about 0.04 in (1 mm) as shown at B in Fig. 6.40. Now move the control lever to 'D' and check that there is a similar gap at A.
4 Check that this clearance remains when the hand control is moved to '1' and 'P'. Make any minor adjustments which may be necessary and then tighten the locknut on the link rod.
5 After making this adjustment, check that the length of visible thread on the linkage rod does not exceed 1.38 in (35.0 mm) - see Fig. 6.41. Note that increasing the rod length decreases the clearance between the selector lever and the gate in position 'D' and increases the clearance in position '2'. With correct adjustment the clearance at position 'D' should be equal to or slightly greater than the clearance at position '2'.

33 Downshift cable - adjustment

1 The downshift cable is fitted with a crimped stop when it is set during production of the car. Should this stop have been removed or if it is loose on the cable, adjustment can only be carried out in the manner described in Section 34.
2 Check that the engine idling speed is correct.
3 Adjust the outer cable threaded adjuster until there is a gap between the end of the crimped stop and the end of the threaded adjuster of 0.04 in (1 mm).
4 Check that with the accelerator pedal fully depressed, the throttle lever is open fully to its stop.

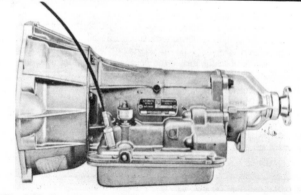

Fig. 6.39. Borg-Warner Automatic Transmission type 35 (Sec. 29)

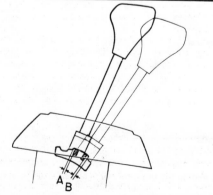

Fig. 6.40. Selector controls adjustment (Sec. 32)

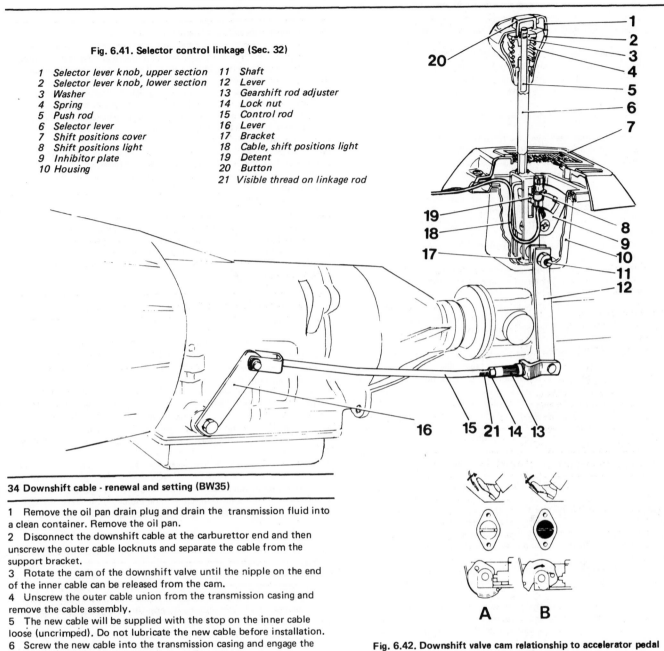

Fig. 6.41. Selector control linkage (Sec. 32)

1	Selector lever knob, upper section	11	Shaft
2	Selector lever knob, lower section	12	Lever
3	Washer	13	Gearshift rod adjuster
4	Spring	14	Lock nut
5	Push rod	15	Control rod
6	Selector lever	16	Lever
7	Shift positions cover	17	Bracket
8	Shift positions light	18	Cable, shift positions light
9	Inhibitor plate	19	Detent
10	Housing	20	Button
		21	Visible thread on linkage rod

34 Downshift cable - renewal and setting (BW35)

1   Remove the oil pan drain plug and drain the transmission fluid into a clean container. Remove the oil pan.

2   Disconnect the downshift cable at the carburettor end and then unscrew the outer cable locknuts and separate the cable from the support bracket.

3   Rotate the cam of the downshift valve until the nipple on the end of the inner cable can be released from the cam.

4   Unscrew the outer cable union from the transmission casing and remove the cable assembly.

5   The new cable will be supplied with the stop on the inner cable loose (uncrimped). Do not lubricate the new cable before installation.

6   Screw the new cable into the transmission casing and engage the inner cable with the downshift valve cam.

7   Attach the upper end of the cable to the throttle lever and the support bracket but leave the locknuts loose.

8   With the accelerator pedal fully released, adjust the locknuts at the upper end of the outer cable so that the cam to valve plunger relationship is as shown at 'A' in Fig. 6.42. Now have an assistant fully depress the accelerator pedal and check that the cam to valve plunger relationship is as shown at 'B'.

9   When adjustment is correct, tighten the cable locknuts and then crimp the stop to the inner cable so that there is a gap between it and the end face of the threaded adjuster of the outer cable of 0.04 in (1 mm).

10 Refit the oil pan and refill the transmission with fluid.

11 See Chapter 13 for the procedure on BW55, AW55, AW70 and AW71 transmissions.

35 Starter inhibitor switch - replacement

1   Disconnect the switch leads and remove the contact.

2   Fit a new gasket on the contact. Screw in the contact and tighten to 10 lb f ft (1.4 kg f m).

3   Connect the leads and check that the engine can only be started

Fig. 6.42. Downshift valve cam relationship to accelerator pedal (Sec. 34)

A   Fully released   B   Fully depressed

with the selector in 'P' and 'N' and that the reversing light is on with the selector in 'R'.

36 Rear brake band - adjustment (BW35)

1   This is not a routine operation and should only require attention if after reference to Fault Diagnosis, Section 41, its adjustment is called for.

2   Access to the rear brake band adjuster is obtained after removing the interior mats from the front compartment, withdrawing the air duct and transmission tunnel cover. Remove the rubber plug from the hole in the transmission tunnel.

3   Release the locknut of the brake band adjuster screw and tighten the screw to 10 lb f ft (1.4 kg f m). Now unscrew the adjuster screw one complete turn and tighten the locknut without disturbing the setting.

4   Refit the transmission tunnel components.

37 Automatic transmission unit - removal and replacement

1   Withdraw the fluid dipstick and drain the fluid. On BW35 remove the drain plug; on BW55 removal of the filler tube drains the transmission. Be careful if the car has just been driven as the fluid will be very hot and can easily scald. Remove the guard plate from underneath the engine.

2   Disconnect the downshift cable at the engine end and detach it from its support bracket.

3   Disconnect the exhaust downpipe from the manifold.

4   Unless the car is on ramps or over an inspection pit it must be raised, and supported very securely, to provide adequate clearance for the torque converter housing to pass beneath the car as the transmission is removed.

5   Unbolt and remove the semi-circular cover plate from the lower front face of the torque converter housing.

6   Disconnect the front of the propeller shaft from the output flange of the transmission.

7   Disconnect the speed selector link rod from the lever on the side of the transmission casing.

8   Unbolt and remove the reinforcing bracket from the rear of the engine sump. Disconnect the oil cooler pipes.

9   Remove the starter motor.

10 Unscrew and remove the bolts which secure the torque converter to the driveplate. These bolts are accessible through the starter motor aperture. Each bolt can be brought into view by turning the crankshaft with a spanner on the pulley bolt.

11 Place a jack and a block of wood as a spreader under the rear end of the engine sump and take the weight of the engine.

12 Disconnect the transmission rear mounting and remove the support member and exhaust bracket.

13 Disconnect the speedometer cable from the transmission.

14 Unscrew the oil filler pipe union (BW35), remove the pipe and plug the hole in the transmission casing.

15 Lower the jack under the engine sump until the transmission is lowered about two inches at its rear end.

16 Disconnect the leads from the starter inhibitor switch and the earth strap.

17 Remove the bolts which secure the torque converter housing to the engine.

18 Using either a trolley jack or the help of two assistants withdraw the transmission rearwards. As soon as the torque converter housing starts to separate from the engine, use a thin lever to keep the torque converter pressed fully to the rear and in engagement with the oil pump drive dogs.

19 If required, the drive plate can be unbolted from the crankshaft rear mounting flange. This may be necessary if the starter ring gear is worn.

20 Installation is the reversal of the removal procedure but before offering the transmission to the engine, make sure that the torque converter is pushed fully to the rear so that the oil pump drive dogs are fully engaged. Keep the torque converter in this position until the torque converter housing is fully engaged with the engine.

21 Refill the unit on completion with the correct grade and quantity of fluid.

22 Adjust the throttle cable, kick-down cable and selector linkage as described in Section 8 of Chapter 13.

38 Fault diagnosis and rectification

1   The test procedure with its accompanying diagnosis and rectification instructions given in Section 40 will enable the owner to decide for himself whether or not the automatic transmission unit is faulty and, if faults are present, whether he himself will be able to rectify them or whether the fault must be corrected by a Volvo agent.

2   Test No 3 in this procedure is described in a little more detail in the remainder of this Section.

3   Before carrying out a stall test, make sure that the engine is developing full power and is properly adjusted. An engine which is not developing full power will affect the stall test reading.

4   Allow the engine and transmission to reach correct working temperatures.

5   Connect a tachometer to the vehicle.

6   Chock the wheels and apply the handbrake and foot brake (an assistant will be needed for this).

7   Select position '1' and run the engine with the accelerator pedal fully depressed. Check the engine speed against the figures specified at the beginning of this Chapter. Repeat the procedure with the selector in position '2'. The implications of speed readings, outside the specification, and other possible symptoms are discussed in Section 40, Test 3.

8   Do not carry out a stall test for a period longer than 10 seconds, otherwise the transmission will overheat.

39 Converter fault diagnosis

1   Inability to start on steep gradients, combined with poor acceleration from rest and low speed, indicate that the converter stator unidirectional clutch is slipping. This permits the stator to rotate in an opposite direction to the impeller and turbine and torque multiplication cannot occur.

2   Poor acceleration in third gear above 30 mph (48 kmph) indicates that the stator unidirectional clutch has seized. The stator will not rotate with the turbine and impeller and the 'fluid flywheel' phase cannot occur. This condition will also be indicated by excessive overheating of the transmission although the stall speed may be correct.

40 Road test procedure

The following test procedure may well be carried out periodically by the owner who is concerned with ensuring that his automatic transmission remains in tip-top condition. It will indicate the necessity for adjustment and may well reveal faults at an early stage, before they make themselves obvious by producing catastrophic failure.

We recommend that, even if you think you have found the cause of any trouble, you carry the tests through completely once you have started. One fault may give rise to another and it is as well to be sure that you know the full extent of the trouble, if any.

The test procedure follows:

Road test	Fault diagnosis	Rectification (see chart overleaf)
1 Check that the starter will operate only with the selector lever in 'P' and 'N' and that the reverse light operates only in 'R'	Starter will not operate in 'P' or 'N' Starter operates in all selector positions	19 20
2 Apply the hand and foot brakes and with the engine idling select 'N—D', 'N—2', 'N—1' and 'N—R'. Gearbox engagement should be felt in each position	Excessive bump on engagement of 'D', '2', '1' or 'R'	4, 3

Road test	Fault diagnosis	Rectification (see chart overleaf)
3 Check the stall speed in '1' and 'R'. Do not stall for more than 10 seconds or transmission will overheat (see Section 38)	High stall speed: a) With slip and squawk in '1'	1, 2, 3, 13a, c, f, 11
	b) With slip and squawk in 'R'	1, 2, 3, 13a, c, f, e, 12
	Low stall speed: more than 600 rev/min below that specified (see Specifications)	21
	Low stall speed: less than 600 rev/min below that specified (see Specifications)	23
4 With transmission at normal running temperature, select 'D' release the brakes and accelerate with minimum throttle. Check for 1—2 and 2—3 shifts. Confirm that third gear has been obtained by selecting '2' when a 3—2 shift should be felt	No drive in 'D', '2' or '1'	1, 2, 3, 13a, 11, 16
	No drive in 'D', drive in '1'	1, 2, 3, 16
	No drive in 'D', '2', '1' or 'R'	1, 2, 3, 13a, 11, 16, 17
	Delayed or no 1—2 shift	3, 14, 13a, 5, 6
	Slip on 1—2 shift	2, 3, 5, 6, 7, 13c, f
	Delayed or no 2—3 shift (if normal drive in 'R', omit 12)	3, 14, 13g, h, c, d, 5, 6, 12
Note: A feature of this transmission is that a slight increase in throttle depression between 15 and 30 mph (25 and 48 kmph) may produce a 3—2 down-shift (part throttle down-shift)	Slip or engine run-up on 2—3 shift	2, 3, 5, 13a, c, 12
	Bumpy gear-shifts	3
	Drag on 'D' and '2'	8
	Drag on binding on 2—3 shift	5, 6
5 From a standing start; accelerate using 'kick-down'. Check for 1—2 and 2—3 shifts at speeds specified at start of Chapter	Slip and squawk or judder on full throttle take-off in 'D'.	1, 2, 3, 13a, c, 11
	Loss of performance and overheating in third gear	21
	Other possible faults are as given in test No. 4	Continue as in test 4
6a At 40 mph (65 kmph) in top gear release the accelerator and select '2' or '1'. Check for 3—2 shift and engine braking. Check for 2—1 roll out	No. 3—2 down-shift or engine braking	1, 5, 6, 7, 12
b At 15 mph (25 kmph) in second gear release the accelerator and select '1'. Check for 2—1 shift	No. 2—1 down-shift and engine braking	8, 9, 10
7a At the speed specified for 3—2 shift, in 3rd gear, depress the accelerator to kick-down, when the gearbox should down-shift to second gear	Transmission will not down-shift	3, 13f, g, 14
b At the speed specified for 3—1 shift, in second gear, depress the accelerator to kick-down when the gearbox should down-shift to first gear	Transmission will not down-shift	3, 13f, g, 14
8a Stop, engage '1' and accelerate to 20 mph (30 kmph), check for clutch slip or breakaway noise (squawk) and that no up-shift occurs	Slip, squawk or judder on take-off in '1'	1, 2, 3, 13, 11
	Transmission up-shifts	1
b Stop, engage 'R' and reverse the vehicle using full throttle if possible. Check for clutch or breakaway noise (squawk)	Slip, squawk or judder on take-off in 'R'	1, 2, 3, 13b, c, e, f, g, 12
	As above, with engine braking available in '1'	1. 2. 3
	Slip but no judder on take-off in 'R'. No engine braking available in '1'	1, 2, 3, 8, 9, 10
	Drag in 'R'	5
	No drive in 'R', no engine braking in '1'	1, 2, 3, 8, 13e, f, g, 9, 10, 12
	As above, with engine braking in '1'	1, 2, 3, 13e, 12
9 Stop the vehicle facing downhill, apply the brakes and select 'P'. Release the brakes and check that the pawl holds. Re-apply the brakes before disengaging 'P'. Repeat facing uphill	Parking pawl inoperative	1, 15
	Miscellaneous: Screech or whine increasing with engine speed	17
	Grinding or grating noise from gearbox	18
	Knocking noise from torque converter area	22
	At high speeds in 'D', transmission down-shifts to second ratio and immediately up-shifts back to third ratio	12

RECTIFICATION CHART

X   1   Check manual linkage adjustment
X   2   Recheck fluid level
X   3   Check adjustment of down-shift valve cable
X   4   Reduce engine idle speed
    5   Check self-adjusting mechanism of front band (BW35)
    6   Check front servo seals and fit of tubes
    7   Check front band for wear (BW35)
    8   Check adjustment of rear band (BW35)
    9   Check rear servo seal and fit of tubes
   10   Check rear band for wear (BW35)
   11   Examine front clutch, check ball valve and seals, also forward sun gear shaft sealing rings. Verify that cup plug in driven shaft is not leaking or dislodged
   12   Examine rear clutch, check ball valve and seals Verify that rear clutch spring seat inner lip is not proud. Check fit of tubes

   13   Strip valve bodies and clean, checking:
        a.   Primary regulator valve sticking
        b.   Secondary regulator valve sticking
        c.   Throttle valve sticking
        d.   Modulator valve sticking
        e.   Servo orifice control valve sticking
        f.   1 to 2 shift valve sticking
        g.   2 to 3 shift valve sticking
        h.   2 to 3 shift valve plunger sticking
   14   Strip governor valve and clean
   15   Examine parking pawl, gear, and internal linkage
   16   Examine one-way clutch
   17   Strip and examine pump and drive tangs
   18   Strip and examine gear train
X 19   Adjust starter inhibitor switch inwards
X 20   Adjust starter inhibitor switch outwards
X 21   Replace torque converter
X 22   Examine torque converter drive plate for cracks or fracture
X 23   Check engine performance

Items marked thus X can be carried out by the owner as they do not involve stripping down the unit.

Chapter 7 Propeller shaft

For modifications, and information applicable to later models, see Supplement at end of manual

Contents

Specifications

Type ... ... Tubular, divided, three universal joints and one support bearing.

Universal joints
Make ... ... Hardy-Spicer
Type ... ... Needle bearings

1 General description

1 The propeller shaft couples two rotating parts which move independently of each other. The engine moves a comparatively small amount in its mounting, while the rear axle has a considerable degree of fore-and-aft displacement. Hence the universally accepted arrangement of universal joints and sliding splines. Because the propeller shaft rotates without being rigidly clamped anywhere, it has to be very carefully balanced or it will vibrate. This balance is lost if the shaft is distorted and runs out of true. Wear in the universal joints will allow it to rotate off centre and this too will produce vibration.

2 The Volvo propeller shaft is made in two parts. The front part is coupled by a universal joint to a flange on the gearbox or, if fitted, the overdrive unit, and is supported at its other end by a ball bearing in a flexible rubber housing. This arrangement takes care of engine movement

3 The rear half has two universal joints. At one end it terminates in a flange which is connected to the rear axle and at the other end the universal joint is connected to a splined shaft which slides into the front part. The spline allows for the fore-and-aft movement of the rear axle.

4 The universal joints are of grease-sealed type and require no regular lubrication.

2 Propeller shaft - removal

1 The easiest way is to remove the two parts separately. Start by removing the bolts between the universal joint and the rear axle flange, lowering the shaft and withdrawing it to the rear. The splined part will pull straight out of the centre bearing (photo).

2 Remove the nuts and bolts joining the gearbox or overdrive flange to the universal joint. Put a couple of bolts back in the holes to take the weight while you undo the two screws fixing the support bearing housing to the chassis (photos).

3 Remove the front half of the propeller shaft with the bearing housing attached.

3 Support bearing - removal

1 Bend back the tab washer and unscrew the nut on the end of the propeller shaft. The bearing and its housing can now be withdrawn from the shaft.

2 Dismantle the housing and take the bearing out. The bearing housing assembly is shown in Fig. 7.2.

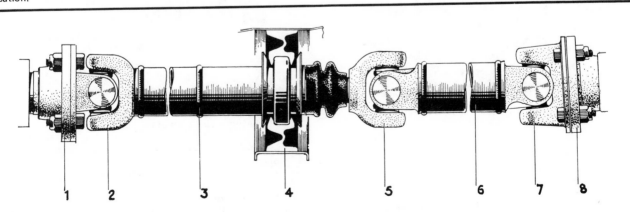

Fig. 7.1. Propeller shaft assembly (Sec. 1)

1 Flange on gearbox	3 Front section of shaft	5 Intermediate universal joint	7 Rear universal joint
2 Front universal joint	4 Support bearing	6 Rear section of shaft	8 Flange on rear axle

2.1 Removing the bolts attaching the universal joint to the rear axle flange

2.2a Bolt fitted temporarily at gearbox flange while removing the support bearing housing screws

2.2b Propeller shaft support bearing

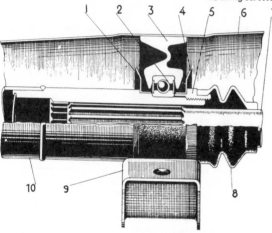

Fig. 7.2. Cut-away view of support bearing (Sec. 3)

1 Dust cover	6 Floor tunnel
2 Ball bearing	7 Splined shaft
3 Rubber housing	8 Rubber cover
4 Dust cover	9 Cap
5 Nut	10 Front section of shaft

Fig. 7.4. Driving bearings through yoke. The bearing on the left has already been driven through (Sec. 4)

Fig. 7.5. When both bearings have been driven through, the yoke will come away (Sec. 4)

Fig. 7.3. Removing circlip which retains bearing cup (Sec. 4)

that the spider can be taken out of the yoke.
5   Drift the bearing cups out of the yoke.

5   Propeller shaft - checking

1   The approved test is to mount the shaft between centres and check for run-out along the whole length. If it is more than 0.010 inches (0.25 mm) out of true it should be replaced. If, like most owners, you don't have measuring equipment of this sort of accuracy, get someone to do it for you if you have any suspicion of vibration. This small tolerance emphasises the importance of correct balancing.
2   It also shows that even minor damage can be a source of trouble. Inspect the shaft for this and renew if necessary.

4   Universal joints - dismantling

1   Remove the circlips which retain the bearings for the spiders.
2   Support one yoke of the joint in a vice. Take care when doing this not to distort the shaft which is hollow.
3   Drive the spider as far as it will go in one direction; this will make the bearing cap stick out of the yoke.
4   Repeat the process in the opposite direction. You will now find

6 Support bearing - inspection

Examine the support bearing by pressing the bearing races against each other by hand and turning them in opposite directions. The bearing should run easily without binding at any point. If it does not, renew it.

7 Universal joints - inspection and reassembly

1   Wash out the needle bearings thoroughly, finishing off with white spirit to remove all traces of cleaning fluid and grease. Check for signs of wear, rust or blueing. Check that their rubber seals are undamaged.
2   Check spiders for signs of wear.
3   If as in paragraph 1 and 2 any imperfection is revealed replace the spiders and the bearings.
4   If the yokes are damaged or the bearing cups are a loose fit in them, replace the shaft concerned. The yokes cannot be removed from the shaft.
5   To reassemble universal joints, fill the bearings half-full of grease and check that the needle rollers are located neatly round the inside of the cup. Push the spider over to the side of the yoke on which you are fitting a bearing so that you can be sure that the bearing cup slides on to the shaft when you fit it (Fig. 7.6). Drive the bearing home gently with a drift just less than a bearing cup diameter and put in the circlip. Do the same on the other end. Take care not to trap the needle rollers.

8 Propeller shaft - refitting

1   Refitting is the reverse of the removal sequence, as described in Section 2.

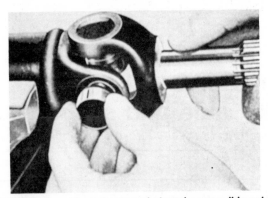

Fig. 7.6. Push the spider as far through the yoke as possible and slide the bearing over it when reassembling (Sec. 7)

2   Alternatively, if you have someone to assist you, there is something to be said for assembling both halves of the propeller shaft and the support bearing housing into a single unit before refitting it to the car. This will ensure that the splines and centre bearing do not collect dirt in the process. The splines should be lubricated with molybdenum disulphide grease before assembling.
3   When assembling, it is important that the yoke on the front section of the propeller shaft and the yoke on the splined shaft are correctly lined up, as shown in Fig. 7.1.

9 Fault diagnosis - propeller shaft

Any trouble occuring in the propeller shaft and the universal joints usually consists of noise caused by vibration and clunking or clicking sounds. Vibration can be recognised by a growling noise which becomes louder as the speed increases. The clunking noise occurs when drive from the engine is transmitted to the rear axle and then conversely changing to the over-run condition.

Symptom	Reason/s	Remedy
Vibration	Support bearing dry or worn	Renew the bearing.
	Support bearing loose in housing	Renew the bearing and housing.
	Propeller shaft bent	Renew the shaft.
Clunking noise	Needle bearings in universal joints worn	Renew the needle bearings.

Chapter 8
Rear axle and suspension; wheels and tyres

For modifications, and information applicable to later models, see Supplement at end of manual

Contents

Specifications

Rear axle

Type	Hypoid, semi-floating
Track	53.15 in (1350 mm)
Reduction ratio	3.73 : 1, 3.9 : 1, 4.10 : 1, or 4.30 : 1
Backlash	0.005 - 0.007 in (0.13 - 0.18 mm)
Oil capacity	2.3 Imp. pints (1.3 litres/2.7 US pints)

Suspension

Type	Trailing arms, torque rods, track rod, coil springs and shock absorbers	
Springs:	**242, 244**	**245**
Wire diameter	0.472 in (12 mm)	0.51 in (12.95 mm)
Coil diameter	5.04 in (128 mm)	5.11 in (129.9 mm)
Number of turns	8	8.35
Shock absorbers:		
Type	Double-acting hydraulic telescopic	

Roadwheels

Type	Disc
Size	5J x 14 or 5.5J x 14

Tyres

Type	Tubeless
Size	175 R 14, 185 R 14 or 185/70 R 14

Torque wrench settings

	lb f ft	kg f m
Flange nut	180 - 220	24 - 30
Differential bearing caps	50	7
Crownwheel bolts*	60	8
Wheel nuts	70 - 100	10 - 14
Hub bearing retaining plate	36	5

Use new bolts

1 Rear suspension - general description

1 A diagram of the rear suspension is given in Fig. 8.1. The rear axle assembly is supported on two arms pivoted to the chassis and sprung against it by coil springs. It is steadied by torque rods attached to the same brackets on the chassis as the support arms but taken to points nearer the middle of the rear axle assembly. All cars except the 245 model are equipped with a rear stabilizer fitted between the support arms.

2 Hydraulic shock absorbers are attached between the body and the support arms and a single tie or 'Panhard' rod extends from an anchorage on the axle casing to a bracket on the opposite side of the body.

2 Shock absorbers and springs - removal and refitting

1 Jack-up the axle and remove the wheel.

2 With the spring under compression (ie. with the axle jacked up after you have removed the wheel) you can remove the shock absorber. If you are only concerned with removing the spring, it is sufficient to let go one end of the shock absorber.

3 To remove the spring, undo the top and bottom attachments while it is still under compression and then take the compression off by jacking-up the body and if necessary letting down the axle, until you are able to take out the spring and its spacers.

4 Refitting is a reversal of removal.

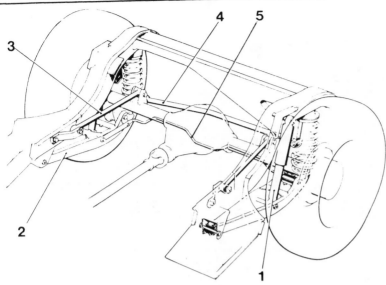

Fig. 8.1. Rear suspension (Sec. 1)

1 Shock absorber
2 Support arm
3 Torque rod
4 Track rod
5 Stabilizer

3 Shock absorbers and springs - checking

1 Shock absorbers and springs may be checked as described in Chapter 11. No maintenance or repair is possible.
2 If you renew a spring, be sure to renew its opposite number even if there is nothing apparently wrong with it. Springs should be obtained in matched pairs.

4 Rubber bushes - renewal

1 Generally speaking, renewal of any of the numerous rubber bushes in the rear suspension is a straightforward business. Press out the old one, give the new one a generous coating of washing-up liquid, press it in. Two bushes need further comment.
2 Bushes for the torque rods are marked and the marks should be placed at right angles to the rod (see Fig. 8.2).
3 The front bushes for the support arms have flats on them. Fit these so that a flat side is at right angles to the length of the support arm (Fig. 8.3).

5 Rear axle - general description

1 The rear axle is entirely conventional, of the hypoid type with the pinion below the centre-line of the crownwheel. It consists of pinion, crownwheel and differential gear. Gear backlash and differential carrier bearing loading are adjusted by shims inside the differential carrier bearings.
2 The differential gears in the differential carrier consist of two level pinions on a trunnion and two side gears in which the halfshafts are carried by internal splines.
3 The differential gears are journalled so that they can rotate, at different speeds. There is a thrust washer under each of the differential gears.
4 The pinion bearings are taper roller bearings. The axial location of the pinion relative to the crownwheel is adjusted by shims under the outer race of the rear pinion bearing.

6 Halfshaft - removal

1 Jack-up the car and remove the wheel. If you are removing the half-shafts as a preliminary to dismantling the back axle, note the remarks on jacking in Section 11, paragraph 1.
2 Unbolt and remove the brake calipers and brake disc (see Chapter 9).
3 Remove the parking brake shoes and their associated mechanism (Chapter 9).
4 Remove the bolts securing the brake backing plate to the back axle casing. You can get at these through holes in the halfshaft flange.

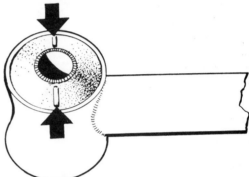

Fig. 8.2. Correct positioning of torque rod bushes (Sec. 4)

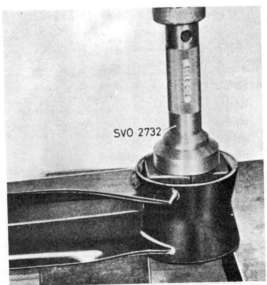

Fig. 8.3. Correct positioning of front bush in support arm (Sec. 4)

5 The halfshaft is now free to be withdrawn, bringing with it its bearing and the retaining plate which was bolted to the rear axle casing. A little judicious tapping with a hammer on a drift applied behind the flange may be necessary to start it off, but generally it presents no difficulty.

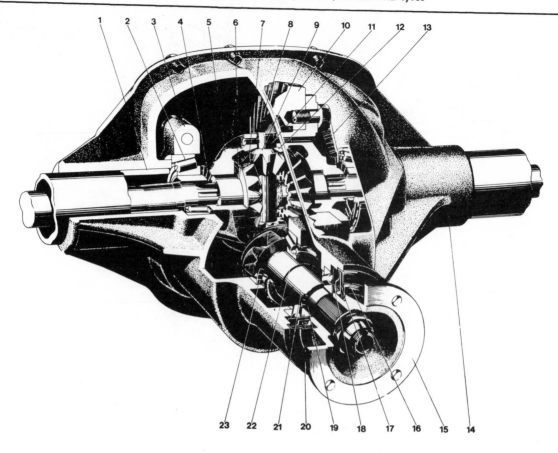

Fig. 8.4. Cut-away view of differential unit (Sec. 5)

1	Tubular shaft	6	Thrust washer	12	Thrust washer
2	Differential carrier	7	Differential side gear	13	Lock cover
	bearing	8	Lock pin	14	Rear axle casing
3	Bearing cap	9	Differential pinion	15	Flange
4	Shims	10	Crown wheel	16	Dust cover plate
5	Differential carrier	11	Shaft	17	Oil seal

18	Oil slinger
19	Shims
20	Front pinion bearing
21	Pinion
22	Rear pinion bearing
23	Shims

7 Halfshafts (broken) - removal

1 If the halfshaft is broken, the splined end will of course remain inside the axle when the outer end is withdrawn. Removal of the broken piece can be done without dismantling the rear axle or removing it from the car.

2 Remove the cover to the differential housing, being careful not to get any dirt into the differential as you do so.

3 With a piece of stiff wire or something similar, push the broken end of the halfshaft (which will still be engaged with the side gear) into the axle casing.

4 When you have got it well clear of the side gear, you will be able to fish it out with a hooked wire inserted at the outside end of the casing.

8 Halfshafts - bearings and oil seals - renewal

1 If halfshaft removal is part of a general overhaul of the rear axle, all oil seals should be renewed. This means that the taper bearing must be removed and renewed, even though it may be entirely satisfactory. If you have no facilities for pressing off the bearing and its locking ring, you can remove the locking ring by drilling and splitting (see Fig. 8.5). Use a ¼ inch (6 mm) drill and be careful you do not drill right through to the halfshaft.

2 Extract the inner seal from the axle casing.

3 Remove the bearing using a press or suitable extractor.

4 Remove the outer seal.

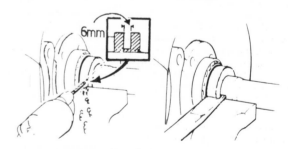

Fig. 8.5. Removing halfshaft bearing locking ring by drilling and splitting (Sec. 8)

5 Clean the bearing, giving it a final wash in white spirit to remove every trace of old grease and cleaning fluid. Examine for signs of wear or blueing. Renew if necessary.

6 Reassemble with new oil seals and (if necessary) a new bearing.

7 **Even if the old locking ring is intact, it must be renewed.**

8 Press or drive on the locking ring, making sure that the whole assembly is as close up as possible to the shoulder on the halfshaft.

9 Check the oil level (see Supplement).

9 Halfshafts - inspection

Clean and examine the halfshaft. The splines must be clean and sharp with no burrs and there must be no trace of twist or warp.

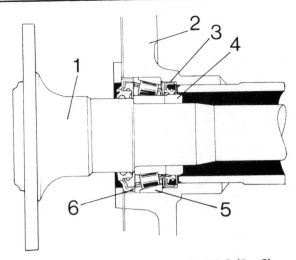

Fig. 8.6. Sectional view of rear hub and halfshaft (Sec. 8)

1 Halfshaft	4 Locking ring
2 Axle casing	5 Taper roller bearing
3 Inner oil seal	6 Outer oil seal

Fig. 8.8. Pulling off the flange (Sec. 12)

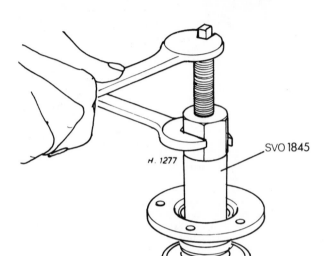

Fig. 8.7. Positioning axle stand correctly (Sec. 11)

Fig. 8.9. Pressing on the flange (Sec. 12)

10 Halfshafts - refitting

1 Pack the bearing with grease and then fit the halfshaft into the axle casing. Hold the halfshaft in a horizontal position and turn it slightly in both directions until the splines at its inner end can be felt to pick up and engage with those of the differential side gears.

2 Refit the bolts securing the backplate and retaining ring, tighten them to the specified torque.

3 Refit the brake mechanism, and bleed the brakes (see Chapter 9).

11 Rear axle - removal and refitting

1 Jack-up the rear of the car and support it securely on axle stands placed just in front of the car jacking point. Do not position the axle stands beyond the dotted line shown in Fig. 8.7. Support the rear axle on a jack, preferably a trolley type.

2 Remove the roadwheels.

3 Disconnect the shock absorber upper mounting bolts.

4 Release the brake pipes from the axle casing.

5 Unbolt and tie up the brake calipers with wire taking care not to bend or twist the pipes.

6 Remove the disc/drum assemblies, the handbrake shoes and other components and disconnect the handbrake cables from their operating levers and from their positioning clips either on the suspension arms or axle casing according to layout. These operations are described in Chapter 9.

7 Disconnect the propeller shaft rear flange from the pinion driving flange.

8 Disconnect the Panhard rod from the bracket on the rear axle housing.

9 Disconnect the roadsprings from the suspension arms.

10 Lower the rear axle and remove the springs.

11 Disconnect the suspension arm pivot bolts from the rear axle, also the bolts holding the torque rods to the axle housing.

12 Lower the jack and withdraw the rear axle from underneath and towards the rear of the car.

13 Refitting is a reversal of the removal operations.

14 Bleed the brakes as described in Chapter 9.

12 Pinion shaft oil seal - renewal

1 This can be done without removing the rear axle from the vehicle. Two simple press tools are needed to remove and refit the flange on the pinion shaft. The special Volvo tools are illustrated, and enough information given to enable you to produce adequate substitutes, in Figures 8.8 and 8.9.

2 Disconnect the rear section of the propeller shaft from the flange on the pinion.

3 Take the opportunity of checking the pinion shaft for looseness. If there is any appreciable play, particularly if the differential is noisy, you should be thinking about a complete overhaul.

4 If all is well, prevent the flange from turning while removing the nut from the shaft.

5 Pull the flange off the shaft.

6 Take off the dust cover and oil slinger and extract the oil seal.

7 Coat the new oil seal generously with grease, particularly all round the coil spring. This will prevent any tendency for the coil spring to come off the seal while you are fitting it. (Fig. 8.10).

8 Fit the oil seal, replace the dust cover and oil slinger, press the flange on to the shaft and tighten the nut to the specified torque.

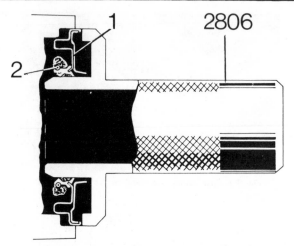

Fig. 8.10. Fitting the pinion shaft oil seal (Sec. 12)

1   Oil seal   2   Coil spring (well greased)

Fig. 8.11. Driving out the locking pin (Sec. 13)

13 Rear axle - overhaul

1   Unless certain tools are available or suitable substitutes can be made up, it is not recommended that the differential is dismantled as damage to unworn components caused by incorrect removal methods or brute force can be very expensive.
2   Before any work can be carried out the axle housing must be stretched to permit extraction of the crownwheel and differential assembly. The Volvo tools (SVO 2394 and 2601) required for this may possibly be borrowed, alternatively expansion struts can be made up using really heavy duty bolts with fine threads at the strut centres to expand the housing in two directions.
3   A micrometer will also be needed and a new set of crownwheel bolts to offset the stretch which has inevitably occurred in the original ones.
4   Remove the rear axle, as described in Section 11.
5   Take off the cover and look for alignment marks on the bearing caps and case which will tell you exactly where and which way round the bearing caps have to go. If there are no marks to be seen, dot punch the components.
6   At this stage it may be a good idea to check the meshing of the crownwheel and pinion as described in paragraph 28. This might give some fault indication which could be helpful later.
7   Remove the bearing caps.
8   Fit the expansion tool SVO 2394 to the axle housing and the axle casing. Then screw up the bolt three and a half turns. This will stretch the axle housing enough to enable the crownwheel and differential assembly to be lifted out.
9   Wash the interior of the housing with paraffin or cleaning fluid.
10 Undo the nut on the centre of the pinion shaft and pull off the coupling flange.
11 Extract the dust cover, oil slinger and oil seal.
12 Drive out the shaft and pinion. The outer ring of the rear bearing and the whole of the front bearing remain in the housing.
13 Between the rear bearing and housing will be found shims. These determine how far the pinion extends inside the case and hence control the meshing of the pinion with the crownwheel.
14 Between the front bearing and the housing will be found another set of shims. These shims fit against the shoulder on the pinion shaft and take up end play in the shaft.
15 Drive out the front bearing, using a drift just small enough to pass through the rear bearing ring. This need be no more than a disc backed up by a suitable length of rod. Clean the shims and put them on one side, making sure that you will know where they came from when you are reassembling.
16 Drive out the rear bearing ring and treat its shims likewise.
17 Mark the crownwheel and cage, take out the securing bolts and remove the cage from the crownwheel.
18 Drive out the locking pin followed by the shaft for the differential gears (Fig. 8.11).
19 Remove the differential gears and thrust washers.

20 Pull the bearings off the ends of the cage. Store them in such a way that you will know on reassembly which bearing and which shims went on which end of the cage.
21 Thoroughly clean all parts. Check all the bearing races and bearings. The races, rollers or roller containers must not be scratched or damaged, and assembled bearings must have no detectable play.
22 Check the crownwheel and pinion teeth for damage. Slight scuff marks may not mean that renewal is essential. The cause may be incorrect running-in, wrong oil, insufficient clearance or faulty tooth contact.
23 Check the teeth and splines of the side gears for damage.
24 Commence reassembly by refitting the differential cage, side gears and pinions. Whether the parts are new or old, they should be clean and dry so that you can check the thickness and loading tolerances accurately. Assemble the side gears in the cage, using the original positions even if you are putting in new gears. Insert the pinions and their washers and their shaft. Do not install the lock pin at this stage.
25 Check the side play of the side gears with feeler gauges, and if this is greater than 0.006 in (0.15 mm), take it up by increasing the thickness of the thrust washers on both sides by the same amount. The ideal condition is when a slight torque is needed to turn the side gears. Use a torque wrench working on something pushed into the splines (a piece of wood would do) and check that this torque does not exceed 14 lb f ft (2 kg f m). Use marker blue to check that the meshing of each of the side gears with the free pinions is the same. If it is not, transfer side washer thickness from one side to the other by increasing one side washer and decreasing the other by the same amount. When all is well, lock in the shaft with the locking pin. Make sure that the locking pin is firm in the cage.
26 Fit the crownwheel, not forgetting the bolt locking plate. Draw it down with the fixing bolts, and if it has been heated allow it to cool. Finally, tighten the fixing bolts to the specified torque wrench setting.
27 We now turn to the pinion. If you are using the original, assemble it with the original shims between the back bearing and the pinion. Be sure the bearing is pressed well home. If it is a new one, observe the marking code. If it is the same as the old one (very unlikely) use the same shims as before. If not, the shim thickness must be altered in accordance with the markings on the pinions. Mark 33 = 0.33 mm (0.013 in).
28 Having fitted the shims and back bearing on the pinion shaft, assemble it in the case, using only the back bearing for the time being. Now put the bearings on the cage without any shims, put the crownwheel and cage assembly in the case and temporarily screw down the bearing caps. **Do not** fit the expansion tool SVO 2394 at this stage. Get the crownwheel meshing with the pinion, and using marker blue observe the pattern made on the crownwheel by the pinion. Fig. 8.3 shows what this should look like and how to tell whether your pinion is set too near or too far from the centre of the crownwheel. You can get the areas of the patterns approximately equal by moving the cage assembly slightly from side to side (ultimately the shims fitted behind the bearings will sort this out), but at this stage you are simply concerned with getting them evenly spaced. If they are not, you will have

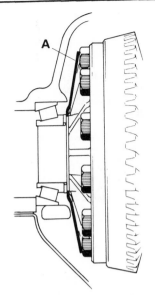

Fig. 8.12. Location of crownwheel bolt lockplate (A) (Sec. 13)

to drive out the pinion shaft and alter the shims until you get it right. Check the patterns at three points on the crownwheel in case it is warped.

29 When these shims are correct, put back the original front shim thickness altered by the same amount as you have altered the back shim thickness. Fit the front bearing and the flange. Do not bother about the oil seal or slinger and dust cover at this stage as this is only a trial run. Use the original fixing nut, and tighten it carefully. If there is a tendency for the pinion to bind before the nut is fully tightened, remove the nut, remove the flange, and drive out the pinion. Increase the shim thickness and try again. If, on the other hand, you get end play, estimate as best you can (eg. by using feeler gauges between the pinion and case) how much end play there is, take out the pinion, remove the front bearing ring and increase the shim thickness. You should aim to get a very slight stiffness, which can be measured by the bar and spring balance method shown in Fig. 8.14 and should be not less than 0.52 lb and not more than 0.95 lb unless you have fitted new bearings, in which case the reading on the spring balance should be between 0.9 and 2.3 lb. If the stiffness is too great, of course, you will have to reduce the shim thickness. If you are unlucky, you may have to have two or three tries, but there is one consolation - when you have got through this stage you are over the worst of it.

30 When the shims are correct, take off the flange again and fit the oil seal, oil slinger and dust cover. This time fix the flange to the shaft with a new fixing nut and tighten to specified torque.

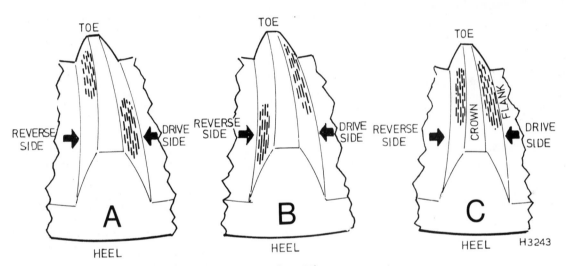

Fig. 8.13. Pinion/crownwheel tooth markings and their interpretation (Sec. 13)

A Pinion too far from centre of crownwheel - increase shim pack
B Pinion too near centre of crownwheel - decrease shim pack
C Pinion to crownwheel mesh correct

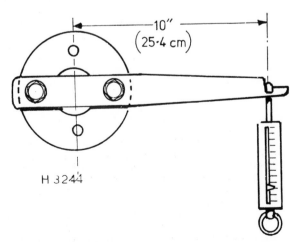

Fig. 8.14. Device for measuring pinion bearing pre-load (Sec. 13)

31 It now remains to adjust the play and centring of the crownwheel/ cage assembly. Start off by choosing a shim thickness 0.003 in (0.076 mm) less than the original shim thickness on each side, putting the appropriate shims behind the bearings and pushing the bearings well home. If, having done this, the assembly will not go into the car, reduce the shim thickness by another 0.002 in (0.05 mm). We suggest that you try this rather than taking out 0.005 in (0.12 mm) straight away because there is quite a chance that the smaller reduction will give the right answer.

32 Check the end play in each direction, and use marker blue to observe the meshing patterns of the pinion and crownwheel as previously described, but this time you are after equality of area. If necessary, alter shim thickness from one side to the other to get the desired result.

33 Once you have got the shims correct, remove the assembly from the casing and add a further 0.003 in (0.076 mm) to each side. Then reassemble, using the expansion tool to stretch the case and enable the assembly to go in. Three or four turns on the screw of the expansion tool should be sufficient.

34 Fit the bearing caps, but do not at this stage tighten the bolts more than fingertight. Remove the expansion tool, tighten the cap bolts to the specified torque.

35 Fit inspection cover with new gasket, bolt down evenly all round.

36 Reinstall the halfshafts as described in Section 10 and the rear axle is ready to to be refitted to the vehicle.
37 Refill the axle with the correct grade and quantity of oil.

14 Wheels and tyres - general

1 The roadwheels are of pressed steel.
2 Periodically remove the wheels, clean dirt and mud from the inside and outside surfaces and examine for signs of rusting or rim damage. Rectify as necessary.
3 Apply a smear of light grease to the wheel studs before screwing on the nuts and finally tighten them to the specified torque.
4 The tyres are of radial construction. Never mix tyres of different construction and regularly check and maintain the pressures.
5 If the wheels have been balanced on the car then it is important that the wheels are not moved round the vehicle in an effort to equalise tread wear. If a wheel is removed, then the relationship of the wheel studs to the holes in the wheel should be marked to ensure exact replacement, otherwise the balance of wheel, hub and tyre will be upset.
6 Where the wheels have been balanced off the car, then they may be moved round to equalise wear. Include the spare wheel in any rotational pattern. With radial tyres, do not move the wheels from one side to the other but only interchange the front and rear wheels on the same side.
7 Balancing of the wheels is an essential factor in good steering and roadholding. When the tyres have been in use for about half their useful life the wheels should be rebalanced, to compensate for the lost tread rubber due to wear.
8 Inspect the tyre walls and treads regularly for cuts and damage and where evident, have them professionally repaired.

15 Fault diagnosis - rear axle and suspension

Symptom	Reason/s
Rear suspension	
Excessive pitching and rolling on corners and during braking	Defective shock absorbers and/or broken spring.
Suspension 'bottoms' on large bumps (car normally loaded)	Weak or broken springs.
Car sags at one 'corner'	Weak or broken springs.
Rear axle	
Noise on drive overrun	Low oil level.
	Loose crownwheel bolts.
	Loose bearing cap bolts.
	General wear in bearing or gear teeth.
Noise on turn	Seized, broken or damaged pinion side gear or thrust washers.
Knock during gearshift or when taking up drive	Excessive crownwheel to pinion backlash.
	Worn gears.
	Worn halfshaft splines.
	Drive pinion nut loose.
	Loose crownwheel bolts or bearing cap bolts.
	Worn side gear splines.

Chapter 9 Braking system

For modifications, and information applicable to later models, see Supplement at end of manual

Contents

Specifications

Front wheel brakes

Type	Discs - Girling or ATE
Brake discs	
Outer diameter	10.35 in (263 mm)
Thickness - new	0.563 in (14.3 mm)
- reconditioned	min. 0.517 in (13.14 mm)
Warp	max. 0.004 in (0.10 mm)
Brake linings	
Thickness - new	0.394 in (10 mm)
Effective area, Girling	26 sq in (166 sq cm)
ATE	22.5 sq in (145 sq cm)
Designation, Girling	DB 818 FG
ATE	Ferodo 2441 FFG
Wheel cylinders	
Area, Girling 1975	1.59 sq in (10.25 sq cm)
1976	1.76 sq in (11.34 sq cm)
ATE	1.58 sq in (10.17 sq cm)

Rear wheel brakes

Type	Discs - Girling or ATE
Brake discs	
Outer diameter	11.06 in (281 mm)
Thickness - new	0.378 in (9.6 mm)
- reconditioned	min. 0.331 in (8.4 mm)
Warp	max. 0.004 in (0.10 mm)
Brake linings	
Thickness - new, Girling	0.31 in (8 mm)
ATE	0.394 in (10 mm)
Effective area, Girling	15.5 sq in (100 sq cm)
ATE	16.3 sq in (105 sq cm)
Designation, Girling	DB 824 FF
ATE	Ferodo 2442 FFG
Wheel cylinders	
Area, Girling	1.77 sq in (11.43 sq cm)
ATE	1.75 sq in (11.33 sq cm)

Master cylinder

Type	Tandem with step piston
Secondary cylinder, nominal diameter	0.621 in (15.75 mm)
Primary cylinder, nominal diameter	0.878 in (22.3 mm)

Brake valve (pressure regulating)	**1975**	**1976**
Make, designation	ATE BRM 18	ATE BRM 18
Cut-out points, 242, 244	427 psi (30 kg/sq cm)	483 psi (34 kg/sq cm)
245	640 psi (45 kg/sq cm)	640 psi (45 kg/sq cm)

Servo cylinder

Type	Direct	
Make, size, B21E	DBA, tandem 8 in	
B20A (auto. transmission)	Girling, 10 in or tandem 8 in	
B21A (auto. transmission)	Girling, 10 in or DBA 9 in	
B20A (manual gearbox)	DBA 9 in	
240 (right-hand steering)	Girling, tandem 8 in	

Reduction ratio

Girling/DBA tandem 8 in	1 : 4	
Girling 10 in	1 : 3.5	
DBA 9 in	1 : 3.5	

Handbrake

Brake drum, diameter	max. 6.32 in (160.45 mm)	
radial throw	max. 0.006 in (0.15 mm)	
out-of-round	max. 0.008 in (0.2 mm)	
Brake linings, effective area	27.28 sq in (176 sq cm)	

Torque wrench settings

	lb f ft	kg f m
Retaining bolts, front brake caliper	65 - 72	9 - 10
Retaining bolts, rear brake caliper	38 - 46	5.2 - 6.4
Retaining bolts, armature	33 - 40	4.5 - 5.5
Retaining nuts, rear guard plate	22 - 36	3 - 5
Wheel nuts	72 - 94	10 - 13
Retaining nuts, master cylinder	22 - 36	3 - 5
Bleeder nipples	2.5 - 4	0.35 - 0.55
Brake pipe unions	5.8 - 8.7	0.8 - 1.2
Brake hoses to brake valve	8.7 - 11.5	1.2 - 1.6
Master cylinder stop screw	6	0.8
Pressure warning switch	15	2.1

1 General description

1 The braking system is a four wheel hydraulic operated disc type. The hydraulic system is of dual circuit layout with each circuit operating two of the front four caliper pistons and a rear brake caliper. This arrangement ensures that half the braking system will be effective in the event of a failure of pressure in one circuit. The master cylinder is step-bored which ensures a braking power that is not noticeably diminished should one brake circuit fail. The driver is, however, warned by an indicator light which is activated by a pressure differential valve in the brake system.

2 The servo cylinder is directly actuated by the brake pedal. Vacuum assistance, obtained from a vacuum pump and the intake manifold, results in reduced pedal pressure being required for braking.

3 Pressure regulating valves are incorporated in each of the rear wheel brake lines to prevent the rear wheels locking in advance of the front wheels during heavy brake application.

4 The handbrake consists of cable operated brake shoes enclosed in small brake drums on the rear hubs.

2 Bleeding the hydraulic system

1 Whenever the hydraulic system has been overhauled, a part renewed or the level in the reservoir has become too low, air will have entered

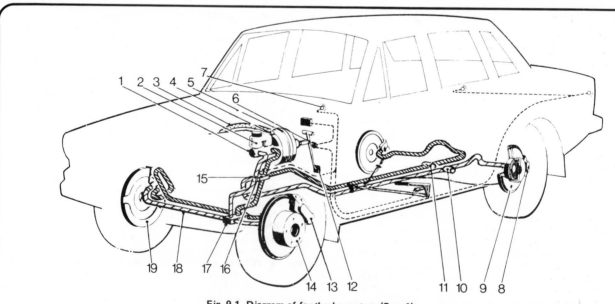

Fig. 9.1. Diagram of footbrake system (Sec. 1)

1	Tandem master cylinder	6	Brake switch	11	Brake valve, primary circuit
2	Brake fluid container	7	Warning lamp	12	Brake pedal
3	Vacuum line	8	Rear brake caliper	13	Front brake caliper
4	Check valve	9	Brake disc with drum	14	Brake disc
5	Servo cylinder	10	Brake valve, secondary circuit	15	Warning switch

16	Warning valve
17	6-branch union, (double 3-branch union)
18	Brake pipe
19	Cover plate

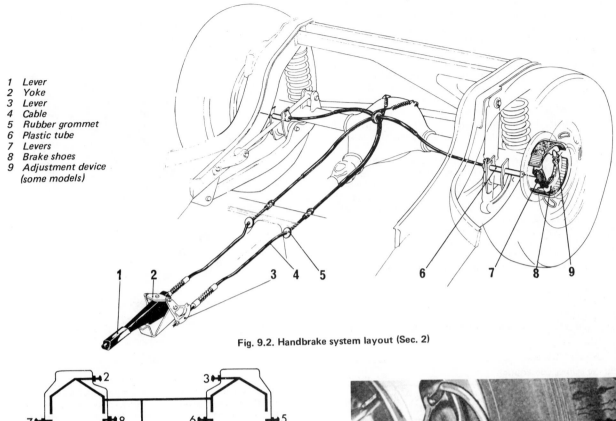

1 Lever
2 Yoke
3 Lever
4 Cable
5 Rubber grommet
6 Plastic tube
7 Levers
8 Brake shoes
9 Adjustment device
   (some models)

Fig. 9.2. Handbrake system layout (Sec. 2)

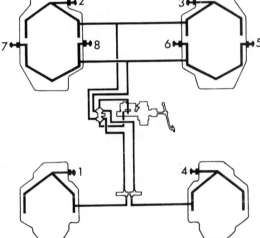

Fig. 9.3. Bleeding sequence (Sec. 2)

1 Left rear wheel
2 Left front wheel, upper,
   inner
3 Right front wheel, upper,
   inner
4 Right rear wheel

5 Right front wheel, outer
6 Right front wheel, lower
   inner
7 Left front wheel, outer
8 Left front wheel, lower
   inner

Fig. 9.4. Bleeding a front wheel brake unit (Sec. 2)

the system. This will cause some or all of the pedal travel to be used
up in compressing air rather than pushing fluid against brake pistons.
If only a little air is present the pedal will have a 'spongy' feel, but if
an appreciable amount has entered, the pedal will not offer any appreciable resistance to the foot and the brakes will hardly work at all.
2   To overcome this, brake fluid must be pumped through the hydraulic system until all the air has been passed out in the form of bubbles
in the fluid. If only one rear brake caliper has been removed and little
brake fluid run out, you may get away with bleeding this brake circuit
only, but otherwise you should bleed the whole system whenever you
have worked on it.
3   The system should be bled in the order shown in Fig. 9.3.
4   One or two points should be watched when bleeding the brakes:
a) Before you start, depress the brake pedal several times in order to

destroy vacuum in the servo cylinder.
b) Make sure that the bleed nipples and their immediate surroundings
are thoroughly clean. Dirt is the deadly enemy of hydraulic systems.
c) Remove the switch from the warning valve.
d) Clean round the cap on the brake fluid container and clean the cap
itself, making sure that the vent hole of the cap is clean. You are going
to have to take the cap on and off to top the reservoir up when you are
bleeding the brakes. If you leave the cap off all the time dirt may
enter the system. You can see the fluid level perfectly well through
the translucent container even when the cap is on.
5   Have a look at Fig. 9.4. This shows a transparent tube fitted over
one of the bleed nipples and fed into a bottle containing brake fluid,
the end of the tube dipping below the brake fluid. This is essential to
avoid air being sucked back into the system as the bleeding procedure

is carried out. The nipple is unscrewed half a turn anticlockwise which enables brake fluid to pass through it from the brake cylinder. Use a 5/16 AF spanner to slacken the nipple.

6   When all is set up, fill the master cylinder reservoir with brake fluid up to the 'Max' mark and have an assistant pump the brake pedal up and down; this will pump fluid through the system and into the bottle. Once you have an inch or so of brake fluid in the bleeding jar, it is essential that the end of the bleed tube remains immersed until the bleed nipple is retightened. Keep the reservoir topped up as the level falls - never let it get as low as the 'Min' mark or air will re-enter the system. The correct method of pumping is to press the brake pedal slowly as far down as it will go, pause a little and then quickly release it.

7   At first, air bubbles will be present in the liquid passing through the tube, but after a while it will be completely free of them. When this is so, press the pedal to the bottom and screw up the bleed nipple. Do not forget to refit the rubber cap on the nipple when you take off the tube and spanner. Recommended tightening torque for the nipple is 12 - 15 lb f ft (1.6 - 2.0 kg f m). Generally it is only necessary to go round the whole car once, but if at the end of this, the brake pedal still feels 'spongy', the process should be repeated until all is well.

8   Finally, fill the brake fluid reservoir up to the 'Max' mark and refit the warning switch, tightening it to a torque of 10-15 lb f ft (1.4-2.0 kg f m).

9   Two final points about the brake fluid itself:
a) Do not let the fluid come in contact with friction surfaces or linings or with paintwork.
b) Do not return any of the fluid pumped out during bleeding to the system - discard it.

3   Disc brake caliper - description

1   Fig. 9.5 shows a diagram of the front wheel brake caliper. This caliper consists of a housing in two halves - referred to as the inner and outer half, Nos 6 and 14 in Fig. 9.5,- bolted together and located on either side of the brake disc. Each half contains two cylinders and pistons. In the diagram the outer half is cut away to show the cylinder and piston assembly.

2   The cut away portion carries a bleed nipple which is additional to those illustrated in the diagram.

3   The two upper cylinders are connected together and fed from one of the hydraulic circuits, while the two lower cylinders are fed from the other one.

4   The sealing rings (1) Fig. 9.5 as well as preventing brake fluid from oozing out act as return springs for the pistons. When hydraulic pressure is released these rings, which distort as the piston moves past them, return to their natural shape and in so doing pull back the piston slightly. The amount of withdrawal of the piston is always the same, so that the system automatically compensates for wear in the brake pads and needs no adjustment.

5   Fig. 9.6 shows a diagram of the rear brake calipers, which operate in just the same manner as the front ones except that they only have one cylinder each. Each rear cylinder is fed by a different hydraulic circuit, so that if one circuit fails half the rear braking effort is still present.

4   Brake pads - removal and replacement

1   At intervals, specified in Routine Maintenance, jack-up and remove each road wheel in turn and examine the thickness of the friction material on the disc pads. This can be judged by the nearness of the pad backing plate to the tension spring but for a really accurate assessment it is necessary to remove the damping spring.

2   If the pads have worn down to between 1/8 and 1/16 in (1.6 and 3.2 mm) they must be renewed.

3   *Girling:* Remove the hairpin-shaped locking clips for the guide pins. Pull out one of the retaining pins while holding the damper spring in place. Remove the springs and the other retaining pin (photos).
ATE: Tap out the upper retaining pin with a drift. Take out the damper spring and tap out the lower retaining pin.

4   Withdraw the disc pads, gripping them with pliers if they prove hard to remove. If the pads are to be used again, mark them to ensure they are restored to their original position (photo).

6   Clean the inside faces of the housings and examine the dust covers

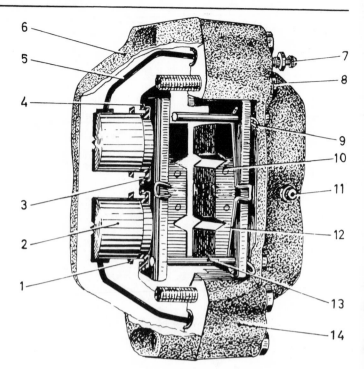

Fig. 9.5. Front brake caliper assembly - Girling (Sec. 3)

1	Seal	8	Bolt
2	Piston	9	Retaining clip
3	Rubber dust cover	10	Brake pad
4	Retaining ring	11	Lower bleeder nipple
5	Channel	12	Damping spring
6	Outer half	13	Retaining pin
7	Upper bleeder nipple	14	Inner half

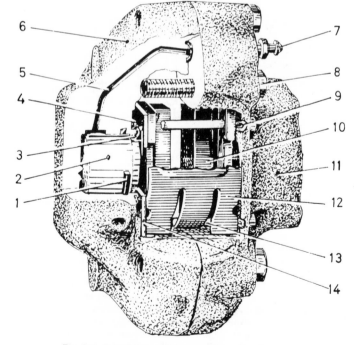

Fig. 9.6. Rear brake caliper assembly - Girling (Sec. 3)

1	Seal	8	Bolt
2	Piston	9	Retaining clip
3	Rubber dust cover	10	Brake pad
4	Retaining ring	11	Inner half
5	Channel	12	Damping spring
6	Outer half	13	Retaining pin
7	Bleeder nipple	14	Washer

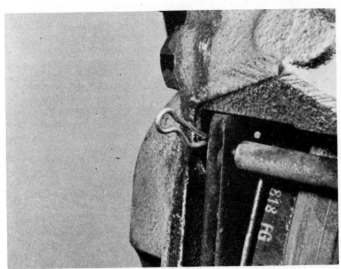
4.3a The hairpin-shaped lock clip (Girling)

4.3b Removing the retaining pin and the springs (Girling)

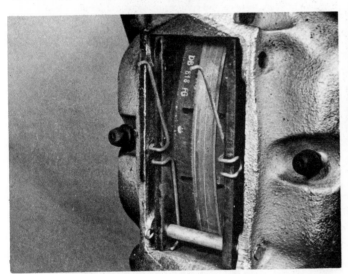
4.3c Remove the other retaining pin and the springs (Girling)

4.4 Withdraw the brake pad (Girling)

protecting the cylinders. Replace any dust covers that are damaged. They are held on to the housing by clip rings and are easily removed.

7   To make room for the new pads, push the pistons down into the cylinders with a screwdriver or the like, taking great care not to damage the dust covers while you do so. Depressing the pistons will cause the fluid level in the master cylinder reservoir to rise. Anticipate this by syphoning out some fluid using an old (clean) hydrometer or syringe.

8   Fitting new pads or refitting the old ones is simply a reversal of the removal procedure.

9   Depress the footbrake pedal several times to position the pads against the disc and then check and top-up the master cylinder fluid reservoir.

10 Disc pads should be renewed in axle sets, not just one wheel only, so repeat the foregoing operations on the opposite wheel.

11 Any nuisance caused by disc pad squeal on the rear brakes may be due to incorrect positioning of the piston cut-out.

5   Front calipers - removal and refitting

1   Jack-up the front end of the car and support it on axle stands placed under the front jack attachments. It is important to do this so that when the hoses are refitted they are free from torsion under normal conditions.

2   Temporarily block the vent hole in the brake fluid container cover to reduce leakage when the brake hoses are disconnected.

Fig. 9.7. Front wheel brake caliper (Sec. 5)

3   Disconnect the brake hoses at the caliper (photo).
4   Remove the two caliper retaining bolts and lift away the caliper (photo).
5   Replacement is in the main simply a reversal of the removal procedure, but it should be done with care. Check that the contact surfaces of the caliper and frame are clean and undamaged.
6   The brake disc should be central in the caliper and parallel to it. This can be checked by measuring the distances between the bosses at the top and bottom of the caliper and the disc, with spacers and feeler gauges. The difference between these distances should not exceed 0.022 in (0.55 mm). The location of the caliper can be adjusted with shims which are available in thicknesses of 0.008 in and 0.016 in (0.2 - 0.4 mm). Coat the fixing bolts with a couple of drops of Loctite, Type AV.
7   When all is finished, do not forget to open the hole in the brake fluid container cover which you blocked up to reduce leakage.
8   Check that the brake discs can rotate easily in the brake pads.
9   Bleed the brake system as described in Section 2.

6   Rear brake calipers - removal and refitting

1   The procedure for rear calipers is basically the same as for the front. The car should be jacked up and supported on its rear axle to ensure that when the hoses are fitted they are not in torsion under normal load conditions. Fig. 9.8 shows the caliper fitted in position.

7   Brake calipers - overhaul

1   Absolute cleanliness is essential when dismantling and reassembling these units. Clean the outside thoroughly before you start. Before dismantling ATE type brake calipers mark the pistons so that you can refit them in the same position with regard to the rim step.
2   Remove the dust cover retaining rings (if fitted) and the dust covers themselves. Place a piece of wood about ½ in (12.5 mm) thick between the pistons and apply compressed air to one of the hoses connected to the caliper to push the pistons out. Only quite low air pressure is required such as is generated by a hand or foot-operated tyre pump. If by any chance the piston is jammed in the housing and will not yield to this treatment, a local garage may be able to apply a high pressure air line for you.
3   Remove the inner sealing rings with a small screwdriver, being very careful not to scratch the bore or damage the groove. It is a good idea to round off the corners of screwdrivers used for this sort of thing.
4   Unscrew the bleed nipples, hose connections etc., from the unit but do not attempt to separate the two halves as reassembling them is a factory job needing specialised equipment.
5   Give the various parts and connecting paths a thorough clean

5.3 Front brake caliper (Girling)

5.4 Removing the rear caliper (Girling)

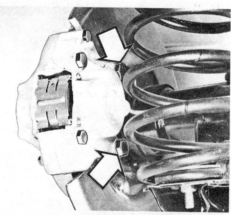

Fig. 9.8. Rear wheel brake caliper - Girling
Arrows show attachment bolts (Sec. 6)

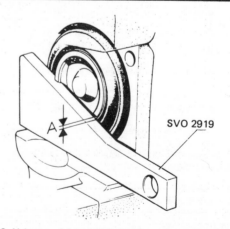

Fig. 9.9. Using special tool SVO 2919 to align ATE caliper piston (Sec. 7)
A (clearance to cut-out step) = 0.04 in (1 mm)

with methylated spirit - about the only fluid which you can guarantee will not affect the rubber seals. Dry the various bits and pieces with a lint-free rag. A hair drier is very useful for the fluid pathways, to make sure - as you must - that all methylated spirit is removed.

6   Thoroughly inspect the various parts. If any of the cylinders is scored or scratched the entire cylinder housing must be replaced complete. Replace any other damaged or worn parts.

7   Reassembly is straightforward. Coat the various parts with brake fluid before assembling them. Fit the inner sealing rings into their grooves, making sure they are the right way round (see Fig. 9.5). Fit the pistons with the large ends inside the housings. In the case of ATE type brakes the outer end of the piston (stepped part) should incline 20° as shown in Fig. 9.9. You will not need a special template if you marked the piston before dismantling as recommended in paragraph 1. If you are replacing the piston with a new one, compare new with old and mark the new one in the same place.

8   Disc - inspection, removal and refitting

1   Each time that the disc pads require renewal, take the opportunity to examine the surfaces of the discs.

2   Light scoring is normal but deep grooves will mean that the disc must be renewed or machined provided that the thickness is not reduced below 0.51 in (13.4 mm), for the front discs and 0.331 in (8.4 mm) for the rear.

3   Disc run-out (out of true) must not exceed 0.004 in (0.1 mm) and should be measured by turning the disc against the plunger of a dial gauge. If this instrument is not available, feeler blades can give an approximate indication if they are used to measure the gap between the disc and a fixed point.

4   *To remove a front disc,* unbolt the caliper and tie it securely to one side to prevent strain on the flexible hoses.

5   Remove the disc/hub securing screws and withdraw the assembly.

6   *To remove a rear disc,* unbolt the caliper, remove the clip which secures the rigid brake line to the rear axle casing and pull the caliper far enough away from the disc to tie it up without bending the brake pipe. Insert a screwdriver in the adjuster hole in the handbrake drum and release the shoe adjustment.

7   Unscrew and remove the two retaining screws and withdraw the disc/drum assembly.

8   Refitting is a reversal of removal but adjust the handbrake shoes on the rear brake so that the drum is stiff to turn and then back off the adjuster by between 4 and 5 teeth, see Section 18.

9   Master cylinder - removal, overhaul and replacement

1   Fig. 9.10 shows the master cylinder fitted on the front face of the vacuum servo booster unit with the fluid reservoir on top.

2   The basic principle on which the cylinder works is perfectly simple. There are two pistons in tandem, the primary piston and the secondary piston. There is no difference in function - and there is certainly no difference in importance - between primary and secondary pistons and the circuits connected to them; the primary piston is so called because it is the one that gets pushed first. If all is working properly, pressure building up in front of the primary piston pushes forward the secondary piston and the same hydraulic pressure is exerted in both primary and secondary circuits. If the primary circuit develops a leak the primary piston is simply carried on until it meets the secondary piston and pushes it forward physically. If there is a leak in the secondary circuit, the secondary piston will carry on until it hits the end of the master cylinder, but pressure will be maintained in front of the primary cylinder and in the primary circuit.

3   To remove the master cylinder, first lift off the brake fluid reservoir. Nothing has to be unscrewed first - it simply sits on top of two rubber seals. If you put your fingers over the bottom holes quickly you will lose very little fluid. A rag placed underneath the cylinder will help to prevent what you do lose from dripping on to places where it is not wanted.

4   Remove the brake lines from the master cylinder and plug them with plastic plugs. Undo the fixing nuts and remove the cylinder.

5   Clean the outside of the cylinder thoroughly.

6   Lever out the rubber seals from the master cylinder.

7   Unscrew and remove the stop screw.

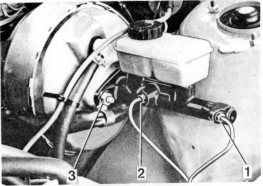

Fig. 9.10. Master cylinder and reservoir (Sec. 9)

1   *Connection for secondary circuit*
2   *Connection for primary circuit*
3   *Retaining bolts*

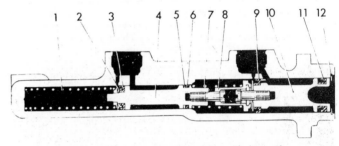

Fig. 9.11. Sectional view of master cylinder (Sec. 9)

1 *Spring*	7 *Spring*
2 *Spring seat*	8 *Connector sleeve*
3 *Seal*	9 *Seal*
4 *Secondary piston*	10 *Primary piston*
5 *Seal*	11 *Seal*
6 *Seal*	12 *Snap ring*

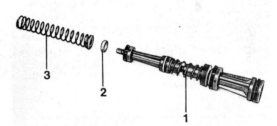

Fig. 9.12. Assembling the master cylinder (Sec. 9)

1   *Piston assembly*   2   *Spring seat*   3   *Spring*

8   Extract the circlip from the end of the master cylinder and withdraw the primary and secondary piston assemblies.

9   At this stage, examine the surfaces of the pistons and cylinder. If they are scored or show any evidence of 'bright' wear areas, the master cylinder should be renewed complete.

10   If these components are in good condition, discard all rubber seals and wash the parts in clean hydraulic fluid or methylated spirit - nothing else.

11   Obtain a repair kit which will contain all the necessary renewable items including new seals.

12   Commence reassembly by installing the seals to the secondary piston. Make sure that the seal lips face the correct way.

13   Install the back-up ring, the thrust washer and the spring to the secondary piston and then dip the assembly in clean hydraulic fluid and insert it into the master cylinder. Take care not to turn over or trap the seal lips.

14   To the primary piston, fit the washer, the piston seal, the plastic washer, the second seal and the second washer. Make sure that the seal

lips face the correct direction.

15 Dip the primary piston assembly in clean hydraulic fluid and insert it into the master cylinder. Take care not to trap or bend back the lips of the seals.

16 Depress the piston far enough to be able to fit the circlip.

17 Fit the stop screw using a new sealing washer. Tighten the screw to a torque of 6 lb f ft (0.8 kg f m).

18 Fit new reservoir to master cylinder sealing collars and push the fluid reservoir firmly into position.

19 Fill the reservoir with clean hydraulic fluid which has remained unshaken for 24 hours and has been stored in an airtight container.

20 Depress the master cylinder piston several times to expel any trapped air and then plug the fluid outlet holes to prevent loss of fluid while the cylinder is being installed.

21 Fit the 'O' ring seal to the master cylinder mounting flange, install the cylinder to the front face of the servo unit, fit the washers and nuts and tighten them to the specified torque.

22 Remove the temporary plugs and connect the fluid lines to the master cylinder.

23 Bleed the complete hydraulic system, as described in Section 2.

Fig. 9.13. Fitting the piston assembly (Sec. 9)

10 Pressure warning valve - resetting

1   The switch is basically a piston assembly which is kept in balance by the equal pressure in the two hydraulic circuits.

2   When a fault causes a drop in pressure in one of the circuits, the piston is displaced and a plunger type switch actuates a warning lamp on the instrument panel.

3   The following operations are necessary before the piston can return to its 'in balance' position.

4   Disconnect the lead from the switch terminal and unscrew the switch from the valve body.

5   Repair the fault or leak and bleed the faulty circuit.

6   The piston assembly will now have returned to its normal setting and the switch should be screwed in and tightened to a torque of 15 lb f ft (2.1 kg f m).

11 Rear brake valves - removal and refitting

1   Any fault in either of the two brake valves which are incorporated in the rear brake lines can only be rectified by renewing the valve complete.

2   To remove a valve, disconnect the rigid brake pipe from the valve and plug the pipe to prevent loss of fluid.

3   Using a close fitting spanner just release the flexible brake hose from the valve. Do not unscrew it more than a quarter of a turn.

4   Unbolt the brake valve and then unscrew the valve body from the flexible hose. Do not twist the hose during this operation.

5   Refitting of the new valve is a reversal of the removal procedure.

6   On completion bleed the hydraulic circuit as described in Section 2.

12 Brake pedal - dismantling and reassembly

1   Remove the panel under the dashboard.

2   Remove the brake stoplamp switch and bracket.

3   Disconnect the pushrod link from the brake pedal.

4   Unscrew and remove the pedal pivot bolt and nut and lift the pedal away.

5   Bushes and sleeves can be fitted to the pedal and linkage by pressing out the old ones and fitting new ones. Apply grease to the bearing surfaces on reassembly.

6   When fitting the stoplamp switch, adjust it as described in Section 13.

13 Brake stoplamp switch - adjustment

1   Make sure that the footbrake pedal is fully released and then measure the distance between the switch and the pedal arm, A in Fig. 9.16.

2   The distance should be 0.16 in (4 mm). Adjust by slackening the retaining screws and moving the switch bracket. Retighten the retaining screws.

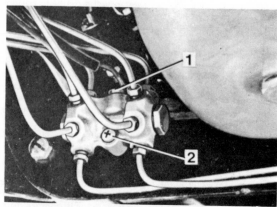

Fig. 9.14. Pressure warning valve (Sec. 10)

1   Pressure warning valve   2   Retaining screw

Fig. 9.15. Removing a brake valve (Sec. 11)

14 Servo brake booster system - general description

1   A vacuum servo unit is fitted in the brake system between the brake pedal and the master cylinder to provide assistance to the driver when the brake pedal is depressed. This reduces the effort required by the driver to operate the brakes under all braking conditions.

2   The unit operates by vacuum from a separate vacuum pump driven from the engine camshaft, B20 engines, or intermediate shaft, B21 engines. It is connected to the engine intake manifold which means that there is still some vacuum available in the event of pump failure.

3   The brake servo booster unit and hydraulic master cylinder are connected together so that the servo unit piston rod acts as the master

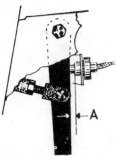

Fig. 9.16. Adjusting the brake stoplamp switch (Sec. 13)

cylinder pushrod. The driver's braking effort is transmitted through another pushrod to the servo unit piston and its built in control system. The servo unit piston does not fit tightly into the cylinder, but has a strong diaphragm to keep its edges in constant contact with the cylinder wall, so assuring an airtight seal between the two parts. The forward chamber is held under vacuum conditions created in the inlet manifold of the engine and, during periods when the brake pedal is not in use, the controls open a passage to the rear chamber so placing it under vacuum conditions as well. When the brake pedal is depressed, the vacuum passage to the rear chamber is cut off and the chamber opened to atmospheric pressure. The consequent rush of air pushes the servo piston forward in the vacuum chamber and operates the main pushrod to the master cylinder.

4 The controls are designed so that assistance is given under all conditions and, when the brakes are not required, vacuum in the rear chamber is established when the brake pedal is released. All air from the atmosphere entering the rear chamber is passed through a small air filter.

5 It is emphasised that the servo unit assists in reducing the braking effort required at the foot pedal and in the event of its failure, the hydraulic braking system is in no way endangered, except that the need for higher pedal pressures will be noticed.

6 The servo unit should not be serviced, overhauled or dismantled and in the event of a fault occurring it should be replaced.

15 Servo booster unit - removal and refitting

1 Remove the master cylinder as described in Section 9.
2 Disconnect the vacuum hose from the booster unit.
3 Disconnect the link arm from the brake pedal.
4 Remove the bracket which supports the clutch pedal stop.
5 Remove the four nuts securing the unit to the bulkhead.

6 Pull the unit forward and then disconnect the pushrod clevis fork from the brake pedal link arm.
7 Refitting is the reverse of the removal procedure.
8 Bleed the hydraulic system as described in Section 2.

16 Servo unit vacuum pump - removal, overhaul and refitting

1 Disconnect both hoses from the vacuum pump.
2 Unscrew and remove the mounting bolts and withdraw the pump.
3 Clean away all external dirt and the secure the pump in a vice. Remove the valve housing cover (Fig. 9.18).
4 Scribe a line across the edges of the upper and lower body flanges to facilitate reassembly.
5 Unscrew the flange screws and separate the upper and lower bodies.
6 Unscrew the centre bolt and remove the diaphragm, washers and spring from the lower housing (Fig. 9.19).
7 Invert the pump and remove the lower cover.
8 Extract the lever shaft, lever and pump rod.
9 Renew worn components by obtaining the appropriate repair kits.
10 Reassembly is a reversal of dismantling but make sure that the diaphragm centre bolt is fitted with its washer and O-ring. Clean the centre bolt threads and coat them with Loctite.
11 Make sure that the raised sides of the diaphragm is upwards and the dished sides of the washers are against the diaphragm.
12 Tighten the centre bolt making sure that the hole in the diaphragm is opposite the one in the housing.
13 Refit the pump to the engine and reconnect the hoses to their respective connections.

17 Non-return valves - removal and refitting

1 Three non-return valves are incorporated in the vacuum system. One is located directly on the servo booster unit, one in the hose to the intake manifold and one in the hose to the vacuum reservoir, see Fig. 9.20.
2 To renew the hoses or non-return valves, release the hose clips and separate the hoses.
3 When fitting the non-return valves, make sure that the arrows on the valve point the right way.

18 Handbrake - description and adjustment

1 The handbrake operates mechanically through cables to shoes and drums at the rear wheels. The layout is shown in Fig. 9.2.
2 The parking brake lever acts on two levers via a yoke. The cables are routed parallel with the propeller shaft tunnel. The cables cross

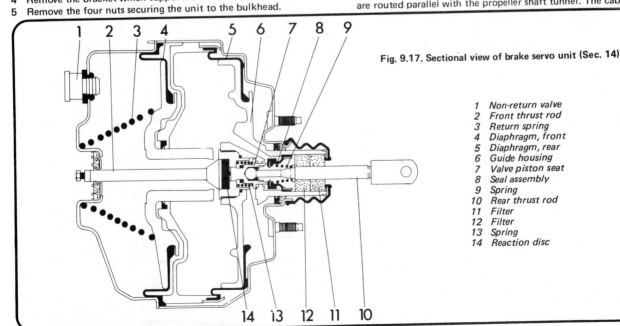

Fig. 9.17. Sectional view of brake servo unit (Sec. 14)

1 Non-return valve
2 Front thrust rod
3 Return spring
4 Diaphragm, front
5 Diaphragm, rear
6 Guide housing
7 Valve piston seat
8 Seal assembly
9 Spring
10 Rear thrust rod
11 Filter
12 Filter
13 Spring
14 Reaction disc

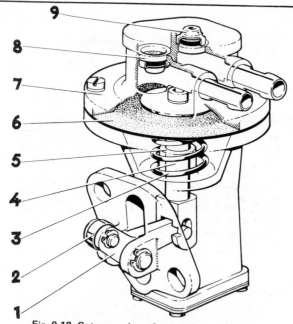

Fig. 9.18. Cut-away view of vacuum pump (Sec. 16)

1   This lever transfers the cam-
     shaft movements to the
     pump rod
2   Roller with needle bearing
3   Pump spring
4   Pump rod

5   Nylon bushing
6   Pump diaphragm
7   Valve housing
8   Suction valve
9   Discharge valve (into the air)

each other on top of the rear axle before being connected to scissor
type levers between the shoe lower ends. An adjuster is provided
between the shoe upper ends on some models.

3   When correctly adjusted the handbrake should give its full effect
when applied between 2 and 8 notches.

4   Handbrake adjustment on models without the adjuster device
between the shoe upper ends differs from the procedure on cars so
equipped.

Models fitted with shoe adjusters

5   Jack-up the rear of the car and remove the road wheels. Remove
the rear ashtray.

6   Screw out the adjustment screw at the rear end of the parking brake
lever so that the cables are slackened, see Fig. 9.21.

7   Align the brake drum so that its hole is opposite the adjuster screw
and adjust with a screwdriver, you will feel the serrations of the
adjuster clicking. Turn the screw until the shoes can be felt to drag
when the drum is rotated then back-off the adjuster 4-5 serrations.
Repeat the procedure on the remaining rear brake.

8   Refit the roadwheels.

Models not fitted with shoe adjusters

9   Jack up the rear of the car. Remove the rear ashtray.

All models

10   Adjust the cable tension with the adjustment screw at the rear
end of the parking brake lever (Fig. 9.21) so that both rear wheels are
locked with the lever applied between 2 and 8 notches.

11   Refit the rear ashtray then lower the car to the ground.

19 Handbrake shoes - inspection and renewal

1   Remove the rear disc/drum assemblies as described in Section 8
paragraphs 6 and 7.

2   Brush away any accumulated dust and inspect the thickness of the
friction linings. If they are worn down, or nearly down, to the securing
rivets (or in the case of bonded linings they are less than 1/16 in (1.6
mm) in thickness) then they must be renewed.

3   If the linings are satisfactory, refit the disc/drum and caliper,
adjust the handbrake, refit the roadwheel and lower the car.

4   If the linings are worn, detach both shoe return springs and remove
the adjuster (if fitted).

Fig. 9.19. Removing the diaphragm (Sec. 16)

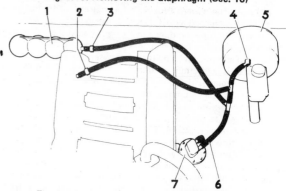

Fig. 9.20. Location of non-return valves (Sec. 17)

1   Vacuum valve
2   Non-return valve (hose
     to intake manifold)
3   Non-return valve (hose
     to vacuum reservoir)

4   Non-return valve
     (on servo unit)
5   Servo unit
6   Hose to vacuum pump
7   Vacuum pump

5   Pull the shoes forward, disconnecting them from the links as they
come.

6   Before installing the new shoes, slacken the handbrake cable at the
handbrake lever.

7   Apply a smear of high melting point grease to the shoe slides on the
brake backplate, also to the adjuster threads (if applicable).

8   Check that the lever and anchor bolt are correctly fitted.

9   Fit the washer and spring to the leading shoe and then fit the shoes,
adjuster (if fitted) and return springs. Note that the shorter section of
the adjuster faces the front of the car on the right-hand brake and
towards the rear on the left-hand brake. Also set the adjuster to its
fully retracted position.

10   Refit the disc/drum and the caliper.

11   Adjust the shoes and the cable, as described in Section 18.

20 Handbrake cable - renewal

1   The handbrake cables can be renewed individually.

2   Remove the handbrake lever cover and disconnect the lead from
the ashtray lamp.

3   Unscrew the adjustment bolt (1) (Fig. 9.24) and remove the nut
(2) at the same time holding the cable in position with a small screwdriver. It should be realised that the cables cross over each other under
the floor and the left-hand cable at the handbrake lever connects with
the right-hand rear brake and the right-hand cable with the left-hand
brake.

4   Lift the front of the rear seat cushion, peel away the carpet and
loosen the clips which hold the cable to the floor.

5   Disconnect the cable end sleeve and grommet from the rear seat
support.

6   Jack-up the rear of the car and support it on stands and then remove
the rear roadwheel.

7   Remove the clamp which attaches the rigid brake line to the rear
axle casing. Unbolt the caliper and without bending the brake line pull
the caliper from the disc and hang it up with a piece of wire.

8   Remove the brake drum and the brake shoes, as described in
Section 8.

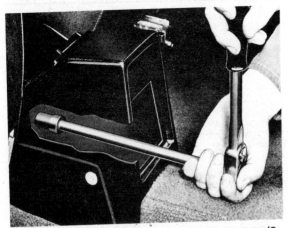

Fig. 9.21. Slackening the adjusting screw at handbrake lever (Sec. 18)

Fig. 9.22. Adjusting the brake shoes (Sec. 18)
(Not all models)

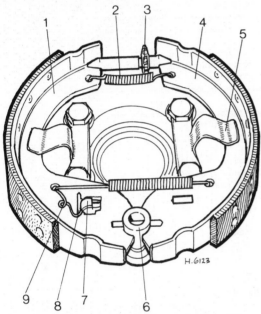

Fig. 9.23. Handbrake shoe arrangement (Sec. 19)

1 Shoe
2 Return spring
3 Adjuster (some models)
4 Shoe
5 Shoe steady clip

6 Anchor bolt
7 Lever
8 Washer
9 Spring

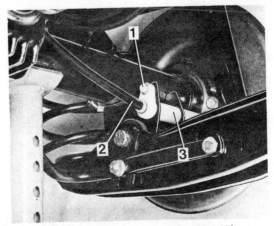

Fig. 9.24. Handbrake cable attachment to control lever (Sec. 20)

1 Adjuster bolt
2 Lockscrew

Fig. 9.25. Disconnecting cable from shoe lever (Sec.20)

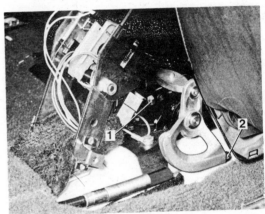

Fig. 9.26. Handbrake cable support (Sec.20)

1 Attaching screw
2 Cable
3 Plastic tube

9 Press out the lock pin which retains the cable to the shoe actuating lever.

10 Remove the bolt from the retainer above the rear suspension arm and pull out the cable, plastic tube and rubber seal.

11 Withdraw the cable from the centre support and channel in the floor of the car.

12 Refit the new cable by reversing the removal procedure and then adjust the cable, see Section 18. When connecting the cable to the handbrake lever check that the cable end protrudes from the nut by equal amounts on each cable. Adjust the nuts as required so that when the handbrake is applied the upper yoke is at right angles to the lever.

21 Fault diagnosis - braking system

Symptom	Reason/s
Brake grab	Excessive run-out of discs.
	Rust on disc.
	Oil stained pads.
Brake drag	Faulty master cylinder.
	Foot pedal return impeded.
	Reservoir breather blocked.
	Seized caliper.
	Incorrect adjustment of handbrake.
	Crushed, blocked or swollen pipe lines.
Excessive pedal effort required	Pads not yet bedded-in.
	Pads or discs contaminated with oil or grease.
	Scored discs.
	Faulty vacuum servo unit.
Brake pedal feels hard	Glazed surfaces of friction material.
	Rust on disc surfaces.
	Seized caliper piston.
Excessive pedal travel	Low reservoir fluid level.
	Disc run-out excessive.
	Worn front wheel bearings.
	Air in system.
	Worn pads.
Pedal creep during sustained application	Fluid leak.
	Internal fault in master cylinder.
	Faulty servo unit non-return valve.
Pedal 'spongy'	Air in system.
	Perished flexible hose.
	Loose master cylinder mounting nuts.
	Faulty breather blocked.
Fall in reservoir fluid level	Normal due to pad wear.
	Leak in hydraulic system.

Chapter 10 Electrical system

For modifications, and information applicable to later models, see Supplement at end of manual

Contents

Specifications

System voltage ... ...   12 volts

Battery
Type	Tudor 6 EX 3 (or equivalent)
Earth connection	Negative terminal
Battery capacity (standard)	60 Ah
Specific gravity of electrolyte:	
Fully charged battery	1.28
When recharging is required	1.21
Recommended charging current	5.5 A

Alternator (SEV Marchal)
Type	SEV Marchal A 14/30 712 712 102
Output	490 W
Maximum amperage	35 A
Maximum speed	15,000 rpm
Direction of rotation	Optional
Ratio: engine speed - alternator speed	1 : 2
Minimum length of brushes	0.2 in (5 mm)
Tightening torque:	
Attaching screws	2.9 lb f ft (0.4 kg f m)
Nut for pulley	29 lb f ft (4 kg f m)
Test values:	
Field winding resistance	4.9 ohm
Output test	30 A at 3,000 rpm and approx. 13 V

Alternator (Bosch K1 - 14V 35A 20)
Type	Bosch K1 - 14V 35A 20
Output	490 W
Maximum amperage	35 A
Maximum speed	13,500 rpm
Direction of rotation	Clockwise
Ratio, engine speed - alternator speed	1 : 2
Minimum diameter of slip rings	1.24 in (31.5 mm)
Maximum radial throw on:	
Slip rings	0.0012 in (0.03 mm)
Rotor body	0.0020 in (0.05 mm)
Minimum length of brushes	0.2 in (5.0 mm)
Brush pressure	0.7 - 0.9 lb (0.3 - 0.4 kg)
Tightening torque, pulley nut	25 - 29 lb f ft (3.5 - 4 kg f m)

Test values:

Resistance in stator	0.26 - 0.29 ohm/phase
Resistance in rotor	4 - 4.4 ohm
Output test	30 A at 3,000 rpm and approx. 14 V

Alternator (Bosch K1 - 14V 55A 20)

Type	Bosch K1 - 14V 55A 20
Output	770 W
Maximum amperage	55 A
Maximum speed	13,500 rpm
Direction of rotation	Clockwise
Ratio: engine speed - alternator speed	1 : 2
Minimum diameter of slip ring	1.24 in (31.5 mm)
Maximum radial throw on:	
Slip rings	0.0012 in (0.03 mm)
Rotor body	0.0020 in (0.05 mm)
Minimum length of brushes	0.2 in (5.0 mm)
Spring pressure	0.7 - 0.9 lb (0.3 - 0.4 kg)
Tightening torque, pulley nut	25 - 32 lb f ft (3.5 - 4.5 kg f m)
Test values:	
Resistance in stator	0.14 to 0.15 ohm/phase
Resistance in rotor	4 - 4.4 ohm
Output test	48 A at 3,000 rpm and approx. 14 V

Voltage regulator

SEV Marchal 727 105 02:	
Control voltage, after driving 10 minutes	13.5 - 14.1 V
Bosch AD - 14V:	
Control voltage, after driving 10 minutes	13.5 - 14.1 V
Load current, two lower contacts	44 - 46 A
Control range (between two upper and lower contacts)	0 - 0.4 V
Load current, two upper contacts	3 - 8 A

Starter motor

Type	Bosch GF 12V 1.1 PS
Voltage	12 V
Earth connection	Negative terminal
Direction of rotation	Clockwise
Output	810 W (1.1 hp)
Number of teeth on pinion	9
Number of brushes	4
Test values:	
Mechanical:	
Armature endfloat	0.0004 - 0.0118 in (0.01 - 0.30 mm)
Brush spring tension	3 - 3.5 lb (1.4 - 1.6 kg)
Distance from pinion to ring gear	0.047 - 0.173 in (1.2 - 4.4 mm)
Frictional torque of rotor brake	2.18 - 3.48 lb in (2.5 - 4 kg cm)
Pinion idling torque	1.22 - 1.91 lb in (1.4 - 2.2 kg cm)
Backlash	0.012 - 0.020 in (0.3 - 0.5 mm)
Minimum diameter of commutator	1.32 in (33.5 mm)
Minimum length of brushes	0.51 in (13 mm)
Electrical:	
Unloaded starter motor (11.5 volts and 30 - 50A)	5,800 - 7,800 rpm
Loaded starter motor (9 volts and 185 - 220A)	1,050 - 1,350 rpm
Locked starter motor (7 volts and 400 - 490A)	0 rpm
Control solenoid, cut-in voltage	Min. 7.5 V

Light bulbs

	Power	Socket
Headlights	60/55 W	H4
Day running lights	5 W/21 W	Ba 15d
Direction indicators:		
Front	21 W or 32 cp	Ba 15s
Rear	21 W or 32 cp	Ba 15s
Tail lights	5 W or 4 cp	Ba 15s
Brake lights	21 W or 32 cp	Ba 15s
Reversing lights	21 W or 32 cp	Ba 15s
Number plate light	5 W	S 8.5
Interior light	10 W	S 8.5
Glovebox light	2 W	Ba 9s
Instrument lighting	2 W	W 2.2d
Engine compartment light	15 W	S 8.5
Lighting:		
Control panel	1.2 W	W 1.8d
Automatic transmission	1.2 W	W 1.8d
Rear ashtray	1.2 W	W 1.8d
Safety belt lock	1.2 W	W 1.8d

Warning lights:		
Charging	1.2 W	W 1.8d
Oil pressure	1.2 W	W 1.8d
Handbrake	1.2 W	W 1.8d
Brake failure	1.2 W	W 1.8d
Bulbs	1.2 W	W 1.8d
Indicator lights:		
Choke	1.2 W	W 1.8d
Direction indicators	1.2 W	W 1.8d
Full beam	1.2 W	W 1.8d
Overdrive	1.2 W	W 1.8d
Hazard warning lights	1.2 W	W 2 x 4.6d
Heated rear window	1.2 W	W 2 x 4.6d
Safety belts	2 W	BA 9S

Heated rear window

Output	150 ± 30 W

* Fuses

Number	Circuit protected	Fuse rating (amps)
1	Cigar lighter	8A
	Tailgate window wiper/washer (245)	
2	Windscreen wipers	16A
	Heater fan	
	Horn	
3	Electrically heated rear window	16A
	Overdrive	
4	Glove compartment light	8A
	Reversing light	
	Electrically heated driver's seat	
5	Instruments	8A
	Indicators	
	Warning light	
	Fasten seatbelt warning light	
6	Hazard warning lights	8A
	Engine compartment light	
7	Clock	16A
	Fuel pump (injection engines)	
8	Brakelight	8A
	Interior light	
9	Daytime running lights (UK only)	8A
	Ignition interlock buzzer, seatbelt (USA only)	
10	Spare	16A
11	Left-hand parking light	8A
	Rear foglight	
12	Right-hand parking light	8A
	Instrument and panel light	

Typical fuse ratings shown. See the handbook for details

1 General description

The electrical system is of the 12 volt type and the major components comprise a 12 volt battery (of which the negative terminal is earthed), voltage regulator, alternator, which is fitted at the front of the engine and is driven from the pulley on the front of the crankshaft, and a starter motor which is mounted on the rear left-hand side of the engine.

The battery supplies a steady amount of current for the ignition, lighting and other electrical circuits, and provides a reserve of electricity when the current consumed by the electrical equipment exceeds that being produced by the alternator.

When fitting electrical accessories to cars with a negative earth system it is important, if they contain silicone diodes or transistors, that they are connected correctly, otherwise serious damage may result to the components concerned. Items such as radios, tape recorders and electronic tachometers should all be checked for correct polarity.

It is important that the battery is always disconnected if it is to be boost charged when an alternator is fitted. This is also applicable when electric welding equipment is to be used.

2 Battery - removal, maintenance, inspection and refitting

1 The battery is fitted on a shelf in the engine compartment (to the left of the radiator) and is held in position by a bar and clamp. When removing it, first disconnect the negative (earth) lead and then the positive lead. This way you avoid any possibility of damage through shorted circuits. The leads are fastened to the battery either by clamps (the normal Volvo practice) or by caps which are screwed to tapped holes in the battery terminals; this type of fitting may be found as a replacement for the original clamps. Removal of the battery is simply a matter of undoing the nuts holding the retaining bar, removing this and lifting the battery out.

2 Every three months the battery should be removed and cleaned - brush it down and give it a rinse with clean luke warm water. At the same time clean the battery shelf and the terminals, wire brushing these if necessary to remove corrosion.

3 Weekly maintenance consists of checking the electrolyte level in the cells to ensure that the separators are covered by ¼ in (6 mm) of electrolyte. If the level has fallen, top up with distilled water only. Do not overfill. If you find it difficult to judge the correct level of electrolyte, you can buy battery fillers which automatically get it right for you, employing a simple valve or cut away in the spout. If the battery is overfilled or any electrolyte spilled, wipe away the electrolyte immediately as it attacks and corrodes any metal it comes into contact with very quickly.

4 Inspect the retaining bar, securing nuts, tray and battery leads for corrosion (white fluffy deposits on the metal which are brittle to touch). If any corrosion is found, clean off the deposit with ammonia and paint over the clean metal with an anti-rust/anti-acid paint.

5 Keep an eye on the battery case for cracks. It is possible to clean and plug these with proprietary compounds made for this purpose. If an appreciable amount of electrolyte has leaked away through a crack or if electrolyte has been spilt out of the battery it should be

replaced with fresh electrolyte; otherwise all topping-up should be done with distilled water.

6   If topping-up becomes excessive and there is no leakage from the case, the battery is being overcharged and the voltage regulator will have to be checked and reset.

7   As part of the three-monthly check, measure the specific gravity of the electrolyte with a hydrometer. A table of specific gravity is given later in this Section. There should be very little variation between different cells. If a variation greater than 0.025 is present, the cause must either be spillage or leakage - which has been topped-up with distilled water, or an internal short circuit in the cell - an indication that the battery will soon need renewal.

8   To check a suspect cell, discharge the battery completely (for example, by leaving the headlights on). Recheck the specific gravities and if the dubious cell is still lower than the others remove some of the electrolyte if necessary and top it up with a mixture of one part sulphuric acid to 2.5 parts of water, repeating this process until the specific gravity comes up to standard. If it is too high to start with, of course, you will top it up with distilled water after removing the electrolyte, but in practice this never seems to happen.

9   Now recharge the battery at about 5 amps until the specific gravity of the electrolyte in the good cells has remained constant for about four hours. It will take you about 18 hours in all. It does not matter if you charge at a lesser rate, but it will take proportionately longer. You can save time by charging at up to 10 amps but do not be tempted to use a rapid charger which claims to restore the power of the battery in one or two hours. They can be dangerous devices to use with batteries that are past their best.

10   In all probability the suspect cell will now have the same specific gravity as the others. Replace the battery in the car and keep a particular eye on this cell. If in a week or two the specific gravity has again dropped below the level of the others, you can resign yourself to the thought that very soon you will have to renew the battery.

11   When mixing sulphuric acid and water **never add water to sulphuric acid** - always pour the acid slowly on to the water in a glass container. **If water is added to sulphuric acid it will explode.**

12   Refitting is a direct reversal of the removal procedure. Connect the positive lead before the negative lead and smear the terminals with petroleum jelly (Vaseline) to prevent corrosion. Never use an ordinary grease as applied to other parts of the car.

13   In wintertime when a heavy demand is placed on the battery it is a good idea to give the battery an occasional charge at about 5 amps. Ideally you should charge at this rate until the specific gravity has remained constant for four hours. We are usually content to observe the vigorous bubbling from the electrolyte which indicates that the battery is fully charged and let this go on for three or four hours.

14   A final hint - in very cold weather, top your battery up just before you start a run. Distilled water is lighter than electrolyte and may float on top of it instead of mixing with it if the car is cold and stationary. In this case it can easily freeze and may ruin your battery by cracking the case.

SPECIFIC GRAVITY TABLE

Specific gravity - fully discharged

1.098 at 100°F or 38°C electrolyte temperature
1.102 at 90°F or 32°C electrolyte temperature
1.106 at 80°F or 27°C electrolyte temperature
1.110 at 70°F or 21°C electrolyte temperature
1.114 at 60°F or 16°C electrolyte temperature
1.118 at 50°F or 10°C electrolyte temperature
1.122 at 40°F or 4°C electrolyte temperature
1.126 at 30°F or-1.5°C electrolyte temperature

Specific gravity - battery fully charged

1.268 at 100°F or 38°C electrolyte temperature
1.272 at 90°F or 32°C electrolyte temperature
1.276 at 80°F or 27°C electrolyte temperature
1.280 at 70°F or 21°C electrolyte temperature
1.284 at 60°F or 16°C electrolyte temperature
1.288 at 50°F or 10°C electrolyte temperature
1.292 at 40°F or 4°C electrolyte temperature
1.296 at 30°F or-1.5°C electrolyte temperature

3 Alternator - general description

1   In an ordinary generator the armature rotates between what are, in effect, the poles of a magnet or may be several sets of these poles. The magnetism is maintained by the field coils. As the position of the armature relative to the magnetic poles varies, the magnetic field passing through the armature changes and it is this change of magnetism which produces current in the armature coils. It is only when the magnetic field is changing that current is produced, (when the armature is not rotating no current appears) and this current, like the changing field that produces it, is changing all the time. In fact, if it were not for the commutator which acts as a reversing switch operated in time with the changing current, the output of the ordinary generator would be alternating current and not direct current.

2   The alternator differs from the ordinary DC generator in that the armature is stationary and the field coils with their magnetic pole pieces rotate. The output from the armature is alternating current because there is now no rotating commutator to keep changing it over, but the current passes through a system of diodes so arranged that whichever way the current is flowing when it leaves the armature it is always flowing in the same direction at the output terminals. It is easy to get an idea of how these diodes operate by looking at the circuit diagrams (Figs. 10.2 and 10.3) and remembering that the electric current only passes through the diodes in the direction indicated by the arrows, so that it is only possible for current to enter and leave the output terminals in the direction shown, whatever is happening in the alternator coils.

3   There is nothing particularly novel about this idea, but it has only become practicable in the last few years because of a technological break through in rectifier design - the development of materials known as semi-conductors. It brings with it some very considerable design advantages. The first of these is that the brushes now only pass the field current - a matter of two or three amps - instead of the total output current of 30-50 amps, and this current needs no commutation but is simply passed into the field coil via slip rings. Because of this the size of the brushes can be greatly reduced and sparking becomes negligible.

4   In a normal generator, excessive current produces overheating of the brushes and commutator leading to complete breakdown of the armature. Because of this the current output has to be limited by an external regulator. With the alternator, provided that the armature is wound with thick enough wire, and in practice this is quite easy, the output current is limited to a safe value by reason of the magnetic effect it produces which cancels out the magnetism produced by the field coil. Because of this, only voltage regulation is needed with an alternator; the current can be allowed to look after itself.

5   Three different alternators are found on the 240 series models. Two of these, the Bosch K1-14 35A 20 and K1-14V 55A 20, are almost identical, the latter providing a larger current output. The third type, SEV Marchal 712 712 12 has slightly different electrical and mechanical arrangements but works on exactly the same principle.

6   The voltage regulator for the alternator is located on the right-hand wheel housing. Fig. 10.9 shows the Bosch regulator: the SEV regulator look very similar.

Fig. 10.1. Location of alternator - B20 engine (Sec. 3)

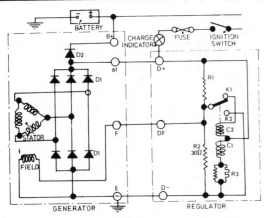

Fig. 10.2. SEV alternator and regulator circuit diagram
(Sec. 3 and 7)

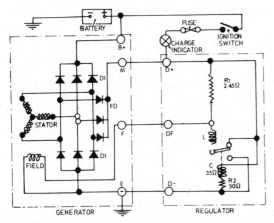

Fig. 10.3. Bosch alternator and regulator circuit diagram (Sec. 3)

5.3 Disconnecting the leads from the alternator

4 Alternator - special precautions

1 The diodes used in alternator equipment are very sensitive to voltages and currents greater than they are designed to withstand, and in particular they are easily damaged by excessive reverse voltages. To avoid any risk of diode failure or shortened life, take the precautions outlined in the next few paragraphs.

2 When replacing or reconnecting the battery, make sure that it is connected with correct polarity, ie. negative earth.

3 Never run the alternator unless the regulator is connected. If the battery is disconnected, be sure that there is some external load - headlamps, for example - connected across the output terminal.

4 No attempt should be made to polarise the alternator. This is not necessary.

5 When charging the battery while installed in the car, the negative battery lead should be disconnected.

6 A rapid charger should not be used as an aid in starting.

7 When using an extra battery as a starting aid, always connect it in parallel.

8 When carrying out electric welding on the vehicle, disconnect the negative battery lead as well as all the alternator leads. The welder should always be connected as near as possible to where the welding is carried out.

5 Alternator - removal and refitting

1 For safety reasons, disconnect the battery.

2 Slacken the belt tensioner and remove the fanbelt.

3 Make a note of, and then disconnect, the leads to the alternator (photo).

4 Undo and remove the alternator securing bolts and remove the alternator from the engine.

5 Refitting the alternator is the reverse sequence to removal. Adjust the fanbelt tension, as described in Chapter 2.

6 Alternator - dismantling, overhaul and reassembly

1 Give the alternator a good clean before starting to take it apart, using paraffin or a proprietary solvent.

2 Figs. 10.4 and 10.5 give exploded views of Bosch and SEV alternators respectively.

3 Remove the screws attaching the brush holder and take off the holder.

4 Using the fanbelt as protection, hold the pulley in a vice with soft jaws. Undo the fixing nut, lift off the pulley key (watch this - its powers of concealment would do credit to a chameleon!) spacing washer or washers (note the order of assembly) and fan.

5 Remove the two bolts holding together the alternator and take off the drive end shield holding the alternator in a vice by the driveshaft. Be careful when using screwdrivers to part the alternator - do not insert them further than 1/16 in (2 mm) or you may damage the stator winding.

6 Remove the retaining plate which holds the rotor bearing in the drive end shield and knock out the bearing by gently tapping on the rotor shaft with a hide mallet or a piece of wood.

7 In the SEV alternator detach the isolation diode holder by removing the nuts and washers on terminal '61' and the corresponding ones on the other side of the isolation diode. This being done, it is a simple matter to detach the rectifier assembly from the slip ring end shield and withdraw the stator winding with the rectifier assembly still connected to it. The end shield may then be detached.

8 For the Bosch alternator, unsolder the stator winding leads from the terminals on the slip ring end shield, marking the leads and terminals so that you know which goes to which. The stator winding can then be withdrawn from the shield. Remove the positive diode assembly, the magnetizing rectifier assembly and the negative diode assembly from the slip ring end shield, which can then be separated from the stator.

Bearings

1 Generally speaking the bearings for the rotor will stay on the rotor shaft when the alternator is dismantled, though sometimes they may remain in the end shields. Where these bearings are of the open type, they should be removed from the end shield or shaft, thoroughly cleaned in White Spirit and examined carefully for signs of scoring, scuffing, wear or blueing. If such signs are present or there is appreciable play in the bearing it should be replaced. Otherwise, pack the bearing with a suitable grease for further use.

2 If the bearings are of the sealed type, check them for play and smoothness of operation and replace them if you are in any doubt about their condition.

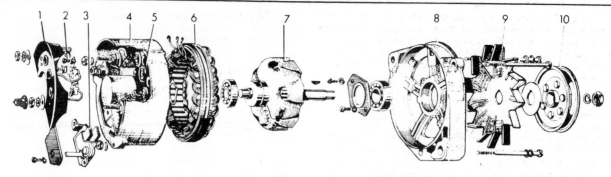

Fig. 10.4. Exploded view of Bosch alternator (Sec. 6)

1 Rectifier (plus diode plate)
2 Magnetizing rectifier
3 Brush holder
4 Slip ring end shield
5 Rectifier (negative diodes)
6 Stator
7 Rotor
8 Drive end shield
9 Fan
10 Pulley

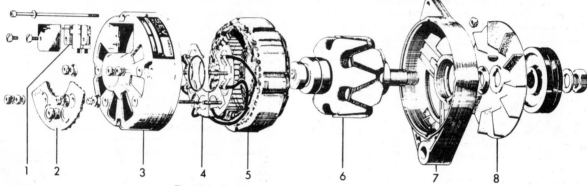

Fig. 10.5. Exploded view of SEV alternator (Sec. 6)

1 Brush holder
2 Isolation diodes with holder
3 Slip ring end shield
4 Rectifier (silicon diodes)
5 Stator
6 Rotor
7 Drive end shield
8 Fan

Brushes and slip rings

1 Using a 12v 2.5w bulb connected to a suitable source (three 4½ volt flat flash lamp batteries are very handy) check that the brushes are isolated from each other (ie. the lamp must not light when connected between the brushes). Check that the connection between the brushes and their respective terminals on the holder are good - ie. the test lamp should light when connected between a brush and its terminal.

2 The minimum length of the brush protruding from the holder should be 0.2 in (5 mm) for SEV alternators and 0.31 in (8 mm) for Bosch.

3 The surface of the slip rings should be smooth. You may give them a polish with very fine sand paper (not emery paper), being careful to remove all traces of the sand paper when you have finished. If the slip rings are burnt or damaged in any other way, there is no reason why they should not be skimmed in a lathe, but a glance at the Specifications for run-out given for the Bosch alternator will show that this is a specialist operation. You should resist the temptation to hold the rotor in an electric drill and take a file to the slip rings.

Checking the rotor

1 Check the slip rings, as described in the previous sub-Section.
2 Examine the winding for breakage or damaged insulation.
3 Check the insulation between the winding and the frame by connecting a test lamp and battery between the frame and one of the slip rings. The lamp should not light.
4 Measure the resistance between the slip rings with an ohmmeter or multi-meter. It should be 4.9 ohms for SEV and 4.0 ohms ± 10% for Bosch.

Checking the stator

1 Examine the winding carefully for signs of burning. If this is found, it means that there is a short circuit in the winding and the stator should be replaced or rewound.
2 Connect a test lamp between one of the winding terminals and the frame, the lamp should not light. If there is the smallest glow, the

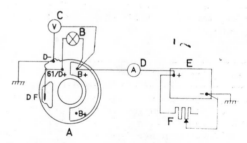

Fig. 10.6. Test circuit for Bosch alternator (Sec. 6)

A Alternator
B Test lamp 12V, 2w
C Voltmeter 0 - 20V
D Ammeter 0 - 50 amps
E Battery 60 Ah
F Load resistance

stator should be replaced.

3 Using an ohmmeter or multi-meter, measure the resistance between each pair of winding terminations (in the case of the Bosch alternator, these are the leads that are connected to the diodes - not the star point which has three wires going to it). The presence of the diodes on the SEV stator windings will not affect these measurements unless the diodes are defective. The three different measurements should give the same value of resistance - certainly within 2%. For the Bosch alternator the resistance value should lie within 0.26 ± 0.03 ohms.

Checking the diodes

1 The diode is simply a device which will allow electric current to pass through it one way and not the other way. In diagrams such as Figs. 10.2 and 10.3 the direction in which current is able to flow through the diode is indicated by the black arrowhead. Electric current flows from positive to negative, so if you connect a positive voltage (for example, the positive lead of your battery/test bulb combination)

to the broad end of the arrow and the negative lead to the other end, current will flow and the lamp will light. If you reverse the connections, the lamp will not light. Normally, you do not have to worry about which way round you connect your lamp, because if the lamp lights when connected one way round and does not light when connected the other way round, the diode must be all right. A faulty diode either lights the lamp both ways or not at all. Note that the positive voltage on a rectifier diode appears at the pointed end of the arrow. The diodes are made up to produce positive voltage at the casing or at the centre lead as required; both types are used in the alternator.

2   Unless specialised apparatus is available, it is necessary to unsolder the leads from the SEV alternator to the diodes mounted on it in order to check them. To someone not experienced in working with electronic equipment, this soldering is a tricky business and best left to a specialist. There is no reason why the local radio shop should not do this for you. Check the diodes as just described with the test lamp and voltage source. In no circumstances should the test voltage exceed 14v. If any defective diodes are found, replace the relevant assembly or have a diode fitted to the existing plate by a specialist. In the Bosch alternator, the diode plate is disconnected from the stator winding when the alternator is dismantled and there is no need to unsolder the diodes themselves. The battery and lamp can be connected across each diode in turn.

Reassembly

1   Reassembly in the main is a reversal of the dismantling process, and presents no special problems. In the Bosch alternator, fit the bearing and retaining plate to the drive end bearing shield before assembling this to the rotor. Coat the slip ring end shield bearing seat with a light layer of 'Molycote' paste or similar and assemble the alternator. Do not forget the spring ring, on the slip ring end shield bearing seat. Fixing screws and nuts should be tightened to a torque of 3.6-4.3 lb f ft (0.50-0.60 kg f m).

2   For the SEV alternator, the fixing screws should be tightened to a torque of 2.0 - 2.2 lb f ft (0.28 - 0.30 kg f m).

3   Be sure that the isolation diode holder on the SEV alternator is fitted with the full complement of plastic tube and isolation washers on its fixing screws.

4   Fit the spacer washer, key, fan, pulley, washer and finally the pulley nut in the order in which you took them off. Tightening torque for the pulley nut is 29 lb f ft (4 kg f m) for both SEV and Bosch alternators.

7   Alternator regulator - checking

1   The SEV regulator does not depend on spring tension, contact clearance etc for its correct operation, being controlled by a voltage sensitive resistor element (R3, Fig. 10.2). No means of adjustment is available and if it does not meet the checking procedure which follows, it should be replaced.

2   To check the SEV regulator, start up the engine and run the alternator at about 5,000 rpm (engine speed 2,500 rpm) for 15 seconds. Switch everything off except the ignition and read the voltage between 'B+' and 'D-' on the alternator. This should lie within the shaded area of Fig. 10.7. Note that the temperature referred to is the air temperature, not the temperature of the regulator itself. The reading should change very little when the alternator is loaded with, for example, full beam headlights. Now drive the vehicle for 45 minutes and repeat the procedure. The readings should now be within the shaded area of Fig. 10.8. If they are not, you will either have to live with it or replace the regulator.

3   To check the Bosch regulator, you will need to load the alternator with 28-30 amps (ie. full beam headlights plus as much again - another pair of bulbs, for example). The check must be carried out quickly, before the regulator has a chance to get really warm. Run the alternator to a speed of 4,000 rpm (engine speed 2,000 rpm) rapidly lower it to about 1,000 rpm (ie. idling speed), raise the speed again to 4,000 rpm and read the voltage between 'B+' and 'D-' on the alternator. This should be 14-15v. Reduce the load on the alternator to 3-8 amps (ie. one dipped headlight equivalent) and read the voltage again. It should now be between 0 and 0.3v less than the first reading. If the voltage is outside specification - particularly if it is too high - the regulator should be adjusted by a specialist or replaced.

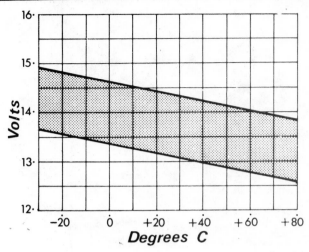

Fig. 10.7. Voltage - temperature diagram, cold regulator (SEV) (Sec. 7)

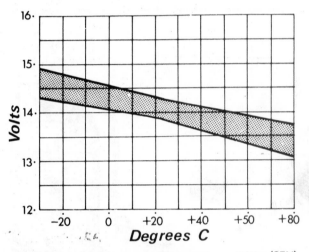

Fig. 10.8. Voltage - temperature diagram, warm regulator (SEV) (Sec. 7)

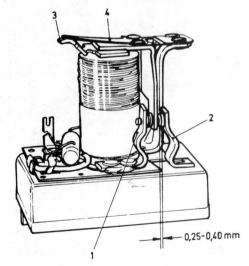

Fig. 10.9. Bosch voltage regulator (Secs. 3 and 7)

1   Contact for lower control range
2   Contact for upper control range
3   Stop arm
4   Spring. Steel upper section
    Bi-metal lower section

10.3a Bolts securing the starter to the flywheel housing (B21 engine)

10.3b Starter motor support bracket (B21 engine)

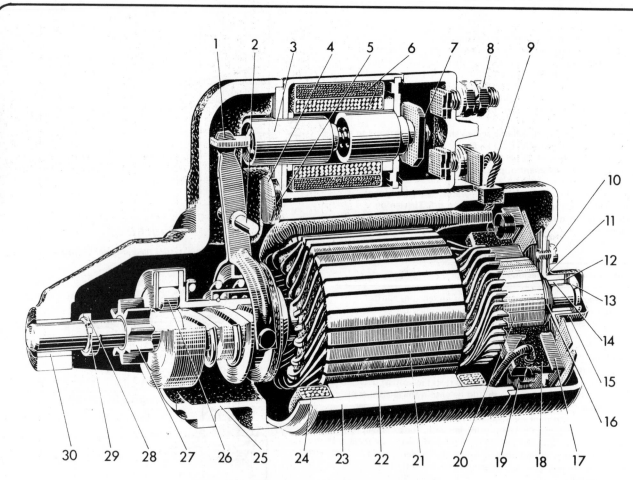

Fig. 10.10. Cut-away view of starter motor (Sec. 11)

1 Shift lever	9 Connection lead to field	17 Brush holder	25 Drive end frame
2 Pivot pin (bearing screw)	10 Screw	18 Brush	26 One-way clutch
3 Plunger	11 Rubber gasket	19 Brush spring	27 Pinion
4 Steel washer	12 Shims	20 Commutator	28 Stop ring
5 Rubber washer	13 Snap ring	21 Armature	29 Snap ring
6 Winding	14 Bush	22 Pole shoe	30 Bush
7 Contact plate	15 Commutator end frame	23 Stator	
8 Terminal for battery lead	16 Adjusting washers	24 Field winding	

8 Starter motor - general description

1   The starter motor is of the pre-engaged type, in which the pinion is mechanically engaged with the flywheel ring gear before the motor is switched on, a roller clutch drive in the pinion assembly allowing the pinion to free-wheel when the engine starts. The mechanical engagement is driven by a solenoid which operates the starter motor switch after it has pushed the pinion into position.

2   If properly lubricated before assembly, the self-lubricating bearings of the starter motor will last as long as the engine.

9 Starter motor - testing on engine

1   If the starter motor fails to operate, first check the condition of the battery by turning on the headlamps. If they shine brightly for several seconds and then gradually dim, the battery needs charging.

2   If the headlights remain bright and it is obvious that the battery is in good condition, check the connections between the battery and the starter - this includes the earth lead from the battery terminal to the bodyframe and the lead from the starter switch to the solenoid.

3   If all the connections are sound, listen for a click from the solenoid when the starter switch is operated. If there is no click, a fault in the solenoid is suggested. If there is a click but the starter motor does not turn, there is probably a fault in the motor itself. In either event the starter motor will have to be removed for inspection.

10 Starter motor - removal and refitting

1   Disconnect the battery, for safety reasons.

2   Make a note of, and then disconnect, the leads from the starter motor solenoid.

3   Undo and remove the bolts and spring washer that secure the starter motor to the flywheel housing. On B21 engines remove the bracket attaching the starter motor to the engine block (photos).

4   Lift away the starter motor.

5   Refitting the starter motor is the reverse of the removal sequence.

11 Starter motor - dismantling, overhaul and reassembly

1   Refer to Fig. 10.10 and remove the small cover located at the front end of the shaft.

2   Lift away the locking washer and the adjustment washer.

3   Suitably mark the drive bearing and commutator bearing brackets.

4   Undo and remove the two through-bolts.

5   Lift off the commutator bearing shield. The brushes and retainers will remain in position on the armature.

6   Remove the brush retaining plate from the armature.

7   Note the position of the washers.

8   The brushes may now be pulled from their holders.

9   Remove the brush gear from the armature taking care not to lose the shims.

10 When the brush gear is removed the negative brushes will also be detached but the positive brushes will remain attached to the field winding.

11 Unscrew the nut that holds the field terminal connection to the solenoid.

12 Undo and remove the screws which hold the solenoid to the drive-shaft end. Lift away the solenoid.

13 Remove the drive end shield and armature from the starter body.

14 Remove the pivot pin from the engagement lever, lift away the rubber washer and also the metal washer.

15 Lift the armature together with the pinion and lever from the drive end shield.

16 Knock back the stop washer and remove the circlip from the armature.

17 Finally pull off the stop ring and drive pinion assembly.

18 Clean off the various components using a compressed air jet.

19 Carefully examine the rotor for signs of mechanical damage such as a worn or bent shaft, scored or burnt commutator or damaged windings. If the rotor shaft is bent or worn, it must be renewed.

20 If the commutator is scored or worn unevenly it may be skimmed on a lathe. Take small cuts each time so that the minimum amount of material is removed. The insulation between the laminations should now be undercut to a depth of 0.016 in (0.4 mm) using a hacksaw blade with the tooth sides ground off.

21 Examine the housing and the field winding for signs of damage caused by the rotor.

22 If possible test the field winding to ensure that it is not earthed by connecting the contact points of a test light and battery to the housing and field winding. If the light comes on, the winding or lead

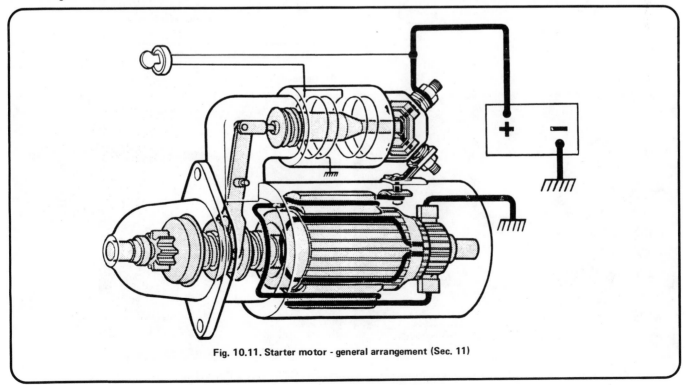

Fig. 10.11. Starter motor - general arrangement (Sec. 11)

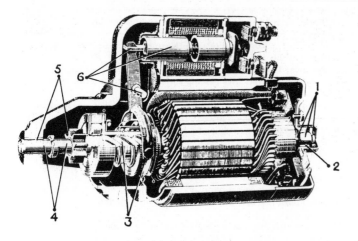

Fig. 10.12. Starter motor - lubrication points (Sec. 11)

1 *Lightly grease insulation washers, shaft end, adjusting washers and lock washer*
2 *Soak bush in oil for 30 minutes*
3 *Well grease rotor thread and engaging lever groove*
4 *Lightly grease rotor shaft*
5 *Soak bush in oil for 30 minutes*
6 *Lightly grease engaging lever joints and iron core of solenoid*

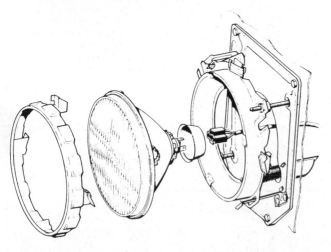

Fig. 10.13. Exploded view of headlamp (Sec. 12)

through the body is damaged. Remove the through lead and re-test. If the light still remains on the field coils are earthed and must be renewed.

23 Carefully examine the brush holders. If any parts are worn or damaged they must be renewed.

24 Generally inspect all other parts and renew any parts that are worn or damaged. During reassembly new circlips should always be used.

25 To remove the brushes they must be unsoldered from their attachments in the brush holder and field winding respectively. Solder the new brushes into position taking care not to allow solder to run down onto the brush leads as this can prevent the necessary movement of the brushes in the brush holders and may also reduce brush spring. Ideally the brushes should be renewed when they have worn down to a length of 0.51 in (13 mm).

26 Reassembly of this starter motor is a direct reversal to the dismantling procedure. Lubricate the starter motor as shown in Fig. 10.12.

12 Headlights - general

1 To remove a headlight pull out the socket connection at the rear and remove the rubber cover. Turn the chromed ring slightly anticlockwise, remove the chromed ring and lift out the headlight (photos).

2 The bulb is removed by releasing the retaining clip and withdrawing the bulb (photo).

3 The beam alignment of the headlights should be adjusted by a service station using modern optical setting equipment.

4 The two adjusting screws are located at the rear of each headlight in the engine compartment.

13 Rear lights - general

1 To change the bulbs remove the lens assembly by undoing the four retaining screws (photos).

2 Disconnect the leads from inside the boot and remove the defective bulb (photo).

3 When refitting the lens ensure the seal is in position.

14 Number plate light - general

1 The rear number plate light is removed by releasing the spring clips, which retain it in position, with a screwdriver (photo).

2 Unclip the cover and remove the bulb (photo).

15 Parking light and direction indicators (front) - general

1 Remove the screws retaining the lens (photo).

12.1a Removing the headlamp socket connection

12.1b Removing the chromed ring

12.2a Bulb retaining clip

12.2b Removing the bulb

13.1a Lens assembly securing screws

13.1b Rear lights cluster with lens removed

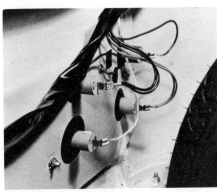
13.2 Rear lights connections in the boot

14.1 Removing the number plate light

14.2 Remove the cover to get at the bulb

15.1 The two screws securing the lens on the front parking light and direction indicator light

15.2 The lens removed exposing the bulbs

2   Lift out the lens and renew the bulb (photo).
3   When refitting the lens ensure the seal is in position.

16 Interior light - general

1   Remove the lens by inserting a screwdriver into the small cut-out and prising out the assembly (photo).
2   The bulb can now be renewed.

17 Flasher unit - general

1   The flasher unit controls the operation of the direction indicators and the hazard warning lights.
2   The unit is located behind the control panel.
3   If a fault occurs in either system, check the wiring and bulbs. If these are in order, pull out the flasher unit from the terminal block and install a new one.

18 Horns and horn switch - general

1   Twin horns are mounted behind the radiator grille (photo).
2   The horns normally require no attention. If they fail to operate, check the circuit fuse and the connecting wiring.
3   To check the horn switch, lever off the crash-pad from the centre of the steering wheel, unscrew the retaining screws and remove the contact bar (photo).
4   If the fuse, wiring and switch is in order but the fault persists, renew the horn.

19 Windscreen wiper blades and arms - removal and refitting

1   Whenever the wiper blades fail to clean the windscreen effectively, they must be renewed.
2   Pull the wiper arm away from the screen until it locks in position. Depress the small locking tab and pull the wiper blade from the wiper

16.1 Changing the interior roof light bulb

18.1 The horns are fitted behind the radiator grille

18.3 Checking the horn switch

19.2 Pulling the wiper blade from the upper arm

19.4 Wiper arm removed from its spindle

20.4 Windscreen wiper motor - location

arm (photo).
3   It may be possible to obtain new rubber inserts otherwise the wiper blade and holder will have to be renewed complete.
4   A wiper arm can be removed by lifting the small locking tab and pulling it from the splines of its driving spindle (photo).
5   Refitting is a reversal of removal but make sure that the wiper arms are fitted to their splines in such a way that the blades are parallel with the bottom edge of the windscreen.

20 Windscreen wiper motor - removal and refitting

1   Disconnect the battery earth terminal. Remove the wiper arms.
2   Remove the panel under the dashboard.
3   Remove the demister hoses.

4   Disconnect the wiper motor leads. Undo and remove the securing screws and linkage. Lift away the motor (photo).
5   Refitting is the reversal of the removal procedure.

21 Windscreen wiper motor - servicing

1   The windscreen wipers are operated by an electric motor which is fitted under the dashboard and drives the wiper arms by linked arms.
2   The electric motor is of the two pole, compound motor type with a parking switch built into the gear housing. The motor has two speeds.
3   Two motors have been fitted, SWF or Electrolux, but their principle of operation is the same.
4   If the motor operation is faulty it is far better to obtain a replacement unit rather than try to repair it as spares can be very difficult to

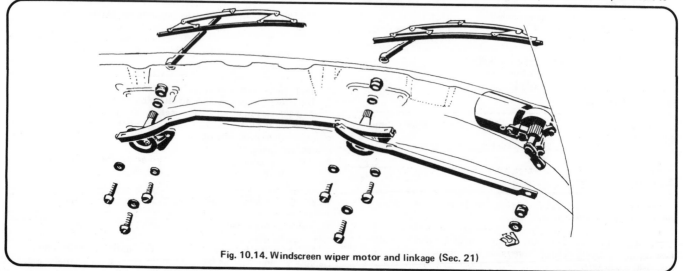

Fig. 10.14. Windscreen wiper motor and linkage (Sec. 21)

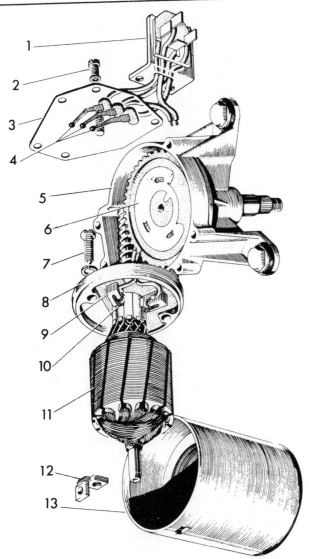

Fig. 10.15. Windscreen wiper motor - exploded view (Sec. 21)

1	Terminal contact	8	End
2	Screw	9	Brush holder
3	Cover	10	Brush
4	Contacts	11	Rotor
5	Housing	12	Nut
6	Gear	13	Stator
7	Screw		

obtain. For the more ambitious, the following notes are given.
5   On the early type of motor the bushes are of the self-lubricating type. When overhauling the motor a few drops of engine oil should be applied to the armature shaft and the gear housing three quarters filled with lithium based grease. If the motor is noisy in operation this is usually caused by excessive endfloat of the armature shaft and this is adjustable by means of a screw. The correct clearance is 0.004-0.012 in (0.1-0.3 mm).
6   On the later type of motor a lubricating wick is used for the bearings. This should be dipped in engine oil. At the same time the gear housing should be filled with lithium based grease. The clearance between the worm screw and the gear wheel should be 0.002-0.006 in (0.05-0.15 mm). Lubricate the linkage joints with a little lithium based grease for refitting.

Self parking position - changing
1   On all models, the windscreen wiper blades are parked on the right when viewed from the driver's seat.
2   The parking position can be changed over, so that the blades park on the left, by turning the contact plate through 180º for Electrolux

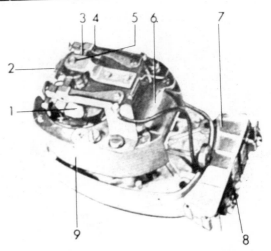

Fig. 10.16. Tailgate window wiper motor (Sec. 22)

1	Rotor	6	Permanent magnet
2	Brush spring	7	Parking switch
3	Brush	8	Diode
4	Brush holder	9	Pole shoe
5	Stop tab for rotor		

Fig. 10.17. Tailgate window wiper drive housing (Sec. 22)

1	Drive on output shaft	3	Rotor shaft drive
2	Intermediate drive, fibre		

wiper motors.
3   The nut, steel washer and fibre washer are first removed after which the contact plate can be lifted up and turned.
4   On cars fitted with the SWF wiper motor the parking position can be changed by removing the shaft and turning it through 180º.

22 Tailgate window wiper (245 models) - general

1   The tailgate window wiper is operated by a single speed permanent magnet electric motor. It is connected to the wiper blade by a link arm.
2   The wiper is removed by taking off the panel on the inside of the tailgate and unscrewing the screws securing the reinforcing plate under the wiper motor which are found under this panel. The battery positive lead should be disconnected before you start as you will have to unscrew leads from terminals on the motor. These leads should, of course, be marked before removal. When the link arm has been disconnected and the reinforcing plate pushed to one side, the motor can be removed.
3   Dismantling and inspecting the motor and gear housing is a simple matter with the guidance of Figs. 10.16, 10.17 and 10.18. Clean all the parts and check them for wear and mechanical damage. Check the armature for short circuiting between commutator and frame and also for short circuiting, and breakage in, the winding coils.
This is usually indicated by signs of overheating in the armature. Signs of burning on the commutator, on the other hand, indicate open circuit armature windings. If you are dubious about the armature, have it tested by a specialist.

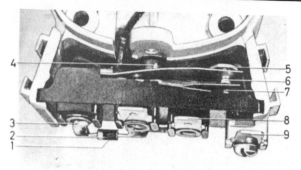

Fig. 10.18. Tailgate window wiper - parking switch (Sec. 22)

1	Connection 31b	6	Contact (2) 53
2	Diode	7	Contact 31b
3	Connection 53	8	Connection 53a
4	Lift tab	9	Connection 31
5	Contact 53a		

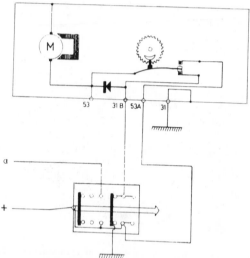

Fig. 10.19. Tailgate window wiper wiring diagram (Sec. 22)

a - connection to window washer

4   On reassembly the drive housing should be well greased. The arma-ture shaft and its bush should be very lightly oiled. Renew the brushes if they are worn.

5   The wiring diagram (Fig. 10.19) illustrates the switching and parking arrangements which are quite different from those for the windscreen wiper. The tailgate wiper switch has three positions - park, wiper operating, wiper and washer operating. The connection 'a' in the diagram takes battery positive to the window washer. When the switch is in the parking position (as shown in the diagram) the wiper motor continues to run until the changeover contact connected to the brush which is not permanently earthed switches over from 12v positive to earth (reached via the switch) and this exerts a braking action on the motor which immediately comes to rest. The normal position of the contact, of course, connects battery positive to the motor brush.

6   When the switch is in one of the running positions, battery positive is connected to terminals '31B' and '53A'. In this case, when the con-tact is actually changing over the current from the battery flows via '31B' through the diode to the motor so that there is no interruption in the supply while the contacts are actually changing over - a compar-atively slow process. When the switch is in the parking position but before the contacts change over, the diode is connected between the motor and earth but does not present a short circuit to the battery because it does not permit current flow in the direction opposite to that indicated by the black arrow head.

7   Failure of this diode would be indicated by some hesitancy in leaving the parking position when the wiper is operating, but in all probability more noticeably by clicks in the car radio each time the wiper passes through this position. This assumes that the diode goes

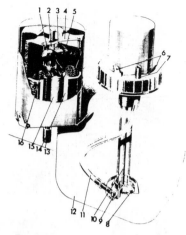

Fig. 10.20. Screen washer (Sec. 23)

1	Brush holder	9	Pump housing
2	Commutator	10	Shaft
3	Brush	11	Hose
4	Thermal fusing	12	Container
5	Spring	13	Flange
6	Terminal pin	14	Stator
7	Water outlet	15	Rotor
8	Pump impeller	16	Field winding

open circuit when it fails; if it goes short circuit it will either burn itself out very quickly (thus going open circuit) or blow the supply fuse.

23 Windscreen and tailgate window washers - general

1   Both these washers are of the same type. They consist of a centri-fugal pump driven by a small permanent magnet motor. They need little maintenance apart from an occasional clean out of the system. Repair of the motor is not a practical proposition.

2   The windscreen washer is located on the right-hand wheel housing, where its position is obvious. The tailgate window washer is placed in a cavity to the right under the floor of the cargo space.

24 Instrument panel - removal and refitting

1   Disconnect the battery earth terminal.

2   Remove the covers round the steering column. Remove the bracket retaining screws and allow the bracket to slip down on the steering column.

3   Remove the retaining screws, disconnect the speedometer cable, then holding the rear of the speedometer press the panel up and out until the upper clip is released. The electrical connections can now be disconnected and warning light bulbs changed. This is a simple opera-tion: the holders may be twisted and removed from the panel and the bulbs pushed into the holders.

4   Dismantling the panel to remove the various instruments is a straightforward process.

25 Speedometer and speedometer cable - general

1   It is most important that the speedometer cable is correctly fitted if the speedometer is to function without trouble. It is vitally important that the cable is not bent too sharply. At no point must the radius of a bend be less than 4 in (100 mm). If the bending radius is less than this, vibration and noises can occur in the instrument. The drive couplings must run true in the outer casing of the cable.

2   This being said, fitting is not difficult. We suggest that you start at the speedometer end, because this is the cleanest. Withdraw the old cable as you go and fit the new one.

3   If a speedometer starts giving trouble, it should be renewed. Faulty operation is almost always the result of wear which cannot really be

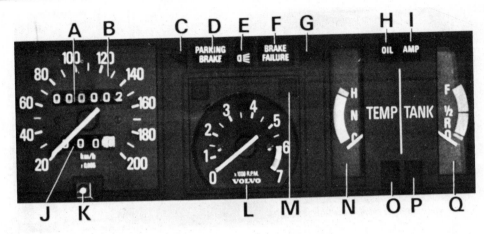

Fig. 10.21. Instrument panel (Sec. 24)

A Odometer
B Speedometer
C Turn left signal light
D Parking brake light
E Headlamp main beams

F Brake circuits failure
   warning light
G Turn right signal light
H Oil pressure failure light
I Battery charging failure light

J Trip, odometer
K Trip meter reset knob
L Tachometer (certain models)
M Bulb failure warning light

N Temperature gauge
O Overdrive light
P Choke light
Q Fuel gauge

compensated by adjustment.

26 Fuel gauge - testing

1 Before removing an apparently faulty fuel gauge always check to see that it is the gauge that is at fault.
2 First check that all terminal connections at the rear of the gauge and and on the top of the tank unit are clean and secure.
3 Switch on the ignition and using a test light check that there is current on the feed side of the gauge.
4 Gauge reads empty:

a) Disconnect the lead on the sender unit and insulate the end so that it cannot earth against the body or tank.
b) Switch on the ignition and the gauge should read 'full'.
c) If the gauge shows 'empty' disconnect the lead on the gauge (the one which connects the gauge to the tank sender unit).
d) Switch on the ignition and if the gauge reads 'full' there is no fault in the gauge and the wiring or sender unit must be suspect.

5 Gauge reads 'full':

a) Disconnect the lead on the tank sender unit.
b) Switch on the ignition and earth the lead to the tank sender unit using a piece of spare wire.
c) If the gauge shows 'empty' the lead and gauge are satisfactory. The fault must therefore be in the tank sender unit.
d) Should the gauge not show 'empty' also disconnect the lead at the terminal on the gauge.
e) Earth the contact screw using a piece of spare wire. If the gauge is satisfactory it should show 'empty'.
f) Should the gauge show anything other than 'empty' the fault is due either to dirty contact on the terminals between the gauge and lead to the sender unit or a breakage in the lead. It is very rare for the gauge to fail.

6 Removal and refitting of the fuel tank sender unit is described in Chapter 3.

27 Voltage stabilizer - general

1 Electric current is supplied to the combined water and oil temperature gauges and the fuel gauge via a voltage stabilizer in order to ensure that the readings given do not fluctuate with the state of charge of the battery.
2 The stabilizer supplies the instruments with a constant voltage of

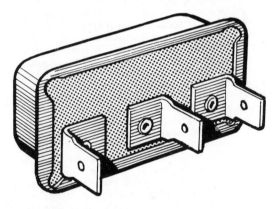

Fig. 10.22. Voltage stabilizer (Sec. 27)

approximately 10 volts.
3 The stabilizer is mounted on the reverse side of the combined instrument. To remove it, pull straight out so that the three pins come loose from their retainers.

28 Seatbelt interlock system - general

1 This system is fitted to cars produced for the North American market. If the front seats are occupied but either seatbelt has not been fastened, the car cannot be started and a warning buzzer (USA only) and lamp are actuated if any attempt is made to do so.
2 Apart from checking the interconnecting wiring and connections, special test equipment is needed to check out a major fault.

29 Bulb failure warning light - general

1 This light comes on if any of the following lights are defective:

One of the lower beams.
One of the tail lights.
One of the number plate lights.
One of the brakelights (when the brake pedal is depressed).

2 The system consists of a Reed relay and a warning light. It indicates a failure of one of the above lights if the light comes on.
3 The relay is located to the left, under the dashboard, and the warning light is located in the instrument panel (Fig. 10.23).

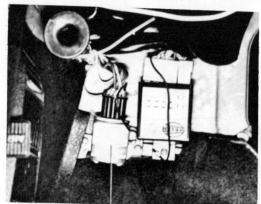

Fig. 10.23. Bulb failure warning light relay - location (Sec. 29)

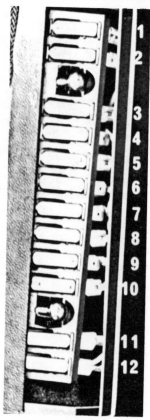

Fig. 10.24. Fuse box with cover removed (Sec. 30)

30 Fuses - general

1   The fusebox is located at the front of the left-hand door. The cover is removed by turning the small knob a quarter-turn.

2   If a fuse blows, temporarily connect a headlamp bulb (main beam) across the fuse holder. If this bulb glows at full strength, you have a complete short circuit. This is certain to be caused by a nipped wire, a broken connection with one end of the wire touching metal, or a connector being bent over to touch metal. If the bulb glows faintly, it may be replaced by an ammeter which will indicate how much the overload current is. Do not leave the ammeter connected for any length of time in case the cause of the overload suffers damage from which it has been protected by the blowing of the fuse.

3   Tracing the cause of a blown fuse is a matter of logic and perseverance. Disconnect each of the switches, lamps etc fed by the fuse in turn until the overload disappears, thus revealing the culprit. If all the items fed by the fuse are dismantled and you are still getting trouble, the fault must lie in the wiring.

4   Intermittent short-circuits are almost invariably due to wiring and connector faults. These are often difficult to trace as they always seem to disappear when you are looking for them, but patience and thoroughness will lead you to them in the end.

5   Always use fuses having the values depicted on the appropriate circuit diagram. This way you can be sure of adequate protection without unnecessary replacement.

31 Faults - tracing (general)

1   Electrical faults fall into three classes:

a) *Failure to generate.*
b) *Failure to start.*
c) *Failure of instrument, accessories or lighting to function properly in an otherwise satisfactory electrical system.*

2   Faults in the first two classes are dealt with in the table that follows. This table concludes with an example of a fault in the third class; this part of the table may be adapted to deal with almost any accessory, and certainly the first two or three possible reasons or remedies are of almost universal application, especially if we take the words 'faulty control switch' to include faulty control relays where applicable.

32 Fault diagnosis - electrical system

Symptom	Reason/s	Remedy
Starter motor turns engine very slowly	Battery in discharged condition	Charge battery.
	Starter brushes badly worn, sticking, or brush wires loose	Examine brushes, renew as necessary, tighten down brush wires.
	Loose wires in starter motor circuit	Check wiring and tighten as necessary.
	Worn bearing bushes in starter motor	Renew starter motor.
Starter motor operates without turning engine	One-way clutch slipping	Clean clutch thoroughly - if this does not prove successful, renew motor.
	Pinion or ring gear teeth broken or worn	Fit new gear ring, and new pinion to starter motor drive.
Starter motor noisy or excessively rough engagement	Pinion or ring gear teeth broken or worn	Fit new ring gear, or new pinion to starter motor drive.
	Starter drive main spring broken	Dismantle and fit new main spring.
	Starter motor retaining bolts loose	Tighten starter motor securing bolts. Fit new spring washer if necessary.
	Worn bearing bushes	Renew starter motor.

Symptom	Reason/s	Remedy
Battery will not hold charge for more than a few days	Battery defective internally	Remove and fit new battery.
	Electrolyte level too low or electrolyte too weak due to leakage	Top-up electrolyte level to just above plates.
	Plate separators no longer fully effective	Remove and fit new battery.
	Battery plates severely sulphated	Remove and fit new battery.
	Drivebelt slipping	Check belt for wear, renew if necessary, and tighten.
	Battery terminal connections loose or corroded	Check terminals for tightness, and remove all corrosion.
	Short in lighting circuit causing continual battery drain	Trace and rectify.
	Regulator unit not working correctly	Check setting, adjust where possible, renew, if defective.
	Faults listed under next heading may also apply	
Ignition light fails to go out, battery runs flat in a few days	Drivebelt loose and slipping, or broken	Check, renew and tighten as necessary.
	Brushes worn, sticking, broken or dirty	Examine, clean, or renew brushes as necessary.
	Brush springs weak or broken	Examine and test. Renew as necessary.
	Commutator or slip rings dirty, greasy, worn or burnt	Clean commutator and undercut segment separators; in alternator, clean slip rings.
	Armature/rotor badly worn or shaft bent	Fit new or reconditioned armature/rotor.
	Faulty regulator unit or isolation diode	Check, renew.
Wipers do not function correctly		
Wiper motor fails to work	Blown fuse	Check and renew fuse if necessary.
	Faulty control switch	Renew.
	Wire connections loose, disconnected or broken	Check wiper wiring. Tighten loose connections.
	Brushes badly worn	Remove and fit new brushes.
	Armature worn or faulty	If electricity at wiper motor remove and overhaul and fit replacement armature.
	Field coils faulty	Purchase reconditioned wiper motor.
Wiper motor works very slowly and takes excessive current	Commutator dirty, greasy or burnt	Clean commutator thoroughly.
	Drive to spindles unlubricated	Examine drive. Lubricate.
	Wheelbox spindle binding or damaged	Remove, overhaul, or fit replacement.
	Armature bearings dry or unaligned	Replace with new bearings correctly aligned.
	Armature badly worn or faulty	Remove, overhaul, or fit replacement armature.
Wiper motor works slowly and takes little current	Brushes badly worn	Remove and fit new brushes.
	Commutator dirty, greasy or burnt	Clean commutator thoroughly.
	Armature badly worn or faulty	Remove and overhaul armature or fit replacement.
Wiper motor works but wiper blades remain static	Driving linkage disengaged	Examine and if faulty, renew.
	Wheelbox gear and spindle damaged or worn	Examine and if faulty, renew.
	Wiper motor gearbox parts badly worn	Overhaul or fit new gearbox.

Fig. 10.15. Wiring diagram (to 1975)

Key to wiring diagram

1 Battery
2 Connection plate
3 Ignition switch
4 Ignition coil
5 Distributor, firing sequence 1-3-4-2
6 Spark plug
7 Starter motor
8 Alternator
9 Charging regulator
10 Fusebox
11 Lighting switch
12 Bulb failure warning unit
13 Step relay for fullbeams, dipped beams and headlight flasher
14 Fullbeams
15 Dipped beams
16 Parking light
17 Day notice light
18 Tail light
19 Side marking light
20 Sign light
21 Stop light contact
22 Stop light
23 Contact on M 40, M 41 gearbox
24 Contact on BW 35 automatic transmission
25 Back-up spotlight
26 Direction indicator lever
27 Hazard warning lights switch
28 Flasher unit
29 Front flasher light

30 Rear flasher light
31 Conn. to instrument
32 Conn. to instrument
33 Conn. to instrument
34 Conn. to instrument
35 Oil pressure warning light
36 Choke light
37 Parking brake warning light
38 Brake warning light
39 EGR - indicator light
40 Battery charging warning light
41 Bulb failure warning light
42 Full beams indicator light
43 Flasher indicator light
44 Overdrive indicator light
45 Fasten seat belt tight
46 Engine compartment
47 Buckle lighting
48 Rear ashtray lighting
49 Gear position lighting
50 Rheostat for instrument panel light
51 Instrument panel light
52 Control panel light
53 Glove locker light
54 Courtesy light
55 Door contact, driver's side
56 Door contact, passenger's side
57 Fuel level sender
58 Temperature sender
59 Oil pressure sensor
60 Choke control contact

61 Parking brake contact
62 Brake warning contact
63 EGR - warning contact
64 Contact, seat belt, pass. seat
65 Contact, seat belt, driver's seat
66 Contact, passenger seat
67 Contact, driver's seat
68 Light buzzer
72 Rev counter
73 Fuel gauge
74 Thermometer
75 Voltage stabilizer
76 Horns
77 Horn ring
78 Cigar lighter
79 Fan
80 Fan switch
81 Windscreen wiper/washer switch
82 Windscreen wipers
83 Windscreen washers
84 Relay for headlight wipers
85 Headlight wipers
86 Switch for tailgate window wiper/washer
87 Tailgate window wiper
88 Tailgate window washer
89 Rear door contact
90 Rear cargo space light
91 Electrically heated rear window switch
92 Electrically heated rear window
93 Switch for overdrive M 41

94 Contact for overdrive on M 41 gearbox
95 Control magnet for overdrive on M 41 gearbox
96 Heater element with thermostat, driver's seat
97 Heater element, driver's seat
98 Clock
99 Diode
100 Joint
101 Relay, start inhibitor
102 Start inhibitor unit
103 Start valve
104 Thermal timer contact
105 Air pressure gauge
106 Main relay, fuel injection
107 Fuel pump relay
108 Fuel pump
109 Pressure regulating valve
110 Auxiliary air valve
111 Resistor
112 Ignition control unit
113 Solenoid on compressor
114 Solenoid valve
115 Switch, AC compressor
116 Thermostat
118 Relay for back-up light

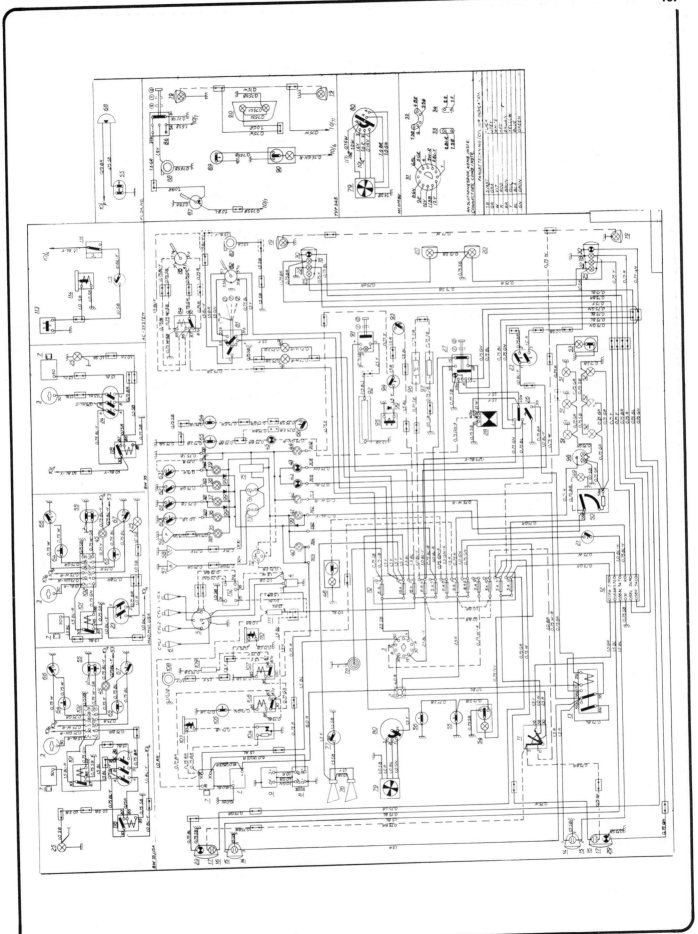

Chapter 11 Front suspension and steering

For modifications, and information applicable to later models, see Supplement at end of manual

Contents

Specifications

Front suspension

Type	Coil spring	
Wire thickness	0.545 in (13.85 mm)	0.553 in (14.05 mm)
Outer diameter	6.531 in (165.9 mm)	6.540 in (166.1 mm)
Number of turns	6.5	6.5
Shock absorbers	Double-acting hydraulic telescopic	

Steering gear (manual)

Type	Rack and pinion
Make	Cam gear or ZF
Cam gear:	
Number of turns, lock-to-lock	4.34
Reduction ratio	21.4 : 1
Rack preload	0.0039 in (0.1 mm)
Preload, rack-pinion	0.4 - 1.2 lb f ft (0.06 - 0.17 kg f m)
Lubricant	Engine oil, SAE 20W-50 or 20W-40
Oil capacity	0.35 Imp. pint (0.2 litre/0.4 US pint)
ZF:	
Number of turns, lock-to-lock	4.34
Reduction ratio	21.4 : 1
Preload, rack-pinion	0.4 - 1.2 lb f ft (0.06 - 0.17 kg f m)
Lubricant	Grease, Calypsol D4024-OK
Grease quantity	1 oz (25 gram)

Power steering

Type	Rack and pinion
Make	Cam gear
Number of turns, lock-to-lock	3.5
Reduction ratio	17.2 : 1
Preload, rack-pinion	0.6 - 1.2 lb f ft (0.09 - 0.17 kg f m)
Checking the servo balance:	
Pump pressure when torque on steering column is checked ...	170 lb f ft (12 kg f m)
Torque on steering column	2.5 - 3.3 lb f ft (0.35 - 0.45 kg f m)
Maximum difference between right and left front wheel turn ...	0.7 lb f ft (0.1 kg f m)
Lubricant	Engine oil SAE 20W-50 or 20W-40
Oil capacity	0.35 Imp. pint (0.2 litre/0.4 US pint)
Power pump:	
Type	Vane type pump
Make	ZF
Maximum pressure	995 - 1,138 psi (70 - 80 kg / sq cm)
Drive	Belt-driven
Ratio, engine speed - pump speed	1 : 1
Hydraulic oil	Automatic Transmission Fluid, Type A or Dexron
Oil capacity (with separate container)	1.9 Imp. pint (1.1 litre/2.3 US pint)

Wheel alignment (vehicle unloaded)

Castor	+2º - +3º
Camber	+1º - +1.5º
Toe-in:	

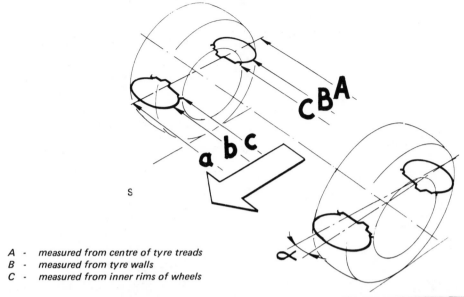

A - *measured from centre of tyre treads*
B - *measured from tyre walls*
C - *measured from inner rims of wheels*

	Angle (2 α)	A — a, mm (in.)	B — b, mm (in.)	C — c, mm (in.)
Mechanical steering	24'±8'	4.5±1.5 (0.18±0.06)	3.5±1 (0.14±0.04)	2.5±1 (0.1±0.04)
Power steering	16'±8'	3.0±1.5 (0.12±0.06)	2.0±1 0.08±0.04)	1.5±1 (0.06±0.04)

Steering axis inclination at a camber of 0° ...   .   12°
Turning angles   ...   .   20° outer wheel, 20.8° inner wheel

Torque wrench settings

	lb f ft	kg f m
Nut, ball joint (on strut) - early type strut	36 - 50	5 - 7
Nut, ball joint stud (later type)	44	6
Bolts, ball joint attachment - later type	15 - 20	2.0 - 2.7
Steering wheel nut	29 - 43	4 - 6
Steering coupling pinch-bolts	18	2.5
Strut upper mounting nuts	18	2.5
Track control arm (front bolt)	60	8.2
Track control arm (rear nut)	40	5.4
Track control arm (bracket bolts)	35	4.8
Roadwheel nuts	70 to 100	10 to 14

1 General description

1   The front suspension is of the MacPherson type with a shock absorber inside the coil spring. It consists of a strut and coil spring assembly, attached at the top to the wheel housing and at the bottom to a control arm. A stabiliser bar, supported in rubber bushings, connects the control arms.
2   The strut assembly contains the shock absorber. The coil spring bottom support and the hub are welded to the strut casing. The shock absorber spindle functions as the strut upper guide and is pivoted in the strut upper attachment.
3   The steering gear is of the rack and pinion type. There are two versions: manual and power-assisted. There are two makes of manual steering gear, one grease-lubricated and the other oil-lubricated.
4   The power pump is a vane-type pump driven by a belt from the crankshaft pulley.
5   The top section of the steering column is provided with a splined sliding joint which, in case of accident, prevents the shaft from being driven into the car. As a further safety measure the steering wheel is connected to the steering column by a steel sleeve which collapses under excessive pressure.

2 Steering mechanism - maintenance and inspection

1   At the intervals specified in 'Routine Maintenance' check and top-up the fluid level in the steering pump. Check the level when the engine is not running. The level should be about ¼ in (6.35 mm) above the mark on the pump reservoir. When the engine is started, the level will fall to the mark (Power steering) (Fig. 11.3).
2   Use only specified (automatic transmission) fluid for topping-up.
3   Wear in the steering gear and linkage is indicated when there is considerable movement in the steering wheel without corresponding movement at the roadwheels. Wear is also indicated when the car tends to 'wander' off the line one is trying to steer. There are three main steering 'groups' to examine in such circumstances, these are the wheel bearings, the linkage joints and bushes and the steering gear itself.
4   First jack-up the front of the car and support it on stands under the side frame members so that both front wheels are clear of the ground.
5   Grip the top and bottom of the wheel and try to rock it. It will not take any great effort to be able to feel any play in the wheel bearing. If this play is very noticeable it would be as well to adjust it straight away as it could confuse further examinations. It is also possible that during this check play may be discovered also in the lower suspension ball joint. If this happens the ball joint will need renewal.
6   Next grip each side of the wheel and try rocking it laterally. Steady pressure will, of course, turn the steering but an alternated back and forth pressure will reveal any loose joint. If some play is felt it would be easier to get assistance from someone so that while one person rocks the wheel from side to side, the other can look at the joints and bushes on the track rods and connections.
7   The most likely places for wear or play to occur are at the track rod end ball joints.

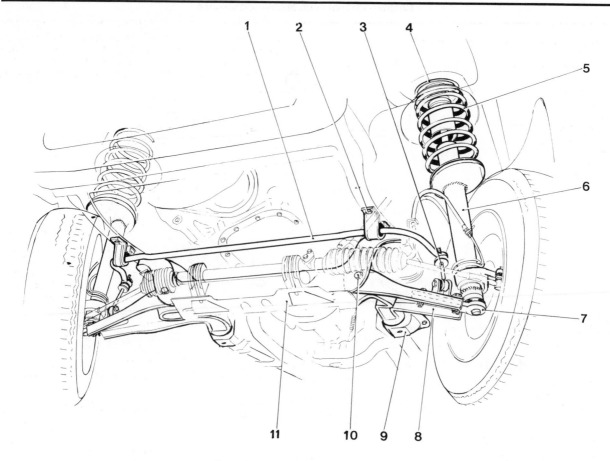

Fig. 11.1. Front suspension (Sec. 1)

1 Stabilizer bar	4 Strut upper pivot point	7 Ball joint	10 Front bracket for control arm
2 Bracket	5 Spring	8 Control arm	11 Front axle member
3 Link	6 Strut assembly	9 Rear bracket for control arm	

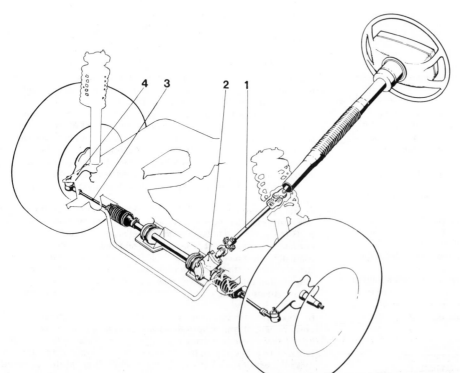

Fig. 11.2. Manual steering gear (Sec. 1)

1 Steering shaft
2 Steering gear
3 Steering rod
4 Steering arm

8 Check the security of the steering box mountings.

3 Front hubs - adjustment

1 Jack-up the front of the car and support the control arm by placing a jack under it.
2 Remove the roadwheel.
3 Tap off the grease cap. This can usually be removed quite easily using a brass drift to drive it off outwards.
4 Extract the split pin.
5 Extract the disc pads (see Chapter 9).

6 Turn the hub in its normal forward direction of rotation and at the same time tighten the nut to a torque of 50 lb f ft (7 kg f m). Unscrew the nut 1/3rd of a turn and insert a new split pin.
7 Half fill the cap with wheel bearing grease and tap it into position.

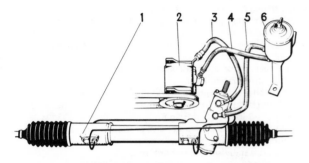

Fig. 11.2A. Power steering system (Sec. 1)

1 Steering gear	4 Oil input
2 Power pump	5 Return oil
3 Oil output	6 Oil reservoir

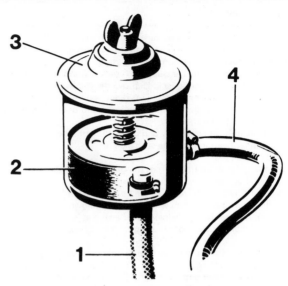

Fig. 11.3. The fluid reservoir (power steering) (Sec. 2)

1 Suction line	3 Cover
2 Filter	4 Return line

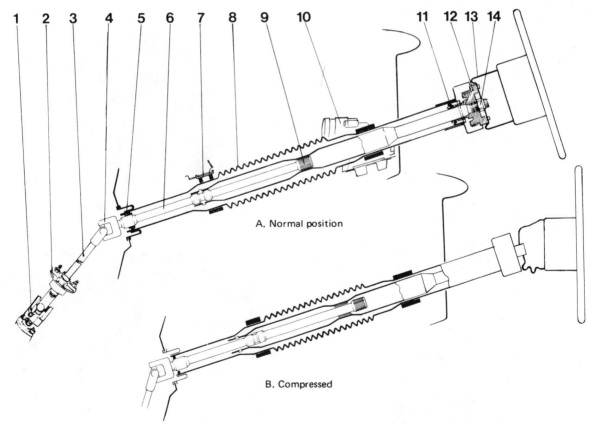

A. Normal position

B. Compressed

Fig. 11.4. Steering column (Sec. 1)

1 Lower U-joint	5 Lower bearing	8 Column jacket (below)	11 Upper bearing
2 Flange	6 Steering shaft, top	9 Serrated sleeve	12 Steering wheel hub
3 Steering shaft, bottom	section	10 Upper attachment	13 Collapsible steel sleeve
section	7 Lower attachment	steering lock	14 Nut, retaining the wheel
4 Upper U-joint			

8   Refit the disc pads.
9   Refit the roadwheel and lower the car to the ground.

4   Front hubs - overhaul

1   If the front wheel bearings become worn, this will usually be indicated by roadwheel rock which cannot be removed even though the wheel bearings have been correctly adjusted.
2   Jack-up the front of the car, support it securely and also support the control arm with a second jack. Remove the roadwheel.
3   Remove the disc caliper assembly, as described in Chapter 9.
4   Remove the grease cap, extract the split pin and unscrew and remove the castellated nut.
5   Pull off the hub/disc assembly and catch the outer bearing.
6   Pull the inner bearing from the stub axle.
7   Extract the oil seal.
8   Drive out the bearing tracks from the hub/disc assembly and wipe out all internal grease.
9   Install the new bearing tracks to the hub/disc assembly.
10 Pack the interior of the hub with grease, leaving an opening in the centre which is equal to the diameter of the stub axle.
11 Fit the oil seal and the inner bearing to the stub axle. Press grease into the bearing.
12 Install the hub/disc to the stub axle, fit the outer bearing having first packed grease into it.
13 Fit the thrust washer and castellated nut and adjust the hub, as described in the preceding Section. Fit the cap.
14 Refit the caliper and bleed the brake hydraulic system.
15 Fit the roadwheel and lower the car to the ground.

5   Control arms and bushings - removal and refitting

1   Jack-up the front end and place stands at the front jack-up points. Remove the wheels.
2   Disconnect the stabiliser bar from the link rod.
3   Remove the three retaining nuts and disconnect the ball joint from the control arm.
4   Remove the control arm front retaining bolt.
5   Remove the bolts securing the rear attachment bracket and lower the control arm. Remove the bracket from the control arm.
6   Press out the bushings from the control arm and bracket.
7   When fitting the new bushing in the control arm the flanged end of the bush is towards the front.
8   When fitting the new bushing in the control arm bracket it should be positioned so that the small slots, Fig. 11.7, point horizontally when fitted on the car.
9   After replacing the bushings fit the bracket to the control arm but do not tighten the nut.
10 Fit the rear end of the control arm in position, fit the three securing bolts but do not tighten them.
11 Fit the front retaining bolt but do not tighten the nut.
12 Attach the ball joint to the control arm and tighten the bolts to a torque of 7 - 9 lb f ft (1 - 1.3 kg f m).
13 Position a jack under the outer end of the control arm, jack-up and compress the spring.
14 Connect the stabiliser bar and link rod.
15 Tighten the front retaining bolt to the specified torque.
16 Tighten the nut for the rear bushing to the specified torque.
17 Tighten the bracket bolts to the specified torque.
18 Fit the roadwheel and lower the car.

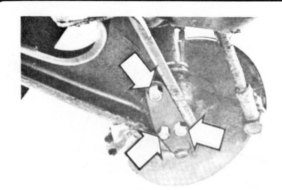

Fig. 11.5. Ball joint to control arm retaining nuts (Sec. 5)

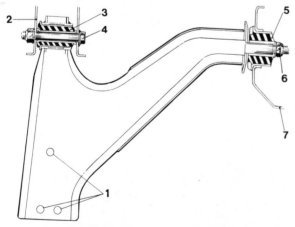

Fig. 11.6. Front control arm (Sec. 5)

1	Hole for ball joint	5	Rear rubber bushing
2	Front axle member	6	Nut
3	Front rubber bushing	7	Rear bracket
4	Bolt		

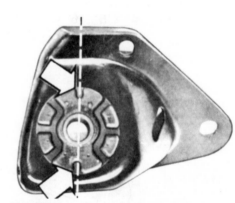

Fig. 11.7. Replacing control arm bracket bushing (Sec. 5)

Fig. 11.8. Compressing the coil spring when refitting the control arm (Sec. 5)

6 Ball joints (later type) - renewal

1 Renewal of early type ball joints is covered in the next Section.
2 Raise the front of the car and support it under its jacking points.
3 Remove the roadwheel.
4 On pre 1978 models, slacken the shock absorber cap nut a couple of turns. To do this will require a peg wrench or special Volvo tool (5039 or 5173 for gas-filled shock absorbers) - Fig. 11.9.
5 Flatten the lockplates, if fitted, and unscrew the four ball joint-to-strut bolts - Fig. 11.10A.
6 Unscrew and remove the three nuts which hold the ball joint to the track control arm - Fig. 11.10B. Remove the ball joint.
7 Unscrew the ball joint retaining nut, and press the ball stud out of the strut attachment plate - Fig. 11.10C.
8 As from 1979, the left and right-hand ball joints are not inter-changeable, so make sure that you have the one for the side being worked on.
9 Refitting is a reversal of removal. Do not grease the ball stud or it may seat too deeply and damage the rubber boot.
10 Use new bolts and tighten the nuts and the bolts to the specified torque.

7 Front suspension strut - removal and refitting

With early type ball joint

1 Raise the front of the vehicle, support under the jacking points and remove the roadwheel.
2 Slacken the cap nut using a peg wrench or special Volvo tool (5039, or 5173 for gas-filled shock absorbers).
3 Support the track control arm using a jack and disconnect the tie-rod ball joint from the steering arm. A ball joint splitter tool (Fig. 11.12) will be required for this.
4 Disconnect the stabilizer bar from the link rod.

5 Prise off the cover from the centre of the strut top mounting - Fig. 11.13.
6 Unscrew the brake pipe bracket bolt.
7 Release, but on no account remove, the strut spindle top nut. When unscrewing the nut, hold the flats on the spindle to prevent it rotating.
8 Mark the position of the strut top mounting, nut reinforcement plate in relation to the inner wing turret and then unscrew and remove the three strut upper mounting nuts.
9 Lower the jack under the track control arm but tie the strut up so that the brake hoses are not strained.
10 Fit clamps to the coil spring. These are available from most motor accessory stores or may be hired. Compress the spring.
11 Unscrew and remove the strut spindle top nut and take off the top mounting components and spring (clamped).
12 Unscrew and remove the cap nut and withdraw the shock absorber from the strut tube.
13 Slacken the ball joint retaining nut using a 19.0 mm socket and long extension inserted into the strut tube. Hold the tube against rotation using grips applied to the tube weld.
14 Release the ball joint stud from the tube using a long drift inserted into the strut tube.
15 A new strut insert (shock absorber) can be fitted by reversing the removal process. If the original coil spring is to be refitted, then the clamps need not be released until it has been fitted to the strut and the top mounting components refitted. If a new coil spring is being fitted then release the clamps very slowly from the old spring before fitting the clamps to the new one.
16 The lower ball joint can be renewed after unbolting it from the track control arm.
17 Refitting is a reversal of removal, align the marks at the turret and tighten all fixings to the specified torque. Failure to align the marks will alter the camber angle.

Fig. 11.9. Slackening the shock absorber cap nut (Sec. 6)

Fig. 11.10A Ball joint-to-strut bolts (arrowed) – later type (Sec 6)

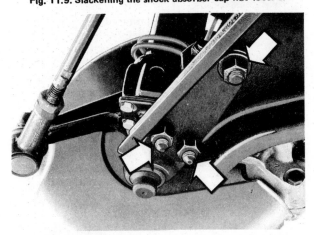

Fig. 11.10B Ball joint-to-track control arm nuts (arrowed) – later type (Sec 6)

Fig. 11.10C Ball joint attachment plate nut (arrowed) – later type (Sec 6)

With ·later type ball joint

18 The operations are very similar to those just described but refer to Section 6 for details of disconnecting the later type ball joint from the base of the strut.

8 Stabiliser bar (front) - removal and refitting

1 Disconnect the stabiliser bar from the link rods.
2 Remove the bolts which secure the stabiliser bar supports to the bodyframe and lift out the bar.
3 Any rubber bushes or mountings which are worn or have deteriorated must be renewed.
4 Refitting is the reverse of the removal procedure.

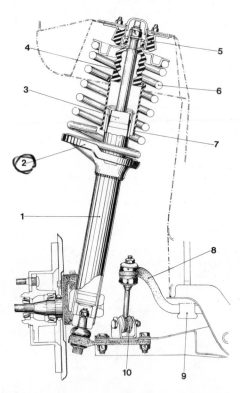

Fig. 11.11 Front strut and spring assembly (Sec. 7)

1 Strut	*6 Coil spring*
2 Spring seat plate	*7 Shock absorber protection*
3 Shock absorber	*8 Stabilizer*
4 Rubber buffer	*9 Stabilizer attachment*
* (rebound stopper)*	*10 Stabilizer link*
5 Upper mounting	

Fig. 11.15. Removing the rubber bumper and shock absorber sleeve (Sec. 7)

9 Steering wheel - removal and refitting

1 Remove the impact pad from the centre of the steering wheel by compressing it sideways and easing off the upper edge.

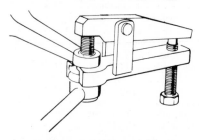

Fig. 11.12. Using a ball joint separator (Sec. 7)

Fig. 11.13. Removing the cover for the upper attachment (Sec. 7)

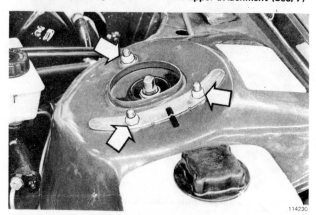

Fig. 11.14 Strut top mounting retaining nuts (arrowed) (Sec 7)

Note the alignment mark

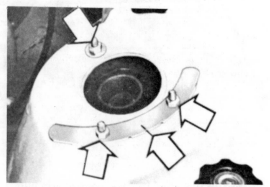

Fig.. 11.16. Slackening the ball joint retaining nut (Sec. 7)

2 Remove the horn ring (see Chapter 10).

3 Remove the centre nut and pull off the steering wheel with a puller.

4 When replacing the wheel check that the roadwheels are in the straight-ahead position. Position the steering wheel spoke horizontally and fit the centre nut. Tighten to the specified torque.

5 Fit the horn ring and the impact pad.

10 Steering column - removal and refitting

1 Disconnect the battery earth terminal.

2 Remove the clamping screw for the upper steering shaft joint in the engine compartment.

3 Remove the steering wheel as described in Section 9.

4 Remove the upper steering column covers. Remove the turn indicator switch and wiper switch and disconnect the leads.

5 Remove the housing for the switches.

6 Remove the spring and column upper bearing.

7 Remove the steering column lock as described in Chapter 13, Section 12.

8 Remove the rubber grommet from the bulkhead, and the lower attachment for the steering column.

9 Push the steering column in through the bulkhead and pull the steering column into the car.

10 Remove the steering lock.

11 The upper and lower bearings can be renewed but any other wear or damage will necessitate a new steering column.

12 Refitting is the reverse of the removal sequence, but the setting dimensions are important; refer to Chapter 13, Section 12.

Turn the steering wheel and check that it can rotate freely. Connect the battery earth cable and check the operation of the horn, indicators and windscreen wipers.

11 Trackrod end ball joints - removal and refitting

1 The trackrod ball joints require no routine lubrication. When wear occurs the ball joints on the trackrods are renewed.

2 Place stands under the front jacking points.

3 Remove the nut and disconnect the ball stud from the steering arm using a suitable ball joint separator.

4 Remove the splash guard from under the car.

5 Slacken the clips at the outboard end of the bellows.

6 Using an open-ended spanner on the flats provided to prevent the trackrod rotating, release the locknut at the trackrod end ball joint.

7 Unscrew the ball joint assembly from the trackrod, counting the number of turns.

8 Screw the new ball joint onto the trackrod by the same number of turns and connect it to the steering arm. Check the wheel alignment as described in Section 23.

9 Tighten the bellows clamp on completion.

12 Steering gear (manual) - removal and refitting

1 Remove the clamp bolt from the universal shaft joint flange. Open the flange slightly with a screwdriver.

2 Raise the front end of the car and put stands under the jacking points. Remove the wheels.

3 Remove the nuts from the trackrod-end ball joints and, using a suitable tool, disconnect the ball joints from the steering arms.

4 Remove the splash guard from under the car.

5 Remove the four bolts securing the steering gear to the front axle member.

6 Disconnect the steering gear from the steering shaft flange and remove the steering gear complete with trackrods.

7 Refitting is the reversal of the removal procedure. Check the wheel alignment, as described in Section 23.

13 Manual steering gear (Cam gear type) - dismantling and inspection

1 Clean off all external dirt. Before dismantling check the inner ball joints for wear.

2 Undo the left side bellows clip, ease off the bellows and drain the oil.

3 Bend up the peening lock on the inner ball joint, and remove the left side trackrod. Remove the right side trackrod.

4 Remove the cover for the pre-loading device and lift out the spring, 'O' ring and piston.

5 Remove the pinion cover and lift out the pinion, top bearing and spacer sleeve. Collect the shims.

6 Pull out the rack towards the pinion side of the steering gear.

7 Clean all the parts in white spirit. Check the rack bush for wear and renew if necessary. Check the pinion lower bearing, if it requires renewing a puller will be required to remove it, see Fig. 11.17. Examine the rack and pinion for wear and damage. Renew all seals and gaskets.

14 Manual steering gear (Cam gear type) - reassembly

1 Oil all the parts before assembly with engine oil (SAE 20W-50 or SAE 20W-40).

2 If new rack bushing is being fitted, position it so that the locks on the bush align with the slots in the housing and drive it in with a drift.

3 Fit the pinion with upper bearing in the housing (no shims) and fit the spacer sleeve. Fit the pinion cover, with a gasket but without the seal.

4 Using a dial gauge check the end play of the pinion. Remove the pinion cover and determine a shim thickness equal to the measured endplay plus 0.0039 in (0.1 mm) for preloading. Shims are available in thicknesses of 0.005-0.0075-0.01 in (0.127-0.191-0.254 mm).

5 Fit a new seal on the pinion cover. Apply a non-hardening gasket compound on the seal and fit the seal on the pinion cover using a suitably sized tube to drive it on.

6 Fit the rack from the pinion side taking care not to damage the bushing.

7 Fit the pinion, with upper bearing, shims and spacer sleeve. Fit the pinion cover gasket and the cover.

8 Fit the preloading piston in the housing without the 'O' ring and spring. Use a steel ruler and feeler gauge to measure the end clearance, see Fig. 11.20. Determine the thickness of shims required. Shims and gasket together should equal the measured end clearance plus 0.0008-0.0059 in (0.02-0.15 mm) for the piston endplay. Shims are available in thicknesses of 0.005-0.01-0.015-0.02 in (0.127-0.254-0.381-0.508 mm).

9 Place the spring and 'O' ring in the piston and fit the gasket and cover.

10 Connect a torque gauge to the pinion shaft and crank the rack back and forward to each end of its travel. The torque should be 5-15 lb f in (0.06 - 0.17 kg f m) if the preloading is correct.

11 Fit the left side trackrod. If fitting the same rod, place a thin shim

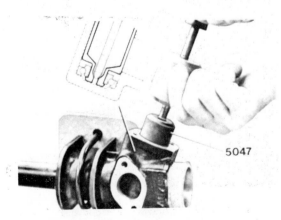

Fig. 11.17. Removing the pinion lower bearing (Sec. 13)

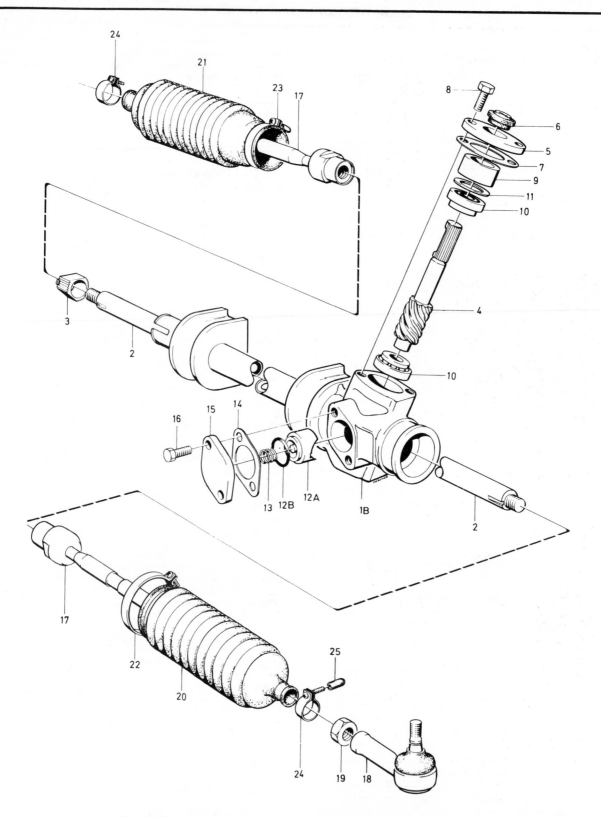

Fig. 11.18. Exploded view of manual steering gear (Cam gear) Sec. 13)

1	Housing	8	Bolt	14	Shim	20	Bellows
2	Rack	9	Spacer	15	Cover	21	Bellows
3	Bearing bushing	10	Ball bearing	16	Bolt	22	Clamp
4	Pinion	11	Shim	17	Steering rod	23	Clamp
5	Cover	12a	Pre-load piston	18	Ball joint	24	Clamp
6	Seal	12b	O-ring	19	Nut	25	Cap
7	Gasket	13	Spring				

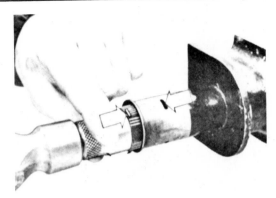

Fig. 11.19. Fitting the rack bushing (Sec. 14)

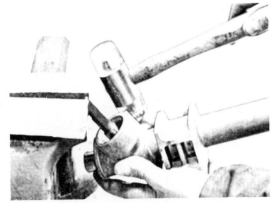

Fig. 11.22. Removing the pinion (Sec. 15)

Fig. 11.20. Measuring the pre-loading piston end clearance (Sec. 14)

Fig. 11.23. Fitting a new O-ring in the pinion nut (Sec. 16)

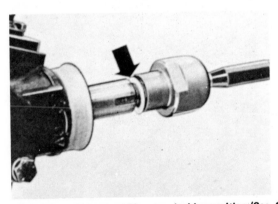

Fig. 11.21. Fitting shim to provide a new locking position (Sec. 14)

between the ball joint and rack shoulder so that an unused part of the ball joint can be used for locking by peening the edge of the ball joint into the rack groove. Fit the bellows and tighten the inner clamp. Fit the right side rod in the same way. Both rods should be the same length within 0.06 in (1.6 mm).

12 Fill the steering gear with specified oil by inserting an oil gun under the lip of the bellows.

15 Manual steering gear (ZF type) - dismantling and inspection

1 Carry out the operations described in Section 13, paragraphs 1-3.
2 Remove the dust seal for the preloading device and remove the split pin (Fig. 11.24).
3 Remove the cover and spring for the preloading device and remove the piston, tapping the rack with the palm of your hand will help to remove it.
4 Remove the pinion dust seal and the circlip. Remove the pinion

nut.
5 To remove the pinion from the housing, clamp the pinion shaft in a vice with soft grips and tap lightly on the housing with a soft-nosed hammer.
6 Pull out the rack towards the pinion side of the housing.
7 Press in the locking tabs for the rack bushing and lever out the bushing.
8 Remove the thrust washer and circlip from the pinion shaft and press off the bearing.
9 Clean all the parts and examine them for wear or damage. Renew 'O' rings and rack bushing.

16 Manual steering gear (ZF type) - reassembly

1 Press the ball bearing on to the pinion shaft and fit the circlip and thrust washer.
2 Fit new 'O' rings on the rack bushing and press it into the housing. Check that the locking tabs for the bearing fit correctly into the recesses in the housing.
3 Grease the rack with Calypsol D4024-OK grease and insert it in the pinion side of the housing. Be careful not to damage the bushing with the rack teeth.
4 Grease and insert the pinion. Pack the bearing with grease. Fit a new 'O' ring on the pinion nut, fit the nut and the locking circlip. Fill the cavity on top of the nut with grease and fit the pinion dust seal.
5 Fit a new 'O' ring on the preloading piston, grease the pinion and fit the piston and spring. Fit the cover but do not finally tighten the cover yet.
6 Connect a torque gauge to the pinion and check the torque. Crank back and forward to each end of travel. The torque should be 5-15 lb f in (0.06 - 0.17 kg f m). To increase the torque, screw in the preload piston cover. When the correct torque is obtained, fit the split pin to lock the cover and fit the dust cover (Fig. 11.25).
7 Crank the rack fully out and fill the tooth spaces with grease. Crank in the rack then out again and apply more grease. The grease charge will be approximately 1 oz (25 gram).
8 Fit the steering rods, as described in Section 14.

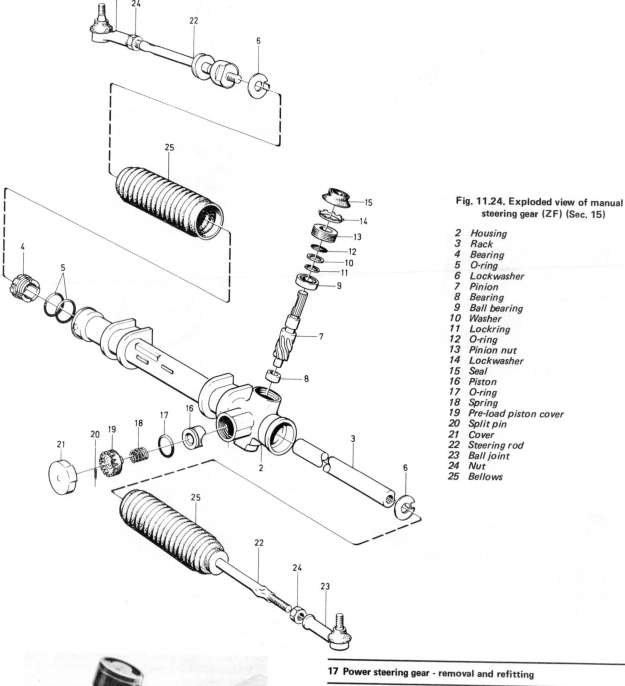

Fig. 11.24. Exploded view of manual
steering gear (ZF) (Sec. 15)

2   Housing
3   Rack
4   Bearing
5   O-ring
6   Lockwasher
7   Pinion
8   Bearing
9   Ball bearing
10 Washer
11 Lockring
12 O-ring
13 Pinion nut
14 Lockwasher
15 Seal
16 Piston
17 O-ring
18 Spring
19 Pre-load piston cover
20 Split pin
21 Cover
22 Steering rod
23 Ball joint
24 Nut
25 Bellows

Fig. 11.25. Checking the pinion torque (Sec. 16)

17 Power steering gear - removal and refitting

Removal and refitting of the steering gear is as described for the
manual steering gear described in Section 12, with the addition of
disconnecting the hoses and plugging them to prevent loss of fluid.
Checking and adjusting after refitting is described in Section 20.

18 Power steering gear - dismantling and inspection

1   Carry out the operations described in Section 13, paragraphs 1-3.
2   Remove the oil pipes.
3   Remove the preloading device cover, the piston, 'O' ring and sleeve.
Do not turn the pinion shaft or you are likely to get an oil spray.
4   Remove the lower cover and spacer sleeve for the pinion. Release
the locking tab and remove the nut. Unscrew the inner bearing race
with ball retainer and outer race.
5   Remove the valve housing cover and the spring. Lift off the valve
housing taking care not to damage the valve housing or valve. Lift out
the pinion.

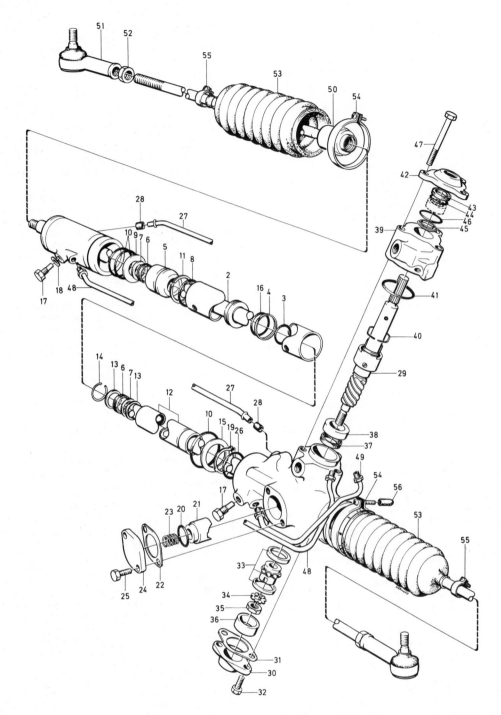

Fig. 11.26. Exploded view of power steering gear (Sec. 18)

2 Rack	16 O-ring	30 Cover	44 O-ring
3 O-ring	17 Dowel	31 Gasket	45 Spring
4 Piston ring	18 Washer	32 Bolt	46 O-ring
5 Bearing housing	19 Circlip	33 Ball bearing	47 Bolt
6 Lead	20 O-ring	34 Lockwasher	48 Pipe
7 Plastic ring	21 Piston	35 Locknut	49 Pipe
8 O-ring	22 Shim	36 Spacer	50 Steering rod
9 Spacer ring	23 Spring	37 Seal ring	51 Ball joint
10 O-ring	24 Cover	38 Bearing	52 Locknut
11 Plastic ring	25 Bolt	39 Valve housing	53 Bellows
12 Inner tabs	26 O-ring	40 Circlip	54 Clamp
13 Spacer ring	27 By-pass	41 O-ring	55 Clamp
14 Circlip	28 Seal	42 Cover	56 Cap
15 Washer	29 Pinion	43 Seal	

6 Remove the lock bolt for the right side housing, pull off the housing and the connecting tube.

7 Pull out the rack and bearing sleeve. Pull the sleeve off the rack.

8 Remove the bolt for the left side housing and pull out the outer tube from the housing, then pull out the inner tube.

9 Remove the upper bushing. For this you will need a puller like the one shown in Fig. 11.17. Use the tool in the middle of the sleeve.

10 Using two thin screwdrivers lever out the upper outer race of the pinion lower bearing.

11 Remove both 'O' rings and spacer from the right side housing. Remove the bearing, 'O' ring and seal from the valve housing cover.

12 Remove the seal, 'O' ring and plastic rings from the rack bearing sleeve.

13 Remove the plastic ring and the 'O' ring under it from the rack.

14 Remove the oil seal, washer and circlip from the inner tube.

15 Clean all parts with white spirit. Examine all the parts for wear or damage. If a pinion, control valve or valve housing is faulty all the assembly parts should be renewed. Also, if the bearing is renewed the bearing sleeve for the rack should be renewed. Renew all seals and 'O' rings.

19 Power steering gear - reassembly

1 Oil all the parts before assembly with engine oil.

2 Fit the oil seal, bearing and 'O' ring on the valve housing cover. Fit the plastic ring and 'O' ring on the rack bearing sleeve.

3 Fit the circlip on the inner tube. Fit the 'O' ring and plastic ring on the rack piston with the 'O' ring under the plastic ring.

4 Fit the spacer sleeve, oil seal and plastic ring on the rack. Fit them from the teeth side of the rack but cover the teeth with a wide tape to protect the oil seal from damage as it is fitted, then remove the tape and fit the spacer sleeve on the rack.

5 In the left side housing fit the oil seal with the lip facing outwards, the bushing (use a suitable drift to drive it in) and the two 'O' rings.

6 Fit the spacer washer and two 'O' rings in the right side housing.

7 On the left side housing fit the inner tube and its spacer washer. Fit the rack, equipped with seal and spacer rings, into the inner tube and press in the seal and spacer rings. Fit the retaining circlip.

8 Fit the outer tube on the left side housing, with the hole for the lock bolt aligned with the hole in the housing, and fit the lock bolt.

9 Fit the bearing sleeve in the outer tube with the holes for the lock bolt in alignment.

10 Fit the seal and plastic ring in the bearing sleeve, use a tape round the sharp edge of the rack to protect the seal.

11 Fit the connecting pipe with rubber seal in the right side housing and then fit the right side housing, so that the holes for the lock bolts and the connecting pipe are in alignment. Fit the lock bolt and connect up the pipe.

12 Fit the outer race for the pinion lower bearing. Fit the pinion taking care not to damage the valve and fit the inner race and ball retainer on the pinion. Fit the lock ring and nut, but do not lock the nut.

13 Fit the outer race and the spacer sleeve.

14 Press down the spacer sleeve so that it bottoms on the bearing and using a feeler gauge and steel ruler measure the distance between the spacer ring and housing (see Fig. 11.20) to determine thickness of gasket required.

15 Fit the selected gasket(s) and the Volvo tool 5054, this represents the cover with the centre removed so that the nut is accessible for adjusting the steering gear when it is fitted in the car, see the following Section.

16 Fit the 'O' ring in the valve housing, fit the housing and then place the coil spring in the valve housing with the big end in first. Fit the valve housing cover making sure that the spring does not get caught between the valve housing and the cover. The pinion shaft shoulder should be 0.06 in (1.5 mm) above the cover face. Adjust the position, if necessary, by moving the lower bearing inner race.

17 Fit the preloading piston, without 'O' ring, in the housing. Using feeler gauge and steel ruler, measure the distance between housing and piston face. Select shims equal to the measured distance plus 0.002-0.006 in (0.05-0.15 mm) for correct end clearance.

18 Fit the 'O' ring and spring for preloading piston, fit selected shims and cover.

19 Connect a torque gauge to the pinion shaft and move the rack back and forward over its full travel. Torque should be 5-15 lb f in (0.09-

0.17 kg f m). If the torque is excessive stop the rack in that position and re-adjust the preloading piston. If the rack jams with the piston removed, the rack is distorted and must be renewed.

20 Fit the oil pipes.

21 Fit the steering rods, as described in Section 14.

22 Valve adjustment, filling power steering oil and lubricating oil is carried out after the steering gear is refitted in the car - see the following Section.

20 Power steering gear - checking and adjusting balance

1 To carry out the following checks and adjustments, special tools are required, the illustrations show the Volvo tools, but suitable equivalents could be used (ie. tool 5054 could be made by cutting the centre out of a pinion cover).

2 Connect the test gauge as shown in Fig. 11.32. Position the gauge in front of the windscreen so that it can be read from the driver's seat.

3 Fill oil almost up to the edge of the reservoir. Start the engine and let it idle. Top-up with oil when the level drops, until the level is stabilised at the correct level. Use ATF Type A or Dexron oil.

4 Turn the steering wheel slowly, from side-to-side several times, topping-up with oil when necessary. Keep turning the steering wheel until the reservoir is almost free of air bubbles. Top-up, if necessary, and fit reservoir cap.

5 Remove the steering wheel impact pad. Turn the steering wheel nearly to the right end position and connect a torque gauge to the steering wheel centre nut with a 27 mm socket and extension. Use the torque gauge to turn slowly to the right and read the torque at the moment the pressure gauge approaches 170 psi (12 kg/sq cm). It is most important that the torque is read exactly when this pressure is reached, as the pressure will remain, even if the torque is lowered in this position.

6 Now check the balance when turning the steering wheel to the left in the same way. The torque should be 2.5-3.3 lb f ft (0.35-0.45 kg f m). The difference between right and left sides must not be more than 0.7 lb f ft (0.1 kg f m).

7 If the torque difference between sides is excessive, switch off the engine and remove the lock nut and lockwasher from the pinion lower bearing. If the torque has to be increased for left side - decreased for right side proceed as follows: Straighten the lockwasher tab which was bent for locking the bearing race (adjustment nut), bend over the next tab to the left. Turn the adjustment nut to the left until its groove fits the lockwasher tab. Fit the lockwasher and locknut. If the torque has to be altered in the opposite direction move one tab to the right. Changing to the next tab alters the torque by 4 lb f in (0.05 kg f m).

8 To check the pump pressure at the left side end position turn the steering wheel fully to the left and hold it there for a maximum of 10 seconds while reading the gauge. The pressure should be 995-1,150 psi (70-80 kg/sq cm). Check the right side end position in the same way.

9 If the pump pressure is incorrect, check the pump by closing the pressure gauge valve for 10 seconds maximum. If the pressure does not reach the figure specified above the pump is faulty.

10 Re-check the balance when turning the steering to the right and then to the left. The torque difference must be within the limit specified in paragraph 6.

11 Switch off the engine and lock the pinion nut with the lockwasher. Remove the adjusting flange taking care not to damage the gasket and fit the pinion cover.

12 Fill the steering gear with lubricating oil, by inserting an oil gun under the lip of the bellows, then carefully compress the bellows so that some oil flows to the other side.

13 Disconnect the test gauge and connect the pressure hose to the steering gear. Fit the steering wheel impact pad.

14 Start the engine. Turn the steering wheel to left and right end positions, check the reservoir oil level and top-up, if necessary.

15 Fit the roadwheels and lower the car.

21 Power steering pump - removal and refitting

1 Place a container to collect the oil below the pump and disconnect the pump hydraulic connections.

2 Remove the nuts on the two long bracket bolts. Remove the

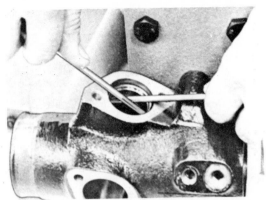

Fig. 11.27. Levering out the upper outer race of the pinion lower bearing (Sec. 18)

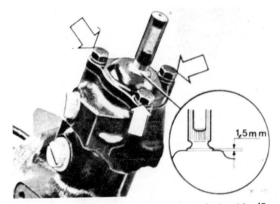

Fig. 11.31. Check the position of the pinion shaft shoulder (Sec. 19)

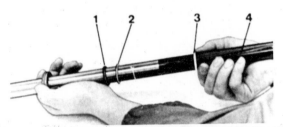

Fig. 11.28. Rack teeth covered with tape when fitting seal (Sec. 19)

1 Spacer   3 Plastic ring
2 Seal   4 Tape

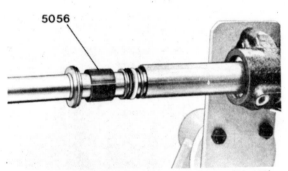

Fig. 11.29. Fitting the rack into the inner tube (Sec. 19)

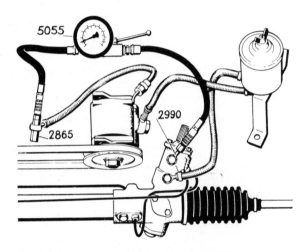

Fig. 11.32. Test equipment connections (Sec. 20)

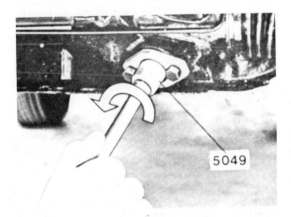

Fig. 11.33. Turning the bearing race (adjustment nut) to the left (Sec. 20)

Tool 5049 inserted through tool 5054

tensioner locking screws on both sides of the pump and lift off the drivebelt.
3   Swing the pump up and remove the three screws securing the bracket to the engine block, then remove the pump and bracket.
4   Separate the bracket from the pump.
5   Refitting is the reverse of the removal procedure. Tension the drivebelt to give a deflection of 0.12 in (5 mm) at the centre of its longest run.
6   Fill and bleed the system, as described in Section 20, paragraphs 3 and 4.

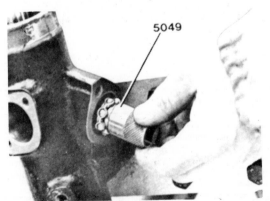

Fig. 11.30. Fitting the inner race and ball retainer on the pinion (Sec. 19)

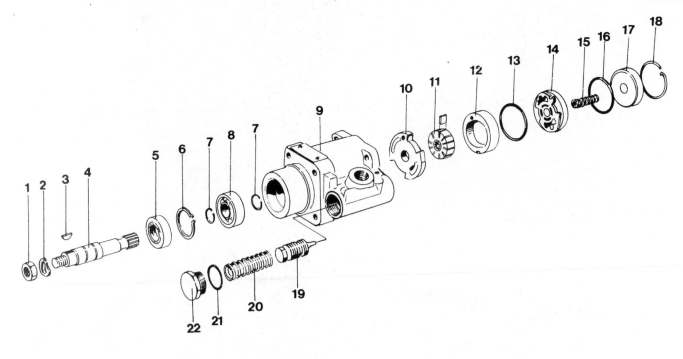

Fig. 11.34 Exploded view of ZF Type power steering pump (Sec. 22)

1	Nut for pulley	9	Housing	16	O-ring
2	Lock washer	10	Thrust plate	17	End plate
3	Shaft key	11	Rotor with vanes	18	Retaining ring
4	Shaft	12	Cam ring	19	Control valve
5	Seal	13	O-ring	20	Spring
6	Retaining ring	14	Pressure plate	21	Copper seal
7	Retaining ring	15	Spring	22	Plug
8	Ball bearing				

22 Power steering pump - overhaul

1   Remove the pulley nut and the pulley. Remove the mounting bracket from the pump. Remove the front seal, Fig. 11.34.

2   Remove the circlip.

3   Using multi-grip pliers remove the spring and pressure plate. Turn the pump over and tap lightly on the end until the rotor and cam ring falls free. If the cam ring does not come loose leave it for now.

4   Remove the ball bearing retaining circlip and push the shaft out of the housing. Push out the thrust plate and, if it did not come out before, the cam ring.

5   Remove the plug, control valve and spring.

6   Renew all 'O' rings. Examine parts for wear and damage. If the pump housing bushing is worn or damaged renew the housing assembly. The rotor, vanes and cam ring are a matched set, if any one is defective they must be renewed as an assembly.

7   Fit the bearing on the shaft and fit the retaining circlips on each side. Press the shaft into the housing.

8   Fit the thrust plate with the dowel located in one of the holes. Fit the cam ring on the dowel with the arrow side upwards, Fig. 11.35. Fit the inner 'O' ring.

9   Fit the rotor with the recess round the shaft hole down towards the drive side. Fit the vanes with the rounded ends towards the cam ring. Fit the pressure plate so that one of the holes locates on the dowel.

10 Fit the outer 'O' ring and spring. Fit the endplate and retaining circlip. It will be necessary to push on the endplate to fit the circlip in its groove.

11 Fit the control valve, spring and plug. Use a new copper washer on the plug.

12 Fit the shaft seal, tap it in lightly until it is properly seated.

13 Fit the pulley and mounting bracket.

14 When overhauling the pump it is a good idea to renew the filter in the reservoir. Remove the cover, spring retaining nut and spring. Lift out the filter and fit a new one. Refit the spring, nut and cover.

Fig. 11.35 Fitting the cam ring and O-ring (Sec. 22)

23 Steering geometry - general

1   Accurate front wheel alignment is essential for good steering and tyre wear. Before considering the steering angle, check that the tyres are correctly inflated, that the front wheels are not buckled, the hub bearings are not worn or incorrectly adjusted and that the steering linkage is in good order, without slackness or wear at the joints.

2   Wheel alignment consists of four factors:

Camber, which is the angle at which the front wheels are set from the vertical when viewed from the front of the car. Positive camber is the amount (in degrees) that the wheels are tilted outwards at the top from the vertical.

Castor, is the angle between the steering axis and a vertical line when viewed from each side of the car. Positive castor is when the steering

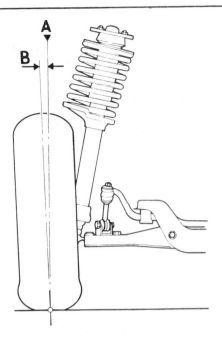

Fig. 11.36. Diagram showing 'A' vertical line and 'B' camber (Sec. 23)

axis is inclined rearward.
Steering axis inclination is the angle, when viewed from the front of the car, between the vertical and an imaginary line drawn between the upper and lower suspension ball joints.

Toe-in is the amount by which the distance between the front inside edges of the front roadwheels (measured at hub height) is less than the diametrically opposite distance measured between the rear inside edges of the front roadwheels.

3   It is recommended that all the steering angles are set by a service station on modern equipment. Castor cannot be adjusted on the 240 series, if it is outside the specification the front suspension must be checked for damage.

4   Camber is adjusted by moving the upper strut attachment in or out. Incorrect camber causes uneven tyre wear.

5   Front wheel alignment can be carried out by the home mechanic if the following operations are followed.

6   Place the car on level ground with the wheels in the straight-ahead position.

7   Obtain or make a toe-in gauge. One may be easily made from tubing, cranked to clear the sump and bellhousing, having an adjustable nut and setscrew at one end.

8   With the gauge, measure the distance between the two inner rims of the front roadwheels, at hub height and at the rear of the wheels.

9   Push the vehicle so that the roadwheel turns through half a turn (180º) and measure the distance between the two inner rims at hub height at the front of the wheel. This last measurement should be less than the first by the specified toe-in which is:

*0.1 ± 0.04 in (2.5 ± 1 mm) for manual steering and
0.06 ± 0.04 in (1.5 ± 1 mm) for power steering.*

10 If the toe-in is incorrect, slacken the trackrod locknuts and the bellows outboard clips and turn the rods into the trackrod-ends to increase the toe-in, or out, to decrease the toe-in. Make sure you turn both rods the same amount so that they are the same length within 0.06 in (1.6 mm).

11 Re-check the toe-in and then tighten the trackrod locknuts and clips.

24 Fault diagnosis - front suspension and steering

Symptom	Reason/s
Excessive movement of steering wheel before roadwheel movement is apparent	Wear in the steering gear and ball joints.
Car difficult to steer in a straight line - wandering	Wear in steering gear and ball joints. Wheel alignment incorrect (indicated by excessive and uneven tyre wear). Front wheel hub bearings loose. Worn strut ball joints.
Steering stiff and heavy	Incorrect wheel alignment. Excessive wear or binding in the steering gear.
Wheel wobble and vibration	Roadwheels out of balance. Wheel alignment incorrect. Wear in steering gear or ball joints.
Excessive pitching or suspension bottoming	Defective shock absorbers and/or coil springs.
Faults usually attributed to the power steering system Car wanders	Low fluid level. Air in the system.
Steering stiff	Low fluid level. Air in system. Pump control valve seized. Reservoir filter blocked. Defective seals in steering gear.
Steering stiff on one lock only	Lack of pressure on one side of the rack piston due to wear.
Front wheel wobble	Air in the system.
Steering heavy if steering wheel is turned rapidly	Pump control valve blocked. Air in system.

Chapter 12 Bodywork

For modifications, and information applicable to later models, see Supplement at end of manual

Contents

1 General description

1 The Volvo 240 series is of integral monocoque construction. The all steel body and frame are welded into one unit. Heat transfer from the exhaust system to the body is reduced by three heat shields and insulation is provided against noise.
2 A heater and ventilating system is fitted as standard but a full air-conditioning system is available as an optional fitting.
3 To assist in the prevention of corrosion the underside is comprehensively rustproofed and undersealed. Hot dipped galvanised (zinc coated) steel is used for many metal components normally subjected to high weather exposures.
4 The grille is made of ABS plastic and retained by spring locks. The front end and front wings are attached by bolts and can be replaced.

2 Maintenance - bodywork

1 The condition of the bodywork is of considerable importance as it is on this, in the main, that the second-hand value of the car depends. Maintenance is easy but needs to be regular and careful. Neglect, particularly after minor damage, can lead quickly to further deterioration and costly repair bills. It is important also to keep watch on those parts of the car not immediately visible, for instance the underside, and inside all the wheel arches.
2 The basic maintenance routine for the bodywork is washing, preferably with a lot of water, from a hose. This will remove all the solids which may have stuck to the car. It is important to flush these off in such a way as to prevent grit from scratching the finish. The wheel arches and underbody need washing in the same way to remove any accumulated mud which will retain moisture and tend to encourage rust. Paradoxically enough, the best time to clean the underbody and wheel arches is in wet weather when the mud is soft.
3 Once a year, or every 12,000 miles, it is advisable to visit a garage equipped to steam clean the body. This facility is available at many commercial vehicle garages. All traces of dirt and oil will be removed and the underside can then be inspected carefully for rust, damaged pipes, frayed electrical wiring and so forth. The car should be greased on completion of this job. The engine compartment should be cleaned in the same way.
4 If steam cleaning is not available, brush 'Gunk' or a similar cleaner over the whole of the engine and engine compartment with a stiff brush, working it well in where there is an accumulation of oil and dirt. Do not forget to cover the ignition system and protect it with oily rags when the 'Gunk' is washed off. As it is washed away, it will take with it all traces of oil and dirt, leaving the engine looking clean and bright.

5 The wheel arches should be given particular attention, as undersealing can easily come away here, and stones and dirt thrown up from the roadwheels can soon cause the paint to chip and flake and so allow rust to set in. If rust is found, clean down to the bare metal with wet and dry paper, paint on an anti-corrosive coating such as 'Kurust' or red lead and renew the undercoating and top coat.
6 The body should be washed once a week or more often if necessary. After washing paintwork, wipe it with a chamois leather to give an unspotted clear finish. If a car is frequently washed, it only needs a very occasional waxing as a protection against chemical pollutants in the air. Wax the chromium plated parts as well as the paintwork. To keep windscreens and windows clear of film wash them with water to which a little ammonia has been added.
  Keep wax polish away from glass - the smallest trace will cause smeariness in wet weather.
7 Spots of tar and grease thrown up from the road can be removed by a rag dampened in petrol. Tar should not be allowed to linger on the paintwork, nor should bird droppings, which sometimes discolour paint.

3 Maintenance - upholstery and floor coverings

1 Mats and carpets should be brushed or vacuum cleaned regularly to keep them free of grit. If they are badly stained remove them for sponging and make sure they are quite dry before replacement. Seats and interior trim panels can be kept clean by a wipe over with a damp cloth. If they do become stained, use a little liquid detergent and a soft nail brush to scour the grime out of the grain of the material.
2 Do not forget to keep the head lining clean in the same way as the upholstery.
3 When using liquid cleaners inside the car do not over-wet the surfaces being cleaned. Excessive damp could get into the seams and padded interior causing stains, offensive odours or even rot. If the inside of the car gets wet accidentally it is worthwhile taking some trouble to dry it out properly, particularly where carpets are involved.

4 Minor body damage - repair

The photographic sequence on pages 190 and 191 illustrates the operations detailed in the following sub-Sections.

Repair of minor scratches in the car's bodywork

  If the scratch is very superficial, and does not penetrate to the metal of the bodywork, repair is very simple. Lightly rub the area of the scratch with a paintwork renovator (eg. T-cut), or a very fine cutting paste, to remove loose paint from the scratch and to clear the surrounding bodywork of wax polish. Rinse the area with clean water.

Apply touch-up paint to the scratch using a thin paint brush, continue to apply thin layers of paint until the surface of the paint in the scratch is level with the surrounding paintwork. Allow the new paint at least two weeks to harden, then, blend it into the surrounding paintwork by rubbing the paintwork, in the scratch area with a paintwork renovator (eg. T-cut or a very fine cutting paste). Finally apply wax polish.

Where the scratch has penetrated right through to the metal of the bodywork, causing the metal to rust, a different repair technique is required. Remove any loose rust from the bottom of the scratch with a penknife, then apply rust inhibiting paint (eg Kurust) to prevent the formation of rust in the future. Using a rubber or nylon applicator fill the scratch with bodystopper paste. If required, this paste can be mixed with cellulose thinners to provide a very thin paste which is ideal for filling narrow scratches. Before the stopper paste in the scratch hardens, wrap a piece of smooth cotton rag around the top of a finger. Dip the finger in cellulose thinners and then quickly sweep it across the surface of the stopper paste in the scratch; this will ensure that the surface of the stopper paste is slightly hollowed. The scratch can now be painted over as described earlier in this Section.

Repair of dents in the car's bodywork

When deep denting of the car's bodywork has taken place, the first task is to pull the dent out, until the affected bodywork almost attains its original shape. There is little point in trying to restore the original shape completely, as the metal in the damaged area will have stretched on impact and cannot be reshaped fully to its original contour. It is better to bring the level of the dent up to a point which is about 1/8 inch (3 mm) below the level of the surrounding bodywork. In cases where the dent is very shallow anyway, it is not worth trying to pull it out at all.

If the underside of the dent is accessible, it can be hammered out gently from behind, using a mallet with a wooden or plastic head. Whilst doing this, hold a suitable block of wood firmly against the impact from the hammer blows and thus prevent a large area of bodywork from being 'belled-out'.

Should the dent be in a section of the bodywork which has a double skin or some other factor making it inaccessible from behind, a different technique is called for. Drill several small holes through the metal inside the dent area - particularly in the deeper sections. Then screw long self-tapping screws into the holes just sufficiently for them to gain a good purchase in the metal. Now the dent can be pulled out by pulling on the protruding heads of the screws with a pair of pliers.

The next stage of the repair is the removal of the paint from the damaged area, and from an inch or so of the surrounding 'sound' bodywork. This is accomplished most easily by using a wire brush or abrasive pad on a power drill, although it can be done just as effectively by hand using sheets of abrasive paper. To complete the preparations for filling, score the surface of the bare metal with a screwdriver or the tang of a file, or alternatively, drill small holes in the affected area. This will provide a really good 'key' to the filler paste.

To complete the repair see the sub-Section on filling and respraying.

Repair of rust holes or gashes in the car's bodywork

Remove all paint from the affected area and from an inch or so of the surrounding 'sound' bodywork, using an abrasive pad or a wire brush on a power drill. If these are not available a few sheets of abrasive paper will do the job just as effectively. With the paint removed you will be able to gauge the severity of the corrosion and therefore decide whether to replace the whole panel (if this is possible) or to repair the affected area. Replacement body panels are not as expensive as most people think and it is often quicker and more satisfactory to fit a new panel than to attempt to repair large areas of corrosion.

Remove all fittings from the affected area except those which will act as a guide to the original shape of damage bodywork (eg. headlamp shells etc.). Then, using tin snips or a hacksaw blade, remove all loose metal and any other metal badly affected by corrosion. Hammer the edges of the hole inwards in order to create a slight depression for the filler paste.

Wire brush the affected area to remove the powdery rust from the surface of the remaining metal. Paint the affected area with rust inhibiting paint (eg. Kurust); if the back of the rusted area is accessible treat this also.

Before filling can take place it will be necessary to block the hole in some way. This can be achieved by the use of zinc gauze or aluminium tape.

Zinc gauze is probably the best material to use for a large hole. Cut a piece to the approximate size and shape of the hole to be filled, then position it in the hole so that its edges are below the level of the surrounding bodywork. It can be retained in position by several blobs of filler paste around its periphery.

Aluminium tape should be used for small or very narrow holes. Pull a piece off the roll and trim it to the approximate size and shape required, then pull off the backing paper (if used) and stick the tape over the hole; it can be overlapped if the thickness of one piece is insufficient. Burnish down the edges of the tape with the handle of a screwdriver or similar, to ensure that the tape is securely attached to the metal underneath.

Bodywork repairs - filling and re-spraying

Before using this Section, see the Sections on dent, deep scratch, rust hole and gash repairs.

Many types of bodyfiller are available, but generally speaking those proprietary kits which contain a tin of filler paste and a tube of resin hardener (eg. Holts Cataloy) are best for this type of repair. A wide, flexible plastic or nylon applicator will be found invaluable for imparting a smooth and well contoured finish to the surface of the filler.

Mix up a little filler on a clean piece of card or board - use the hardener sparingly (follow the maker's instructions on the packet) otherwise the filler will set very rapidly.

Using the applicator, apply the filler paste to the prepared area; draw the applicator across the surface of the filler to achieve the correct contour and to level the filler surface. As soon as a contour that approximates the correct one is achieved, stop working the paste - if you carry on too long the paste will become sticky and begin to 'pick-up' on the applicator. Continue to add thin layers of filler paste at twenty-minute intervals until the level of the filler is just 'proud' of the surrounding bodywork.

Once the filler has hardened, excess can be removed using a Surform plane or Dreadnought file. From then on, progressively finer grades of abrasive paper should be used, starting with a 40 grade production paper and finishing with 400 grade 'wet-and-dry' paper. Always wrap the abrasive paper around a flat rubber, cork, or wooden block - otherwise the surface of the filler will not be completely flat. During the smoothing of the filler surface the 'wet-and-dry' paper should be periodically rinsed in water. This will ensure that a very smooth finish is imparted to the filler at the final stage.

At this stage the dent should be surrounded by a ring of bare metal, which in turn should be encircled by the finely 'feathered' edge of the good paintwork. Rinse the repair area with clean water, until all of the dust produced by the rubbing-down operation is gone.

Spray the whole repair area with a light coat of grey primer - this will show up any imperfections in the surface of the filler; repair these imperfections with fresh filler paste or bodystopper, and once more smooth the surface with abrasive paper. If bodystopper is used, it can be mixed with cellulose thinners to form a really thin paste which is ideal for filling small holes. Repeat this spray and repair procedure until you are satisfied that the surface of the filler, and the feathered edge of the paintwork are perfect. Clean the repair area with clean water and allow to dry fully.

The repair area is now ready for spraying. Paint spraying must be carried out in a warm, dry, windless and dust free atmosphere. This condition can be created artificially if you have access to a large indoor working area, but if you are forced to work in the open, you will have to pick your day very carefully. If you are working indoors, dousing the floor in the work area with water will 'lay' the dust which would otherwise be in the atmosphere. If the repair area is confined to one body panel, mask off the surrounding panels; this will help to minimise the effects of a slight mis-match in paint colours. Bodywork fittings (eg. chrome strips, door handles etc) will also need to be masked off. Use genuine masking tape and several thicknesses of newspaper for the masking operation.

Before commencing to spray agitate the aerosol can thoroughly, then spray a test area (an old tin, or similar) until the technique is mastered. Cover the repair area with a thick coat of primer; the thickness should be built up using several thin layers of paint rather than one thick one. Using 400 grade 'wet-and-dry' paper, rub down the surface of the primer until it is really smooth. While doing this, the work area should be thoroughly doused with water, and the 'wet-and-dry' paper periodically rinsed in water. Allow to dry before spraying on more paint.

Spray on the top coat, again building up the thickness by using several thin layers of paint. Start spraying in the centre of the repair area and then, using a circular motion, work outwards until the whole repair area and about 2 inches of the surrounding original paintwork is covered. Remove all masking material 10 to 15 minutes after spraying on the final coat of paint.

Allow the new paint at least 2 weeks to harden fully; then, using a paintwork renovator (eg. T-cut) or a very fine cutting plaste, blend the edges of the new paint into the existing paintwork. Finally, apply wax polish.

7.1 Front grille lock

5   Major body damage - repair

Where serious damage has occurred or large areas need renewal due to neglect, it means certainly that completely new sections or panels will need welding in and this is best left to professionals. If the damage is due to impact it will also be necessary to completely check the alignment of the body shell structure. Due to the principle of construction the strength and shape of the whole can be affected by damage to a part. In such instances the services of a Volvo agent with specialist checking jigs are essential. If a body is left misaligned it is first of all dangerous as the car will not handle properly and secondly uneven stresses will be imposed on the steering, engine and transmission, causing abnormal wear or complete failure. Tyre wear may also be excessive.

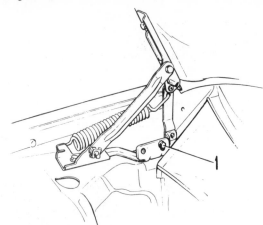

Fig. 12.1. Adjusting bonnet hinges (Sec. 9)

1   Lock bolt

6   Door rattles - tracing and rectification

The most common cause of door rattles is a misaligned, loose or worn latch plate but other causes may be:

a) *loose door handles, window winder handles or door hinges;*
b) *loose, worn or misaligned door lock components;*
c) *loose or worn door locking linkages;*
d) *any combination of the above three.*

Worn parts should be renewed as described in later parts of this Chapter.

7   Replacing the grille

1   Depress and turn the spring locks 90° then lift up the spring locks. (photo).
2   Pull the grille forward to free it from the upper member and lift it out.
3   Transfer the springs to the new grille.
4   Position the grille and the spring locks, depress the locks and turn so that they lock. Check that the grille is held securely.

8   Front wing - removal and replacement

1   Raise the front of the vehicle and remove the roadwheel.
2   Remove the plastic shield from under the wing.
3   Remove the radiator grille, headlamp, front parking/direction indicator lamp cluster and headlamp wash/wipe if fitted.
4   Disconnect the bumper end fixing from the wing.
5   Remove the wing front fixing screws and those at the rear after opening the door fully for access.
6   Chisel through the spot welds at the bottom fixing plate.
7   Unscrew the top row of wing fixing bolts and remove the wing. The flange seal will have to be cut with a sharp knife to release the wing.
8   Refitting is a reversal of removal, spot welding is not essential. Apply undersealing compound and finish the exterior surface to match the body colour.

9   Bonnet - removal, refitting and adjustment

1   Open the bonnet to its fullest extent.
2   Mark the location of the hinge plates on the underside of the bonnet to facilitate refitting.
3   Obtain the help of an assistant to support the bonnet and then unscrew and remove the bolts which secure the hinges to the bonnet. Lift the bonnet from the car.
4   Any adjustment can be made when refitting the bonnet by moving it within the limits of the hinge plate elongated bolt holes.
5   Positive closure of the bonnet can be provided by moving the positions of the bonnet lock and spring-loaded lock bolt within

the limits of their mounting plate bolts. The lock bolt is also adjustable in length so that the bonnet when closed will be flush with the tops of the front wings. If the lock bolt is adjusted then the two rubber buffers at the corners of the bonnet will also probably need screwing in or out (photo).

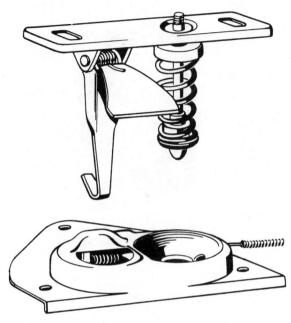

Fig. 12.2. Bonnet lock (Sec. 9)

10 Front door lock - removal and refitting

1   Take out the two plastic plugs from the arm rest and remove the attaching screws located on the inside (photos).
2   Turn the plastic ring at the front edge of the armrest several turns to the left, push the arm rest forwards and the hook at the front edge disengages, allowing the arm rest to be removed (photo).
3   Remove the window winding handle by removing the cover, then the retaining screw and the handle (photos).
4   Unscrew the door lock button and the screws at the top edge of the door interior trim panel.
5   Remove the interior trim panel by inserting a screwdriver, or similar flat tool, between the panel and door and then carefully prise off the trim panel.
6   Remove the lock cylinder attaching screw from the rear edge of the door, Fig. 12.4.
7   Release the securing clip and remove the pushrod from the door lock knob.
8   Disconnect the pullrod from the door interior handle.
9   Disconnect the pullrod from the door exterior handle.
10 Unscrew and remove the three screws which secure the door lock assembly to the edge of the door. Withdraw the lock from the door cavity.
11 The exterior handle may be removed, if required, after removing the two securing screws, accessible with the window lowered.
12 If the lock is worn or damaged, renew it as an assembly.
13 Refitting the lock assembly is the reverse of the removal procedure. Make any necessary adjustment by altering the length of the exterior handle pullrod, Fig. 12.3.

11 Rear door lock - removal and refitting

1   Carry out the operations described in Section 10, paragraphs 1 to 5 and 7 to 9.

9.5 Bonnet lock

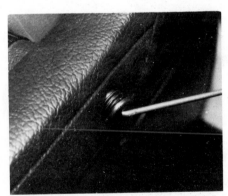

10.1a Removing a plastic plug from arm rest

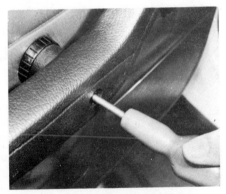

10.1b Removing the arm rest attaching screws

10.2 Disengaging the arm rest

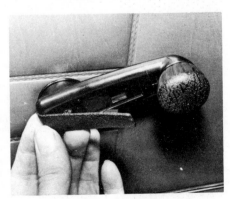

10.3a Taking off the window winding handle cover

10.3b Removing the winding handle retaining screw

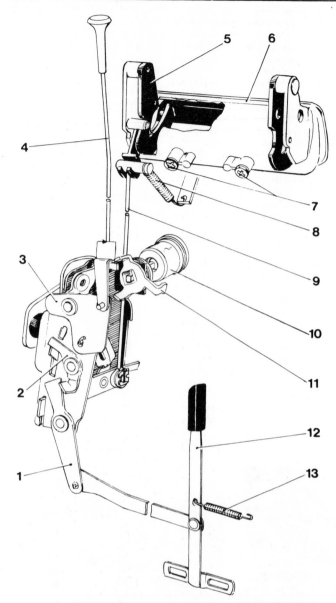

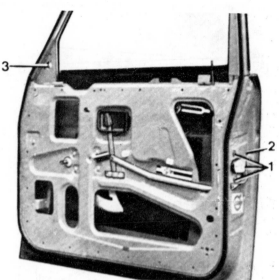

Fig. 12.4. Front door lock attaching screws (Sec. 10)

1 Door lock screws
2 Hole for the lock cylinder attaching screw
3 Hole for rear view mirror installation

Fig. 12.3. Front door lock components (Sec. 10)

1 Lever
2 Lever
3 Lever
4 Pull rod for lock button
5 Outer handle
6 Cover for outer handle
7 Screws for outer handle
8 Return spring for outer handle
9 Pull rod for outer handle
10 Lock cylinder
11 Lock device
12 Inner door opener
13 Return spring for inner door opener

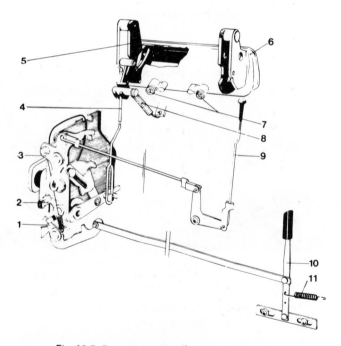

Fig. 12.5. Rear door lock components (Sec. 11)

1 Lever for remote control
2 Lever for child safety door lock
3 Lever
4 Pull rod for outer handle
5 Outer handle
6 Cover for outer handle
7 Screws for outer handle cover
8 Return spring for outer handle
9 Pull rod for lock button
10 Inner door opener
11 Return spring for inner door opener

2   Disconnect the interior lock plunger rod by removing the locking clip.

3   Remove the screw from the rear window guide channel and the lock securing screws, all of which are located on the rear edge of the door.

4   The exterior handle can now be removed, if necessary, after removing the securing screws.

5   Refitting is the reverse of the removal procedure but adjust the rod for the exterior handle to provide a clearance, 'A' in Fig. 12.5, of 0.04 in (1 mm) between the pullrod eyelet and the pin in the lock lever.

12 Door stop - removal and refitting

The door stop is shown in detail in Fig. 12.6. It is fastened to the door by two bolts and to the pillar by a single bolt. When these are removed the complete assembly comes away. When replacing it, do not forget the rubber seal.

13 Other locks and latch plates

1   Figs. 12.7, 12.8 and 12.9 give sufficient detail of these to enable the owner to carry out whatever adjustment or replacement is necessary.
2   An interesting example of Volvo thoroughness is their specification for the tilt of the latch plate, which is actually the same plate whether fitted to front or rear doors.

14 Front door window - removal and replacement

1   Lower the window to its bottom position.
2   Remove the interior trim as described in Section 10.
3   Remove the lock springs and washers on the inside of the winding arms. Bend the arms outwards and separate them from the window channel.
4   Remove the window by lifting and turning it towards the car as shown in Fig. 12.10.

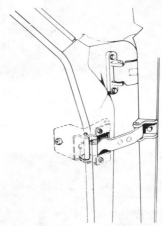

Fig. 12.6. Door stop (Sec. 12)

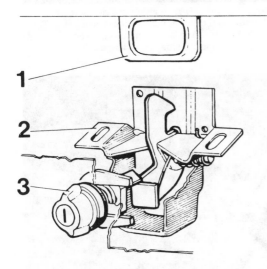

Fig. 12.7. Luggage compartment lock (Sec. 13)

1   *Lock catch, fitted in lid*
2   *Lock mechanism, fitted in rear section*
3   *Lock knob, fitted in rear section*

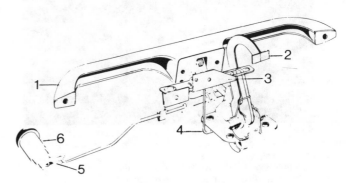

Fig. 12.8. Tailgate lock, 245 (Sec. 13)

1   *Outer handle*
2   *Inside opener*
3   *Latching device for inner opener*
4   *Control for latching device*
5   *Eccentric*
6   *Lock cylinder*

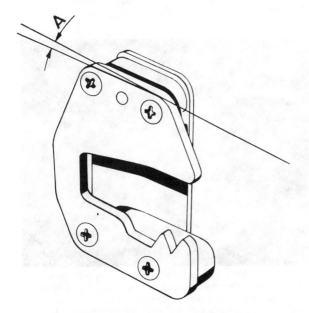

Fig. 12.9. Latch plate (Sec. 13)

A = 1.5° - Front door
A = 2.5° - Rear door

Fig. 12. 10. Lifting out the front door window (Sec. 14)

This sequence of photographs deals with the repair of the dent and paintwork damage shown in this photo. The procedure will be similar for the repair of a hole. It should be noted that the procedures given here are simplified — more explicit instructions will be found in the text

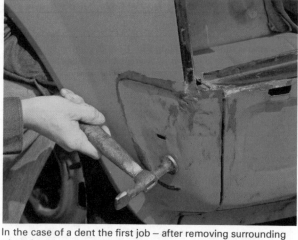

In the case of a dent the first job — after removing surrounding trim — is to hammer out the dent where access is possible. This will minimise filling. Here, the large dent having been hammered out, the damaged area is being made slightly concave

Now all paint must be removed from the damaged area, by rubbing with coarse abrasive paper. Alternatively, a wire brush or abrasive pad can be used in a power drill. Where the repair area meets good paintwork, the edge of the paintwork should be 'feathered', using a finer grade of abrasive paper

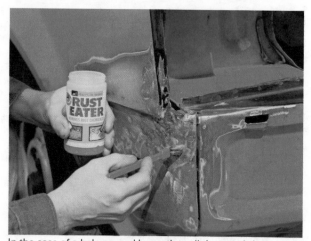

In the case of a hole caused by rusting, all damaged sheet-metal should be cut away before proceeding to this stage. Here, the damaged area is being treated with rust remover and inhibitor before being filled

Mix the body filler according to its manufacturer's instructions. In the case of corrosion damage, it will be necessary to block off any large holes before filling — this can be done with aluminium or plastic mesh, or aluminium tape. Make sure the area is absolutely clean before ...

... applying the filler. Filler should be applied with a flexible applicator, as shown, for best results; the wooden spatula being used for confined areas. Apply thin layers of filler at 20-minute intervals, until the surface of the filler is slightly proud of the surrounding bodywork

Initial shaping can be done with a Surform plane or Dreadnought file. Then, using progressively finer grades of wet-and-dry paper, wrapped around a sanding block, and copious amounts of clean water, rub down the filler until really smooth and flat. Again, feather the edges of adjoining paintwork

The whole repair area can now be sprayed or brush-painted with primer. If spraying, ensure adjoining areas are protected from over-spray. Note that at least one inch of the surrounding sound paintwork should be coated with primer. Primer has a 'thick' consistency, so will find small imperfections

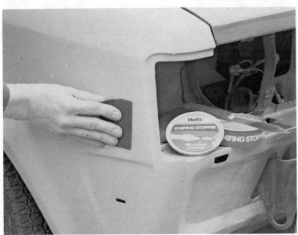

Again, using plenty of water, rub down the primer with a fine grade wet-and-dry paper (400 grade is probably best) until it is really smooth and well blended into the surrounding paintwork. Any remaining imperfections can now be filled by carefully applied knifing stopper paste

When the stopper has hardened, rub down the repair area again before applying the final coat of primer. Before rubbing down this last coat of primer, ensure the repair area is blemish-free – use more stopper if necessary. To ensure that the surface of the primer is really smooth use some finishing compound

The top coat can now be applied. When working out of doors, pick a dry, warm and wind-free day. Ensure surrounding areas are protected from over-spray. Agitate the aerosol thoroughly, then spray the centre of the repair area, working outwards with a circular motion. Apply the paint as several thin coats

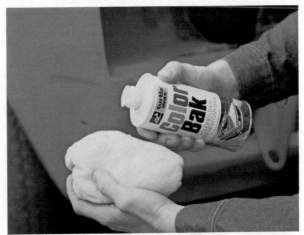

After a period of about two weeks, which the paint needs to harden fully, the surface of the repaired area can be 'cut' with a mild cutting compound prior to wax polishing. When carrying out bodywork repairs, remember that the quality of the finished job is proportional to the time and effort expended

5   Replacement is the reverse of the removal procedure.

15 Front door window winding mechanism - removal and replacement

1   Carry out operations 1 to 3 in Section 14.
2   Remove the clip at one of the winding arm's securing points in the door, see Fig. 12.11.
3   Remove the winding mechanism four retaining screws and withdraw the mechanism from the cavity in the door.
4   Replacement is the reverse of the removal sequence, but after refitting the retaining screws, wind the window up to the fully closed position before tightening the screws.

16 Rear door window and winding mechanism - replacement

The procedure for replacing the window and door winding mechanism is the same as described in Sections 14 and 15.

17 Doors and tailgate - removal, refitting and adjustment

1   To remove the doors, take out the upholstery panels (Section 10) you have to do this to get at the nuts on the hinge bolts - remove the door stops (Section 12), disconnect the heated rear window and unscrew the bolts between the hinges and the door. Elongated holes in the hinges where they fit to the door and oversized holes in the pillar where the hinges are attached provide for adjustment of the door position.

18 Tailgate - removal and replacement

1   To remove the tailgate, you will have to take off the upholstery panel on the inside. Then remove the left-hand number plate lamp and its cable, disconnect the other out-going cables from the tailgate, remove the gas spring, undo the bolts connecting the hinges to the tailgate and lift it off. The tailgate hinges can be removed from the body by easing the hinge out of its groove at the rear, pushing the electric cables out of the way and thus enabling yourself to get at the nuts holding the hinge bolts. Replacement is straightforward, the only problem being to compress the gas spring. To keep it compressed a simple bracket, like that shown in Fig. 12.12, is very little trouble to make.

19 Luggage compartment lid

1   The luggage compartment lid is mounted on two hinges both of

which are attached by two bolts to the inner plate of the lid and by three bolts to the pillar under the rear window.
2   The lid is counterbalanced by a spring support. When fitting a new spring support use a clamp as shown in Fig. 12.12. The holes in the hinges are elongated to provide adjustment when refitting the lid.

20 Windscreen glass - removal and refitting

1   This is a job for specialists. Due to the method of sealing the glass, the old windscreen must be released using a hot soldering iron of special shape.
2   Fitting the new screen requires special adhesive and butyl tape and when one considers the cost involved if the windscreen should get broken during fitting it is recommended that you leave this job to your Volvo agent.

21 Rear window glass - removal and refitting

1   Disconnect the leads from the heated rear window. Move the bright trim clips aside and prise off the time (Fig. 12.13).
2   Release the rubber surround from the glass and the body flange by sliding a thin plastic blade round the joint.
3   Working inside the car but with an assistant outside to catch the glass, prise the lip of the rubber surround from the body starting at the top left-hand corner and pushing the glass outwards at the same time.
4   Clean all old sealant from the glass, body flange and the rubber surround. If the latter is damaged, hardened or sealant is stuck to it, renew the surround.
5   Cut a piece of strong cord greater in length than the periphery of the glass and insert it into the body flange locating channel of the rubber surround (Fig. 12.14).
6   Apply a thin bead of sealant to the face of the rubber channel which will eventually mate with the body.
7   Offer the glass to the body aperture and pass the end of the cord, previously fitted and located at bottom centre into the vehicle interior.
8   Press the glass into place, at the same time have an assistant pulling the cords to engage the lip of the rubber channel over the body flange (Fig. 12.15).
9   Remove any excess sealant with a paraffin soaked rag.
10 Refit the bright trim. This is best done by inserting a 5/32 in (4 mm) diameter cord (or leather thong) in the groove in the rubber surround. Soak the cord in paraffin or soapy solution beforehand. Press the trim into position at the same time pulling the cord out and upwards. Fit the trim joint clips (Fig. 12.16).

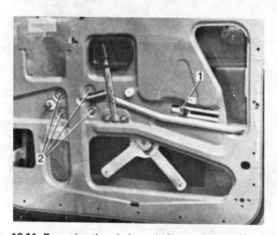

Fig. 12.11. Removing the window winding mechanism (Sec. 15)

1   Lock   2   Winding mechanism retaining
                                           screws

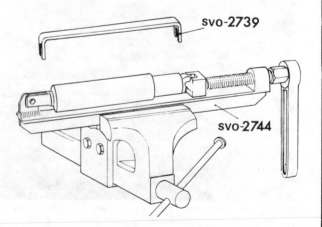

**Fig. 12.12. Compressing the gas spring for luggage compartment lid
or tailgate (Sec. 18)**

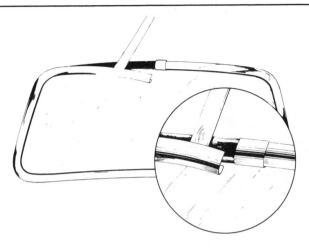

Fig. 12.13. Removing the trim from rear window surround (Sec. 21)

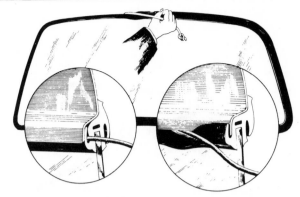

Fig. 12.15. Pulling the edge of the rubber strip over the surround (Sec. 21)

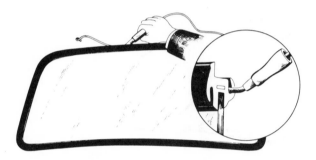

Fig. 12.14. Fitting the cord in rubber strip (Sec. 21)

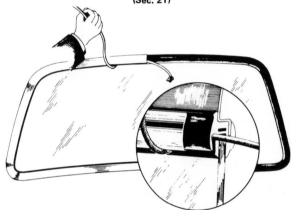

Fig. 12.16. Fitting the metal trim (Sec. 21)

22. Rear quarter glass - removal and refitting

1   The method of replacing these windows is very similar to the procedure described in Section 21.

23 Sun roof

1   Enough details are given in Fig. 12.17 to enable anyone looking at it, in conjunction with an actual sun roof, to see how the whole thing works. It can be removed as follows.
2   Open the sun roof and release the clips securing the roof upholstery at the front end. Move the upholstery back to leave an opening.
3   Crank the sun roof forwards and slacken the screws at its four attachments (9 and 11, Fig. 12.17). Bend the blade springs (10) to one side and remove the reinforcing plates (13) at the rear attachments. The sun roof can now be lifted off.

24 Sun roof - replacing cables

1   Remove the sun roof as described in Section 23.
2   Remove the wind deflector (2, Fig. 12.17).
3   Remove the intermediate pieces (8) covering strip (3) and holders above the drive. Release the front guide rails (6) and pull out the cables (5).
4   Fit replacement cables so that the attachments for the sun roof come opposite each other at the rear end of the roof opening. Screw the front guide rails on securely.
5   Refit the intermediate pieces, holders, covering plate and the wind deflector.
6   Screw on the roof securely and put back the leaf springs.
7   Crank the sun roof forwards until it is completely closed and check that it is level with the main roof. If necessary adjust at the front and rear attachments (7 and 12, Fig. 12.17). Check that the lifts on the rear attachments are pushed up when the roof is closed. (B, Fig. 12.17).

8   When the roof is closed the crank should point straight forwards in the vehicle. If it does not, unscrew the crank and gear housing, turn the crank to the stop position and replace.

25 Bumpers - removal and refitting

1   Various types of bumper section may be encountered, also different methods of mounting them.
2   On some cars the bumpers are mounted on rigid brackets while on others, including those destined for North America, the mountings may be of coil spring, hydraulic or gas-filled type. These impact absorbing type bumpers are removed as with the other designs, simply by releasing the mounting nuts or bolts.
3   Where the gas-filled shock absorbing type mountings are installed, do not attempt to open them or weld or heat them as the gas can explode.
4   Before discarding a defective impact absorber it should be emptied by drilling holes to release the gas. Use safety glasses while drilling the holes.

26 Driver's seat heater pads - renewal

1   On some cars, an electrically heated driver's seat is fitted.
2   Disconnect the leads to the seat heating pads at the junction box (Fig. 12.18).
3   Unbolt and remove the seat, complete with runners, from the car floor.
4   Disconnect the leads between the seat back panel and the seat cushion pad.
5   Remove the screws which secure the seat cushion and remove the cushion (Fig. 12.19).
6   Place the seat upside down on the bench and cut and remove the upholstery front retaining clamps.
7   Release the plastic hooks and pull out the heater pad from the seat back (Fig. 12.20).
8   When installing the new heater pad to the seat back, make sure

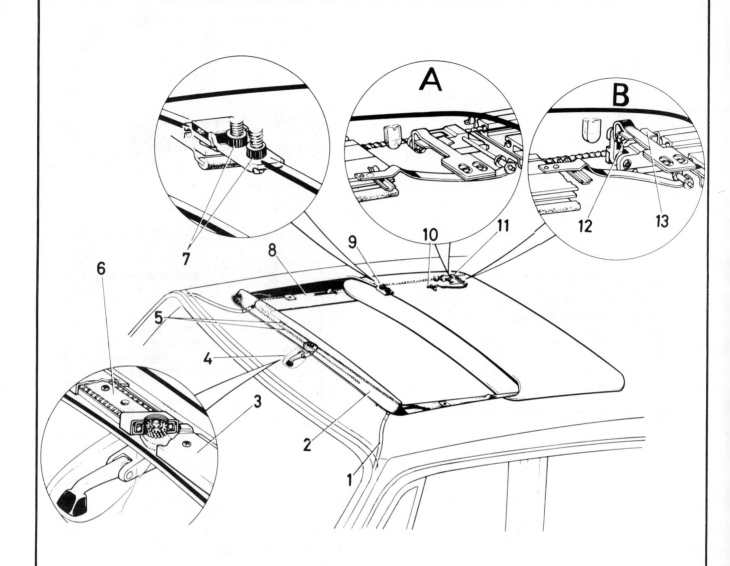

Fig. 12.17. Sun roof (Secs. 23 and 24)

A. Rear attachment when roof is open
B. Rear attachment when roof is closed

1 Drain hose
2 Wind deflector
3 Cover strip
4 Crank housing with crank
5 Cables
6 Front guide rail
7 Front adjustment

8 Intermediate piece
9 Front attachment
10 Leaf spring
11 Rear attachment
12 Rear adjustment
13 Reinforcing plate

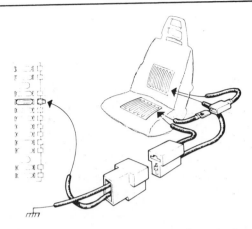

Fig. 12.18. Leads and connectors for driver's seat heater pads
(Sec. 26)

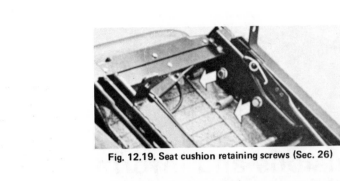

Fig. 12.19. Seat cushion retaining screws (Sec. 26)

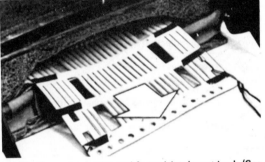

Fig. 12.20. Removing heater pad from driver's seat back (Sec. 26)

Fig. 12.21. Fitting heater pad to driver's seat cushion (Sec. 26)

that the barbed side of the elements faces the seat padding and the electrical leads run on the inner side of the seat back (nearer the transmission terminal).

9   To renew the pad in the seat cushion, place the cushion upside down and remove the cover plate.

10 Cut and remove the clamp at the rear end of the cushion. With-

draw the heater pad. Note that a thermostat is fitted in the cushion heater pad.

11 When installing the new pad, make sure that the barbed side of the heater element is towards the padding, and the electrical leads run on the inner side of the cushion (nearer the transmission tunnel).

12 Connect the upholstery using new clamps.

Chapter 13
Revisions and information on later models

Contents

1 Introduction

1   Since its introduction in 1974, the 240 Series has been the subject of continuous development and modification with detailed design changes to many components. It is not the intention of this Supplement to list these changes unless their inclusion affects the specifications or the original overhaul operations given in this manual.
2   In order to use this Supplement to the best advantage, it is suggested that it is referred to before the main Chapters of the manual, where the date of production of the vehicle being worked upon falls within the years 1977 to 1986.

2 Specifications

Note: *The information given below is supplementary to the Specifications in the twelve main Chapters of the manual*

Engine – B17A, B19, B21 and B23
B17A engine (special territories only)
As B19 engine except for the following:

Stroke	2.829 in (71.85 mm)
Capacity	1784 cc (108.8 cu in)
Compression ratio	8.3 to 1
Max output @ rpm, DIN:	
1979, 1980	66 kW (90 hp) @ 5750 rpm
1981	66 kW (90 hp) @ 5500 rpm
Max torque @ rpm. DIN:	
1979, 1980, 1981	97 lbf ft (132 Nm) @ 2500 rpm

B19 engine (special territories only)
As B21 engine except for the following:

Bore	3.50 in (88.9 mm)
Capacity	1986 cc (121.2 cu in)
Compression ratio:	
B19A (carburettor engines)	8.8 to 1 (to 1978) 8.5 to 1 (1979 on)
B19E (fuel injection engines)	8.8 to 1 (to 1981) 9.2 to 1 (1982 on)
Max output @ rpm DIN:	
B19A (8.8 to 1 CR)	71 kW (97 hp) @ 5400 rpm
B19A (8.5 to 1 CR)	66 kW (90 hp) @ 5000 rpm, 71 kW (97 hp) @ 5400 rpm or 71 kW (97 hp) @ 5500 rpm
B19E	86 kW (117 hp) @ 6000 rpm
Max torque @ rpm DIN:	
B19A (8.8 to 1 CR)	116 lbf ft (157 Nm) @ 3200 rpm
B19A (8.5 to 1 CR)	112 lbf ft (152 Nm) @ 2500 rpm, 116 lbf ft (157 Nm) @ 3200 rpm or 114 lbf ft (154 Nm) @ 2500 rpm
B19E (8.8 to 1 CR)	116 lbf ft (157 Nm) @ 4500 rpm
B19E (9.2 to 1 CR)	111 lbf ft (150 Nm) @ 4500 rpm

B21 ET (Turbo) engine

As B21 engine except for the following:

Compression ratio	7.5 to 1
Max output @ rpm, DIN	114 kW (155 hp) @ 5500 rpm
Max torque @ rpm, DIN	177 lbf ft (240 Nm) @ 3750 rpm

B21F engine

As B21 engine except for the following:

Compression ratio	9.3 to 1
Max output @ rpm, DIN	
Canada	86 kW (117 hp) @ 5250 rpm
USA	83 kW (113 hp) @ 5250 rpm
Max torque @ rpm, DIN	
Canada	124 lbf ft (168 Nm) @ 4500 rpm
USA	118 lbf ft (160 Nm) @ 2500 rpm

B21F Turbo engine

As B21 engine except for the following:

Compression ratio	7.5 to 1
Max output @ rpm, DIN	98 kW (133 hp) @ 5400 rpm
Max torque @ rpm, DIN	155 lbf ft (210 Nm) @ 3750 rpm

B21F – MPG engine

As B21 engine except for the following:

Compression ratio	9.3 to 1
Max output @ rpm, DIN	77 kW (105 hp) @ 5000 rpm
Max torque @ rpm, DIN	118 lbf ft (160 Nm) @ 3000 rpm

B23 engine

As B21 engine except for the following:

Bore	3.780 in (96.0 mm)
Capacity	2315 cc (141.2 cu in)
Compression ratio:	
B23A (carburettor engines)	10.3 to 1 or 9.0 to 1
B23E (fuel injection engines)	10.0 to 1 or 10.3 to 1
Max output @ rpm, DIN:	
B23A (10.3 to 1 CR)	82 kW (112 hp) @ 5000 rpm
B23A (9.0 to 1 CR)	78 kW (106 hp) @ 5000 rpm
B23E (to 1980)	103 kW (140 hp) @ 5750 rpm
B23E (1981 on)	100 kW (136 hp) @ 5500 rpm
Max torque @ rpm, DIN:	
B23A (10.3 to 1 CR)	137 lbf ft (185 Nm) @ 2500 rpm
B23A (9.0 to 1 CR)	132 lbf ft (179 Nm) @ 2500 rpm
B23E (to 1980)	141 lbf ft (191 Nm) @ 4500 rpm
B23E (1981 on)	140 lbf ft (190 Nm) @ 4500 rpm

Pistons

Length:	
B17	2.9724 in (75.5 mm)
B19, B21A, B21E	2.7953 in (71.0 mm)
B21ET (Turbo)	2.8150 in (71.5 mm)
B23	3.1654 in (80.4 mm) or 3.0079 in (76.4 mm)
Clearance in bore:	
B17, B19, B21A, B21E	0.0004 to 0.0016 in (0.01 to 0.04 mm)
B19ET (Turbo)	0.0012 to 0.0024 in (0.03 to 0.06 mm)
B21ET (Turbo)	0.0008 to 0.0016 in (0.02 to 0.04 mm)
B23E	0.0020 to 0.0028 in (0.05 to 0.07 mm) or 0.004 to 0.0016 in (0.01 to 0.04 mm)

Cylinder head

Height:	
New	5.752 in (146.1 mm)
Minimum	5.732 in (145.6 mm)
Maximum warp:	
Longitudinally	0.040 in (1.0 mm)
Crosswise	0.020 in (0.5 mm)

Crankshaft

Endfloat	0.010 in (0.25 mm)

Camshaft

Marking/max lift height:	
B17A, B19A	A/0.413 in (10.5 mm)
B19E	D/0.441 in (11.2 mm)

B19ET (Turbo)	T/0.390 in (9.9 mm)
B21ET (Turbo)	T/0.390 in (9.9 mm)
B23A	A/0.413 in (10.5 mm)
B23E (1979 to 1980)	H/0.472 in (12.0 mm)
B23E (1981 on)	K/0.471 in (11.95 mm)

Inlet valve opening timing (cold):	Valve clearance	°BTDC
B17A, B19A	0.028 in (0.7 mm)	13
B19E	0.028 in (0.7 mm)	15
B19ET, B21ET (Turbo)	0.020 in (0.5 mm)	11
B23A	0.028 in (0.7 mm)	13
B23E (1979 to 1980)	0.020 in (0.5 mm)	28
B23E (1981 on)	0.020 in (0.5 mm)	22.6

Lubrication system

Oil capacity (B21ET with oil cooler)	Add additional 1.1 Imp pt; 0.63 US qt; 0.6 litre if completely drained

Torque wrench settings

Cylinder head bolts (hexagon head):	lbf ft	Nm
Stage 1	15	20
Stage 2	44	60
Stage 3	Angle tighten 90°	

B200 Engine (low friction)
General

As B21 engine except for the following:	
Bore	3.5 in (88.9 mm)
Stroke	3.15 in (80.0 mm)
Displacement	1986 cc (121 cu in)
Compression ratio	10 to 1 except B200K special territories 8.5 to 1
Output (DIN):	
B200K	101 bhp (74 kW) @ 5400 rpm
B200K (special territories)	98 bhp (72 kW) @ 5400 rpm
B200E	117 bhp (86 kW) @ 6000 rpm
Torque (DIN):	
B200K	118 lbf ft (160 Nm) @ 2400 rpm
B200E	117 lbf ft (158 Nm) @ 3000 rpm

Cylinder head

Material	Light alloy
Height	5.752 in (146.1 mm)
Minimum height after refacing	5.732 in (145.6 mm)

Cylinder block

Material	Cast-iron
Bore grade:	
C	3.5000 to 3.5004 in (88.90 to 88.91 mm)
D	3.5004 to 3.5008 in (88.91 to 88.92 mm)
E	3.5008 to 3.5012 in (88.92 to 88.93 mm)
G	3.5016 to 3.5020 in (88.94 to 88.95 mm)
Wear limit	0.004 in (0.1 mm)

Pistons

Length:	
High compression	2.752 in (69.9 mm)
Low compression	2.665 in (67.7 mm)
Weight difference between pistons	0.56 oz (16.0 g)
Clearance in bore:	
1985 models	0.0004 to 0.0011 in (0.010 to 0.027 mm)
1986 models	0.0001 to 0.0012 in (0.003 to 0.030 mm)

Piston rings

Width:	
Top compression	0.0681 to 0.0685 in (1.728 to 1.740 mm)
Second compression	0.0681 to 0.0685 in (1.728 to 1.740 mm)
Oil scraper	0.1368 to 0.1374 in (3.475 to 3.490 mm)
Piston ring-to-groove clearance:	
Top compression	0.0024 to 0.0036 in (0.060 to 0.092 mm)
Second compression	0.0012 to 0.0025 in (0.030 to 0.062 mm)
Oil scraper	0.0008 to 0.0022 in (0.020 to 0.055 mm)
Piston ring end gap:	
Top compression	0.012 to 0.020 in (0.30 to 0.50 mm)
Second compression	0.012 to 0.022 in (0.30 to 0.55 mm)
Oil scraper	0.010 to 0.020 in (0.25 to 0.50 mm)

Gudgeon pin

Diameter:
    Standard .... 0.9055 in (23.00 mm)
    Oversize .... 0.9075 in (23.05 mm)
Length .... 2.36 in (60.0 mm)

Valves

Exhaust valve stem diameter .... 0.3128 to 0.3134 in (7.945 to 7.960 mm)

Valve springs

Free length:
    B200K and B200E .... 1.77 in (45.0 mm)
    B200ET .... 1.79 in (45.5 mm)

Camshaft

B200K:
    Marking .... Y
    Maximum lift height .... 0.407 in (10.35 mm)
    Inlet valve opens .... 8° BTDC
B200E:
    Marking V
    Maximum lift height .... 0.448 in (11.37 mm)
    Inlet valve opens .... 11° BTDC
B200ET:
    Marking .... T
    Maximum lift height .... 0.390 in (9.9 mm)
    Inlet valve opens .... 7° BTDC

Crankshaft

Endfloat .... 0.0032 to 0.0106 in (0.080 to 0.270 mm)
Main bearing running clearance .... 0.0009 to 0.0028 in (0.024 to 0.072 mm)
Big-end bearing running clearance .... 0.0009 to 0.0026 in (0.023 to 0.067 mm)
Main bearing journals:
    Diameter (standard) .... 2.1654 in (55.0 mm)
    Undersize:
        1 .... 2.1555 in (54.75 mm)
        2 .... 2.1457 in (54.50 mm)
Big-end crankpins:
    Diameter (standard) .... 1.9291 in (49.0 mm)
    Undersize:
        1 .... 1.9193 in (48.75 mm)
        2 .... 1.9094 in (48.50 mm)

Connecting rods

Endfloat on crankshaft .... 0.001 to 0.018 in (0.25 to 0.45 mm)
Length between centres .... 5.98 (152.0 mm)
Maximum weight difference between connecting rods .... 0.7 oz (20.0 g)

Lubrication

Oil capacity (Turbo models) .... Add 1.1 Imp pint (0.63 US qt, 0.6 litre) if oil cooler drained
Oil pump:
    Gear endfloat .... 0.0008 to 0.0047 in (0.02 to 0.12 mm)
    Radial clearance .... 0.0008 to 0.0035 in (0.02 to 0.09 mm)
    Backlash .... 0.006 to 0.014 in (0.15 to 0.35 mm)

B230 engine
General

Specifications as for B200 engine plus the following differences:
Bore .... 3.780 in (96.0 mm)
Displacement .... 2316 cc (141.2 cu in)
Compression ratio:
    B230A .... 10.3 to 1
    B230 (special territories) .... 9.0 to 1
    B230E .... 10.3 to 1
    B230F .... 9.8 to 1
Output (DIN):
    B230A .... 110 bhp (81 kW) @ 5000 rpm
    B230 (special territories) .... 106 bhp (78 kW) @ 5000 rpm
    B230E .... 131 bhp (96 kW) @ 5400 rpm
    B230F .... 113 bhp (83 kW) @ 5400 rpm
Torque (DIN):
    B230A .... 138 lbf ft (187 Nm) @ 2500 rpm
    B230 (special territories) .... 132 lbf ft (179 Nm) @ 2500 rpm
    B230E .... 140 lbf ft (190 Nm) @ 3600 rpm
    B230F .... 137 lbf ft (185 Nm) @ 2750 rpm

Cylinder block

Bore grade:

C	3.7795 to 3.7799 in (96.00 to 96.01 mm)
D	3.7799 to 3.7803 in (96.01 to 96.02 mm)
E	3.7803 to 3.7807 in (96.02 to 96.03 mm)
G	3.7811 to 3.7815 in (96.04 to 96.05 mm)

Pistons

Length	2.5472 in (64.7 mm)
Clearance in bore	0.0001 to 0.0012 in (0.003 to 0.030 mm)

Piston rings

Piston ring-to-groove clearance:

Top compression	0.0024 to 0.0036 in (0.060 to 0.092 mm)
Second compression	0.0016 to 0.0028 in (0.040 to 0.072 mm)
Oil scraper	0.0012 to 0.0025 in (0.030 to 0.065 mm)

Piston ring end gap:

Top compression	0.012 to 0.022 in (0.30 to 0.55 mm)
Second compression	0.012 to 0.022 in (0.30 to 0.55 mm)
Oil scraper	0.012 to 0.024 in (0.30 to 0.60 mm)

Gudgeon pin

Length	2.56 in (65.0 mm)

Valve springs

Free length:

B230A, K, E and ET	1.77 in (45.0 mm)
B230F and FT	1.79 in (45.5 mm)

Camshaft

B230A:

Marking	A
Maximum lift height	0.413 in (10.5 mm)
Inlet valve opens	13° BTDC

B230K:

Marking	X
Maximum lift height	0.419 in (10.65 mm)
Inlet valve opens	10° BTDC

B230E:

Marking	V
Maximum lift height	0.448 in (11.37 mm)
Inlet valve opens	11° BTDC

B230ET:

Marking	A
Maximum lift height	0.413 in (10.5 mm)
Inlet valve opens	13° BTDC

B230F:

Marking	M
Maximum lift height:	
Inlet	0.374 in (9.5 mm)
Exhaust	0.413 in (10.5 mm)
Inlet valve opens	6° ATDC
Exhaust valve opens	44° BBDC

B230FT:

Marking	T
Maximum lift height	0.390 in (9.9 mm)
Inlet valve opens	4° BTDC

B200 and B230 engines
Torque wrench settings

	lbf ft	Nm
Cylinder head bolts (oiled)*:		
Stage 1	15	20
Stage 2	44	60
Stage 3	Turn through 90°	
Main bearing cap bolts	81	110
Big-end cap bolts:		
Stage 1	15	20
Stage 2	Turn through 90°	
Flywheel (use new bolts)	52	70
Camshaft sprocket bolt	37	50
Intermediate shaft sprocket bolt	15	20
Camshaft bearing cap bolts	15	20
Crankshaft sprocket bolt:		
Stage 1	44	60
Stage 2	Turn through 60°	

* Renew after five removals and refittings or if bolt length exceeds 2.185 in (55.5 mm); indicating stretched condition.

Cooling system
Capacity 1983 on
Manual transmission .... 16.5 Imp pt (9.9 US qt, 9.4 litre)
Automatic transmission .... 16.2 Imp pt (9.7 US qt, 9.2 litre)

Expansion tank pressure cap
Pressure relief valve opens .... 14 lbf/in² (0.97 bar)
Vacuum valve opens .... 1.0 lbf/in² (0.069 bar)

Thermostat

Marking	**82**	**87**	**92**
Starts to open	82°C	87°C	92°C
Fully open	92°C	97°C	102°C

Radiator fan thermal switch
Cuts in .... 212°F (100°C)
Switches off .... 203°F (95°C)

Torque wrench settings

	lbf ft	**Nm**
Fixed fan bolt (B20A)	15 to 19	20 to 25
Fixed fan bolt (B17, 19, 21 and 23)	7	9

Fuel system
Zenith-Stromberg 175 CD-2SE carburettor
Application .... B20A and B21A engines
B20A engine, 1975/76 .... Needle B1CC
B21A engine:
   1975 .... Needle B2BB
   1976 .... Needle B1ED
   1977 .... Needle B1EE
CO%, B20A engine:
   1975 .... 2.5
   1976 .... 1.5
CO% B21A engine 2.5

SU HIF-6 carburettor
Application .... B17A, B19A, B21A and B23A engines
B21A engine:
   Early .... Needle BCJ
   Late .... Needle BDJ
Idling adjustments:

	CO%	Idling speed
B17A (1979 on)	2.0	900 rpm
B19A (1977)	3.0	850 rpm
B19A (1978 on)	2.0	900 rpm
B21A (1975 to 1977)	2.5	850 rpm
B21A (1978)	2.5	900 rpm
B21A (1979 on)	2.0	900 rpm
B23A (1981 on)	2.0	900 rpm

Solex-Cisac carburettor
Application .... B200K and B230AK engines
Float level .... 1.332 in (33.8 mm)
Idle speed .... 900 rev/min
CO% .... 1.0 to 2.5

Pierburg DVG 175 CDSU carburettor
Application .... B230A engine
Float level .... 1.064 to 1.143 in (27.0 to 29.0 mm)
Idle speed .... 900 rpm
CO% .... 1.5 to 3.0 with Pulsair system disconnected and plugged

Pierburg 2B5 carburettor

Application	B230K engine
Float level:	
Primary	1.064 to 1.143 in (27.0 to 29.0 mm)
Secondary	1.14 to 1.22 in (29.0 to 31.0 mm)
Idle speed:	
Manual transmission	800 rpm
Automatic transmission	900 rpm
CO%	0.5 to 2.0

Fuel injection (Continuous Injection) system

Application	B200E and B230E engines
Idle speed (B200E):	
Manual transmission	800 rpm
Automatic transmission	900 rpm
Idle speed (B230E)	900 rpm
CO%	0.5 to 2.0

Fuel injection (Motronic ignition) system

Application	B200ET and B230ET engines
Idle speed	900 rpm
CO%:	
B200ET	1.0 to 2.5
B230ET	0.5 to 2.0

Revised CO levels and idle speeds

	CO%	Idle speed
B19/21E (1975 to 1980)	2.0	900 rpm
B19/21E (1981 on)	1.0	900 rpm
B19/21ET (Turbo) (1981 on)	2.0	900 rpm
B23E (1979 to 1980)	2.0	950 rpm
B23E (1981 on)	1.0	900 rpm
B21F and Turbo	1.0	900 rpm
B21F – MPG	1.0	750 rpm

LH Jetronic fuel injection system

Application	B230F and B230FT engines
Idle speed:	
Air conditioner off	750 rpm
Air conditioner on	900 rpm
CO%	0.4 to 0.8

Fuel system coding

Engine number suffix:	
A	Carburettor (variable choke)
E	Fuel injection (except North America)
ET	Fuel injection turbo (except North America)
F	Fuel injection (North America)
FT	Fuel injection turbo (North America)
K	Carburettor (fixed jet)

Torque wrench settings

	lbf ft	Nm
Turbo mounting bolts:		
Stage 1	0.7	1
Stage 2	22	30
Stage 3	Angle tighten 120°	
Lambda-sond sensor	40	54

Ignition system
Ignition timing (contact breaker type ignition)

Vacuum disconnected, engine at idling speed

Engine	Year	Degrees BTDC	International variations
B17A	1979 to 84	12	
B19A	1977	15	
	1978	15	Italy
	1978 to 80	12	
	1981 to 84	10	

Engine	Year	Degrees BTDC	International variations
B19K	1984	7	
B20A	1975 to 76	10	
B21A	1975	12	
	1976 to 77	15	
	1978	12	Sweden
		15	Except Sweden
	1979 to 80	12	
	1981	10	Scandinavia and Australia
		12	Except Scandinavia and Australia
	1982 to 83	10	Scandinavia and Australia
		7	Canada
		12	Except Scandinavia, Australia and Canada
	1984	10	Scandinavia and Australia
		7	Except Scandinavia and Australia
B23A	1981 to 82	7	Scandinavia
	1982	5	Except Scandinavia
	1983 to 84	7	Europe
		5	Except Europe

Ignition timing (breakerless type ignition)
Vacuum disconnected, engine at idling speed

Engine	Year	Degrees BTDC	International variations
B19E	1977 to 83	8	
	1984	10	
B19ET	1982 to 84	15	
B21E	1975 to 82	8	
B21ET	1981 to 84	15	
B23E	1978 to 82	5	
	1983	10	Canada
		5	Except Canada
	1984	10	
B20F	1975	5	
B21F	1976	15	
	1977	12	USA
		15	Except USA
	1978	12	
	1979	8	California and Japan
		10	Except California and Japan
	1980	10	Canada
		8	Except Canada
	1981 to 84	8	
B21FT	1981 to 84	12	

Ignition timing (computerised ignition system)

Engine	Year	Degrees BTDC	International variations
B200K	1985 to 86	7	
B200E	1985 to 86	10	
B230A	1985 to 86	7	
B230E	1985 to 86	10	
B230F	1985 to 86	12	North America
B230FT	1985 to 86	12	North America

Spark plugs

Engine	Bosch	Champion
B17A	W7DC	N9YC
B19A	W7DC	N9YC
B19E	W6DC	N7YC
B19ET	W6DC	N7YC
B19K	W7DC	None specified
B20A	W7DC	L82YC
B20F	W6DC	None specified
B21A	W7DC	N7YC
B21E	W6DC	N7YC
B21ET	W6DC	N7YC
B21F	W6DC	None specified
B21FT	W6DC	None specified
B23A	W7DC	N9YC
B23E	W6DC	N7YC
B23ET	W6DC	None specified
B200E	W6DC	None specified
B200K	W7DC	None specified
B230A	W7DC	N9YC
B230E	W6DC	N7YC

B230F	WR7DC	None specified
B230FT	WR7DC	None specified
Electrode gap	0.028 to 0.032 in (0.7 to 0.8 mm)	

Torque wrench setting	**lbf ft**	**Nm**
Spark plug	15 to 22	20 to 30

Clutch
1983 and later
Throw-out for fork free travel:
All cable operated clutches	0.04 to 0.12 in (1.0 to 3.0 mm)

Clutch pedal travel:
Turbo models	6.1 to 6.8 in (155 to 170 mm)

Manual gearbox
Types M45 and M46
Clearances:
Reverse gear-to-selector	0.004 to 0.040 in (0.1 to 1.0 mm)
Input shaft axial clearance	0.0004 to 0.008 in (0.01 to 0.20 mm)
Mainshaft axial clearance	0.0004 to 0.008 in (0.01 to 0.20 mm)

Layshaft axial clearance:
Iron casing	0.0009 to 0.0039 in (0.025 to 0.10 mm)
Aluminium casing	0.001 to 0.003 in (0.03 to 0.08 mm)

Type M47
Ratios:
1st	4.03 to 1
2nd	2.16 to 1
3rd	1.37 to 1
4th	1.0 to 1
5th	0.83 to 1
Reverse	3.68 to 1

Clearance:
Reverse gear-to-selector lever	0.004 to 0.10 in (0.1 to 2.5 mm)

Endfloat:
Input shaft	0.0004 to 0.008 in (0.01 to 0.20 mm)
Layshaft	0.0004 to 0.004 in (0.01 to 0.10 mm)
Mainshaft	0.0004 to 0.008 in (0.01 to 0.20 mm)
5th gear synchro-hub	0.0004 to 0.008 in (0.01 to 0.20 mm)
Oil capacity	2.3 Imp pt (1.4 US qt, 1.30 litre)

Torque wrench settings	**lbf ft**	**Nm**
Clutch housing	26 to 37	35 to 50
Rear cover	26 to 37	35 to 50
Gearlever bracket bolts	35	47
Top cover bolts	20	27
Layshaft screw	30	41
Output flange nut:		
M16	60	82
M20	80	109

Overdrive
Oil pressure
Early models	384 to 427 lbf/in² (27 to 30 kgf/cm²)
Later models (except Turbo)	469 to 512 lbf/in² (33 to 36 kgf/cm²)
Turbo models	526 to 711 lbf/in² (37 to 50 kgf/cm²)

Automatic transmission
Type AW70/71
Reduction ratios:
1st gear	2.45 to 1
2nd gear	1.45 to 1
3rd gear	1.1 to 1
Overdrive	0.69 to 1
Reverse	2.21 to 1
Torque converter size	9.8 in (248 mm)
Fluid capacity	13.2 Imp pt (9.8 US qt; 7.5 litre) including 4.4 Imp pt (2.6 US qt; 2.5 litre) in torque converter

Torque wrench settings

	lbf ft	Nm
Type BW55		
Converter housing to engine	26 to 37	35 to 50
Driveplate to converter:		
M12 bolts	41 to 66	55 to 90
M10 bolts	30 to 37	41 to 50
Converter housing cover:		
M6 bolts	4 to 6	6 to 9
M8 bolts	13 to 19	18 to 25
Sump (oil pan):		
Yellow gasket	4 to 7	6 to 10
Blue gasket	6 to 9	8 to 12
Output flange	30 to 37	41 to 50
Oil cooler pipe union	15 to 22	20 to 30
Oil filler pipe nut	59 to 74	80 to 100
Type AW70/71		
Driveplate to torque converter	30 to 36	41 to 49
Sump (oil pan)	3 to 3.5	4 to 5
Drain plug	13 to 17	18 to 23

Rear axle
Final drive ratios

With 4-speed gearbox	3.31 to 1 or 3.54 to 1
With 4-speed gearbox and overdrive	3.54 to 1 or 3.73 to 1
With 5-speed gearbox	3.91 to 1
With automatic transmission:	
Type BW35	3.91 to 1 or 4.10 to 1 depending upon engine
Type BW55	3.54 to 1, 3.73 to 1 or 3.91 to 1 depending upon engine
Type AW55	3.73 to 1, 3.91 to 1 or 4.10 to 1 depending upon engine
Type AW70/71	3.73 to 1 or 3.91 to 1

Oil capacity

Type 1031 (Heavy duty rear axle)	2.8 Imp pt (1.6 litre, 1.7 US qt)

Wheels and tyres
Roadwheels

Type (GT and GLT models)	Aluminium
Size (GT and GLT models)	6J x 15

Tyres

Size (GT and GLT models)	195/60 HR 15

Torque wrench settings

	lbf ft	Nm
Rear axle		
Speedometer sensor locknut	35	48
Limited slip differential case bolts (left-hand thread)	50	68
Rear suspension		
Torque rod	62	84
Panhard rod to axle	44	59
Panhard rod to body	62	84
Coil spring upper fixing	32	44
Coil spring lower fixing	14	19
Shock absorber mountings	62	84
Trailing arm to axle	90	122
Trailing arm to body	80	109
Stabilizer bar front fixing	62	84
Stabilizer bar rear fixing	32	44
Roadwheel nuts	100	136

Braking system
Front brake discs (ventilated type – 1983 on)

Thickness (new)	0.94 in (24.0 mm)
Thickness – minimum after regrind	0.82 in (20.8 mm)

Pressure regulating valve (1983 on)

Cut-put point:	
Saloon	483 lbf/in² (33.3 bar)
Estate	710 lbf/in² (49.0 bar)

Electrical system

Battery

Type	Tudor 6EX4F (or equivalent)

Alternator

SEV-Marchal C14/55A

Maximum amperage	55A
Maximum wattage	770W
Minimum diameter, slip rings	1.34 in (34.0 mm)
Minimum brush length	0.20 in (5.0 mm)
Tightening torque – pulley nut	30 lbf ft (41 Nm)
Test values:	
Rotor winding resistance	3.5 to 4.3 ohms
Stator resistance	0.17 to 0.23 ohm/phase
Output at 14V	48A at 3000 rpm

SEV-Marchal D14/70A

Maximum amperage	70A
Maximum wattage	980W
Minimum diameter, slip rings	1.34 in (34.0 mm)
Minimum brush length	0.20 in (5.0 mm)
Tightening torque – pulley nut	30 lbf ft (41 Nm)
Test values:	
Rotor winding resistance	3 to 5 ohms
Stator resistance	0.08 to 0.18 ohm/phase
Output at 14V	62A at 3000 rpm

Bosch N1 14V 70A 20

Maximum amperage	70A
Maximum wattage	980W
Minimum diameter, slip rings:	
With remote regulator	1.24 in (31.5 mm)
With integral regulator	1.06 in (27.0 mm)
Minimum brush length	0.20 in (5.0 mm)
Tightening torque – pulley nut	26 lbf ft (35 Nm)
Test values:	
Rotor winding resistance	4 to 4.4 ohms
Stator resistance	0.1 ohm/phase
Output at 14V	58A at 3000 rpm

Transistorized remote regulator

Regulator temperature with fully charged battery	77°F (25°C)
Test voltage between B + and D − terminals (engine at 3000 rpm, alternator load 5 to 10A):	
Except Part No 1308030:	
Cold	13.7 to 14.5V
Warm (30 minutes running)	13.5 to 14.1V
Part No 1308030:	
Cold	14.3 to 15.0V
Warm (15 minutes running)	14.05 to 14.35V

Integral regulator

Regulator temperature with fully charged battery	77°F (25°C)
Test voltage between B + and D − terminals (engine at 3000 rpm, alternator load 5A):	
Cold	14.4 to 14.8V
Warm (15 minutes running)	13.8 to 14.3V

Starter motor

Bosch JF 12V 2kW

Output	2kW (2.7 hp)
Armature axial clearance	0.004 to 0.012 in (0.1 to 0.3 mm)
Pinion clearance	0.014 to 0.024 in (0.35 to 0.60 mm)
Minimum commutator diameter	1.673 in (42.5 mm)
Minimum length of brushes	0.335 in (8.5 mm)
Minimum solenoid cut-in voltage	7.5V

Hitachi 12V 1.4 kW

Output	1.4 kW (1.9 hp)
Armature axial clearance	0.001 to 0.004 in (0.03 to 0.1 mm)
Minimum diameter of commutator	1.535 in (39.0 mm)

Minimum length of brushes .... 0.433 in (11.0 mm)
Minimum solenoid cut-in voltage 8.0V

Light bulbs
	Wattage
Rear foglights	21
Number plate light:	
1979 on (except 245)	4
1981 245	5
Luggage compartment	15

Fuses (1986) – typical

Fuse number	Circuits protected	Rating (A)
1	Cigar lighter, exterior mirror, radio, tailgate wash/wipe, cruise control governor	8
2	Windscreen wiper/washer, horn	16
3	Heater blower	16
4	Fuel pump	8
5	Spare	8
6	Main fuel pump	8
7	Stop-lamps, cruise control switch	16
8	Interior lamp, glovebox lamp, boot lamp, engine compartment lamp, central locking system, radio aerial	8
9	Hazard warning system, gearchange indicator lamp	8
10	Power-operated windows	16
11	5th speed o/d gear (manual), 4th speed o/d gear (automatic), heated rear window, seat heaters	16
12	Reversing lamps, power window relay, air conditioner blower, heated rear window relay	8
13	Instruments, seat belt warning lamp, direction indicators, fuel injection system relay	8
14	Rear fog warning lamps	8
15	Left-hand parking lamps, rear number plate lamp	8
16	Right-hand parking lamps, panel and control illumination	8

Front suspension and steering
Power steering
Cam Gear steering gear with aluminium housing

Oil capacity (ATF) .... 1.2 Imp pt (0.74 US qt, 0.7 litre)

ZF steering gear

Number of turns, lock-to-lock 3.5
Reduction ratio .... 17.2 to 1
Pinion to rack pre-tension (fixed valve housing type) .... 1.3 to 2.2 lbf in (15 to 25 Ncm)
Pre-tension piston to cover clearance .... 0.004 to 0.006 in (0.1 to 0.15 mm)
Oil capacity (ATF) .... 1.2 Imp pt (0.74 US qt, 0.7 litre)

Power steering pump
Maximum pressure (ZF type) .... 824 lbf/in² (58 kgf/cm²)
Maximum pressure (Saginaw type) .... 853 to 996 lbf/in² (60 to 70 kgf/cm²)
Ratio, engine to pump (Saginaw type) .... 1 to 0.9

Wheel alignment (vehicle unladen)
Castor:
   1979 on models with power steering .... 3 to 4° positive
Camber:
   DL, GL models .... 1° to 1° 30′ positive
   All other models .... 0° 15′ to 0° 45′ positive
   Maximum side-to-side variation .... 0° 30′
King pin inclination .... 12°
Toe-in (measured at wheel rim):
   Manual steering .... 0.06 to 0.138 in (1.5 to 3.5 mm)
   Power steering .... 0.02 to 0.10 in (0.5 to 2.5 mm)
Roadwheel turning angles:
   Outer wheel .... 20°
   Inner wheel .... 20° 48′

Bodywork
Kerb weights (1984 on)
Saloon .... 2844 to 2921 lb (1290 to 1325 kg)
Estate .... 2965 to 3009 lb (1345 to 1365 kg)
Maximum roof rack load .... 220 lb (100 kg)
Maximum trailer weight .... 3300 lb (1500 kg)

3 Engine

B17A type engine – description

1 This engine was introduced in 1979 exclusively for vehicles destined for operation in Israel and Nigeria.

2 The engine is very similar to the B19 engine mentioned in this Supplement apart from its smaller capacity, achieved by reducing the stroke.

B19 type engine – description

3 This engine was introduced in 1977 for use in cars destined for operation in a few special territories only. Three versions are available: one fuel injection model (B19E) and two carburettor versions (B19A).

4 Apart from its displacement, achieved by reducing the cylinder bore, the engine is identical to the B21 Series engine.

B21 engine – description

5 As from 1980 models, the B21F engine is available in North America and is similar to the B21E. The USA version incorporates a 'Lambda-sond' oxygen sensor feed-back system and catalytic converter.

6 The B21F-MPG engine was introduced in 1981 and is an economy version with an electronic spark control system and low rear axle ratio.

7 The B21F-Turbo (B21FT) engine was also introduced in 1981.

B23 type engine – description

8 This engine was introduced in 1981 and is available in three versions; B23A, B23E, and B23F according to territory.

9 The engine is similar to the B21 series engine, its increased displacement being obtained by increasing the cylinder bore, although the block is different.

B200 and B230 type engines – description

10 Based upon the B21 power unit, these engines are described as low friction power units largely due to lighter weight internal components with reduced bearing surfaces.

11 The engine capacity of the B230 is achieved by increasing the cylinder bore.

12 Both engines have cylinder heads of crossflow design.

13 Carburettor, fuel injection and turbo versions are available depending upon operating territory.

Engine sump pan (1979 on) – removal and refitting

14 A deeper type of sump pan was introduced early in 1979 and if it is to be removed from the car with the engine in position, the following operations must be adhered to.

15 Raise the front end and support the car under the jacking points.

16 Drain the engine oil.

17 Remove the splash shield from under the engine.

18 Remove the engine mounting nuts from the underside of the crossmember.

19 Release both pinch-bolts from the universal joint coupling on the steering shaft and slide the coupling up the splines on the shaft.

20 The engine must now be raised slightly. Do this by attaching a hoist to the lifting lugs or by using a crossbar and threaded hook similar to the arrangement shown (Fig. 13.3).

21 Unscrew and remove the bolts which secure the crossmember and lower it.

22 Unbolt and remove the engine mounting from the left-hand side.

23 Unbolt the bracing brackets from the rear corners of the sump pan.

24 Unbolt the sump pan, lower it and turn it to remove it.

25 Refitting is a reversal of removal. Use a new gasket and tighten the steering coupling pinch-bolts to the specified torque.

26 Fill the engine with oil.

Cylinder head bolts (overhead camshaft engines) tightening

27 On later models the cylinder head bolts have normal hexagon heads instead of socket heads, and the tightening procedure is different. The bolt threads should be clean and oiled, and tightened in three stages with reference to the Specifications.

28 Retightening the head bolts after running the engine is not necessary with the new type bolts.

Fig. 13.1 Engine mounting nuts (Sec 3)

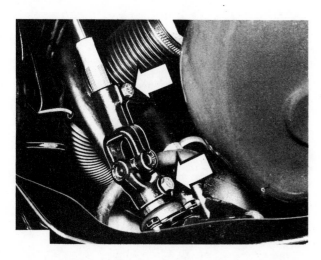

Fig. 13.2 Steering shaft pinch-bolts (Sec 3)

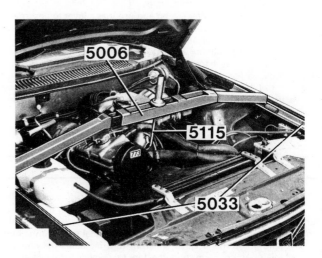

Fig. 13.3 Volvo engine supporting tools (Sec 3)

Turbo engine exhaust valves

29 On Turbo engines the exhaust valve heads have a coating of stellite, and the valves are filled with sodium. The valve heads must not be machined although careful grinding in with paste is permitted.
30 Sodium filled exhaust valves should be disposed of carefully and not exposed to high temperatures otherwise they may explode.

Crankshaft vibration damper/pulley

31 This is fitted instead of the normal drivebelt pulley to B200 engines.
32 The crankshaft timing belt sprocket incorporates a dowel pin onto which the damper/pulley fits so that it can only be fitted in one position.

Engine mountings – renewal

33 The engine mountings may be renewed in the following way.
34 Disconnect the battery.
35 Support the weight of the engine on a hoist or by placing a jack and a block of wood under the sump pan (anti-splash shield removed).
36 Unbolt the mounting and remove it. Renew one mounting at a time and, if the left-hand one is being removed, then the power steering hose will have to be unclipped and moved aside.
37 On E engines, disconnect the brace at the intake manifold.
38 Refitting is a reversal of removal.

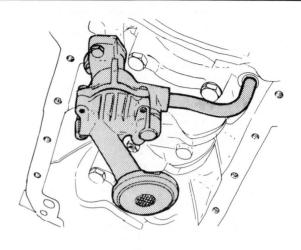

Fig. 13.4 Oil pump and delivery pipe (Sec 3)

Oil pump – removal and refitting (engine in vehicle)

39 Remove engine sump pan as described in Chapter 1, Section 38 or this Section, paragraphs 14 to 26, according to vehicle model year.
40 Unscrew the two mounting bolts and withdraw the pump, complete with delivery pipe.
41 When refitting the pump, use new seals and make sure that the oil separator drain hose clip is located under the oil pump fixing bolt.

Engine – removal and refitting

42 The removal operations for later models are similar to those described in Chapter 1, but the splash shield must be removed from under the engine compartment and, on Turbo versions, the exhaust pipe must be disconnected from the turbo compressor.
43 On B200 and B230 engines, the distributor is located at the rear end of the cylinder head, so before lifting the engine from its compartment, remove the distributor cap to prevent it making contact with the bulkhead; there is very little clearance.

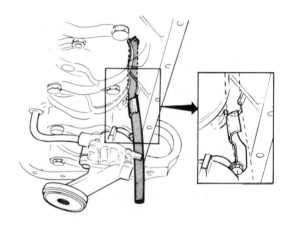

Fig. 13.5 Oil trap drain hose and clip (Sec 3)

Engine oil – renewal

44 Always drain the engine oil hot after a run. Unscrew the sump pan drain plug and catch the oil in a suitably large container.
45 While the oil is draining, unscrew the filter and discard it. A filter removal tool will possibly be needed to do this and various types are available from motor accessory stores. If all else fails, drive a large screwdriver through the filter casing and use it as a lever to unscrew it.
46 Refit the drain plug, oil the rubber gasket of the new filter and screw it on using hand pressure only.
47 Pour the correct quantity and type of oil into the rocker cover filler. Start the engine, run it for a few minutes. The oil pressure warning lamp will take a few seconds to go out due to the time taken for the new filter to fill. Check and top up the oil level. To do this, withdraw the dipstick, wipe it clean, reinsert it, withdraw it for the second time and read off the level.

---

4   Cooling system, heater and air conditioner

Fan coupling

1   The slip coupling type radiator cooling fan has been modified on certain models. As well as being speed sensitive, the fan is also temperature sensitive by the inclusion of a bi-metal spring in its hub.
2   The spring controls a valve which in turn regulates the coupling internal oil flow, so permitting the fan to revolve faster or slower according to the cooling requirements of the engine.

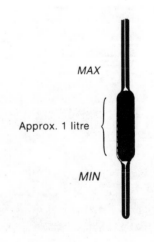

MAX

Approx. 1 litre

MIN

Fig. 13.6 Typical engine oil dipstick (Sec 3)

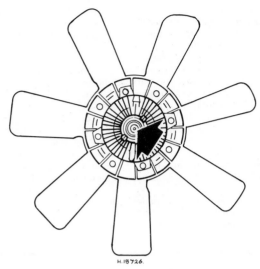

Fig. 13.7 Modified radiator cooling fan with bi-metal spring (arrowed) (Sec 4)

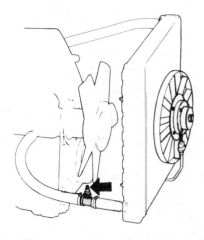

Fig. 13.8 Electric fan and thermal switch (arrowed) (Sec 4)

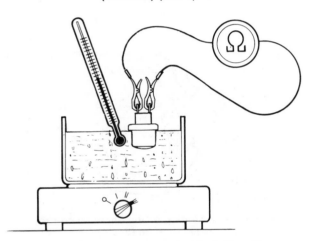

Fig. 13.9 Checking thermal switch (Sec 4)

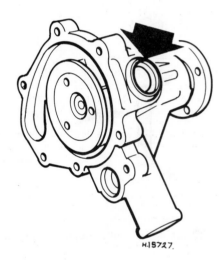

Fig. 13.10 Water pump on B17, B19, B21 and B23 engines showing single upper outlet (arrowed) (Sec 4)

Electric cooling fan

3   This is fitted to 1984 and later models which are equipped with a turbo intercooler or air conditioner.

4   A thermal switch is located in the lower radiator hose. A relay is fitted into the wiring circuit.

5   To test the circuit and relay, bridge the terminals of the thermal switch and turn on the ignition. The fan should operate.

6   The functioning of the thermal switch may be checked by warming it then cooling it and observing whether it cuts in and out at the specified levels when connected as part of a test lamp circuit.

Water pump (B17, B19, B21 and B23 engines) – removal and refitting

7   The water pump on the above engines incorporates only one upper outlet into the head, and the heater return pipe locates in the rear face of the pump adjacent to the bottom hose inlet.

8   Before fitting the sealing ring to the outlet, half fill the groove with anti-corrosion liquid such as Dinitrol.

Drivebelts – tensioning and renewal

9   Adjustment of the fanbelt is described in Chapter 2, Section 7.

10 As many vehicles are equipped with power steering or air conditioning a multi-belt arrangement may be encountered.

11 The correct tension of all belts is that it should deflect between 0.2 and 0.4 in (5.0 and 10.0 mm) when depressed by moderate thumb pressure at the centre of the longest run of the belt.

12 Adjustment is carried out by moving the compressor (air conditioner), alternator or power steering pump on its mounting bolts.

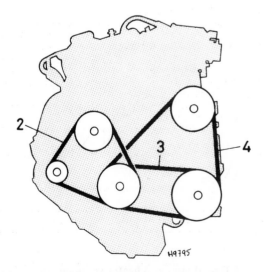

Fig. 13.11 Typical drivebelt arrangement (Sec 4)

2   Alternator and water pump   4   Power-assisted steering
3   Air conditioner compressor   pump

13 On configurations having two belts running off the crankshaft pulley for the power steering pump and a/c compressor, belt tension is adjusted by increasing or decreasing the number of shims fitted between the halves of the crankshaft pulley.

Heater unit (standard) – removal and refitting

14 Disconnect the battery negative lead.

15 Move the heater controls to minimum and remove the heater side cover panels. Drain the cooling system.

16 Disconnect the defroster and air vent hoses.

17 Pull back the carpet and position a container beneath the heater to catch any spilled water.

18 On the type A heater (Fig. 13.13) disconnect the coolant hoses noting their position, then remove the control valve from the bracket and disconnect the cable.

19 On the type B heater (Fig. 13.14) disconnect the coolant hoses noting their position, then pull the control valve capillary tube from the housing leaving the control valve on the bracket.

20 Unscrew the lower mounting screws and disconnect the air duct from the unit.

21 Disconnect the temperature control cable, and remove the housing mounting screws; noting the location of the fan motor earth lead.

22 Remove the glove compartment and the facia centre air vents, then remove the vent duct.

23 Disconnect the defroster hose.

24 Remove the screws and lower the rear floor air duct, then remove the lower mounting screw and the drain hose.

25 Pull off the fan motor switch knob, unscrew the nut and withdraw the switch from the facia panel. Disconnect the positive wire.

26 Disconnect the control cables from the floor and defroster flaps.

27 Unscrew the upper mounting screws and withdraw the heater unit.

28 To dismantle the unit remove the drain hose and the intake seal, and prise off all the clips. Separate the casing halves and on the type A heater unclip the capillary tube. Remove the matrix and motor assembly, and if necessary separate the motor from the bracket (two screws).

29 Reassembly and refitting is a reversal of removal and dismantling, but apply sealing compound to the casing half mating faces and adjust the control cables as required. Top up the cooling system with reference to Chapter 2.

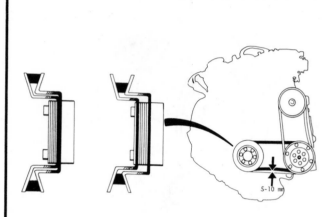

Fig. 13.12 Crankshaft pulley adjustment shims (Sec 4)

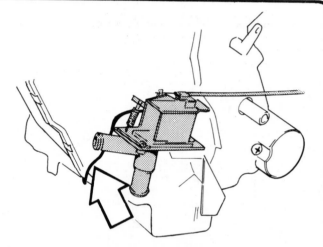

Fig. 13.13 Type A standard heater showing control valve capillary tube (Sec 4)

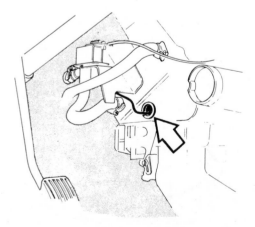

Fig. 13.14 Type B standard heater showing control valve capillary tube (Sec 4)

Fig. 13.15 Removing the matrix and motor assembly from the standard heater (Sec 4)

Motor assembly holder arrowed

Heater unit (combined/vacuum controlled) – removal and refitting

30 Disconnect the battery negative lead.

31 Move the heater controls to minimum and remove the heater side cover panels.

32 Remove the radio (if applicable) and the centre control panel. Disconnect the wiring and cables and, if air conditioning is fitted, take care not to damage the heat sensor capillary tube.

33 Remove the glove compartment and prise off the strips below the air vents.

34 Remove the steering column shrouds and the choke control or cover plate.

35 Remove the knobs from the instrument lighting rheostat and lighting switch.

36 On 1981 models remove the instrument panel.

37 Remove the storage compartment, centre air vents, and instrument panel frame.

38 Disconnect the wiper multi-plug, centre vent air duct, glove compartment light wiring and defroster vent straps.

39 On 1981 models remove the facia complete.

40 Remove the screws and lower the rear floor air duct.

41 Unscrew the heater lower mounting screws.

42 Disconnect the vacuum tank hose and the control valve cable.

43 Remove the centre console upper and lower screws, and centre support screws.

44 Disconnect the motor wiring.

45 Drain the cooling system (Chapter 2) then disconnect the control valve hose and upper hose.

46 Disconnect the vacuum hoses and air ducts.

47 Unscrew the upper mounting screws then remove the screws and lower the rear floor duct.

48 Unbolt the lower mounting and centre console.

49 Remove the right-hand mounting and support, and disconnect the fan wiring and positive lead.

50 Disconnect the control panel vacuum hose and floor flap vacuum hoses.

51 On models with air conditioning remove the evaporator clips and move the cover to one side to release the evaporator. If necessary disconnect the heat sensor capillary tube.

52 Remove the upper mounting screws and withdraw the heater unit.

53 To dismantle the unit remove the upper hose, inlet seal, and defroster seals.

54 Unclip and remove the side covers and prise off the flap clips.

55 Prise off the fan locking clips.

56 Remove the drain hose, vacuum tank, bracket, flap return spring and casing half clips.

57 Remove the fan motor screws and control valve capillary tube.

58 Disconnect the flap hose.

59 Separate the halves and withdraw the matrix and motor.

60 Reassembly and refitting is a reversal of removal and dismantling, but apply sealing compound to the casing half mating faces. If the fan motor is being renewed on a pre-1980 model, the new motor will be a permanent magnet type whereas the existing motor is a field wound type. The existing casing must be filed to accept the new motor and the wiring adapted as shown in Fig. 13.230. Refill the cooling system as described in Chapter 2.

Air conditioner – drier

61 The drier is located next to the radiator on 1978 and later models.

---

5 Fuel system

Zenith 175 CD-2SE (tamperproof) carburettor – idle (CO) mixture adjustment

1 Generally known as the Zenith-Stromberg, this type of carburettor can be recognised by the fact that a plug is not fitted to the underside of the float chamber. The idle mixture is normally set during production and unless the carburettor is completely overhauled or has new internal parts fitted, it should not require adjustment.

2 A special tool (No 999 5159) will be required to adjust the jet on this type of carburettor.

3 Have the engine at normal operating temperature and adjust the idle speed to 900 rpm (refer to paragraph 32).

Fig. 13.16 The combined/vacuum controlled heater (Sec 4)

1	Upper hose	4	Demister seals
2	Inlet seal	5	Side cover clips
3	Flap clips		

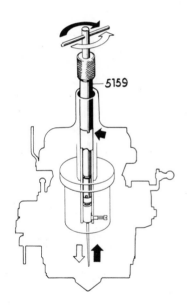

Fig. 13.17 Zenith-Stromberg 175 CD-2SE carburettor jet adjusting tool (Sec 5)

4 Using an exhaust gas analyser or other device such as a 'Colortune', connected in accordance with the maker's instructions, check that the CO level is between 1.5 and 3.5% or that the combustion flame colour is correct.

5 Where adjustment is required, remove the damper and insert the special tool, pushing it down until the lugs on the tool engage with the notches in the air valve spindle. If the engine is inclined to stall during installation of the tool, hold the throttle open until the tool is engaged.

6 Now turn the inner member of the tool to adjust the jet and the mixture. Clockwise rotation of the tool enriches the mixture, anticlockwise weakens it.

7 Make sure that the outer member of the tool is not allowed to rotate during the adjustment operation, otherwise the flexible diaphragm within the carburettor will tear.

8 After each movement of the adjusting tool, rev up the engine to

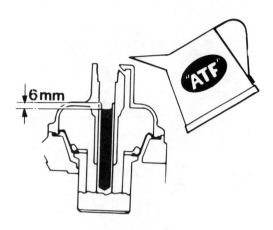

Fig. 13.18 Topping-up the carburettor damper (Sec 5)

Fig. 13.19 Carburettor metering needle, guide screw and special jet adjusting tool (Sec 5)

Fig. 13.20 Carburettor flexible diaphragm locating lug (arrowed) (Sec 5)

about 3000 rpm before checking the mixture evaluating instrument.
9   When the mixture is correct, withdraw the tool, top up the damper cylinder and refit the damper.
10   Remove the analysing device.

Zenith 175 CD-2SE carburettor metering needle – removal and refitting

11   Remove the carburettor from the engine and clean its external surfaces.
12   Remove the suction chamber cover, extract the coil spring and lift out the air valve piston and flexible diaphragm.
13   Insert the special adjusting tool (inner member) and turn the metering needle until it releases from the adjuster screw.
14   Unscrew the spring-loaded guide screw and remove the needle and retainer if required.
15   To fit the needle/retainer, insert the assembly into the base of the air valve piston and then insert the guide screw so that it engages in the groove in the needle retainer.
16   Again using the special tool, screw up the needle until its floating washer is flush with the base of the piston. This is the basic mixture setting position and the mixture must be finally adjusted as described above (paragraphs 3 to 10) once the carburettor is installed on the engine.
17   Refit the air valve and diaphragm, making sure that the alignment projection on the diaphragm engages in the recess in the carburettor body.
18   Fit the coil spring and the suction chamber cover.
19   Fill the damper with oil of the specified type and fit the damper piston.
20   Install the carburettor on the engine using new flange gaskets.

Zenith DVG 175 CDSU carburettor – description

21   Introduced in 1978, this unit was known later as a Pierburg carburettor. It differs from other Zenith carburettors fitted to the range mainly by a special fuel nozzle. The mixture is varied by an adjustable fuel nozzle which incorporates temperature-variable bi-metal washers (temperature compensator).
22   When the fuel is cold, these washers come together, causing the coil spring to force the fuel nozzle downward so creating a greater

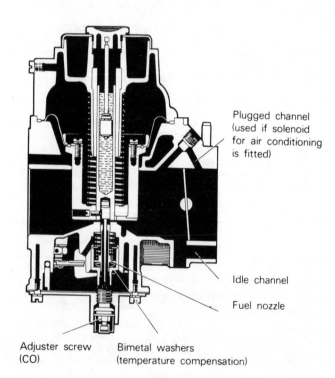

Plugged channel (used if solenoid for air conditioning is fitted)

Idle channel

Fuel nozzle

Adjuster screw (CO)

Bimetal washers (temperature compensation)

Fig. 13.21 Sectional view of Zenith DVG 175 CDSU carburettor (Sec 5)

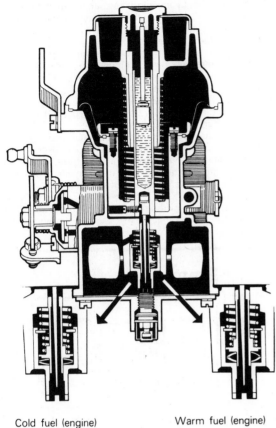

Cold fuel (engine)   Warm fuel (engine)

Fig. 13.22 Position of spring-loaded fuel nozzle at different temperatures (Sec 5)

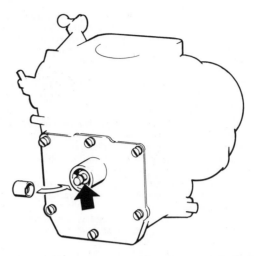

Fig. 13.23 Mixture screw (arrowed) on Zenith DVG 175 CDSU carburettor (Sec 5)

Fig. 13.24 Adjusting idle speed on Zenith DVG 175 CDSU carburettor (Sec 5)

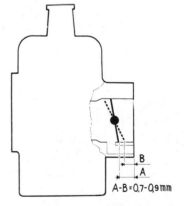

A–B = 0.7–0.9 mm

Fig. 13.25 Throttle butterfly valve basic setting on Zenith DVG 175 CDSU carburettor (Sec 5)

space between nozzle and metering needle to permit a larger fuel flow and in consequence a richer mixture.

23 As the fuel temperature increases, the bi-metal washers separate, causing a smaller space between nozzle and metering needle to give a weaker mixture.

24 The fuel nozzle/washer/spring assemblies are only supplied as complete units.

25 This carburettor also incorporates a manually-operated cold start device (choke).

Zenith DVG 175 CDSU carburettor – idle mixture (CO) adjustment

26 The mixture (CO) is set during production of this carburettor and should not be tampered with unless the unit has been the subject of major overhaul with the renewal of some internal components.

27 Have the engine at normal operating temperature with the idle speed set to the specified level (refer to paragraph 32).

28 Connect an exhaust gas analyser or combustion flame viewer such as a 'Colortune' in accordance with the manufacturer's instructions. Check that the CO level is between 1.5 and 3.5% or that the combustion flame colour is correct.

29 Where adjustment is required, prise out the plastic plug which seals the mixture adjusting screw and turn the screw – clockwise to enrich the mixture and anti-clockwise to weaken it.

30 On completion, refit the plastic plug.

Carburettors – idle speed adjustment

31 The later type of carburettors described in this Supplement have an independent idling circuit which provides a smoother idle and eliminates run-on by means of a solenoid-operated valve.

32 Idle speed adjustment should normally be carried out only by means of the screw located in the intake manifold connecting flange. With the engine at normal operating temperature, turn the screw in or out to bring the idle speed to between 850 and 950 rpm.

33 The basic setting of the throttle butterfly is adjusted during production and it should not be altered unless the normal adjusting method proves unsatisfactory or new carburettor components have been fitted.

34 To alter the basic setting, first remove the carburettor from the engine. Close the butterfly valve fully and measure the dimension A shown in Fig. 13.25.

35 Now adjust the butterfly so that when it is fully closed, dimension B will be between 0.028 and 0.036 in (0.7 and 0.9 mm) less than A previously measured. Adjustment on Zenith-Stromberg carburettors is made by bending the spindle, while on SU carburettors a screw and locknut are fitted.

DVG 175 CDSU carburettor – dismantling and reassembly

36 Remove the carburettor from the intake manifold and clean external dirt and grease from it.
37 Remove the damper piston, the suction chamber and the return spring. Carefully lift out the air valve and the diaphragm.
38 Remove the float chamber cover and its gasket.
39 Remove the adjuster screw from the float chamber cover. Extract the O-ring from the screw.
40 Remove the fuel nozzle with temperature compensator and spring.
41 Remove the fuel inlet needle valve and its washer.
42 Remove the cold start device.
43 Clean, examine and renew components as necessary. If the butterfly valve is dismantled, refit it so that the engraved face is downwards and towards the float chamber.

44 Check the float level by inverting the chamber so that the fuel inlet valves are depressed by the weight of the floats only. Measure as shown in Fig. 13.27, adjusting if necessary by bending the tongues which bear on the fuel inlet valves.
45 When fitting the metering needle, make sure that it is not worn, bent or scored (an unevenly running engine is an indication of a worn needle). The needle must be marked PN. Locate the flat side of the needle against the end of the retaining screw.
46 When fitting the float chamber adjuster screw, remember the O-ring and screw it into the cover until the nozzle is 0.10 in (2.5 mm) under the carburettor housing bridge.
47 Make sure that the diaphragm is not perforated and engage the pip on the diaphragm in the recess in the carburettor housing.
48 Align the suction chamber then tighten its fixing screws. Lift the piston with a finger and allow it to drop unaided. It should fall smoothly without any tendency to stick. It should strike the bridge with a distinct metallic click.
49 Check that the damper piston has an endfloat on its rod of between 0.020 and 0.060 in (0.5 and 1.5 mm). Lack of clearance can cause delay in acceleration.

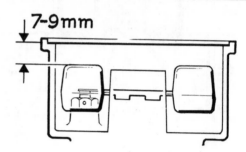

Fig. 13.27 Float level adjustment diagram for Zenith DVG 175 CDSU carburettor (Sec 5)

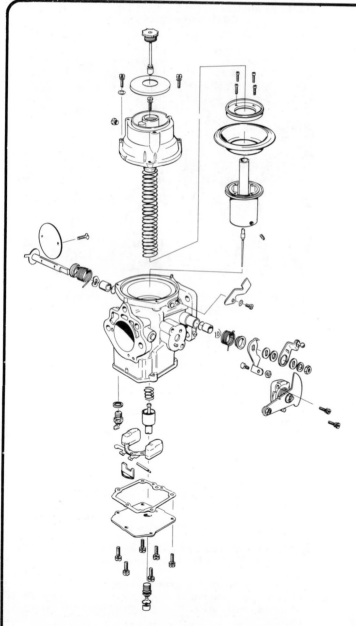

Fig. 13.26 Exploded view of Zenith DVG 175 CDSU carburettor (Sec 5)

Fig. 13.28 Suction chamber alignment marks on Zenith DVG 175 CDSU carburettor (Sec 5)

Fig. 13.29 Carburettor damper piston endfloat (Sec 5)

A = 0.020 to 0.060 in (0.5 to 1.5 mm)

50 Fill the damper with automatic transmission fluid.

51 When installing the carburettor, use a new gasket and make sure that its straight edges are located as shown in Fig. 13.30.

Zenith DVG carburettor – modification

52 The DVG carburettor fitted to 1981 on models incorporates an oil reservoir to ensure that the correct oil level is maintained in the damper spindle. If the oil level is low, the downward movement of the damper draws oil from the reservoir at the top of the carburettor.

Constant idle speed valve (air conditioned models with carburettor)

53 On later models equipped with an air conditioner, an additional solenoid valve is incorporated in the carburettor in order to maintain the engine idle speed when the air conditioner compressor is switched on. This is achieved by opening a passage to admit extra fuel/air mixture as soon as the solenoid valve is energised by completion of the air conditioner electrical circuit.

Manifold pre-heating (carburettor models)

54 The intake manifold is coolant-heated on models built after 1978 to ensure more rapid warm-up. All later models are also equipped with an automatic temperature-controlled air cleaner.

Solex-Cisac carburettor – description

55 This carburettor is fitted to B19K and B200 engines (1984 on) and is of fixed jet, dual barrel, downdraught type.

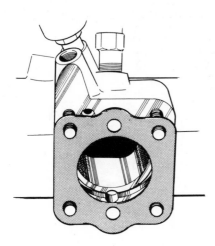

Fig. 13.30 Correctly fitted carburettor flange gasket (Sec 5)

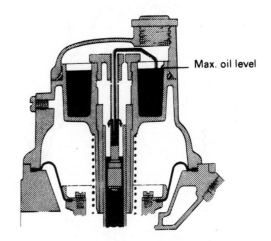

Max. oil level

Fig. 13.31 Sectional view of Zenith DVG 175 CDSU carburettor showing damper oil reservoir fitted from 1981 (Sec 5)

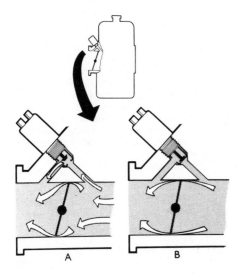

Fig. 13.32 Diagram showing operation of constant idle speed valve on air conditioned models (Sec 5)

A   Air conditioner on   B   Air conditioner off

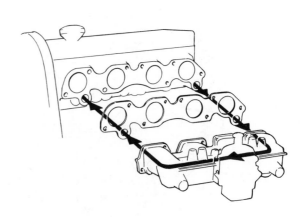

Fig. 13.33 Coolant heated intake manifold. Coolant flow arrowed (Sec 5)

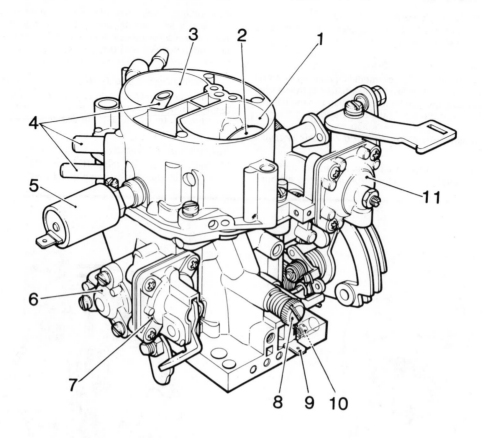

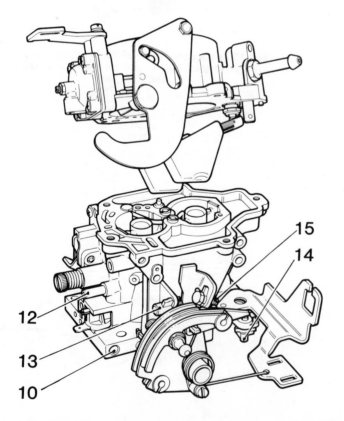

Fig. 13.34 Views of Solex-Cisac carburettor (Sec 5)

1   Primary venturi
2   Choke (cold start) valve plate
3   Secondary venturi
4   Float chamber vents
5   Fuel cut-off solenoid valve
6   Part throttle enrichment device
7   Accelerator pump
8   Idle speed (air volume) screw
9   Thermister heater for idling channels
10 Mixture (CO) adjustment screw
11 Choke control vacuum unit
12 Vacuum take off for distributor
13 Primary throttle valve plate adjustment screw
14 Secondary throttle valve plate adjustment screw*
15 Fast idle adjustment screw*
*   Preset – do not alter

Solex-Cisac carburettor – idle speed and mixture adjustment

56 Have the engine at normal operating temperature and idling. Turn the idle speed (air volume screw) until the engine speed recorded on the tachometer is as specified; see Specifications.

57 The mixture is adjusted during production and should not normally require alteration. However, if the carburettor has been overhauled or if the engine requirements have changed due to carbon build-up or wear then ideally the mixture should be set using an exhaust gas analyser.

58 With the engine still at operating temperature, prise out the mixture screw tamperproof plug and turn the screw in or out until the exhaust emission CO level stabilises within the specified tolerance. If the adjustment is prolonged, rev the engine at one minute intervals to clear the intake before continuing with the adjustment.

59 If an exhaust gas analyser is not available, turn the mixture screw in until the idle quality is poor then unscrew it until the engine is at its smoothest idle. The idle speed may now require slight readjustment.

60 Switch off the engine and fit a new tamperproof cap.

Solex-Cisac carburettor – removal and refitting

61 Remove the air cleaner.

62 Disconnect the fuel and ventilation hoses.

63 Disconnect the throttle and choke cables.

64 Disconnect the lead from the solenoid anti-run on valve.

65 Unscrew the four mounting nuts and lift the carburettor from its mounting flange on the inlet manifold.

66 Before refitting the carburettor, clean the mating surfaces and use a new gasket on each side of the insulating block.

67 Observe the warm start and crankcase ventilation hose arrangement which must not be altered (Fig. 13.35).

68 Adjust the throttle cable at the carburettor by turning the cable threaded end fitting so that, when the accelerator pedal is fully depressed, the throttle quadrant at the carburettor is against its stop. Check that, when the pedal is released, the quadrant is against its idle stop.

69 Check that the choke valve flap in the primary barrel is fully open when the choke knob is pushed in and fully closed when it is pulled out.

Solex-Cisac carburettor – overhaul

70 The work described should be regarded as the limit of overhaul operations. If the carburettor has had a long life and wear is now evident in throttle valve spindles and other components, it should be changed for a new or factory rebuilt unit.

71 Before commencing, obtain a repair kit for the specific carburettor. This will contain gaskets, seals and other renewable items.

72 With the carburettor removed from the engine, clean away external dirt and grease.

73 Extract the top cover screws and lift off the cover with floats. Remove the flange gasket.

74 Tip out the fuel and clean any sediment from the bowl.

75 Unscrew and remove the jets and clean them by blowing air through them from a tyre pump. Never probe the jets with wire as this will ruin their calibration.

76 Before refitting the jets, clean the carburettor body passages with air, again using a tyre pump.

77 Extract the fuel inlet filter and clean it.

78 Carefully drive out the float pivot pin, remove the float and check that the fuel inlet valve body is tight. A leak here will have the effect of bypassing the needle valve with consequent high fuel level in the fuel bowl.

79 Examine the tip of the fuel inlet needle valve. If it is scored or worn, renew the complete valve assembly.

80 Refit the float.

81 If the carburettor adjustment screws have been removed, set them in the following way so that the engine will start. Carry out final adjustment when the carburettor is back on the engine (see paragraph 56).

> Idle speed screw – five turns out from seated
> Idle mixture screw – eight turns out from seated

82 Where necessary, the diaphragms for the enrichment device and vacuum-operated choke control and accelerator pump may be renewed after taking off their respective covers.

83 As reassembly progresses, carry out the following checks and adjustments.

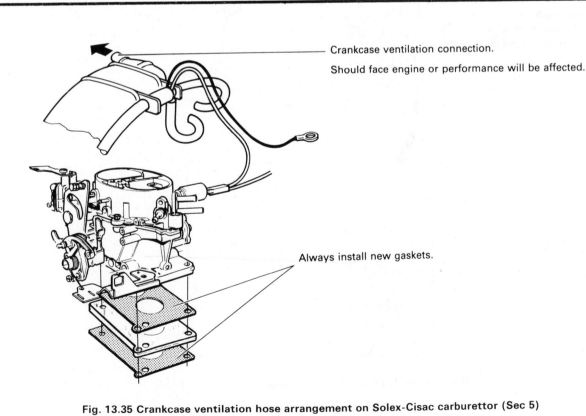

Crankcase ventilation connection.

Should face engine or performance will be affected.

Always install new gaskets.

Fig. 13.35 Crankcase ventilation hose arrangement on Solex-Cisac carburettor (Sec 5)

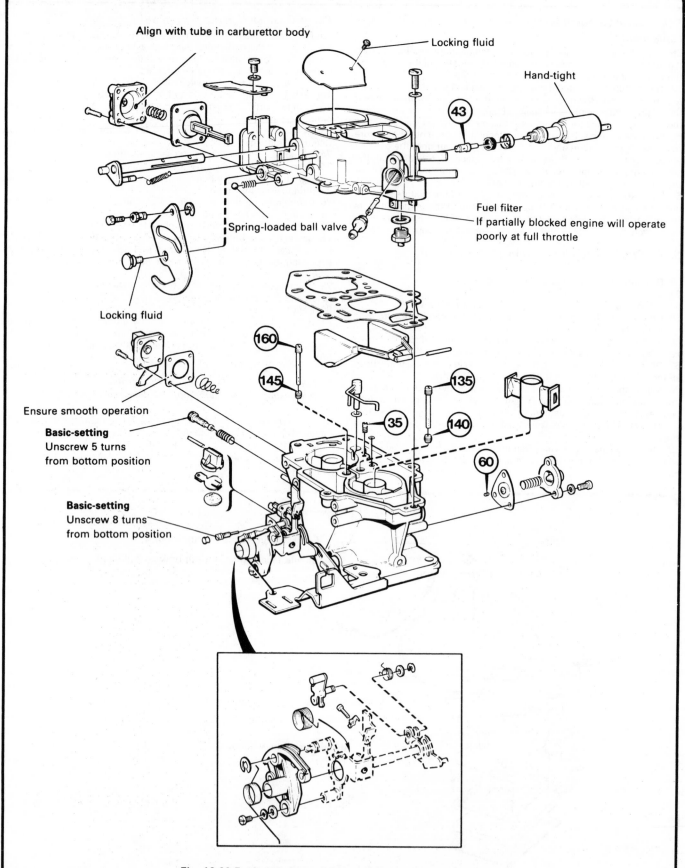

Align with tube in carburettor body

Locking fluid

Hand-tight

43

Fuel filter
If partially blocked engine will operate
poorly at full throttle

Spring-loaded ball valve

Locking fluid

Ensure smooth operation

Basic-setting
Unscrew 5 turns
from bottom position

Basic-setting
Unscrew 8 turns
from bottom position

160

145

135

35

140

60

Fig. 13.36 Exploded view of Solex-Cisac carburettor (Sec 5)

Numbers circled indicate jet sizes

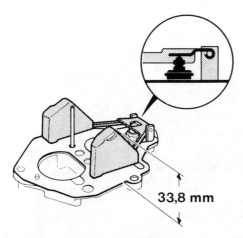

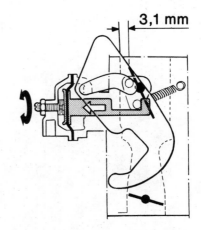

Fig. 13.37 Float level setting diagram for Solex-Cisac carburettor (Sec 5)

Fig. 13.38 Choke vacuum control adjustment diagram for Solex-Cisac (Sec 5)

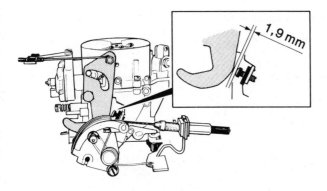

Fig. 13.39 Fast idle adjustment diagram for Solex-Cisac carburettor (Sec 5)

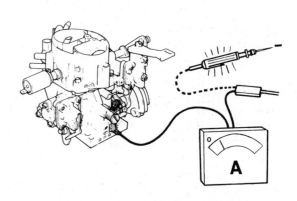

Fig. 13.40 Idle channel heater test circuit (Sec 5)

Float adjustment
84 Invert the top cover so that the weight of the floats depresses the needle valve ball. Check that the floats are level and then measure between the surface of the flange gasket and the highest point of the float. If outside specified dimensions, bend the tab which rests on the needle valve.

Choke vacuum control – adjustment
85 Operate the choke control lever to fully close the choke valve flap.
86 Depress the choke vacuum unit pullrod until it bottoms, then check the gap between the edge of the valve plate and the carburettor wall. This should be 0.122 in (3.1 mm). A twist drill is useful for checking this. If adjustment is required, turn the screw on the vacuum unit.

Fast idle – adjustment
87 The gap between the cam and the head of the adjuster screw should be 0.075 in (1.9 mm) with the choke valve flap fully open. Adjust as necessary by turning the screw after releasing the locknut.

Anti-run on valve
88 The anti-run on valve should be screwed in using hand pressure only. Once the carburettor has been refitted to the engine, connect the lead to the valve and turn on the ignition. A serviceable valve will be heard to click.

Idle channel heater
89 This is a thermister type heating element which keeps the idling channels warm to prevent icing.
90 To check the operation of the device, an ammeter will be required. Switch on the ignition, connect the ammeter between the connector plug and the thermister (Fig. 13.40).
91 At 68°F (20°C) the ammeter should read 1 amp. As the thermister warms up, the reading should drop. If there is no initial reading, withdraw the thermister retaining roll pin and cap and thoroughly clean all contact surfaces.

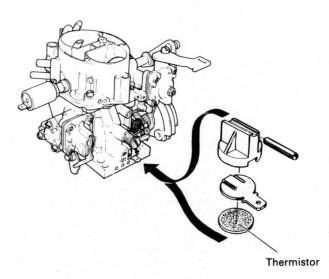

Thermistor

Fig. 13.41 Idle channel heater components (Sec 5)

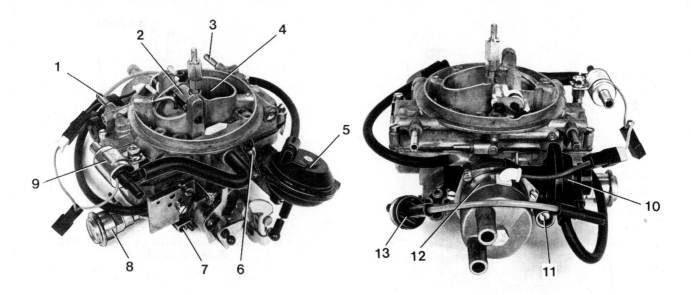

Fig. 13.42 Pierburg 2B5 carburettor (Sec 5)

1 Return fuel line
2 Primary venturi
3 Fuel inlet
4 Secondary venturi

5 Secondary venturi valve
   plate vacuum unit
6 Accelerator pump lever

7 Mixture (CO) adjustment
   screw
8 Fuel cut-off valve
9 Hot start valve

10 Choke vacuum unit
11 Idle speed adjustment screw
12 Bi-metallic spring
13 Non-return valve

Pierburg 2B5 carburettor – description

92 The carburettor is of fixed jet, dual barrel, down draught type and fitted to B230 engined models from 1985. A coolant-heated automatic choke is fitted incorporating an electrically-heated bi-metallic spring.

Pierburg 2B5 carburettor – idle speed and mixture adjustment

93 The operations are similar to those described in paragraphs 56 to 60. If the vehicle is equipped with air conditioning, then a combined vacuum valve/idle screw is fitted which should be turned to alter the idle speed. The air conditioner should be switched off and the Pulsair system (if fitted) disconnected.

Pierburg 2B5 carburettor – removal and refitting

94 Remove the air cleaner.
95 Disconnect the leads from the hot start valve and the choke bi-metallic spring.
96 Disconnect the fuel, vacuum and warm-up hoses.
97 Disconnect the throttle and kick-down cables.
98 Clamp the coolant hoses near the carburettor using self-locking grips or similar and disconnect the hoses from the automatic choke housing.
99 Unscrew the four socket-headed mounting screws and remove the carburettor, with the insulator block and gaskets.
100 Before refitting the carburettor, clean the mating surfaces and use a new gasket on each side of the insulator block.
101 Reconnect all hoses and leads and top up the cooling system expansion tank.
102 Check the adjustment of the throttle cable as described in paragraph 68.
103 On vehicles equipped with automatic transmission, check the adjustment of the kick-down cable. Do this by depressing the accelerator pedal fully. The distance from the end of the outer cable threaded sleeve to the crimped stop should be between 2.0 and 2.1 in (50.4 and 52.6 mm). Adjust if necessary by turning the cable threaded sleeve.
104 Set the choke fast idle cam so that it is in the idle position. The throttle valve lever should be in contact with the stop screw.
105 Adjust the link rod to give a clearance of between 0.020 and 0.040 in (0.5 and 1.0 mm) between the throttle lever and the pulley stop screw.
106 Renew the O-ring seal on the air inlet duct on the carburettor top cover unless it is in perfect condition.

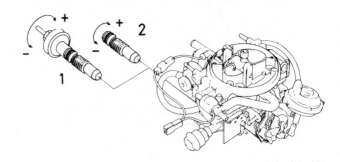

Fig. 13.43 Adjustment screws on Pierburg 2B5 carburettor (Sec 5)

1 Idle speed screw (vehicle without air conditioner)
2 Idle speed screw/vacuum valve (vehicle with air conditioner)

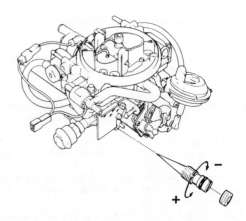

Fig. 13.44 Idle mixture screw with tamperproof cap on Pierburg 2B5 carburettor (Sec 5)

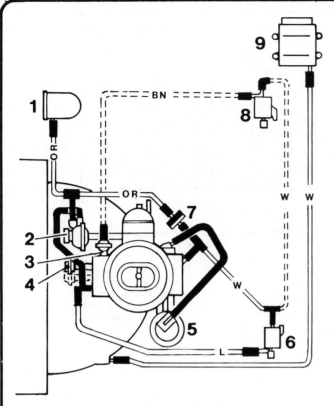

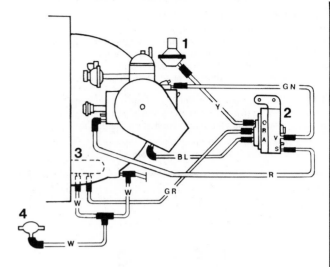

Fig. 13.46 Pierburg 2B5 EGR and Pulsair system
connections (Sec 5)

1 EGR valve
2 Vacuum amplifier
3 Thermostat valve

4 Shut-off valve (Pulsair
   system)

For colour code see Fig. 13.45

Fig. 13.45 Pierburg 2B5 vacuum line connecting diagram
(Sec 5)

1 Vacuum tank
2 Choke vacuum diaphragm
   unit
3 Vacuum valve/idle screw
   (vehicle with air conditioner)
4 Fuel cut-off valve
5 Secondary valve plate
   vacuum unit

6 Fuel cut-off solenoid valve
7 Non-return valve
8 Solenoid valve/idle speed
   compensation system
   (vehicle with air conditioner)
9 Ignition system control unit

Colour code

OR	orange	GR	grey
BN	brown	R	red
W	white	BL	blue
L	lilac	GN	green
Y	yellow		

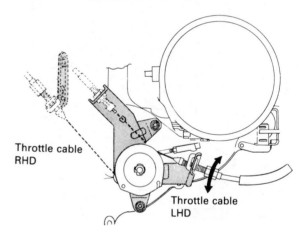

Fig. 13.47 Throttle cable adjustment diagrams
(Sec 5)

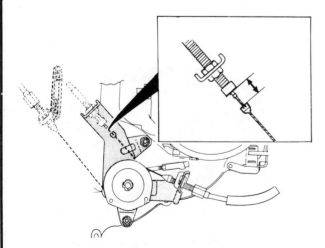

Fig. 13.48 Kick-down cable adjustment diagram (Sec 5)

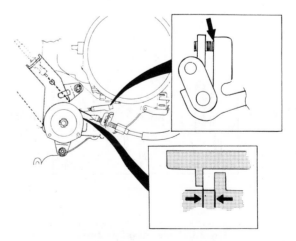

Fig. 13.49 Throttle lever-to-pulley stop screw gap on
Pierburg 2B5 carburettor (Sec 5)

Pierburg 2B5 carburettor – overhaul

107 Refer to paragraphs 70 to 73.

108 Unscrew and remove all jets and clean them and their carburettor body passages with air pressure from a type pump. Do not probe the jets with wire as this will ruin their calibration.

109 Check and tighten the fuel inlet valves as described in paragraphs 78 to 80.

110 If the carburettor adjustment screws have been removed, set them in the following way so that the engine will start. Carry out final adjustment when the carburettor is back on the engine.

> *Idle speed screw – 2.5 turns out from seated*
> *Idle mixture screw – 3.5 turns out from seated*

111 As reassembly progresses, carry out the following checks and adjustments.

Float adjustment

112 Invert the carburettor top cover. The weight of the floats should not depress the needle valve spring-loaded pin. Measure between the cover flange (no gasket) and the highest point of the floats. No adjustment is provided so, if the float setting is outside that specified, renew the valve assembly or floats.

Fast idle speed

113 Open the primary throttle valve flap fully and at the same time set the fast idle screw in number 6 cam step. Close the throttle valve flap.

114 Measure the gap between the throttle valve lever and stop screw

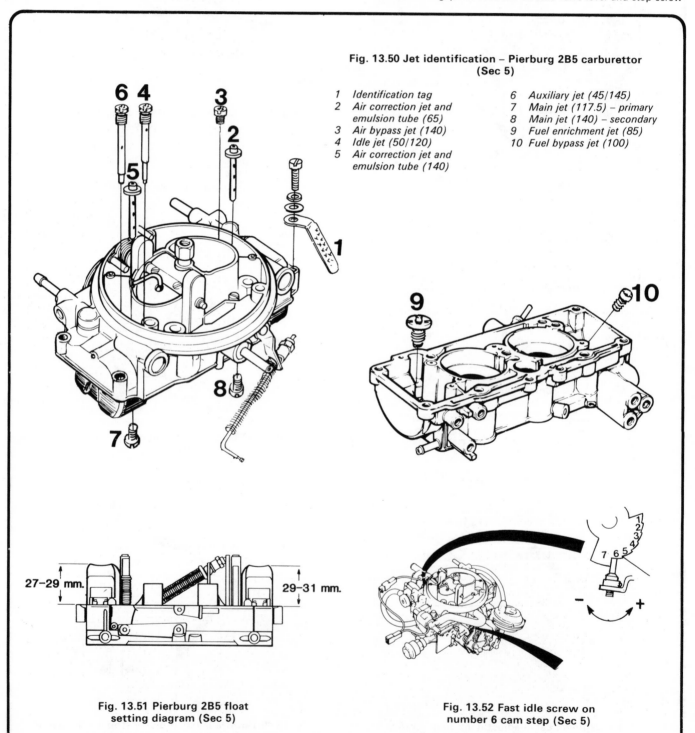

Fig. 13.50 Jet identification – Pierburg 2B5 carburettor (Sec 5)

1	Identification tag	6	Auxiliary jet (45/145)
2	Air correction jet and emulsion tube (65)	7	Main jet (117.5) – primary
3	Air bypass jet (140)	8	Main jet (140) – secondary
4	Idle jet (50/120)	9	Fuel enrichment jet (85)
5	Air correction jet and emulsion tube (140)	10	Fuel bypass jet (100)

27–29 mm.   29–31 mm.

Fig. 13.51 Pierburg 2B5 float setting diagram (Sec 5)

Fig. 13.52 Fast idle screw on number 6 cam step (Sec 5)

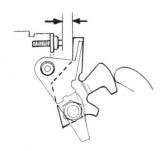

Fig. 13.53 Throttle valve lever-to-stop screw gap (Sec 5)

Fig. 13.54 Choke vacuum link rod clearance (Sec 5)

(Fig. 13.53). The gap should be 0.16 in (4.0 mm), in Switzerland 0.19 in (4.8 mm). If adjustment is required, turn the fast idle screw.

The following checks and adjustments should be carried out in the order in which they are listed.

Choke link adjustment
115 Move the choke link so that the choke valve flap is fully closed.
116 Open and close the throttle valve and check that the fast idle screw rests on the highest cam (7).
117 With the choke fully closed, the link to vacuum unit link rod clearance should be between 0.020 and 0.039 in (0.5 and 1.0 mm). If necessary, bend the link rod tag.

Choke housing – alignment
118 Alignment marks are present on the housing and cover as an aid to reassembly. At room temperature – 68°F (20°C) – the choke valve plate gap should be between 0.022 and 0.081 in (0.55 and 2.05 mm). Turn the housing cover if necessary to adjust.

Full load enrichment tube
119 The tube should be located so that its end is 0.020 in (0.5 mm) above the throttle valve plate. Too high a level can cause cold starting difficulties, too low a level causes high fuel consumption.

Accelerator pump – adjustment
120 Fill the carburettor bowl with fuel.
121 Hold the fast idle cam out of contact with the fast idle screw.
122 Place the carburettor on a funnel inserted into a measuring jar. Open and close the throttle valve fully at a rate of one cycle per second. Allow a three minute dwell between each movement.
123 Measure the volume of fuel caught after ten throttle valve movements. Divide the volume by ten when the result should be between 1.0 and 1.4 cc. Adjust if necessary by turning the accelerator pump link rod nut.

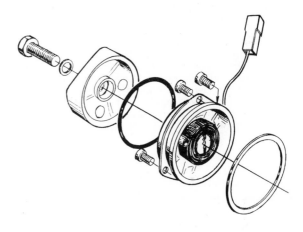

Fig. 13.55 Pierburg 2B5 choke housing components (Sec 5)

Fig. 13.56 Choke housing alignment marks (Sec 5)

Fig. 13.57 Enrichment tube setting (Sec 5)

Fuel injection system (1978 on) – idle speed and mixture adjustment

124 The idle speed should be adjusted when the engine is at normal operating temperature. Start the engine and turn the screw in or out as necessary to set the engine speed to 900 rpm (manual transmission) or 800 rpm (automatic transmission).

125 To check the CO level, insert an exhaust gas analyser probe into the end of the exhaust pipe on vehicles without a catalytic converter or into the exhaust pipe (plug provided) just forward of the catalytic converter on vehicles provided with this device.

126 Using the special tool (5015) inserted into the hole in the airflow sensor, adjust the screw until the CO reading is within the specified tolerance (see Specifications, Chapter 3, Part B).

Air injection system (Pulsair type)

127 This type of emission control system is fitted to engines on some models, depending upon operating territory.

128 The purpose of the system is to inject air into the exhaust manifold to promote the combustion of unburnt gases leaving the cylinders.

129 The main difference between this and other air injection systems is that an air pump is not required. Pressure changes in the exhaust system are used to inject the air.

Constant idle speed system – description

130 This system is fitted to North American models to regulate the idling speed and bypass air under different engine operating conditions. The system consists of an electronic control unit, air control valve, throttle switch, coolant temperature sensor and ignition coil.

131 The air control valve regulates the quantity of air to the intake manifold on a bypass circuit and has three separate air flow modes. Under deceleration with the throttle closed the valve allows reduced air flow. With the throttle depressed under normal and slow driving the valve allows high air flow. At idle speed with the throttle closed the valve regulates the air flow to maintain a steady idle speed.

132 The electronic control unit is located forward of the right-hand front door, below the control unit for the Lambda-sond system.

Constant idle speed system throttle switch – checking and adjustment

133 Connect a voltmeter across terminals 1 and 2 (Fig. 13.62).

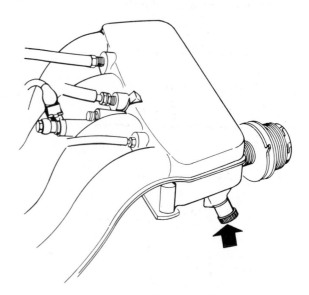

Fig. 13.58 Idle speed adjustment screw on fuel injection models 1978 on (Sec 5)

134 With the ignition on and the throttle in the idle position a reading of 2 to 8 volts should be obtained.

135 With the throttle above idle speed there should be no reading

136 If the switch requires adjustment refer to Figs. 13.63 and 13.64. Using a 0.016 in (0.4 mm) feeler blade, position the switch so that the voltmeter just shows a reading indicating that the contacts have just separated.

137 For checking purposes the voltmeter should show a reading using a 0.008 in (0.2 mm) feeler blade, but should not show a reading using a 0.036 in (0.9 mm) feeler blade on B21F and B21F – MPG engines, or a 0.045 in (1.1 mm) feeler blade on B21F – Turbo engines.

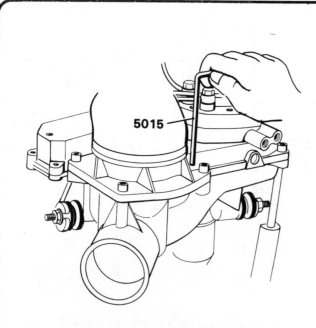

Fig. 13.59 Mixture adjustment tool 5015 on fuel injection models 1978 on (Sec 5)

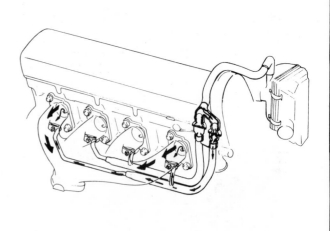

Fig. 13.60 Pulsair air injection system (Sec 5)

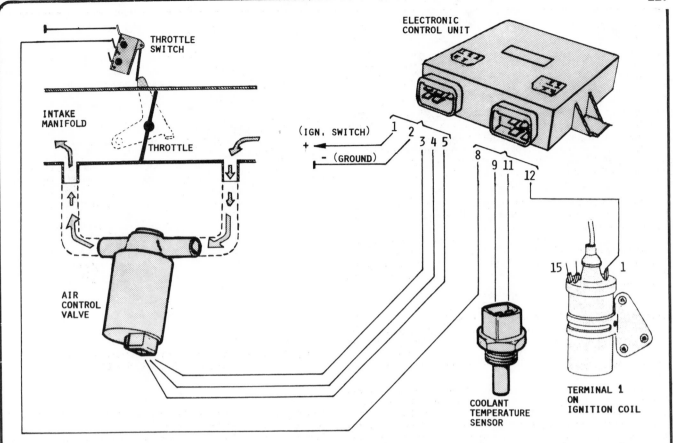

Fig. 13.61 Constant idle speed system components (Sec 5)

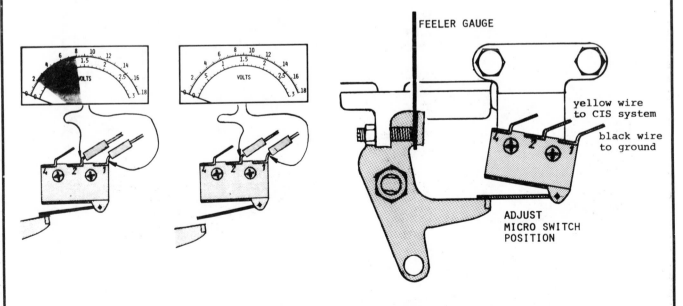

Fig. 13.62 Constant idle speed system throttle switch checking circuit (Sec 5)

Fig. 13.63 Constant idle speed system throttle switch adjustment diagram for B21F and B21F – MPG engines (Sec 5)

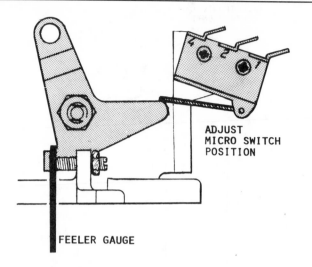

Fig. 13.64 Constant idle speed system throttle switch adjustment diagram for B21F engine (Sec 5)

LH Jetronic 2 fuel injection system (up to 1984) – description

138 This fuel system is fitted to the B23F and B21F engines. It is fully computerised and incorporates the constant idle speed system described in earlier paragraphs. The same engines are also fitted with a computer controlled ignition system.

139 The fuel system is an updated version of the LH-Jetronic system introduced in 1981 and on the B21F engine and the components are shown in Figs. 13.65 and 13.66.

140 The electronic control unit controls the injectors as well as the constant idle speed air valve.

141 On B21F engines a vacuum switch is fitted instead of a throttle switch and the injectors operate two at a time instead of all at the same time as on B23F engines.

142 The new system does not incorporate a cold start injector or thermal time switch.

143 A 25 amp blade type fuse protects the system circuit and is located on the left of the engine compartment.

144 A line pressure regulator located in the fuel supply line to the injectors senses inlet manifold pressure and regulates the fuel pressure at an increased pressure of 35.5 lbf/in² (2.4 bar).

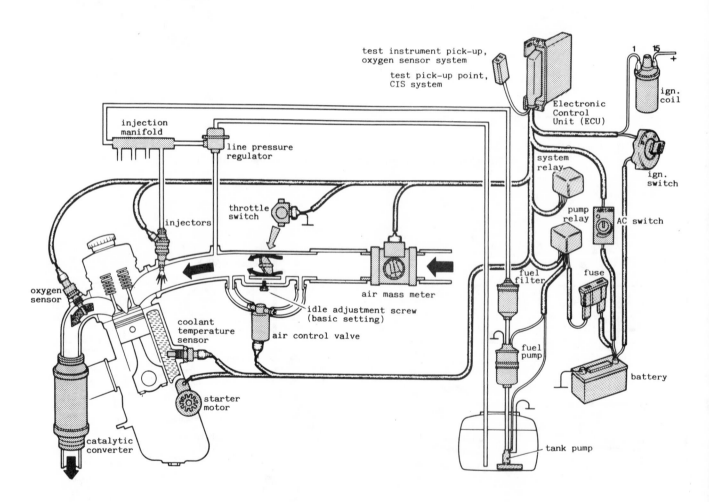

Fig. 13.65 LH Jetronic 2 fuel system (Sec 5)

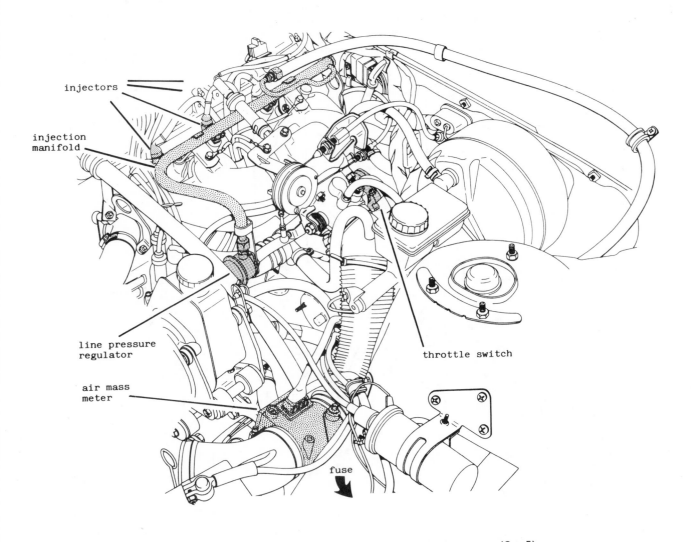

injectors

injection
manifold

line pressure
regulator

air mass
meter

throttle switch

fuse

Fig. 13.66 Location of LH Jetronic 2 fuel system components (Sec 5)

LH Jetronic 2 fuel system – maintenance and checks
145 To adjust the idle speed run the engine to normal operating
temperature then ground the blue/white test point lead at the front left
of the engine compartment. With a tachometer connected and the
engine idling turn the idle adjustment screw to adjust the speed to 720
rpm. After disconnecting the ground lead the idle speed should
increase to 750 rpm.
146 The throttle switch adjustment is correct if an audible click is heard
as soon as the throttle valve starts to open.
147 The injectors incorporate O-ring seals retained by clamps. When
renewing the O-rings smear them with a little petroleum jelly prior to
fitting them.

LH Jetronic 2.2 fuel injection system (1985 on) –
description
148 This 'second generation' system is fitted to B230F engines.
Changes to system components include a different control unit and
modified ignition system connections.

LH Jetronic 2.2 fuel injection system components –
removal and refitting
149 Individual components should not be dismantled, but any fault
rectified by renewal of the item concerned.

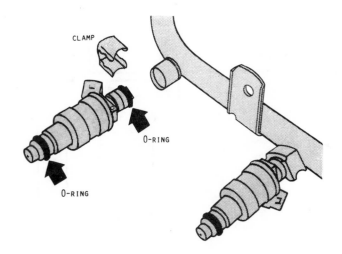

CLAMP

O-RING

O-RING

Fig. 13.67 Fuel injector O-ring seals on later models (Sec 5)

150 Location of the components is shown in Fig. 13.68.
151 Always check the fuses for the pump relay and tank pump before assuming that there is a more serious fault.
152 Earth connections are particularly important.
153 The fuel injectors should always be removed and refitted complete with the manifold.
154 It is important that no air leaks occur at the throttle housing or the fuel mixture will be lean. A dirty throttle housing indicates a clogged air cleaner element.
155 Always use a new gasket when refitting the throttle housing.

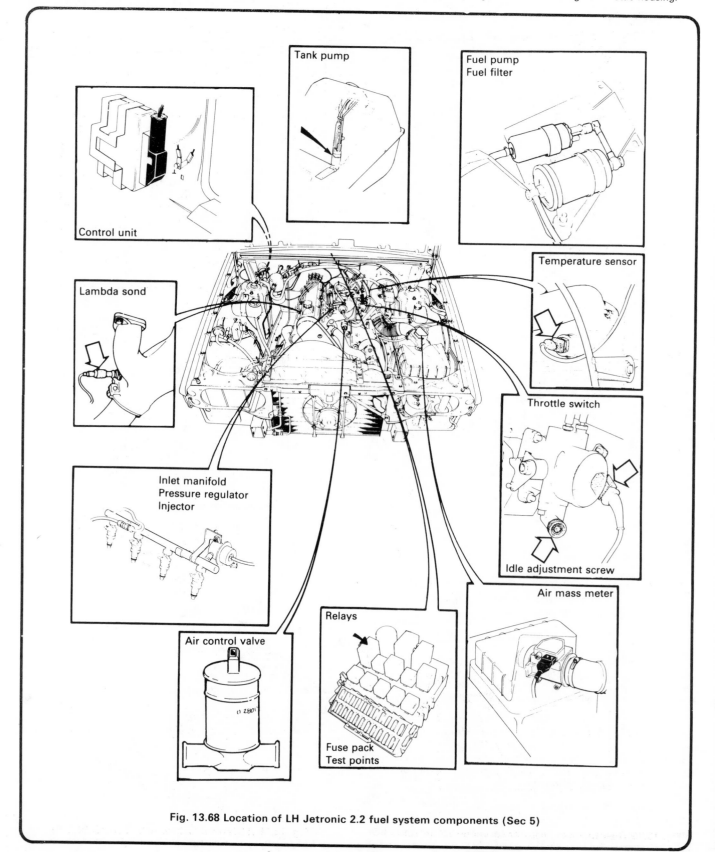

Fig. 13.68 Location of LH Jetronic 2.2 fuel system components (Sec 5)

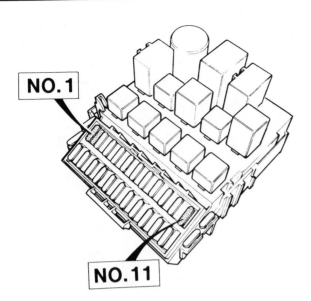

Fig. 13.69 Fuel pump and pump relay fuses for LH Jetronic
2.2 fuel injection system (Sec 5)

LH Jetronic 2.2 fuel injection system – adjustments

Throttle lever

156 Slacken the adjuster screw locknut and unscrew the screw until the throttle is fully closed.

157 Turn the adjuster screw until it just contacts the link arm and then give it a further quarter of a turn. Tighten the locknuts without moving the screw.

Throttle switch

158 Open the throttle slightly and listen for the idle switch to click. If this is not heard, adjust in the following way. Slacken the switch socket-headed mounting screws and turn the switch slightly clockwise then turn it anti-clockwise until a click is heard. Tighten the mounting screws and retest.

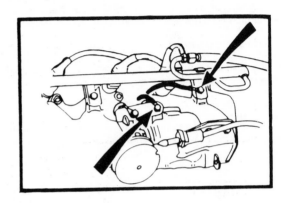

Fig. 13.70 Earth connections on inlet manifold of LH
Jetronic 2.2 fuel injection system (Sec 5)

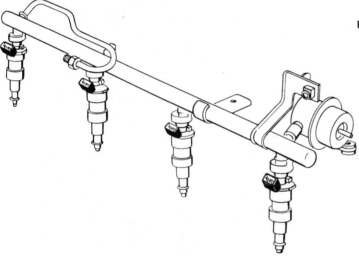

Fig. 13.71 Fuel injector/manifold assembly on LH Jetronic
2.2 fuel injection system (Sec 5)

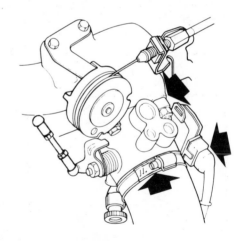

Fig. 13.72 LH Jetronic 2.2 throttle housing (Sec 5)

Connecting clip, plug and flange gasket arrowed

Fig. 13.73 Throttle lever adjuster screw on LH Jetronic 2.2
fuel injection system (Sec 5)

Fig. 13.74 LH Jetronic 2.2 throttle switch (Sec 5)

Idle speed and mixture

159 Have the engine at normal operating temperature then earth the red/white wire from the test plug. This will close the air control valve.
160 If air conditioning is fitted, switch it off. Allow the engine to idle.
161 Turn the idle speed screw until the idle speed is 700 rpm.
162 Disconnect the red/white wire from earth and the idle speed should rise to between 730 and 770 rpm.
163 Check the ignition timing is 12° BTDC using a stroboscope (refer to Chapter 4).
164 Disconnect the Lambda-sond.
165 An exhaust gas analyser will now be required, connected in accordance with the maker's instructions. The exhaust gas CO level should be between 0.4 and 0.8%.
166 If adjustment is required, switch off the engine and remove the tamperproof plug from the adjuster screw hole. The best way to remove the plug is to drill two holes in it and extract it using circlip pliers.
167 Turn the screw clockwise to enrich the mixture, or anti-clockwise to weaken it.
168 Once adjustment is complete, reconnect the Lambda-sond and tap a new plug into the mixture screw hole.

Evaporative emission control system
Roll-over valve
169 Commencing with 1980 models, a valve is fitted to prevent fuel spillage through the charcoal filter in the event of the vehicle turning over.

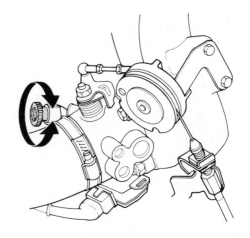

Fig. 13.75 LH Jetronic 2.2 idle speed screw (Sec 5)

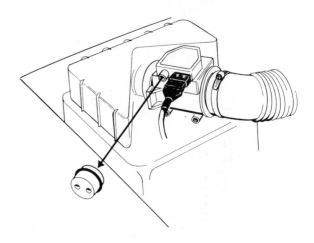

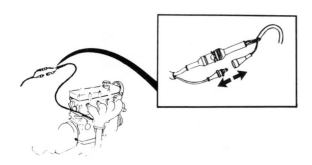

Fig. 13.76 LH Jetronic 2.2 Lambda-sond connecting plug (Sec 5)

Fig. 13.77 Mixture screw tamperproof plug on LH Jetronic 2.2 fuel injection system (Sec 5)

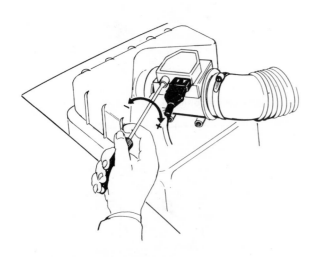

Fig. 13.78 Adjusting mixture screw (Sec 5)

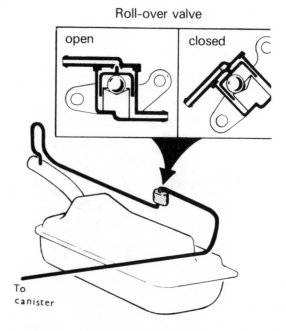

Fig. 13.79 Roll-over fuel valve (Sec 5)

170 The valve closes once it is tipped more than 45° from horizontal.
Carbon canister
171 Commencing with 1980 models, a larger carbon canister is fitted with integral vacuum valve operated by the engine intake manifold vacuum.
172 The new canister is located under the left-hand front wing.
173 Always keep the drain hole at the base of the canister clear by probing periodically.
Fuel tank cap
174 On later models with a fuel evaporative control system, a special fuel tank filler cap is used. The cap has two integral valves to control excess pressure or vacuum within the tank.
175 It is important that the cap seal is kept in good condition.

Turbo-compressor – description
176 The turbo-compressor consists of a turbine, driven by the exhaust gases, connected by a shaft which drives a compressor wheel in the induction system. The shaft rotates at up to 120 000 rpm and therefore the turbines must be finely balanced, also adequate lubrication of the bearings is important. The engine oil should be changed twice as often as for non-turbo models and the engine should always be allowed to idle for a short period after starting and before stopping the engine.

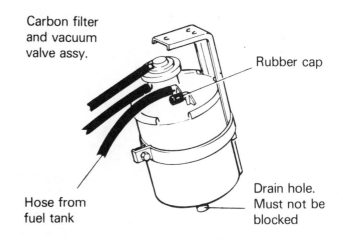

Carbon filter and vacuum valve assy.

Rubber cap

Hose from fuel tank

Drain hole. Must not be blocked

Fig. 13.80 Later type carbon canister (Sec 5)

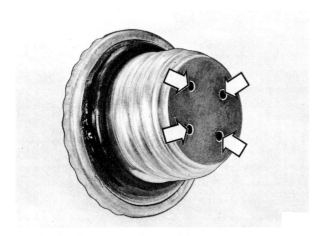

Fig. 13.81 Later type fuel filler cap (Sec 5)
Vent holes arrowed

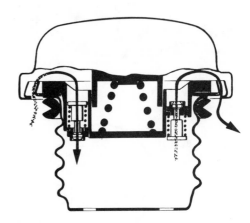

Fig. 13.82 Sectional view of later type fuel filler cap (Sec 5)

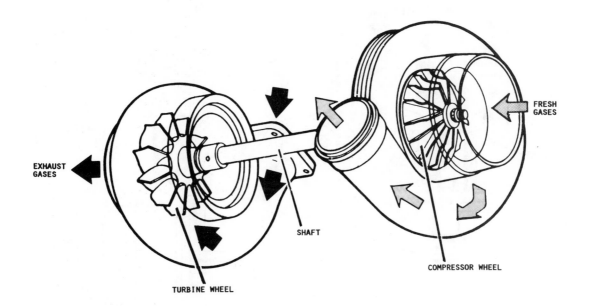

EXHAUST GASES

FRESH GASES

SHAFT

TURBINE WHEEL

COMPRESSOR WHEEL

Fig. 13.83 Diagrammatic view of turbocharger (Sec 5)

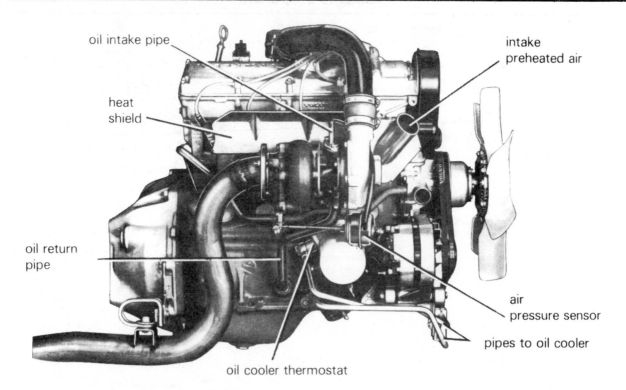

oil intake pipe

intake
preheated air

heat
shield

oil return
pipe

air
pressure sensor

pipes to oil cooler

oil cooler thermostat

Fig. 13.84 Turbocharger components (Sec 5)

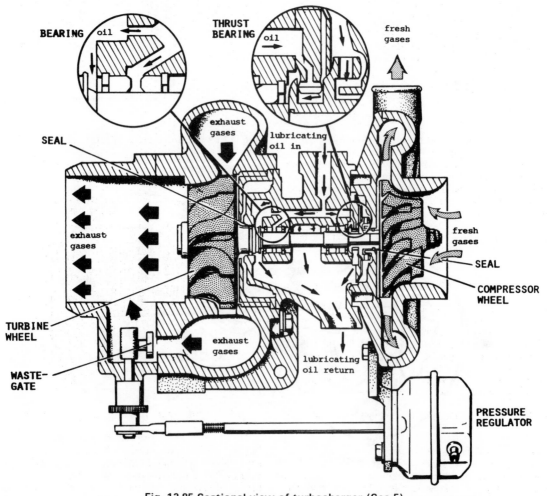

BEARING oil

THRUST
BEARING oil

fresh
gases

exhaust
gases

lubricating
oil in

SEAL

exhaust
gases

fresh
gases

SEAL

COMPRESSOR
WHEEL

TURBINE
WHEEL

exhaust
gases

lubricating
oil return

WASTE-
GATE

PRESSURE
REGULATOR

Fig. 13.85 Sectional view of turbocharger (Sec 5)

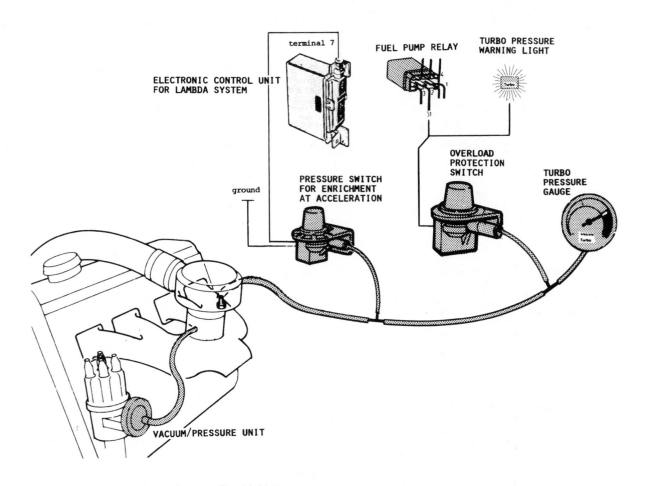

Fig. 13.86 Turbocharger controls (Sec 5)

177 The turbo compressor is designed to provide relatively high pressure at mid-range engine speed, and a wastegate valve system is incorporated to prevent excessive pressure at high speeds. For acceleration, a pressure switch senses when the induction pressure drops to 2.9 lbf/in² (0.2 bar) and a signal is sent to the Lambda-sond electronic module.

178 An overload protection switch cuts the fuel pump in the event of the wastegate system not functioning.

179 The distributor vacuum control unit on turbo models has a double function. Under normal conditions it can advance the ignition by 15°, but with an induction pressure of 5 lbf/in² (0.35 bar) the timing is retarded by 8°.

180 Turbo engines are fitted with low compression pistons (7.7 to 1) with concave crowns, and the piston clearances are increased to compensate for the high internal temperatures.

181 An oil cooler is located by the radiator and an internal thermostat diverts engine oil through the cooler at temperatures above approximately 165°F (75°C).

182 The CIS air/fuel control unit is attached to the top of the air cleaner and the air temperature control is on the bottom of the air cleaner.

183 The catalytic converter is located in the downpipe from the turbo-compressor.

Turbo-compressor – removal and refitting

184 Disconnect the battery negative lead.

185 Remove the coolant expansion tank and bracket.

186 Remove the air cleaner pre-heater hose and the hoses from the turbo unit. Disconnect the crankcase ventilation hose.

187 Unscrew the nuts and move the exhaust pipe to one side.

Fig. 13.87 Air/fuel control unit (Sec 5)

188 Disconnect the spark plug HT leads.

189 Unbolt the upper heat shield, remove the turbo-to-manifold bracket, then remove the lower heat shield.

190 Unbolt the return oil pipe from the turbo unit and cylinder block, unscrew all but one of the manifold nuts, then remove the delivery oil pipe.

191 Unscrew the clamps and position the air/fuel control unit to one side, then remove the air cleaner filter.

192 Unscrew the remaining nut and withdraw the turbo unit and exhaust manifold from the engine. Remove the manifold gaskets and detach the oil return O-ring from the cylinder block.

193 Unbolt the turbo unit from the manifold.

194 Before fitting the turbo unit check that the actuating rod clearance (rod disconnected) is as shown in Fig. 13.88.

195 To refit the unit use a new gasket positioned as shown in Fig. 13.89 and tighten the bolts evenly in three stages as given in the Specifications. Refer also to Fig. 13.90 for assembly torque wrench settings.

196 Fit the turbo unit and manifold using new gaskets positioned with the letters UT away from the engine.

197 Fit the oil return pipe together with a new O-ring, then fit the air cleaner filter and air/fuel control unit.

198 Inject engine oil in the oil inlet hole and fit the delivery pipe together with a new O-ring.

199 Fit the heat shields and bracket.

200 Reconnect the spark plug HT leads.

201 Refit the exhaust pipe, hoses and expansion tank.

202 Reconnect the battery lead.

203 Disconnect terminal 15 on the ignition coil and spin the engine on the starter for 30 seconds to ensure that the oil is circulating through the unit, then reconnect the lead and allow the engine to idle for several minutes.

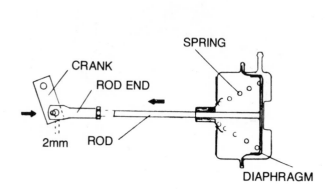

Fig. 13.88 Turbo actuating rod clearance (Sec 5)

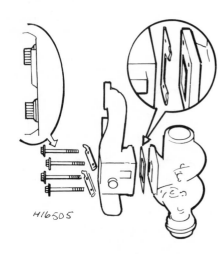

Fig. 13.89 Location of turbocharger gaskets (Sec 5)

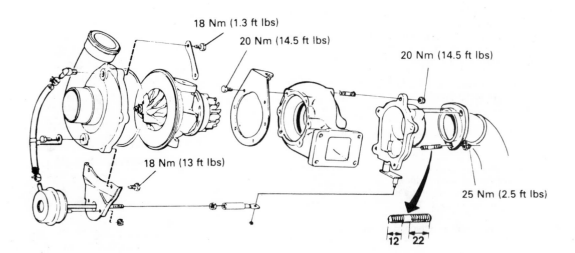

Fig. 13.90 Turbo torque wrench setting diagram (Sec 5)

Crankcase ventilation system

204 On Turbo models the crankcase ventilation system is as shown in Fig. 13.91. The crankcase gases are taken to the inlet duct on the entry to the turbo unit. As there is always vacuum at this point with the engine running there is no direct connection with the inlet manifold, and there is no need for a flame trap at the oil separator.

205 As from 1981 models the crankcase ventilation system on non-Turbo engines has been modified as shown in Figs. 13.92, 13.93 and 13.94. The oil separator has also been modified in the interests of oil consumption.

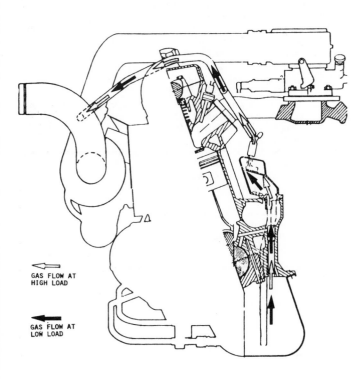

GAS FLOW AT HIGH LOAD

GAS FLOW AT LOW LOAD

Fig. 13.91 Sectional view of crankcase ventilation system on Turbo models (Sec 5)

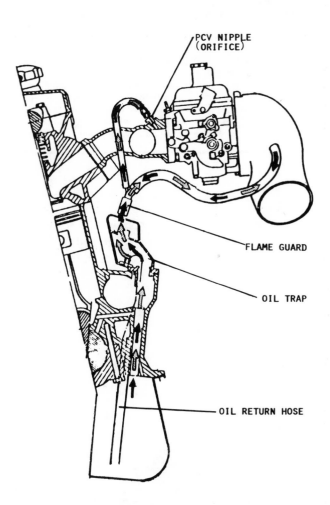

PCV NIPPLE (ORIFICE)

FLAME GUARD

OIL TRAP

OIL RETURN HOSE

Fig. 13.92 Sectional view of crankcase ventilation system on Type A engines (Sec 5)

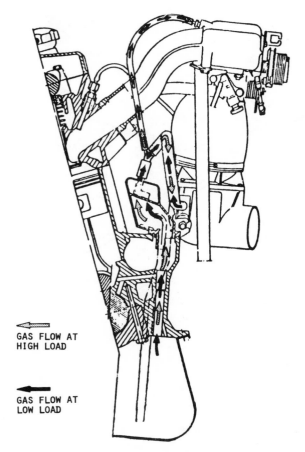

GAS FLOW AT HIGH LOAD

GAS FLOW AT LOW LOAD

Fig. 13.93 Sectional view of crankcase ventilation system on Type E and F engines (Sec 5)

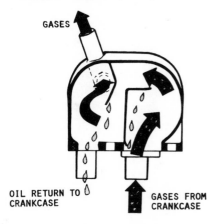

GASES

OIL RETURN TO CRANKCASE

GASES FROM CRANKCASE

Fig. 13.94 Sectional view of later type crankcase ventilation system oil separator (Sec 5)

Cruise control system (up to 1984) – description and adjustment

206 The cruise control system is designed to enable the driver to select and maintain a constant roadspeed (over 30 mph – 48 km/h) without the need to continually adjust the position of the accelerator pedal. The system is immediately overriden if the brake or clutch pedals are depressed.

207 Earlier versions incorporated a mechanically controlled system but later models are electronically controlled.

208 The system should not be engaged in heavy traffic or when driving on wet or slippery roads.

209 If the system is in use and the gearchange lever is inadvertently knocked into the neutral position, quickly depress the clutch or brake pedal which will switch the system off to prevent over-revving of the engine.

210 If the system is disengaged by a depression of the clutch or brake pedal, the set speed can be re-introduced if the control switch is momentarily moved to the RESUME position, but anticipate violent acceleration if the speed differential between the actual roadspeed and the set speed is excessive. Momentary rapid acceleration for overtaking will not interrupt the set speed setting which will be resumed on completion of the acceleration without having to touch the RESUME switch.

211 To set the desired roadspeed, move the switch on the steering column stalk to ON. Accelerate to the desired roadspeed and when it is reached, depress the button. If a lower set speed is subsequently desired, depress the button and hold it depressed until the speed has dropped to the required level, then release it.

212 The main components of the cruise control system are:

(a) Steering column switch (slide and push-button) to select ON-OFF-RESUME-SET SPEED

(b) Speed pick-up coil, located in the speedometer to sense speedo revolutions and relay to governor

(c) Governor, receives signals from the pick-up coil and then controls the throttle actuator

(d) Throttle actuator, receives signals from the governor and in turn controls the throttle setting

(e) Clutch and brake switches, interrupt the system when clutch or brake pedals are depressed

(f) Retard switch, cuts out system when deceleration exceeds a pre-determined value

(g) Vacuum valve, opens when brake pedal depressed to open throttle cable actuator motor to atmospheric pressure so removing tension from throttle operating cable.

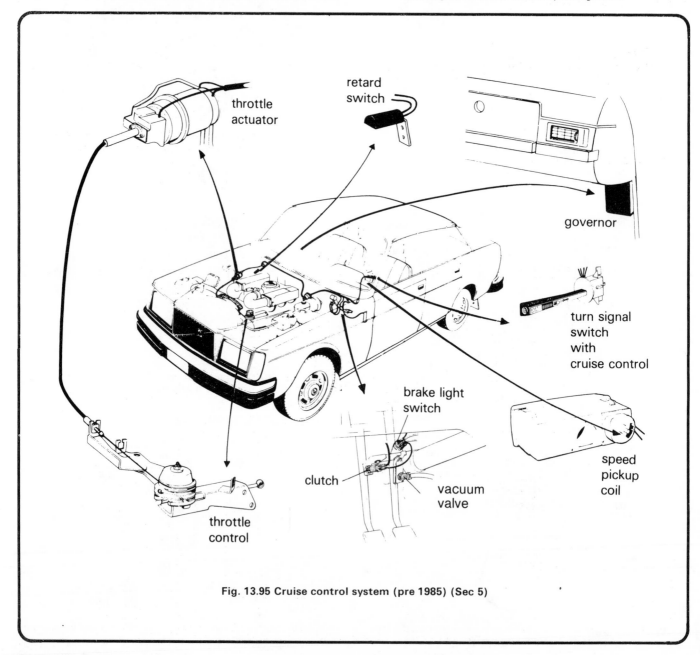

Fig. 13.95 Cruise control system (pre 1985) (Sec 5)

213 If a fault occurs in the system, the following simple checks can be carried out. More extensive investigation should be left to your dealer:

(a) Check the circuit fuse
(b) Check for secure wiring connections
(c) Check for loose or perforated vacuum hoses
(d) Check that the retard switch is set at an angle of 17° to the horizontal. This is a mercury switch and the correct setting is very important

214 It should be noted that the governor is earthed through the brake stop-lamp bulbs and if both these bulbs blow, the governor will be inoperative.

215 Failure of the system to operate at the specified speed levels may indicate that the governor requires adjustment. Adjustment is carried out while the vehicle is being road tested and an assistant should be engaged for this purpose.

216 Remove the governor from its mounting but do not disconnect its electrical leads. If the engaging speed is out of line with the indicated roadspeed, insert a screwdriver in the LOW SPEED hole and turn the screw clockwise to increase, or anti-clockwise to decrease, the engaging speed. If the set speed is not maintained to within ± 3 mph (4.8 km/h), insert a screwdriver into the CENTRING holes and turn the screw clockwise to increase the engaging speed or anti-clockwise to decrease it.

217 The governor is adjusted during production for maximum sensitivity which ensures that the throttle control is continuously adjusted to take care of variations in road and other conditions. The sensitivity can be reduced to improve fuel economy for vehicles driven almost entirely with driver only and no luggage, by inserting a screwdriver into the SENSITIVITY hole and turning the screw anti-clockwise. Turning the screw clockwise increases the sensitivity of the governor.

Cruise control system (1985 on) – description and adjustment
218 This later system incorporates some different components, as shown in Fig. 13.98.

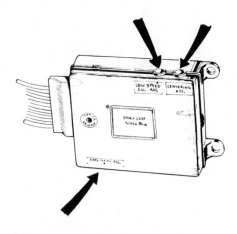

Fig. 13.97 Cruise control governor adjustment points (arrowed) on pre 1985 system (Sec 5)

Fig. 13.96 Cruise control retard switch setting (Sec 5)

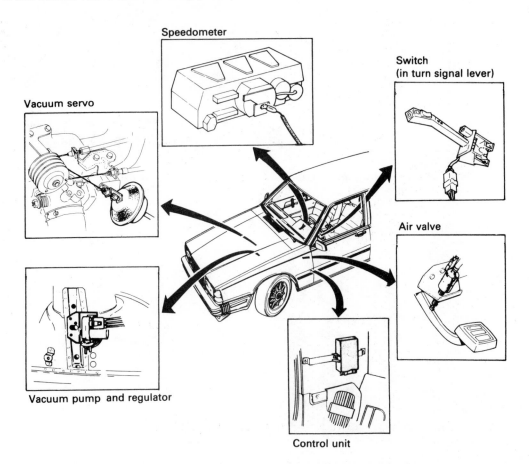

Speedometer

Switch (in turn signal lever)

Vacuum servo

Air valve

Vacuum pump and regulator

Control unit

Fig. 13.98 Cruise control system (1985 on) (Sec 5)

219 Apart from the adjustments described in the following paragraphs, any other work or fault tracing should be left to checking the wiring and connections (see wiring diagram Fig. 13.231) also the vaccuum hoses.

Brake stop-lamp switch

220 This should be adjusted so that the stop-lamps light when the pedal is depressed through between 0.31 and 0.55 in (8.0 and 14.0 mm).

Pedal air valves

221 These should be adjusted at the brake and clutch pedals so that when the pedal arms are in the fully released (upward) position, the switch plunger is exposed by between 0.39 and 0.59 in (1.0 and 1.5 mm).

Throttle cable – adjustment

222 On type A (carburettor) engines first check that the control turret spring is in the correct position for the type of transmission (Fig. 13.102) then adjust the throttle cable so that the inner cable is slightly tensioned with the control turret against the idle stop. Now adjust the link rod to give the clearance shown in Fig. 13.103.

223 On type E (fuel injection) engines check the control turret spring position as described in paragraph 222 on pre 1980 models. Later models have a modified turret. Disconnect the link rod from the throttle lever and the throttle cable from the turret. Slacken the locknut then fully back off the throttle lever adjustment screw, screw it in until it just touches the lever plus one complete turn and tighten the locknut. With a 0.04 in (1.0 mm) feeler blade between the turret and stop the adjuster screw clearance should be between 0.004 and 0.012 in (0.1 and 0.3 mm) with the link rod reconnected. Adjust the link rod as

required. Refit the cable and adjust it so that the inner cable is slightly tensioned with the control turret against the idle stop.

224 After adjusting the throttle cable adjust the downshift cable as described in Section 8.

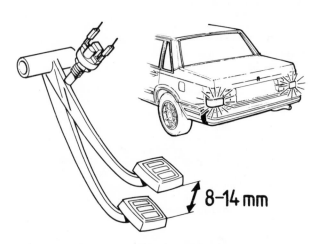

Fig. 13.99 Brake pedal stop-lamp switch adjustment diagram for later type cruise control system (Sec 5)

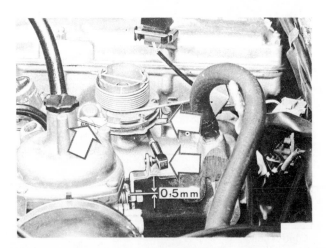

Fig. 13.100 Pedal air valve adjustment diagram for later type cruise control system (Sec 5)

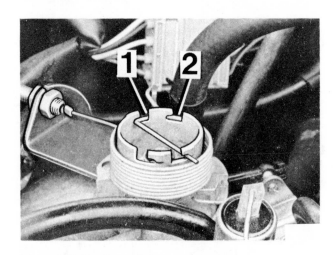

Fig. 13.101 Throttle cable control turret positions (Sec 5)

1   With automatic transmission

2   With manual gearbox

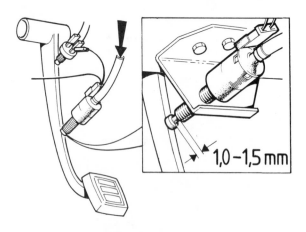

Fig. 13.102 Throttle control link rod adjustment on Type A engine (Sec 5)

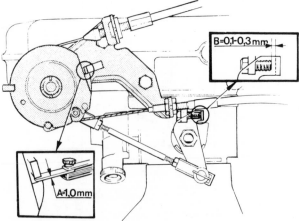

Fig. 13.103 Adjuster screw clearance on Type E engine (Sec 5)

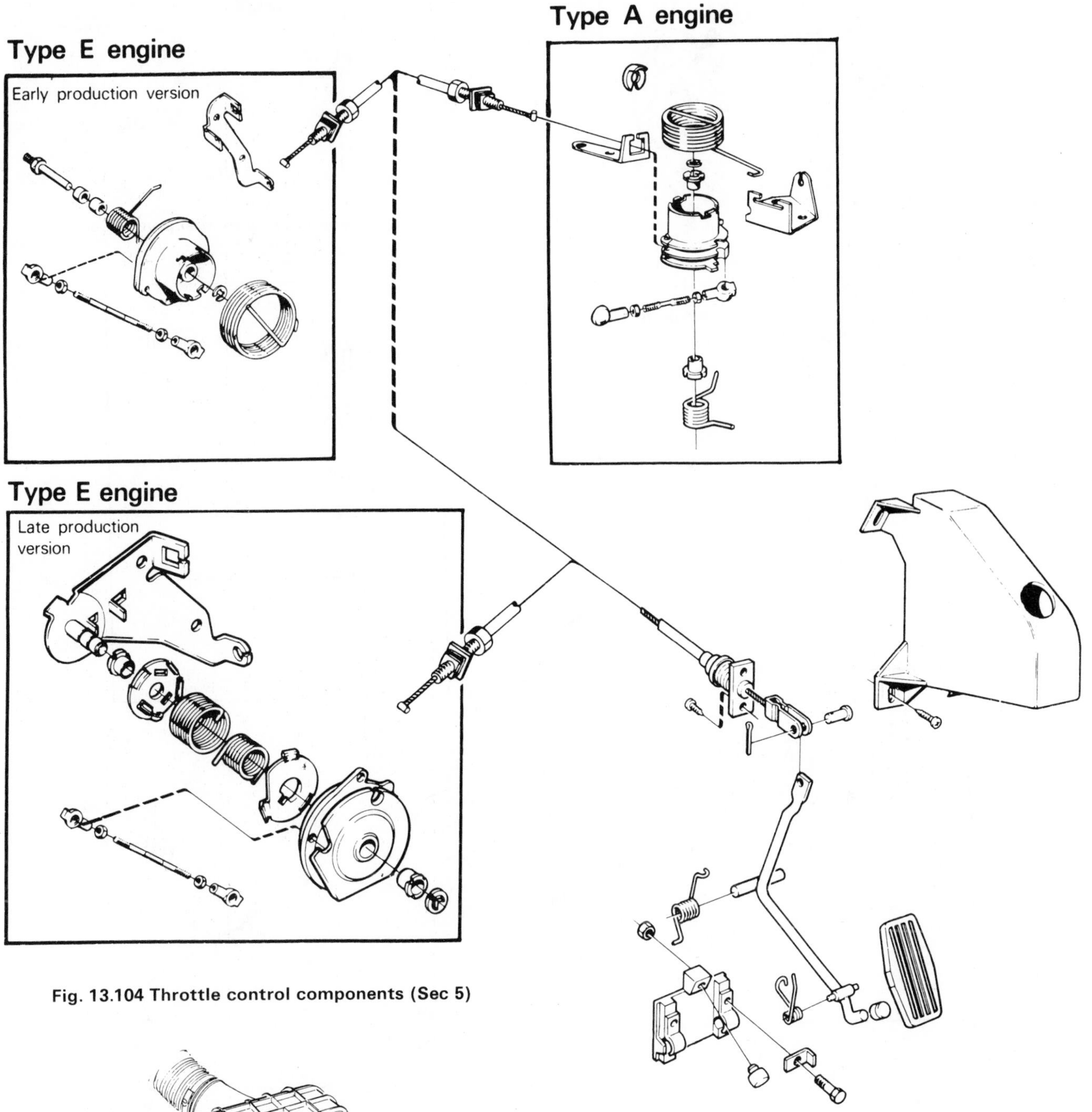

Type E engine

Early production version

Type A engine

Type E engine

Late production version

Fig. 13.104 Throttle control components (Sec 5)

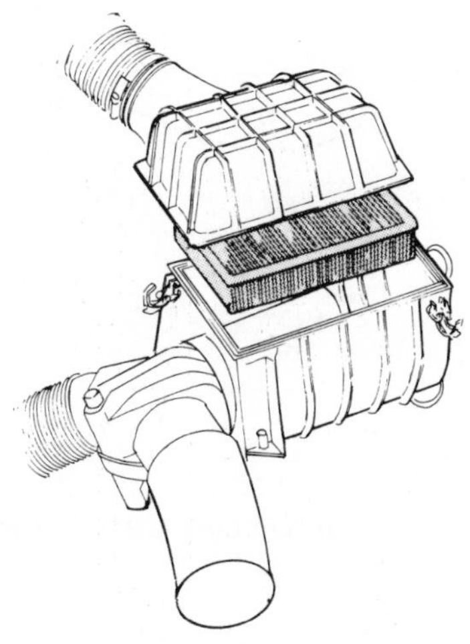

Fig. 13.105 Typical later type air cleaner (Sec 5)

Air cleaner
225 The air cleaner on later models is of remotely-sited type. The cover can be removed after releasing the toggle clips to expose the filter element.

Fuel filter (carburettor engines)
226 On later engines, a larger capacity fuel filter is located on the engine compartment rear bulkhead. The filter is a snap-on fit to its bracket.

Fuel pump (carburettor engines)
227 In addition to the Pierburg fuel pump described in Chapter 3, Part A, pumps of AC and Sofabex make may be fitted.
228 The cover on both these pumps may be removed and the filter cleaned, but more extensive overhaul is not possible due to spares not being available or the pump being of semi-sealed type.

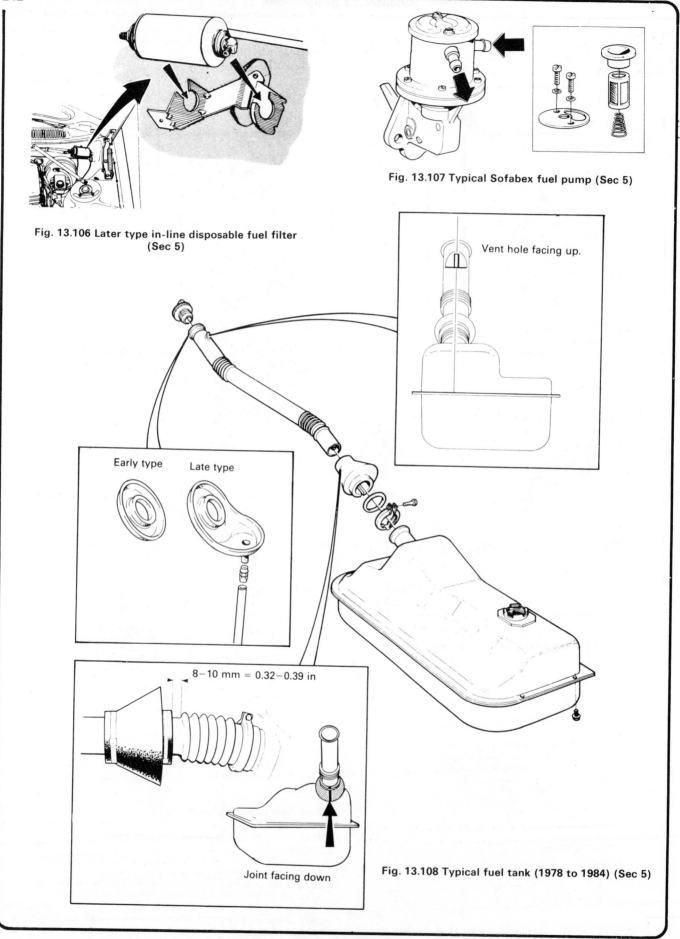

Fig. 13.106 Later type in-line disposable fuel filter
(Sec 5)

Fig. 13.107 Typical Sofabex fuel pump (Sec 5)

Vent hole facing up.

Early type   Late type

8–10 mm = 0.32–0.39 in

Joint facing down

Fig. 13.108 Typical fuel tank (1978 to 1984) (Sec 5)

Fuel tank

229 The design of later type fuel tanks has changed two or three times and when renewing an earlier type tank, only the later design is available as a spare part.

230 This will cause a certain number of modifications to be carried out in order to install the new tank and include the following:

Drilling a hole in the floor panel next to the fuel filler hose hole
Connecting a filler hose with sealing grommet
Shaping a new fuel evaporative system hose to fit the appropriate control system with which the vehicle is equipped

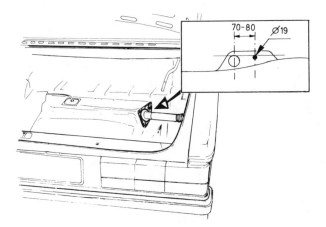

Fig. 13.109 Fuel filler pipe hole drilling diagram (Sec 5)

Dimensions in mm

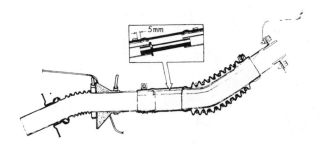

Fig. 13.110 Later type fuel filler hose arrangement (Sec 5)

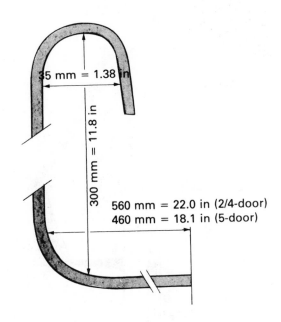

Fig. 13.111 Later type fuel evaporative hose shaping diagram (Sec 5)

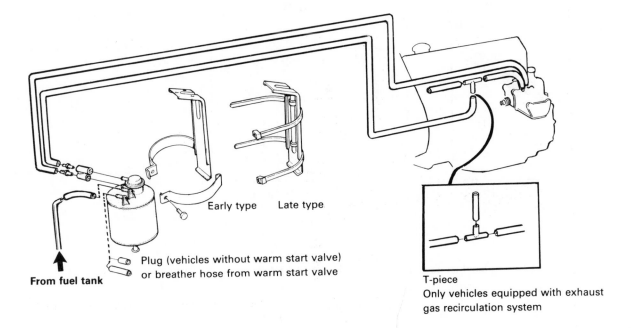

Fig. 13.112 Fuel evaporative system components on 1980 to 1981 models (Sec 5)

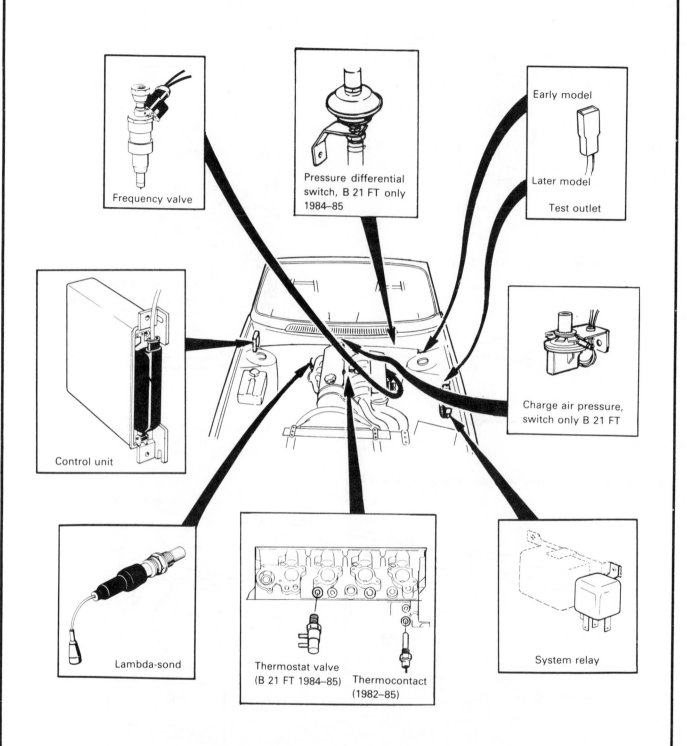

Frequency valve

Pressure differential switch, B 21 FT only 1984–85

Early model

Later model

Test outlet

Control unit

Charge air pressure, switch only B 21 FT

Lambda-sond

Thermostat valve (B 21 FT 1984–85)

Thermocontact (1982–85)

System relay

Fig. 13.113 Lambda-sond system on B21F and B21FT engines with CI fuel injection (Sec 5)

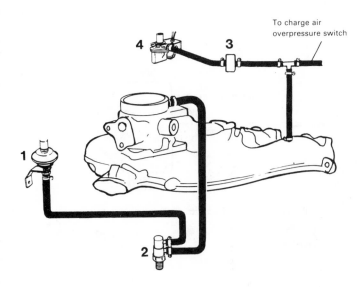

Fig. 13.114 Vacuum hose arrangement on Lambda-sond system (Sec 5)

*1 Pressure differential switch
  on B21FT engine 1984 to
  1985
2 Thermostatic valve
3 Delay valve (automatic
  transmission 1982)
4 Charge air overpressure
  switch*

Lambda-sond system (later models)

231 Certain system components and their locations have been changed (Fig. 13.113).

232 It is important that the vacuum hoses are connected to their switches correctly (Fig. 13.114).

6 Ignition system

Ignition coil

1 As from 1979 models the ignition system on type A engines incorporates a ballast resistor fitted in series with the ignition coil.

2 When the starter motor is operated, full battery voltage is applied to terminal 15 of the coil, the power coming directly from terminal 16 on the starter motor solenoid.

3 As soon as the engine starts, reduced voltage reaches the coil through the ballast resistor.

4 The arrangement provides better cold starting and prevents the flow of excessive current through the coil.

Computer controlled ignition system – description and adjustments

5 As from 1981 certain models are equipped with a computer controlled ignition system. The three main components of the system are an electronic control unit, distributor and ignition coil.

6 The electronic control unit is fed information on engine speed and load, and determines the correct ignition timing and dwell angle. It incorporates an emergency mode which enables the car to be driven to a service station in the event of a failure in the microprocessor.

7 The distributor does not incorporate any advance mechanism, but it includes an engine speed pick-up unit in addition to the HT function of the rotor arm and distributor cap.

8 Although the ignition coil is similar in appearance to the conventional ignition type, it is specifically designed for the computer controlled ignition.

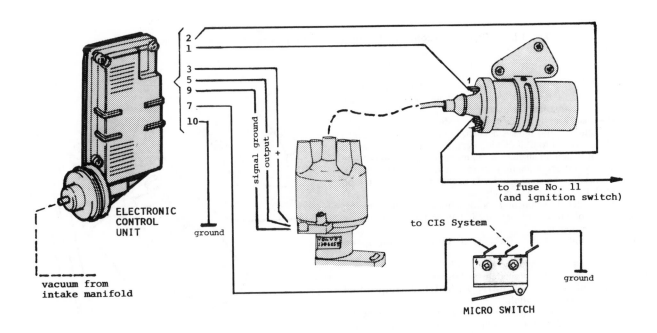

Fig. 13.115 Typical computer-controlled ignition system components (Sec 6)

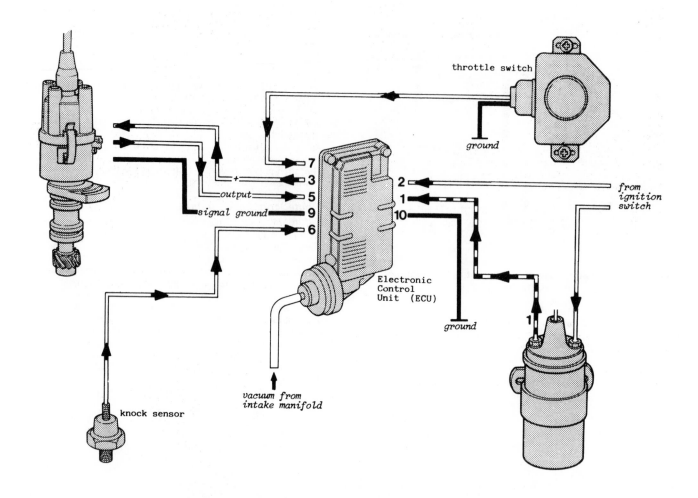

Fig. 13.116 Computer-controlled ignition system incorporating knock sensor (Sec 6)

9 The system incorporates a microswitch on the throttle to cut out the vacuum signal to the control unit during idling and deceleration. On B200 and B230 engines, the distributor is located on the rear end of the cylinder head and driven by the camshaft.

10 On certain later engines the system incorporates a knock sensor to retard the ignition by up to 6° if pinking occurs, even momentarily. To check the sensor switch off all auxiliary equipment, increase the engine speed above idle and use a timing light to record the ignition timing. Now tap the boss on the right-hand side of the engine above the oil filter and check that the ignition is retarded.

11 Apart from regularly inspecting the distributor cap and rotor for cracks or erosion of the cap contacts, the following adjustment may be required very infrequently.

Microswitch adjustment – B21F with constant idle speed system

12 Refer to Section 5, Paragraphs 133 to 137.

13 Carry out the adjustment procedure as described.

Microswitch adjustment – B21F with LH Jetronic fuel injection system (1982 models)

14 Disconnect the wiring plug from the vacuum switch. Connect a test lamp between the battery (+) terminal and the orange wire on the switch. Start the engine; the test lamp should light with the engine idling.

15 Increase the engine speed when the light should go out. If it does not, check the vacuum hose, if satisfactory then the switch must be faulty.

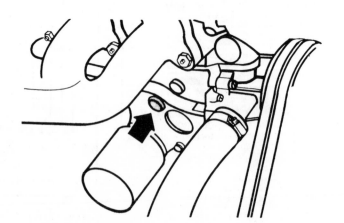

Fig. 13.117 Knock sensor boss above engine oil filter (Sec 6)

Fig. 13.118 Checking microswitch on B21F; 1982 with LH Jetronic fuel injection (Sec 6)

Fig. 13.119 Checking microswitch operations on B21F; 1983 with LH Jetronic fuel injection (Sec 6)

Microswitch adjustment – B23F with LH Jetronic fuel injection system (1983 models)

16 With the engine switched off, turn the throttle pulley slowly and listen for the click of the microswitch.

17 If a click is not heard, release the switch fixing screws and turn the switch until it just contacts its stop. Tighten the screws and recheck operation.

Ignition timing

18 The ignition timing may be checked on all types of ignition system using a stroboscope or special Volvo mono-tester (see Chapter 4, Sections 12 and 13).

19 Checking should be carried out with the engine at normal operating temperature and air conditioning (if fitted) switched off.

20 Any adjustment required is made by turning the distributor after having released its clamp bolt.

Distributor – removal and refitting

Mechanical breaker type

21 Remove the distributor cap and leads to one side.

22 Disconnect the LT leads and vacuum hose.

23 Turn the crankshaft until the contact end of the rotor is aligned with the mark on the rim of the distributor body.

24 Remove the distributor fixing bolt and lift the distributor from the crankcase.

25 To refit the distributor, hold it over its mounting hole so that the clamp plate bolt hole is central in the clamp plate elongated slot.

26 Turn the rotor arm (contact end) clockwise 60° from the body rim mark. Insert the distributor when the meshing of the drivegears will turn the rotor so that it aligns with the rim mark. Turn the distributor body until the points just begin to open.

27 Screw in the fixing bolt finger tight until the timing has been checked and adjusted (Chapter 4, Section 12).

Breakerless type

28 The operations are as described for the mechanical breaker type but ignore reference to contact points.

Computerised ignition system type

29 The distributor is driven from the rear end of the camshaft on B200 and B230 engined models.

Chrysler distributor

30 Remove the cap with HT leads and place to one side.

31 Turn the crankshaft until the rotor (contact end) is aligned with the rubber grommet and then unscrew the clamp plate bolt and remove the distributor.

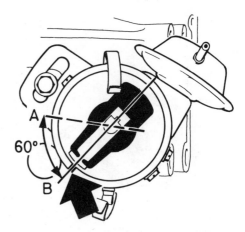

Fig. 13.120 Refitting mechanical breaker type distributor (Sec 6)

A Rotor position before   B Rotor position after
   installation   installation

Fig. 13.121 Rotor aligned with rubber grommet on breakerless type distributor (Sec 6)

32 To refit the distributor, turn the shaft so that the gear roll pin greater protruding end is aligned with the groove in the distributor body.

33 Hold the distributor over its mounting hole so that the clamp plate bolt hole is central in the clamp plate elongated slot.

34 Push the distributor into position. The gears will mesh and turn the rotor to line up with the rubber grommet. Check the ignition timing.
Bosch distributor

35 The operations are as described in paragraphs 21 to 27 but ignoring reference to vacuum hose and contact points.

Distributor (computerised ignition) – overhaul

The following overhaul operations should be regarded as the limit of economic work. Many internal components are not supplied as spares and a generally well worn distributor is better renewed.

Chrysler type

36 Remove the distributor as previously described.

37 Take off the rotor and springs which hold the Hall pick-up.

38 Disconnect the wiring plug and remove the Hall pick-up.

39 Reassembly is a reversal of removal but make sure that the leads are positioned out of the way of the rotor.

Bosch type

40 Remove the distributor as previously described.

41 Extract the screws and remove the cap fixing clips. Remove the rotor arm and the dust cover.

42 Extract the circlip from around the distributor shaft and remove the two retaining screws from around the body.

43 Using two screwdrivers as levers, prise out the rotor, taking care not to lose the lockpin.

44 Extract the second circlip and remove the Hall pick-up.

45 Reassembly is a reversal of removal.

Fig. 13.122 Gear roll pin aligned with groove before installing breakerless type distributor (Sec 6)

Fig. 13.123 Reluctor circlip on Bosch distributor (Sec 6)

Fig. 13.124 Reluctor lockpin on Bosch distributor (Sec 6)

Fig. 13.125 Hall pick-up circlip on Bosch distributor (Sec 6)

Fig. 13.126 Hall pick-up removed from Bosch distributor (Sec 6)

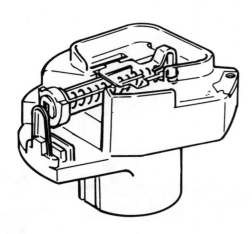

Fig. 13.127 Distributor rotor arm speed limiter (Sec 6)

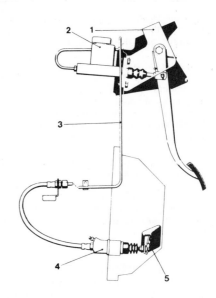

Fig. 13.128 Hydraulic clutch actuating system components
(Sec 7)

1 Pedal bracket   4 Slave cylinder
2 Master cylinder   5 Release arm
3 Hydraulic pipeline

Engine speed limiter

46 B200 and B230 engines (except B230F) are fitted with an engine
rev limiter. This takes the form of a spring-loaded weight on top of the
distributor rotor arm. At 6200 rpm, the weight overcomes spring
resistance due to centrifugal force and shorts the ignition circuit by
making an electrical contact.
47 Engine speed is limited on B230F models by the control unit which
cuts fuel supply to the injectors.

7 Clutch

General description

1 From 1975 onwards, right-hand drive models are fitted with a
hydraulically actuated clutch. This is basically the same as the cable
operated clutch system, except in the method of clutch actuation. The
pendant clutch pedal is connected to the clutch master cylinder and
hydraulic fluid reservoir by a short pushrod. The master cylinder and
hydraulic reservoir are mounted on the engine side of the bulkhead in
front of the driver. Depressing the clutch pedal moves the piston in the
master cylinder forwards, so forcing hydraulic fluid through the
hydraulic pipe to the slave cylinder. The piston in the slave cylinder
moves forward on the entry of the fluid and actuates the clutch release
arm by means of a short pushrod. From this point on the clutch is
disengaged in the same manner as the cable actuated clutch. It must be
noted, however, that owing to the fact that a cable pulls the release arm
and hydraulic pressure can only push it, the arm used in conjunction
with the hydraulically actuated system is of different design to that
used in the cable operated system. Instead of the release arm pivot
being on the opposite side of the release bearing to the actuated end of
the arm as in the cable actuated system, it is situated *between* the
release bearing and the actuated end of the arm.
2 All left-hand drive models are fitted with a cable actuated clutch,
however on Turbo versions the arrangement differs from that described
in Chapter 5 as follows. The release bearing is in constant contact with
the pressure plate diaphragm fingers, the preload being applied by the
clutch pedal return spring. There is no return spring at the release arm
end of the cable.

Clutch cable – adjustment

3 The throw-out fork free travel on all cable operated clutches has
been amended to the dimension given in the Specifications.
4 To check the free travel on Turbo models pull the throw-out fork
(release arm) rearwards and measure the dimension shown in Fig.
13.129. Loosen the locknut and turn the adjustment ferrule as required
then tighten the locknut.

Clutch cable – removal and refitting

5 The procedure is basically as given in Chapter 5, but on Turbo
models a return spring must never be fitted to the release arm.

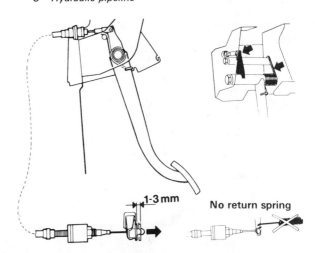

1-3 mm   **No return spring**

Fig. 13.129 Clutch cable components and free travel on
Turbo models (Sec 7)

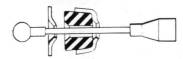

Fig. 13.130 Correctly fitted clutch cable vibration damper
(Sec 7)

6 On some models a rubber vibration damper may be fitted at the
release arm end of the cable. Make sure that the taper locates correctly
in the arm.

Clutch hydraulic system – bleeding

7 Whenever the clutch hydraulic system has been overhauled, a part
renewed, or the level in the reservoir is allowed to get low, air will enter
the system, necessitating bleeding. During this operation the level of
hydraulic fluid in the reservoir should not be allowed to fall below
half-full, otherwise air will be drawn in again.

8   Obtain a clean dry jar, plastic tubing at least 12 in (305 mm) long and able to fit tightly over the bleed screw of the slave cylinder, and a supply of the specified hydraulic fluid. The services of an assistant will be required.

9   Check that the master cylinder reservoir is full, and if not, fill it. Cover the bottom 1 in (25 mm) of the jar with hydraulic fluid.

10   Place one end of the tube securely over the end of the bleed screw after removing the dust cap (if fitted) and insert the other end in the jar so that the tube end is below the level of the fluid.

11   With a suitable spanner, open the bleed screw one turn.

12   An assistant should now depress the clutch pedal and allow it to return slowly.

13   Repeat this sequence, until no more air bubbles appear. Tighten the bleed screw during the next pedal downstroke.

14   Do not forget to check the reservoir frequently to ensure that the hydraulic fluid does not drop too far, so letting air into the system.

15   Refit the rubber dust cap over the bleed screw after removing the bleeding tube. **Note: Never re-use the fluid bled from the hydraulic system.** Refer also to Section 11 for alternative bleeding methods.

Clutch master cylinder – removal, overhaul and refitting

16   Connect up the end of a suitable length of tubing to the bleed screw of the slave cylinder and place the other end in a jar. Undo the bleed screw one turn and pump the clutch pedal up-and-down until the clutch fluid reservoir is empty of fluid. Remove the tube and tighten the bleed screw.

17   Disconnect the fluid outlet pipe from the master cylinder.

18   Remove the panel under the dashboard and then disconnect the pushrod from the clutch pedal by removing the clevis pin.

19   Unscrew and remove the bolts from the master cylinder mounting flange and remove the master cylinder.

20   Clean away all external dirt before taking the master cylinder to a totally clean working area.

21   Pull off the dust excluding cover and withdraw the pushrod.

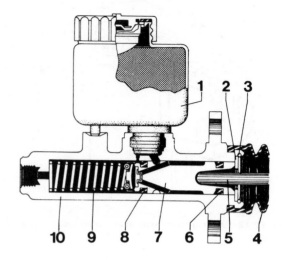

Fig. 13.131 Sectional view of clutch master cylinder (Sec 7)

1	Fluid reservoir	6	Piston seal
2	Washer	7	Piston
3	Circlip	8	Piston seal
4	Dust cover	9	Spring
5	Pushrod	10	Cylinder body

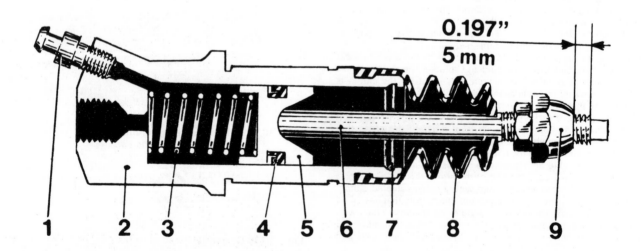

Fig. 13.132 Sectional view of clutch slave cylinder (Sec 7)

1	Bleed screw	4	Seal	7	Stop ring
2	Cylinder body	5	Piston	8	Dust cover
3	Spring	6	Pushrod	9	Domed nut

22 Extract the circlip now visible at the end of the master cylinder and remove the washer, piston, seals and return spring.
23 Examine the surfaces of the piston and the cylinder bore for scoring or bright wear areas. If such conditions are evident, renew the master cylinder complete.
24 If these components are unmarked and in good condition, discard the rubber seals and wash each part in clean hydraulic fluid or methylated spirit. **Do not use any other fluid.**
25 Obtain a repair kit which will contain all the necessary seals and other renewable items.
26 Dip the new seals in clean hydraulic fluid and position them on the piston using the fingers only.
27 Insert the spring, piston and seals and washer carefully into the master cylinder and secure with the circlip.
28 Insert the pushrod and refit the dust cover.
29 Refitting the master cylinder is a reversal of the removal procedure.
30 Check that there is a clearance of 0.04 in (1 mm) between the pushrod and the piston. If not, adjust the clearance by turning the adjusting nuts on each side of the pushrod yoke that connects to the pedal.
31 Refit the pedal mounting cover panel under the dashboard.
32 Fill up the master cylinder reservoir with hydraulic fluid and bleed the system as described in paragraphs 7 to 15.

Clutch slave cylinder – removal and refitting

33 Disconnect the flexible hose from the rigid hydraulic pipe by unscrewing the union nut from the latter.
34 Disconnect the hose from its securing bracket and plug the open end of the fluid line to avoid loss of fluid.
35 On early models extract the circlip and withdraw the slave cylinder from the clutch housing. On later models unbolt and remove the slave cylinder.
36 Clean away all external dirt from the slave cylinder and remove the rubber dust cover and pushrod.
37 Extract the circlip (which is now visible at the end of the cylinder) and withdraw the piston assembly and spring.
38 Inspect the surfaces of the piston and cylinder bore for scoring or bright wear areas. If these are evident, the complete slave cylinder must be renewed.
39 If the components are in good condition, wash them in clean hydraulic fluid or methylated spirit. **Do not use any other fluid.**
40 Obtain a repair kit which will contain a new seal and other renewable items.
41 Dip the new piston seal in clean hydraulic fluid and manipulate into position on the piston using the fingers.
42 Refit the spring and piston assembly into the cylinder and secure with the circlip. Refit the pushrod and dust cover.
43 On early models check that the domed nut is located on the pushrod as shown in Fig. 13.132 and if necessary loosen the locknut, re-position the domed nut then tighten the locknut.
44 Refitting is a reverse of the removal procedure. The system must be topped up with the specified hydraulic fluid and then bled, as described in paragraphs 7 to 15.

Clutch pedal – removal, overhaul and refitting

45 This is basically similar to the method described for the cable-actuated mechanism in Chapter 5. Detail differences will be apparent, notably that the master cylinder pushrod must be disconnected from the pedal by removal of the clevis pin instead of detaching the clutch cable.

Clutch release arm – removal and refitting

46 On early models slide the thrust bearing from the sleeve, then slide the locating pins from the groove in the bearing and withdraw the arm. The thrust bearing may be retained by clips.
47 On later models the thrust bearing can be removed from the sleeve separate to the arm. Pull the arm outward to release it from the pivot ball.
48 Lubricate the sleeve and pivot ball with a little grease.
49 Refitting is a reversal of removal, but on later models make sure that the spring clip is correctly located on the pivot ball as shown in Fig. 13.133.

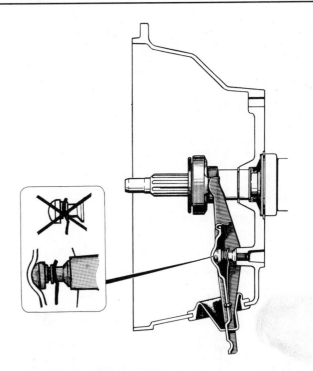

Fig. 13.133 Correctly located clutch release arm spring clip on later models (Sec 7)

8 Manual gearbox, overdrive and automatic transmission

Manual gearbox – oil changing and oil type

1 Commencing with 1979 models, the transmission is 'filled for life' and routine oil changes are no longer specified by the manufacturer.
2 However, in the light of operating experience, it is still advisable to renew the oil periodically to remove accumulations of metallic swarf and to make good the inevitable deterioration in the oil additives and anti-friction qualities.
3 It is suggested that the oil is renewed whenever the clutch driven plate is changed. Drain the oil hot after a run by removing the drain and filler/level plugs. Where overdrive is fitted, unbolt and remove the oil strainer cover and clean the strainer. Refill with oil, allowing time for the oil (common supply) to flow into the overdrive before checking that the oil just starts to flow out of the filler/level hole. Refit the plug and recheck the oil level after a few miles road operation. The recommended lubricant has been changed from automatic transmission fluid on later models operating in temperate climates; it is important that one type of lubricant only is used, not intermixed.

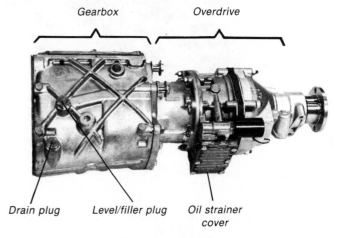

Fig. 13.134 Oil filler/level and drain plugs on manual gearbox (Sec 8)

Manual gearbox – modifications to Type M45/46 gearboxes

4 On later gearboxes (1979 on); only one selector shaft is used instead of the three previously used. Two shift forks and the gearchange selector dog are attached to the selector shaft.

5 Two selector plates are retained in position by a spring and the transmission cover.

6 Movement of the plates by the selector shaft/dog is controlled by three projecting guides which allows them to move sideways when the gearchange control lever is moved.

7 A leaf spring is incorporated in the gearbox cover to keep the reverse selector in position. Also cast into the underside of the cover are three stop lugs for the selector plates.

8 It is emphasised that many components of this modified gearbox have been redesigned and are not interchangeable with earlier models. These include:

  (a) *Input shaft with 22 splines (different type of clutch driven plate required in consequence)*
  (b) *3rd/4th gears and synchroniser*
  (c) *Steel shift forks with renewable brass friction pads*

9 The gearchange control lever used with this later type of gearbox has been modified at its lower end as shown (Fig. 13.139). The reverse gear slot is now on the left-hand side instead of at the rear. The gear lever extension support is now of square section steel tubing.

10 As from 1981 models the first, second and third gears run on needle bearings instead of bushes, and also the gear lever on M46 versions incorporates a pushbutton instead of the previous switch control for the overdrive.

11 Also from 1981 models the M46 gearbox incorporates automatic disengagement of the overdrive when changing down from 4th gear. The circuit is shown in Fig. 13.141 and consists of an electronic relay and gearbox switch. As from 1985 a vibration damper is incorporated in 1st speed gear similar to that used in the Type 47; see paragraph 64.

Gear lever pullrod – renewal

12 Unclip the gear lever gaiter and pull it up the lever, taking care not to damage the overdrive wiring on M46 models.

13 Hold the lever stationary and use a punch to drive the pin from the bottom of the lever.

14 On M46 models remove the centre console side panel where

Fig. 13.135 Single selector shaft on 1979 and later M45 and M46 gearboxes (Sec 8)

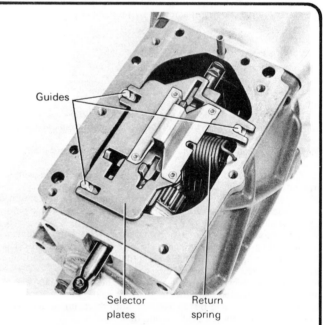

Fig. 13.136 Selector plates on 1979 and later M45 and M46 gearboxes (Sec 8)

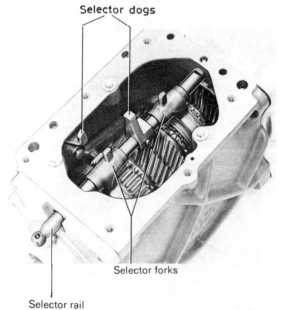

Fig. 13.137 Interior of M45 and M46 gearbox (1979 and later) (Sec 8)

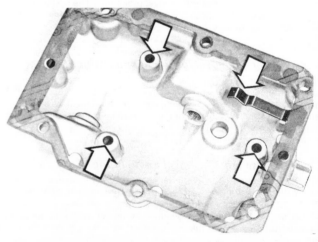

Fig. 13.138 Reverse selector leaf springs and selector plate stop lugs (arrowed) on 1979 and later M45 and M46 gearboxes (Sec 8)

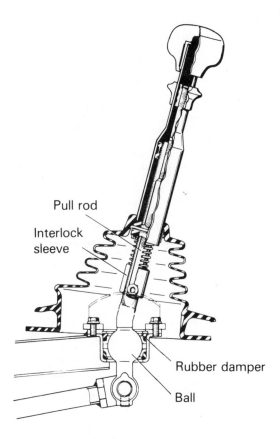

Pull rod

Interlock
sleeve

Rubber damper

Ball

Fig. 13.139 Later type gear lever (Sec 8)

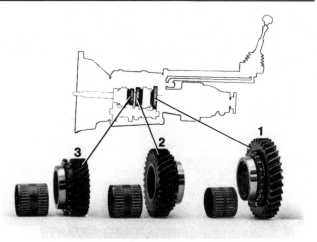

Fig. 13.140 1981 and later gears and needle roller
bearings (Sec 8)

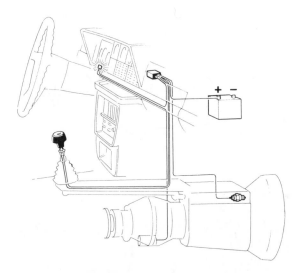

Fig. 13.141 Overdrive disengagement circuit (Sec 8)

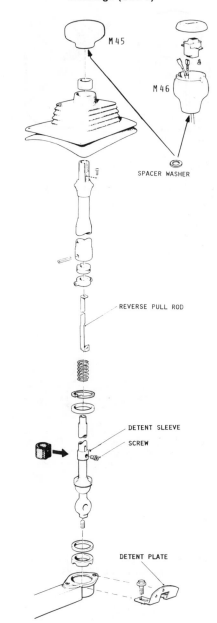

M45

M46

SPACER WASHER

REVERSE PULL ROD

DETENT SLEEVE

SCREW

DETENT PLATE

Fig. 13.142 Components of later type gearchange lever
(Sec 8)

applicable and disconnect the plugs. Also remove the top of the gear
lever knob.
15 Remove the gear lever.
16 Grip the gear lever in a soft jawed vice then use a soft mallet to tap
off the knob.
17 Remove the screw and withdraw the reverse detent knob.
18 Remove the pullrod, spring and interlock sleeve.

19 Remove the screw and separate the sleeve from the pullrod. Note that the sleeve has been modified (Fig. 13.143) and the later type should always be fitted together with a 0.08 in (2.0 mm) thick, 0.63 in (16.0 mm) diameter washer beneath the gear lever knob to ensure that the sleeve clears the detent bracket.

20 Bend the end of the pullrod as shown in Fig. 13.144 to prevent it rattling.

21 Fit the spring and interlock sleeve to the pullrod, apply locking fluid to the screw then tighten it.

22 Grease the pullrod and fit the reverse detent knob to the rod and secure it with the screw.

23 Fit the pullrod to the lever then grip the lever in a soft jawed vice and tap the knob into position.

24 Fit the lever to the stub on the gearbox and secure by tapping in the pin.

25 Engage 1st gear and use a feeler gauge to check that the clearance between the reverse detent plate and the detent screw is between 0.02 and 0.06 in (0.5 and 1.5 mm). Engage 2nd gear and check that the clearance is the same. If necessary loosen the bolts and adjust the

detent plate as required.

26 On M46 models reconnect the overdrive wiring, refit the top of the gear lever knob, and where applicable refit the centre console side panel.

27 Clip the gear lever gaiter into position.

Five-speed manual transmission (M47) – description

28 Commencing 1984, a five-speed manual gearbox is fitted as an option to the four-speed unit with overdrive.

29 The gearbox is virtually identical to the Type M45 four-speed except that 5th gear and synchromesh are located within a housing at the rear of the gearbox.

30 5th speed synchromesh was originally located on the end of the mainshaft, but in 1986 it was moved to the layshaft (countershaft).

5th speed gear and synchro – removal from and refitting to mainshaft (up to 1985)

31 With the gearbox removed, drain the oil.

32 Unbolt and remove the top cover and gasket.

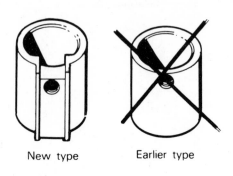

Fig. 13.143 Later type of pullrod interlock sleeve (Sec 8)

New type   Earlier type

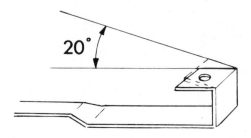

Fig. 13.144 Pullrod bending diagram (Sec 8)

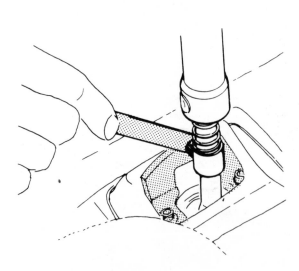

Fig. 13.145 Checking reverse detent clearance with a feeler blade (Sec 8)

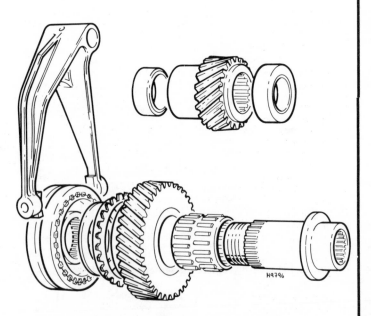

Fig. 13.146 5th speed gear arrangement 1986 models (Sec 8)

Fig. 13.147 Exploded view of M47, five-speed gearbox (Sec 8)

1 End casing
2 Oil seal
3 Cover
4 Gasket
5 Leaf spring
6 Selector plate
7 5th gear housing
8 Gasket
9 Roller bearing
10 Bearing track
11 Speedometer drive
12 Bearing track
13 Inner race
14 Adjusting shim
15 Cover plate
16 Selector arm
17 Roll pin
18 Selector shaft
19 Selector fork
20 Reverse gear selector fork
21 Pivot pin
22 Selector fork
23 Selector arm
24 Pad
25 Spring
26 Interlock ball
27 Selector shaft
28 Washer
29 Dowel pin
30 Circlip
31 Adjusting shim
32 Ball-bearing
33 Roller bearing
34 Casing
35 Gasket
36 Oil seal
37 Ball-bearing
38 Adjusting shim
39 Sealing plate
40 Gear wheel
41 Roller bearing
42 Countershaft
43 Reverse idler gear
44 Shaft
45 Synchronizer hub
46 Collar
47 Spring ring
48 Sliding key
49 Synchro sleeve
50 Spring ring
51 Baulk ring
52 Circlip
53 Spacer
54 Needle bearing
55 5th gear wheel
56 Spacer
57 Spigot bearing
58 Input shaft
59 Needle bearing
60 Circlip
61 Baulk ring
62 Spring ring
63 Synchro sleeve
64 Synchronizer hub
65 Baulk ring
66 3rd gear wheel
67 Sliding key
68 Mainshaft
69 2nd gear wheel
70 Baulk ring
71 Synchro sleeve

72 Spring ring
73 Synchronizer hub
74 Sliding key
75 Synchronizer cone
76 Circlip
77 Washer
78 1st gear wheel
79 Vibration damper
80 Springs
81 Plate
82 Thrust washer

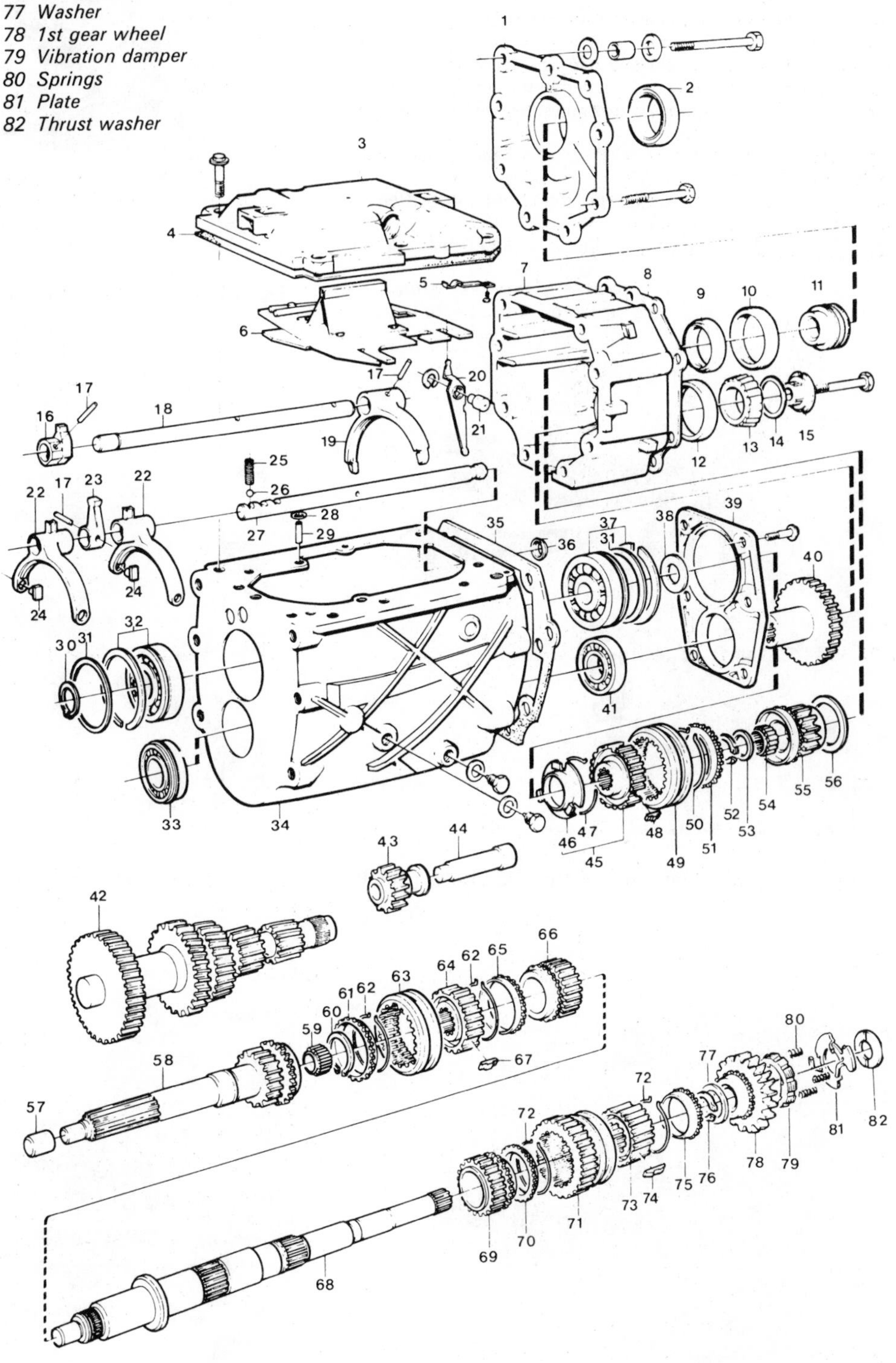

33 Remove the gear selector plate now exposed, lift off the washers, spring and ball.

34 Unbolt and remove the gearchange lever support bracket and remote control rod.

35 Lock up two gears at once by moving the rods within the top cover aperture and then unbolt and remove the drive flange. A puller will be needed for this.

36 Remove the speedometer driven gear.

37 Unbolt and remove the end cover plate and gasket.

38 Unscrew and remove the screw from the end of the countershaft. Take off the washer and the shim.

39 Refit the screw (5 or 6 turns) and use as a pressure point for a two-legged puller which should be engaged in the square cut-outs in the 5th gear housing. Pull off the housing and remove the gasket and selector rod oil seal.

40 Pull the speedometer drivegear, washer, roller bearing and washer from the mainshaft.

41 Using a puller, remove 5th speed gear from the layshaft. Remove the shaft end screw.

42 Remove 5th speed gear, needle bearing, bush and baulk ring from the mainshaft.

43 Drive the roll pin from 5th speed selector fork, extract the synchro-hub circlip and slide the synchro, with the fork as an

Fig. 13.148 Gear selector plate, washers and spring on M47 gearbox (Sec 8)

Fig. 13.149 Gearchange lever support bracket bolts (Sec 8)

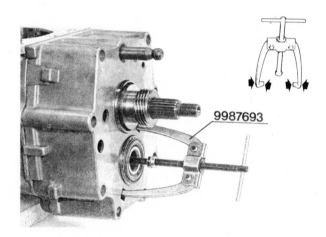

9987693

Fig. 13.150 Removing 5th gear housing (Sec 8)

Fig. 13.151 Removing speedo drive gear from mainshaft (Sec 8)

Fig. 13.152 Removing 5th speed gear from the layshaft (Sec 8)

assembly, from the main and selector shafts. The synchro sleeve will probably come away, leaving the hub on the shaft. Remove the hub with a puller, take off the adjusting shim and retain it.

Refitting

44 If a new synchro unit is to be fitted, the hub will have to be pressed onto the shaft and the clearance between the hub face and the circlip measured. If the clearance is greater than 0.0079 in (0.20 mm) then it must be reduced by inserting a shim behind the hub. Shims are available in four thicknesses.

45 If the original synchro is to be refitted, use the original shim.

46 Fit the synchro-hub circlip.

47 Locate the three synchro sliding keys in the synchro-hub. Engage the 5th speed selector fork in the groove of the synchro sleeve so that the chamfered teeth are towards the sliding keys.

48 Fit the sleeve and fork simultaneously, at the same time holding the synchro springs engaged in the sliding keys. The ends of the springs should engage in the same key but run in opposite directions.

49 Secure the selector fork to the shaft with a roll pin.

50 Grease the needle bearings and insert them with the spacer, in 5th speed mainshaft gear.

51 Fit the synchro baulk ring and fit both 5th speed gears to their shafts. Screw in the layshaft screw with washer.

52 Fit the washer, roller bearing (taper towards end of shaft) the thrust washer ring and speedo gear to the mainshaft.

53 Fit the bearing tracks (if renewed) and selector shaft seal into 5th gear housing.

54 Grease a new gasket and fit it with 5th gear housing to the end of the gearbox.

55 Fabricate some tubular distance pieces and fit them to the rear cover plate bolts. Screw in the bolts to 35 lbf ft (50 Nm) to hold the 5th gear housing tightly.

56 Fit the layshaft rear bearing (without shim), the cover washer, with the splines engaged, and tighten the screw.

57 Check the layshaft endfloat, preferably using a dial gauge. The endfloat must be between 0.0004 and 0.004 in (0.01 and 0.10 mm). Select shims from the five thicknesses available to give the specified endfloat. Fit the shim, washer and new self-locking screw. Tighten the screw to 32 lbf ft (45 Nm).

58 Remove the bolts and temporary spacers, fit the seals and speedo driven gear to the end cover.

Fig. 13.153 5th speed synchro-hub circlip (Sec 8)

Fig. 13.154 Checking 5th speed synchro-hub-to-circlip clearance (Sec 8)

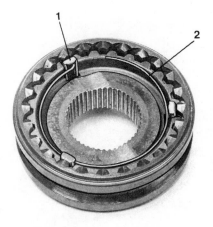

Fig. 13.155 Synchromesh unit (Sec 8)

1   Sliding key   2   Spring

Fig. 13.156 Mainshaft 5th speed gear components (Sec 8)

1   Needle roller bearing   2   Spacer

Fig. 13.157 Tightening drive flange nut (Sec 8)

Fig. 13.158 1st speed gear and vibration damper (Sec 8)

59 Grease a new gasket and locate the rear cover. Fit the gearchange rod and support bracket screw in the bolts and tighten to the specified torque.
60 Lock up two gears at once by moving the selector rods within the top cover aperture. Fit the drive flange and tighten a new nut to specified torque. Return the gears to neutral.
61 Fit the washers, selector plate, interlock ball and the spring.
62 Grease a new gasket and fit the top cover to the gearbox. Tighten the bolts to specified torque.

5th speed gear and synchro – removal from and refitting to layshaft (1986)

63 The operations are virtually identical to those described in the preceding sub-section, except that the components are located on the layshaft.

Vibration damper (Type M4 gearbox)

64 This is fitted to 1st speed gear to reduce vibration at idling speed. The device comprises a spring-loaded tapered braking ring which slows 1st speed gear when the engine is idling. The action of a spring pulls the damper from the gear at higher input shaft speeds. The vibration damper springs are located and held in the braking ring by a washer. A press or extractor will be required to remove or refit the vibration damper from or to the mainshaft.

Automatic transmission (AW55, AW70 and AW71) – general description

65 The AW type transmissions are manufactured in Japan by Aisin-Warner under licence from Borg-Warner.
66 The AW55 transmission is fitted in conjunction with the North American B21F engine and is similar to the BW55 transmission.
67 Fitted to later models, the AW70 and AW71 transmissions are 4-speed units; 1st, 2nd and 3rd speeds being as on earlier 3-speed units with 4th speed as an overdrive.
68 It should be noted that the automatic transmissions have been modified a number of times especially in respect of the valve bodies.
69 AW70 and AW71 transmission incorporate a solenoid valve on the left-hand side. When removing the transmission the wiring plug must be disconnected.

Automatic transmission (BW55, AW55, AW70 and AW71) downshift cable – renewal and adjustment

70 Cut the inner cable at the throttle end and disconnect the loose end from the throttle lever.
71 Loosen the locknut and disconnect the outer cable ferrule from the bracket.
72 At the transmission end clean the surrounding area then pull out the outer cable.
73 Drain the transmission oil and remove the oil pan.
74 Using long-nosed pliers, pull the inner cable down from inside the transmission, then pull the inner cable to move the cam into view. Use a screwdriver to retain the cam in this position.

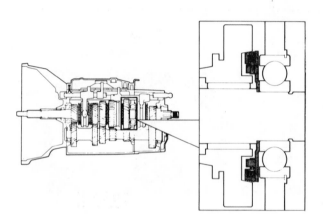

Fig. 13.159 Sectional view of 1st speed gear vibration damper (Sec 8)

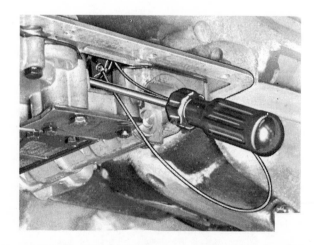

Fig. 13.160 Retaining downshift cable cam with screwdriver (Sec 8)

75 Disconnect the inner cable then withdraw the complete cable.
76 Fit the new cable in reverse order but fit a new O-ring seal where the cable end enters the transmission.
77 To adjust the inner cable stop, loosen the locknuts and position the outer cable ferrule to take up the play and provide a light preload. Re-position the locknuts to retain the ferrule then crimp the cable stop 0.01 to 0.04 in (0.25 to 1.0 mm) from the end of the ferrule.
78 Have an assistant fully depress the throttle pedal, then check that the distance between the cable stop and ferrule end is between 1.98 and 2.07 in (50.4 and 52.6 m). Adjust the locknuts as necessary. In the idle position there should be no play on the inner cable, and in the full throttle position it should be possible to pull out the inner cable a further 0.08 in (2.0 mm).
79 Refit the oil pan and fill the transmission with oil.

Automatic transmission starter inhibitor switch – adjustment

80 Remove the selector lever cover and check that the inhibitor switch lever aligns correctly with the N and P marks. If not, loosen the bolts, reposition the switch then tighten the bolts.
81 Move the selector lever through all positions and check that the contact pin does not slide out of the switch lever. Check that the engine can only be started with the selector lever in positions P and N and that the reversing lights come on in position R. If the reversing light flashes when the car is reversed move the switch forward 0.04 in (1.0 mm), but check that the engine can only be started in positions P and N.

Automatic transmission fluid cooler – cleaning

82 The transmission fluid is cooled by passing it through a cooler incorporated in the right-hand side of the radiator. On some models an auxiliary cooler is also mounted in front of the radiator. After removing the transmission or draining the fluid for any reason it is worthwhile cleaning the old fluid from the cooler.
83 To clean the standard cooler first overfill the transmission by approximately 0.5 Imp pt (0.3 US qt, 0.3 litre).
84 Disconnect the fluid return pipe from the rear of the transmssion and positon a container beneath it.
85 With P selected and the handbrake applied, have an assistant start the engine and let it idle.
86 Switch off the engine when clean fluid comes out, then reconnect the return pipe and top up the fluid level as described in Chapter 6.
87 To clean the auxiliary cooler disconnect the pipes at the standard cooler then use a pump to force new fluid through the cooler until it emerges from the return pipe.
88 Re-connect the pipes then top up the fluid level as described in Chapter 6.

Automatic transmission – fluid changing

89 As from 1984 models the transmission fluid should be changed at the revised intervals. However, it is only necessary to drain the fluid from the transmission sump then add fresh fluid and check the level – the fluid remaining in the torque converter and hydraulic lines cannot be drained.

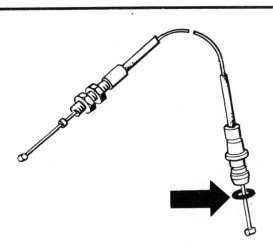

Fig. 13.161 Downshift cable O-ring seal (Sec 8)

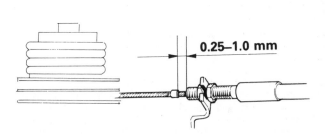

Fig. 13.162 Downshift cable stop setting diagram with accelerator pedal released (Sec 8)

Fig. 13.163 Downshift cable stop setting with accelerator pedal fully depressed (Sec 8)

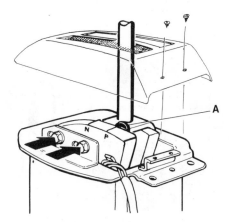

Fig. 13.164 Inhibitor switch adjustment bolts (Sec 8)

A Lever

9 Propeller shaft

Modification

1   As from 1979 the rear section of the propeller shaft is modified on certain models. The section is sleeved with rubber damping inserts between the sleeves, in order to reduce transmission noises.

10 Rear axle and rear suspension

General description

1   Later models can be fitted with a limited slip differential rear axle as an option. The axle is identical to the standard type axle except for the differential. The purpose of this type of axle is to limit the differences in rotational speed between the two halfshafts by means of internal clutches. With this type of axle, never jack up one rear wheel and turn it while the opposite wheel is still on the ground. Always jack up both wheels together, otherwise damage may be caused to the unit.

2   As from 1979 certain models are fitted with gas pressurized shock absorbers. The shock absorbers still contain oil, but this is pressurized at all times by gas sealed in a chamber at the bottom of the unit.

3   As from 1979, aluminium wheels are fitted to certain models together with low profile tyres as given in the Specifications.

Limited slip differential – overhaul

4   The overhaul operations are as described for the standard axle in Chapter 8, except for the following special work which must be done once the differential carrier is removed.

5   With a suitable tool, remove the differential case bearings.

6   Using quick-drying paint, mark the ends of the differential gear shafts in relation to their holes in the case. Also mark the two halves of the differential case.

7   Unscrew and remove the bolts which hold the differential case together. *These bolts have left-hand threads.*

8   Lift the case from the crownwheel and extract the clutch discs and gears, keeping them all in fitted order.

9   If the crownwheel is to be removed, unscrew the retaining bolts and discard them. Purchase new ones for reassembly.

10 Commence reassembly by fitting the crownwheel, using new bolts and thread locking fluid applied to their threads, and tighten them to the specified torque.

11 With the teeth of the crownwheel towards you, insert the shafts, gears and the discs correctly aligned. Apply specified oil to all the components as they are fitted.

12 Fit the differential case, screw in the bolts *(left-hand thread)* and tighten to the specified torque.

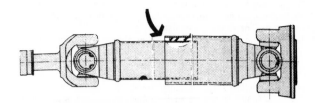

Fig. 13.165 Propeller shaft with rubber damping inserts (arrowed) (Sec 9)

Fig. 13.166 Sectional view of gas-filled rear shock absorber (Sec 10)

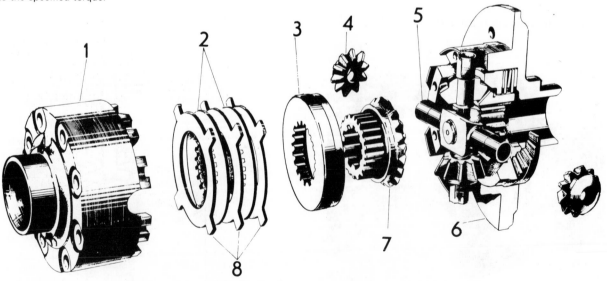

Fig. 13.167 Limited slip differential components (Sec 10)

1 Differential case	3 Gear retainer	5 Shafts	7 Side gear
2 Clutch discs	4 Pinion gear	6 Differential case	8 Clutch discs

Fig. 13.168 Differential case alignment marks (Sec 10)

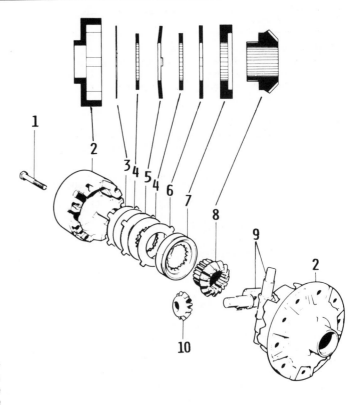

Speedometer drive

13 The 1986 models have an impulse sender screwed into the rear axle cover which transmits to the speedometer head through an electrical wire instead of the rotating mechanical drive cable from the gearbox used on earlier vehicles. The sensor-to-pulse wheel clearance must be maintained at between 0.020 and 0.047 in (0.5 and 1.2 mm)

Rear axle lubricant

14 Attention is drawn to the need for special lubricant in limited slip rear axles. This must conform to standard AP1-GL-5 (MIL-L-2105 B or C).

15 1986 vehicles without limited slip rear axles should use a low friction rear axle oil in the interest of fuel economy (Volvo Part No 1161276-9).

16 The rear axle is 'filled for life' and should normally only require topping-up. However, for those wishing to renew the oil after an extended service interval (say 50,000 miles – 80,000 km) drain the oil hot after a run by removing the drain and filler/level plugs.

17 Refit the drain plug and fill with the specified oil until it runs out of the filler/level plug hole.

Fig. 13.169 Assembly sequence of limited slip differential (Sec 10)

1 Bolt	6 Flat disc (0.1 in/2.4 mm)
2 Differential case	7 Gear retainer
3 Disc (0.06 in/1.5 mm)	8 Side gear
4 Flat discs	9 Shafts
5 Dished disc (0.1 in/2.4 mm)	10 Pinion gear

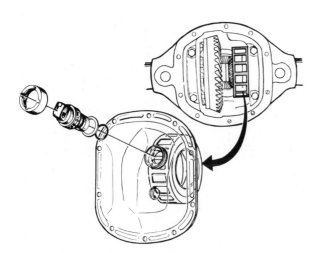

Fig. 13.170 Rear axle speedometer impulse sender (Sec 10)

Drain plug   Filler plug

Fig. 13.171 Rear axle drain and filler/level plugs (Sec 10)

11 Braking system

Front brake discs

1   The front brake discs on certain later models are of the ventilated type. Reference should be made to the Specifications in this Supplement for details of new and refinishing dimensions for these later type discs.

Handbrake ratchet

2   On later models (1980 on), the handbrake control lever ratchet pawl is of double-toothed type to provide an additional safety feature.

Caliper units

3   Both Girling and ATE type brake calipers are fitted, and the type fitted can be determined by the code numbers 1 and 2 which respectively refer to Girling and ATE. The code numbers are located on a plate. On early models the plate is on the pillar behind the right-hand front door, from March 1978 to July 1979 it is on the right-hand front door, on 1980 models it is in front of the radiator, and on 1981 on models it is in the engine compartment (Saloons) or luggage compartment (Estates). Note that for 1976 and 1977 models the code applies only to the rear calipers, as all front calipers are manufactured by Girling.

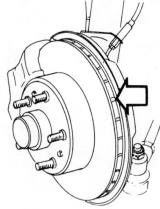

Fig. 13.172 Ventilated type brake disc (Sec 11)

Fig. 13.173 Components of ATE type front caliper (Sec 11)

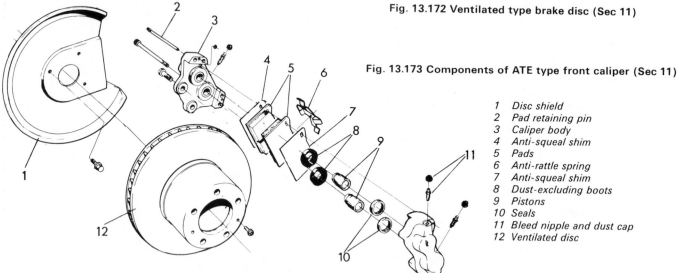

1   Disc shield
2   Pad retaining pin
3   Caliper body
4   Anti-squeal shim
5   Pads
6   Anti-rattle spring
7   Anti-squeal shim
8   Dust-excluding boots
9   Pistons
10 Seals
11 Bleed nipple and dust cap
12 Ventilated disc

Fig. 13.174 Components of ATE type rear caliper (Sec 11)

1   Disc shield
2   Disc/drum
3   Caliper body
4   Piston seal
5   Piston
6   Dust-excluding boot
7   Boot retaining clip
8   Pad
9   Anti-rattle spring
10 Anti-squeal shims (if fitted)
11 Bleed nipple and dust cap
12 Pad retaining pin
13 Guard plate (USA models only)

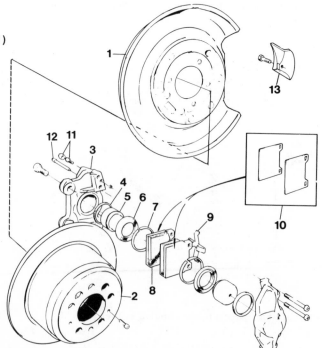

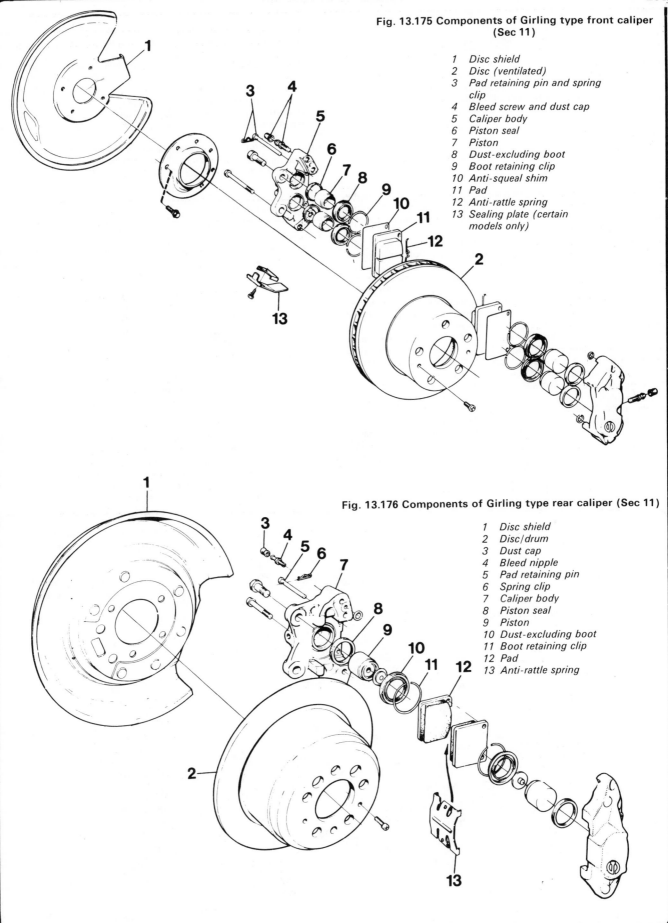

Fig. 13.175 Components of Girling type front caliper (Sec 11)

1 Disc shield
2 Disc (ventilated)
3 Pad retaining pin and spring clip
4 Bleed screw and dust cap
5 Caliper body
6 Piston seal
7 Piston
8 Dust-excluding boot
9 Boot retaining clip
10 Anti-squeal shim
11 Pad
12 Anti-rattle spring
13 Sealing plate (certain models only)

Fig. 13.176 Components of Girling type rear caliper (Sec 11)

1 Disc shield
2 Disc/drum
3 Dust cap
4 Bleed nipple
5 Pad retaining pin
6 Spring clip
7 Caliper body
8 Piston seal
9 Piston
10 Dust-excluding boot
11 Boot retaining clip
12 Pad
13 Anti-rattle spring

Hydraulic system – bleeding

4 If the services of an assistant are not available to bleed the brakes, as described in Chapter 9, then one of the two following methods may be used. If the master cylinder or pressure regulating valve have been disconnected and reconnected, then the complete system (both circuits) must be bled. If only one circuit has been disturbed, then only that particular circuit need be bled. Note that Volvo now recommend bleeding the brakes in the following order:

1 Front left wheel
2 Front right wheel
3 Rear left wheel
4 Rear right wheel

Bleeding using a one-way valve kit

5 There are a number of one-man brake bleeding kits currently available from motor accessory shops. These devices simplify the bleeding process and reduce the risk of expelled air or fluid being drawn back again into the system.

6 To use this type of kit, connect the outlet tube to the bleed nipple and then open the nipple half a turn. If possible, position the union so that it can be viewed from inside the car. Depress the brake pedal to the floor and slowly release it. The one-way valve in the bleed kit will prevent expelled air or fluid from returning to the system at the end of each pedal return stroke. Repeat this operation until clean hydraulic fluid, free from air bubbles, can be seen coming through the bleed tube. Tighten the bleed nipple and remove the tube.

7 Repeat the operations on the remaining bleed nipples in the correct sequence. Make sure that throughout the process the fluid reservoir level never falls so low that air can be drawn into the master cylinder, otherwise the work up to this point will have been wasted.

Bleeding using a pressure bleeding kit

8 These, too, are available from motor accessory shops and are usually operated by air pressure form the spare tyre.

9 By connecting a pressurised container to the master cylinder fluid reservoir, bleeding is then carried out by simply opening each bleed nipple in turn and allowing the fluid to run out, rather like turning on a tap, until air bubbles are no longer visible in the fluid being expelled.

10 Using this system, the large reserve of hydraulic fluid provides a safeguard against air being drawn into the master cylinder during the bleeding process.

11 This method is particularly effective when bleeding 'difficult' systems and when bleeding the entire system at the time of routine fluid renewal.

12 When the bleeding operations are completed, check and top up the fluid level in the master cylinder. Check the feel of the brake pedal, which should be firm and free from any sponginess which would indicate air still being present in the system.

13 Discard any expelled hydraulic fluid as it is likely to be contaminated with moisture, air and dirt, which makes it unsuitable for further use.

14 Hydraulic fluid should always be stored in an airtight container as it absorbs moisture from the air which tends to lower its boiling point. Never shake a tin of hydraulic fluid before using it.

12 Electrical system

Alternator

1 As from 1981 models, the voltage regulator is integral with the brush holder and not mounted separately in the engine compartment.

Fig. 13.177 Later type brush holder/voltage regulator (Sec 12)

Starter motor

2 Additional makes of starter motor may be encountered (see Specifications at the beginning of this Supplement). Although the design of individual components may vary, the procedures described in Chapter 10 will still apply in general.

3 After 1978, the front starter motor mounting bracket is no longer fitted to cars having B19 or B21 series engines.

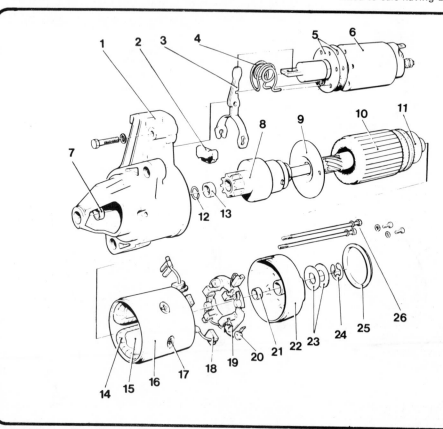

Fig. 13.178 Exploded view of Hitachi starter motor (Sec 12)

1   Drive end bearing housing
2   Rubber packing piece
3   Shift arm
4   Spring
5   Shims
6   Solenoid
7   Bush
8   Drive
9   Centre bearing
10 Armature
11 Commutator
12 Lock ring
13 Stop ring
14 Field coil
15 Pole shoe
16 Starter body
17 Screw
18 Brush
19 Brush holder
20 Spring
21 Bush
22 End cover
23 Shims
24 Lock ring
25 Seal
26 Tie-bolts

Headlamps (except North America)

4 On 1978 models, the headlamps project further forward to accommodate a new design of radiator grille. A spacer and mounting plate are used to achieve this.

5 Adjustment of the headlamp beam is carried out by inserting a screwdriver into the cut-outs in the headlamp trim.

6 Rectangular headlamps were introduced in 1979, and in 1981 they were modified together with the wrap-around direction indicators, each unit being retained by four nuts.

7 Halogen type bulbs or sealed beam units have been progressively introduced from 1981.

Running lights

8 On 1976 models, daytime running lights are fitted in the front parking and tail lamps. The circuit is fused and is operative when the ignition is switched on.

Rear lights (Saloon)

9 Wrap-around rear lights were introduced in 1979 incorporating a printed circuit board. The bulbs can be removed from inside the luggage compartment and it is not now necessary to disconnect any leads.

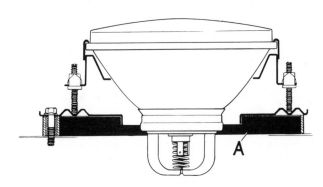

Fig. 13.179 Later type headlamp mounting with spacer (A)
(Sec 12)

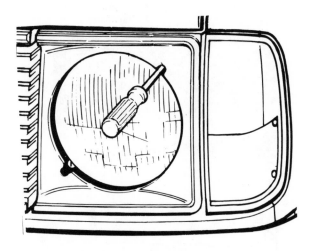

Fig. 13.180 Adjusting later type headlamp beam (Sec 12)

Fig. 13.181 Rectangular headlamp (Sec 12)

Fig. 13.182 North American type headlamps (Sec 12)

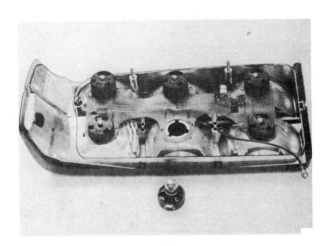

Fig. 13.183 Later type rear lamp cluster (Sec 12)

Rear lights (Estate)

10 The bulbs are accessible from within the load area.
11 If the bulb is to be renewed on the left-hand side, unclip the side cover and remove the spare wheel. If the right-hand side, lift the floor cover and then unclip and remove the side trim panel.
12 Turn the bulbholder anti-clockwise and remove it. The bulb is of bayonet fitting type.

Number plate lights (Saloon)

13 As from 1979, bayonet type bulbs are fitted to the number plate lights.

Number plate light (Estate)

14 Access to the festoon type bulb is obtained after depressing the spring tab at the side of the lamp lens and removing the lamp body.

Engine compartment lamp

15 Access to the festoon type bulb is obtained by loosening the fixing screw and withdrawing the lamp body.

Side repeater lamps

16 Access to the bulb is obtained by sliding the lens towards the front of the vehicle and prising the rear edge of the lens away from the body panel.
17 Pull the wedge base bulb from the bulbholder.

Fig. 13.184 Rear lamp cluster, Estate models (Sec 12)

1   Stop-lamp   3   Direction indicator lamp
2   Reversing lamp   4   Tail lamp

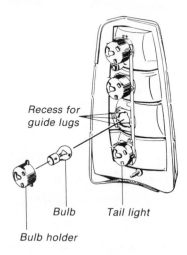

Fig. 13.185 Rear lamp bulb and holder arrangement on Estate models (Sec 12)

Fig. 13.186 Prising out rear number plate lamp on Estate models (Sec 12)

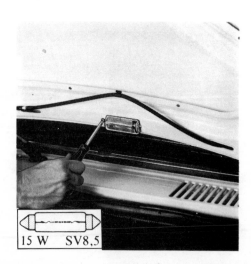

Fig. 13.187 Releasing engine compartment lamp lens screw (Sec 12)

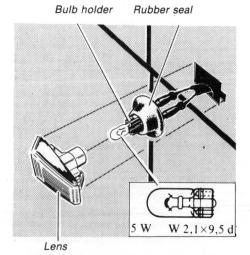

Fig. 13.188 Side repeater lamp (Sec 12)

Boot interior lamp

18 A luggage boot lamp is fitted on DL models after 1978. Access to the bulb is obtained after extracting the securing screw and separating the lens.

Headlamp wipers/washers

19 These were introduced in 1979. Each headlamp has an independent motor. The washer jet is located in the wiper arm and fed by a flexible pipe.

20 Removal and refitting is quite straightforward once the radiator grille and the headlamp trim panel have been withdrawn but on completion, the following adjustment must be carried out.

21 Pull back the cover to expose the wiper arm-to-motor spindle locknut. Release the locknut so that the arm is free and then set the wiper blade immediately below the lower stop lug(s). Reconnect the wiper arm to spindle and tighten the locknut. Finally lift the wiper blade and locate it above the stop lug(s).

22 As from 1981 models the wiper motors are attached to the bottom plate instead of the side, and although the motors are the same as previously fitted the blades and arms are different.

23 To renew a headlamp wiper blade, pull the wiper arm from its pivot point and pull the blade from its arm.

24 Snap the new blade into position making sure that the longer of the two support arms is towards the radiator grille.

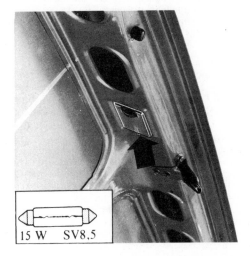

Fig. 13.189 Luggage boot lamp (Sec 12)

Fig. 13.190 Earlier type headlamp wash/wipe mechanism (Sec 12)

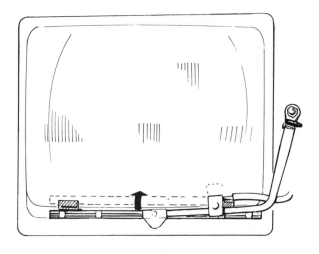

Fig. 13.191 Headlamp wiper blade adjustment diagram (earlier models) (Sec 12)

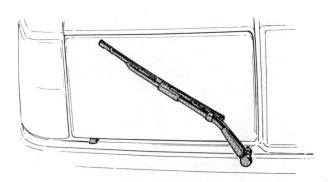

Fig. 13.192 Later type headlamp wiper (Sec 12)

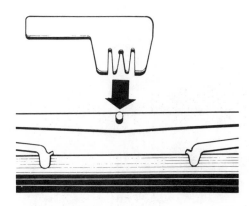

Fig. 13.193 Headlamp wiper arm-to-blade connection (Sec 12)

Tailgate window washer

25 On 1981 on models a single fluid reservoir is provided for both the windscreen washer and tailgate washer.

26 The pumps are located on the side of the reservoir, and the tailgate pump is identified with a blue dot.

Windscreen wiper arms

27 As from 1981 models the windscreen wiper arms are secured to the spindles with nuts. To remove an arm, lift the cover, unscrew the nut and pull the arm from the splines on the spindle. When refitting the arm, align it as described in Chapter 10.

Heated rear window

28 The element on the inside of the heated rear window (or tailgate) glass should be treated with care. Do not allow luggage to rub against it during journeys. Clean the glass with water and detergent only, wiping the glass in the direction of the elements, and avoid scratching them with rings on the fingers.

29 Do not stick labels across the heater element.

30 It is possible to repair a broken element by using a special conductive paint available from your Volvo dealer.

Relays

31 A relay panel is located on the engine compartment rear bulkhead and may include relays to actuate any of the following components and accessories according to the particular model and date of production (see wiring diagram):

    (a) Fuel injectors
    (b) Fuel pump
    (c) Window regulator
    (d) Headlamp relay
    (e) Emission control (Lambda-sond)
    (f) Spotlamp
    (g) Central locking system
    (h) Air conditioning delay
    (i) Windscreen wiper interval

32 The air conditioning delay relay prevents the compressor from engaging until approximately 10 seconds after the alternator has commenced to charge. This enables the engine to be started more easily when the air conditioning is switched on.

33 The interval relay for the windscreen wipers is fitted to later models and located under the facia panel on the left-hand support.

34 As from 1981 models, the overdrive disengagement relay is located behind the instrument panel.

Fuses

35 The fuses are of 8A, 16A and on certain later models 25A rating. The circuits protected vary according to the year of production of the vehicle and the extent of its equipment.

36 Refer to the fusebox cover for fuse and circuit details.

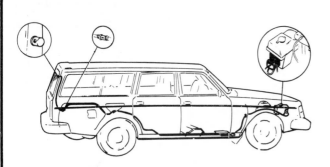

Fig. 13.194 Tailgate washer system – Estate 1981 on (Sec 12)

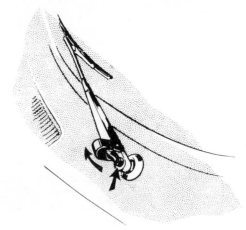

Fig. 13.195 Wiper arm attachment – 1981 and later models (Sec 12)

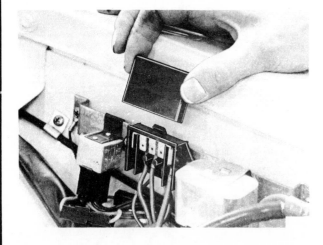

Fig. 13.196 Typical relay panel and junction box (Sec 12)

Fig. 13.197 Windscreen wiper interval relay (arrowed) (Sec 12)

Instrument panel
37 As from 1981 models the instrument panel has been revised as shown in Figs. 13.198 to 13.200.

Battery
38 Later models are fitted with a low maintenance battery on which the electrolyte level needs checking only once a year. However the terminals and battery exterior should be maintained as described in Chapter 10.

Electrically-operated boot lid lock
39 Some later models are fitted with an electrically-operated boot lid lock in addition to the normal key operation. The control button is located inside the glovebox.

Electrically-operated window regulator – description
40 On later models, some versions are equipped with an electrically-operated window lift mechanism.

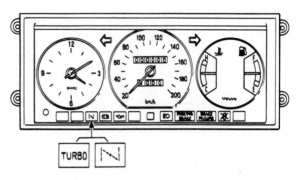

Fig. 13.198 Revised instrument panel (UK 1981 on) (Sec 12)

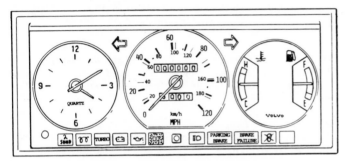

Fig. 13.199 Revised instrument panel (North American models 1981 on) (Sec 12)

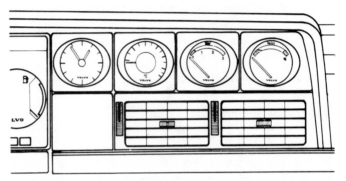

Fig. 13.200 Supplementary instruments on North American models (Sec 12)

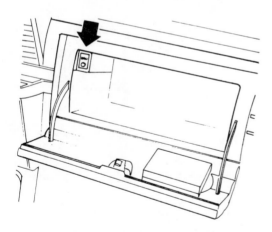

Fig. 13.201 Boot lid lock switch (Sec 12)

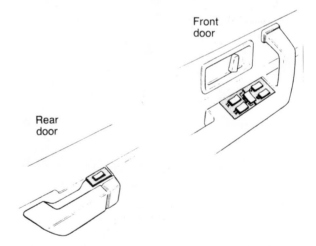

Fig. 13.202 Power-operated window control switches (Sec 12)

41 Access to the motors is obtained as described for manually-operated regulators in Chapter 12.
42 Failure of the system may be due to a blown fuse, check this first.
43 The control switches are located in the door armrests, those at the driver's door being of master type to control and override all the other switches.

Electrically-operated window regulator – removal, refitting and adjustment
44 With the door interior panel removed as described in Chapter 12, peel away the waterproof sheet.
45 Fully lower the window to its stop.
46 Release the regulator arms from the glass rail. Do this by pushing the safety brackets to loosen them, extracting the washers and levering the arms towards you.

47 Raise the glass fully by hand and prop or wedge it.
48 Disconnect the battery negative lead.
49 Remove the panel from under the end of the fascia, also the side panel from just forward of the front pillar.
50 Disconnect the electrical leads from the regulator motor. On some models this will mean dismounting the fusebox to disconnect the leads. In this case it is recommended that the leads are cut and a suitable connecting plug fitted to facilitate the operation on any future occasion.
51 Release the lifting arm from the side of the rail in the door, extract the regulator mounting screws and withdraw the mechanism through the access hole in the door.
52 To dismantle the mechanism, secure it in a vice and remove the electric motor.
53 Release the vice only very slowly and keep the fingers away from the mechanism as it is under spring tension.

54 When reassembling, grip the toothed ratchet quadrant in the vice and tension the regulator spring again, before fitting the electric motor.
55 Refitting to the door is a reversal of removal. Adjust in the following way.
56 Raise the window to its stop and then release the stop lug.
57 Try to raise the window further by operating the lift button. Adjust the stop lug against the toothed quadrant, then tighten the lug locknut.
58 Lower the window fully to its stop and then check that the lifting arm does not bottom in the slide fork. Adjust the stop lug if necessary to provide a clearance in the fork of approximately $1/32$ in (1.0 mm).

Central door locking system
59 On later models, a central door locking system is fitted either as standard or as an option depending upon the version.
60 Either by turning the cylinder lock on the driver's door or by depressing the interior lock plunger knob, all other doors are automatically locked. All doors are unlocked simultaneously when the driver's door is unlocked.
61 On five-door Estate models, the tailgate is included in the central locking circuit.
62 Actuation is accomplished by relays and solenoids (in the doors). The opening and closure of the driver's door is mechanical, simultaneous with the electrical switching of the other door locks.
63 The relays are mounted behind the clock on the facia panel. Access to the door lock solenoids is obtained after removing the door interior trim panel as described in Chapter 12.

Gearchange indicator
64 Some later models are equipped with a gearbox which incorporates a microprocessor-controlled gearchange indicator system as an aid to fuel economy.
65 A lamp indicates to the driver that a change to a higher gear is required.
66 The main components of the system are a control unit and a clutch pedal switch.
67 The control unit receives engine speed signals from terminal 1 on the injection coil and roadspeed information from the speedometer transmitter on the rear axle and, on vehicles so equipped, from the overdrive relay.
68 At engine start, the warning lamp comes on but goes out as soon as the vehicle is driven away.
69 By taking into account engine and roadspeeds, the control unit calculates the most desirable gear ratio and if changing to another gear is required, the indicator lamp illuminates. Operation of the clutch pedal switch signals the control unit that a change of gear has occurred.

Memory reprogramming
70 If the battery is disconnected or the power supply to the control unit is interrupted, then the memory will be erased.
71 To reprogramme, drive the vehicle in 2nd gear and each higher gear for an eight second period (each gear). The indicator lamp will flicker once as each gear programming is completed. Make sure that the foot is lifted completely from the clutch pedal after each gearchange.
72 Refer to wiring diagram (Fig. 13.232).

Headlamp bulbs and wiring circuit (North America)
73 1986 North American models are fitted with rectangular headlamps with renewable bulbs. Refer to wiring diagram (Fig. 13.233).

High level stop-lamp
74 This is fitted to 1986 North American Saloon models and is located inside the rear window.

Fig. 13.203 Power-operated window stop lug adjustment (arrowed) – window raised (Sec 12)

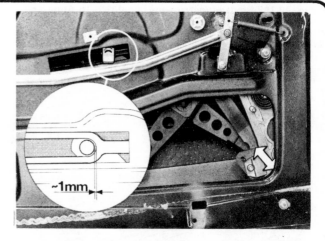

Fig. 13.204 Power-operated window stop lug adjustment (arrowed) – window lowered (Sec 12)

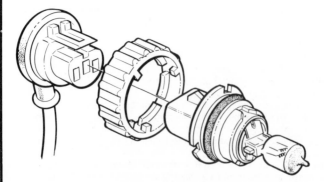

Fig. 13.205 Headlamp bulbs (North American models 1986) (Sec 12)

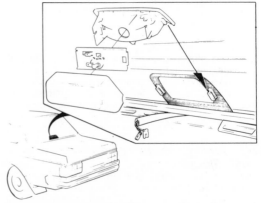

Fig. 13.206 High level brake stop-lamp (Sec 12)

Electronic speedometer

75 This is fitted in conjunction with the electric sensor on the rear axle ... 1986 models and referred to earlier in this Supplement. Refer to wiring diagram (Fig. 13.234).

Heated front seats

76 The driver's and passenger's front seats are electrically heated on some later models. A control switch is located in the centre console and the temperature is regulated by a thermostat.

Mobile radio equipment – interference-free installation

Aerials – selection and fitting

The choice of aerials is now very wide. It should be realised that the quality has a profound effect on radio performance, and a poor, inefficient aerial can make suppression difficult.

A wing-mounted aerial is regarded as probably the most efficient for signal collection, but a roof aerial is usually better for suppression purposes because it is away from most interference fields. Stick-on wire aerials are available for attachment to the inside of the windscreen, but are not always free from the interference field of the engine and some accessories.

Motorised automatic aerials rise when the equipment is switched on and retract at switch-off. They require more fitting space and supply leads, and can be a source of trouble.

There is no merit in choosing a very long aerial as, for example, the type about three metres in length which hooks or clips on to the rear of the car, since part of this aerial will inevitably be located in an interference field. For VHF/FM radios the best length of aerial is about one metre. Active aerials have a transistor amplifier mounted at the base and this serves to boost the received signal. The aerial rod is sometimes rather shorter than normal passive types.

A large loss of signal can occur in the aerial feeder cable, especially over the Very High Frequency (VHF) bands. The design of feeder cable is invariably in the co-axial form, ie a centre conductor surrounded by a flexible copper braid forming the outer (earth) conductor. Between the inner and outer conductors is an insulator material which can be in solid or stranded form. Apart from insulation, its purpose is to maintain the correct spacing and concentricity. Loss of signal occurs in this insulator, the loss usually being greater in a poor quality cable. The quality of cable used is reflected in the price of the aerial with the attached feeder cable.

The capacitance of the feeder should be within the range 65 to 75 picofarads (pF) approximately (95 to 100 pF for Japanese and American equipment), otherwise the adjustment of the car radio aerial trimmer may not be possible. An extension cable is necessary for a long run between aerial and receiver. If this adds capacitance in excess of the above limits, a connector containing a series capacitor will be required, or an extension which is labelled as 'capacity-compensated'.

Fitting the aerial will normally involve making a $^7/_8$ in (22 mm) diameter hole in the bodywork, but read the instructions that come with the aerial kit. Once the hole position has been selected, use a centre punch to guide the drill. Use sticky masking tape around the area for this helps with marking out and drill location, and gives protection to the paintwork should the drill slip. Three methods of making the hole are in use:

(a) Use a hole saw in the electric drill. This is, in effect, a circular hacksaw blade wrapped round a former with a centre pilot drill.

(b) Use a tank cutter which also has cutting teeth, but is made to shear the metal by tightening with an Allen key.

(c) The hard way of drilling out the circle is using a small drill, say $^1/_8$ in (3 mm), so that the holes overlap. The centre metal drops out and the hole is finished with round and half-round files.

Whichever method is used, the burr is removed from the body metal and paint removed from the underside. The aerial is fitted tightly ensuring that the earth fixing, usually a serrated washer, ring or clamp, is making a solid connection. *This earth connection is important in reducing interference.* Cover any bare metal with primer paint and topcoat, and follow by underseal if desired.

Aerial feeder cable routing should avoid the engine compartment and areas where stress might occur, eg under the carpet where feet will be located. Roof aerials require that the headlining be pulled back and that a path is available down the door pillar. It is wise to check with the vehicle dealer whether roof aerial fitting is recommended.

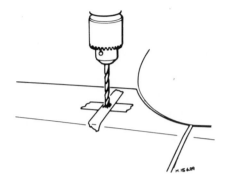

Fig. 13.207 Method of drilling the body (Sec 12)

Loudspeakers

Speakers should be matched to the output stage of the equipment, particularly as regards the recommended impedance. Power transistors used for driving speakers are sensitive to the loading placed on them.

Before choosing a mounting position for speakers, check whether the vehicle manufacturer has provided a location for them. Generally door-mounted speakers give good stereophonic reproduction, but not all doors are able to accept them. The next best position is the rear parcel shelf, and in this case speaker apertures can be cut into the shelf, or pod units may be mounted.

For door mounting, first remove the trim, which is often held on by 'poppers' or press studs, and then select a suitable gap in the inside door assembly. Check that the speaker would not obstruct glass or winder mechanism by winding the window up and down. A template is often provided for marking out the trim panel hole, and then the four fixing holes must be drilled through. Mark out with chalk and cut cleanly with a sharp knife or keyhole saw. Speaker leads are then threaded through the door and door pillar, if necessary drilling 10 mm diameter holes. Fit grommets in the holes and connect to the radio or tape unit correctly. Do not omit a waterproofing cover, usually supplied with door speakers. If the speaker has to be fixed into the metal of the door itself, use self-tapping screws, and if the fixing is to the door trim use self-tapping screws and flat spire nuts.

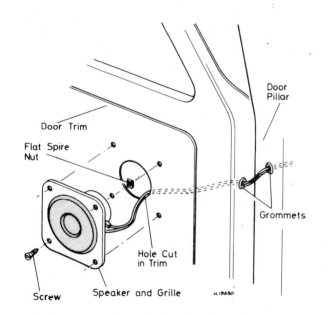

Fig. 13.208 Door mounted speaker installation (Sec 12)

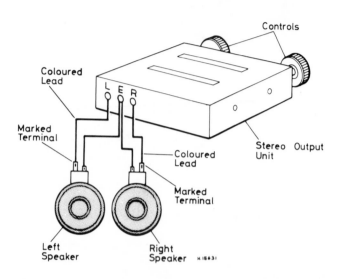

Fig. 13.209 Typical speaker connections (Sec 12)

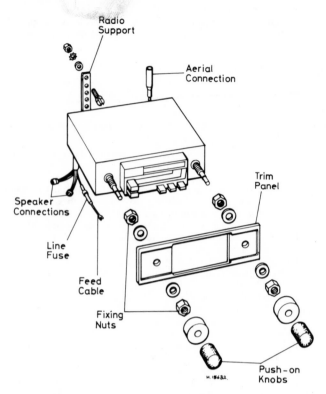

Fig. 13.210 Typical radio/cassette mounting components (Sec 12)

Rear shelf mounting is somewhat simpler but it is necessary to find gaps in the metalwork underneath the parcel shelf. However, remember that the speakers should be as far apart as possible to give a good stereo effect. Pod-mounted speakers can be screwed into position through the parcel shelf material, but it is worth testing for the best position. Sometimes good results are found by reflecting sound off the rear window.

Unit installation

Many vehicles have a dash panel aperture to take a radio/audio unit, a recognised international standard being 189.5 mm x 60 mm. Alternatively a console may be a feature of the car interior design and this, mounted below the dashboard, gives more room. If neither facility is available a unit may be mounted on the underside of the parcel shelf; these are frequently non-metallic and an earth wire from the case to a good earth point is necessary. A three-sided cover in the form of a cradle is obtainable from car radio dealers and this gives a professional appearance to the installation; in this case choose a position where the controls can be reached by a driver with his seat belt on.

Installation of the radio/audio unit is basically the same in all cases, and consists of offering it into the aperture after removal of the knobs (*not* push buttons) and the trim plate. In some cases a special mounting plate is required to which the unit is attached. It is worthwhile supporting the rear end in cases where sag or strain may occur, and it is usually possible to use a length of perforated metal strip attached between the unit and a good support point nearby. In general it is recommended that tape equipment should be installed at or nearly horizontal.

Connections to the aerial socket are simply by the standard plug terminating the aerial downlead or its extension cable. Speakers for a stereo system must be matched and correctly connected, as outlined previously.

Note: *While all work is carried out on the power side, it is wise to disconnect the battery earth lead.* Before connection is made to the vehicle electrical system, check that the polarity of the unit is correct. Most vehicles use a negative earth system, but radio/audio units often have a reversible plug to convert the set to either + or – earth. *Incorrect connection may cause serious damage.*

The power lead is often permanently connected inside the unit and terminates with one half of an in-line fuse carrier. The other half is fitted with a suitable fuse (3 or 5 amperes) and a wire which should go to a power point in the electrical system. This may be the accessory terminal on the ignition switch, giving the advantage of power feed with ignition or with the ignition key at the 'accessory' position. Power to the unit stops when the ignition key is removed. Alternatively, the lead may be taken to a live point at the fusebox with the consequence of having to remember to switch off at the unit before leaving the vehicle.

Before switching on for initial test, be sure that the speaker connections have been made, for running without load can damage the output transistors. Switch on next and tune through the bands to ensure that all sections are working, and check the tape unit if applicable. The aerial trimmer should be adjusted to give the strongest reception on a weak signal in the medium wave band, at say 200 metres.

Interference

In general, when electric current changes abruptly, unwanted electrical noise is produced. The motor vehicle is filled with electrical devices which change electric current rapidly, the most obvious being the contact breaker.

When the spark plugs operate, the sudden pulse of spark current causes the associated wiring to radiate. Since early radio transmitters used sparks as a basis of operation, it is not surprising that the car radio will pick up ignition spark noise unless steps are taken to reduce it to acceptable levels.

Interference reaches the car radio in two ways:

(a) by conduction through the wiring.
(b) by radiation to the receiving aerial.

Initial checks presuppose that the bonnet is down and fastened, the radio unit has a good earth connection (*not* through the aerial downlead outer), no fluorescent tubes are working near the car, the aerial trimmer has been adjusted, and the vehicle is in a position to receive radio signals, ie not in a metal-clad building.

Switch on the radio and tune it to the middle of the medium wave (MW) band off-station with the volume (gain) control set fairly high. Switch on the ignition (but do not start the engine) and wait to see if irregular clicks or hash noise occurs. Tapping the facia panel may also produce the effects. If so, this will be due to the voltage stabiliser, which is an on-off thermal switch to control instrument voltage. It is located usually on the back of the instrument panel, often attached to the speedometer. Correction is by attachment of a capacitor and, if still troublesome, chokes in the supply wires.

Switch on the engine and listen for interference on the MW band. Depending on the type of interference, the indications are as follows.

A harsh crackle that drops out abruptly at low engine speed or when the headlights are switched on is probably due to a voltage regulator.

A whine varying with engine speed is due to the dynamo or alternator. Try temporarily taking off the fan belt – if the noise goes this is confirmation.

Regular ticking or crackle that varies in rate with the engine speed is due to the ignition system. With this trouble in particular and others in general, check to see if the noise is entering the receiver from the wiring or by radiation. To do this, pull out the aerial plug, (preferably shorting out the input socket or connecting a 62 pF capacitor across it). If the noise disappears it is coming in through the aerial and is *radiation noise*. If the noise persists it is reaching the receiver through the wiring and is said to be *line-borne*.

Interference from wipers, washers, heater blowers, turn-indicators, stop lamps, etc is usually taken to the receiver by wiring, and simple treatment using capacitors and possibly chokes will solve the problem. Switch on each one in turn (wet the screen first for running wipers!) and listen for possible interference with the aerial plug in place and again when removed.

Electric petrol pumps are now finding application again and give rise to an irregular clicking, often giving a burst of clicks when the ignition is on but the engine has not yet been started. It is also possible to receive whining or crackling from the pump.

Note that if most of the vehicle accessories are found to be creating interference all together, the probability is that poor aerial earthing is to blame.

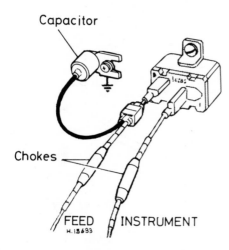

Fig. 13.211 Voltage stabiliser interference suppression (Sec 12)

Component terminal markings

Throughout the following sub-sections reference will be found to various terminal markings. These will vary depending on the manufacturer of the relevant component. If terminal markings differ from those mentioned, reference should be made to the following table, where the most commonly encountered variations are listed.

Alternator	Alternator terminal (thick lead)	Exciting winding terminal
DIN/Bosch	B +	DF
Delco Remy	+	EXC
Ducellier	+	EXC
Ford (US)	+	DF
Lucas	+	F
Marelli	+ B	F

Ignition coil	Ignition switch terminal	Contact breaker terminal
DIN/Bosch	15	1
Delco Remy	+	–
Ducellier	BAT	RUP
Ford (US)	B/+	CB/–
Lucas	SW/+	–
Marelli	BAT/+ B	D

Voltage regulator	Voltage input terminal	Exciting winding terminal
DIN/Bosch	B + /D +	DF
Delco Remy	BAT/+	EXC
Ducellier	BOB/BAT	EXC
Ford (US)	BAT	DF
Lucas	+/A	F
Marelli		F

Suppression methods – ignition

Suppressed HT cables are supplied as original equipment by manufacturers and will meet regulations as far as interference to neighbouring equipment is concerned. It is illegal to remove such suppression unless an alternative is provided, and this may take the form of resistive spark plug caps in conjunction with plain copper HT cable. For VHF purposes, these and 'in-line' resistors may not be effective, and resistive HT cable is preferred. Check that suppressed cables are actually fitted by observing cable identity lettering, or measuring with an ohmmeter – the value of each plug lead should be 5000 to 10 000 ohms.

A 1 microfarad capacitor connected from the LT supply side of the ignition coil to a good nearby earth point will complete basic ignition interference treatment. *NEVER fit a capacitor to the coil terminal to the contact breaker – the result would be burnt out points in a short time.*

If ignition noise persists despite the treatment above, the following sequence should be followed:

(a) Check the earthing of the ignition coil; remove paint from fixing clamp.

(b) If this does not work, lift the bonnet. Should there be no change in interference level, this may indicate that the bonnet is not electrically connected to the car body. Use a proprietary braided strap across a bonnet hinge ensuring a first class electrical connection. If, however, lifting the bonnet increases the interference, then fit resistive HT cables of a higher ohms-per-metre value.

(c) If all these measures fail, it is probable that re-radiation from metallic components is taking place. Using a braided strap between metallic points, go round the vehicle systematically – try the following: engine to body, exhaust system to body, front suspension to engine and to body, steering column to body (especially French and Italian cars), gear lever to engine and to body (again especially French and Italian cars), Bowden cable to body, metal parcel shelf to body. When an offending component is located it should be bonded with the strap permanently.

(d) As a next step, the fitting of distributor suppressors to each lead at the distributor end may help.

(e) Beyond this point is involved the possible screening of the distributor and fitting resistive spark plugs, but such advanced treatment is not usually required for vehicles with entertainment equipment.

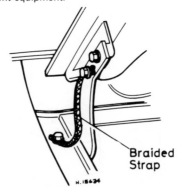

Fig. 13.212 Bonnet earth strap (Sec 12)

Electronic ignition systems have built-in suppression components, but this does not relieve the need for using suppressed HT leads. In some cases it is permitted to connect a capacitor on the low tension supply side of the ignition coil, but not in every case. Makers' instructions should be followed carefully, otherwise damage to the ignition semiconductors may result.

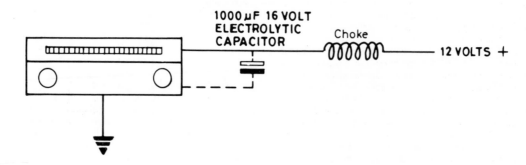

Fig. 13.213 Suppressor in radio supply line (Sec 12)

Suppression methods – generators

Alternators should be fitted with a 3 microfarad capacitor from the B+ main output terminal (thick cable) to earth. Additional suppression may be obtained by the use of a filter in the supply line to the radio receiver.

It is most important that:

(a) *Capacitors are never connected to the field terminals of the alternator.*

(b) *Alternators must not be run without connection to the battery.*

Suppression methods – voltage regulators

Alternator regulators come in three types:

(a) *Vibrating contact regulators separate from the alternator. Used extensively on continental vehicles.*

(b) *Electronic regulators separate from the alternator.*

(c) *Electronic regulators built-in to the alternator.*

In case (a) interference may be generated on the AM and FM (VHF) bands. For some cars a replacement suppressed regulator is available. Filter boxes may be used with non-suppressed regulators. But if not available, then for AM equipment a 2 microfarad or 3 microfarad capacitor may be mounted at the voltage terminal marked D+ or B+ of the regulator. FM bands may be treated by a feed-through capacitor of 2 or 3 microfarad.

Electronic voltage regulators are not always troublesome, but where necessary, a 1 microfarad capacitor from the regulator + terminal will help.

Integral electronic voltage regulators do not normally generate much interference, but when encountered this is in combination with alternator noise. A 1 microfarad or 2 microfarad capacitor from the warning lamp (IND) terminal to earth for Lucas ACR alternators and Femsa, Delco and Bosch equivalents should cure the problem.

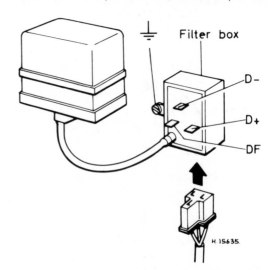

Fig. 13.214 Typical filter box for vibrating contact voltage regulator (alternator) (Sec 12)

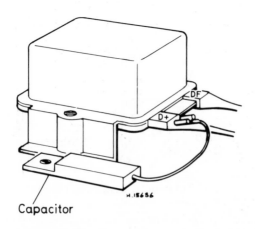

Fig. 13.215 Suppression of AM interference by vibrating contact voltage regulator (Sec 12)

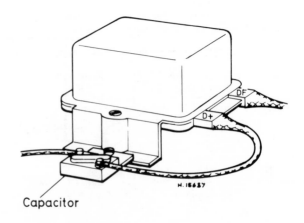

Fig. 13.216 Suppression of FM interference by vibrating contact voltage regulator (Sec 12)

Suppression methods – other equipment

Wiper motors – Connect the wiper body to earth with a bonding strap. For all motors use a 7 ampere choke assembly inserted in the leads to the motor.

Heater motors – Fit 7 ampere line chokes in both leads, assisted if necessary by a 1 microfarad capacitor to earth from both leads.

Electronic tachometer – The tachometer is a possible source of ignition noise – check by disconnecting at the ignition coil CB terminal. It usually feeds from ignition coil LT pulses at the contact breaker terminal. A 3 ampere line choke should be fitted in the tachometer lead at the coil CB terminal.

Horn – A capacitor and choke combination is effective if the horn is directly connected to the 12 volt supply. The use of a relay is an alternative remedy, as this will reduce the length of the interference-carrying leads.

Electrostatic noise – Characteristics are erratic crackling at the receiver, with disappearance of symptoms in wet weather. Often shocks may be given when touching bodywork. Part of the problem is

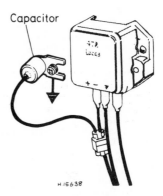

Fig. 13.217 Suppression of electronic voltage regulator (Sec 12)

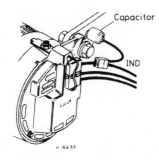

Fig. 13.218 Suppression of alternator integral type electronic voltage regulator (Sec 12)

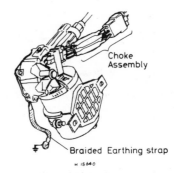

Fig. 13.219 Suppression of wiper motor (Sec 12)

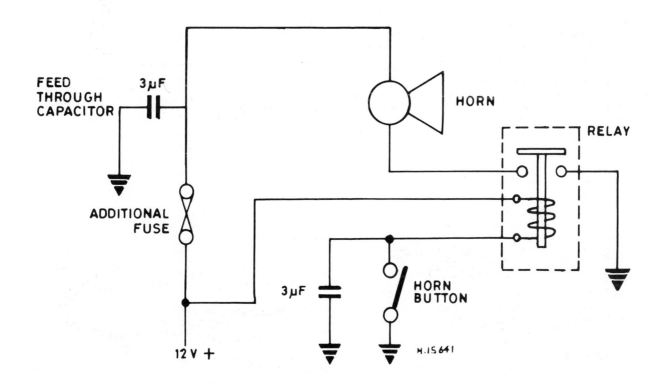

Fig. 13.220 Relay used to reduce horn interference (Sec 12)

the build-up of static electricity in non-driven wheels and the acquisition of charge on the body shell. It is possible to fit spring-loaded contacts at the wheels to give good conduction between the rotary wheel parts and the vehicle frame. Changing a tyre sometimes helps – because of tyres' varying resistances. In difficult cases a trailing flex which touches the ground will cure the problem. If this is not acceptable it is worth trying conductive paint on the tyre walls.

Fuel pump – Suppression requires a 1 microfarad capacitor between the supply wire to the pump and a nearby earth point. If this is insufficient a 7 ampere line choke connected in the supply wire near the pump is required.

Fluorescent tubes – Vehicles used for camping/caravanning frequently have fluorescent tube lighting. These tubes require a relatively high voltage for operation and this is provided by an inverter (a form of oscillator) which steps up the vehicle supply voltage. This can give rise to serious interference to radio reception, and the tubes themselves can contribute to this interference by the pulsating nature of the lamp discharge. In such situations it is important to mount the aerial as far away from a fluorescent tube as possible. The interference problem may be alleviated by screening the tube with fine wire turns spaced an inch (25 mm) apart and earthed to the chassis. Suitable chokes should be fitted in both supply wires close to the inverter.

Radio/cassette case breakthrough

Magnetic radiation from dashboard wiring may be sufficiently intense to break through the metal case of the radio/cassette player. Often this is due to a particular cable routed too close and shows up as ignition interference on AM and cassette play and/or alternator whine on cassette play.

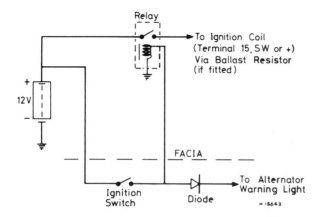

Fig. 13.221 Ignition coil relay used to suppress case breakthrough (Sec 12)

The first point to check is that the clips and/or screws are fixing all parts of the radio/cassette case together properly. Assuming good earthing of the case, see if it is possible to re-route the offending cable – the chances of this are not good, however, in most cars.

Next release the radio/cassette player and locate it in different positions with temporary leads. If a point of low interference is found, then if possible fix the equipment in that area. This also confirms that local radiation is causing the trouble. If re-location is not feasible, fit the radio/cassette player back in the original position.

Alternator interference on cassette play is now caused by radiation from the main charging cable which goes from the battery to the output terminal of the alternator, usually via the + terminal of the starter motor relay. In some vehicles this cable is routed under the dashboard, so the solution is to provide a direct cable route. Detach the original cable from the alternator output terminal and make up a new cable of at least 6 mm² cross-sectional area to go from alternator to battery with the shortest possible route. *Remember – do not run the engine with the alternator disconnected from the battery.*

Ignition breakthrough on AM and/or cassette play can be a difficult problem. It is worth wrapping earthed foil round the offending cable

run near the equipment, or making up a deflector plate well screwed down to a good earth. Another possibility is the use of a suitable relay to switch on the ignition coil. The relay should be mounted close to the ignition coil; with this arrangement the ignition coil primary current is not taken into the dashboard area and does not flow through the ignition switch. A suitable diode should be used since it is possible that at ignition switch-off the output from the warning lamp alternator terminal could hold the relay on.

Connectors for suppression components

Capacitors are usually supplied with tags on the end of the lead, while the capacitor body has a flange with a slot or hole to fit under a nut or screw with washer.

Connections to feed wires are best achieved by self-stripping connectors. These connectors employ a blade which, when squeezed down by pliers, cuts through cable insulation and makes connection to the copper conductors beneath.

Chokes sometimes come with bullet snap-in connectors fitted to the wires, and also with just bare copper wire. With connectors, suitable female cable connectors may be purchased from an auto-accessory shop together with any extra connectors required for the cable ends after being cut for the choke insertion. For chokes with bare wires, similar connectors may be employed together with insulation sleeving as required.

VHF/FM broadcasts

Reception of VHF/FM in an automobile is more prone to problems than the medium and long wavebands. Medium/long wave transmitters are capable of covering considerable distances, but VHF transmitters are restricted to line of sight, meaning ranges of 10 to 50 miles, depending upon the terrain, the effects of buildings and the transmitter power.

Because of the limited range it is necessary to retune on a long journey, and it may be better for those habitually travelling long distances or living in areas of poor provision of transmitters to use an AM radio working on medium/long wavebands.

When conditions are poor, interference can arise, and some of the suppression devices described previously fall off in performance at very high frequencies unless specifically designed for the VHF band. Available suppression devices include reactive HT cable, resistive distributor caps, screened plug caps, screened leads and resistive spark plugs.

For VHF/FM receiver installation the following points should be particularly noted:

(a) Earthing of the receiver chassis and the aerial mounting is important. Use a separate earthing wire at the radio, and scrape paint away at the aerial mounting.

(b) If possible, use a good quality roof aerial to obtain maximum height and distance from interference generating devices on the vehicle.

(c) Use of a high quality aerial downlead is important, since losses in cheap cable can be significant.

(d) The polarisation of FM transmissions may be horizontal, vertical, circular or slanted. Because of this the optimum mounting angle is at 45° to the vehicle roof.

Citizens' Band radio (CB)

In the UK, CB transmitter/receivers work within the 27 MHz and 934 MHz bands, using the FM mode. At present interest is concentrated on 27 MHz where the design and manufacture of equipment is less difficult. Maximum transmitted power is 4 watts, and 40 channels spaced 10 kHz apart within the range 27.60125 to 27.99125 MHz are available.

Aerials are the key to effective transmission and reception. Regulations limit the aerial length to 1.65 metres including the loading coil and any associated circuitry, so tuning the aerial is necessary to obtain optimum results. The choice of a CB aerial is dependent on whether it is to be permanently installed or removable, and the performance will hinge on correct tuning and the location point on the vehicle. Common practice is to clip the aerial to the roof gutter or to employ wing mounting where the aerial can be rapidly unscrewed. An alternative is to use the boot rim to render the aerial theftproof, but a popular solution is to use the 'magmount' – a type of mounting having a strong magnetic base clamping to the vehicle at any point, usually the roof.

Aerial location determines the signal distribution for both transmission and reception, but it is wise to choose a point away from the engine compartment to minimise interference from vehicle electrical equipment.

The aerial is subject to considerable wind and acceleration forces. Cheaper units will whip backwards and forwards and in so doing will alter the relationship with the metal surface of the vehicle with which it forms a ground plane aerial system. The radiation pattern will change correspondingly, giving rise to break-up of both incoming and outgoing signals.

Interference problems on the vehicle carrying CB equipment fall into two categories:

(a) Interference to nearby TV and radio receivers when transmitting.
(b) Interference to CB set reception due to electrical equipment on the vehicle.

Problems of break-through to TV and radio are not frequent, but can be difficult to solve. Mostly trouble is not detected or reported because the vehicle is moving and the symptoms rapidly disappear at the TV/radio receiver, but when the CB set is used as a base station any trouble with nearby receivers will soon result in a complaint.

It must not be assumed by the CB operator that his equipment is faultless, for much depends upon the design. Harmonics (that is, multiples) of 27 MHz may be transmitted unknowingly and these can fall into other user's bands. Where trouble of this nature occurs, low pass filters in the aerial or supply leads can help, and should be fitted in base station aerials as a matter of course. In stubborn cases it may be necessary to call for assistance from the licensing authority, or, if possible, to have the equipment checked by the manufacturers.

Interference received on the CB set from the vehicle equipment is, fortunately, not usually a severe problem. The precautions outlined previously for radio/cassette units apply, but there are some extra points worth noting.

It is common practice to use a slide-mount on CB equipment enabling the set to be easily removed for use as a base station, for example. Care must be taken that the slide mount fittings are properly earthed and that first class connection occurs between the set and slide-mount.

Vehicle manufacturers in the UK are required to provide suppression of electrical equipment to cover 40 to 250 MHz to protect TV and VHF radio bands. Such suppression appears to be adequately effective at 27 MHz, but suppression of individual items such as alternators/dynamos, clocks, stabilisers, flashers, wiper motors, etc, may still be necessary. The suppression capacitors and chokes available from auto-electrical suppliers for entertainment receivers will usually give the required results with CB equipment.

Other vehicle radio transmitters

Besides CB radio already mentioned, a considerable increase in the use of transceivers (ie combined transmitter and receiver units) has taken place in the last decade. Previously this type of equipment was fitted mainly to military, fire, ambulance and police vehicles, but a large business radio and radio telephone usage has developed.

Generally the suppression techniques described previously will suffice, with only a few difficult cases arising. Suppression is carried out to satisfy the 'receive mode', but care must be taken to use heavy duty chokes in the equipment supply cables since the loading on 'transmit' is relatively high.

Wiring diagrams

Owing to the large number of diagrams produced for these cars, it has only been possible to include a typical selection.

Wiring diagrams commence overleaf

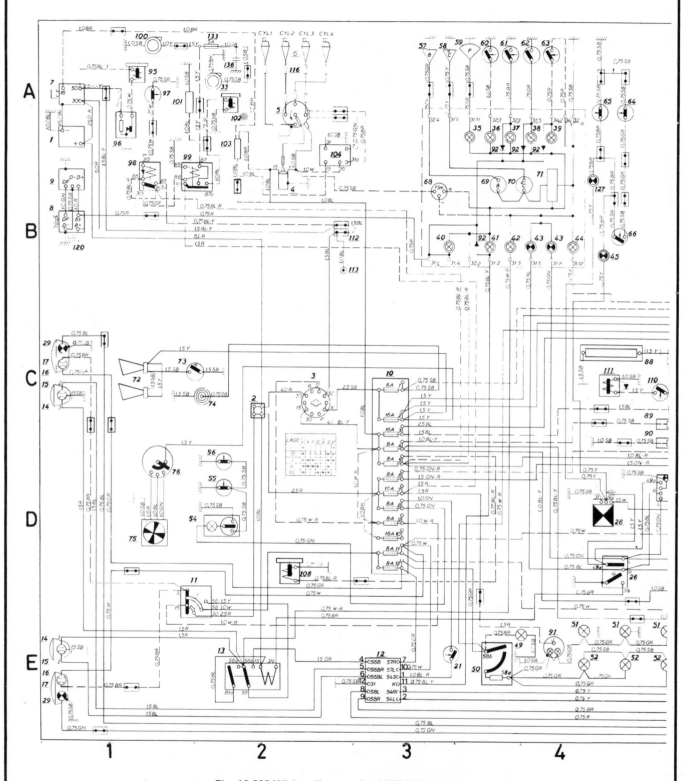

Fig. 13.222 Wiring diagram for 1977 UK models

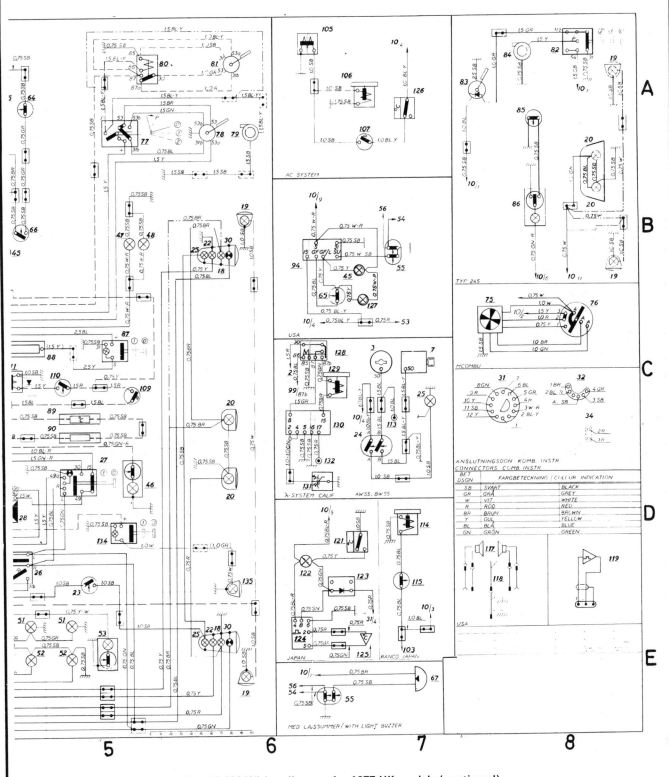

Fig. 13.222 Wiring diagram for 1977 UK models (continued)

Key to Fig. 13.222. Wiring diagram for 1977 UK models

Diagram for 1976 UK models similar

1	Battery	A1	37	Parking brake indicator light, 1.2 W	A4
2	Connection plate	C2	38	Brake warning light, 1.2 W	A4
3	Ignition switch	C2,C7	39	EGR indicator light, 1.2 W	A4
4	Ignition coil 1.2 A	B2	40	Battery charging warning light, 1.2 W	B3
5	Distributor	A2	41	Bulb failure warning light, 1.2 W	B4
6	Spark plugs	A2	42	Mainbeam indicator light, 1.2 W	B4
7	Starter motor, 800 W	A1,C7	43	Direction indicator panel light, 1.2 W	B4
8	Alternator, 760 W	B1	44	Overdrive indicator light, 1.2 W	B4
9	Charging regulator	B1	45	Fasten seat belt warning light, 1.2 W	B4,B7
10	Fusebox	C3	46	Engine compartment light, 15 W	D5
11	Lighting switch	D2	47	Fasten seat belt light, 1.2 W	B5
12	Bulb failure warning sensor	E3	48	Ashtray light, 1.2 W	B5
13	Step relay for full beams and dipped beams		49	Selector lever light, 1.2 W	E4
	and headlight flasher	E2	50	Rheostat for instrument panel light	E3
14	Mainbeam 60 W max	C1,E1	51	Instrument panel light, 2 W	E4,E5
15	Dipped beams, 55 W max	C1,E1	52	Control panel light, 1.2 W	E4,E5
16	Parking lights, 5 W	C1,E1	53	Glove locker light, 2 W	E5
17	Day running lights, 21 W	C1,E1	54	Courtesy light bulb, 10 W	D2
18	Tail lights, 5 W	B6,E6	55	Door switch, driver's side	B7,D2,E6
19	Side marker lights, 3 W	A8,B6	56	Door switch, passenger's side	D2
20	Number plate light, 5 W	C6,B8	57	Fuel gauge sender	A3
21	Stop-light switch	E3	58	Temperature gauge sender	A3
22	Stop-light, 21 W	B6, E6	59	Oil pressure sensor	A3
23	Switch on gearbox	D5	60	Choke contact	A3
24	Switch on automatic transmission	C7	61	Parking brake switch	A4
25	Reversing lights, 21 W	B6,C7	62	Brake warning switch	A4
26	Direction indicator stalk	D4	63	EGR/EXH warning switch	A4
27	Switch for hazard warning lights	D5	64	Switch, seat belt, passenger's seat	A4
28	Flasher device	D4	65	Switch, seat belt, driver's seat	A4
29	Front direction indicator light, 21 W	C1,E1	66	Switch, passenger's seat	B4
30	Rear direction indicator light, 21 W	B6,E6	67	Headlights on reminder buzzer	E7
31	Connection at instrument	C8	68	Rev counter	B3
32	Connection at instrument	C8	69	Fuel gauge	B3
33	Tank pump, 1.6 A	A2	70	Thermometer	B4
34	Connection at instrument	C8	71	Voltage stabilizer	B4
35	Oil pressure warning light, 1.2 W	A3	72	Horn 7.5 A	C1
36	Choke light, 1.2 W	A4	73	Horn pad	C2

Key to Fig. 13.222. Wiring diagram for 1977 UK models (continued)

74	Cigar lighter, 7 A	C2
75	Fan, 115 or 170 W	C8,D1
76	Fan switch	C8,D1
77	Switch for windscreen wipers/washers	A5
78	Windscreen wipers, 3.5 A	A6
79	Windscreen washer, 2.6 A	A6
80	Relay for headlight wipers	A5
81	Headlight wipers	A6
82	Switch for tailgate wiper/washer	A8
83	Tailgate wiper, 1 A	A7
84	Tailgate washer, 2.6 A	A8
85	Rear door switch	A8
86	Rear cargo space light, 10 W	B8
87	Switch for electrically heated rear window	C5
88	Electrically heated rear window, 150 W	C5
89	Heater element with thermostat, driver's seat cushion, 30 W	C5
90	Heater element, driver's seat backrest	C5
91	Clock	E4
92	Diode	
93	Joint	
94	Fasten seat belt reminder	A1
95	Cold start valve	A1
96	Thermal timer switch	A1
97	Fan, combined system	A1
98	Fan switch, fan combined system	A1
99	Relay for fuel pump	A1
100	Fuel pump, 6.5 A	A1
101	Control pressure regulator	A2
102	Auxiliary air valve	A1
103	Resistance, 0.4 to 0.6 ohm	A2
104	Control unit, ignition system	A6

105	Control magnet, compressor	A7
106	Solenoid valve	A7
107	Switch for air conditioning	D2
108	Solenoid valve, carburettor	C5
109	Switch for overdrive	C5
110	Switch for overdrive on gearbox M 46	C4
111	Control magnet for overdrive 2.2 A on gearbox M 46	B3
112	Coupling	B3,C7
113	Power output	D7
114	Thermostat	D7
116	Suppressor	A2
117	Loudspeaker, front doors, 4 ohms	D7
118	Antenna, windscreen	D8
119	Top dead centre sender	D8
120	Capacitor, 2.2μ F	B1
121	Thermostat, floor, 149°C	D6
122	Exhaust temp. indicator light	D6
123	Diode box	D7
124	Temperature sensor, 850°C	E6
125	Thermoelement, catalyst	E7
126	Thermostat AC	A7
127	Fasten seat belt warning light	B4
128	Switch for rear foglights	C6
129	Relay for Lambda system	E1
130	Control unit, Lambda system	C6
131	Lambda-sond	D6
132	Test point, Lambda-sond	D6
133	Cable fusing, tank pump	A2
134	Motor for window winder, RH side front	D5
135	Rear foglights	D6
136	Condenser, tank pump	A2

Colour code

BL	Blue	R	Red
BR	Brown	SB	Black
GN	Green	W	White
GR	Grey	Y	Yellow

Key to Fig. 13.223. Wiring diagram for 1980 UK models

Diagrams for 1978 and 1979 UK models similar

1	Battery	B1
2	Connection plate	C3
3	Ignition switch	A2,C3
4	Ignition coil	C2
5	Distributor	C1
6	Spark plugs	C1
7	Starter motor	A1,A2,B1
8	Alternator	A2
9	Charging regulator	B2
10	Fusebox	C3
11	Light switch	B4
12	Bulb failure warning sensor	C5
13	Step relay for full beams and dipped beams and headlight flasher	B5
14	Full beams	A3,A4,A5
15	Dipped beams	A3,A5
16	Parking lights	A3,A5
17	Day running lights	A3,A5
18	Tail lights	F2,F5,G5
19	Side marker lights	G5
20	Number plate lights	F3,G5
21	Stop-light switch	D5,G2
22	Stop-light	F2,F5,G5
23	Reversing lights contact, manual gearbox	E4
24	Reversing lights contact, automatic transmission	A2
25	Reversing lights	A2,F2,F5
26	Direction indicator stalk	E4
27	Switch for hazard warning flashers	E3
28	Flasher device	E4
29	Front direction indicator light	A3,A5
30	Rear direction indicator light	F2,F5,G5
31	Connection at instrument	L3
32	Connection at instrument	L3
33	Tank pump	B1
34	Connection at instrument	L3
35	Oil pressure warning light	D1
36	Choke light	D1
37	Parking brake indicator light	D1
38	Brake warning light	D1
40	Battery charging warning light	D2
41	Bulb failure warning light	D2
42	Full beams indicator light	D2
43	Direction indicator panel light	D2
44	Overdrive indicator light	E2
45	Fasten seat belt warning light, front	E2,L2
46	Engine compartment light	B3
47	Belt lock light	E2
48	Ashtray light	E2
49	Selector lever light	D5
50	Rheostat for instrument panel light	D5
51	Instrument panel light	E5

52	Control and panel light	E5
53	Glove locker light	E5
54	Courtesy light bulb	B4
55	Door switch, driver's side	B4,C1,L2
56	Door switch, passenger's side	B3,B4,G1
57	Fuel gauge sender	D1
58	Temperature gauge sender	D1
59	Oil pressure sensor	D1
60	Choke contact	D1
61	Parking brake switch	D1
62	Brake warning switch	D1
63	Lambda-sond switch	D1
64	Switch, seatbelt, passenger's seat	E1
65	Switch, seatbelt, driver's seat	E1,K2
66	Switch, passenger's seat	E2
67	Headlights ON ignition key IN reminder buzzer	C4
68	Rev counter	D2
69	Fuel gauge	D2
70	Temperature gauge	D2
71	Voltage stabilizer	D2
72	Horn	B3
73	Horn pad (button)	B3
74	Cigar lighter	C2
75	Car heater (standard)	B4
76	Switch for car heater blower	B3
77	Switch for windscreen wipers/washers	F1
78	Windscreen wipers	F1
79	Windscreen washers	F1
80	Relay for headlight wipers	K2
81	Headlight wipers	K3
82	Switch for tailgate wiper/washer	G2
83	Tailgate wiper	G2
84	Tailgate washer	G3
85	Rear door switch	G4
86	Rear cargo space light	F4
87	Switch for electrically heated rear window	E3
88	Electrically heated rear window	E3
89	Heater element and thermostat, driver's seat cushion	E3
90	Heater element, driver's seat, backrest	E3
91	Clock	D5,H1,L1
92	Diode	D1,D2,E3
93	Connector	
94	Fasten seat belt reminder	L2
95	Cold start injector	B1
96	Thermal timer switch	B1
97	Fan heater, combined system	K5
98	Switch for fan combined system	L5
99	Relay for fuel pump	B1
100	Fuel pump	B1
101	Control pressure regulator	B1
102	Auxiliary air valve	B1

Key to Fig. 13.223. Wiring diagram for 1980 UK models (continued)

103	Resistance	B1	161	Control unit, Lambda system	L3
104	Control unit, ignition system	C1	162	Lambda-sond	K3
105	Control magnet, compressor	H5	163	Interval wipe relay, rear window	G3
106	Solenoid valve	K5	164	Control unit, preheating, diesel	H4
107	Switch for air-conditioning (with thermostat)	H5	165	Relay, preheating (glow) current	K4
109	Switch for overdrive M46	E3	166	For glow plugs	K4
110	Switch for overdrive on gearbox M46	E3	167	Relay, delayed courtesy lighting	G4
111	Control magnet for overdrive on gearbox M46	E3	168	Relay for elec. cooling fan	H5
112	Coupling	C2	169	Thermostat for elec, cooling fan	G5
113	Power socket, starter motor	A2,C2	170	Motor for elec. cooling fan	G5
114	Thermostat	L4	171	Heater element with thermostat, passenger's	
116	Damper resistance	C1		seat cushion	G2
117	Loudspeaker, front doors	L5	172	Heater element, passenger's seat backrest	G2
118	Antenna, windscreen	L5	173	Switch, heater element, passenger's seat	F1
119	Top dead centre sender	K3	174	Cigar lighter, rear	G1
120	Capacitor	B2	175	Switch, rear cargo space light	G1
122	Exhaust temperature indicator light	L4	176	Courtesy light, left	G1
123	Diode box	L4	177	Courtesy light, right	G1
124	Temperature sensor	L4	178	To switch for motor-driven antenna	G1
125	Thermo element, catalyst	K4	179	Motor-driven antenna	G1
126	Relay for window winders	H3	180	Headlamp wipers	E1,F1
127	Rear foglights	F2,F4,F5	181	Solenoid valve, carburettor, or fuel valve diesel	C4
128	Switch for rear foglights	E4	182	Diode, Lambda-sond indicator light	D1
129	Delay relay for air-conditioning	K5	183	Lambda-sond indicator light or indicator light	
130	Rear cargo space light	E3		for glow current, diesel	D1
135	Fasten seatbelt warning light, rear	E2,L2	184	Switch for window winder, driver's side	H2,K2
136	Main switch for window winders, rear	H2	185	Switch for window winder, passenger's side,	
137	Switch for window winder, LH side rear	G4		front	H4,K4
138	Motor for window winder, LH side rear	G4	186	Motor for window winder, passenger's side,	
139	Switch for window winder, RH side rear	H4		front	H4
140	Motor for window winder, RH side rear	G5	187	Motor for window winder, driver's side	H3,K3
141	Switch for electrically operated rear view mirror, LH side	K2	188	Relay for central lock, opening all doors	H1,K1
142	Electrically operated rear view mirror, LH side	H2	189	Relay for central lock, locking all doors	K1,L1
143	Switch for electrically operated rear view mirror, RH side	K2	190	Switch for central lock, link rod	H1,L1
144	Electrically operated rear view mirror, RH side	K2	191	Switch for central lock, key	K1,L1
147	Fusebox, headlights, Italy	B5	192	Motor for central lock, passenger's side	H1,L1
148	Relay for windscreen interval wipe	E1	193	Motor for central lock, LH side, rear	K1
149	Test point, Lambda-sond	L4	194	Motor for central lock, RH side, rear	K1
150	Side direction indicators	B3,B5	195	Motor for central lock, tailgate (245, 265)	K1
152	Spotlights	G4	196	Motor for central lock, driver's door 262 C	H1
153	Relay for spotlights	H4	197	Switch for central lock, armrest 262 C	K1
154	Switch, spotlights	H4	198	Switch for cruise holder	G1
155	Road bend and foglights	G4,G5	199	Control unit for cruise holder	H2
156	Relay for road bend and foglights	H5	200	Pick-up coil for cruise holder	H2
157	Switch for road bend and foglights	H4	201	Retardation switch for cruise holder	G2
158	Temperature gauge sensor	H4	202	Switch, clutch pedal, for cruise holder	H2
159	Relay for Lambda-sond	L3	203	Servo for cruise holder	H2
160	Frequency valve	L4	204	Microswitch, Lambda-sond	K4
			210	Relay for control unit, diesel	K4
			211	Cable fusing 4 A	G2

For colour code see key to Fig. 13.222

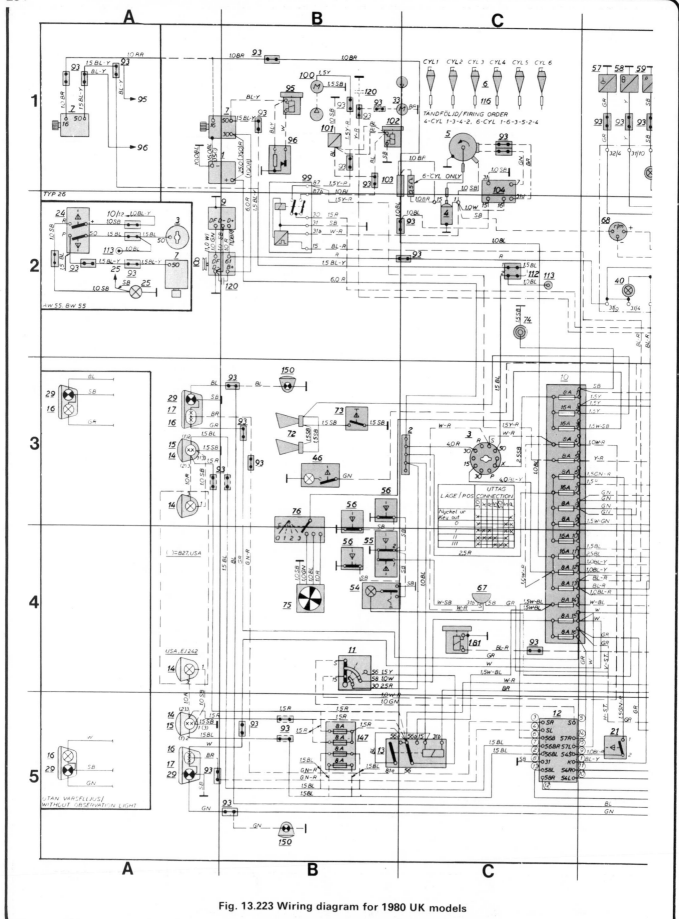

Fig. 13.223 Wiring diagram for 1980 UK models

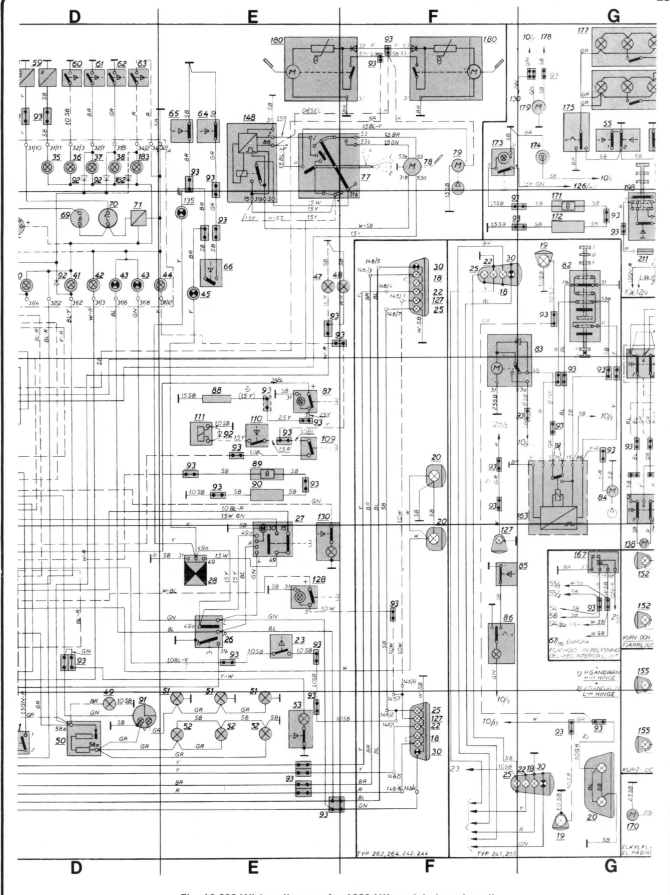

Fig. 13.223 Wiring diagram for 1980 UK models (continued)

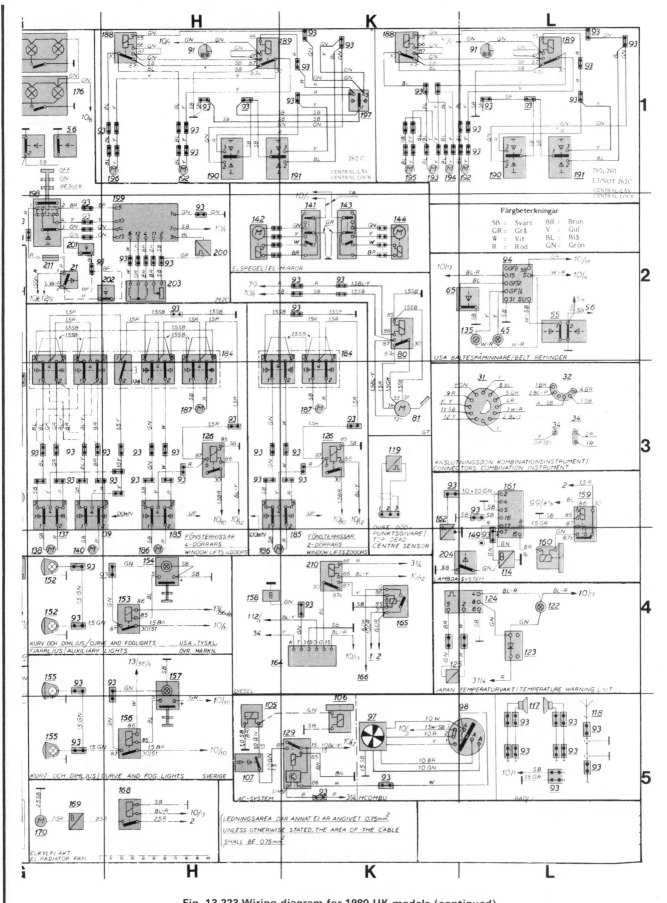

Fig. 13.223 Wiring diagram for 1980 UK models (continued)

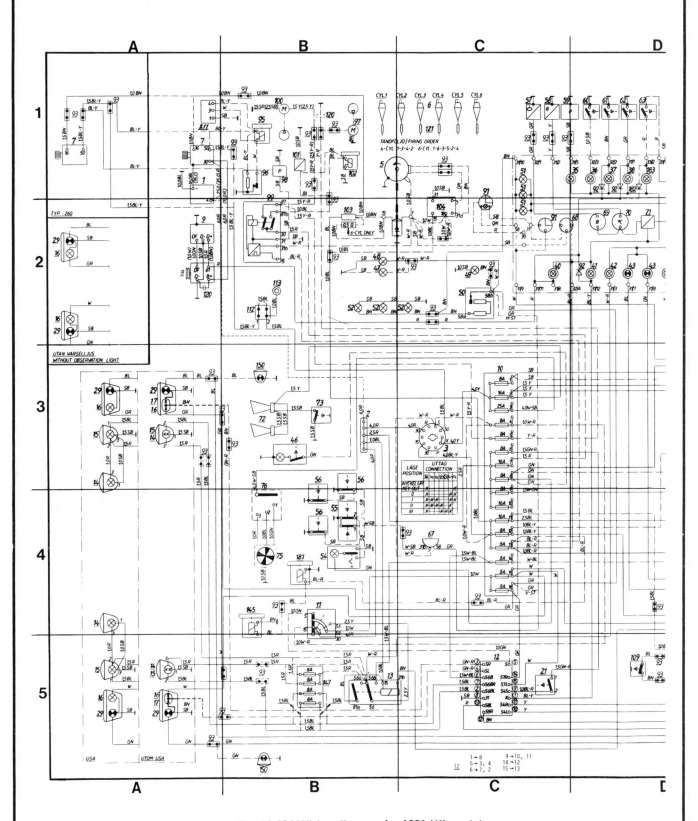

Fig. 13.224 Wiring diagram for 1981 UK models

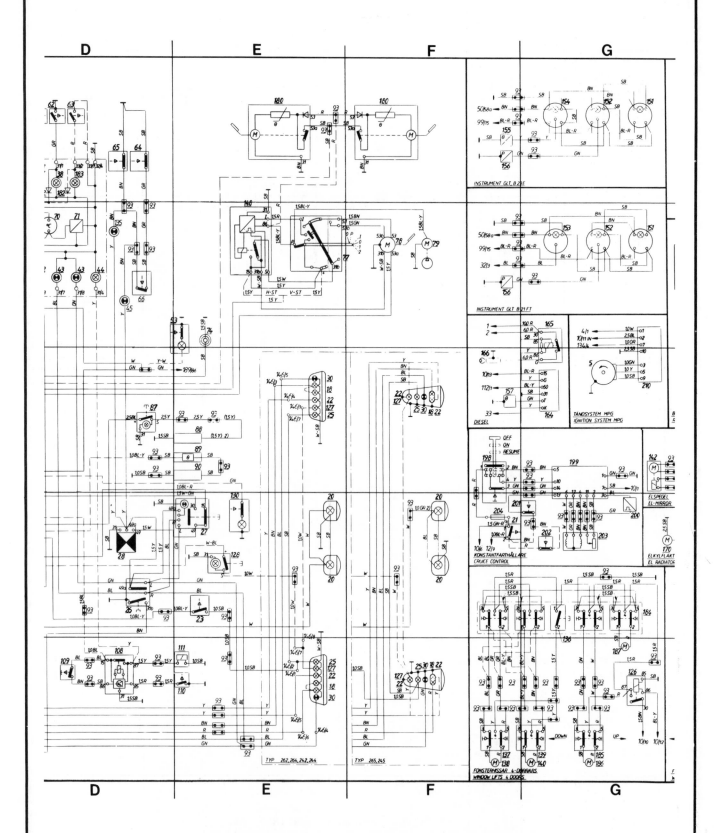

Fig. 13.224 Wiring diagram for 1981 UK models (continued)

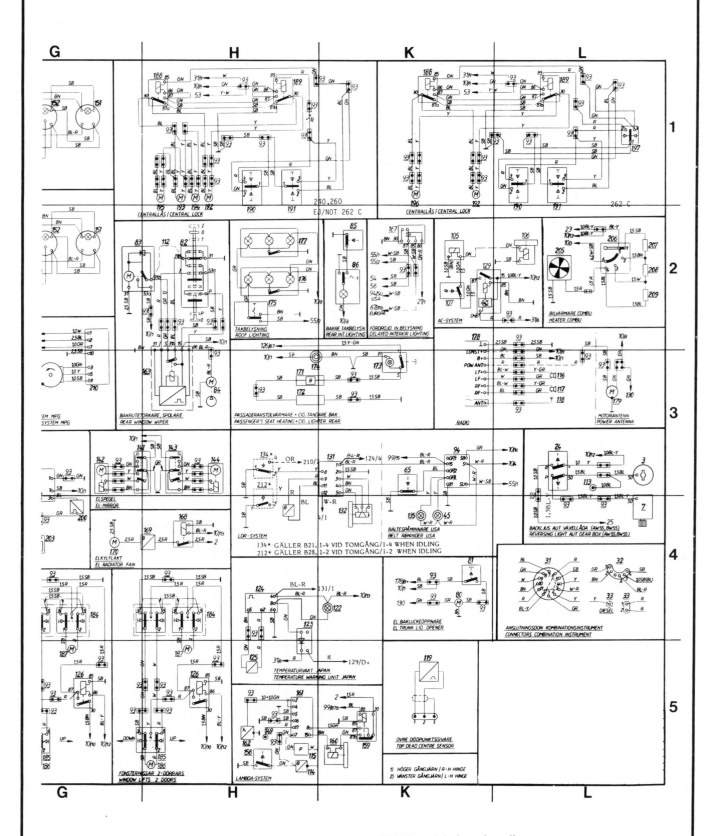

Fig. 13.224 Wiring diagram for 1981 UK models (continued)

Key to Fig. 13.224. Wiring diagram for 1981 UK models

Diagrams for 1982 to 1984 UK models similar

1	Battery	A1
2	Junction box	B3
3	Ignition switch	C3,L3
4	Ignition coil	B2
5	Distributor	B1,G3
6	Spark plugs	C1
7	Starter motor	A1,L4
8	Alternator	A2
9	Charging regulator	A2
10	Fusebox	C3
11	Light switch	B4
12	Bulb failure warning sensor	C5
13	Step relay for full/dipped beams and headlight flasher	B5
14	Full beams	A3,A4,A5
15	Dipped beams	A3,A5
16	Parking light	A2,A3,A5
17	Day running lights	A3,A5
18	Tail light	E3,E5,F3,F5
20	Number plate light	E4,F4
21	Brake light switch	C5,F4
22	Brake light	E3,E5,F3,F5
23	Reversing light contact, man. gearbox	E4
24	Reversing light contact, auto transmission	L3
25	Reversing light	E3,E5,F3,F5
26	Direction indicator stalk	D4
27	Switch, hazard warning flasher	E4
28	Flasher device	D4
29	Front direction indicator	A2,A3,A5
30	Rear direction indicator	E3,E5,F3,F5
31	Connection at instrument	L4
32	Connection at instrument	L4
33	Connection at instrument	L4
35	Oil pressure warning light	D1
36	Choke light	D1
37	Parking brake indicator light	D1
38	Brake warning light	D1
40	Battery charging warning light	C2
41	Bulb failure warning light	D2
42	Full beams indicator light	D2
43	Direction indicator panel light	D2
44	Overdrive indicator light	D2
45	Fasten seat belt warning light	D2,K4
46	Engine compartment light	B3
47	Seat belt lock light	B2
48	Ashtray light	B2
49	Gear selector light	C2
50	Rheostat for instrument panel light	C2
51	Instrument panel light	C1,C2
52	Control and panel light	B2,C2
53	Glove compartment light	E2
54	Courtesy light	B4
55	Door switch, driver's side	B4
56	Door switch, passenger's side	B3,B4
57	Fuel level sender	C1

58	Temperature sender	C1
59	Oil pressure sensor	C1
60	Contact: choke control	D1
61	handbrake	D1
62	brake warning	D1
63	Lambda-sond	D1
64	seat belt, passenger's seat	D1
65	seat belt, driver's seat	D1,K3
66	passenger's seat	D2
67	Headlights ON ignition key IN reminder buzzer	C4
68	Rev counter	D2
69	Fuel gauge	D2
70	Temperature gauge	D2
71	Voltage stabilizer	D2
72	Horn, 7.5A	B3
73	Horn pad (button)	B3
74	Cigar lighter 7A	E2
75	Heater fan (standard) 115W	B4
76	Switch for heater fan	B3
77	Switch for windscreen wash/pipe	E2
78	Windscreen wiper 3.5A	F2
79	Windscreen washer 3.4A	F2
80	Boot lock motor 0.6A	K4
81	Boot lock contact	K4
82	Switch for tailgate wash/wipe	H2
83	Tailgate wiper 1A	G2
84	Tailgate washer 2.6A	H3
85	Rear door switch	K2
86	Rear courtesy light	K2
87	Switch, heated rear window	D3
88	Heated rear window 150W	E3
89	Heater element and thermostat, driver's seat cushion 30W	E3
90	Heater element, driver's seat backrest 30W	E3
91	Clock	C1,C2
92	Diode	D1,D2
93	Connector	
94	Fasten seat belt reminder	K3
95	Cold start device	B1
96	Thermal timer switch cold start device	B1
97	Tank pressure 1.6A	B1
98	Air pressure sensor for turbo	B1
99	Relay for fuel pump	B1
100	Fuel pump 6.5A	B1
101	Control pressure regulator	B1
102	Auxiliary air valve	B1
103	Resistance 0.9 Ω/4cyl. 0.5 Ω/6 cyl	B2
104	Control unit, ignition system	C2
105	Control solenoid, for compressor, air cond. 3.9A	K2
106	Solenoid valve	L2
107	Switch for air conditioning (with thermostat)	K2

Key to Fig. 13.224. Wiring diagram for 1981 UK models (continued)

108	Relay for overdrive	D5	162	Lambda-sond	H5
109	Switch for overdrive, M46	D5	163	Intermittent wipe relay, tailgate	H3
110	Contact for overdrive on M46	E5	164	Control unit, preheating, diesel	G3
111	Control magnet for overdrive on M46		165	Relay, preheating (glow) current – diesel	G2
	2.2A	E5	166	Glow plug – diesel	F3
112	Coupling	B2,H2	167	Relay, delayed courtesy light	K2
113	Power socket for running starter motor	B2,L3	168	Relay for elec. cooling fan	H4
114	Thermostat, Lambda system	H5	169	Thermostat for elec. cooling fan 100°C	H4
115	Pressure contact, Lambda system	H5	170	Motor for elec. cooling fan 13A	G4
116	Loudspeaker, LH front door 4	L3	171	Heater element with thermostat, passenger's	
117	Loudspeaker, RH front door 4	L3		seat cushion 30W	H3
118	Antenna, windscreen	L3	172	Heater element, passenger's seat backrest	H3
119	TDC sender for monotester	K5	173	Switch, heater element, passenger's seat	K3
120	Capacitor 2.2mF	A2,B1	174	Cigar lighter, rear 7A	H3
121	Damper resistance, spark plugs	C1	175	Switch, courtesy light	H2
122	Exhaust temperature indicator light		176	Courtesy light, left	H2
	(Japan)	K4	177	Courtesy light, right	H2
123	Diode box (Japan)	H4	178	Radio	K2
124	Temperature sensor (Japan) 850°C	H4	179	Elec. antenna 3A	L3
125	Thermal element, catalyst (Japan)	H5	180	Headlamp wiper 1A	E1,F1
126	Relay for window winders	G5,H5	181	Solenoid valve, carburettor, or fuel valve diesel	B4
127	Rear foglight	E3,E5,F3,F5	182	Diode, Lambda-sond indicator light	D1
128	Switch, rear foglight	E4	183	Lambda-sond indicator light or indicator light	
129	Delay relay for air-conditioning	K2		for flow current – diesel	D1
130	Boot light	E4	184	Switch for window winder, driver's side	G4,H4
131	Control unit CIS (constant idle speed system)	K3	185	Switch for window winder, passenger's side,	
132	Idle valve CIS	K4		front	G5,H5
133	Temp. sender CIS	H4	186	Motor for window winder, passenger's side,	
134	Microswitch CIS	H3		front 5A	G5,H5
135	Fasten seatbelt warning, rear	D2,K4	187	Motor for window winder, driver's side 5A	G5,H5
136	Main switch for window winders, rear	G4	188	Relay for central lock, opening	H1,K1
137	Switch for window winder, LH side rear	F5	189	Relay for central lock, locking	H1,L1
138	Motor for window winder, RH side, rear 5A	F5	190	Switch for central lock, link rod	H2,L1
139	Switch for window winder, RH side, rear	G5	191	Switch for central lock key	H2,L1
140	Motor for window winder, RH side, rear 5A	G5	192	Motor for central lock, passenger's side	H1,K1
141	Switch for elec. rear view mirror, LH side	G3	193	Motor for central lock, LH side, rear	H1
142	Elec. rear view mirror, LH side	G3	194	Motor for central lock, RH side, rear	H1
143	Switch for elec. rear view mirror, RH side	H3	195	Motor for central lock, rear door (245/265)	H1
144	Elec. rear view mirror, RH side	H3	196	Motor for central lock. driver's side 262C	K1
145	Hot start valve	B4	197	Switch for central lock, arm rest 262C	L1
146	Junction 8 poles	E3,E5	198	Switch for cruise control	F3
147	Fusebox, headlamps Italy	B5	199	Control unit for cruise control	G3
148	Relay for intermittent windscreen wipe	E2	200	Pick-up coil for cruise control	G4
149	Test point, Lambda-sond	H5	201	Retardation switch for cruise control	F4
150	Side direction indicators	B3,B5	202	Switch, clutch pedal, for cruise control	G4
151	Voltmeter	G1,G2	203	Servo for cruise control	G4
152	Oil pressure gauge	G1,G2	204	Fuse, cruise control 4A	F4
153	Charge pressure gauge for Turbo	G2	205	Heater fan CU	L2
154	Ambient temp. gauge	G1	206	Switch, Heater fan CU	L2
155	Ambient gauge sender	F1	207	Resistance 1.9 ohms	L2
156	Oil pressure sender	F1,F2	208	Resistance 0.7 ohms	L2
157	Temperature sender, diesel	F3	209	Resistance 0.2 ohms	L2
158	Microswitch Lambda-sond	H5	210	Control unit, ignition system MPG	G3
159	Relay for Lambda-sond	K5	211	Impulse relay, cold start device	A1
160	Frequency valve	K5	212	Microswitch	L5
161	Control unit, Lambda system	H5			

Colour code

BL	Blue	R	Red	
BN	Brown	SB	Black	
GN	Green	VO	Violet	
GR	Grey	W	White	
OR	Orange	Y	Yellow	

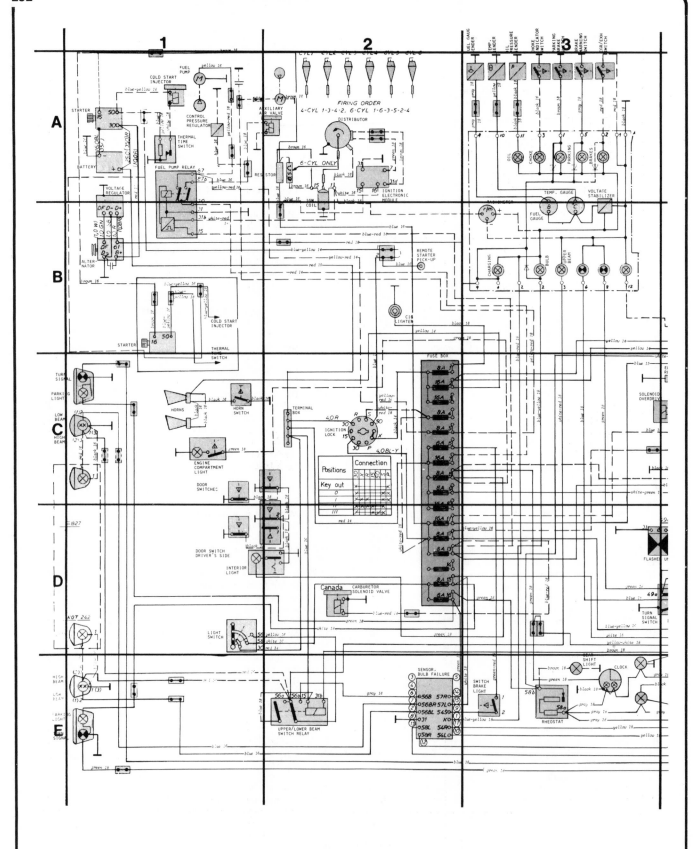

Fig. 13.225 Wiring diagram for 1979 North American models

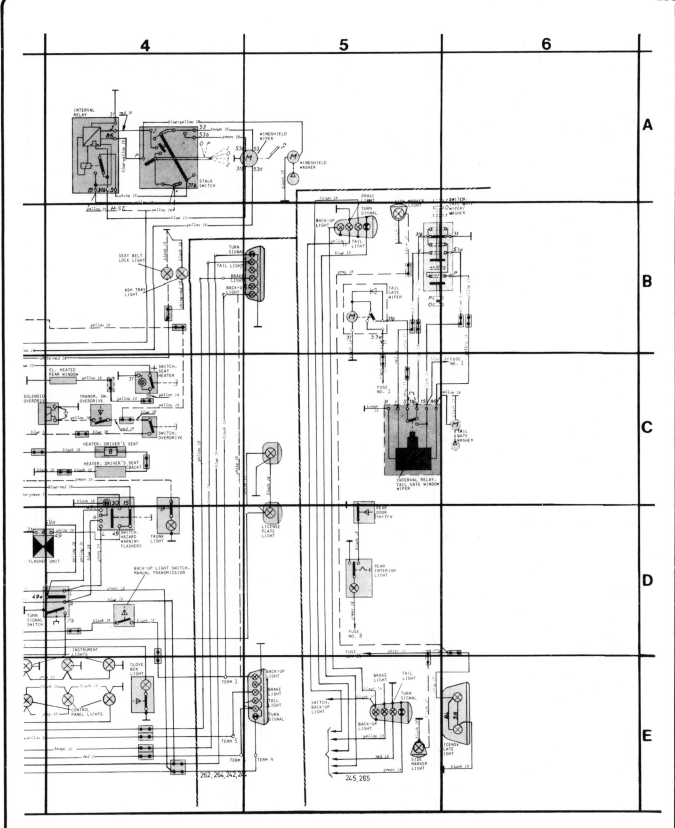

Fig. 13.225 Wiring diagram for 1979 North American models (continued)

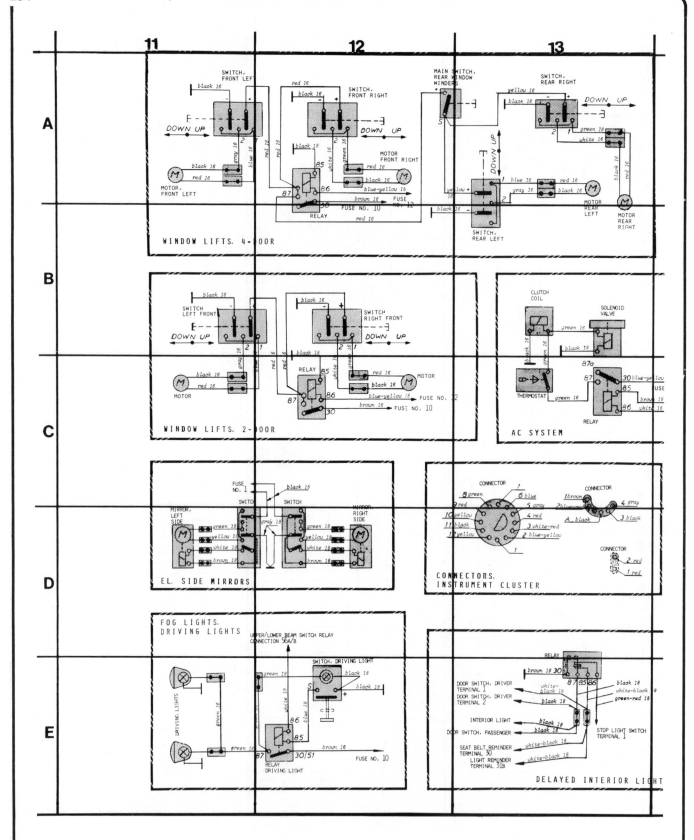

Fig. 13.225 Wiring diagram for 1979 North American models (continued)

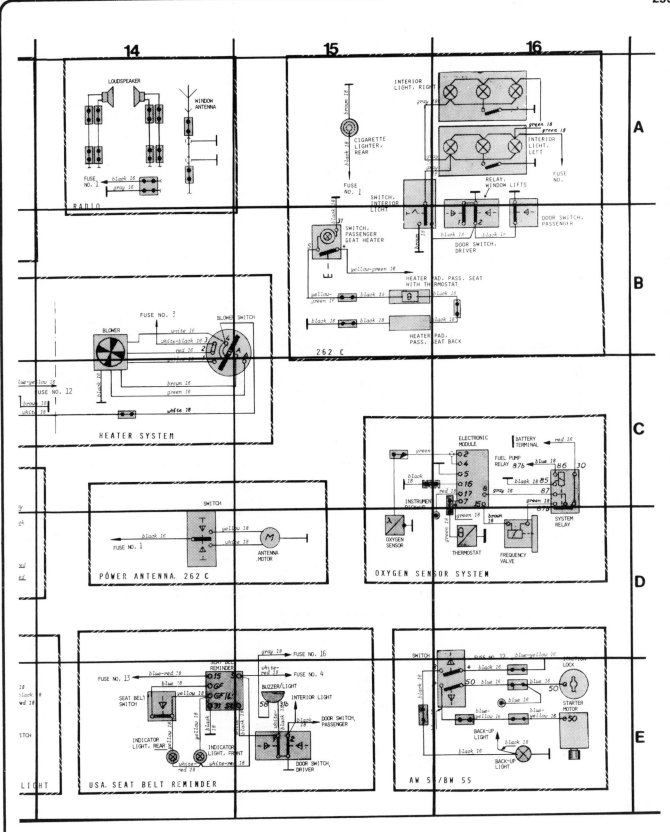

Fig. 13.225 Wiring diagram for 1979 North American models (continued)

Key to Fig. 13.225. Wiring diagram for 1979 North American models

Diagrams for 1980 and 1981 North American models similar

AC system	C13	Parking lights: front	C1,E1
Alternator	B1	rear	B5,E5
Ashtray light	B4	Power antenna, 262C	D14
Automatic transmission	E15	Radio	A14
Auxiliary air valve	A2	Relay, upper/lower beam	E2
Battery	A1	Remote starter pick-up	B2
Brake lights	B5,E5	Rheostat, instrument lights	E3
Carburettor solenoid relay (Canada)	D2	Seat belt lock light	B4
Cigarette lighter	B2	Seat belt reminder	E14
Clock	E3	Seat heater	C4
Cold start injector	A1	Sender, for gauges	A3
Connectors, instrument cluster	D12	Sensor, bulb failure	E2
Control panel lights	E4	Side mirrors	D11
Control pressure regulator	A1	Spark plugs	A2
Delayed interior light	E13	Starter	B1
Distributor	A2	Switch: back-up lights	D4
Door switches	D2	brake lights	E3
Electrically heated rear window	C4	door	D2
Engine compartment light	C1	hazard warning flashers	D4
Flasher unit	D4	overdrive	C4
Fuel pump relay	B1	rear door	D5
Fuse box	C1	seat heater	C4
Gauges: fuel	B3	stalk	A4
temperature	B3	tailgate wiper/washer	B6
Gear shift light	E3	turn signal	D4
Glovebox light	E4	Tachometer	B3
Heater system	C14	Tail lights	B5,E5
Horns	C1	Tail lights, 245/265	B6,E6
Ignition coil	B2	Thermal time switch	A1
Ignition electronic module	B2	Trunk light	D4
Ignition lock	C2	Turn signal: front	C1,E1
Indicator lights	A3,B3	rear	B5,E5
Instrument lights	E6	switch	D4
Interior light	D2	Voltage regulator	B1
Interior light, rear 245	D5	Voltage stabilizer	B3
Interval relay: tailgate window wiper	C5	Washer: tailgate window	C5
wiper	A4	windshield	A4
License plate light	C5,E5	Window lifts: 2-door	C11
Light switch	D1	4-door	B11
Overdrive solenoid	C4	Wiper: tailgate window	B5
Overdrive switch	C4	windshield	A4
Oxygen sensor system	D15		

Key to Fig. 13.226. Wiring diagram for 1982 North American models

Alternator	B2
Auxiliary air valve	A3
Back-up lights	D9,F9
Wagon	F10,G10
Ballast resistor	B3
Battery	B2
Brake lights	D9,G9
Brake light switch	G5
Bulb failure sensor	G5
Carburettor solenoid (Canada)	F3
Cigarette lighter	C8
Cold start injector	A2
Control pressure regulator	A3
Distributor	A4
Door switches	E3
Electrically heated rear window	D8
Flasher unit	E7
Fuel pump	A3
Fuel pump relay	B2
Fuel tank pump	A3
Fusebox	E5
Glovebox light	C8
Horns	D2
Ignition coil	B4
Ignition switch	D4
Ignition electronic module	B4
Impulse relay	A2
Interval relay, wiper	B8
License plate light	E9
Wagon	E10
Light switch	F3
Parking lights, front	D1,G1

Rear demist	D7
Relay, upper/lower beam	G3
Remote starter pick-up	C2
Seat belt control light:	
Front	C7
Rear	B7
Seat heater	D8
Sensor, bulb failure	G5
Spark plugs	A4
Starter motor: 4-cylinder	A2
6-cylinder	A1
Switches:	
Back-up light:	
Manual transmission	F8
Brake light	G5
Door	E3
Hazard warning	E8
Ignition	D4
Pressure (Turbo)	A2
Rear demist	D7
Seat belt	A7
Seat heater	D8
Turn signal	F7
Windshield wiper/washer	B9
Tail lights	D9,G9
Wagon	D10,G10
Thermal time switch	B2
Trunk light	E8
Turn signal, front	D1,G1
Rear	D9,G9
Rear, Wagon	D10,G10

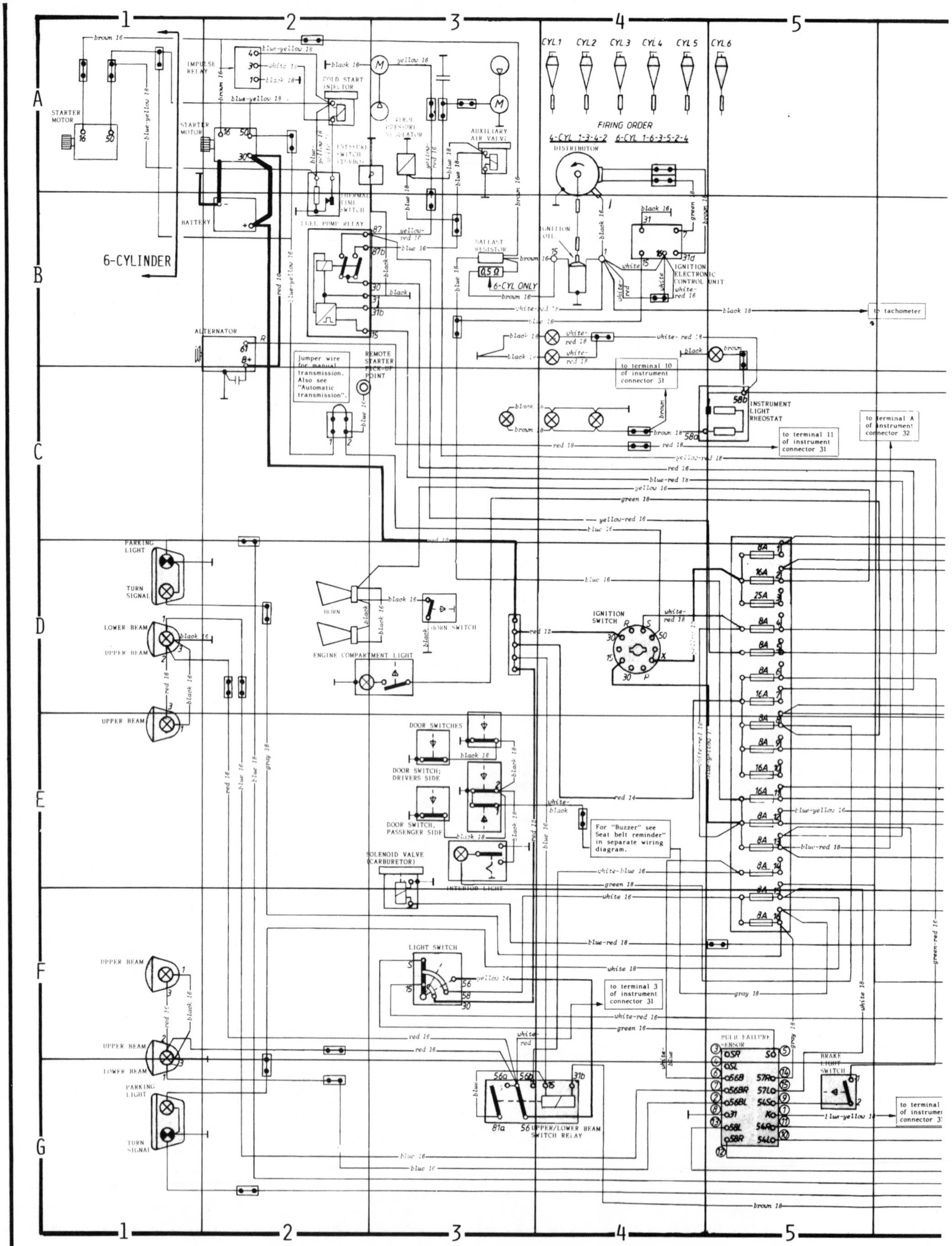

Fig. 13.226 Wiring diagram for 1982 North American models

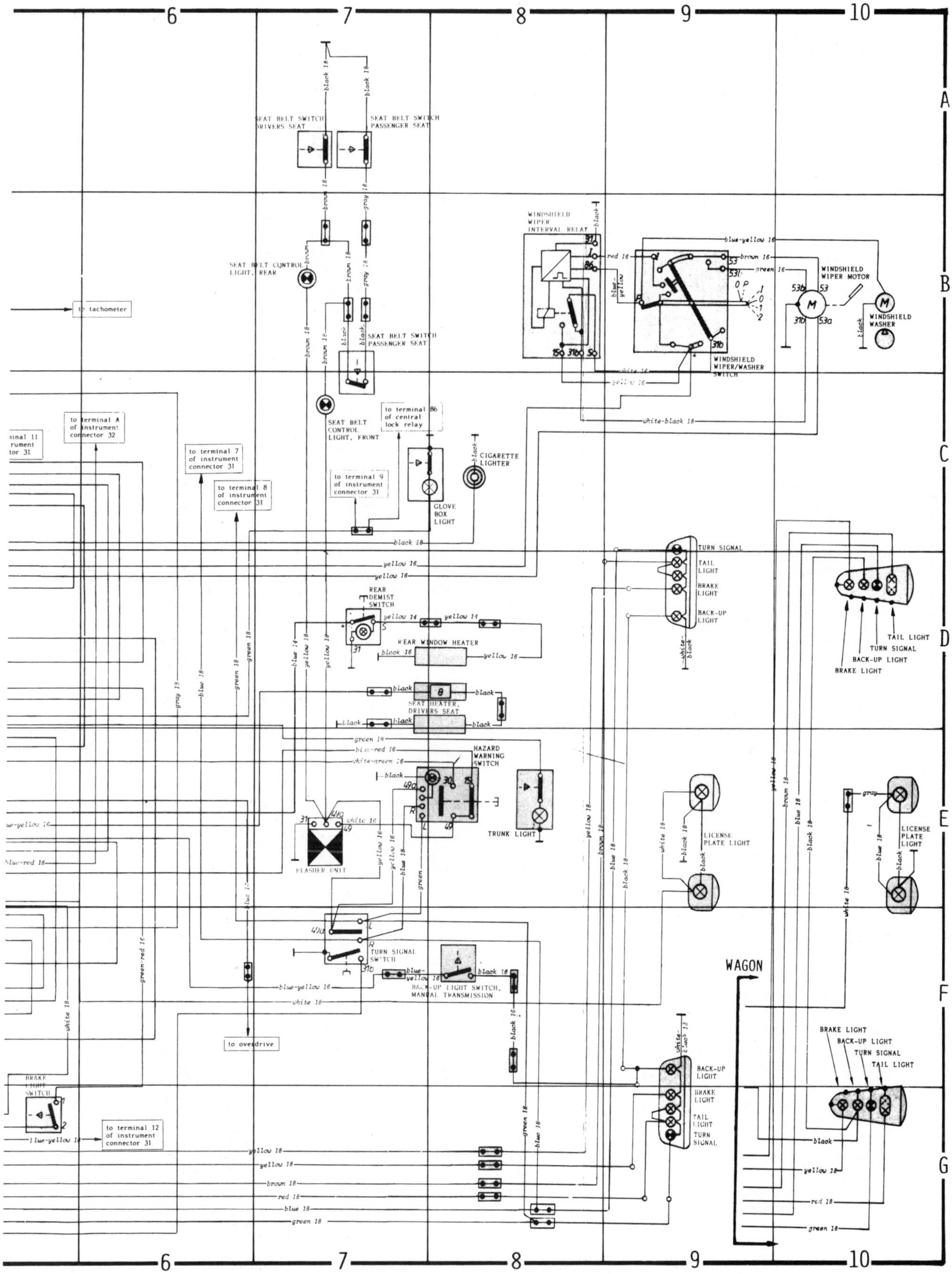

Fig. 13.226 Wiring diagram for 1982 North American models (continued)

Key to Fig. 13.227. Wiring diagram for 1983 North American models

Diagram for 1984 North American models similar

1	Battery	B1	63	Switch, Lambda-sond	E1
2	Junction box	C3	64	Switch, seat belt, passenger seat	E1
3	Ignition switch	C3,N2	65	Switch, seat belt, driver seat	E1,N1
4	Ignition coil 12A	C2	66	Switch, seat belt, passenger seat	E2
5	Distributor	C1,N3	67	Buzzer for lights and key	C4
6	Spark plug	C1	68	Tachometer	D2
7	Starter motor	A1,B1,	69	Fuel gauge	D2
8	Alternator	A2 N3	70	Temperature gauge	E2
10	Fusebox	D3,K5	71	Voltage stabilizer 10 ± 0.2 V	E1
11	Light switch	B4	72	Horn, 7.5 A	B3
12	Bulb failure warning sensor	D5	73	Horn switch	B3
13	Headlamp relay	C5	74	Cigar lighter 7 A	F2
14	High beam 75 W max	A3,A4,A5	75	Heater fan (standard) 115 W	B4
15	Low beam 55 W max	A3,A5	76	Fan switch	B3
16	Parking light 4 cp/5 W	A2,A3,A5	77	Windshield wash/wipe switch	G2
17	Day running lights 32 cp/21 W	A3,A5	78	Windshield wiper 3.5A	G2
18	Tail light 4 cp/5 W	G3,G5	79	Windshield washer 2.6 A	G2
20	License plate light 4 cp/5 W	G3,G4	80	Trunk lock motor 0.6 A	N5
21	Brake light switch	D5,H4	81	Trunk lock switch	B4,N4
22	Brake light	G3,G5	82	Tailgate washer/wipe switch	H1
23	Back-up light contact, man. gearbox	F4	83	Tailgate wiper 1A	H1
24	Back-up light contact, auto. gearbox	N2	84	Tailgate washer 3.4 A	H2
25	Rear spotlight 32 cp/21 W	G3,G5	85	Rear door switch	J1
26	Direction indicator stalk	E4	86	Rear courtesy lighting 10 W	J1
27	Hazard warning light switch	F4	87	Heated rear window switch	E3
28	Flasher device	A4	88	Heated rear window 150 W	F3
29	Direction indicator, front	A2,A3	89	Heater pads + thermostat, driver's seat	
30	Direction indicator, rear	G3,G5		cushion 30 W	F3
31	Instrument panel connection	M4	90	Heated pads, driver's seat, backrest 30 W	F3
32	Instrument panel connection	M4	91	Clock	D1, D2
33	Instrument panel connection	M5	92	Diode	D1,D2,E1
35	Indicator light, oil pressure	D1	94	Seat belt reminder	N1
36	Indicator light, choke	D1	95	Start injector	B1
37	Indicator light, parking brake	E1	96	Thermal timer switch, start injector	B1
38	Indicator light, brake failure	E1	97	Tank pump 1.6 A	C1
40	Indicator light, battery charging	D2	98	Pressure sensor for Turbo cars	B1
41	Indicator light, bulb failure	D2	99	Fuel pump relay	B1
42	Indicator light, main beams	D2	100	Fuel pump 6.5 A	B1
43	Indicator light, direction indicator	E2	101	Control pressure regulator	B1
44	Indicator light, overdrive	E2	102	Auxiliary air valve	C1
45	Indicator light, seat belts 2 W	E2, N1	103	Resistance 0.9 ohm/4 cyl.	C1
46	Engine compartment light 15 W	B3	104	Control unit, ignition system	C1
47	Seat belt lock	C2	105	Control solenoid, for compressor, AC 3.9 A	M4
48	Ashtray light	C2	106	Solenoid valve	N4
49	Gear selector light	C2	107	AC switch (+ thermostat)	M4
50	Rheostat for instrument panel light	C2	108	Overdrive relay	E5,M3
51	Instrument lighting 2 W	D1	109	Overdrive switch M46	E5,M3
52	Instruments and panel lighting	C2	110	Overdrive gearbox switch M46	E5
53	Glove compartment light 2 W	E2	111	Overdrive solenoid on gearbox M46 2.2 A	E5
54	Courtesy light 10 W	B4	112	Coupling	B2,H1
55	Door switch, driver side	C4	113	Power socket for running starter motor	B2,N2
56	Door switch, passenger side	B3,B4,C3	114	Thermostat, Lambda system	N2
57	Fuel level sender	D1	115	Pressure switch, Lambda system	N2
58	Temperature sensor	D1	116	Loudspeaker, LH front door 4	M2
59	Oil pressure sensor	D1	117	Loudspeaker, RH front door 4	M2
60	Switch, choke	D1	118	Antenna, windshield	M3
61	Switch, parking brake	D1	119	TDC sensor for monotester	N4
62	Switch, brake failure	E1	120	Capacitor 2.2 μF	B1,B2

Key to Fig. 13.227. Wiring diagram for 1983 North American models (continued)

121	Spark plug suppressor	C1
122	Indicator light, exhaust gas temperature (Japan) 2 W	M1
123	Diode box (Japan)	M2
124	Temperature sensor (Japan) 850°C	L1
125	Thermal element, catalyst (Japan)	L2
126	Window winder relay	15
127	Rear foglight 32 cp/21 W	F3,G3,G5
128	Rear foglight switch	F4
129	Delay relay for AC	M4
130	Trunklight	F3
131	Idle valve CIS (Constant Idle)	M1
132	Idle valve CIS	K5,M1
133	Temp. sensor CIS	M1
134	Microswitch CIS	M1
135	Indicator light, rear seat belts 2 W	E2,N1
136	Master switch for rear window winders	H5
137	Window winder switch, rear left	H5
138	Motor for window winder, rear left 5A	H5
139	Window winder switch, rear right	H5
140	Motor for window winder, rear right 5A	H5
141	Switch for door mirrors LH	J3
142	Door mirror, left	J3
143	Switch for door mirror RH	J3
144	Door mirror, right	K3
145	Hot start valve	B4
146	Junction 8 poles	F3,F5
148	Windshield relay for intermittent wipe	F1
149	Test point Lambda-sond	N2
150	Side marker lights	B3,B5
151	Voltmeter	L1
152	Oil pressure gauge	L1
153	Boost pressure gauge, Turbo cars	K1
154	Ambient temperature gauge	K1
155	Ambient temperature sensor	K1
156	Oil pressure sensor	K1,K2
157	Temp. sensor, diesel	L4
158	Microswitch Lambda-sond	N2
159	Relay for Lambda-sond	N2
160	Frequency valve	N2
161	Control unit, Lambda-sond system	N1
162	Lambda-sond	K5,N2
163	Relay for tailgate intermittent wipe	H2
164	Control unit, preheating diesel	M4
165	Relay, glow current	M4
166	Glow plug	L4
167	Relay for delayed courtesy light	J1
168	Relay for cooling fan	J4
169	Thermostat for cooling fan 100°C	J4
170	Motor for cooling fan 13 A	J4
171	Heater pads + thermostat, passenger seat cushion 30 W	J2
172	Heater pads, passenger seat backrest, 30 W	J2
173	Switch, heater pads, passenger seat	J2
174	Cigar lighter, rear 7A	J2

175	Courtesy light switch	J1
176	Courtesy light, left	J1
177	Courtesy light, right	J1
178	Radio	L2
179	Electric antenna 3 A	M3
181	Solenoid valve, carburettor, or fuel valve diesel	B4
182	Indicator light, diode Lambda-sond	E1
183	Lambda-sond or glow current diesel, lamps	E1
184	Window winder switch, driver side	J4,K4
185	Window winder switch, passenger side front	H5,J5
186	Motor for window winder, passenger side, front 5 A	H5,J5
187	Motor for window winder, driver side 5 A	J5
188	Relay for central lock, opening	H2,K2
189	Relay for central lock, locking	J2,L2
190	Switch for central locking, push rod	H3,J3,K3
191	Switch for central locking, key	J3,L3
192	Motor for central lock, passenger side	H3,K3
193	Motor for central locking, rear left	K3
194	Motor for central locking, rear right	K3
195	Motor for central locking, tailgate	K3
196	Motor for central locking, driver door 2-door models	H3
197	Armrest switch for central locking 2-door models	J3
198	Cruise control, switch	H3
199	Cruise control, control unit	H3
200	Cruise control, pick-up coil	J4
201	Cruise control, retardation switch	H4
202	Cruise control, clutch pedal switch	H4
203	Cruise control, power assist	H4
204	Cruise control, 4A fuse	H4
205	Heater fan CU	N4
206	Switch, heater fan CU	N4
207	Resistor 1.9	N4
208	Resistor 0.7	N4
209	Resistor 0.2	N4
210	Control unit, ignition system B23F	N3
211	Impulse relay, start injector	B1
212	Microswitch	M1
213	Microswitch	M4
214	Control unit B23F LH-Jetronic 2	K4
215	Air mass meter	L5
216	Fuel pump relay B23F LH-Jetronic 2	K5
217	System relay B23F LH-Jetronic 2	L5
218	Idle speed and full throttle cut-out switch, B23F LH-Jetronic 2	L4
220	Overdrive control solenoid AW71 1.3A	M3
221	Temperature sensor B23F LH-Jetronic 2	K4
222	Idle speed adjustment	L4,M1
223	Pressure differential valve	N2
224	Knock sensor	N3
225	Injector 0.75 A	K4

Colour code

BL	Blue		R	Red
BN	Brown		SB	Black
GN	Green		VO	Violet
GR	Grey		W	White
OR	Orange		Y	Yellow
P	Pink			

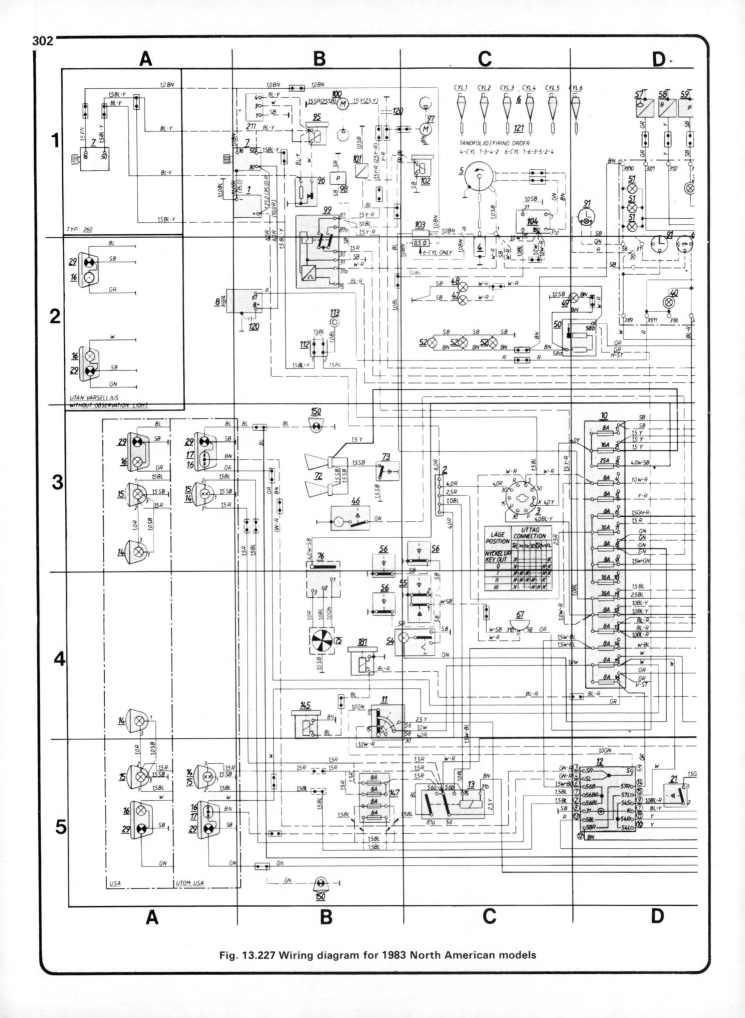

Fig. 13.227 Wiring diagram for 1983 North American models

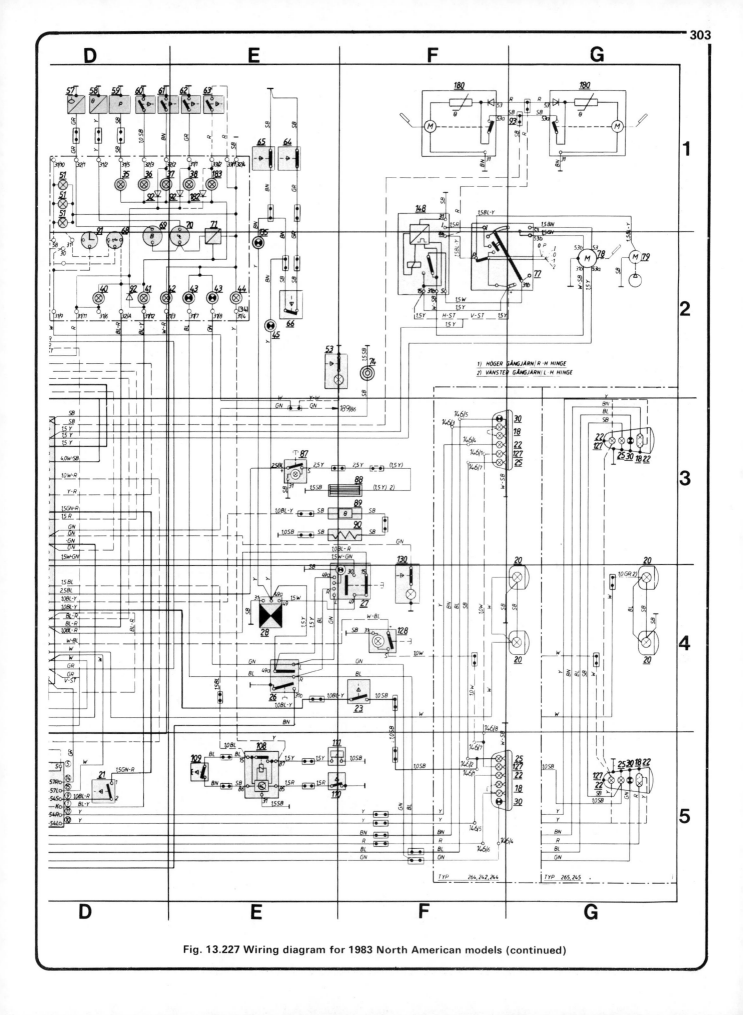

Fig. 13.227 Wiring diagram for 1983 North American models (continued)

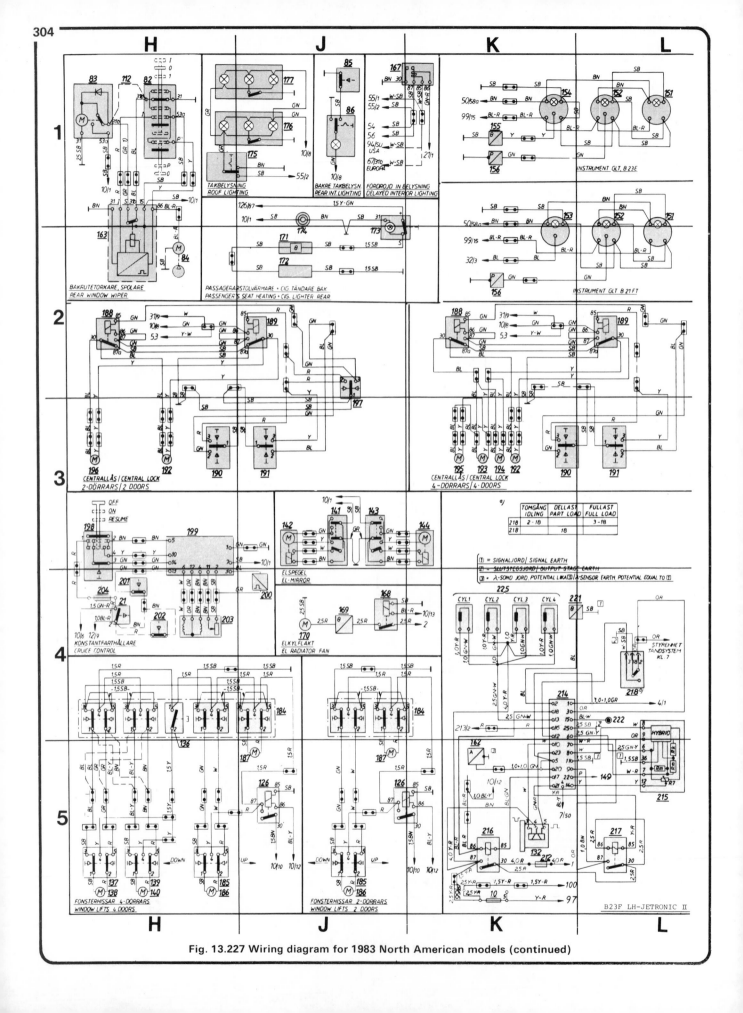

Fig. 13.227 Wiring diagram for 1983 North American models (continued)

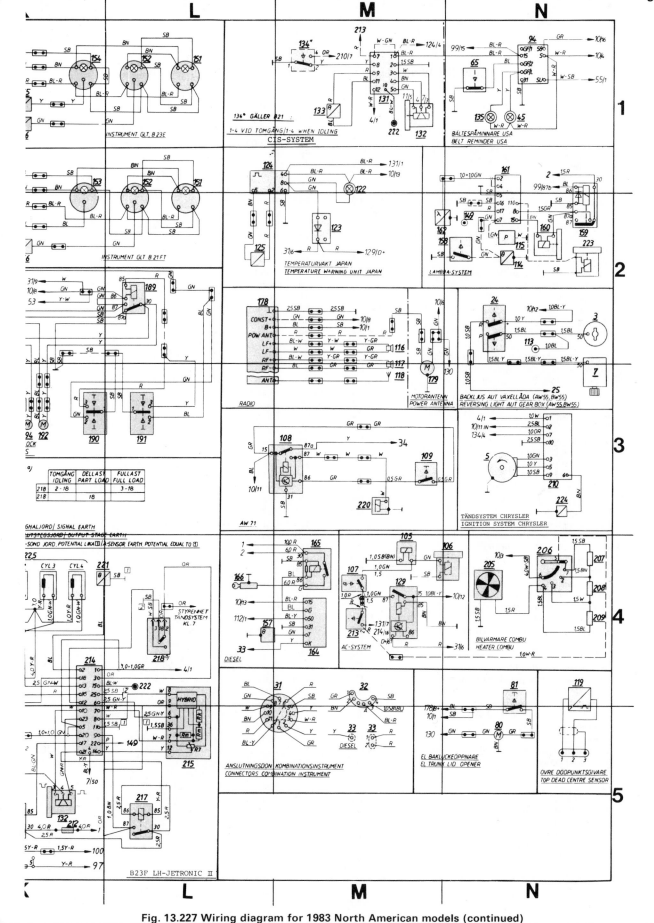

Fig. 13.227 Wiring diagram for 1983 North American models (continued)

Key to Fig. 13.228. Wiring diagram for 1985 UK and North American models

1	Battery	B1	65	Seat belt switch driver	E1,N1
2	Fusebox	C3	66	Seat belt switch passenger	E2
3	Ignition switch	C3,N2	67	Reminder buzzer for key and lights	C4
4	Ignition coil 12 A	C1	68	Tachometer	D1
5	Distributor	C1,L3,M2	69	Fuel gauge	D1
6	Spark plug	C1	70	Temperature gauge	E1
7	Starter motor	A1,B1	71	Voltage stabilizer 10 ± 0.2 V	E1
8	Alternator	A2	72	Horn, 7.5 A	B3
10	Fusebox	D3,K5,L2	73	Horn switch	B3
11	Light switch	B4,J1	74	Cigar lighter 7 A	F2
12	Bulb failure warning sensor	D5	75	Standard heater fan 115 W	B4
13	Step relay for main and dipped beams and flash	C5	76	Heater fan switch	B3
14	Main beam bulb 75 W max	A3,A4,A5	77	Windscreen wash/wipe switch	G2
15	Dipped beam bulb 55 W max	A3,A5	78	Windscreen wipe 3.5 A	G2
16	Parking light 4cp/5 W	A2,A3,A5	79	Windscreen washer 2.6 A	G2
17	Day running light 32 cp/21 W	A3,A5	80	Boot release motor 0.6 A	F3,K3
18	Tail light 4 cp/5 W	G3,G5	81	Boot release switch	K4
20	Number plate light 4 cp/5 W	G3,G4	82	Tailgate wash/wipe switch	H1
21	Brake light switch	D5,H4	83	Tailgate wiper 1A	H1
22	Brake light	G3,G5	84	Tailgate washer 3.4 A	H2
23	Reversing light switch, manual gearbox	F4	85	Rear door switch	J1
24	Reversing light switch, automatic gearbox	N2	86	Rear courtesy lighting 10 W	J1
25	Reversing light 32 cp/21 W	G3,G5	87	Heated rear window switch	E3
26	Direction indicator switch	E4	88	Heated rear window 150 W	F3,J1
27	Hazard warning light switch	F4	89	Heater pads + thermostat, driver seat 30 W	F3
28	Flasher device	E4	90	Heater pad driver backrest 30 W	F3
29	Direction indicator, front	A2,A3,A5	91	Clock	D1
30	Direction indicator, rear	G3,G5	92	Diode	D1,D2,E1
31	Instrument connection	N4	94	Fasten belt reminder light	C3,N1
32	Instrument connection	N4	95	Start injector	B1
33	Instrument connection	N3	96	Thermal timer switch, start injector	B1
34	Instrument connection, AW71	N4	97	Tank pump 1.6 A	C1
35	Oil pressure indicator lamp	D1	98	Charge air overpressure switch (turbo)	B1
36	Choke indicator lamp	D1	99	Fuel pump relay	B1
37	Parking brake indicator lamp	D1	100	Fuel pump 6.5 A	B1
38	Brake failure warning lamp	E1	101	Control pressure regulator	B1
39	Overdrive (AW71) indicator lamp	D2	102	Auxiliary air valve	C1
40	Battery charging indicator lamp	D2	103	Resistance 0.9Ω/4 cyl, 0.5Ω/6 cyl	L2
41	Bulb failure warning sensor lamp	D2	104	Ignition system control unit	L2
42	Main beam indicator lamp	D2	105	AC compressor solenoid 3.9 A	M4
43	Direction indicator indicator lamp	E2	106	Solenoid	L4
44	Overdrive indicator lamp	E2	107	AC switch (thermostat type)	L4
45	Seat belt reminder light	E2, N1	108	Overdrive relay	E5,M3
46	Engine compartment light 15 W	B3	109	Overdrive switch M46	E5,M3
47	Seat belt buckle light	C2	110	Overdrive casing switch M46	E5
48	Ashtray light 1.2 W	C2	111	Overdrive solenoid (M46) 2.2 A	E5
49	Gear selector panel light	C2	112	Bridge connector	B2,H1
50	Adjustment knob, panel light intensity	C2	113	Service socket for cranking starter motor	B2,N3
51	Instrument lighting 2 W	D1	114	Lambda-sond cut-out device	N2
52	Instrument and panel lighting	C2	115	Pressure switch, Lambda system	L1,N2
53	Glove compartment light 2 W	E2	116	Loudspeaker 4 ohms, front left door	M3
54	Courtesy light 10 W	B4	117	Loudspeaker 4 ohms, front right door	M3
55	Door switch, driver side	C4	118	Aerial, (windscreen pillar)	M3
56	Door switch, passenger side	B3,B4,C3	119	TDC transmitter for monotester	H2
57	Fuel level sensor	D1	120	Capacitor 2.2μF	B2,H2
58	Temperature sender	D1	121	Spark plug suppressor	C1
59	Oil pressure sender	D1	126	Power window relay	J5
60	Choke switch	D1	127	Rear foglight 32 cp/21 W	G3,G5
61	Parking brake switch	D1	128	Rear foglight switch	F4
62	Brake failure warning switch	E1	129	AC delay relay	E4,M4
63	Lambda-sond switch	E1	130	Boot light	F3
64	Seat belt switch, passenger	E1	131	CIS control unit	M1
			132	CIS air control valve	K5,M1

Key to Fig. 13.228. Wiring diagram for 1985 UK and North American models (continued)

133	CIS temperature sender	M1	181	Carburettor solenoid valve (fuel valve diesel)	B4
134	CIS microswitch	L1	182	Lambda-sond diode lamp 1.2 W	E1
135	Rear seat belt light 2 W	E1,N1	183	Lambda-sond lamp (glow lamp diesel) 1.2 W	E1
136	Power window switch (main), rear	H4	184	Power window switch, driver side	J4,K4
137	Power window winder switch, rear left	H5	185	Power window switch, passenger side	H5,J5
138	Power window motor, rear left 5 A	H5	186	Power window motor 5 A, passenger side	H5,J5
139	Power window switch, rear light	H5	187	Power window motor 5 A, driver side	J5
140	Power window motor, rear right 5 A	H5	188	Central lock motor, unlocking	H2
141	Power door mirror switch, left	J3	189	Central lock motor, locking	E2,J2
142	Power door mirror, left	J3	190	Central lock link rod switch	J3
143	Power door mirror switch, right	J3	191	Central door lock switch	J3
144	Power door mirror, right	K3	192	Central lock motor, passenger side	H3
145	Warm start injector	B4	193	Central lock motor, rear left	H3
146	Connector 8-pole	F3,F5	194	Central lock motor, rear right	H3
147	Fusebox, headlights, Italy	B5	195	Central lock motor, tailgate	H3
148	Windshield wiper relay	F1	196	Central lock motor, driver door	H3
149	Lambda-sond test socket	N2,L4	197	Central lock motor armrest 242	K3
150	Side marker light 2-4 W	B3,B5	198	Cruise control, switch	H3
151	Voltmeter	L2	199	Cruise control, control unit	H3
152	Oil pressure gauge	L2	200	Cruise control, pick-up	J4
153	Boost pressure gauge, (turbo)	K2	201	Cruise control, deceleration switch	H4
154	Fuel valve (diesel)	B2	202	Cruise control, clutch switch	H4
155	Heated seat switch	E3	203	Cruise control, servo unit	H4
156	Oil pressure sender	K2	204	Fuse	H4
157	Coolant temperature sender	K3	205	Heater fan CU	M4
158	Solex carburettor PTC resistor	B4	206	Heater fan switch CU	M4
159	Lambda-sond relay	N2	207	Resistor 1.9 ohms	N4
160	Frequency valve	N2	208	Resistor 0.7 ohm	N4
161	Lambda-sond control unit	N1	209	Resistor 0.2 ohm	N4
162	Lambda-sond (heated = B230F)	K4,M2	210	TZ-28H ignition system control unit	C1
163	Tailgate wipe relay	H2	211	Impulse relay	B1
164	Control unit (diesel)	K3	212	Fuse 25 A	L5
166	Glow plug	K4	213	AC Microswitch	M4
167	Delayed courtesy light relay	C3,J1	214	Control unit B 230 FLH Jetronic 2.2	K4
168	Electric cooling fan relay	C3,C4,J4,K1	215	Air mass meter	L5
169	Electric cooling fan thermostat 100°C	J4,K1	216	Gearbox switch	L4
170	Electric cooling fan motor 13 A	J4	217	Main relay B 230 F	K5
171	Shift indicator control unit	C2,D2,E2,L3	218	Microswitch (idling and full load)	L4
172	Rear axle impulse sender	K3	220	Overdrive (AW 71) solenoid	M4
173	Clutch switch	K3	221	Temperature sender B 230 F	K4
174	Headlamp relay	C4	222	Idle speed adjustment	L4,M1
175	Heated rear window delay relay	J1	223	AC receiver/driver	L4
176	Switch, delay relay	J1	224	Knock sensor	L3
177	Pressure differential switch	N1	225	Injector	K4
178	Radio	D2,L2	226	Altitude compensation pressure switch	J1
179	Power aerial 3 A	M3	227	Altitude compensation solenoid valve	J1
180	Headlamp wiper 1 A	F1,G1	230	Engine rpm relay	L1
			232	On-off valve	L1

For colour code see key to Fig. 13.227

308

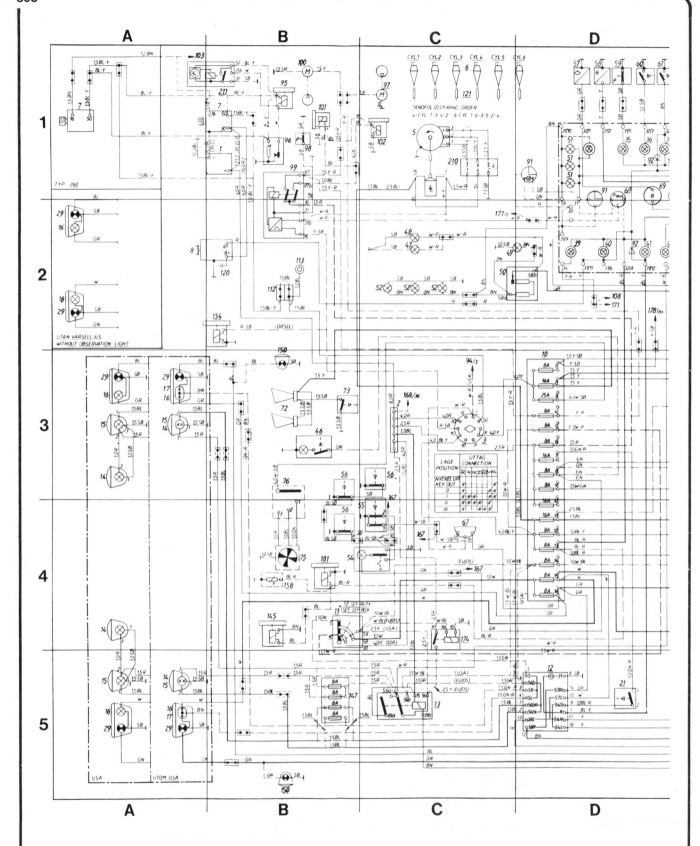

Fig. 13.228 Wiring diagram for 1985 UK and North American models

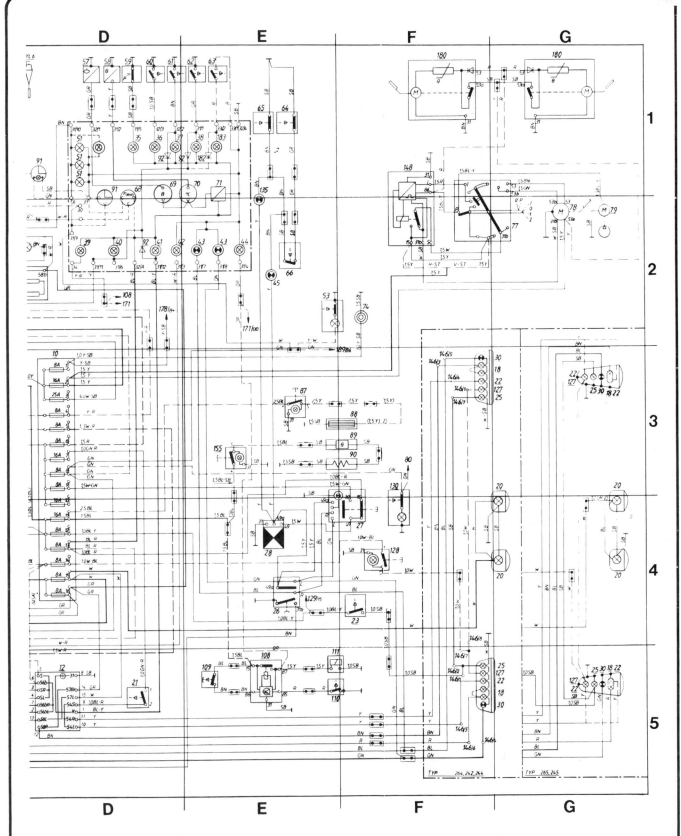

Fig. 13.228 Wiring diagram for 1985 UK and North American models (continued)

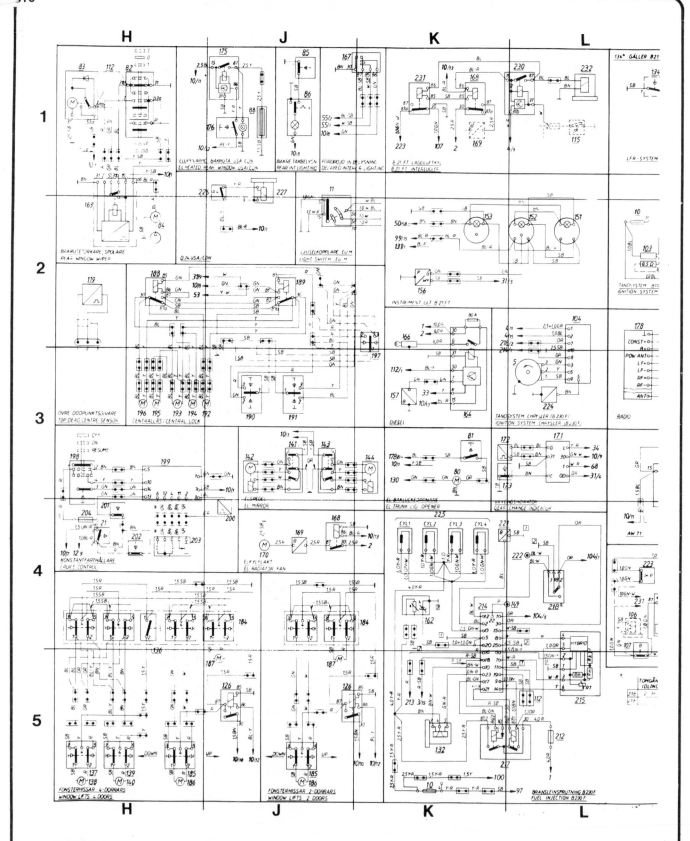

Fig. 13.228 Wiring diagram for 1985 UK and North American models (continued)

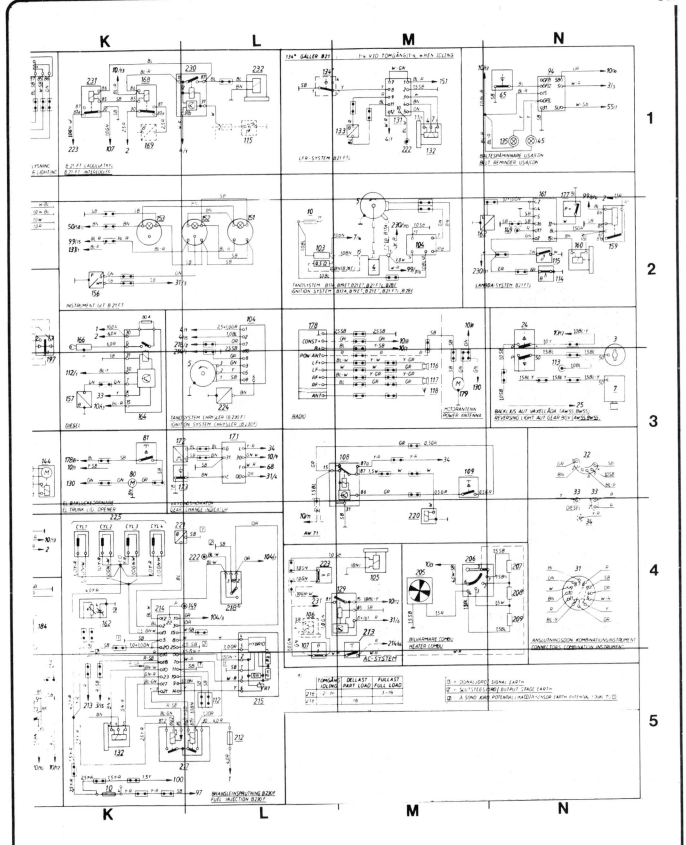

Fig. 13.228 Wiring diagram for 1985 UK and North American models (continued)

Key to Fig. 13.229. Wiring diagram for 1986 UK and North American models

1	Battery
2	Fusebox
3	Ignition switch
4	Ignition coil 12 A
5	Distributor
6	Spark plug
7	Starter motor
8	Alternator
10	Fusebox
11	Light switch
12	Bulb failure warning sensor
13	Step relay for main and dipped beams and flash
14	Main beam bulb 75 W max
15	Dipped beam bulb 15 W max
16	Parking light 4cp/5 W
17	Day running light 4cp/5 W
18	Tail light 4cp/5 W
20	Number plate light 4cp/5 W
21	Brake light switch
22	Brake light
23	Reversing light switch, manual gearbox
24	Reversing light switch, automatic gearbox
25	Reversing light 32 cp/21 W
26	Direction indicator switch
27	Hazard warning light switch
28	Flasher device
29	Direction indicator, front
30	Direction indicator, rear
31	Instrument connection
32	Instrument connection
33	Instrument connection
34	Instrument connection, AW71
35	Oil pressure indicator lamp
36	Choke indicator lamp
37	Parking brake indicator lamp
38	Brake failure warning lamp
39	Overdrive (AW71) indicator lamp
40	Battery charging indicator lamp
41	Bulb failure warning sensor lamp
42	Main beam indicator lamp
43	Direction indicator indicator lamp
44	Overdrive indicator lamp
45	Seat belt reminder light
46	Engine compartment light 15 W
47	Seat belt buckle light
48	Ashtray light 1.2 W
49	Gear selector panel light
50	Adjustment knob, panel light intensity
51	Instrument lighting 2 W
52	Instrument and panel lighting
53	Glove compartment light 2 W
54	Courtesty light 10 W
55	Door switch, driver side
56	Door switch passenger side
57	Fuel level sensor
58	Temperature sender
59	Oil pressure sender
60	Choke switch
61	Parking brake switch
62	Brake failure warning switch
63	Lambda-sond switch
64	Seat belt switch, passenger
65	Seat belt switch, driver
66	Seat belt switch, passenger
68	Tachometer
69	Fuel gauge
70	Temperature gauge
71	Voltage regulator 10±0.2 V
72	Horn 7.5 A
73	Horn switch
74	Cigar lighter 7 A
75	Standard heater unit 115 W
76	Heater fan switch
77	Windscreen wash/wipe switch
78	Windscreen wipe 3.5 A
79	Windscreen washer 2.6 A
82	Tailgate wash/wipe switch
83	Tailgate wiper 1 A
84	Tailgate washer 3,4 A
85	Rear door switch
86	Rear courtesy lighting 10 W
87	Heated rear window switch
88	Heated rear window 150 W
89	Heater pads + thermostat, driver seat 30 W
90	Heater pad, driver backrest 30 W
91	Clock
92	Diode
94	Fasten seat belt reminder light
95	Start injector
96	Thermal time switch, start injector
97	Tank pump 1.6 A
99	Fuel pump relay
100	Fuel pump 6.5 A
101	Control pressure regulator
102	Auxiliary air valve
105	AC compressor solenoid 3.9 A
106	Solenoid
107	AC switch (thermostat type)
108	Overdrive relay
109	Overdrive switch M 46
110	Overdrive casing switch M 46
111	Overdrive solenoid (M 46) 2.2 A
112	Bridge connector
113	Service socket for cranking starter motor
114	Lambda-sond cut-out device
115	Pressure switch, Lambda system
116	Loudspeaker 4 ohms, front left door
117	Loudspeaker 4 ohms, front right door
118	Aerial, (windscreen pillar)
120	Capacitor 2.2 µF
121	Spark plug suppressor
122	Heater pad, passenger backrest
123	Heater pad, passenger seat cushion
124	Main light relay
125	Rear foglight relay
126	Power window relay
127	Rear foglight 32 cp/21 W
128	Rear foglight switch

Key to Fig. 13.229. Wiring diagram for 1986 UK and North American models (continued)

129	AC delay relay
130	Boot light
132	CIS air control valve
135	Rear seat belt light 2 W
136	Power window switch (main), rear
137	Power window switch, rear left
138	Power window motor, rear left 5 A
139	Power window switch, rear right
140	Power window motor, rear right 5 A
141	Power door mirror switch, left
142	Power door mirror, left
143	Power door mirror switch, right
144	Power door mirror, right
145	Warm start injector
146	Connector 8-pole
148	Windscreen wiper relay
149	Lambda-sond test socket
150	Side marker light 2-4 W
154	Fuel valve (diesel)
155	Heated seat switch
157	Coolant temperature sender
158	Solex carburettor PTC resistor
162	Lambda-sond (heated = B 230 F)
163	Tailgate wipe relay
164	Control unit (diesel)
166	Glow plug (diesel)
167	Delayed courtesy light relay
171	Shift indicator control unit
173	Clutch switch
175	Heated rear window delay relay
176	Switch, delay relay
178	Radio
179	Power aerial 3 A
180	Headlamp wiper 1 A
181	Carburettor solenoid valve (fuel valve diesel)
183	Lambda-sond lamp (glow lamp diesel 1.2 W)

184	Power window switch, driver side
185	Power window switch, passenger side
186	Power window motor 5 A, passenger side
187	Power window motor 5 A, driver side
188	Central lock motor, unlocking
189	Central lock motor, locking
190	Central lock link rod switch
191	Central lock door lock switch
192	Central lock motor, passenger side
193	Central lock motor, rear left
194	Central lock motor, rear right
205	Heater fan CU
206	Heater fan switch CU
207	Resistor 1.9 ohms
208	Resistor 0.7 ohm
209	Resistor 0.2 ohm
210	TZ-28 H ignition system control unit
212	Fuse 25 A
213	AC Microswitch
214	Control unit B 230 F LH Jetronic 2.2
215	Air mass meter
216	Gearbox switch
217	Main relay B 230 F
218	Microswitch (idling and full load)
220	Overdrive (AW 71) solenoid
221	Temperature sender B 230 F
222	Idle speed adjustment
223	AC receiver/driver
224	Knock sensor
225	Injector
228	Speedometer
229	Impulse sender, rear axle
233	Instrument connection
234	Parking lights, indicator lamp
235	Instrument connection
236	Glow plug indicator lamp (Diesel)

For colour code see key to Fig. 13.227

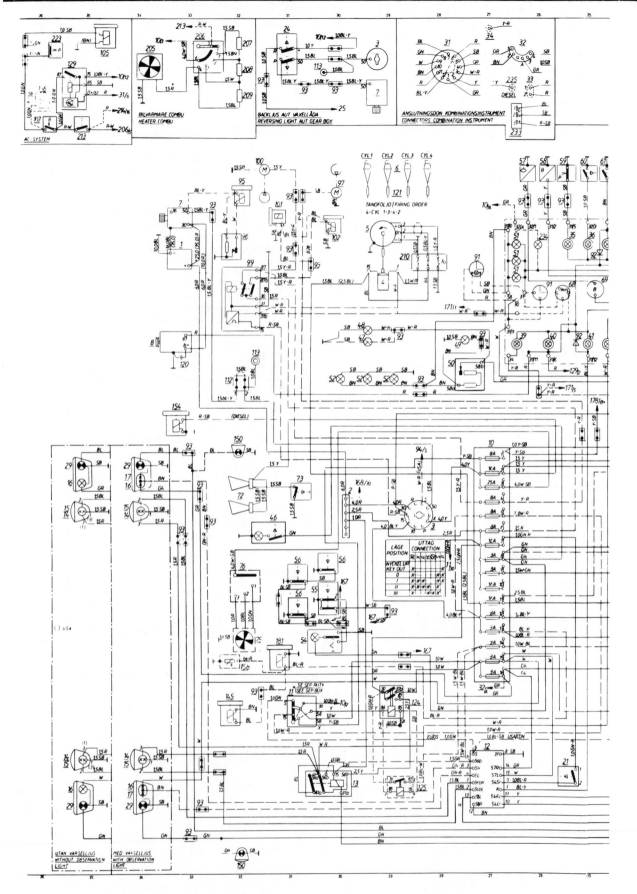

Fig. 13.229 Wiring diagram for 1986 UK and North American models

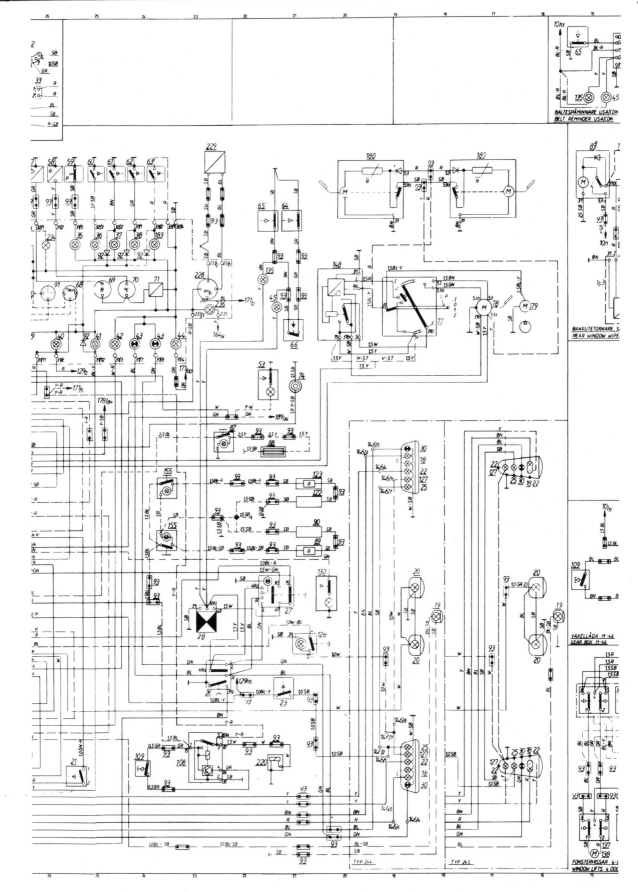

Fig. 13.229 Wiring diagram for 1986 UK and North American models (continued)

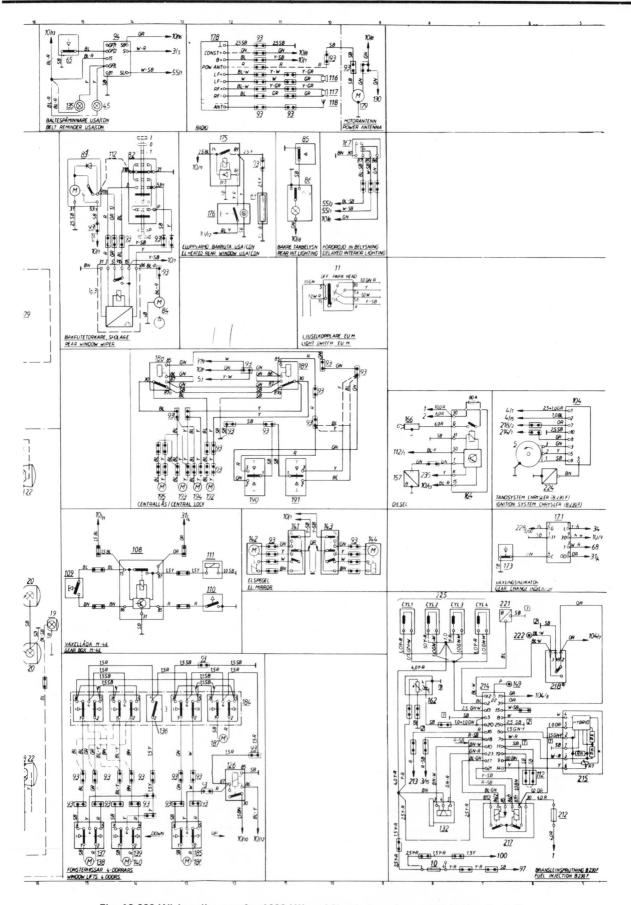

Fig. 13.229 Wiring diagram for 1986 UK and North American models (continued)

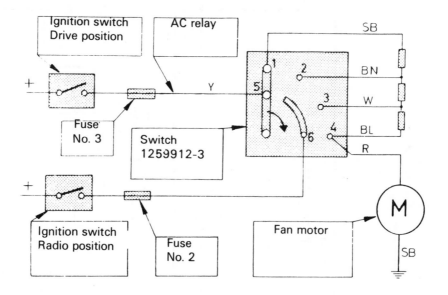

Fig. 13.230 Wiring diagram – later type heater blower motor

For colour code see key to Fig. 13.227

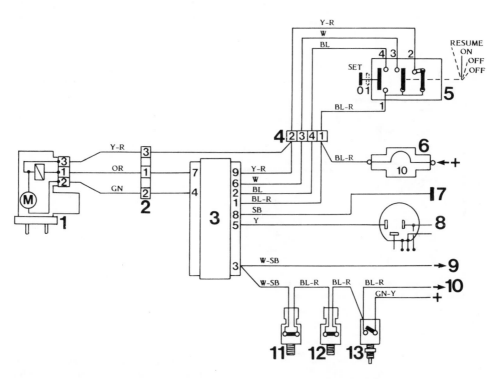

Fig. 13.231 Wiring diagram – cruise control system – 1985 on

1	Vacuum pump and regulator	7	Earth connection (in central electrical unit)
2	11-pole connector at right A-pillar (housed in black retainer containing three connectors)	8	Speedometer
3	Control unit	9	To change indicator relay (manual gearboxes only)
4	Switch connector	10	To brake lights
5	Switch (in turn signal lever)	11	Air valve switch at clutch pedal
6	Fuse no. 10 (in central electrical unit)	12	Air valve switch at brake pedal
		13	Brake light switch

For colour code see key to Fig. 13.227

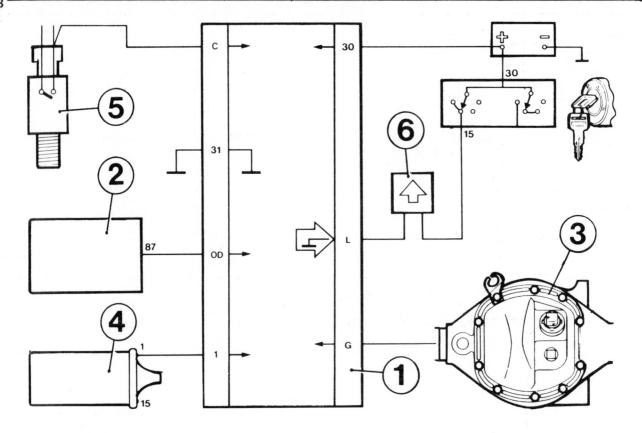

Fig. 13.232 Wiring diagram – gearchange indicator (fuel economy system)

1	Control unit, gear change indicator	4	Ignition coil
2	Overdrive relay	5	Clutch pedal switch
3	Speedometer transmitter	6	Indicator lamp

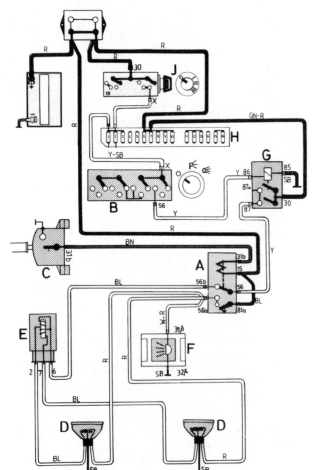

Fig. 13.233 Wiring diagram – headlamps wired through ignition switch to prevent leaving on when parked

A	Step relay	F	Main beam indicator lamp
B	Main light switch	G	Headlamp relay
C	Turn signal switch	H	Fusebox
D	Headlamps	J	Ignition switch
E	Bulb failure sensor		

For colour code see key to Fig. 13.227

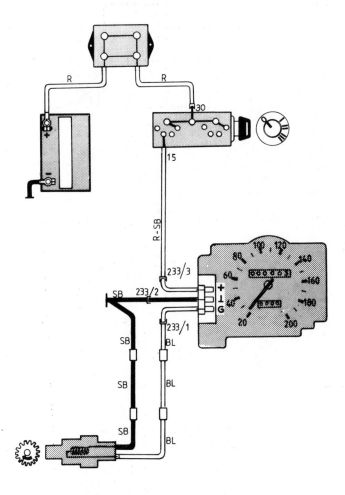

Fig. 13.234 Wiring diagram for electronic speedometer

For colour code see key to Fig. 13.227

13 Front suspension and steering

Steering wheel – removal and refitting

1 On later models (1979 on) a puller is no longer required to remove the steering wheel. This has been achieved by altering the taper angle at the upper end of the steering shaft.

2 The advantage of this modification is somewhat offset by the need for a special tool (No 1158146) in order to reach the steering wheel nut on these models.

Steering shaft – adjustment

3 As from 1979 the steering shaft incorporates splines for adjustment of length. On manual steering models the lower universal joint is protected by a cover.

4 The steering shaft should be adjusted on the splines so that the gap shown in Fig. 13.236 is between 0.39 and 0.75 in (10.0 to 19.0 mm). Tighten the bolts after making an adjustment.

Power steering pump

5 A Saginaw steering pump is fitted to some models produced between 1975 and 1984 as an alternative to the ZF type pump.

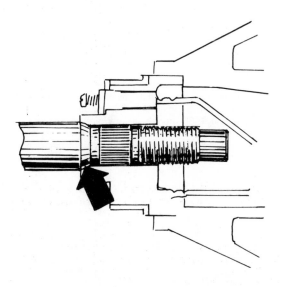

Fig. 13.235 Modified steering shaft taper on 1979 and later models (Sec 13)

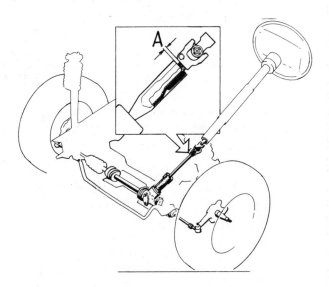

Fig. 13.236 Steering shaft coupling position (Sec 13)

A = 0.39 to 0.75 in (10.0 to 19.0 mm)

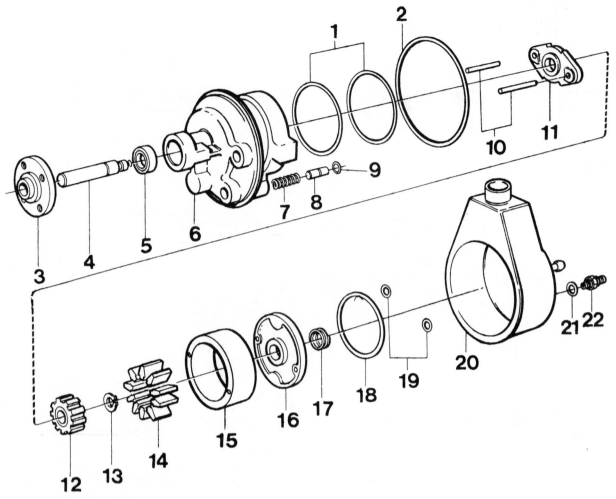

Fig. 13.237 Exploded view of Saginaw type power steering pump (1975 to 1984) (Sec 13)

1	O-rings	7	Spring	13	Circlip	18	Lock ring
2	O-ring	8	Valve	14	Vanes	19	O-rings
3	Hub	9	O-ring	15	Ring	20	Reservoir
4	Driveshaft	10	Pins	16	Plate	21	O-ring
5	Seal	11	Plate	17	Spring	22	Union
6	Housing	12	Rotor				

6   Overhaul procedures are similar to those described in Chapter 11, Section 22, but refer to Fig. 13.237 for component differences.

7   Introduced on 1985 models, a new, lighter Saginaw pump with remotely-sited plastic fluid reservoir is fitted to vehicles with B200 and B230 engines. If a fault develops in this type of pump, renew it as a complete assembly.

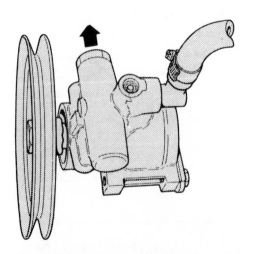

Fig. 13.238 1985 and later type of Saginaw power steering pump (Sec 13)

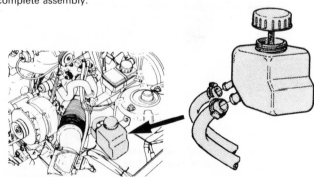

Fig. 13.239 Remotely-sited power steering fluid reservoir (Sec 13)

Power steering pump fluid – level checking

8   Later pump fluid reservoirs have a dipstick attached to the reservoir cap. When the engine is cold, unscrew and withdraw the cap. The fluid level should be between the MIN and MAX marks. If necessary, top up with automatic transmission fluid.

Power steering gear

9   As from 1979 models the different power steering gear units have been introduced as shown in Figs. 13.241, 13.242 and 3.243.

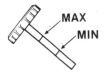

Fig. 13.240 Power steering fluid dipstick (Sec 13)

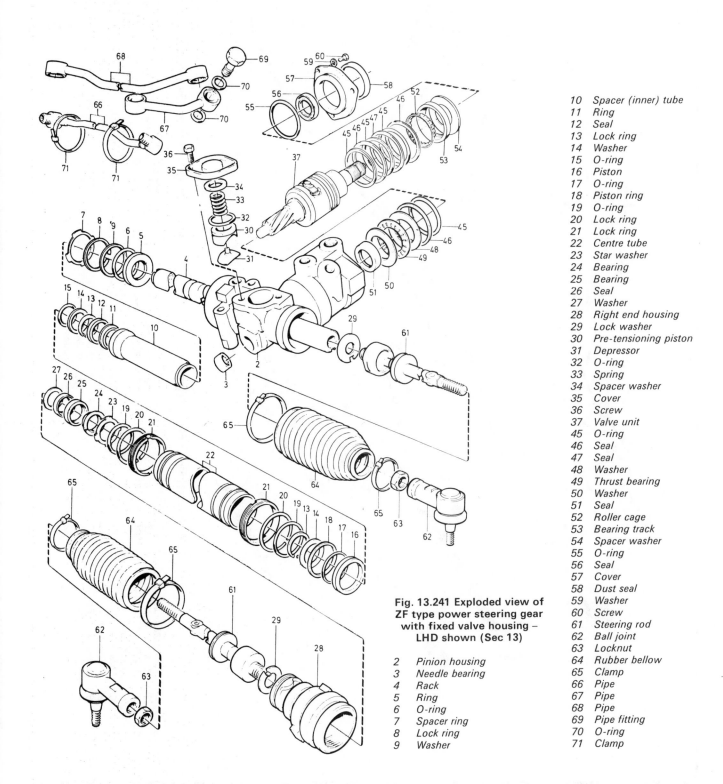

10	Spacer (inner) tube
11	Ring
12	Seal
13	Lock ring
14	Washer
15	O-ring
16	Piston
17	O-ring
18	Piston ring
19	O-ring
20	Lock ring
21	Lock ring
22	Centre tube
23	Star washer
24	Bearing
25	Bearing
26	Seal
27	Washer
28	Right end housing
29	Lock washer
30	Pre-tensioning piston
31	Depressor
32	O-ring
33	Spring
34	Spacer washer
35	Cover
36	Screw
37	Valve unit
45	O-ring
46	Seal
47	Seal
48	Washer
49	Thrust bearing
50	Washer
51	Seal
52	Roller cage
53	Bearing track
54	Spacer washer
55	O-ring
56	Seal
57	Cover
58	Dust seal
59	Washer
60	Screw
61	Steering rod
62	Ball joint
63	Locknut
64	Rubber bellow
65	Clamp
66	Pipe
67	Pipe
68	Pipe
69	Pipe fitting
70	O-ring
71	Clamp

Fig. 13.241 Exploded view of ZF type power steering gear with fixed valve housing – LHD shown (Sec 13)

2	Pinion housing
3	Needle bearing
4	Rack
5	Ring
6	O-ring
7	Spacer ring
8	Lock ring
9	Washer

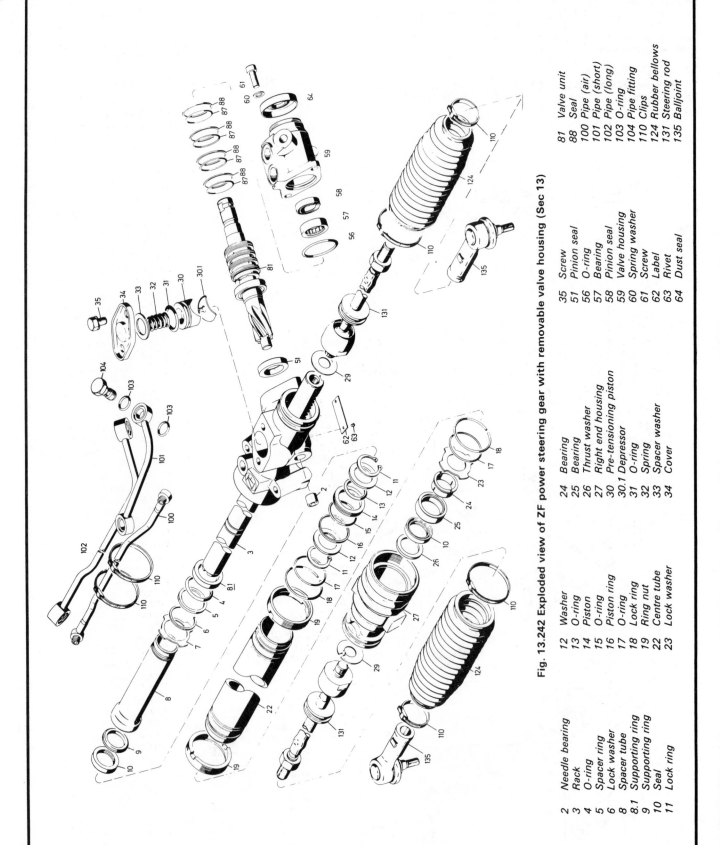

Fig. 13.242 Exploded view of ZF power steering gear with removable valve housing (Sec 13)

2	Needle bearing	12	Washer	24	Bearing	35	Screw	81	Valve unit
3	Rack	13	O-ring	25	Bearing	51	Pinion seal	88	Seal
4	O-ring	14	Piston	26	Thrust washer	56	O-ring	100	Pipe (air)
5	Spacer ring	15	O-ring	27	Right end housing	57	Bearing	101	Pipe (short)
6	Lock washer	16	Piston ring	30	Pre-tensioning piston	58	Pinion seal	102	Pipe (long)
8	Spacer tube	17	O-ring	30.1	Depressor	59	Valve housing	103	O-ring
8.1	Supporting ring	18	Lock ring	31	O-ring	60	Spring washer	104	Pipe fitting
9	Supporting ring	19	Ring nut	32	Spring	61	Screw	110	Clips
10	Seal	22	Centre tube	33	Spacer washer	62	Label	124	Rubber bellows
11	Lock ring	23	Lock washer	34	Cover	63	Rivet	131	Steering rod
						64	Dust seal	135	Balljoint

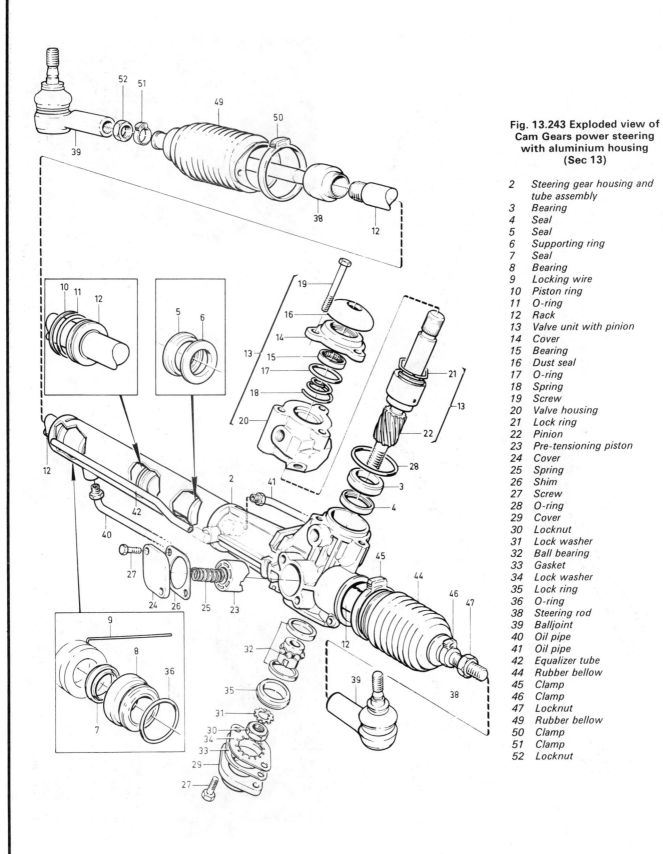

Fig. 13.243 Exploded view of Cam Gears power steering with aluminium housing (Sec 13)

2 Steering gear housing and tube assembly
3 Bearing
4 Seal
5 Seal
6 Supporting ring
7 Seal
8 Bearing
9 Locking wire
10 Piston ring
11 O-ring
12 Rack
13 Valve unit with pinion
14 Cover
15 Bearing
16 Dust seal
17 O-ring
18 Spring
19 Screw
20 Valve housing
21 Lock ring
22 Pinion
23 Pre-tensioning piston
24 Cover
25 Spring
26 Shim
27 Screw
28 O-ring
29 Cover
30 Locknut
31 Lock washer
32 Ball bearing
33 Gasket
34 Lock washer
35 Lock ring
36 O-ring
38 Steering rod
39 Balljoint
40 Oil pipe
41 Oil pipe
42 Equalizer tube
44 Rubber bellow
45 Clamp
46 Clamp
47 Locknut
49 Rubber bellow
50 Clamp
51 Clamp
52 Locknut

Steering column lock

10 Disconnect the battery earth lead.

11 Remove the steering wheel (using a puller on pre 1979 models).

12 Remove the steering column shrouds.

13 Disconnect the wiring plugs for the ignition and steering column switches.

14 Unclamp and remove the column switches.

15 Drill out the shear-head lock fixing screws or drill holes in them and then use a screw extractor.

16 Extract the lock-to-column tube clamp screws and then insert the ignition key to release the lock.

17 Remove the lock assembly, noting that the ignition switch is located at the end of the lock body.

18 Refitting is a reversal of removal but position the lock on the column tube as shown in Fig. 13.246, screw in new shear bolts but do not fully tighten them at this stage.

19 Measuring from Position II on the face of the lock to the facia panel check that the dimension is between 0.53 and 0.65 in (13.5 and 16.5 mm). If it is not, then the column will have to be moved on its mountings.

20 For 1978 models with ZF power steering and all 1979 and later vehicles, check that distance (A) – Fig. 13.236 is as specified. If not, release the shaft coupling pinch-bolts and move the couplings on the splines.

Fig. 13.244 Access to steering lock shear-head bolts (arrowed) (Sec 13)

Fig. 13.245 Steering lock-to-column tube locating screws (Sec 13)

97mm

Fig. 13.246 Steering column lock positioning diagram (Sec 13)

Fig. 13.247 Ignition switch positions (Sec 13)

0	Locked (key withdrawn	II	Ignition and all electrical
I	Radio, cigar lighter,		components on
	headlamp and blower on	III	Starter energised

21 Finally, check the steering wheel hub to column clearance (Fig. 13.249). Adjust if necessary by moving the steering lower shaft.

22 When all the settings are correct, tighten the lockbolts until their heads shear off.

23 If the complete steering column has been removed, before refitting it, check that there is no play between the upper and lower splined sections, then check that the overall length is as shown in Fig. 13.250. If the length is outside the limits, the collapsible section of the column is damaged and therefore the complete column should be renewed.

15 ±1,5 mm

Fig. 13.248 Measuring switch face-to-facia projection (Sec 13)

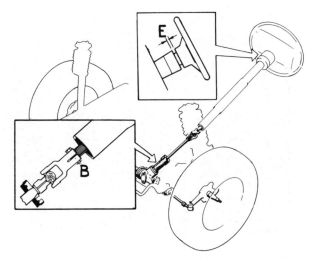

Fig. 13.249 Steering column-to-steering wheel hub clearance diagram (Sec 13)

E = 0.039 to 0.079 in (1.0 to 2.0 mm)   B   Coupling pinch-bolt

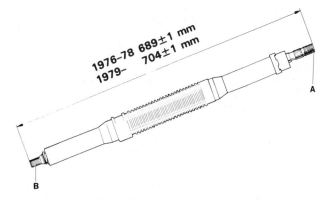

Fig.13.250 Collapsible type steering column checking dimension (Sec 13)

A   Upper shaft   B   Lower shaft

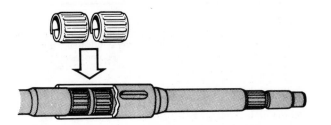

Fig. 13.251 Sleeves on torque limited steering lock (Sec 13)

Steering shaft lock (1986)

24 On 1986 models, the upper steering shaft has been modified to accept a torque-limited steering lock.

25 This comprises a strong outer sleeve pressed onto spring sleeves attached to the shaft.

26 The tongue of the steering lock engages in the grooves of the outer sleeve and if unreasonable force is applied to the steering wheel in an attempt to shear the lock tongue, the sleeve assembly slips in order to reduce the shear force.

Front suspension struts

27 Commencing with 1979 models, the fluid in the suspension struts is gas-pressurised to provide better damping action.

Roadwheel hub caps

28 On certain 1980 models equipped with pressed steel roadwheels, a new type of hub cap is fitted. The cap is secured on three wide spring clips.

29 Before removing the main hub cap, prise out the small emblem disc from its centre as this acts as a wedging device to keep the spring clips apart. Refit in the reverse order.

Front hubs

30 As from 1981 the front hub nut and thrust washer has been replaced by a combined nut incorporating an increased number of castellations.

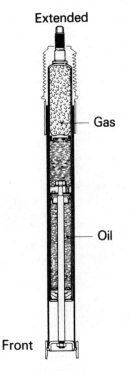

Fig. 13.252 Sectional view of later type gas-filled suspension strut (Sec 13)

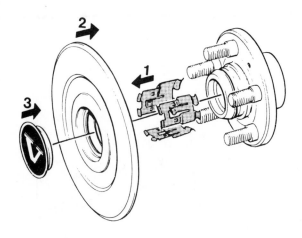

Fig. 13.253 Later type roadwheel hub cap (Sec 13)

1   Spring clips   3   Motif
2   Hub cap

ls and tyres – general care and maintenance

Wheels and tyres should give no real problems in use provided that a close eye is kept on them with regard to excessive wear or damage. To this end, the following points should be noted.

Ensure that tyre pressures are checked regularly and maintained correctly. Checking should be carried out with the tyres cold and not immediately after the vehicle has been in use. If the pressures are checked with the tyres hot, an apparently high reading will be obtained owing to heat expansion. Under no circumstances should an attempt be made to reduce the pressures to the quoted cold reading in this instance, or effective underinflation will result.

Underinflation will cause overheating of the tyre owing to excessive flexing of the casing, and the tread will not sit correctly on the road surface. This will cause a consequent loss of adhesion and excessive wear, not to mention the danger of sudden tyre failure due to heat build-up.

Overinflation will cause rapid wear of the centre part of the tyre tread coupled with reduced adhesion, harsher ride, and the danger of shock damage occurring in the tyre casing.

Regularly check the tyres for damage in the form of cuts or bulges, especially in the sidewalls. Remove any nails or stones embedded in the tread before they penetrate the tyre to cause deflation. If removal of a nail *does* reveal that the tyre has been punctured, refit the nail so that its point of penetration is marked. Then immediately change the wheel and have the tyre repaired by a tyre dealer. Do *not* drive on a tyre in such a condition. In many cases a puncture can be simply repaired by the use of an inner tube of the correct size and type. If in any doubt as to the possible consequences of any damage found, consult your local tyre dealer for advice.

Periodically remove the wheels and clean any dirt or mud from the inside and outside surfaces. Examine the wheel rims for signs of rusting, corrosion or other damage. Light alloy wheels are easily damaged by 'kerbing' whilst parking, and similarly steel wheels may become dented or buckled. Renewal of the wheel is very often the only course of remedial action possible.

The balance of each wheel and tyre assembly should be maintained to avoid excessive wear, not only to the tyres but also to the steering and suspension components. Wheel imbalance is normally signified by vibration through the vehicle's bodyshell, although in many cases it is particularly noticeable through the steering wheel. Conversely, it should be noted that wear or damage in suspension or steering components may cause excessive tyre wear. Out-of-round or out-of-true tyres, damaged wheels and wheel bearing wear/maladjustment also fall into this category. Balancing will not usually cure vibration caused by such wear.

Wheel balancing may be carried out with the wheel either on or off the vehicle. If balanced on the vehicle, ensure that the wheel-to-hub relationship is marked in some way prior to subsequent wheel removal so that it may be refitted in its original position.

General tyre wear is influenced to a large degree by driving style – harsh braking and acceleration or fast cornering will all produce more rapid tyre wear. Interchanging of tyres may result in more even wear, but this should only be carried out where there is no mix of tyre types on the vehicle. However, it is worth bearing in mind that if this is completely effective, the added expense of replacing a complete set of tyres simultaneously is incurred, which may prove financially restrictive for many owners.

Front tyres may wear unevenly as a result of wheel misalignment. The front wheels should always be correctly aligned according to the settings specified by the vehicle manufacturer.

Legal restrictions apply to the mixing of tyre types on a vehicle. Basically this means that a vehicle must not have tyres of differing construction on the same axle. Although it is not recommended to mix tyre types between front axle and rear axle, the only legally permissible combination is crossply at the front and radial at the rear. When mixing radial ply tyres, textile braced radials must always go on the front axle, with steel braced radials at the rear. An obvious disadvantage of such mixing is the necessity to carry two spare tyres to avoid contravening the law in the event of a puncture.

In the UK, the Motor Vehicles Construction and Use Regulations apply to many aspects of tyre fitting and usage. It is suggested that a copy of these regulations is obtained from your local police if in doubt as to the current legal requirements with regard to tyre condition, minimum tread depth, etc.

14 Bodywork

General

1 Changes to bodywork and trim on later models are generally cosmetic and include such items as a larger windscreen, greater use of corrosion resistant panels, impact absorbing bumpers and re-designed trim.

Front wing liners

2 Commencing with 1978 models, protective plastic liners are fitted under the front wings. They are retained by small set bolts.

Door locks

3 On later models (1978 on), modified door locks are fitted and are the only type supplied as spares for earlier versions.
4 To renew the earlier type of lock, it will only be necessary to carry out a direct substitution, but note that the newer type of lock cylinder is retained by a spring clip.
5 To renew a later type of lock, carry out the following operations. If a front door lock is being removed, withdraw the stowage compartment first from the inner surface of the door.
6 Remove the window regulator handle, the lock interior handle, the armrest and the lock plunger knob.
7 Remove the door interior trim panel and the waterproof sheet.
8 Extract the spring retainers from the interior and exterior handle linkage and the plunger rod (Fig. 13.255).

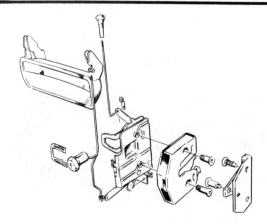

Fig. 13.254 Later type door lock components (Sec 14)

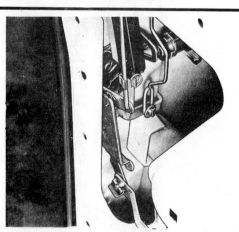

Fig. 13.255 Spring retainers on door lock link rod (Sec 14)

9 . Using an Allen key, unscrew the two socket-headed screws from the lock at the door edge. Withdraw the lock outer section and then remove the inner section from the door interior.

10 If a front door is being worked on, the lock cylinder can be removed if the retaining clip is first prised out with a screwdriver.

11 Refitting is a reversal of removal, but make sure that there is a gap of 0.040 in (1.0 mm) at the exterior handle link rod to lever (Fig. 13.257) before fitting the securing spring clip.

Luggage boot lid lock (1979 to 1985)

12 A key opening lock is fitted to 1979 and later models which cannot be opened by turning with the fingers as was the case on earlier models.

13 The lock is retained by a forked clip as is used on later type door lock cylinders. Volvo recommend using their tool 5174 to extract the clip, but a lever may be used instead.

14 To dismantle the lock, prise out the E-clip and remove the latch and the return spring.

15 When reassembling, engage the end of the return spring in the recess in the latch, connect the latch/return spring to the lock cylinder and then pre-tension the spring by one notch by turning the latch clockwise. Refit the E-clip.

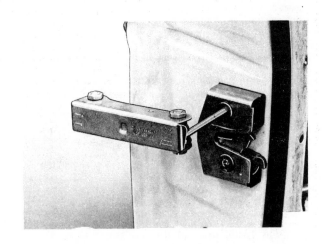

Fig. 13.256 Using an Allen key to extract door lock screw (Sec 14)

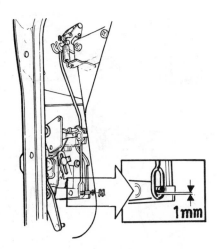

Fig. 13.257 Exterior handle link rod adjustment diagram (Sec 14)

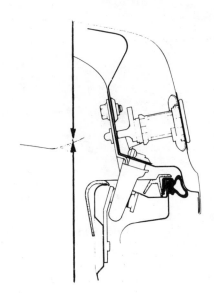

Fig. 13.258 Later type boot lock (Sec 14)

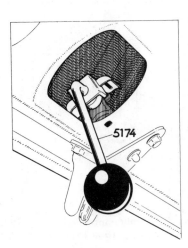

Fig. 13.259 Using special tool to remove boot lid lock (Sec 14)

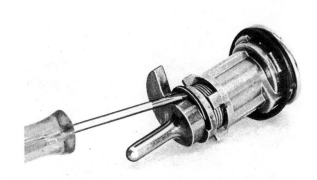

Fig. 13.260 Extracting lock cylinder E-clip (Sec 14)

...ge boot lid lock (1986)
16 The lock is integrated in the central locking system and can be removed and refitted in the following way.
17 Remove the lock protective cover and unscrew the three lock fixing bolts. Depress the lock button and withdraw the lock.
18 If the lock cylinder is to be removed, unscrew the fixing bolt,

disconnect the link rod from the central door lock system motor and withdraw the cylinder.
19 Refitting is a reversal of removal.

Exterior rear view mirrors
20 On certain later models the exterior mirrors are remotely controlled

Fig. 13.261 Boot latch return spring (Sec 14)

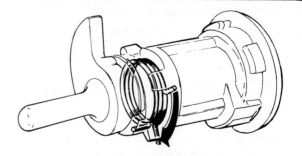

Fig. 13.262 Pre-tensioning boot latch return spring (Sec 14)

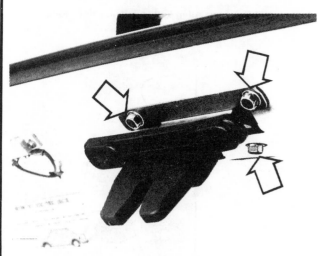

Fig. 13.263 1986 boot lid lock protective cover and fixing bolts (Sec 14)

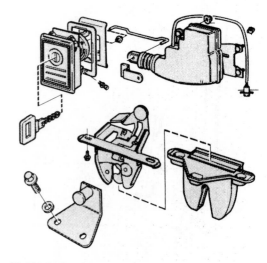

Fig. 13.264 Boot lock components with central locking system (Sec 14)

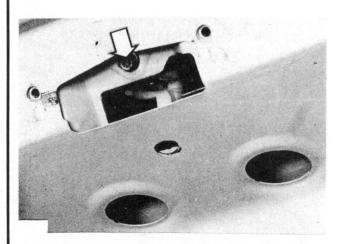

Fig. 13.265 Boot lock cylinder fixing bolt (Sec 14)

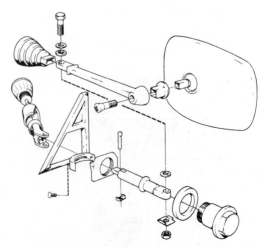

Fig. 13.266 Remotely controlled mirror 1975 to 1980 (Sec 14)

from inside the car. On DL and GL models the control is manual, but on GLE and Coupe models an electrically operated control is provided.

21 Although the mounting components differ slightly according to production date of the vehicle, typical procedure is as follows:

22 Remove the door trim panel and prise off the mirror trim cover.

23 Pull out the forked spring clip (A) and unscrew the two retaining bolts (B) – Fig. 13.270.

24 Withdraw the mirror.

25 To change the mirror glass (which can also be done without removing the mirror assembly), press the lower edge of the glass inwards so that the teeth are exposed through the hole in the lower part of the mirror housing. Prise the teeth to the right using a small screwdriver and remove the glass.

26 Refitting is a reversal of removal; when fitting the glass, prise the teeth to the left.

Rear quarter windows (four-door models)

27 As from 1981 models the rear quarter window glasses are bonded to the body panel with butyl tape, and the window surrounds retained with cross-head screws.

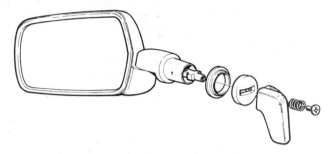

Fig. 13.267 Remotely controlled mirror 1980 to 1985 (Sec 14)

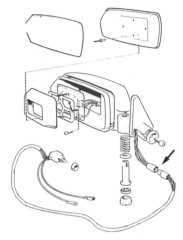

Fig. 13.268 Electrically-operated mirror (Sec 14)

Wiring plug (arrowed) early models

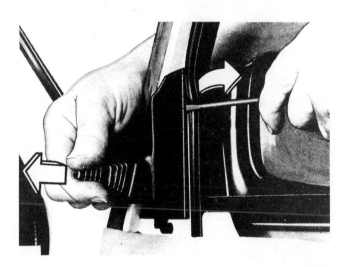

Fig. 13.269 Removing mirror control trim cover (Sec 14)

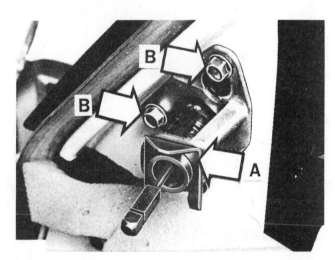

Fig. 13.270 Mirror fixings (Sec 14)

A Clip   B Setscrews

Fig. 13.271 Removing exterior mirror glass (Sec 14)

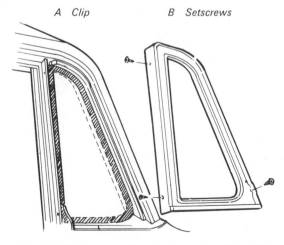

Fig. 13.272 Rear quarter fixed window (Sec 14)

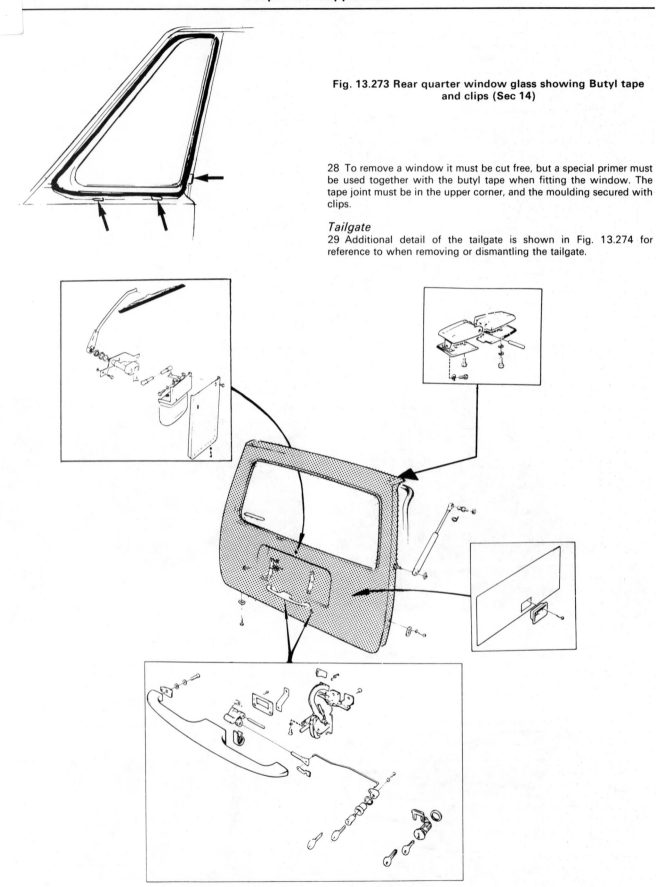

Fig. 13.273 Rear quarter window glass showing Butyl tape and clips (Sec 14)

28 To remove a window it must be cut free, but a special primer must be used together with the butyl tape when fitting the window. The tape joint must be in the upper corner, and the moulding secured with clips.

Tailgate

29 Additional detail of the tailgate is shown in Fig. 13.274 for reference to when removing or dismantling the tailgate.

Fig. 13.274 Tailgate components (Sec 14)

Routine maintenance – models 1984 on

As from 1984, maintenance intervals and tasks have been revised.

VEHICLES OPERATING IN TERRITORIES OTHER THAN NORTH AMERICA

Every 6000 miles (9600 km) or six months

Check and top up transmission lubricant
Check and top up rear axle lubricant
Renew engine oil and filter
Check and top up power steering fluid
Check and top up cooling system
Check battery level and terminals
Top up carburettor dashpot
Renew spark plugs (not long life type)
Renew contact breaker points
Check ignition timing
Check idle speed and mixture
Lubricate all controls, hinges and locks
Check damping action of shock absorbers

Every 12 000 miles (19 000 km) or 12 months

Check handbrake adjustment
Check adjustment of front hub bearings
Check all steering and suspension components for wear
Check disc pad wear
Check condition of brake hydraulic hoses
Check clutch adjustment (LHD)
Check propeller shaft joints for wear
Check exhaust system for corrosion
Check front wheel alignment
Check headlamp beam alignment
Check condition of brake and fuel pipe lines
Clean fuel filter (carburettor)
Check condition and tension of drivebelts
Renew spark plugs (long life type)

Every 24 000 miles (38 000 km) or two years

Renew automatic transmission fluid
Renew fuel filter (injection models)
Renew air cleaner element
Renew fuel filter (carburettor)
Clean crankcase vent hoses
Check valve clearances
Adjust timing belt
Adjust rear brake band (BW35 automatic transmission)
Renew coolant
Renew brake fluid by bleeding

Every 36 000 miles (58 000 km) or three years

Renew timing belt (B17 engine)

Every 48 000 miles (77 000 km) or four years

Renew timing belt (all engines except B17)
Renew rear axle oil (optional)
Renew manual gearbox oil (optional)

VEHICLES OPERATING IN NORTH AMERICA 1984 TO 1985

Every 3750 miles (6250 km) or three months

Renew engine oil and filter (B21F only)

Every 5000 miles (8000 km)

Renew engine oil and filter (not B21F)

500 miles (12 000 km) or six months

Inspect condition of brake hoses and pipe lines
Check handbrake adjustment
Check clutch adjustment
Check adjustment of automatic transmission controls
Check propeller shaft joints for wear
Check all suspension and steering components for wear
Check shock absorber damping action
Check exhaust system for corrosion
Check rear axle oil level
Check transmission lubricant level
Check coolant level
Check brake fluid level
Check power steering fluid level
Check battery level and terminals for corrosion
Check carburettor damper oil level (Canada)
Check breaker points and dwell angle (Canada)
Check Pulsair system (Canada)
Check tightness of turbo/exhaust nuts (B21F)
Check turbo seal
Check turbo system functioning

Every 15 000 miles (25 000 km) or 12 months

Clean positive crankcase vent system
Renew spark plugs (except B21F and B23F)
Lubricate distributor
Check ignition timing
Check EGR valve operation and clean
Check exhaust CO emission level
Check disc pad wear
Renew Lambda-sond oxygen sensor
Reset 'EXH' warning light switch

Every 30 000 miles (48 000 km) or two years

Renew automatic transmission fluid
Renew coolant
Renew air cleaner element (B21F)
Check condition and tension of drivebelts
Check valve clearances
Renew EGR valve
Renew spark plugs (B21F, B23F and B230F)
Renew fuel filter (B21F and B23F)
Check ignition timing
Renew brake fluid by bleeding

Every 45 000 miles (72 000 km) or three years

Renew timing belt
Clean fuel pump
Renew air cleaner element (except B21F)
Check idle speed and mixture adjustment
Renew rear axle oil (optional)
Renew manual gearbox oil (optional)

VEHICLES OPERATING IN NORTH AMERICA – 1986

The service intervals have been altered as follows:

Every 5000 miles (8000 km) or six months

Renew engine oil and filter
Check brake fluid level
Check level of automatic transmission fluid
Check power steering fluid level
Check rear axle oil level
Check propeller shaft joints for wear
Check manual transmission lubricant level

Every 10 000 miles (16 000 km) or 12 months

Check condition of wiper blades
Check condition of brake hoses and pipe lines
Check disc pad wear
Check fluid level in power steering
Check steering and suspension components for wear
Check front hub bearing adjustment
Check front wheel alignment
Check damping action of shock absorbers
Check clutch adjustment
Check exhaust system for corrosion
Adjust kick-down cable (automatic transmission)
Check coolant level
Check battery electrolyte level and terminals for corrosion
Check condition of drivebelts and tension

Every 20 000 miles (32 000 km) or two years

Renew automatic transmission fluid

Every 30 000 miles (48 000 km) or three years

Renew coolant
Renew air cleaner element
Renew spark plugs
Check valve clearances
Renew brake fluid by bleeding

Every 50 000 miles (80 000 km) or four years

Renew timing belt
Renew rear axle oil (optional)
Renew manual gearbox oil (optional)

Every 60 000 miles (96 000 km) or five years

Clean PCV system
Renew fuel filter.

General repair procedures

Whenever servicing, repair or overhaul work is carried out on the car or its components, it is necessary to observe the following procedures and instructions. This will assist in carrying out the operation efficiently and to a professional standard of workmanship.

Joint mating faces and gaskets

Where a gasket is used between the mating faces of two components, ensure that it is renewed on reassembly, and fit it dry unless otherwise stated in the repair procedure. Make sure that the mating faces are clean and dry with all traces of old gasket removed. When cleaning a joint face, use a tool which is not likely to score or damage the face, and remove any burrs or nicks with an oilstone or fine file.

Make sure that tapped holes are cleaned with a pipe cleaner, and keep them free of jointing compound if this is being used unless specifically instructed otherwise.

Ensure that all orifices, channels or pipes are clear and blow through them, preferably using compressed air.

Oil seals

Whenever an oil seal is removed from its working location, either individually or as part of an assembly, it should be renewed.

The very fine sealing lip of the seal is easily damaged and will not seal if the surface it contacts is not completely clean and free from scratches, nicks or grooves. If the original sealing surface of the component cannot be restored, the component should be renewed.

Protect the lips of the seal from any surface which may damage them in the course of fitting. Use tape or a conical sleeve where possible. Lubricate the seal lips with oil before fitting and, on dual lipped seals, fill the space between the lips with grease.

Unless otherwise stated, oil seals must be fitted with their sealing lips toward the lubricant to be sealed.

Use a tubular drift or block of wood of the appropriate size to install the seal and, if the seal housing is shouldered, drive the seal down to the shoulder. If the seal housing is unshouldered, the seal should be fitted with its face flush with the housing top face.

Screw threads and fastenings

Always ensure that a blind tapped hole is completely free from oil, grease, water or other fluid before installing the bolt or stud. Failure to do this could cause the housing to crack due to the hydraulic action of the bolt or stud as it is screwed in.

When tightening a castellated nut to accept a split pin, tighten the nut to the specified torque, where applicable, and then tighten further to the next split pin hole. Never slacken the nut to align a split pin hole unless stated in the repair procedure.

When checking or retightening a nut or bolt to a specified torque setting, slacken the nut or bolt by a quarter of a turn, and then retighten to the specified setting.

Locknuts, locktabs and washers

Any fastening which will rotate against a component or housing in the course of tightening should always have a washer between it and the relevant component or housing.

Spring or split washers should always be renewed when they are used to lock a critical component such as a big-end bearing retaining nut or bolt.

Locktabs which are folded over to retain a nut or bolt should always be renewed.

Self-locking nuts can be reused in non-critical areas, providing resistance can be felt when the locking portion passes over the bolt or stud thread.

Split pins must always be replaced with new ones of the correct size for the hole.

Special tools

Some repair procedures in this manual entail the use of special tools such as a press, two or three-legged pullers, spring compressors etc. Wherever possible, suitable readily available alternatives to the manufacturer's special tools are described, and are shown in use. In some instances, where no alternative is possible, it has been necessary to resort to the use of a manufacturer's tool and this has been done for reasons of safety as well as the efficient completion of the repair operation. Unless you are highly skilled and have a thorough understanding of the procedure described, never attempt to bypass the use of any special tool when the procedure described specifies its use. Not only is there a very great risk of personal injury, but expensive damage could be caused to the components involved.

Professional motor mechanics are trained in safe working procedures. However enthusiastic you may be about getting on with the job in hand, do take the time to ensure that your safety is not put at risk. A moment's lack of attention can result in an accident, as can failure to observe certain elementary precautions.

There will always be new ways of having accidents, and the following points do not pretend to be a comprehensive list of all dangers; they are intended rather to make you aware of the risks and to encourage a safety-conscious approach to all work you carry out on your vehicle.

Essential DOs and DON'Ts

DON'T rely on a single jack when working underneath the vehicle. Always use reliable additional means of support, such as axle stands, securely placed under a part of the vehicle that you know will not give way.

DON'T attempt to loosen or tighten high-torque nuts (e.g. wheel hub nuts) while the vehicle is on a jack; it may be pulled off.

DON'T start the engine without first ascertaining that the transmission is in neutral (or 'Park' where applicable) and the parking brake applied.

DON'T suddenly remove the filler cap from a hot cooling system – cover it with a cloth and release the pressure gradually first, or you may get scalded by escaping coolant.

DON'T attempt to drain oil until you are sure it has cooled sufficiently to avoid scalding you.

DON'T grasp any part of the engine, exhaust or catalytic converter without first ascertaining that it is sufficiently cool to avoid burning you.

DON'T allow brake fluid or antifreeze to contact vehicle paintwork.

DON'T syphon toxic liquids such as fuel, brake fluid or antifreeze by mouth, or allow them to remain on your skin.

DON'T inhale dust – it may be injurious to health (see *Asbestos* below).

DON'T allow any spilt oil or grease to remain on the floor – wipe it up straight away, before someone slips on it.

DON'T use ill-fitting spanners or other tools which may slip and cause injury.

DON'T attempt to lift a heavy component which may be beyond your capability – get assistance.

DON'T rush to finish a job, or take unverified short cuts.

DON'T allow children or animals in or around an unattended vehicle.

DO wear eye protection when using power tools such as drill, sander, bench grinder etc, and when working under the vehicle.

DO use a barrier cream on your hands prior to undertaking dirty jobs – it will protect your skin from infection as well as making the dirt easier to remove afterwards; but make sure your hands aren't left slippery.

DO keep loose clothing (cuffs, tie etc) and long hair well out of the way of moving mechanical parts.

DO remove rings, wristwatch etc, before working on the vehicle – especially the electrical system.

DO ensure that any lifting tackle used has a safe working load rating adequate for the job.

DO keep your work area tidy – it is only too easy to fall over articles left lying around.

DO get someone to check periodically that all is well, when working alone on the vehicle.

DO carry out work in a logical sequence and check that everything is correctly assembled and tightened afterwards.

DO remember that your vehicle's safety affects that of yourself and others. If in doubt on any point, get specialist advice.

IF, in spite of following these precautions, you are unfortunate enough to injure yourself, seek medical attention as soon as possible.

Asbestos

Certain friction, insulating, sealing, and other products – such as brake linings, brake bands, clutch linings, torque converters, gaskets, etc – contain asbestos. *Extreme care must be taken to avoid inhalation of dust from such products since it is hazardous to health.* If in doubt, assume that they *do* contain asbestos.

Fire

Remember at all times that petrol (gasoline) is highly flammable. Never smoke, or have any kind of naked flame around, when working on the vehicle. But the risk does not end there – a spark caused by an electrical short-circuit, by two metal surfaces contacting each other, by careless use of tools, or even by static electricity built up in your body under certain conditions, can ignite petrol vapour, which in a confined space is highly explosive.

Always disconnect the battery earth (ground) terminal before working on any part of the fuel or electrical system, and never risk spilling fuel on to a hot engine or exhaust.

It is recommended that a fire extinguisher of a type suitable for fuel and electrical fires is kept handy in the garage or workplace at all times. Never try to extinguish a fuel or electrical fire with water.

Fumes

Certain fumes are highly toxic and can quickly cause unconsciousness and even death if inhaled to any extent. Petrol (gasoline) vapour comes into this category, as do the vapours from certain solvents such as trichloroethylene. Any draining or pouring of such volatile fluids should be done in a well ventilated area.

When using cleaning fluids and solvents, read the instructions carefully. Never use materials from unmarked containers – they may give off poisonous vapours.

Never run the engine of a motor vehicle in an enclosed space such as a garage. Exhaust fumes contain carbon monoxide which is extremely poisonous; if you need to run the engine, always do so in the open air or at least have the rear of the vehicle outside the workplace.

If you are fortunate enough to have the use of an inspection pit, never drain or pour petrol, and never run the engine, while the vehicle is standing over it; the fumes, being heavier than air, will concentrate in the pit with possibly lethal results.

The battery

Never cause a spark, or allow a naked light, near the vehicle's battery. It will normally be giving off a certain amount of hydrogen gas, which is highly explosive.

Always disconnect the battery earth (ground) terminal before working on the fuel or electrical systems.

If possible, loosen the filler plugs or cover when charging the battery from an external source. Do not charge at an excessive rate or the battery may burst.

Take care when topping up and when carrying the battery. The acid electrolyte, even when diluted, is very corrosive and should not be allowed to contact the eyes or skin.

If you ever need to prepare electrolyte yourself, always add the acid slowly to the water, and never the other way round. Protect against splashes by wearing rubber gloves and goggles.

When jump starting a car using a booster battery, for negative earth (ground) vehicles, connect the jump leads in the following sequence: First connect one jump lead between the positive (+) terminals of the two batteries. Then connect the other jump lead first to the negative (–) terminal of the booster battery, and then to a good earthing (ground) point on the vehicle to be started, at least 18 in (45 cm) from the battery if possible. Ensure that hands and jump leads are clear of any moving parts, and that the two vehicles do not touch. Disconnect the leads in the reverse order.

Mains electricity

When using an electric power tool, inspection light etc, which works from the mains, always ensure that the appliance is correctly connected to its plug and that, where necessary, it is properly earthed (grounded). Do not use such appliances in damp conditions and, again, beware of creating a spark or applying excessive heat in the vicinity of fuel or fuel vapour.

Ignition HT voltage

A severe electric shock can result from touching certain parts of the ignition system, such as the HT leads, when the engine is running or being cranked, particularly if components are damp or the insulation is defective. Where an electronic ignition system is fitted, the HT voltage is much higher and could prove fatal.

Fault diagnosis

Introduction

The vehicle owner who does his or her own maintenance according to the recommended schedules should not have to use this section of the manual very often. Modern component reliability is such that, provided those items subject to wear or deterioration are inspected or renewed at the specified intervals, sudden failure is comparatively rare. Faults do not usually just happen as a result of sudden failure, but develop over a period of time. Major mechanical failures in particular are usually preceded by characteristic symptoms over hundreds or even thousands of miles. Those components which do occasionally fail without warning are often small and easily carried in the vehicle.

With any fault finding, the first step is to decide where to begin investigations. Sometimes this is obvious, but on other occasions a little detective work will be necessary. The owner who makes half a dozen haphazard adjustments or replacements may be successful in curing a fault (or its symptoms), but he will be none the wiser if the fault recurs and he may well have spent more time and money than was necessary. A calm and logical approach will be found to be more satisfactory in the long run. Always take into account any warning signs or abnormalities that may have been noticed in the period preceding the fault – power loss, high or low gauge readings, unusual noises or smells, etc – and remember that failure of components such as fuses or spark plugs may only be pointers to some underlying fault.

The pages which follow here are intended to help in cases of failure to start or breakdown on the road. There is also a Fault Diagnosis Section at the end of each Chapter which should be consulted if the preliminary checks prove unfruitful. Whatever the fault, certain basic principles apply. These are as follows:

Verify the fault. This is simply a matter of being sure that you know what the symptoms are before starting work. This is particularly important if you are investigating a fault for someone else who may not have described it very accurately.

Don't overlook the obvious. For example, if the vehicle won't start, is there petrol in the tank? (Don't take anyone else's word on this particular point, and don't trust the fuel gauge either!) If an electrical fault is indicated, look for loose or broken wires before digging out the test gear.

Cure the disease, not the symptom. Substituting a flat battery with a fully charged one will get you off the hard shoulder, but if the underlying cause is not attended to, the new battery will go the same way. Similarly, changing oil-fouled spark plugs for a new set will get you moving again, but remember that the reason for the fouling (if it wasn't simply an incorrect grade of plug) will have to be established and corrected.

Don't take anything for granted. Particularly, don't forget that a 'new' component may itself be defective (especially if it's been rattling round in the boot for months), and don't leave components out of a fault diagnosis sequence just because they are new or recently fitted. When you do finally diagnose a difficult fault, you'll probably realise that all the evidence was there from the start.

Electrical faults

Electrical faults can be more puzzling than straightforward mechanical failures, but they are no less susceptible to logical analysis if the basic principles of operation are understood. Vehicle electrical wiring exists in extremely unfavourable conditions – heat, vibration and chemical attack – and the first things to look for are loose or corroded connections and broken or chafed wires, especially where the wires pass through holes in the bodywork or are subject to vibration.

All metal-bodied vehicles in current production have one pole of the battery 'earthed', ie connected to the vehicle bodywork, and in nearly all modern vehicles it is the negative (–) terminal. The various electrical components – motors, bulb holders etc – are also connected to earth, either by means of a lead or directly by their mountings. Electric current flows through the component and then back to the battery via the bodywork. If the component mounting is loose or corroded, or if a good path back to the battery is not available, the circuit will be incomplete and malfunction will result. The engine and/or gearbox are also earthed by means of flexible metal straps to the body or subframe; if these straps are loose or missing, starter motor, generator and ignition trouble may result.

Assuming the earth return to be satisfactory, electrical faults will be due either to component malfunction or to defects in the current supply. Individual components are dealt with in Chapter 10. If supply wires are broken or cracked internally this results in an open-circuit, and the easiest way to check for this is to bypass the suspect wire temporarily with a length of wire having a crocodile clip or suitable connector at each end. Alternatively, a 12V test lamp can be used to verify the presence of supply voltage at various points along the wire and the break can be thus isolated.

If a bare portion of a live wire touches the bodywork or other earthed metal part, the electricity will take the low-resistance path thus formed back to the battery: this is known as a short-circuit. Hopefully a short-circuit will blow a fuse, but otherwise it may cause burning of the insulation (and possibly further short-circuits) or even a fire. This is why it is inadvisable to bypass persistently blowing fuses with silver foil or wire.

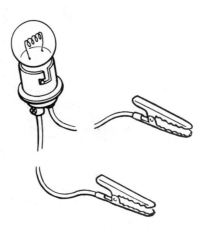

A simple test lamp is useful for tracing electrical faults

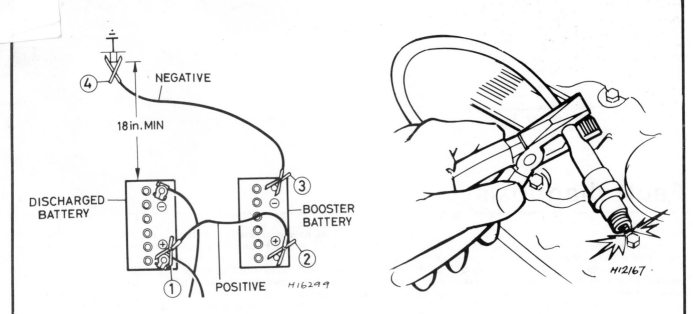

Jump start lead connections for negative earth vehicles — connect leads in order shown

Crank engine and check for spark. Note use of insulated tool

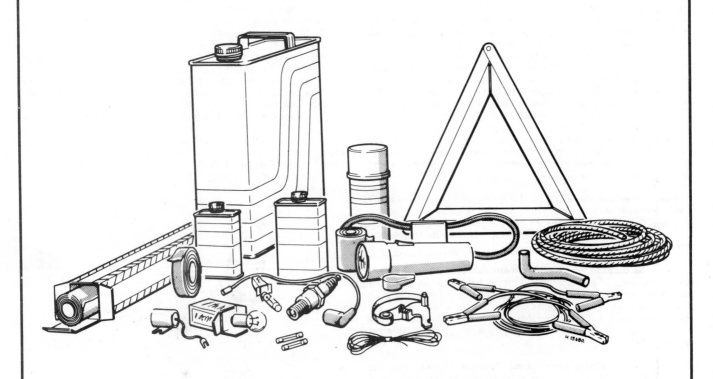

Carrying a few spares can save you a long walk

Spares and tool kit

Most vehicles are supplied only with sufficient tools for wheel changing; the *Maintenance and minor repair* tool kit detailed in *Tools and working facilities*, with the addition of a hammer, is probably sufficient for those repairs that most motorists would consider attempting at the roadside. In addition a few items which can be fitted without too much trouble in the event of a breakdown should be carried. Experience and available space will modify the list below, but the following may save having to call on professional assistance:

Spark plugs, clean and correctly gapped
HT lead and plug cap – long enough to reach the plug furthest from the distributor
Distributor rotor, condenser and contact breaker points
Drivebelt(s) – emergency type may suffice
Spare fuses
Set of principal light bulbs
Tin of radiator sealer and hose bandage
Exhaust bandage
Roll of insulating tape
Length of soft iron wire
Length of electrical flex
Torch or inspection lamp (can double as test lamp)
Battery jump leads
Tow-rope
Ignition waterproofing aerosol
Litre of engine oil
Sealed can of hydraulic fluid
Worm drive clips
Tube of filler paste

If spare fuel is carried, a can designed for the purpose should be used to minimise risks of leakage and collision damage. A first aid kit and a warning triangle, whilst not at present compulsory in the UK, are obviously sensible items to carry in addition to the above.

When touring abroad it may be advisable to carry additional spares which, even if you cannot fit them yourself, could save having to wait while parts are obtained. The items below may be worth considering:

Clutch and throttle cables
Cylinder head gasket
Alternator brushes
Fuel pump repair kit or spare pump
Tyre valve core

One of the motoring organisations will be able to advise on availability of fuel etc in foreign countries.

Engine will not start

Engine fails to turn when starter operated
Flat battery (recharge, use jump leads, or push start)
Battery terminals loose or corroded
Battery earth to body defective
Engine earth strap loose or broken
Starter motor (or solenoid) wiring loose or broken
Automatic transmission selector in wrong position, or inhibitor switch faulty
Ignition/starter switch faulty
Major mechanical failure (seizure)
Starter or solenoid internal fault (see Chapter 10)

Starter motor turns engine slowly
Partially discharged battery (recharge, use jump leads, or push start)
Battery terminals loose or corroded
Battery earth to body defective
Engine earth strap loose or broken
Starter motor (or solenoid) wiring loose
Starter motor internal fault (see Chapter 10)

Starter motor spins without turning engine
Flat battery
Starter motor pinion sticking on sleeve
Flywheel gear teeth damaged or worn
Starter motor mounting bolts loose

Engine turns normally but fails to start
Damp or dirty HT leads and distributor cap (crank engine and check for spark)
Dirty or incorrectly gapped distributor points (if applicable)
No fuel in tank (check for delivery at carburettor)
Excessive choke (hot engine) or insufficient choke (cold engine)
Fouled or incorrectly gapped spark plugs (remove, clean and regap)
Other ignition system fault (see Chapter 4)
Other fuel system fault (see Chapter 3)
Poor compression
Major mechanical failure (eg camshaft drive)

Engine fires but will not run
Insufficient choke (cold engine)
Air leaks at carburettor or inlet manifold
Fuel starvation (see Chapter 3)
Ballast resistor defective, or other ignition fault (see Chapter 4)

Engine cuts out and will not restart

Engine cuts out suddenly – ignition fault
Loose or disconnected LT wires
Wet HT leads or distributor cap (after traversing water splash)
Coil or condenser failure (check for spark)
Other ignition fault (see Chapter 4)

Engine misfires before cutting out – fuel fault
Fuel tank empty
Fuel pump defective or filter blocked (check for delivery)
Fuel tank filler vent blocked (suction will be evident on releasing cap)
Carburettor needle valve sticking
Carburettor jets blocked (fuel contaminated)
Other fuel system fault (see Chapter 3)

Engine cuts out – other causes
Serious overheating
Major mechanical failure (eg camshaft drive)

Engine overheats

Ignition (no-charge) warning light illuminated
Slack or broken drivebelt – retension or renew (Chapter 2)

Ignition warning light not illuminated
Coolant loss due to internal or external leakage (see Chapter 2)
Thermostat defective
Low oil level
Radiator clogged externally or internally
Electric cooling fan not operating correctly
Engine waterways clogged
Ignition timing incorrect or automatic advance malfunctioning
Mixture too weak

Note: *Do not add cold water to an overheated engine or damage may result*

Low engine oil pressure

Gauge reads low or warning light illuminated with engine running
Oil level low or incorrect grade
Defective gauge or sender unit
Wire to sender unit earthed
Engine overheating
Oil filter clogged or bypass valve defective

Oil pressure relief valve defective
Oil pick-up strainer clogged
Oil pump worn or mountings loose
Worn main or big-end bearings
Note: *Low oil pressure in a high-mileage engine at tickover is not necessarily a cause for concern. Sudden pressure loss at speed is far more significant. In any event, check the gauge or warning light sender before condemning the engine.*

Engine noises

Pre-ignition (pinking) on acceleration
Incorrect grade of fuel
Ignition timing incorrect
Distributor faulty or worn
Worn or maladjusted carburettor
Excessive carbon build-up in engine

Whistling or wheezing noises
Leaking vacuum hose
Leaking carburettor or manifold gasket
Blowing head gasket

Tapping or rattling
Incorrect valve clearances
Worn valve gear
Worn timing belt
Broken piston ring (ticking noise)

Knocking or thumping
Unintentional mechanical contact (eg fan blades)
Worn drivebelt
Peripheral component fault (generator, water pump etc)
Worn big-end bearings (regular heavy knocking, perhaps less under load)
Worn main bearings (rumbling and knocking, perhaps worsening under load)
Piston slap (most noticeable when cold)

Conversion factors

Length (distance)

Inches (in)	X	25.4	= Millimetres (mm)	X	0.0394	= Inches (in)
Feet (ft)	X	0.305	= Metres (m)	X	3.281	= Feet (ft)
Miles	X	1.609	= Kilometres (km)	X	0.621	= Miles

Volume (capacity)

Cubic inches (cu in; in^3)	X	16.387	= Cubic centimetres (cc; cm^3)	X	0.061	= Cubic inches (cu in; in^3)
Imperial pints (Imp pt)	X	0.568	= Litres (l)	X	1.76	= Imperial pints (Imp pt)
Imperial quarts (Imp qt)	X	1.137	= Litres (l)	X	0.88	= Imperial quarts (Imp qt)
Imperial quarts (Imp qt)	X	1.201	= US quarts (US qt)	X	0.833	= Imperial quarts (Imp qt)
US quarts (US qt)	X	0.946	= Litres (l)	X	1.057	= US quarts (US qt)
Imperial gallons (Imp gal)	X	4.546	= Litres (l)	X	0.22	= Imperial gallons (Imp gal)
Imperial gallons (Imp gal)	X	1.201	= US gallons (US gal)	X	0.833	= Imperial gallons (Imp gal)
US gallons (US gal)	X	3.785	= Litres (l)	X	0.264	= US gallons (US gal)

Mass (weight)

Ounces (oz)	X	28.35	= Grams (g)	X	0.035	= Ounces (oz)
Pounds (lb)	X	0.454	= Kilograms (kg)	X	2.205	= Pounds (lb)

Force

Ounces-force (ozf; oz)	X	0.278	= Newtons (N)	X	3.6	= Ounces-force (ozf; oz)
Pounds-force (lbf; lb)	X	4.448	= Newtons (N)	X	0.225	= Pounds-force (lbf; lb)
Newtons (N)	X	0.1	= Kilograms-force (kgf; kg)	X	9.81	= Newtons (N)

Pressure

Pounds-force per square inch (psi; lbf/in^2; lb/in^2)	X	0.070	= Kilograms-force per square centimetre (kgf/cm^2; kg/cm^2)	X	14.223	= Pounds-force per square inch (psi; lbf/in^2; lb/in^2)
Pounds-force per square inch (psi; lbf/in^2; lb/in^2)	X	0.068	= Atmospheres (atm)	X	14.696	= Pounds-force per square inch (psi; lbf/in^2; lb/in^2)
Pounds-force per square inch (psi; lbf/in^2; lb/in^2)	X	0.069	= Bars	X	14.5	= Pounds-force per square inch (psi; lbf/in^2; lb/in^2)
Pounds-force per square inch (psi; lbf/in^2; lb/in^2)	X	6.895	= Kilopascals (kPa)	X	0.145	= Pounds-force per square inch (psi; lbf/in^2; lb/in^2)
Kilopascals (kPa)	X	0.01	= Kilograms-force per square centimetre (kgf/cm^2; kg/cm^2)	X	98.1	= Kilopascals (kPa)

Torque (moment of force)

Pounds-force inches (lbf in; lb in)	X	1.152	= Kilograms-force centimetre (kgf cm; kg cm)	X	0.868	= Pounds-force inches (lbf in; lb in)
Pounds-force inches (lbf in; lb in)	X	0.113	= Newton metres (Nm)	X	8.85	= Pounds-force inches (lbf in; lb in)
Pounds-force inches (lbf·in; lb in)	X	0.083	= Pounds-force feet (lbf ft; lb ft)	X	12	= Pounds-force inches (lbf in; lb in)
Pounds-force feet (lbf ft; lb ft)	X	0.138	= Kilograms-force metres (kgf m; kg m)	X	7.233	= Pounds-force feet (lbf ft; lb ft)
Pounds-force feet (lbf ft; lb ft)	X	1.356	= Newton metres (Nm)	X	0.738	= Pounds-force feet (lbf ft; lb ft)
Newton metres (Nm)	X	0.102	= Kilograms-force metres (kgf m; kg m)	X	9.804	= Newton metres (Nm)

Power

Horsepower (hp)	X	745.7	= Watts (W)	X	0.0013	= Horsepower (hp)

Velocity (speed)

Miles per hour (miles/hr; mph)	X	1.609	= Kilometres per hour (km/hr; kph)	X	0.621	= Miles per hour (miles/hr; mph)

*Fuel consumption**

Miles per gallon, Imperial (mpg)	X	0.354	= Kilometres per litre (km/l)	X	2.825	= Miles per gallon, Imperial (mpg)
Miles per gallon, US (mpg)	X	0.425	= Kilometres per litre (km/l)	X	2.352	= Miles per gallon, US (mpg)

Temperature

Degrees Fahrenheit = (°C x 1.8) + 32   Degrees Celsius (Degrees Centigrade; °C) = (°F - 32) x 0.56

*It is common practice to convert from miles per gallon (mpg) to litres/100 kilometres (l/100km), where mpg (Imperial) x l/100 km = 282 and mpg (US) x l/100 km = 235

Index

Printed by
J H Haynes & Co Ltd
Sparkford Nr Yeovil
Somerset BA22 7JJ England